Open Source ESBs in Action

Open Source ESBs in Action

EXAMPLE IMPLEMENTATIONS IN MULE AND SERVICEMIX

TIJS RADEMAKERS
JOS DIRKSEN

MANNING

Greenwich
(74° w. long.)

Manning Publications Co.
Sound View Court 3B
Greenwich, CT 06830

Development Editor: Jeff Bleil
Copyeditors: Liz Welch, Tiffany Taylor
Typesetter: Denis Dalinnik
Cover designer: Leslie Haimes

ISBN: 1933988215
Printed in the United States of America
1 2 3 4 5 6 7 8 9 10 – MAL – 12 11 10 09 08

brief contents

v

contents

foreword

Getting different applications to work together has never been fun. It's not sexy, the rewards are limited, and there is no glory. Throughout my career, it seemed as if a stigma was associated with integration—that it was a dirty job, and you pulled the short straw if you were working in this area. Personally, I always enjoyed working in integration, and because enterprises never throw anything away, getting different applications to work together has become an increasingly essential element of IT.

Things really became interesting when the enterprise service bus (ESB) made its debut.

The concepts on which the ESB is founded have changed over time. Since IBM first released MQSeries, enterprises have been sold on the benefits of decoupling systems using point-to-point message queues. When TIBCO brought Rendezvous to the market, it expanded the horizons of messaging by introducing the publish-subscribe model. The Java Message Service (JMS)—born through Sun's Java Community Process (JCP)—set out to unify the point-to-point and publish-subscribe messaging models. It wasn't long before enterprises required more than just messaging; they also needed a way to orchestrate messages between systems and perform transformations.

To address this need, major vendors such as IBM, Oracle, and Microsoft built enterprise application integration (EAI) brokers that added message brokering and centralized transformation engines on top of their existing messaging servers. The problem with the EAI approach was that it adopted a hub-and-spoke architecture where all data had to flow through the EAI broker. Although this worked for many applications, enterprises were soon pushing the boundaries of these systems; it became clear that something more flexible, scalable, and distributed was required. Enterprises needed connectivity, transaction management, security, and message routing, and they needed to host services that operated on data moving around their systems. The industry needed the ESB.

With the advance of service-oriented architecture (SOA) in the last several years, we've seen confusion unfold about what SOA really is. One affirmation that has resonated well in the industry is that the ESB is the foundation of SOA. The term *SOA* covers a much broader topic than just technology, but we need technologies like ESBs to realize the benefits of what service orientation has to offer. The ESB provides an anchor point for many enterprises that are braving the nebulous ocean of SOA marketing, vendor claims, and vaporware. The ESB bridges the gap between old and new. It acts as a mediator between application integration and service orientation, enabling enterprises to build new applications and processes from existing technology.

The ESB has gained in popularity because there is a general understanding of what an ESB is; but if you're still confused, this book will definitely provide clarity. The notion of an ESB involves a common messaging *bus* that is used to communicate between different systems within an enterprise. Typically, there is a shared messaging format on the bus, and adapters between the bus and back-end applications translate data from the proprietary data formats to the shared message bus format. The power of this model is that applications can share information while being totally decoupled from one another. Additionally, the ESB provides a common platform for handling security, transformations, message routing, transactions, and monitoring. This book does a great job of covering each of these topics and dives deep into the detail of how to apply these features in the real world.

I founded the Mule project in 2003 because I was frustrated by the proprietary nature of products available for building ESB solutions. In 2001, I was working as an architect for a tier-1 investment bank. I was tasked with building a custom ESB-like solution to integrate hundreds of legacy and custom applications. Back then, the term *enterprise service bus* hadn't been coined (although by 2002, Sonic Software, Fiorano, and SpiritSoft all staked claim to the term), but what we built was in fact an ESB. At the time, the technology choices were limited; you used either an application server or a heavyweight EAI solution that required a huge upfront investment in infrastructure, money, and human resources. We wanted something lightweight and easy to deploy and manage. Like many enterprises at the time, we built our own abstraction on top of JMS. We discovered early on that building our own was an extreme undertaking and a huge burden on our developers. After that experience, I realized that the industry needed an open source solution built on open standards.

The open source model is the perfect choice for developing an ESB. More accurately, open source is perfect for integration. After all, ESBs are about surfacing, manipulating, and moving data between applications. Application integration is complex on many levels. The permutations of applications, protocols, message formats, environment restrictions, and nuances in the way an application (or even a standard) has been implemented cause system integrators an unholy amount of grief. No single vendor can realistically claim to understand the intricacies of your application environment, so all the proprietary vendors have instead chosen to offer products that make their customers abide by their rules when building an ESB solution. I can say from experience that this quickly becomes a problem when the vendor's approach doesn't suit your needs. Sometimes, you want to get into the code and customize for the problem at hand.

By providing access to the source code, open source ESBs can alleviate these problems—but the benefits don't stop there. By nature, open source projects are developed to be lean and modular. Developers working on the project don't have time to maintain a huge product, and they want the code base to be accessible to their community to encourage contributions. Given that the use cases for ESBs and integration are so varied, it's impossible to have one vendor test every scenario. It's far better to give the code to a community of active users who provide testing and feedback about their experience with the ESB. That same user community has connectivity and message-format requirements far beyond what is provided, so it makes sense to enable the users to build support for the more exotic protocols. These extensions can then be committed back to the project for the benefit of the rest of the community.

Since the Mule project was founded in 2003, many open source ESBs have emerged. Each has its own way of doing things, and each focuses on different areas. As examples, Apache ServiceMix is built on Java Business Integration (JBI), whereas Apache Synapse is built around the Web Services (WS) standards, and Apache Tuscany uses the Service Component Architecture (SCA) standard. Mule takes a pragmatic approach by embracing these standards without forcing the use of any of them, giving the user a great deal of flexibility when building an ESB solution.

Choice is usually a good thing for consumers, but with so many choices, it can be difficult to navigate the landscape of open source ESBs. I believe this book is a valuable resource for those looking to choose an ESB and wanting a stronger grasp on how to implement an ESB using open source projects. I found the case studies in section 3 particularly useful because they pull together many of the concepts learned throughout the book.

This book guides you through a logical journey of discovery and demonstration to deliver a solid understanding of the core ESB concepts and how you can use them in the real world. I think that armed with this book and the wealth of open source projects available, you'll be ready to take on any ESB project. Open source has made ESBs a lot more interesting. Go and enjoy yourself!

ROSS MASON
Co-Founder & CTO, MuleSource, Inc.
Founder of the Mule Project

foreword

Enterprise service bus is a loosely defined term, and lots of products are claiming to implement the ESB concept. This concept is covered in depth in the first chapter of this book; in short, the goal is to provide a distributed and reliable mediation framework that the different systems in an IT environment can use to communicate, thus removing the need for a given system to know how to talk to the others in a specific way. Integration, which is what ESBs are about, is complicated: Each time you add a system, it needs to talk to all the other systems, and ad-hoc integration between the systems has long been considered a bad solution.

The concept of EAI emerged as a solution, but it led to another set of problems related to using a hub-and-spoke architecture, where a single system, the EAI broker, becomes the center of the system and a single point of failure. The next step of this evolution led to what is now known as an ESB: Data and exchanges are conveyed from system to system in a single logical bus, decoupling all the systems from each other. This leads to a much more maintainable system and can save a lot of time in the long term.

Integration technologies are becoming commodity software, and the rise of open source integration frameworks is becoming increasingly important. Open source is now unavoidable; who would think about paying for an XML parser? ESBs aren't at this point yet, but most of the underlying technologies in the integration world are available as open source projects, from JMS brokers to SOAP stacks to ESBs. Companies generally use ESBs to convey sensitive data, and they sometimes need advice when they're developing the applications hosted in the ESBs or when they're putting these applications in production. Even if you don't immediately think of commercial support and open source together, this is one of the main reasons it's important to have companies that can provide consulting, training, and support for such projects; this requirement is now filled by a huge number of open source projects.

In this book, you'll learn how to use two different open source products classified as ESBs. Having committed on both Mule and ServiceMix, I think both projects are awesome and mature, have good communities, and are backed by vendors that can provide the needed support. By reading this book, you'll see that even if the two projects have different configurations and sometimes different ways of solving the same problem, you'll be able to solve your problems with both.

One of the key differentiators is that ServiceMix implements the Java Business Integration (JBI) specification. JBI defines a framework to connect components and make them talk together in a standard way. In the JBI world, components can host business logic (a BPEL engine or a rules engine) or handle a particular protocol (HTTP, JMS, and so on). The key benefit of JBI is that new components can be wired easily on the bus, because they all abide by the JBI specification. For example, ServiceMix doesn't provide a BPEL engine by itself; instead, you can plug in any JBI-compliant component for BPEL (such as the one provided by Apache Ode).

Even after you've learned how to configure and use ServiceMix, at the end of this book, you won't dive too far into the JBI API. The JBI specification doesn't target end users, but rather is intended to be implemented by ESB vendors and other software vendors that want to integrate their products in a JBI-compliant environment, such as a BPEL engine, a business rules engine, a transformation engine, or another specific technology. This is, in my mind, the key benefit of JBI.

JBI 1.0 has some shortcomings: the JBI packaging and classloader architecture, the mandatory use of XML everywhere in the bus, and the fact that writing a JBI component isn't easy. But being part of the Expert Group for JBI 2.0, my hope is that those shortcomings will be addressed in the next version of the specification—or even earlier, in ServiceMix 4, which is briefly discussed in the appendixes of this book.

That's why open source is so attractive: The feedback from the community provides vital input for the next major version of a product, and this usually leads to better and more innovative products. Enjoy this book and learning from Tijs and Jos how to work with Mule and ServiceMix in a wide variety of integration challenges. You're also invited to work with the community on making these open source ESBs even better!

GUILLAUME NODET
Principal Engineer IONA
Project Lead Apache ServiceMix

preface

Working on integration projects used to mean working with EAI products, each of which implemented its own stack of tools with proprietary technology. To switch from one EAI product to another meant learning the proprietary technology and toolset from that new product. Then, the market changed from EAI to SOA and ESB products, with more focus on open standards that emerged in the integration market. Examples of these open standards are Java Message Service (JMS), SOAP, XML, and WS-*. With open standards available, more and more open source projects began to implement these specifications.

Because we enjoyed working with open source frameworks in JEE application development, we watched the progress of integration frameworks with a lot of interest. Mule was one of the first projects that provided a large set of integration functionality; after a while, it was called an ESB. When we had the chance to design an SOA architecture of a new solution for our current employer in 2005, we chose Mule as the foundation product. It was delightful to work with an open source ESB to solve our integration needs, because it offered a rich set of integration functionality out of the box. Even when we had to add nonexistent functionality, the ease of development was striking.

At the same time, the JBI specification (JSR 208) was released. It was intended to standardize the ESB infrastructure and had the potential to implement an ESB with products from several vendors, with each product suited for its specific task, such as routing, transformation, or service orchestration. Although the JBI specification didn't really take off, some interesting products were created. Apache ServiceMix is an excellent example of a JBI implementation; because it makes working with the JBI specification simple, we think ServiceMix is a great alternative to Mule. Mule focuses on ease of development with support for all kinds of payloads, and it uses an architecture and design model, which isn't based on a specification. ServiceMix implements the JBI specification and therefore focuses on XML payload and the implementation of binding components and service engines.

Mule and ServiceMix have a lot of differences, but they also have common ground that's focused on integration functionality. We noticed the lack of books in the open source integration area, and it occurred to us that we could write a book that covered both Mule and ServiceMix; it would provide a good overview of the current state of open source integration products. Because we're developers and are working on client projects all the time, we decided to provide a lot of examples in the book.

Writing this book has been an intense, but interesting and enjoyable experience. It took a lot of time to implement every example, but the result is material that's freely available to everyone and a good starting point for a Mule or ServiceMix project. While we were writing this book, we had a hard time keeping up with the fast development pace of the Mule and ServiceMix projects and emerging frameworks like Apache Camel and Spring Integration. But we kept up: This book uses Mule 2.0.2 and Service-Mix 3.2.1. Please note that there has been a new release of ServiceMix with version 3.2.2. This is just a maintenance release which does not change the contents of this book, nor the example implementations.

We provide a fully implemented development environment with many additional frameworks and libraries, and functionality to build and test integration solutions. This book provides a complete approach to working with Mule and ServiceMix, and we hope you'll enjoy reading it and working with the examples.

acknowledgments

We appreciate the contributions of many people who have helped us make this book a reality. We couldn't have written it without the discussions, enthusiasm, remarks, and code and chapter reviews of these individuals.

Special thanks to Andy Verberne, who provided invaluable feedback about the chapters and the code examples. We were also happy with the support and feedback we received from the Mule team, especially Ross Mason and Daniel Feist; and from the ServiceMix team, particularly Guillaume Nodet and Bruce Snyder. We also want to thank Guy Crets for his comments in the early stages of writing this book and for his enthusiasm and support throughout our writing period. We don't have enough space to mention all the people involved, but your help is appreciated.

At Manning Publications, we're grateful to our development editor Jeff Bleiel. Jeff was great to work with, and his work improved the readability of our manuscript a lot. We also want to thank publisher Marjan Bace for giving us the opportunity to write this book and for his no-nonsense comments and remarks, which made this book what it is. Thanks to the Manning production team for turning our manuscript into a real book. Finally, we want to thank the reviewers who gave valuable feedback at all stages during manuscript development: Edmon Begoli, Martyn Fletcher, Valentin Crettaz, Lajos Moczar, Andrew Oswald, Davide Piazza, Rick Wagner, Christian Siegers, Craig Borysowich, Jeff Davis, Holger Hoffstätte, Rodney Biresch, Jeroen Benckhuijsen, John Reynolds, Doug Warren, Steve Smith, Hugh Taylor, Dmitri Maximovich, Andrew Perepelytsya, Ross Mason, Dave Corun, Glenn Stokol, Scott Stirling, Andrew Cooke, Emmanuel B. Sangalang, and Dan Alford.

And very special thanks to Ross Mason and Guillaume Nodet for taking the time out of their busy schedules to look at the manuscript and to write forewords to our book.

TIJS RADEMAKERS

I would like to thank my girlfriend Ankie, who recently gave birth to our first child, Liv. Without your support during all the hours of writing, this book would have never been written. I promise to be more involved in our little family from now on. I also want to thank my parents Wil and Fieke and in-laws Fer and Annie for their love and understanding. Jos, thanks for all your commitment, enthusiasm, and knowledge during the years of writing and discussing this book. Also thanks to my managers Diego and Hugo for providing time and freedom in my day-to-day job.

JOS DIRKSEN

Many people have supported me during the writing of this book. In particular I'd like to thank Tijs for keeping me on my toes during the writing of this book. I'd also like to thank the team at Manning for helping us to write and produce this book: specifically Jeff, for reviewing and tidying up the chapters, and of course all the reviewers for taking the time to offer comments and feedback.

I also want to express my gratitude to Diego, my boss at Atos Origin, for giving me time to write parts of this book during office hours. Another colleague I'd like to thank is Andy, who provided us with an extensive review and also spent much of his time doing the final technical review of the book.

Finally, I want to thank my girlfriend Brigitte—who when this book comes out will be my wife—for not complaining too much about the evenings and weekends spent working on the book (and my occasional bad temper).

about this book

This book is for everyone interested in open source ESBs in general and Mule and ServiceMix in particular. For consultants and architects, this book provides an excellent overview of the functionality provided by Mule and ServiceMix and other open source–based integration frameworks. For developers, this book provides numerous code examples and a ready-to-go development environment that you can use to start your projects.

We use Mule 2.0.2 and ServiceMix 3.2.1 in this book. New versions of Mule and ServiceMix will be released at a constant rate; for example when this book went to press, ServiceMix had a new maintenance release, version 3.2.2. If you are looking for updated examples that will work with newer versions of Mule or ServiceMix, please visit our website at http://www.esbinaction.com.

Roadmap

Part 1 of the book starts by explaining the core functionalities of an ESB and the project structure and architecture of Mule and ServiceMix, including some basic examples. Be sure you don't skip this part!

- *Chapter 1* introduces the functionality that an ESB is expected to provide. We explain seven core functionalities in detail. We also provide an overview of the currently available open source ESBs with a detailed comparison. We finish the chapter with a hello world example that uses Mule and ServiceMix.

- *Chapter 2* explores the architecture of both Mule and ServiceMix. We describe Mule concepts like endpoints, routers, transformers, and components and work through examples. With ServiceMix, we introduce the JBI specification and discuss service engines, binding components, and the Normalized Message Router (NMR). In this chapter we also provide some examples of how to implement service Units to be deployed on ServiceMix.
- *Chapter 3* introduces three technologies that complement the Mule and Service-Mix open source ESBs: Spring, JiBX, and ActiveMQ. We also set up a development environment that includes all the tools and libraries you'll need throughout the book. The chapter ends with Mule and ServiceMix examples that use the three new technologies and test the development environment.
- *Chapter 4* describes how to develop simple integration solutions with Mule and ServiceMix. We finish this chapter with a description of a message flow and a more complex example implementation.

Part 2 discusses the core functionalities of Mule and ServiceMix in more detail, with lots of examples including routing, transformation, connectivity, web services, and error handling:

- *Chapter 5* shows how to implement routing, validation, and transformation in Mule and ServiceMix. We also show an alternative implementation for routing and validation that uses Apache Synapse.
- *Chapter 6* discusses the most common connectivity options for Mule and Service-Mix. They include JMS, FTP, File, JDBC, and Mail, and we demonstrate their use with lots of practical examples.
- *Chapter 7* is dedicated to web services functionality. Mule and ServiceMix use Apache CXF (the successor of XFire) as their main web services platform. We show examples that use a top-down approach (WSDL to Java) and a bottom-up approach (Java to WSDL).
- *Chapter 8* explores more complex ESB functionality. We present a number of examples that involve error handling, showing you Mule's and ServiceMix's extensive ability to handle exceptions. We also discuss security and transactions.

In part 3, we introduce a pattern-based design approach and implement a full case study using Mule and ServiceMix. We also present a monitoring and management environment, and we use a case study to demonstrate integration with a process engine:

- *Chapter 9* starts with an introduction to Enterprise Integration patterns and provides a pattern-based design approach you can use in open source ESB projects. We also describe a case study with full example implementations in both Mule and ServiceMix.
- *Chapter 10* talks about the management and monitoring parts of an open source ESB, related to the case study from chapter 9. We explain how to use JMX and JConsole to manage your Mule and ServiceMix environment, and we show how to use MC4J to monitor these open source ESBs.

- *Chapter 11* introduces the use of a process engine together with an ESB. We show how you can use jBPM as a process engine, together with Mule as an ESB, to implement a process-driven integration solution. We also explain how to use Apache ODE as a process engine, together with ServiceMix as an ESB, for the same example integration solution.

Code conventions

All source code in listings or in text is in a `fixed-width font like this` to separate it from ordinary text. We use two dominant languages and markups in this book— Java and XML—and we try to adopt a consistent approach. Method and function names, object properties, XML elements, and attributes in text are presented using this same font.

In many cases, the original source code has been reformatted; we've added line breaks and reworked indentation to accommodate the available page space in the book. In rare cases even this was not enough, and listings include line-continuation markers. Additionally, many comments have been removed from the listings. Where appropriate, we've also cut implementation details that distract rather than help tell the story, such as JavaBean setters and getters, `import` and `include` statements, and namespace declarations.

Code annotations accompany many of the listings, highlighting important concepts. In some cases, numbered bullets link to explanations that follow the listing.

Code downloads

Source code for all of the working examples in this book is available for download from www.manning.com/OpenSourceESBsinAction. Basic setup documentation is provided with the download.

Because this book covers a wide range of topics related to open source ESBs, we also introduce many tools and frameworks, including databases, process engines, LDAP servers, and XML serialization. To make it easier for you to set up the environment, we've provided an Ant build script that downloads all the necessary tools and frameworks and creates the right directory structure. For a full explanation of the project structure, read chapter 3.

Author Online

The purchase of *Open Source ESBs in Action* includes free access to a private web forum run by Manning Publications, where you can make comments about the book, ask technical questions, and receive help from the authors and from other users. To access the forum and subscribe to it, point your web browser to www.manning.com/OpenSourceESB sinAction. This page provides information about how to get on the forum once you're registered, what kind of help is available, and the rules of conduct on the forum.

Manning's commitment to our readers is to provide a venue where a meaningful dialogue between individual readers and between readers and the authors can take place. It isn't a commitment to any specific amount of participation on the part of the authors, whose contribution to the forum remains voluntary (and unpaid). We suggest you try asking the authors some challenging questions lest their interest stray! The Author Online forum and the archives of previous discussions will be accessible from the publisher's website as long as the book is in print.

About the authors

TIJS RADEMAKERS is a software architect with more than six years of experience in designing and developing Java and EE applications. He works for Atos Origin, a large European system integrator, where he is responsible for SOA and BPM services and knowledge development. Tijs has designed and implemented large process- and application-integration solutions, primarily focused on open standards. He has extensive product knowledge of open source as well as closed source SOA and enterprise integration tools, including Mule, ServiceMix, jBPM, and WebSphere Process Server. Tijs is a regular speaker at Java conferences, where he talks about open source integration topics like Mule and ServiceMix. Tijs lives in the Netherlands near Eindhoven with his girlfriend and his new daughter, Liv.

JOS DIRKSEN has been working with Java and J2EE applications for more than six years as a software architect. The last couple of years, his focus topics have been open source, security, and quality. He has worked with various open source and commercial integration solutions, mostly in the areas of government and healthcare. Jos has a lot of project experience working with Mule, Apache Synapse, and Apache Axis2 and has also completed projects based on the integration tooling from IBM. Jos regularly gives presentation on open source, Mule, and other related topics. He lives in Eindhoven, the Netherlands, with his wife.

About the title

By combining introductions, overviews, and how-to examples, the *In Action* books are designed to help learning and remembering. According to research in cognitive science the things people remember are things they discover during self-motivated exploration.

Although no one at Manning is a cognitive scientist, we're convinced that for learning to become permanent it must pass through stages of exploration, play, and, interestingly, retelling of what is being learned. People understand and remember new things, which is to say they master them, only after actively exploring them. Humans learn in action. An essential part of an *In Action* book is that it's example-driven. It encourages the reader to try things out, to play with new code, and explore new ideas.

There is another, more mundane, reason for the title of this book: Our readers are busy. They use books to do a job or solve a problem. They need books that allow them to jump in and jump out easily and learn just what they want just when they want it. They need books that aid them *in action*. The books in this series are designed for such readers.

About the cover illustration

The figure on the cover of *Open Source ESBs in Action* is captioned "A traveling sales-man" and it is taken from a 19th century edition of Sylvain Maréchal's four-volume compendium of regional dress customs published in France. Each illustration is finely drawn and colored by hand.

The rich variety of Maréchal's collection reminds us vividly of how culturally apart the world's towns and regions were just 200 years ago. Isolated from each other, people spoke different dialects and languages. In the streets or in the countryside, it was easy to identify where they lived and what their station in life was just by their dress.

Dress codes have changed since then and the diversity by region, so rich at the time, has faded away. It is now hard to tell apart the inhabitants of different continents, let alone different towns or regions. Perhaps we have traded cultural diversity for a more varied personal life—certainly for a more varied and fast-paced technological life.

At a time when it is hard to tell one computer book from another, Manning celebrates the inventiveness and initiative of the computer business with book covers based on the rich diversity of regional life of two centuries ago, brought back to life by Maréchal's pictures.

Part 1

Understanding ESB functionality

An enterprise service bus (ESB) is a confusing topic in the modern world of IT. Sometimes it's referred to as an architectural pattern, which describes a flexible and constructive way to approach integration challenges. The ESB seen as a pattern can and will be implemented with several different products, each excelling in its own domain like routing, transformation, security, and orchestration.

An ESB from an integration vendor perspective is a product offering that provides integration functionality, a developer toolset, and a management environment. These product offerings often have a background in the enterprise application integration (EAI) domain.

Another perspective of an ESB is as an important part of a service-oriented architecture (SOA). From the SOA perspective, an ESB can be used as an integration platform that enables existing IT assets and applications to be exposed as services. Because the ESB is based on open standards, the proprietary technology of legacy applications can be exposed as services based on open and modern technologies like web services and messaging.

In part 1, we will show the functionality an ESB can offer to solve integration challenges. We take a close look at open source ESBs and provide an overview of the open source ESBs currently available. We also introduce two open source ESBs, Mule and Apache ServiceMix, and show you how to set up a development environment to work with these ESBs and the examples in this book. Finally, we take a first look at how to implement integration functionality and message flows in Mule and ServiceMix.

The world of open source ESBs

If you ask integration specialists and architects to supply one buzzword used in the integration market today, enterprise service bus (ESB) would be one of the predominant answers. Concepts like service-oriented architecture (SOA) and business process management (BPM) would also be mentioned. These buzzwords sound interesting, but are they just part of the hype in the integration market or do they represent real business value?

As with every buzzword in the integration industry, a sales pitch is involved, but these concepts have a business case. Other books are available that focus on SOA (such as *Understanding Enterprise SOA* by Eric Pulier and Hugh Taylor [Manning, 2005]). In this book we focus on the enterprise service bus, but we also discuss some interesting open source products related to SOA and BPM.

There's a lot of confusion about what an ESB is, so let's start off with an overview of the most important functionality that should be present in a product calling itself an ESB. Many ESB products are available in the market, from vendors like

IBM, TIBCO, Microsoft, and Oracle. Most ESB vendors offer products that have a background in the enterprise application integration (EAI) market. As we'll see in section 1.1, this is not so strange, because ESB functionality has a lot in common with the *older* EAI products.

But there are also a number of products available that have been built from the ground up. In this group of products we see not only commercial vendors but also open source projects that deliver the functionality needed in an ESB.

In section 1.5 we examine two open source ESBs (Mule and ServiceMix) that we use in the examples and case studies presented in this book. These two open source ESBs have gained a lot of attention in the market and are the two most used open source ESBs in businesses around the world today. This means that this book is not a typical cookbook for a specific ESB. Because we show examples involving two ESBs, we're confident that you'll gain the knowledge and experience you need to use any open source ESB.

1.1   *Why do you need an ESB?*

We can't begin a book about open source ESBs without a good discussion about the use of an ESB within an enterprise. Maybe you've already read articles or books that introduced the concept of an ESB. If you want to have a solid background, we recommend you check out *Enterprise Service Bus* by David A. Chappell (O'Reilly Media, 2004).

A lot of the early ESB products had a history in the enterprise application integration market. It was sometimes hard to tell the difference between some ESB products and their EAI predecessors!

However, we can identify two main differences between EAI and ESB products. The first is the change from the hub-and-spoke model in EAI products to a bus-based model in ESB products. The hub-and-spoke model is a centralized architecture, where all data exchange is processed by a hub, or broker. The hub-and-spoke model can be seen as the successor of the point-to-point model (which we discuss in figure 1.1 in a moment). The bus model, on the other hand, uses a distributed architecture, in which the ESB functionality can be implemented by several physically separated functions.

A second main difference between EAI and ESB products is the use of open standards. EAI products like WebSphere Message Broker, TIBCO BusinessWorks, and Sonic XQ were mainly based on proprietary technology to implement messaging functionality and transformation logic. ESB products are based on open standards, such as Java Message Service (JMS), XML, J2EE Connector Architecture (JCA), and web services standards.

As we mentioned earlier, many current ESB products have a background in the EAI space. So newer versions of WebSphere Message Broker (version 6), TIBCO Business-Works (version 5), and Sonic ESB (yes, the name has changed) are now marketed as ESBs but still have a strong foundation in EAI. In addition, a number of ESBs have been built from the ground up, like WebSphere ESB, Cordys, and TIBCO ActiveMatrix Service Grid.

Because open source ESBs were not yet available during the EAI period, they don't have a history in the implementation of proprietary technology. Many integration specifications like JMS and Java Business Integration (JBI) are available, and open source ESBs use these specifications as the foundation for their open source product implementations.

But why do you need an ESB? Let's take some time to explore the benefits of an ESB. Then, in section 1.1.2 we look in greater detail at the ESB from an application perspective.

1.1.1 Benefits of an ESB

In any discussion of the implementation of an ESB within an organization or department, there's a need for a management-level overview of an ESB. In essence, an ESB is a technical product that solves integration problems. But let's try to step back from the technical aspects of an ESB and talk about some high-level benefits. To show the advantages of an ESB, we start with an overview of how applications are integrated *without* the use of an EAI broker or an ESB. This model (see figure 1.1) is known as point-to-point architecture.

The application landscape example shown in figure 1.1 is still a common way of dealing with integration problems. In this example, four existing applications are integrated via point-to-point integration solutions. For example, the enterprise resource planning (ERP) system needs to have billing information from the COBOL application.

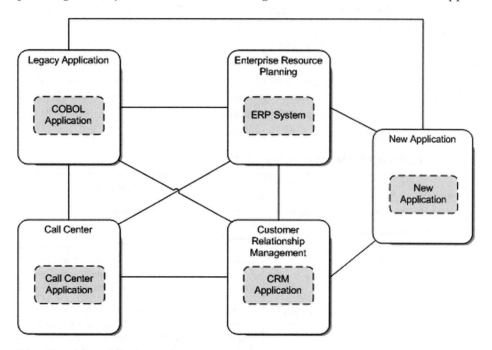

Figure 1.1 The point-to-point model describes an environment where applications are integrated with a unique and custom-made integration solution.

Because the COBOL application is only capable of exporting a file in a batch, a custom-made integration solution is being used to transfer the billing information from the exported file to the ERP system. The information also has to be transformed to a data format that the ERP system is able to process. For every line drawn between the four existing applications in figure 1.1, a custom integration solution is developed. So an important downside to the point-to-point model is the number of custom-made integration solutions that must be developed and maintained.

The complexity and maintenance cost increase when we add a new application to this application landscape. Imagine that this new application must communicate with the ERP, customer relationship management (CRM), and COBOL application as depicted in figure 1.1. This means that we need to implement three new integration solutions to be able to integrate this new application into the existing environment.

In this kind of application environment, there are many reasons to think about an integration solution like an ESB (summarized in table 1.1). Is there a business driver to integrate applications? In most organizations a real business need exists for integrating applications. New products have to be delivered to the market today, not tomorrow. And the IT environment must be able to facilitate the business to be able to do this. An ESB can help to increase the flexibility of an IT environment, and therefore can help to improve the time-to-market for new products.

Here's another reason to consider ESBs: the application landscape is heterogonous when it comes to technologies and protocols. When you have to deal with many different protocols—for example, JMS, FTP, HTTP, SOAP, SMTP, and TCP—it's difficult to implement new integration solutions between applications. An ESB provides protocol or technology adapters, which make it easy to deal with a heterogonous IT environment.

A third reason is the reduction of the total cost of ownership of the full application landscape. In a point-to-point model, the management and maintenance of all the integration points can be time-consuming and therefore expensive. It would be less time-consuming to have an ESB solution to deal with integration problems so that management and maintenance becomes easier.

Table 1.1 Reasons to start thinking about an ESB

Reason	Description
Necessity to integrate applications	There must be a clear business need to integrate applications. Time-to-market and real-time reports are examples of business drivers.
Heterogonous environment	When you have to deal with lots of different technologies and protocols, there is a clear need for a central solution that's made to deal with these challenges.
Reduction of total cost of ownership	IT departments are forced to cut maintenance costs to be able to satisfy demands for new products by the business departments. A central integration solution can help decrease the management and maintenance costs of the full application landscape.

We've discussed the point-to-point model and explained the disadvantages of this model. The introduction of an ESB to an application landscape could help to deal with the maintenance nightmare and make it easier to add new applications. Let's go back to the application environment example described in figure 1.1. The addition of an ESB to this environment is depicted in figure 1.2.

What's most striking in figure 1.2 is the reduction in the number of integration connections among the various applications. Every application is connected to the ESB, and the integration logic needed to integrate the COBOL application with the CRM application is implemented within the ESB. Note that the ESB landscape shown in figure 1.2 is just a high-level picture. The picture hides the complexity of implementing the integration logic by drawing an ESB layer, but complexity remains inside this layer that should be dealt with. The big difference with the point-to-point model is that the ESB is designed to deal with integration challenges. Because an ESB provides all kinds of integration functionality, workbenches, and management environments out of the box, implementing a new integration flow between applications is made much easier.

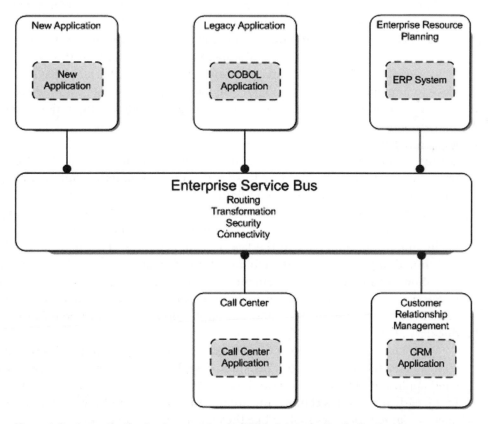

Figure 1.2 An application landscape using an ESB to integrate the applications

As shown in figure 1.2, adding a new application is also simpler than ever before. The new application is connected to the ESB with the transport protocol and technology adapter suited for this application. The integration flows that connect the new application with the three existing applications can be handled within the ESB.

This concludes our discussion about the benefits of an ESB on a high level. Let's focus a bit more on the technology aspects of an ESB, as we take a look at the ESB from an application perspective.

1.1.2   *Using an ESB from an application perspective*

With the rise of Java Message Service (JMS) as a messaging standard, most of the integration products that are currently available in the market are built with Java technology. The integration vendors, however, hide this Java technology from the integration specialist by offering fancy integration workbenches, which let you use drag-and-drop development. Therefore, integration architects and specialists working with these integration products often don't have a background in Java and Java Enterprise Edition (JEE) development.

This book focuses on a specific kind of ESB, the open source ESB. Open source ESBs are also built on JMS and other Java technologies. Although graphical tools are also available for most of the open source ESBs, as we'll see later in this book, open source ESBs are more focused on Java and XML development. In this book we show many code examples that include Java and XML snippets, because that's the typical place to implement integration logic within an open source ESB. This means that you shouldn't be afraid of doing a bit of Java coding and XML configuration when using an open source ESB.

A COMMON JEE APPLICATION ARCHITECTURE

Because you likely have a Java background, we'll look at the use of an ESB from a Java or JEE application in this section. To start this discussion, let's examine a typical JEE application architecture, as shown in figure 1.3.

The three-tier architecture approach shown in figure 1.3 is common in JEE or Microsoft .NET applications developed in business-critical environments. The division of the application logic into three layers promotes the scalability of an application and should improve the maintainability. All the functionality needed for the application shown in figure 1.3 is implemented in the three layers. The only external part necessary is a relational database to retrieve and store the information that's maintained in the application. So would this application architecture benefit from introducing an ESB?

Well, knowing that the logic implemented in this application isn't used by other applications, the answer is no. This kind of application can be categorized as an isolated application that doesn't have the need to communicate with other applications. In the early years of this century, the architecture of most applications that were developed for large businesses looked like the example shown in figure 1.3.

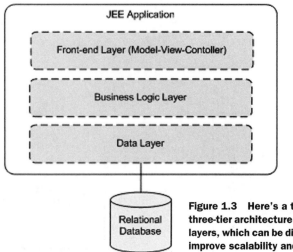

Figure 1.3 Here's a typical example of an application with a three-tier architecture. The application logic is divided into three layers, which can be distributed over multiple physical servers to improve scalability and performance if necessary.

DESCRIBING THE NEED FOR AN INTEGRATION SOLUTION

However, with the demand to improve the flexibility of business processes and the time-to-market for new products and other business drivers, applications have to be integrated. The need for a single-client view is an example of the need for application integration. Information about clients exists in many businesses scattered across different applications, like CRM applications, ERP systems, and legacy applications. When the call center of such a business needs a complete client overview, information from all these applications is necessary. And most likely, the call center application is not the only party interested in the client view. Figure 1.4 shows an overview of this single-client view example.

The example given in figure 1.4 requires a solution that's capable of retrieving the information of a specific client from the ERP, CRM, and COBOL applications and that's able to consolidate this information into a single-client view and return it to the call center application. We have multiple options for implementing such an integration solution.

ADDING AN ADDITIONAL LAYER TO THE APPLICATION

One option is to enrich the call center application with logic necessary to create the single-client view. This would mean that the application architecture shown in figure 1.3 should be extended with an integration layer. This integration layer is responsible for the retrieval of the client information from the three other applications. Although only three applications need to be integrated, a lot of integration logic is necessary. You can imagine that the connectivity necessary to integrate the legacy COBOL application is different from the connectivity needed for the ERP system. This means that the integration layer of the call center application also needs to support different connectivity protocols and likely different message formats as well. The architecture of the call center application would then look like the overview in figure 1.5.

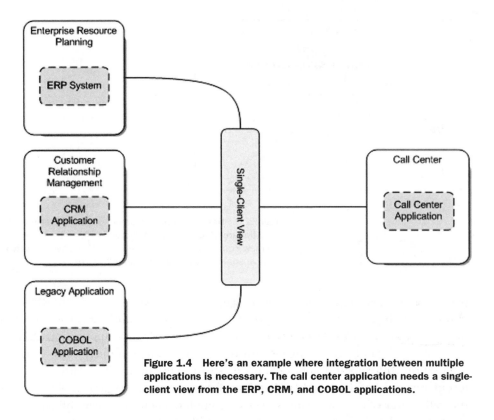

Figure 1.4 Here's an example where integration between multiple applications is necessary. The call center application needs a single-client view from the ERP, CRM, and COBOL applications.

The architecture shown in figure 1.5 is not bad per se. If the logic or data of the applications that needs to be integrated won't be needed in any other application within a department or enterprise, a separate integration solution may not be necessary. But implementing different connectivity protocols; supporting various message formats; and providing messaging, routing, and transformation functionality is a time-consuming exercise. Furthermore, dedicated software is available to solve an integration problem. This is where the ESB product comes into the picture.

USING AN ESB TO IMPLEMENT THE INTEGRATION SOLUTION

When we look at the possibilities for adding an ESB to the architecture shown in figure 1.5, it's clear that the main difference involves the size of the integration layer and the abstraction that an ESB can provide. The integration logic needed for the ERP, CRM, and COBOL applications can be implemented in the ESB solution. Furthermore, the ESB can implement the logic needed to create a single-client view. What remains in the integration layer is connectivity logic to communicate with the ESB. The advantage is that ESBs support a wide range of connectivity protocols, including industry standards like SOAP over JMS or SOAP over HTTP. Figure 1.6 shows the architecture of the call center application with the addition of an ESB for the integration with the three back-end applications.

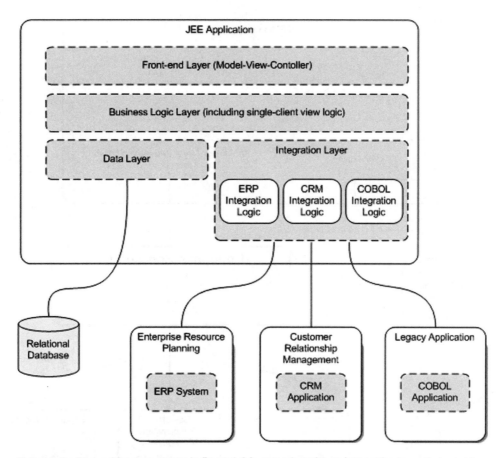

Figure 1.5   The architecture shown in figure 1.3 is extended with an integration layer that provides the logic needed to integrate with other applications.

If we compare figures 1.5 and 1.6, the main difference is where the integration logic for the back-end applications is implemented. In figure 1.5, the integration layer of the call center application implements the integration logic, which translates to a lot of custom development. With the addition of an ESB in figure 1.6, the integration logic is centralized in a software component that isn't part of the call center application. Because ESBs offer an environment that's focused on providing integration functionality, there's no need for much custom development to implement the integration with the three back-end applications.

In figure 1.6 we show a simplified overview of a call center application that's integrated with three back-end applications via an ESB. The advantages of using an ESB become clearer if we consider multiple applications that need to be integrated with, for example, the ERP system and the CRM application. The ESB has already implemented integration logic with these applications, and this logic can be reused for other applications that need information from the ERP system or to update data in the CRM application.

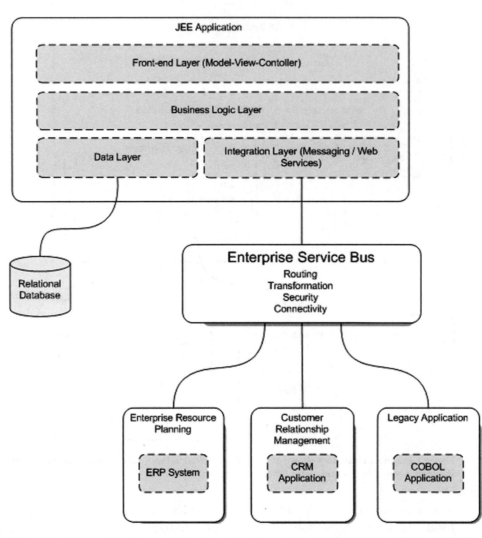

Figure 1.6   Here we introduce an ESB to the call center architecture. The ESB provides functionality to communicate with the three back-end applications and to route the message to the right back-end application.

But before we can decide when and when not to use an ESB, let's first look at the core functionality of an ESB.

1.2   *Explaining the core functionalities of an ESB*

ESB is a common integration buzzword nowadays, and there are a lot of definitions used by integration vendors, market analysts, and business users. If you want to look for these definitions, just Google "enterprise service bus" and you'll definitely find enough resources for a couple of hours' reading. We provide you with a practical overview, not an exhaustive list, of what we think are the core functionalities of an ESB. You can then use this overview to create your own definition of an ESB. Table 1.2 provides a short overview of the seven core functionalities.

Table 1.2 Overview of the core functionalities necessary in an ESB

ESB core functionality	Description
Location transparency	The ESB helps with decoupling the service consumer from the service provider location. The ESB provides a central platform to communicate with any application necessary without coupling the message sender to the message receiver.
Transport protocol conversion	An ESB should be able to seamlessly integrate applications with different transport protocols like HTTP(S) to JMS, FTP to a file batch, and SMTP to TCP.
Message transformation	The ESB provides functionality to transform messages from one format to the other based on open standards like XSLT and XPath.
Message routing	Determining the ultimate destination of an incoming message is an important functionality of an ESB that is categorized as message routing.
Message enhancement	An ESB should provide functionality to add missing information based on the data in the incoming message by using message enhancement.
Security	Authentication, authorization, and encryption functionality should be provided by an ESB for securing incoming messages to prevent malicious use of the ESB as well as securing outgoing messages to satisfy the security requirements of the service provider.
Monitoring and management	A monitoring and management environment is necessary to configure the ESB to be high-performing and reliable and also to monitor the runtime execution of the message flows in the ESB.

Next we explore each of these seven core functionalities. The first functionalities that we discuss, location transparency and transport protocol conversion, are typical examples of ESB functionality. The ordering of the other core functionalities is not really relevant.

1.2.1 *Location transparency*

When a service consumer communicates with a service provider (you can also think of an application here) via the ESB, the consumer doesn't need to know the actual location of the service provider. This means that the service consumer is decoupled from the service provider and that a service provider's new server location has no impact on the service consumer. The core functionality of an ESB that provides this capability is known as *location transparency.*

You can implement the location transparency within the ESB with a simple XML configuration, a database, or a service registry. Your approach depends on your requirements, such as dynamic configuration capabilities and the need for additional information about service providers (e.g., quality of service). The simplest implementation of location transparency is the configuration of service provider endpoints in a static XML file. This is a common way to implement location transparency in an open source ESB. When you need dynamic configuration of service provider locations, you require more advanced configuration options. Dynamic configuration can be implemented with a hot-deployment model for location configuration files or with locations stored in a database. When you have even more requirements, such as the definition of quality of service and business information about a specific service provider, a service registry can provide the necessary capabilities. In this book, we focus on the static XML file and the hot-deployment options. Figure 1.7 shows a graphical overview of the options you have available when implementing location transparency with an ESB.

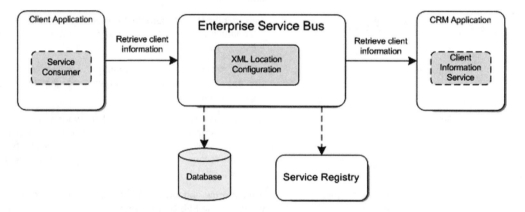

Figure 1.7   The ESB can use several options to configure and store the location of the CRM client information service. A common option is an XML file configuration, but there are alternatives, such as a database or a service registry.

Figure 1.7 shows a simple case in which an application needs client information from a CRM application. Because an ESB is used, the location of the client information service within the CRM application is transparent to the service consumer. Notice that when the location of the client information service changes, only the location configuration within the ESB has to be updated.

1.2.2   *Transport protocol conversion*

Another common scenario is one in which we have a service consumer that's using a different transport protocol than the service provider is. You can probably think of a number of cases where you have seen this in practice. Let's use an example in which we have a service consumer that's communicating via JMS. The service provider is a

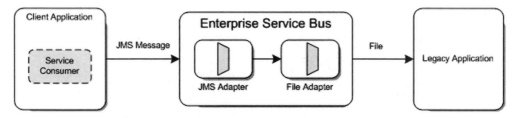

Figure 1.8 In this example a client application sends a JMS message to the ESB. A JMS adapter accepts the JMS message and forwards it to the file adapter, which writes the content of the JMS message to the file system of a legacy application.

legacy system that's only capable of importing and exporting files in a batch. Of course, we can write our own transport protocol conversion logic, but wouldn't it be great if it were offered out of the box? An ESB is capable of converting incoming transport protocols to different outgoing transport protocols; we call this ESB core functionality *transport protocol conversion.* The components in an ESB offering transport protocol conversion are typically referred to as *protocol adapters.* Figure 1.8 shows the transport protocol conversion of the example we have just discussed: JMS to File.

When dealing with environments with many different transport protocols, an ESB can offer transport protocol conversion, as shown in figure 1.8. Of course, a typical ESB doesn't support all of the transport protocols you may come across in complex integration environments, but it does support a wide variety. For protocols that aren't supported out of the box, you can purchase an adapter from third parties or develop a custom adapter.

1.2.3 *Message transformation*

Besides the support for a set of transport protocols, implementing the integration between a service consumer and a service provider often requires a transformation of the message format. In the example shown in figure 1.8, the content of the JMS message can't be forwarded as is to the legacy application. There is a need for logic that transforms the message format to the expected format of the service provider. The ESB core functionality that helps with changing the message format is known as the *message transformation* functionality.

A common technology to transform a message from the source to the target format is Extensible Stylesheet Language Transformation (XSLT). XSLT is a World Wide Web Consortium (W3C) recommendation widely adopted in the integration industry, which ensures that message transformations written in XSLT are usable in most of the ESBs available in the market. Before the age of open standards like XSLT and the use of ESBs, the EAI products, often referred to as brokers, implemented message transformation most often with proprietary technology. So message transformation is a good example of the evolution of open standards used in integration products. Let's take a look at a graphical representation of message transformation as a core functionality of an ESB in figure 1.9.

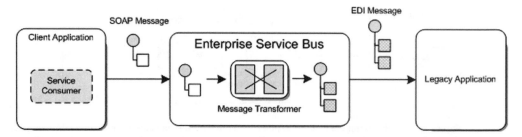

Figure 1.9   An ESB provides the capability to transform the message format of an incoming message to the format expected by the target application. In this example the ESB transforms the SOAP message to an EDI message by using a message transformer.

Message transformation, as shown in figure 1.9, is one of the most used capabilities in ESBs. It's rare that the message format of an incoming message exactly matches the format expected by the target application. The example used in figure 1.9 shows a transformation from a SOAP message to an electronic data interchange (EDI) message. The message transformer that performs the message transformation can be implemented with an XSLT style sheet as we already mentioned, but it can also be a transformation tool from a third party that's dedicated to supporting all kinds of EDI-related transformations. Alternatively, you can write your own with the application programming interface (API) provided with your ESB product. In chapter 5, we explore how message transformation can be implemented with a number of examples.

1.2.4   *Message routing*

In our examples so far, the target destination of the incoming message was just one possible service provider. But in most integration projects, multiple applications are involved that could be the target application of a particular incoming message. Based on many kinds of rules and logic, the ESB has to determine which service provider(s) a message must be sent to. The core functionality involved with dealing with this kind of logic is known as *message routing*.

This message routing functionality is a classification for different kinds of routing capabilities. There is, for example, content-based routing, which is used for routing messages to their ultimate destination based on their content. But there is also the message filter routing functionality, which is used to prevent certain messages from being sent to a particular destination. A third example is the recipient list routing capability, which can be used to send a particular message to multiple destinations. Message routing is the ESB core functionality needed in almost every integration implementation. Figure 1.10 shows an example of message routing based on the content of an incoming message.

Message routing can be complex and difficult to implement because knowledge of the routing rules and logic involved is often spread across different people. It's difficult to explain the use of routing rules to businesspeople, although their business

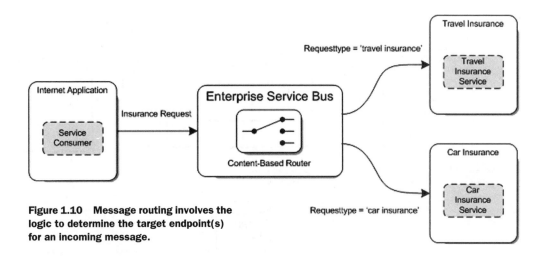

Figure 1.10   Message routing involves the logic to determine the target endpoint(s) for an incoming message.

domain is essential for the definition of a routing rule. The rules and logic involved with message routing is, however, related to the functionality of the applications that are integrated. Therefore, a deep understanding of the applications involved in an integration project is often necessary to specify the proper routing rules. The example given in figure 1.10 is just a simple one, designed to show what we mean by message routing and content-based routing. In figure 1.10 the insurance request consists of an element named requesttype that specifies the kind of insurance request applied for by the customer using the internet application. Based on the value of this element, the message is routed to the travel or the car insurance service. We'll look at different routing examples in greater detail later in this book, starting with chapter 5.

1.2.5   *Message enhancement*

The message transformation process can change a source message format to a target message format. But to be able to create the correct outgoing message that will be sent to the target application, you may have to add additional data or convert the existing data. A common way to add data to a message is by retrieving it from a database based on certain element values of the incoming message. An example of such an element is a *client identifier.* The destination of the incoming message with the client identifier can be an application that requires some extra client information that's not available in the incoming message. The ESB can then retrieve this information from a database based on the client identifier in the incoming message. For data conversion, more custom development is needed in most cases. A data conversion example is where the length of the client name has to be reduced to a maximum length of 40 characters. This functionality requires a clear message-handling API so that the retrieval and update of a particular message element is made easy for a developer.

The functionality described here can be categorized as a *message enhancement* capability and is closely related to message transformation. The main difference between these functionalities is that message transformation deals with data that's already

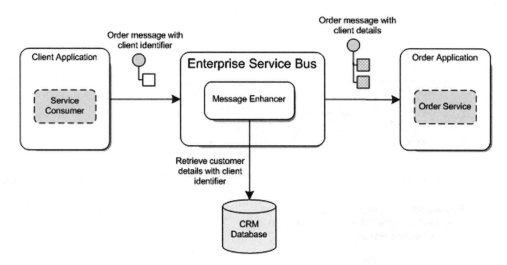

Figure 1.11   In this example of message enhancement, an order message with a client identifier is sent by a client application. The ESB retrieves the customer details from the CRM database using the client identifier with message enhancement capability.

available in the incoming message, and message enhancement deals with data that must be retrieved from a (external) data source, for example a database. Figure 1.11 shows an example of message enhancement.

The example shown in figure 1.11 uses a message enhancer that retrieves client information from a database based on the client identifier provided by the incoming message. In this typical example, the ESB needs to provide functionality to connect to a database and perform a query with parameters provided in the configuration settings. Another functionality that's used often and that's part of message enhancement is that some custom logic is performed against the incoming message. This custom logic can be implemented with, for example, Java code to retrieve data from an external database. We'll discuss the functionality of message enhancement in greater detail in chapter 5.

1.2.6   *Security*

Because ESBs often deal with business-critical integration logic that involves a substantial number of applications, an ESB must provide ways to authenticate and authorize incoming messages. For messages that may be intercepted for malicious purposes, encryption is an important feature that an ESB must be able to provide. When an ESB doesn't apply a security model for its environment, everybody who can send messages to the starting point of an integration flow, such as a message queue or a web service, is able to start this flow with possibly malicious messages. In most situations, an ESB is an internally oriented environment, which means that it's not accessible from outside the organization boundaries, due to firewall settings. This means that possible malicious

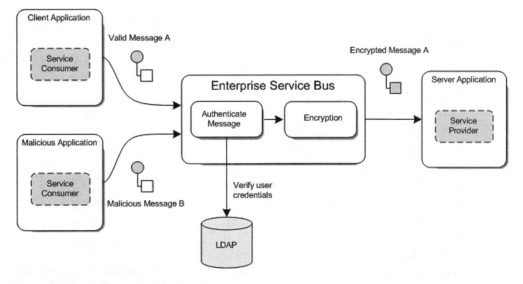

Figure 1.12   Security involves the confidentiality, integrity, and availability of messages sent over the ESB. This example shows an implementation of confidentiality via an authentication mechanism.

messages can only arrive from within the IT environment of the organization. But when an ESB also offers starting points of integration flows to applications outside the boundaries of the organization, security is even more important.

Let's first look at an example of security within an ESB (see figure 1.12).

The example in figure 1.12 shows how the authentication inside an ESB can be implemented. Besides authentication, authorization can also be configured for an integration flow. By using authorization, the functionality of a service provider can be secured on a method level so that, for example, a group of users can be granted different access than an administrator user. Our example also implements encryption for the outgoing message before it's sent to the service provider. This is another part of the security functionality an ESB should be able to implement. Service providers can have all kinds of security measures implemented, and an ESB should be able to construct an outgoing message that has the right security values set. For example, to ensure that a message can't be read by other parties, a message can be encrypted with the public key of the service provider in the ESB, as in the example in figure 1.12. As you can see, security is a broad topic. In chapter 8 we discuss how security can be implemented in an ESB with a number of practical examples.

1.2.7   *Monitoring and management*

The last ESB core functionality that we examine involves managing an ESB environment. This core functionality is different from the ones we've discussed, as the others were focused on development and runtime capabilities of an ESB. This section focuses on the ability to maintain and manage an ESB.

Because an ESB is a critical piece in a system landscape, the environment must be managed and monitored. This is not that different from application servers hosting JEE applications, but an ESB usually integrates a large set of applications not only limited to a Java domain. Therefore, if the message size in a queue is exceeding a certain limit, for example, that must be detected as early as possible. We categorize this functionality as *monitoring and management*. A graphical representation of this ESB core functionality appears in figure 1.13.

Managing and monitoring an ESB environment can become complex because of the large set of capabilities an ESB provides. Therefore, the management and monitoring functionality consists of multiple parts, and each is responsible for a component of the ESB. For the messaging layer in the ESB, the management and monitoring environment will, for instance, involve managing the queues and monitoring the message size and message throughput of queues. For web services provided by the ESB, monitoring will involve such things as whether the web service is up and running and how many calls are made per minute; management will address the number of instances that are running for a web service. In chapter 10, we explore examples involving the management and monitoring capabilities of an ESB.

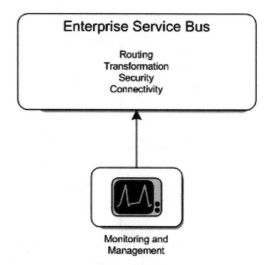

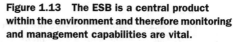

Figure 1.13   The ESB is a central product within the environment and therefore monitoring and management capabilities are vital.

1.2.8   *Core functionality overview*

Well, we covered quite a bit of ground in this section; we hope we didn't overwhelm you with a theoretical discussion of the core functionality of an ESB. We wrote this book with a practical goal in mind: to show how ESBs and, in particular open source ESBs, can be used for your own purposes. But we think that a book about ESBs should begin with a clear definition of what an ESB is and what it should do. This section defines seven core functionalities an ESB should provide at the very least. These core functionalities are by no means a complete list; we didn't yet mention orchestration and transaction handling. These functionalities are important, but we chose the keep the list of core functionalities short—just enough to provide a good picture of what an ESB is. In the remaining chapters, we discuss other functionalities.

You should now be able to arrive at your own opinion as to what an ESB is and how it compares to the definition you found on the internet. You can see that some definitions are difficult to understand, and some define an ESB as the ultimate integration solution. But let's end our theoretical discussion of ESB functionality and move on to practical implementations. Next we present an overview of available open source ESBs.

1.3　*Researching the open source ESB market*

A lot of definitions you find on the internet are from vendors who are selling ESBs for a substantial license fee. Because this book is about open source ESBs, we first discuss the differences between *closed source* (products with a license fee and a confidential source) and open source ESBs based on the core functionalities we've discussed.

As we see in section 1.3.2, quite a few options are available in the open source market. To provide a good overview of the available open source ESBs, we introduce the most important ones in short sections. But let's begin with a discussion of some open source ESBs myths. We include this short discussion because there's a lack of clarity within the integration market about open source products.

1.3.1　*Demystifying the open source ESB*

Let's first specify what we mean by open source and so-called closed source ESBs. When we talk about closed source ESBs, we're referring to ESB products that have a usage-based license fee and for which the source code is not freely available. Open source ESBs do have a license (like the Apache or GPL license), but don't have a usage-based license fee and the source code is freely available. Although the open source ESB itself is available for free, services and support can be provided for a fee.

Therefore, open source ESBs can be provided by a commercial vendor just like closed source ESBs. Good examples of companies making money with open source ESBs are MuleSource (the company behind Mule) and IONA Technologies (which offers support and training for Apache ServiceMix with its FUSE ESB product). So let's explode the myth that open source ESBs lack support and training options. The open source ESBs discussed in this book, Mule and ServiceMix, have company backing that provides 24/7 support and can offer training.

A second myth is that open source projects in general, including open source ESBs, are led by geeks who are developing interesting pieces of software, but lack a quality assurance (QA) model, a decent release roadmap, and a delivery process. Of course, open source development means that developers are often working full-time in their day-to-day job and are developing the open source projects in their spare time. However, there's a movement in which full-time open source developers work for a company to offer support and training for an open source project. Again, good examples include MuleSource and IONA; in addition, WSO_2 (with Apache Synapse) and Sun Microsystems (with Open ESB) fit this picture.

Because all decent open source projects use a bug-tracking environment like Atlassian's JIRA (which identifies all closed and open bugs and also provides information about the release schedule), a solid foundation for QA is laid. In addition, good unit tests, a continuous build environment, and an active community pave the way to well-tested and community-driven releases. With a release roadmap, which consists of several release candidates, the quality of the open source ESB can be guaranteed. The community behind the open source ESB is involved in the delivery process of a new version. So in conclusion, the great thing about open source projects is that the QA model is open for everyone and that you are able to test new releases early in the release process.

The last myth that we want to discuss is that open source ESBs lack tool support for development and testing. Closed source ESBs provide integration workbenches to give developers an abstraction layer that hides the technical implementation. The integration workbench provides drag-and-drop development interfaces and wizards to create integration flows. This means that the developer is more or less guided in the design and implementation of an integration flow. For open source ESBs, the tool support is more basic, with a focus on XML configuration and Java development. This means more or less that there's no abstraction layer to hide the technical implementation. Developers working with open source ESBs therefore need to have more development knowledge to implement integration flows. But this also gives developers greater freedom in implementing integration logic for their integration solution. And because enterprise integration is difficult and often requires custom integration logic, this can be very welcome.

But does this mean that the myth about tool support is true? No, tool support is available that can ease the development effort when working with open source ESBs. In appendix C we show two examples of tool projects that provide graphical support for constructing message flows for Mule and ServiceMix. And in chapter 11 we examine two tools that provide graphical drag-and-drop support to construct processes that can be deployed on Mule and ServiceMix. So the tool support is growing and will be enhanced in the near future, but admittedly there's some catching up to do when compared to the closed source ESB product offerings. In table 1.3 the myths about open ESBs are summarized.

Table 1.3   Overview of the myths about open source ESBs

Myth	Short description
Lack of support and training	Just like the closed source ESBs, 24/7 support and training are available for open source ESBs. Companies like MuleSource, IONA, WSO2, Sun, JBoss, and EBM Websourcing provide support and training for specific open source ESBs.
Lack of QA, a decent release calendar, and a delivery process	Open source ESBs that we examine in section 1.3.2 have an excellent bug-tracking system, provide unit tests, and are backed by an active community. In addition, a core team of developers is often working full-time on the development of the open source ESB. Therefore, the QA model and release process are well implemented and also open to everyone who is interested.

Table 1.3   Overview of the myths about open source ESBs *(continued)*

Myth	Short description
Lack of tool support	Open source projects are not famous for their tool support. This is not different for most open source ESBs, so Java and XML skills are mandatory for open source integration developers. Tool support is, however, growing, and the NetBeans support for open ESB is a great example of an open source ESB with good tool support.

Now, let's look at the best-of-breed open source ESBs currently available.

1.3.2   Overview of open source ESBs

In just a couple of years, we've seen quite a few open source ESBs arrive on the market. The adoption of open standards and Java specifications like JMS, JCA, XML, JBI, SOAP, and others paved the way for the development of open source ESBs. With the specifications available for everyone who is interested, the only things lacking were implementations of these specifications. A number of open source projects started to implement specifications like JMS and JBI. These projects provided the foundation to build open source ESBs, and eventually several open source ESB projects were launched.

The problem with providing an overview of open source projects for a particular technology or functionality is that there are so many projects out there. This isn't different for open source ESBs. Therefore, we have only listed the open source ESBs that received a lot of attention on the internet and in the integration market. Another criterion is that we focused on the open source projects provided by a substantial community, such as Apache, Codehaus, Java.net, and JBoss.

MULE

After doing the same donkey work at a number of integration projects for setting up an integration infrastructure, Ross Mason decided to define a reusable integration platform named Mule (http://mule.codehaus.org). Basing his work on Gregor Hohpe and Bobby Woolf's book *Enterprise Integration Patterns* (Addison-Wesley Professional, 2003), Mason implemented a lightweight messaging framework. The central part of Mule is the service definitions, which implement the integration logic.

These services can consist of an inbound and outbound element to configure the input and output connectivity. A service can also consist of a component, which can be implemented with all kinds of technologies, including Java and Spring beans. This is a big selling point for Java developers who are looking for an integration framework. Most of the development work with Mule can be implemented with Java classes, and the messages that flow through the Mule container can be Java messages. Figure 1.14 gives an overview of the functionality provided by Mule.

Mule offers connectivity for more than 20 transport protocols and integrates with a large number of integration projects, including Spring, ActiveMQ, Joram, CXF, Axis,

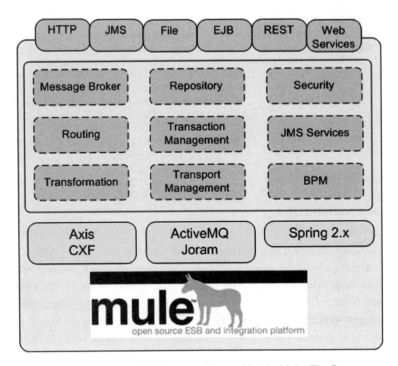

Figure 1.14   Overview of the functionality provided by Mule. The figure shows some examples of open source frameworks that can be integrated with Mule, including CXF and ActiveMQ.

and Drools. Mule chose to not build their architecture on JBI, but implemented their own flexible and lightweight model, focusing on productivity and ease of development. After the 1.0 release of Mule in 2005, Mule received more and more market attention over the years, resulting in the creation of MuleSource (http://www.mulesource.com), which provides professional services and support for Mule. This product is currently used by a large number of companies around the world, including WalMart, Hewlett-Packard, Sony, Deutsche Bank, and CitiBank.

Mule provides connectivity with JBI containers via a JBI adapter implementation. But the next open source ESB, Apache ServiceMix, is fully based on the JBI specification.

APACHE SERVICEMIX
The foundation for Apache ServiceMix is the JBI specification delivered by the Java Community Process (JCP) under Java Specification Request (JSR) 208 in 2005. The purpose of JBI is to define a standard for an integration platform that consists of components from multiple vendors and open source projects (in order to prevent vendor lock-in). For integration products adhering to the JBI specification, it should be possible to build JBI components that can be deployed on all these JBI-based products. A salient detail of the JSR 208 vote was that IBM and BEA abstained, and even today these companies have no integration product adhering to the JBI specification.

For more details about the JBI specification, see chapter 2, where we discuss the architecture of ServiceMix. Figure 1.15 gives an overview of the functionality provided by ServiceMix.

After the JBI specification was accepted by the JCP, in late 2005 the Apache Service-Mix project was introduced as an incubator project at Apache. The goal of ServiceMix is to provide an ESB that implements the JBI specification, with a focus on flexibility, reliability, and breadth of connectivity. ServiceMix includes a large set of JBI components that together supply the ESB core functionalities listed in section 1.2. Included are JBI components that support protocols like JMS, HTTP, and FTP, as well as components that implement Hohpe's patterns of enterprise integration, rules, and scheduling.

In September 2007 the Apache ServiceMix project became a top-level Apache project. The ServiceMix product can be integrated with a number of other Apache projects. Apache ActiveMQ is the messaging foundation, which provides reliability and makes possible a distributed environment and clustering. ServiceMix can also be integrated with Apache CXF, Apache ODE, Apache Camel, Apache Geronimo, JBoss, and any web container. ServiceMix is deployed in many large enterprises around the world, including Raytheon, British Telecom, CVS/Pharmacy, Cisco Systems, and Sabre Holdings, just to name a few.

LogicBlaze was the professional services, support, and training company behind Apache ServiceMix and Apache ActiveMQ. Some of the core developers of ActiveMQ and ServiceMix were employed by LogicBlaze. In 2006, LogicBlaze was acquired by IONA Technologies, which now provides support, services, and training for ServiceMix and other Apache projects via its FUSE ESB product. The FUSE ESB is an open source

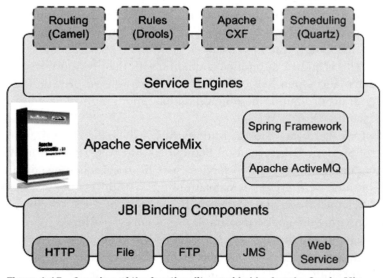

Figure 1.15   Overview of the functionality provided by Apache ServiceMix

product based on ServiceMix and includes other products based on Apache ActiveMQ, Apache Camel, and Apache CXF.

OPEN ESB

The two previous examples of open source ESBs currently available are hosted by open source communities, Mule at Codehaus and ServiceMix at Apache. Open ESB is an ESB initiative started by Sun Microsystems and is hosted as a Java.net project. All of the committers of the Open ESB project are employees of Sun Microsystems. Like the ServiceMix ESB implementation, Open ESB is also an implementation of the JBI specification. The Open ESB project is an umbrella project that includes a number of subprojects. One subproject implements a JBI runtime environment that was started to provide a JBI implementation for Sun's Glassfish application server. Other subprojects provide JBI components such as a JMS binding component and a Business Process Execution Language (BPEL) service engine.

This kind of functionality is also provided by ServiceMix, but one difference is that Open ESB is focused on the Glassfish application server and ServiceMix can be easily deployed on the Apache Geronimo or the JBoss application servers. However, the main difference between Open ESB and other ESB implementations like ServiceMix is the tooling support. Because Sun can build upon its NetBeans IDE, it can provide wizards for building JBI components and design the dependencies between these components. In 2007 the NetBeans IDE was enriched quite impressively as part of Sun's open source strategy. An Enterprise package is available that, among other things, provides a BPEL editor, a Web Services Description Language (WSDL) editor, and a Composite Application Service Assembly (CASA) editor. The CASA editor provides a drag-and-drop interface for designing a JBI service assembly.

APACHE SYNAPSE

One can question if Apache Synapse actually is a true ESB, but based on the core functionalities that we list in section 1.2, Synapse *can* be called an ESB. In essence, Synapse is a web services mediation framework that is built upon Apache Axis2, the web services container. This is quite a difference compared with the previously discussed ESBs (Mule, ServiceMix, and Open ESB). The focus of Synapse is to provide functionality such as routing, transformation, message validation, and a registry based on web services and XML standards.

As a part of standardization organizations such as OASIS (Organization for the Advancement of Structured Information Standards) and W3C (the World Wide Web Consortium), an enormous set of web services specifications is being standardized. A few examples of these web services specifications are WS-Addressing, WS-Security, WS-Policy, and WS-Reliable Messaging. Based on the naming of these specifications, you can pretty much extract the goal: for example, WS-Security provides a specification for things like message encryption and authentication, and WS-Reliable Messaging shows how messages between web services can be exchanged in a reliable way. These web services standards are quite complex in general, and as a developer, you aren't always interested in dealing with the exact syntax and semantics of a web services standard.

So besides offering ESB core functionalities such as routing, transformation, and a registry, Synapse can provide the necessary abstraction to use complex web services standards. Here's an example of this abstraction layer: with only two lines of XML configuration, Synapse is able to execute a message exchange with a WS-Reliable messaging enabled web service. The same abstraction is provided for WS-Security and other web services standards.

The primary connectivity options are SOAP over HTTP and JMS, but other options such as SMTP are also possible. Early in 2007, Synapse graduated from the incubator status to become a full member of the Apache web services project. When dealing with integration problems in a web services area, Synapse provides the necessary functionality.

JBoss ESB

JBoss ESB is widely known for its popular application server and successful open source projects such as Hibernate, an object relational mapping (ORM) framework; Seam, an application framework for building Web 2.0 applications; and jBPM, a process engine. In the area of enterprise integration, JBoss provides a JMS provider called JBossMQ and a rules engine, JBoss Rules. In mid-2006, JBoss acquired an ESB product, Rosetta, that was used as a messaging backbone for a large insurance provider in Canada. Based on Rosetta, JBoss developed a product called JBoss ESB, which provides most of the core functionalities listed in section 1.2.

With the addition of the JBoss ESB product, a complete integration architecture can be implemented based on JBoss products. The messaging layer of JBoss ESB is called JBoss Messaging (the successor of JBossMQ), a JMS provider implementation. The routing functionality of JBoss ESB is based on the rules engine, JBoss Rules, and the orchestration functionality is provided by the jBPM process engine. For custom logic and web services support, Enterprise JavaBeans (EJB) 3 or Plain Old Java Object (POJO) components can be developed that can be deployed on a JBoss application server.

OW2 PETALS

We've discussed three open source ESBs that implement the JBI specification. With PEtALS we introduce the fourth and last JBI-based open source ESB. PEtALS, which was officially JBI certified by Sun Microsystems in March 2008, provides many connectivity options out of the box. In 2005, architects and EAI experts from EBM Websourcing were unsatisfied with existing integration solutions and decided to launch an open source project named PEtALS. In the following years, the open source ESB gradually supported more connectivity options like JMS, SMTP, file, SOAP, and FTP support.

The PEtALS architecture is focused on providing a distributed environment where different PEtALS instances are seamlessly integrated into one ESB environment. This means that services hosted on different instances are able to access one another without additional configuration. Another selling point is the web-based monitoring tool, whereby JBI components can be managed and your message flows can be deployed and managed. We show an example of this monitoring application in chapter 10.

APACHE TUSCANY

Apache Tuscany is a good example of a product that doesn't use the term *ESB* in its project description but that does provide many of the core functionalities listed in section 1.2. This Apache project is an implementation of the Service Component Architecture (SCA) specification, which is hosted by 18 companies, among them BEA, IBM, Interface21, Oracle, and Sun (http://www.osoa.org). The SCA specification is currently being standardized by OASIS. The goal of the SCA specification is to define services in a vendor-, technology-, and protocol-neutral way.

The specification describes a Service Component Definition Language (SCDL) XML configuration in which you can define service components. A service component has a particular implementation (Java, PHP, BPEL, Ruby script, and so on) and exposes this functionality via service interfaces. A service component is able to communicate with other components and services through service references. Figure 1.16 provides a schematic overview of service components as defined in the SCA specification.

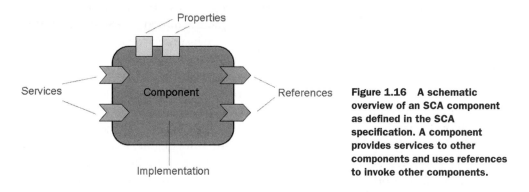

Figure 1.16   A schematic overview of an SCA component as defined in the SCA specification. A component provides services to other components and uses references to invoke other components.

Until this point we haven't seen a lot of overlap with ESB functionality. However, the service interfaces and service references have a binding type attached to them. A binding type can, for example, be a web service, a JMS component, an EJB, or a JCA adaptor. This means that you are able to expose a Java component as a web service. This provides all kinds of connectivity options that can also be seen in ESB products. When we compare this functionality with the JBI specification, it is similar to the binding components concept. On the other hand, an SCA component could be perfectly suited as a JBI service engine implementation.

We decided not to include SCA and Apache Tuscany in the remaining chapters of the book, although SCA is an interesting specification. We consider SCA to be a specification that is focused on implementing services as part of a SOA. Therefore, it doesn't fit in the open source ESB topic of this book.

SPRING INTEGRATION

Another interesting open source integration framework initiative is the Spring Integration framework, which was announced by SpringSource, the company that provides support and services for the Spring Framework, in December 2007 (http://www.spring-source.com/web/guest/2007/springintegration). Spring already provided support for integration projects with JMS templates and web services, but with the Spring Integration project, the strength of the integration functionality is centralized within an abstraction layer, which eases development.

The integration functionality provided by Spring Integration is based on the patterns found in the *Enterprise Integration Patterns* book. With a simple Spring XML and annotations-based model, Spring beans can be utilized in an integration environment. At the time of this writing, there is no 1.0 release yet, but when this book hits the shelves we feel certain there will be a first production release available. In chapter 4 we offer a sneak preview of what you can expect from the Spring Integration framework.

OTHER OPEN SOURCE ESBS

A number of open source ESBs are part of an offering from companies with a smaller community. We've mentioned FUSE ESB (provided by IONA), but there are other examples, such as WSO2's Enterprise Service Bus, which is based on the Apache Synapse product.

Other open source ESBs that we did not mention yet are ChainBuilder ESB, a project by Bostech focused on tool support, and the OpenAdapter platform, which provides support for all kinds of transport protocols and enterprise integration functionality like transformation, validation, and data filtering. Table 1.4 offers an overview of the open source ESBs.

Table 1.4   Open source ESB overview

Open source ESB	Website	Short description
Apache ServiceMix	http://servicemix.apache.org	Apache JBI implementation with a lot of JBI components
Apache Synapse	http://ws.apache.org/synapse	ESB focused on web services support based on Apache Axis2
Apache Tuscany	http://tuscany.apache.org/	Implementation of the (SCA) specification
ChainBuilder ESB	http://www.chainforge.net/	A JBI-based ESB that focuses on providing graphical tools to ease the development effort
FUSE ESB	http://open.iona.com/products/fuse-esb/	IONA's open source ESB offering based on Apache ServiceMix
JBoss ESB	http://labs.jboss.com/jbossesb/	The JBoss implementation of an ESB based on JBoss messaging
Mule	http://www.mulesource.org	Lightweight ESB with a custom implementation model

Table 1.4   Open source ESB overview *(continued)*

Open source ESB	Website	Short description
OpenAdapter	https://www.openadaptor.org/	EAI-based platform that provides a number of adaptors to implement integration solutions
Open ESB	https://open-esb.dev.java.net	JBI implementation provided by Sun that provides great tool support with NetBeans
PEtALS	http://petals.objectweb.org/	Another JBI-based ESB, hosted by OW2 (formerly ObjectWeb)
Spring Integration	http://www.springframework.org/spring-integration	An integration framework that is provided by the well-known Spring Framework
WSO2 ESB	http://wso2.com/products/esb/	WSO2's open source ESB offering based on Apache Synapse

As you can see in table 1.4, the open source ESB options are substantial. Now that we've taken a quick look at a number of open source ESBs, it's time to discuss why we chose Mule and ServiceMix for this book.

1.4   *Why did we choose Mule and ServiceMix?*

To make an objective choice, we define the criteria that we've found are important when choosing an open source ESB.

1.4.1   *Defining selection criteria*

The first criterion is quite obvious; we defined a list of core functionalities that should be present in an ESB in section 1.2, so the ESB of our choice has to provide support for all these capabilities.

An important criterion that's often neglected by open source projects is the quality of the documentation available. Of course, the source is available for everyone to look into, but developers need good-quality documentation when using an ESB.

Another criterion is the market visibility of the open source ESB. This includes the availability of articles on the internet as well as the number of implementations in businesses.

When working with an open source product, you may run into bugs or enhancement requests. Therefore, it's important that an open source product be able to rely on an active community that can provide support for questions and solve bugs and that's capable of including enhancement requests in future releases.

Another important criterion for open source ESBs is the flexibility and the development effort needed to implement custom logic. Integration projects often need to deal with unique requirements, due to the specific environment for a particular business, so custom logic may be necessary for an integration solution. It should therefore be a minimal effort to implement your own piece of Java code.

Because an ESB is a central component that must be able to integrate applications implemented with different technologies, the transport and connectivity options provided by an ESB are key. An important criterion when selecting an ESB is whether it can provide the connectivity you need in your own IT environment. Developing custom transports requires a lot of expertise and development effort that could be provided out of the box.

This criterion has some common ground with another important capability of an ESB: the ability to integrate with other open source projects. Because there's a wide variety of open source projects available that provide solutions for all kinds of integration challenges, it's important that the ESB of your choice be able to integrate with these projects. There are, for example, ESBs that integrate with the Spring framework out of the box, which can provide you with a lot of additional functionality you may need.

Another criterion that we want to share with you is the support for implementing your integration solution via an IDE. The tool support for open source projects is something that has room for improvement. However, with the availability of Eclipse and NetBeans as IDE platforms, this support is improving more and more. The development effort needed to build a robust interface capable of configuring an ESB is quite extensive. Therefore, many open source ESBs are focusing more on the runtime functionality than on increasing developer productivity via GUIs. Having said this, a drag-and-drop user interface doesn't necessarily improve a developers' productivity.

1.4.2 Assessing the open source ESBs

We should now be able to classify five of the open source ESBs listed in section 1.3.2 with the eight criteria that we have discussed. Notice we don't include Tuscany, Spring Integration, or any of the vendor-based ESBs like FUSE and WSO2 ESB. We consider the open source ESBs listed here as the best-of-breed products currently available. The following list discusses the eight criteria (two criteria are discussed together) for the five open source ESBs:

- *ESB core functionality*—Mule and ServiceMix provide good support for the core functionalities. Open ESB isn't yet there with message routing and message enhancement. In the areas of monitoring and management, there is still room for improvement in all ESBs.
- *Quality of documentation*—The documentation of Mule is the most complete. The examples in ServiceMix's documentation are sometimes outdated. Open ESB's documentation is excellent and offers screenshots and clear examples, but they are focused on BPEL. Synapse provides good examples and documentation.

- *Market visibility*—The number of implementations at businesses around the world is starting to increase. Mule has a head start, because it can rely on a large number of implementations of its product and is receiving a lot of attention in the market. ServiceMix has also received a lot of attention, because it is the best-known open source JBI implementation and an Apache project. For the other ESBs, the market visibility is increasing but has some catching up to do compared with Mule and ServiceMix.

- *Active development and support community*—The communities of the five open source ESBs are in general quite active, and support is available from commercial parties as well as forums. Mule has an active development community and is able to provide support via MuleSource. The same is true for ServiceMix, with support offered by IONA. The community for the other open source ESBs is a bit smaller but is growing.

- *Custom logic*—Most of the reviewed ESBs provide good support for adding custom logic. Mule, ServiceMix, and Synapse make it easy to add your own piece of logic, because you can easily integrate POJOs. With Open ESB the focus is not yet on supporting developers to write custom logic, but on writing binding components and service engines.

- *Transport protocols and connectivity options and integration capabilities with open source frameworks*—Most of the transport protocol and connectivity support is offered by integrating other open source products with the ESB. ServiceMix and Mule provide the widest range of connectivity and open source product support. Synapse and PEtALS also offer a nice set of transport protocols and open source products. For Open ESB, the capabilities and support is increasing but is not so impressive yet.

- *Tool support*—Open ESB has excellent IDE support with NetBeans. Some of the other ESBs provide some Eclipse plug-ins, like the Mule 2.0 IDE and the Eclipse STP Enterprise Integration Designer, but these tools don't offer the same level of quality as the Open ESB IDE support.

Table 1.5 shows an overview of five open source ESBs that meet these criteria.

Table 1.5 An assessment summary of the five open source ESBs related to the selection criteria. The notation used in this classification is simple: ++ is very good, + is good, +/– is average, – is not well supported, and — is not supported at all.

Selection criterion	Mule	ServiceMix	Open ESB	Synapse	PEtALS
1. Support for ESB core functionality: location transparency, transport protocol conversion, transformation, routing, message enhancement, security, and monitoring and management	+	+	+/–	+	+
2. Well-written documentation	+	+/–	+	+	+/–

Table 1.5 An assessment summary of the five open source ESBs related to the selection criteria. The notation used in this classification is simple: ++ is very good, + is good, +/– is average, – is not well supported, and — is not supported at all. *(continued)*

Selection criterion	Mule	ServiceMix	Open ESB	Synapse	PEtALS
3. Market visibility	++	+	+/–	+/–	+/–
4. Active development and support community	++	+	+/–	+	+
5. Flexible and easily extendable with custom logic	++	+	+/–	++	+
6. Support for a wide range of transport protocols and connectivity options	+	+	+/–	+/–	+
7. Integration with other open source projects	++	++	+/–	+	+
8. Productivity with IDE support	+	+	++	+/–	+

Notice that the classification is a snapshot in time of these open source ESBs and has some subjective parts in it. Based on the selection criteria we have used, Mule is the winner and ServiceMix is a good second. Because we think that both ESBs provide a unique implementation model and complement each other, we use both Mule and ServiceMix in the examples for this book. We've also seen that a number of open source ESBs are based on JBI. So with the choice of ServiceMix as a JBI implementation example and of Mule as a Java-based model example, we have representatives for both models that currently dominate the open source ESB products. We don't limit this book to only Mule and ServiceMix; we also give short examples of the other ESBs mentioned in section 1.3.2 when appropriate.

Up to this point, we've talked quite a bit about the theory of an ESB, the difference between open source and closed source ESBs, and our choice to use two open source ESBs in this book, Mule and ServiceMix. It's time to see some action, don't you think?

1.5 *Hello world with Mule and ServiceMix*

We wrap up this chapter with a simple example of both Mule and ServiceMix as a teaser for the examples we give in later chapters. This example isn't about a complex integration challenge; rather, it polls for new files in one directory and writes the polled file to another directory. We use this simple file polling and writing example to illustrate the basics of Mule and ServiceMix without having to go into detail about difficult and challenging steps of the integration solution. A graphical representation of the "hello world" style example is shown in figure 1.17.

In this section, we begin by downloading the Mule and ServiceMix distributions to implement the basic example shown in figure 1.17. You're welcome to join us when

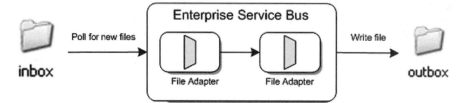

Figure 1.17   A hello world example with an ESB that polls for new files in the inbox directory and writes the polled files to a directory named outbox.

configuring the simple file integration solution, but you can also just look at the code listings. The idea is just to show you a bit of Mule and ServiceMix before we take a deep dive in chapter 2.

1.5.1   Taking a donkey ride with Mule

Our donkey ride starts with the setup of the book's environment by downloading the source code file from the Manning website (or you can use our own website, http://www.esbinaction.com).

Setting up the environment

Once you've downloaded the source code file, you'll notice that there is no actual source code in the downloaded file. The downloaded file contains an Ant build file that will download Mule, ServiceMix, and a lot of other tools and frameworks used in this book. The Ant script will also download the source code of the book and set up the Eclipse projects. Note that the script's execution takes quite some time, due to necessary downloads.

Unpack the downloaded file in a directory like c:/osesbinaction for Windows or /osesbinaction for Unix. Now execute the ant command from the root directory of the unpacked file. Mule, ServiceMix, other tools and frameworks, and the source code of this book will be downloaded for you. For detailed information about Java and Ant versions and the resulting environment of this script, you should read chapter 3, but for this chapter you will be good to go.

In this book we use Mule version 2.0.2 (the current production release of Mule version 2). For an overview of the differences between Mule 1.*x* and 2.*x*, check out appendix B of this book.

INSTALLING MULE
In the previous step, by running the Ant script provided in the source code of this book, we already installed the Mule ESB by unpacking the Mule 2.0.2 distribution in the esb/mule-2.0.2 directory. The unpacked distribution should look like the directory structure shown in figure 1.18.

The directory structure shown in figure 1.18 isn't complex. The bin directory consists of scripts to start and stop Mule. For settings like log levels and internal configurations, the files in the conf directory should be explored. Then there are two directories to get more information on how Mule works: in docs, the Javadoc is available, and in the examples directory, you find examples of Mule in use. The lib directory contains the libraries that make up Mule and possibly custom JARs. The licenses directory holds the licenses of the libraries used by Mule, the logs directory contains logging information, and the src directory contains the Mule sources.

Now that we've discussed the contents of the Mule distribution, we've almost finished with the installation. We only have to set the MULE_HOME environment variable to the Mule installation directory before we can run Mule from the command line.

📁 bin
📁 conf
📁 docs
📁 examples
📁 lib
📁 licenses
📁 logs
📁 src
📄 INSTALL.txt
📄 LICENSE.txt
📄 USAGE.txt

Figure 1.18 The directory structure of the unpacked Mule distribution

TESTING THE MULE INSTALLATION
When you've configured the MULE_HOME environment variable, you can verify your installation by opening a command line or a console and going to the examples/echo directory within your Mule installation directory. Use the echo shell script (for Unix/Linux) or the batch file (for Windows) to start a simple example that will ask for input via System.in and will forward your input to System.out. When you run the echo script or batch file, you should see the following question once Mule starts up:

```
Please enter something:
```

When you enter the text of your choice and press Enter, the text is output to the console. This means you have succeeded in installing Mule!

IMPLEMENTING A FILE POLLING EXAMPLE WITH MULE
Now that you've installed Mule, you're ready to implement the simple example shown in figure 1.17. We don't go into much detail about the Mule configuration at this point, because we intend to just give you a first look at Mule. In chapter 2 we talk in greater detail about the Mule architecture and how you can configure Mule. Mule is configured with an XML configuration file that is commonly named mule-config.xml. Without further delay, let's take a look at the mule-config.xml for the file polling example (listing 1.1).

Listing 1.1 The file poller Mule configuration: mule-config.xml

```xml
<?xml version="1.0" encoding="UTF-8"?>
<mule xmlns="http://www.mulesource.org/schema/mule/core/2.0"
      xmlns:spring="http://www.springframework.org/schema/beans"
      xmlns:file="http://www.mulesource.org/schema/mule/file/2.0">

  <model name="FileExample">
    <service name="FileService">    <—  Describe service
```

```
    <inbound>
      <file:inbound-endpoint path="inbox"          ◁─┐  Poll directory
           fileAge="500" pollingFrequency="100"/>
    </inbound>
    <outbound>
      <outbound-pass-through-router>
        <file:outbound-endpoint path="outbox"       ◁─┐  Set file output
             outputPattern="output.xml"/>              │  directory
      </outbound-pass-through-router>
    </outbound>
  </service>
 </model>
</mule>
```

The configuration of a Mule implementation starts with a service declaration. The root element of the mule-config.xml file is the `mule` element, which has the namespace declaration Spring (showing the out-of-the-box integration of Mule with the Spring Framework). We don't use any Spring functionality in this short example, however.

The service shown in listing 1.1 configures the name `FileService`. This simple Mule service accepts an incoming message from a configured address and passes it on to a configured outgoing address. Because we don't have to implement any logic for our file polling example, no Mule component is needed.

Within the `service` element we configure two child elements: an inbound router and an outbound router. The inbound router is configured to poll for new files in the inbox directory that is relative to the directory where Mule is started.

The outbound router is configured to write files to the outbox directory, also relative to the directory where Mule is started. The router that we use here is called `OutboundPassThroughRouter`. This Mule component routes the file to one configured endpoint address, in this case the outbox directory, without any filtering.

The remaining part of the configuration instructs Mule which filename to use for the file written to the outbox directory. With a single attribute on the endpoint configuration called `outputPattern`, a filename can be configured. For our hello world example, we use the static filename output.xml, but we could add dynamic parts to the filename such as the current date.

TESTING THE FILE POLLING EXAMPLE WITH MULE

We have now implemented our simple file example for Mule, so let's start Mule with the configuration shown in listing 1.1. In the workspace/workspace-mule/mule/resources/chapter1 folder, you find the file example implementation. Now you can start Mule with the configuration shown in listing 1.1 by issuing a console command from the chapter1 folder.

For Windows:

```
%MULE_HOME%\bin\mule.bat -config file-config.xml
```

For Unix:

```
$MULE_HOME/bin/mule –config file-config.xml
```

Mule now starts with the file polling example configuration. In the current directory (resources/chapter1) you find a file named test-file.xml. To test the file polling example, you can copy this file to the inbox directory within the resources/chapter1 directory in your Mule project. When you've copied the file, you see that an output.xml file containing the same XML content is written to the outbox directory. Congratulations—you have made the first step toward understanding the basics of the open source Mule ESB.

1.5.2   *Taking a JBI dive with ServiceMix*

The second open source ESB that will be discussed in this book is ServiceMix. We start this section by discussing the ServiceMix distribution before implementing the file polling example described in figure 1.17. The ServiceMix 3.2.1 distribution is already downloaded and installed with the execution of the Ant script as described in the previous Mule section.

INSTALLING SERVICEMIX

The ServiceMix 3.2.1 distribution is available as zip and tar.gz, and a separate download is available as a web application archive. We use the binary distribution, whose contents should look like figure 1.19.

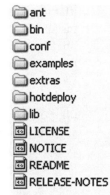

Although we don't go into detail in this section about JBI and the functionality that ServiceMix implements, let's take a quick look at ServiceMix. The ant directory contains Ant scripts that you can use to, for example, install a JBI component or stop and start a JBI component. In other words, these Ant scripts are an easy way to administer the JBI container. The bin directory contains the start and stop scripts for ServiceMix.

Figure 1.19
An overview of the directories within the ServiceMix distribution

The conf directory contains all kinds of configuration settings for ServiceMix, including the messaging platform and security parameters. The data directory is used by ServiceMix for the log files of the JBI container, the JBI components, ActiveMQ, and the ActiveMQ data files, and also serves as a repository for tracking installed JBI components and service assemblies. The data directory is created when you run ServiceMix for the first time. The examples directory contains a set of examples to demonstrate some of the ServiceMix features. The hotdeploy directory is used to install JBI components or JBI service assemblies, which we also talk about in chapter 2. The last directory, lib, contains the libraries necessary to run ServiceMix.

TESTING THE SERVICEMIX INSTALLATION

Before we go further, you need to set an environment variable called SERVICEMIX_ HOME that points to the ServiceMix installation root directory, esb/apache-servicemix-3.2.1. Next, go to ServiceMix's root directory in a console or command prompt and use the following command.

For Windows:

```
bin\servicemix.bat
```

For Unix:

```
bin/servicemix
```

The console or command prompt should now start ServiceMix, and the log messages should include this message:

```
ServiceMix JBI Container (ServiceMix) started
```

When this log message appears, you can consider the ServiceMix installation to be successful. Because ServiceMix lacks a simple example like Mule's echo example, we go ahead with the implementation of the file polling example as shown in figure 1.17. Before we can configure the file polling and writing logic within ServiceMix, we first have to deploy the file JBI component.

IMPLEMENTING A FILE POLLING EXAMPLE WITH SERVICEMIX

When you look in the hotdeploy directory where you installed ServiceMix, you see that it contains a JBI component named servicemix-file-3.2.1-installer.zip. Inside this installer file a JAR named servicemix-file-3.2.1.jar is available. Extract this library to the lib directory of your ServiceMix installation. "Wait," you might say, "didn't you just say that the hotdeploy directory is the place where JBI components can be deployed?" Well, you're absolutely right about that, but there's a small caveat to this.

To keep the example as simple as possible, we use a static configuration for our file polling implementation. This means that we don't make a JBI-compliant service assembly for this example, but we just use a XML configuration file. Making a JBI-compliant service assembly takes a few extra steps that we don't discuss here, but in later chapters we examine this process in detail. So for our static configuration file polling example, place the JAR file in the lib directory.

ServiceMix static configuration

ServiceMix supports the use of a static configuration in addition to the common service assembly deployment model. Note that the static configuration should not be used in projects, as this is not a JBI-compliant way to deploy a ServiceMix configuration. We only use the static configuration here to reduce the amount of knowledge that's necessary for our simple example.

All JBI components of ServiceMix also need a set of base classes available within the servicemix-shared-3.2.1-installer.zip file. All the JAR files inside this shared installer, including servicemix-common-3.2.1.jar and servicemix-shared-3.2.1.jar, should also be extracted to the lib directory. With the addition of these libraries, the file JBI component is ready to use.

To implement the file polling and writing logic as described in figure 1.17, we have to configure two components within ServiceMix: a file poller and a file sender. Like

Mule, ServiceMix needs an XML configuration for this. The big difference is that this XML configuration file follows the JBI specification. You can compare the differences between the Mule configuration and the ServiceMix configuration based on listing 1.2.

Listing 1.2   The file poller ServiceMix configuration: servicemix.xml

```xml
<?xml version="1.0" encoding="UTF-8"?>
<beans xmlns:sm="http://servicemix.apache.org/config/1.0"
    xmlns:file="http://servicemix.apache.org/file/1.0"
    xmlns:esb="http://esbinaction.com/helloworld">

  <bean id="jndi"
     class="org.apache.xbean.spring.jndi.SpringInitialContextFactory"
     factory-method="makeInitialContext" singleton="true" />

  <sm:container id="jbi" useMBeanServer="true"          ⟵  Configure the ServiceMix
                                                            container
       createMBeanServer="true">
    <sm:endpoints>
      <file:poller  service="esb:poller"    ⟵┘  Poll directory
                    endpoint="pollerEndpoint"
                    targetService="esb:sender"
                    file="file:inbox" />
      <file:sender  service="esb:sender"    ⟵┐  Set file output
                    endpoint="senderEndpoint"    directory
                    directory="file:outbox">
        <file:marshaler>
          <sm:defaultFileMarshaler>
            <sm:fileName>
              <bean class="org...ConstantExpression">
                <constructor-arg value="output.xml"/>
              </bean>
            </sm:fileName>
          </sm:defaultFileMarshaler>
        </file:marshaler>
      </file:sender>
    </sm:endpoints>
  </sm:container>
</beans>
```

We don't cover the ServiceMix configuration in much detail, because we do this extensively in chapter 2. Note that JBI requires a basic structure that's pretty much the same for every JBI configuration. There's an element named `container` that belongs to a ServiceMix namespace. The `container` element represents the JBI container for which several endpoints can be configured. Every endpoint represents a component within your JBI implementation solution. In this case, we have two endpoints: a file poller and a file sender. Multiple endpoints can be configured, but for this example we have a file poller and a file sender endpoint. The `poller` element references a poller implementation within the file JBI component. Because we can set some additional attributes for the poller, the JBI container can be instructed to listen for new files in the inbox directory with the `file` attribute and knows that it must forward the file contents to the `esb:sender` service with the `targetService` attribute.

The esb:sender configured as the target service for the file poller must be able to write the file to the outbox directory with the static filename output.xml. To implement this, we have to configure a separate endpoint with the same semantics as the file poller except for some configuration details. For this file sender component, we can also configure the necessary attributes. The service name must be esb:sender, so that the JBI container can forward the file contents to this component. The directory attribute, which configures the destination of the file contents, is set to the outbox directory. Because we want the filename to be output.xml, we have to configure a marshaler with a filename element. We use a constant expression implementation class, because the filename is a static name.

TESTING THE FILE POLLING EXAMPLE WITH SERVICEMIX

Don't try to understand every detail of the configuration as we go into greater depth in upcoming chapters. With our configuration in place, we should now be able to test the file polling example. To execute the test, open a console or command prompt to the directory where you unpacked the source distribution of this book. There's a directory called workspace/workspace-servicemix/servicemix in this distribution with a resources/chapter1 directory inside it. The directory structure here is pretty much the same as for the Mule example, except for the servicemix directory (which holds the servicemix.xml configuration in listing 1.2). In the resources/chapter1 directory, execute the following command to start ServiceMix with the file polling implementation.

For Windows:

```
%SERVICEMIX_HOME%\bin\servicemix.bat servicemix\servicemix.xml
```

For Unix:

```
$SERVICEMIX_HOME/bin/servicemix servicemix/servicemix.xml
```

You can now copy test-file.xml, which is available in the resources/chapter1 directory, to the inbox directory. The file will be picked up by ServiceMix and the file contents will be written to the outbox directory in the file output.xml.

Well, you've done it! While reading just a few pages in this first chapter, you have seen a file polling implementation of Mule as well as ServiceMix.

1.6 *Summary*

With the need to increase the flexibility of the IT environments within organizations, applications have to be integrated and easily adaptable to new requirements. An ESB is an excellent product for integrating applications and helps you avoid having to write your own integration logic for every application over and over again. Using an ESB, you can overcome a number of the challenges seen in every integration project, such as location transparency, transport protocol conversion, message transformation, message routing, message enhancement, security, and monitoring and management.

Because this book is specifically about open source ESBs, we discussed some myths about open source ESBs in an integration market that is dominated by closed source ESBs. One of the main reasons why companies choose the common integration vendors is the support and training. But we've shown that the open source ESBs discussed in section 1.3.2 all have support and training options provided by open source integration vendors such as MuleSource and IONA. The open source ESB projects have become competitive with the well-known integration products and have teams of full-time developers, a great QA, a release model, and an active community. And of course, the products are free, and the source and test code as well as the bug tracking status is open to everyone interested in the open source ESB product.

Architecture of
Mule and ServiceMix

In chapter 1 we defined an ESB, explored its features, and showed you how an ESB can be used to solve integration problems. We also introduced two popular open source ESBs, Mule and Apache ServiceMix, and you saw a hello world example of these two ESBs in action.

In this chapter we look deeper into these two technologies. More specifically, we examine the architecture of Mule 2.0.2 and ServiceMix 3.2.1. We start by explaining Mule and show you its main concepts and how they work together.

Next, we explore ServiceMix in two distinct sections. In section 2.2 we address Java business integration (JBI), since that's the foundational specification of Service-Mix. Then, we investigate ServiceMix in more detail in section 2.3.

At the end of this chapter you'll have learned the architecture of both Mule and ServiceMix and how the basic components of these two ESBs are designed. You'll also have a good knowledge of JBI and how that specification is used in ServiceMix.

Just a reminder: you can download all the source code for the examples in this book from the book's website. In the next chapter we explain in more depth how you can set up a local environment in which you can run these examples.

2.1 *Mule architecture and components*

In this section we give you more in-depth information on the ideas behind Mule 2.0. This section provides a good overview of how messages flow through the Mule ESB and thus forms a good foundation for the examples in upcoming chapters.

In the following subsections we explain the main architectural concepts of Mule and show you how they all work together by diving into a complete Mule configuration file. For the moment we only focus on the most important parts of Mule and tackle the more advanced topics in the following chapters.

2.1.1 *Mule components overview*

Mule's architecture consists of a number of components that work together to provide all the features an ESB should provide. Figure 2.1 shows the main parts and how they interact.

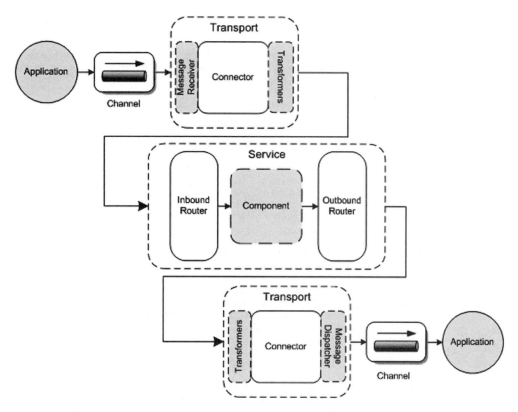

Figure 2.1 This figure illustrates the main concepts of the Mule ESB that enable it to process incoming messages to the proper target applications.

Figure 2.1 shows most of the foundational concepts of Mule. The figure is designed to illustrate the logic order of processing, from receiving an incoming message to sending the message to the right destination. Mule uses transports to receive and send messages from and to all kinds of sources, including Java Message Service (JMS), HTTP, FTP, and files. Another important concept of Mule is the service definition, which consists of an inbound router, a component, and an outbound router. The service definition is where you as a Mule developer will implement the integration logic necessary to solve your integration challenge.

In the next sections, we discuss the various concepts shown here and things will become a lot clearer. Before we delve into each component, we begin by introducing them. Table 2.1 describes the Mule components shown in figure 2.1.

To be able to comprehend all the concepts from table 2.1, let's look at the example shown in figure 2.2.

Table 2.1   The main concepts of the Mule architecture

Name	Description
Application	This identifies the application we're integrating with. It can be anything—an old legacy Cobol system, a .NET application, a J2EE application, or even another Mule instance.
Channel	A channel (an Enterprise Integration pattern) provides a way for external applications to communicate with Mule. Channels can also be used inside Mule to wire services together.
Message receiver	As the name implies, this component can receive information from a certain channel. Mule provides receivers for a lot of common standards and technologies.
Connector	A connector understands how to send and receive data from certain channels. As you can see in the previous figure, the connector is present both at the receiving and the sending ends. The message receiver and message dispatcher are part of the connector.
Transformer	We've already seen this component in chapter 1. A transformer transforms data from one format to another.
Inbound router	An inbound router determines what to do with a message once it's received from a channel.
Component	The component is the logical place within the Mule architecture to implement integration logic not provided by other Mule parts. A component can be implemented with a number of technologies: POJO, Groovy Script, REST service, and BPM, among others.
Outbound router	This is much the same as the inbound router, but this component determines where a message is sent to after it's processed by the component.
Message dispatcher	This is the opposite of the message receiver. This component knows how to send information over a specific channel.

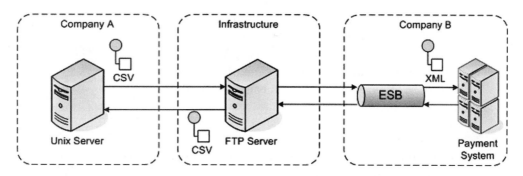

Figure 2.2   This example shows the use of the main concepts of Mule. A CSV file is sent to Mule with an FTP server, and Mule transforms the message to XML and sends it on to the payment system.

In the example shown in figure 2.2, a comma-separated values (CSV) message is read from an FTP server, transformed into an XML message, and then sent to the payment service. After the payment service finishes processing the message, the message is again transformed to CSV and dropped on the file system.

If we implement this using Mule and look at the various components we need, we can list the following actions taking place:

1   The *application* of company A puts the CSV file in a specified FTP directory.

2   This directory serves as a *channel* into the running Mule instance.

3   Mule uses a *message receiver*, which is part of the incoming *connector*, to read the file from the file channel, so that it can be processed further.

4   The *transformer* converts the incoming message to the XML format required by the payment service.

5   The *inbound router* checks where the message needs to be sent to. In this case the message is sent to the payment service.

6   The payment service is declared as a *component*, implemented as a POJO that can receive messages from Mule.

7   After the message has been processed by the payment service, Mule uses an *outbound router* to determine where the message needs to be sent to next.

8   A *message dispatcher*, which is part of the outgoing *connector*, is now used to send the message to a *channel*. In this case this channel is once again a file directory on the FTP server, where the *application* from company A can pick it up again.

As you can see, the Mule architecture provides all the basic components that are needed for application integration. Before we look at the various parts in more detail, let's quickly look at how you as a developer configure Mule. Configuring Mule is done using XML. You create a file that specifies the transformers you want to use, which routers need to be used, and so forth. Let's look at the parts this file contains in figure 2.3 before we move on to the code examples.

As you can see in figure 2.3, a lot of the already mentioned Mule concepts are configured in this file. If you want to use message filters, specific transformers, and connectors for technologies, they are all configured in this XML file. We must also define a Mule model to contain all our Mule services. A Mule service is a simple container component that specifies on which channels we're listening (the inbound router), how the routing is handled (the outbound router), and which component is invoked.

Now that we've introduced you to the basic architecture and concepts of Mule, let's look somewhat deeper into these concepts.

2.1.2 *Mule endpoints*

Channels provide a way for external systems to communicate with Mule and to let components interact with one another. However, an application needs to have a way to connect to a channel, and this can be done by creating an *endpoint*. The channels, connectors, senders, and receivers work together to accomplish this.

The configuration of an endpoint changed between Mule version 1.4 and Mule version 2.0. To understand the use of endpoints in Mule, let's first look at the old definition of endpoints, which can still be used in Mule 2.0. In the next subsection we focus on Mule 2.0–style endpoints.

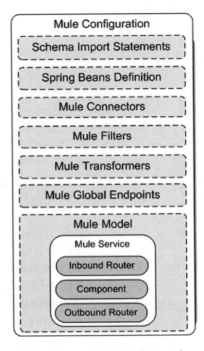

Figure 2.3 An overview of the main parts of a Mule configuration file. This figure also shows that Spring beans can be easily integrated in the Mule configuration.

MULE ENDPOINTS, OLD STYLE

Before explaining how Mule works with these endpoints, let's look at a couple of these endpoints. The ones listed here are examples of basic endpoint definitions:

```
<endpoint address="pop3://user:password@mail.mycompany.com"/>
<endpoint address="jms://topic:myTopic"/>
<endpoint address="http://mycompany.com/mule"/>
<endpoint address="file:///tmp/data/in"/>
<endpoint address="axis:http://mycompany.com/mule/services/MyUMO"/>
```

As you can see from this list, Mule endpoints are easy to read and understand. They describe the technology used (for example, `pop3://` for email, `file://` for access to the file system) and where to read or send a message to. Let's look a bit more closely at the POP3 endpoint of the previous list:

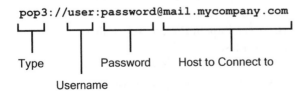

So what does the endpoint from this illustration tell us?

1 We're connecting using POP3, a protocol for accessing your email.

2 Next we see the username and password that are required to connect to this endpoint.

3 The final part from this endpoint is the host that we're connecting to.

Some endpoints have additional parameters or specific naming conventions (e.g., the topic part of the JMS URL), but generally an endpoint looks like this example.

Now let's see what can be configured on a Mule endpoint. The following shows how an endpoint in Mule is defined:

scheme://[username][:password][host][:port]/

[endpoint name]/[address]?[params]

The fields from this URI are explained in table 2.2.

Table 2.2 Mule URI fields description

Name	Description	Required?
scheme	This is the type of connection we want to make. If we want to connect using a JMS broker, the scheme would be `jms`. If we need to write something to the file system, the scheme would be `file`. Mule already provides support for over 20 different schemes.	Yes
username	If a connection to a certain host requires a username, it can be provided in this part.	No
password	If we need to specify more than just the username, a password can also be provided by using this part.	No
host	Here we specify to which host we connect. If both a username and a host are used, they should be separated by a @.	Yes*
port	Here we specify to which port on the server we need to connect. If this isn't filled in, the default port for the service is used.	No*
endpoint name	It's possible to create reusable endpoints. These endpoints can be defined globally and used throughout the configuration file.	Yes*
address	The address specifies where we need to connect to on the previously defined host. This can, for instance, be a specific URL on an HTTP server, a specific queue name for a JMS broker, or a certain location on the file system.	Yes
params	Some schemes allow additional parameters that you can use to customize the behavior of this endpoint. A file endpoint, for instance, allows you to specify whether a file is deleted after it's picked up, or that a file should be moved to a certain directory.	Yes

* Either a host, an endpoint name, or both is required. Usually, though, you won't use an endpoint and a host:port together. It's possible, however. If it's done, the host:port specified will override the host and port specified in the global endpoint.

You've now seen how Mule allows you to connect to various systems by using these endpoints. However, we haven't told you everything you need to know about these endpoints. As you'll see in later chapters, it's also possible to define a transformer directly on an endpoint. We explain that in more detail in the following section.

A couple of more complex endpoint addresses are listed next, and with the information provided in this section you should be able to know what they do:

```
smtp://mule:secret@smtp.gmail.com?subject=HelloWorld&to=info@world.com
file://work/incoming?pollingFrequency=10000&moveToDirectory=work/processed
jms://topic:information?username=mule&password=secret
ejb://localhost:1099/SomeService?method=remoteMethod
```

If you can understand what these endpoints do, you understand one of the most important concepts of the Mule architecture.

MULE ENDPOINTS, NEW STYLE

Starting with Mule 2.0, the configuration of endpoints has become easier with the introduction of transport-specific namespaces and attributes. For instance, when we look at the JMS endpoint configuration from the previous section, we can also configure it with an endpoint specific to the JMS transport in Mule 2.0. It would look like this:

```
<jms:inbound-endpoint queue="order.queue"/>
<jms:outbound-endpoint topic="order.topic"/>
```

The main advantage is that you get code completion for the configuration of an endpoint related to a specific transport. This also makes it simpler to determine which properties you can use for an endpoint of a specific transport. Because this style of configuring endpoints is more powerful, we use the transport-specific namespaces in this book.

Another important difference is the use of inbound-endpoint and outbound-endpoint elements in Mule 2.0 instead of the endpoint element in Mule 1.4. This means that the inbound and outbound endpoint definitions are clearly separated and that the attributes and child elements for these endpoint definitions can be different. Let's look at a couple of examples of more complex endpoint definitions, to be able to compare them with the Mule 1.4 complex endpoints of the previous section:

```
<file:inbound-endpoint path="inbox" fileAge="1000"
    pollingFrequency="2000" />
<smtp:outbound-endpoint host="localhost" port="1234"
    to="info@esbinaction.com" subject="hello" />
```

Now that you know how Mule interacts with incoming and outgoing messages, let's go ahead and look at the way incoming and outgoing messages can be transformed.

2.1.3   *Transformers*

The next concept we discuss is the *transformer*. As we mentioned earlier, transformers are used to transform data from one format to another. For instance, if you decide to use a common data format for all your ESB message flows, you can use transformers to create the mappings for that format.

If you look back at figure 2.1 earlier in this chapter, you can see that transformers are applied after the message receiver has received a message. The main question here is, what does the source message look like when we receive it for transformation? If we receive one message from a JMS queue, and another one from a mail provider, you can assume the format in which we receive the messages is different.

Well, you're partly right. Although Mule tries to hide the transport and its technical implementation as much as possible, there are some factors you need to take into account. Mule applies a sensible default transformation to an incoming and outgoing message based on the type of transport on which we receive or send the message. When we receive a message over JMS, Mule automatically transforms it based on the JMSMessage received. If a TextMessage is received, it's transformed into a String, an ObjectMessage is transformed into an Object, and the other JMS message types also have their Java object equivalents. This is all done automatically and doesn't require you to specify anything.

You can, of course, specify your own transformations that can override the default transformations or be applied together with them. One thing to keep in mind, though, is that when you specify your own transformers, the internal Mule transformers aren't executed by default anymore. So if you want to also execute the default transformers, you have to configure them explicitly.

Let's assume we want to convert a message, received from a JMS queue, from one XML format to another. To transform this message, we need the transformers specified in figure 2.4.

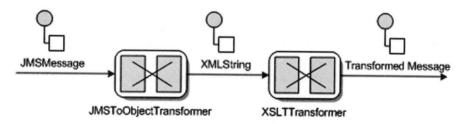

JMSMessage   XMLString   Transformed Message

JMSToObjectTransformer   XSLTTransformer

Figure 2.4 An example of stacked transformations, which shows how a message is transformed in two steps. First, the default JMS transformer is executed, and then an XSLT transformation converts the incoming message into a different XML format.

When the message is received, the following take place:

- The message is transformed by the default JMSToObjectTransformer, which we now have to specify explicitly because we're also using another transformer. A JMS TextMessage goes into this transformer and a String object comes out.
- The String object is passed into the XSLT transformer, the style sheet is applied, and the message is transformed into the required XML format.

You've seen in the previous section that endpoints are an important part of the Mule configuration. Configuring transformers is also partly done using those endpoints. It consists of two steps. The first step is to define the transformers and assign a logical name. The XML configuration to define the transformers is shown in listing 2.1.

Listing 2.1   Transformers configuration in Mule

```
<jms:jmsmessage-to-object-transformer      <--- ❶
    name="JMSToStringTransformer"/>

<xml:xslt-transformer name="XSLT" xsl-file="yourfile.xslt"/>   <--- ❷

<custom-transformer name="Custom" class="esb.YourTransformer"/>   <--- ❸
```

The JMS transformer ❶ and the XSLT transformer ❷ are provided by Mule, so we can easily define these transformers using the transport-specific namespace. For this example, we don't need any additional transformers, but to show how to configure your own developed transformer, we include the `custom-transformer` element ❸. For more details about the implementation of a custom transformer, check out chapters 4 and 5.

The second step involves configuring these transformers on an endpoint. In this example, they're added to an inbound endpoint:

```
<jms:inbound-endpoint queue="query.response">
  <transformer ref="JMSToStringTransformer"/>
  <transformer ref="XSLT"/>
</jms:inbound-endpoint>
```

As you can see, the transformers can be configured using the `transformer` element with a `ref` attribute, which can be set on an inbound and outbound endpoint. To configure multiple transformers, you can just use multiple `transformer` elements.

We're halfway there! You've seen how Mule can connect to various technologies and how the messages received from and sent to those technologies can be transformed. Let's now explore the most interesting and powerful part of Mule: the routers.

2.1.4   Routers

Looking back again at figure 2.1, you can see that there are two different types of routers: inbound and outbound. You can also see that the inbound router is applied after the transformation of a message and the outbound router is applied before the transformation. As the name implies, routers allow you to determine what to do with a message when it's received and before it's sent. Let's look at an example of an inbound and an outbound router provided by Mule, so you can see how they work. In the following chapters, when we discuss routing in more depth, we also look at some of the other routers Mule provides.

INBOUND ROUTER

The inbound router we'll be looking at is called the *selective consumer*. With the selective consumer, we can use a filter to specify the types of messages we want to receive.

For instance, we could specify that we only want to receive messages that contain a String or that match a certain XPath expression. Listing 2.2 shows a simple inbound router configuration.

Listing 2.2 Sample inbound router definition for Mule

```
<inbound>
  <forwarding-catch-all-strategy>
    <jms:outbound-endpoint queue="failure.queue" />
  </forwarding-catch-all-strategy>
  <selective-consumer-router>
    <jxpath-filter pattern="(//resultcode)='success'"/>
  </selective-consumer-router>
  <jms:inbound-endpoint queue="list.in" />
</inbound>
```
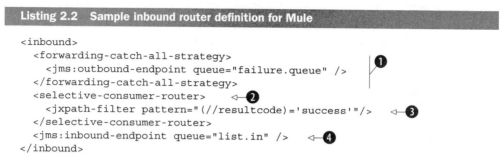

This configuration gives a glimpse of what's possible with Mule. In the next chapter we explain what you see in this example in greater depth. For now, this list will give you a high-level overview of what the configuration does:

- A catchall strategy ❶ allows you to define an endpoint to which messages are sent when they aren't matched by any of the filters. In this case, they're routed to a JMS endpoint.
- The router defined here is a SelectiveConsumer ❷. The filter in this section defines whether a message is received by this service. In this example we define an out-of-the-box JXPath filter as an element of the selective router. Another option would be to define your own filter with the custom-filter element.
- The filter expression is a JXPath expression ❸, which is applied to the incoming message on the endpoint that's specified ❹. If the result is true, the message is accepted by this service.

The previous example was just a short introduction to the inbound routers. Mule has a number of standard routers that you can use. Table 2.3 lists most of the inbound routers, which we come back to in later chapters.

Table 2.3 The most common inbound routers provided by Mule

Router name	Description
Idempotent receiver	This router ensures that only messages are received that contain an unique ID.
Aggregator	The aggregator router combines two or more messages together and passes them on as a single message.
Resequencer	The resequencer will hold back messages and can reorder the messages before they are sent to the component.
Selective consumer	With a selective consumer, you can easily specify whether or not you want to receive a certain event.

Table 2.3   The most common inbound routers provided by Mule *(continued)*

Router name	Description
Wiretap router	With the wiretap router, it's possible to route certain incoming events to a different endpoint as well as to the component.
Forwarding consumer	This router forwards the message directly to the outbound router without invoking the component.

OUTBOUND ROUTER

In addition to inbound routers, Mule has a large set of standard outbound routers. Let's look at one in detail before listing them all. The outbound router we examine, called the the list message splitter, is a bit more complex than the previous inbound router, but you should get a good idea of how routers work. This particular router accepts a list of objects and, based on their type, routes them to one of the specified endpoints. Listing 2.3 shows how this outbound router is configured.

Listing 2.3   Configuration showing how to use an outbound router

```
<outbound>                                        ❶  Defines type        ❷  Defines
  <list-message-splitter-router>         ⟵┘     of router                 expected
    <payload-type-filter expectedType="java.util.List"/>    ⟵             payload
    <jms:outbound-endpoint queue="order.queue">
      <payload-type-filter expectedType="esb.chapter2.Order"/>       ⟵
    </jms:outbound-endpoint>
    <jms:outbound-endpoint queue="item.queue">
      <payload-type-filter expectedType="esb.chapter2.Item"/>
    </jms:outbound-endpoint>
    <jms:outbound-endpoint queue="customer.queue">
      <payload-type-filter expectedType="esb.chapter2.Customer"/>
    </jms:outbound-endpoint>                              Determines target
  </list-message-splitter-router>                    queue on payload type  ❸
</outbound>
```

We see a number of new things here. The first thing, of course, is the whole outbound router definition. As you can see, we define a `list-message-splitter-router` ❶. This router allows us to specify multiple endpoints, each with its own filter. In our example we specify three endpoints on this router, and each endpoint once again has its own filter ❸. So based on the type of object in the supplied list, the message is sent to a specific endpoint. An interesting thing to notice here is that we can also specify a filter on the router itself ❷, to make sure the message is of the expected type before we attempt to split it up.

This router was just one of the many routers that Mule provides. In the following chapters we look at most of the others in detail. Table 2.4 describes the outbound routers that Mule provides.

As with all the components we discuss in this chapter, you can also write your own inbound and outbound routers; you'll learn how in chapter 9. With the routers we've discussed the most complex part of Mule; the final concept we discuss is the component.

Table 2.4 The most common outbound routers provided by Mule

Router name	Description
Filtering outbound router	This is a simple router that routes based on the content of the message.
Recipient list	This router can be used to send a message to multiple endpoints.
Multicasting router	A multicasting router can be used to send the same message to multiple endpoints.
Chaining router	A chaining router can be used to tie various endpoints together.
Message splitter	This router can be used to split an outgoing message into separate messages and to send each to a certain endpoint.
Filtering XML message splitter	This router is much the same as the one we discussed in this section, but it works on XML documents.
Exception-based router	This router is used for sending messages over unreliable endpoints. It allows you to specify a set of endpoints that the router tries until one succeeds.
List message splitter	This router allows you to split an incoming list of objects into separate messages.

2.1.5 *Component*

A component is invoked when a message is received by an inbound router and has passed all the filters. This default component is just a POJO without any dependencies to the Mule framework. It can be a simple POJO, but it's also possible to use external containers to manage these components for you. For instance, it's possible to use Spring (as we do throughout this book) to manage these components. Additionally, these components can be implemented with other technologies, such as a Groovy script or a REST component. The component implementation is extensible, so any technology of interest can be plugged in.

To show you how easy it is to implement a Java component in Mule, check out listing 2.4.

Listing 2.4 Example of a simple component with Java implementation

```
public class ExampleComponent {

    public void processCustomer(Customer customer) {
        // do something interesting with the customer
    }
}
```

Listing 2.4 contains a valid component implementation that can be used in a Mule configuration. The following code snippet shows all you have to do to configure the Java class in Mule:

```
<component class="esb.chapter2.ExampleComponent"/>
```

The one question that always remains is, if these components have no dependencies to Mule, how can Mule tell which method to invoke on these components? Well, there are three possible options:

- *Let Mule decide*—Normally Mule decides for itself what method to invoke on your component. It does so by enumerating all the available public methods on the component and checks to see whether one of those matches the payload type of the message that's received.
- *Specify a method name*—We've already seen that some endpoints allow the specification of properties. If we specify a property with the name "method," the value of that parameter is used as method name on the component you want to invoke.
- *Use the entry point–resolving functionality of Mule*—The first two options use the default entry point–resolving functionality. The `ReflectionEntryPointResolver` is used for the first option and the `ExplicitMethodEntryPointResolver` is used for the second. There are, however, more options, including the `CallableEntryPointResolver` (which invokes the `onCall` method of the `Callable` interface that the component implements) and the custom entry point resolver that you can write yourself by implementing the `EntryPointResolver` interface.

Once a component has processed the message, the result of the invoked method is used as the new message. If that method returns void, the method's parameters are sent to the outbound router. One thing to keep in mind is that when a component returns null from an invoked message, the message processing stops. So keep this in mind when calling your own custom components.

2.1.6 *Mule deployment models*

Thus far we've talked about how Mule works and the architecture of Mule. We haven't yet discussed the different ways you can run Mule, so we focus on that next.

RUN MULE AS A STAND-ALONE SERVER
In this book we use Mule as a stand-alone server. With this model, we start Mule from the command line and Mule itself is responsible for managing it resources (such as JDBC data sources, JMS connection factories, and transactions). If you want a lightweight ESB, this is usually the best way to run Mule. It's easy to start and manage, but you'll lose some of the functionality provided by the container.

RUN MULE FROM A SERVLET ENGINE
You can also run Mule from a servlet engine such as Tomcat or Jetty. That way, you can easily deploy Mule as part of a web application and make use of all the resources managed by the web container. Getting Mule started from a servlet engine requires some configuration in your servlet's `web.xml`. When you run Mule as a stand-alone server, you use command-line arguments to specify the configuration with which Mule should start. For a servlet, this isn't possible. So if you want to start Mule from a servlet, you have to do two things. First, you must define the configuration files you want to use. You can do this by setting a servlet context parameter:

```
<context-param>
  <param-name>org.mule.config</param-name>
  <param-value>
      mule-configuration-1.xml,
      mule-configuration-2.xml
  </param-value>
</context-param>
```

As you can see in this code snippet, you can use this parameter to specify the configuration files you'd like Mule to load when it's started. The second thing you need to do is add a context listener, which will start up the Mule ESB. Mule has already provided a listener for this purpose, so you all you have to do is configure Mule's context listener in your web.xml:

```
<listener>
  <listener-class>
    org.mule.config.builders.MuleXmlBuilderContextListener
  </listener-class>
</listener>
```

With both the context parameters and the listener in place, Mule will start automatically when your web application is deployed.

RUN AND CONNECT TO MULE FROM AN APPLICATION SERVER

When you want to run Mule in an application server, you've got a couple of options. You can use the method we described earlier where you package Mule in a web application and deploy Mule as a web archive (WAR) to the application server, or you can deploy Mule as a resource adapter. Mule has a JCA 1.5–compatible resource adapter, so if your application server supports JCA 1.5, you can use JCA to communicate with the Mule resource adapter from your application server.

Resource adapter configuration is specific for each application server, so we don't go into detail here. Mule has support for Geronimo, JBoss, Oracle, WebLogic, and WebSphere, and provides extensive documentation online explaining how to configure these application servers.

2.1.7 *Mule wrap-up*

In the last couple of sections, we've examined the Mule architecture. As you've probably seen for yourself, Mule isn't that difficult to work with. As long as you understand the core concepts, working with this ESB is easy.

Let's quickly summarize these main concepts by walking through the process of how Mule receives and sends a message:

- Mule receives messages by listening on a *channel*; a *message receiver* will receive the message using the specific technology required by this channel.
- After the message is received by the *channel*, it's passed on to the next Mule concept in the process: the *transformer*. If the message needs to be modified before it's passed into the *component*, this is the place to do it.

- Before our custom login in the *component* is invoked, we first have to pass through the *inbound router*, which decides whether we want to process this message in the *component*.

- The next step in the process is passing the message on to the place where we can put our custom integration logic: the *component*. After we've applied our custom integration logic, we repeat the incoming process, only in the reverse direction.

- So the message is now passed on to the *outbound router*, which determines where the message is sent to. After that, another *transformer* is invoked and the message is sent to the *message dispatcher* that puts it onto the destination channel.

Next we take a look at ServiceMix, beginning with an exploration of its underlying architecture, JBI.

2.2   *JBI, the foundation for ServiceMix*

Java business integration (JBI) is the standard on which ServiceMix is built. JBI defines a standards-based architecture that can be used as the basis for Java-based integration products, in particular an ESB. Besides ServiceMix, a couple of other open source ESBs are based on this standard: OpenESB and PEtALS. Since the focus of this book is on open source ESBs and not the JBI specification, we only show you the important parts of this specification. To learn more, check out the complete specification, available at http://jcp.org/en/jsr/detail?id=208. Even though this is a 240-page document, it's very well written and readable. In figure 2.5 you can see a simplified overview of what JBI defines.

JBI defines an architecture that allows integration products to be built based on components that can be plugged into the JBI environment. These components can then provide additional services, consume services, or do both. For instance, component A could provide XSLT transformation functionality, while component B could consume incoming JMS messages. This provides a high degree of flexibility and also allows components to be reused by multiple JBI environments. In other words, JBI-compliant components that work in ServiceMix will also work in other JBI environments.

There are a number of concepts described by the JBI specification that you need to understand. In this section we describe those concepts and explain how they're

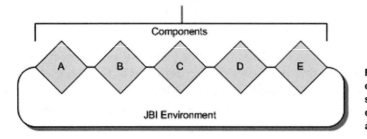

Figure 2.5 A high-level overview of the JBI specification with a focus on the component-based architecture

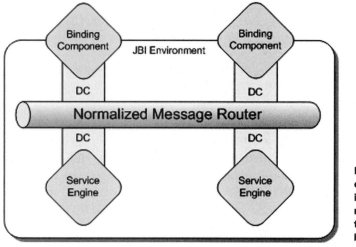

Figure 2.6 A high-level JBI container showing the most important concepts: the normalized message router, the service engines, and the binding components

used. In upcoming chapters, when we show you more about ServiceMix, we again visit these concepts.

Let's start by looking at a detailed overview of the JBI specification (see figure 2.6).

In the following sections wel explain the concepts shown in figure 2.6 in more detail. First, we look at the binding components, which handle the communication with external systems, and service engines, which contain your business logic.

2.2.1 Service engines and binding components

Service engines (SEs) and binding components (BCs) are the components in the JBI environment that provide services to other components and that allow external systems to communicate with the JBI environment. An SE provides functionality to other components and can consume services provided by other components. If you already have custom Java components that provide reusable functionality, you can easily make them available as a service engine. What you need to keep in mind, though, is that when you make a service available through an SE, only other JBI services can access this service.

Consumers and providers

In this section on JBI and the next on ServiceMix, we talk a lot about consumers and providers. *Consumers* and *providers* are the two roles a component inside a JBI container can have. If a component provides services to another component, the component's role is the provider. If a component uses a service provided by another component, it consumes this service, and the component is called a consumer.

A good example of a provider is an XSLT service engine. This component's role is provider, since it provides transformation services to other components. If you look at a BPEL component, a component that can orchestrate various services, you've got a good example of a consumer. The BPEL process consumes various services provided by other components. The BPEL process itself also provides a service to other components.

The binding component (BC) is a JBI component that provides connectivity to existing applications and services that are located outside the JBI environment. For instance, if you want to communicate with existing applications, you have to do that by using binding components. The same is true if you want to integrate with non-Java-based protocols or communication protocols (such as JMS and HTTP). Besides providing access to external services, BCs can be used to expose internal JBI services to the outside world. For instance, if you've got a transformation service running in an XSLT SE, you can't access it from outside the JBI container. If you want to make this service available to the world outside the JBI container, you'll have to use a BC to expose this service. You could, for instance, use a JMS BC to expose this service on a JMS queue.

The main thing to remember is that if you want to communicate with services outside the JBI environment or you want to allow an external application to communicate with the JBI environment, you must use binding components. For components that only provide and consume services in the JBI environment, you can use service engines.

Service engines vs. binding components

If you dive somewhat deeper into the various interfaces and deployment descriptors associated with JBI, you'll find out the implementation differences between an SE and a BC are minimal. It's merely a pragmatic and conceptual distinction. The BC contains the infrastructure specific logic and the SE contains the business logic. This provides a good separation between the two different types of JBI components on a JBI container.

Besides this pragmatic distinction, there's also an administrative distinction. JBI defines a set of Ant tasks that you can use to list information about the deployed component in your JBI environment. You can use one of these tasks to list all the SEs deployed, and another one to list the BCs deployed.

Before we go into more detail on how the components communicate with one another, take a look at figure 2.7.

Figure 2.7 shows a JBI container on which a couple of JBI components are installed. In this container three BCs are installed: an HTTP BC, a JMS BC, and a File BC. As you can see, each of these BCs allows communication over a certain technology. A BC doesn't just allow incoming communications; it also provides a way for the other components in the container to communicate with external technologies.

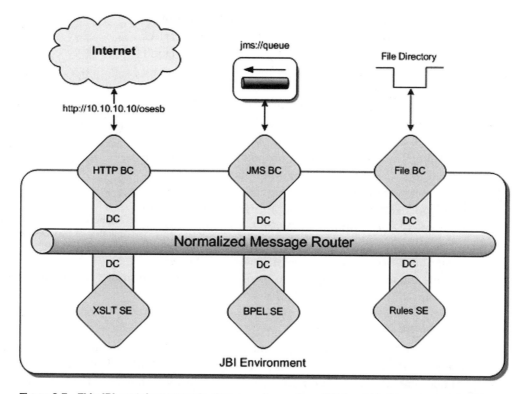

Figure 2.7 This JBI container example shows service engines (SEs) and binding components (BCs) linked to the normalized message router via a delivery channel (DC).

Inside the container you see three SEs:

- An XSLT SE that can transform XML
- A BPEL SE that can be used to orchestrate services and implement a business process
- A Rules SE, which provides the functionality to execute a set of business rules

Now that we've seen the type of components that can exist inside a JBI container, let's see how these components can interact with one another.

2.2.2 Services and endpoints

The following is a high-level summary of services and endpoints. This should help you grasp these concepts without having to dive too deep into the JBI specification.

We've mentioned that a JBI container contains a number of JBI components (BCs and SEs). What we haven't mentioned yet is that each of these components in itself can act as a container. Let's look again at the architecture described in figure 2.7, but now we zoom in on the XSLT SE (see figure 2.8). Remember that this SE provides us with XML transformation functionality.

Figure 2.8 shows the XSLT SE, which is the JBI component as it's installed in the JBI container. Four services (S1, S2, S3, and S4) are running inside this SE. Don't worry now how to deploy services to a service engine; we explain that later in this chapter.

Each of these services executes some specific XSLT functionality. For instance, in this example S1 might transform an XML message based on a static configured XSLT file, while S2 might use a property from a message header to select the transformation to be applied.

A service can't be accessed directly. To access a service, you need to use an endpoint. Each service must have at least one endpoint, but it can have many more. So when you want to consume a service provided by a JBI component, you need to know the name of the service

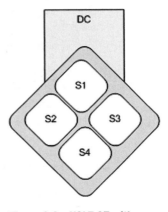

Figure 2.8   XSLT SE with a number of services (XSLT style sheets) deployed

and the name of the endpoint to invoke. This combination of a service and a specific endpoint on that service is called a service endpoint.

2.2.3   *Normalized message router*

If you look back at figure 2.6, you can see that at the center of all the components is a component called the normalized message router (NMR). This means that the JBI components (SE or BC) don't directly communicate with each other—they communicate using the NMR. The components don't connect directly to this NMR, but instead use a delivery channel (DC). It's the NMR's job to make sure that the messages are exchanged correctly among the various components in the JBI environment.

The NMR can exchange messages in a number of ways, or *patterns*. The following is the list of patterns that must be supported by each JBI implementation. Note that you should consider each pattern from the provider's point of view.

- *In-Only*—With this pattern the consumer makes a request but doesn't expect a response back. This also means that should a fault occur, this fault isn't sent back to the consumer.
- *Robust-In-Only*—This pattern is similar to the previous one, only this time the provider can send a fault message if something goes wrong.
- *In-Out*—In this traditional request/reply scenario, the consumer sends a request and expects a response from the provider. If an error occurs, the provider is free to send a fault message.
- *In-Optional-Out*—This pattern is similar to the previous one, only this time the response is optional, and during the message interaction both parties can send a fault message.

Let's look a bit closer at one of these exchanges. In figure 2.9 the interaction between a consumer, a provider, and the NMR is shown for an In-Out message exchange.

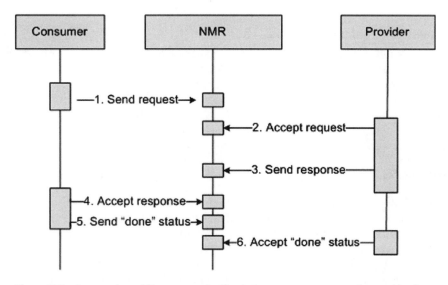

Figure 2.9 An overview of the communication between a consumer and a provider for an In-Out message exchange, including the communication with the normalized message router.

The following steps are executed here:

1 The consumer creates a message exchange for a specific service and endpoint (this combination of service name and endpoint is called the ServiceEndpoint). The consumer sets the "in" part of the message exchange with the request body. After this step, it sends the message by putting it on its delivery channel, and thus sending it to the NMR.

2 The NMR determines to which provider this exchange needs to be sent and queues it for delivery to the provider. The provider accepts this message exchange and executes its business logic.

3 After the provider has finished processing, the response message is added to the "out" part of the message exchange and the message exchange is again presented to the NMR.

4 The NMR once again queues the message for delivery to the consumer. The consumer accepts the message exchange.

5 After the response is accepted, the consumer ends this exchange by setting the status to "done." The consumer sends the "done" response status to the NMR.

6 Finally, the provider accepts this "done" status and the complete exchange is finished.

This might look a bit complex just to send a simple message from one component to the other, but ServiceMix and the other JBI implementations as well will hide most of this complexity for you. Besides that, with the number of available service engines and binding components, you won't often have to deal with the internals.

Message exchange patterns

The message exchange patterns described here aren't specific to JBI. The patterns are the same ones defined in the Web Services Description Language (WSDL) 2.0 specification. JBI only uses the four patterns we described earlier. However, the specification defines a couple of extra patterns (http://www.w3.org/TR/2004/WD-wsdl20-patterns-20040326) that aren't used in JBI. As you can see from the previous patterns, they're all written from the perspective of the provider. For instance, when we look at the In-Out pattern, the provider receives an incoming message and sends a message back to the consumer. Alternatively, the provider only receives a message and doesn't send anything back (the In-Only pattern).

The WSDL 2.0 specification also specifies message exchange patterns the other way around. These are exchanges that are initiated by the provider and, just like the other patterns, are written from the provider point of view. So instead of the In-Only pattern, you also get the Out-Only pattern. You should consider these kinds of messages to be event messages; for instance, a certain service provider can notify its consumers that it's going offline for an hour, or send out warnings or other events.

2.2.4   *Service description, invocation, and message exchanges*

We've talked a bit about message exchanges and you've seen how messages are exchanged from a high-level point of view. In this section, we dive a bit deeper into the message exchanges and explore how they're defined and how a consumer can create a message exchange.

We've already talked about consumers and providers. A provider provides a certain service, and a consumer can consume that service. But how can the consumer tell what kind of operations you can invoke on a certain provider, what do the messages look like that need to be sent, and what kind of errors can you expect? There are two possible sources to get more details about the interface of a service provider. The first one is the obvious one: just look closely at the documentation and determine which operation is provided and what kind of messages can be sent. There is, however, also a more dynamic way of doing this: *self-describing services.*

Let's quickly look at what the JBI specs have to say about this:

> *[S]ervice providers declare to the NMR the particular services they provide. Each declaration must be accompanied by a corresponding metadata definition, which describes the declaration. (This metadata definition is supplied by a Component-supplied SPI.) JBI requires that WSDL 1.1 or WSDL 2.0 be used for all such declarations. The NMR presumes (but does not enforce) that all such declarations are compliant with the WSDL specifications. However, if the metadata is malformed, it is a likely consequence that service consumers will be unable to properly invoke the service.*

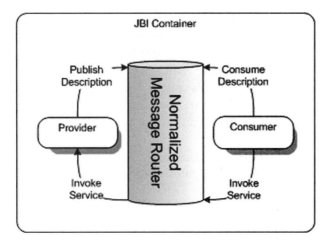

Figure 2.10 An overview of the publication and consumption of services via the normalized message router. A provider publishes a service on the NMR and a consumer can consume this service.

What this says is that each provider should publish its service description to the normalized message router as a WSDL 1.1 or WSDL 2.0 document. However, the NMR doesn't check whether or not they are valid. Figure 2.10 illustrates the publication and consumption of services.

As you can see in figure 2.10, a provider can publish a service on the NMR and a consumer can consume this service. Knowing this, you can simply tell a consumer to look up the service description for a certain service endpoint and the consumer will know what kind of operations are supported and the type of messages that can be sent.

Abstract and concrete WSDL

A WSDL 2.0 document is split into an *abstract* part and a *concrete* part. The abstract part defines the operations, the messages, and the XML structures a service implements. The concrete part shows how the operations can be called (such as SOAP over JMS, or by using a file in a certain directory). You can view the abstract WSDL as a Java interface definition and the concrete part as the implementation.

When you consider this from the JBI point of view, the abstract part of the WSDL is used inside the NMR. When you look up a certain description for a provider, you'll only need the abstract part to determine how to invoke a certain service. The concrete part is often used to configure business components and service engines. For instance, Open ESB uses the concrete part of a WSDL to configure its JBI components.

Now that you know how to determine what kind of operations and messages a service provides, let's see how a consumer can create a message exchange with a certain provider.

Invoking a certain operation on a provider isn't that hard. You simply create a new `MessageExchangeFactory` for a certain service or interface. Using this factory, you create an exchange for a specific operation. Once you have the message exchange, just set the correct message and pass it on the NMR. The NMR will route the message to the correct service. This might all seem a bit complex, but you don't have to worry. All the JBI-based ESBs out there provide a large set of components so usually you don't have to be concerned with these internals, unless you're writing your own SEs or BCs.

You've now seen how the services can communicate with one another, which roles services can have, and what service engines and binding components do. In the next section we show how you can deploy artifacts to service engines and binding components.

2.2.5 *Service unit and service assembly*

We've talked about service engines and binding components and explained that they can be containers themselves to which resources can be deployed. For instance, you could have a service engine that provides validation services and allows you to deploy XML Schemas that can be used for validation.

The resources that you can deploy to such a container are called *service units* (SUs). If you group these service units together, you can create a *service assembly* (SA), as shown in figure 2.11.

In figure 2.11 a service assembly is shown that contains multiple service units. Once this service assembly is deployed to a JBI container, each of the service units is deployed to its specific SE or BC.

The JBI specification doesn't specify a format for these SUs and SAs, so each service engine and binding component is free to handle those in its own way. We come back to SUs and SAs in section 2.3.

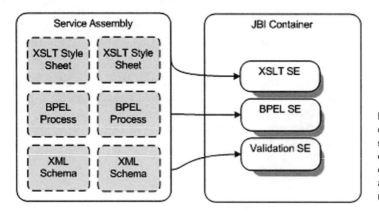

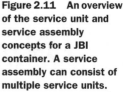

Figure 2.11 An overview of the service unit and service assembly concepts for a JBI container. A service assembly can consist of multiple service units.

2.2.6 *JBI wrap-up*

Let's quickly summarize what we've learned about JBI so far. Table 2.5 summarizes the most important parts.

Table 2.5 The main concepts of the JBI specification

Component	Description
Service engine	A JBI component that can provide services to other JBI components and can also consume services provided by other JBI components.
Binding component	A JBI component used to consume and provide services to services outside the JBI container.
Normalized message router	This component of a JBI environment takes part in delivering a message from one component to another component. This exchange always follows one of the standard message exchange patterns.
Delivery channel	The delivery channel connects a JBI component (a service engine or a binding component) to the normalized message router.
Service unit	This is an artifact that can be deployed into a running service engine or binding component.
Service assembly	A group of service units is called a service assembly.

Remember, though, that JBI implementations take away much of the complexity from JBI. But it's still important to know how JBI works internally, in case you have to solve some JBI container–related problem when implementing your integration solution.

2.3 *ServiceMix architecture and components*

ServiceMix is a JBI container, and therefore it provides all the infrastructure and tools required by the JBI specification. We don't have the space to explain exactly how ServiceMix implements the JBI specification, but instead we focus on how ServiceMix allows you to easily create your own services and enables those services to communicate with one another.

2.3.1 *ServiceMix overview*

ServiceMix provides a list of JBI components that you can use to solve your integration problems, as you can see in figure 2.12.

The ServiceMix JBI components as shown in figure 2.12 are binding components as well as service engines. The binding components, shown above the NMR, include the `servicemix-http` and `servicemix-file` components. The service engines, shown below the NMR, include the `servicemix-bean` and `servicemix-eip` components.

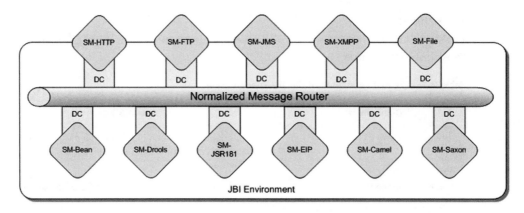

Figure 2.12   Overview of a number of service engines and binding components provided by ServiceMix

Table 2.6 describes the JBI components provided by ServiceMix.

In section 2.2.5 we mentioned that service units are artifacts that can be deployed to a certain JBI component. All the components in table 2.6 support this. If you want to use the SE or BC functionality, you can deploy a service unit (which is nothing more than a JAR file containing a standard file layout) that contains an xbean.xml file.

Table 2.6   The most-used JBI components provided by ServiceMix

Component	Description
servicemix-bean	This service engine allows you to use POJOs as components within the JBI container.
servicemix-eip	ServiceMix's EIP service engine provides various router implementations that can be used to allow more dynamic routing than the default NMR allows. The patterns in the component are based on the patterns from Hohpe and Woolf's *Enterprise Integrations Patterns* book.
servicemix-file	This binding component allows easy access to the file system.
servicemix-http	This binding component allows easy access to SOAP and HTTP-based services.
servicemix-jms	This binding component provides access to JMS implementations like Apache ActiveMQ.
servicemix-camel	Camel is a routing library that contains many of the EIP patterns. This service engine allows you to use Apache Camel functionality for the routing of messages between services.
servicemix-cxf	Apache CXF provides us with web services support. This component, which provides an SE as well as a BC implementation, allows us to easily consume and provide web services.

The service unit JAR file, including the xbean.xml configuration, can be deployed to a JBI component, which will use the information configured in the service unit to create new services and register endpoints to those services. The XML data shown in listing 2.5 shows a complete xbean.xml file that can be deployed as part of a service unit to the `servicemix-file` binding component.

Listing 2.5 Sample XBean configuration for the ServiceMix file BC

```
<beans xmlns:file="http://servicemix.apache.org/file/1.0"
       xmlns:esb="http://esbinaction.com/architecture">
  <file:poller service="esb:poller"        <--❶
    endpoint="pollerEndpoint"        <--❷
    targetService="esb:sender"
    targetEndpoint="senderEndpoint"          ❸
    file="inbox"        <--❹
    period="10000" />        <--❺
</beans>
```

This configuration will create a new service in the file BC with the service name esb:poller ❶. It will also make the file BC register an endpoint with the name poller-Endpoint, through which the service can be invoked ❷. This service endpoint combination must be unique inside the JBI container. After this service unit is deployed, it will be started and will monitor the inbox directory for files ❹; it will poll every 10 seconds ❺. Once a file is found there, it's picked up and sent as an InOnly message exchange to the service and endpoint ❸ specified as target service and target endpoint.

If you look back at the examples from the Mule architecture, you'll immediately see a big difference. Mule has chosen a generic configuration that's used by all the different services. For Mule, it doesn't matter whether you're connecting over JMS or over HTTP—the configuration you use is pretty much the same. ServiceMix, however, through the means of the service units in combination with XBeans, has a unique, XML Schema–backed configuration for each technology. Apache XBean is a subproject of the Apache Geronimo application server project, which provides integration with the Spring framework. With Apache XBean you can easily define your own XML configuration language, and this is exactly what Apache ServiceMix does.

2.3.2 Routing and transformations in ServiceMix

In Mule, routing and transformation are an integral part of the architecture. Because ServiceMix itself is based on JBI, and JBI doesn't specify anything about complex routing and transformations, it isn't part of ServiceMix's architecture.

Luckily, the developers of ServiceMix have provided us with a couple of options that fill in this gap. In this section, we show you a high-level overview of these options and explain how you can use them. In later chapters we describe these approaches in greater detail.

ROUTING USING THE **EIP** SERVICE ENGINE

The EIP service engine provides an implementation of a number of Enterprise Integration patterns that can be used for routing. These components are used just like any of the other service engines used in ServiceMix: via an XML-based configuration. Listing 2.6 shows an XML fragment from such a configuration.

Listing 2.6   Content-based routing using the EIP service engine

```
<eip:content-based-router service="esb:simplerouter"
    endpoint="routerEndpoint">                        ❶ Defines type
  <eip:rules>                                              of router
    <eip:routing-rule>              ❷ Adds routing
      <eip:predicate>                  rule
        <eip:xpath-predicate
            xpath="/esb:order/esb:type=1"     ❸ Evaluates incoming
            namespaceContext="#nsContext" />       message
      </eip:predicate>
      <eip:target>
        <eip:exchange-target
            service="esb:orderService1" />    ❹ Targets service
      </eip:target>                              for routing rule
    </eip:routing-rule>       ❺ Adds another
    <eip:routing-rule>           routing rule
      <eip:predicate>
        <eip:xpath-predicate
            xpath="count(/esb:order/esb:type)=2"
            namespaceContext="#nsContext" />
      </eip:predicate>
      <eip:target>
        <eip:exchange-target
            service="esb:orderService2" />
      </eip:target>
    </eip:routing-rule>       ❻ Targets service
    <eip:routing-rule>           for default rule
      <eip:target>
        <eip:exchange-target service="esb:orderService3" />
      </eip:target>
    </eip:routing-rule>
  </eip:rules>
</eip:content-based-router>
                                          Defines namespace for
<eip:namespace-context id="nsContext">    XPath expression
  <eip:namespaces>
    <eip:namespace
        prefix="esb">http://opensourceesb/architecture
    </eip:namespace>
  </eip:namespaces>
</eip:namespace-context>
```

In listing 2.6 we define a content-based router service ❶. If a message is sent to this service, the service uses routing rules ❷ and ❺ to determine what to do with the message. In a routing rule, a number of predicates ❸ are defined. If all the predicates match, the message is sent to the specified target ❹. If no routing rules match, the message is sent to the routing rule with no predicates ❻.

This is just one of the many routing patterns available in ServiceMix and the EIP service engine. Table 2.7 describes the routing patterns provided.

Table 2.7 The routing patterns supported by the EIP service engine provided with ServiceMix

Router name	Description
Content-based router	Routes a message to a certain service based on its content.
Message filter	Drops a message if it doesn't match a certain criterion.
Pipeline	Serves as a bridge between an In-Only message exchange pattern (MEP) and an in-out MEP.
Static recipient list	Sends a message to a number of different services (multicast).
Static routing slip	Routes a message to a number of services in sequence.
Wire tap	Listens in on the messages being sent on the line.
XPath splitter	Splits a message based on an XPath expression and routes the resulting messages to the specified service.
Splitter/aggregator	Combines the messages from the XPath splitter back into a single message.
Content enricher	Enriches the message with information from an additional service.
Resequencer	Resequences the order of the messages before sending them on to the target.

ROUTING USING CAMEL

Besides routing using the EIP service engine, ServiceMix can use the Apache Camel project to handle its routing. Apache Camel is a subproject of Apache ActiveMQ that implements a full set of Enterprise Integration patterns that can be configured in either Java or XML. We don't go too deep into Apache Camel in this section; we save that for the later chapters, including chapter 5 (where we examine routing support). Just to give you a taste of the functionality of Apache Camel, the following is a quick example of how it works in combination with ServiceMix.

Apache Camel has two different configuration types. You can either write the routing rules in Java using a Java Domain Specific Language (DSL), or you configure the rules in XML. First we see how the most basic routing rule looks in Java (listing 2.7).

Listing 2.7 Camel route using Java

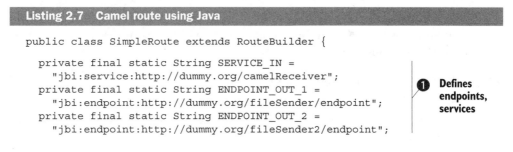

```
public class SimpleRoute extends RouteBuilder {

    private final static String SERVICE_IN =
        "jbi:service:http://dummy.org/camelReceiver";
    private final static String ENDPOINT_OUT_1 =
        "jbi:endpoint:http://dummy.org/fileSender/endpoint";
    private final static String ENDPOINT_OUT_2 =
        "jbi:endpoint:http://dummy.org/fileSender2/endpoint";
```

❶ Defines endpoints, services

```
public void configure() throws Exception {
    from(SERVICE_IN).to(ENDPOINT_OUT_1,ENDPOINT_OUT_2);
}
}
```

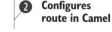 **Configures route in Camel**

In listing 2.7 we use plain Java to configure a route. We first define a number of fully qualified names (names with namespaces) ❶, and in the `configure` method, we tell Apache Camel how it should route a message. The route described in ❷ is a basic route; it listens for messages that are sent to the service specified as `SERVICE_IN` and sends those messages to the endpoints defined as `ENDPOINT_OUT_1` and `ENDPOINT_OUT_2`. So with this simple configuration we've implemented the recipient list pattern, where each incoming message is sent to multiple targets.

Doing this in XML is pretty much the same as in Java, except we use a different notation (listing 2.8).

Listing 2.8   Camel route using XML

```
<route>
    <from uri="jbi:service:http://dummy.org/camelReceiver" />
    <to>
        <uri>jbi:endpoint:http://dummy.org/fileSender/endpoint</uri>
        <uri>jbi:endpoint:http://dummy.org/fileSender2/endpoint</uri>
    </to>
</route>
```

As you can see in listing 2.8, the XML is very readable and easy to understand. You once again specify where the message is coming from, and where you want it to be sent to.

With the EIP and Camel options for routing, ServiceMix provides good support for routing messages from one service (or endpoint) to the other. Next we show you how ServiceMix deals with applying transformations to messages.

APPLYING TRANSFORMATIONS

Transforming messages from one format to another is less important in ServiceMix (or in any other JBI container) than it is in Mule. Since the internal format used has to be XML, all the messages that are sent between the various components are guaranteed to be XML. However, XML messages also come in a lot of different flavors, so we still need message transformation. To implement transformations in ServiceMix, you can use the Saxon service engine, which uses XSLT style sheets, as shown here:

```
<saxon:xslt service="esb:xslt-transformation"
            endpoint="trans-endpoint"
            resource="classpath:OrderTypeAToOrderTypeB.xsl">
```

In addition to the Saxon service engine, ServiceMix provides an Xquery-based transformation component.

2.3.3   *ServiceMix deployment models*

So far we've mainly talked about how JBI and ServiceMix work and how all the various concepts are related to one another. Now let's take a quick look at the various ways you can run ServiceMix.

RUNNING SERVICEMIX AS A STAND-ALONE SERVER

In this book we use ServiceMix as a stand-alone server. We've created an Ant target *start* that starts up ServiceMix and allows you to deploy artifacts to it. In this model you have to manage all resources yourself by configuring them in the `servicemix.xml` configuration file or by adding them to the ServiceMix-provided jndi.xml file.

RUNNING SERVICEMIX FROM A SERVLET ENGINE

ServiceMix can easily be run from a servlet engine such as Apache Tomcat since it already provides a complete web application that can be used to deploy ServiceMix as a web application to a servlet engine. In the ServiceMix distribution you'll find an example folder; in this folder is a project named servicemix-web. This folder contains all the information you need to create a web application that starts ServiceMix.

If you want to play around with servicemix-web, you only have to use Maven to package ServiceMix into a WAR. Use the `mvn package` command in the root directory of this example to create a WAR file, which you can deploy to Tomcat or any other servlet engine.

The ServiceMix web application is also provided as a separate distribution download on the ServiceMix website. This WAR file can be deployed directly to a servlet engine such as Tomcat.

RUNNING AND CONNECTING TO SERVICEMIX FROM AN APPLICATION SERVER

There are two options for deploying ServiceMix to an application server. The first approach is to use ServiceMix's support for Geronimo and JBoss. In this case, ServiceMix will be tightly integrated with Geronimo and JBoss. The ServiceMix website provides tutorials that will help you to complete this integration. For the other application servers, you can use the servlet option we just explained in the servlet engine section.

2.3.4 *ServiceMix wrap-up*

ServiceMix makes working with JBI easier by hiding much of JBI's complexity and providing a simple way to configure and deploy service units. In the following chapters, you'll learn how to work with ServiceMix and create your own custom components.

2.4 *Summary*

This chapter showed you how easy it is to create your own components in Mule. There's a lot more to learn about Mule, and we explore this functionality in the following chapters. Rest assured, though, that with the examples from this chapter, you now have a solid foundation to build on.

You also learned the basic concepts of JBI and explored how ServiceMix implements this specification. We promise that in the following chapters things will get easier, since we'll start using ServiceMix and won't have to worry much about the JBI specification details.

In the next chapter we introduce you to three technologies that we use throughout the book in our examples—Spring, JiBX, and Apache ActiveMQ—and show you how to set up an environment in which you can play around with the examples from this book.

Setting up the Mule and ServiceMix environments

In this chapter:

- Using Spring, JiBX, and ActiveMQ
- Setting up the development environment
- Example implementation with Mule
- Example implementation with ServiceMix

When you work with open source ESBs, you can use other tools and frameworks to help you solve common problems. In this chapter we introduce three tools: Spring, which we use as a component container; JiBX, to help in transforming XML to Java and back again; and Apache ActiveMQ, which we use as our JMS broker to provide reliable messaging.

We also explain how to set up the development environment we'll be working with. We provide you with an easy-to-use environment to test the examples in this book.

Finally, we show you some examples that illustrate how the technologies described in this chapter are used. You can find all this chapter's examples in the source code at the book's website.

When you're working through this chapter, you'll have a complete environment that you can use both for our examples and for your own projects. You'll also gain a basic understanding of the tools that we use to solve some common integration problems and how they're used with the open source ESBs Mule and ServiceMix.

3.1　*Three technologies enhancing the ESB functionality*

For our examples we use technologies (see table 3.1) that will make our work easier and allow for more reuse.

Table 3.1　The technologies we use to enhance the ESB functionality

Name	Description
Spring	Spring is a component framework that makes it easy to work with Plain Old Java Objects (POJOs). We use this framework to create and configure our custom components. Spring is also integrated out of the box in both ServiceMix and Mule 2, so having a basic understanding of this technology is useful.
JiBX	JiBX is an XML-to-Java mapping framework that we use to transform the message format (XML) to an object that we can use in our POJOs. JiBX is able to transform Java objects back to XML.
Apache ActiveMQ (JMS broker)	An important part of an ESB is a message broker. A message broker provides functionality such as asynchronous message exchange and reliable messaging. In this book we use Apache ActiveMQ as a JMS broker implementation.

We have chosen these three technologies because they extend the basic functionality of the ESBs Mule and ServiceMix and make solving integration problems easy by providing some additional functionality.

Some of you might already know how to use these technologies. The reason we introduce them here is to make sure everyone is on the same page and feels confident with these tools. Of these three tools, the first one we look at is Spring.

3.1.1　*Using Spring as an object container*

Spring is a component framework that lets you manage all your components. Spring was introduced in 2002 with Rod Johnson's *Expert One-on-One J2EE Design and Development* (Wrox, 2002). In this book Johnson described a framework that could be used to make lightweight Java applications. The general response to this framework was so overwhelming that Johnson decided to make it open source, and this became the first version of the Spring framework. Nowadays, Spring is used by many tools and other frameworks, including ServiceMix and Mule, which use Spring for their configuration. The Spring framework has evolved from a dependency injection framework to a mature Java application framework that includes, among others, Model-View-Controller (MVC), Data Access Object (DAO), security, and web services modules.

There are many good books on Spring, and there is also a lot of great information to be found online. So if you want to know more about Spring, check out the Spring-Source website at www.springframework.org. *Spring in Action, Second Edition* (Manning, 2007), by Craig Walls with Ryan Breidenbach, serves as a great guideline for working with Spring.

WHAT IS SPRING AND HOW DOES IT WORK?

We introduce you to the most important aspects of the Spring framework and explain how we use it in this book's examples. The goals of Spring are to

- *Simplify J2EE development*—J2EE development is complex. You have to know a lot of different standards before you can start developing. Those of you who have worked with J2EE already know that it's difficult to work with J2EE's component model. Spring aims to make J2EE simpler, without sacrificing any of its power. So you will still have access to transactions, persistency, and messaging, but the development effort is much less. Remember that when Spring was started, J2EE wasn't as easy as it is now. When you needed to write an EJB in those days, you had to write a whole lot of boilerplate code and XML deployment descriptors to expose a simple bean as an EJB.

- *Facilitate best practices*—Besides simplifying J2EE development, Spring makes it easy to follow best practices. It provides a clean separation between your business logic and the enterprise services such as persistency, transactions, and security (which Spring applies using aspect-oriented programming (AOP) techniques (for more information, see *AspectJ in Action* [Manning 2003]).

- *Provide a simple POJO-based programming model*—The last goal of Spring, and the one that we come back to in this book's examples, is the programming model. Spring's programming model is based on POJOs. This means we don't need to write session beans following the rules set out by the J2EE specification or implement all kinds of lifecycle interfaces—we can just create a simple, testable POJO and use Spring to glue everything together.

The previous goals can easily be summarized with a well-known quote from Alan Kay (an American computer scientist known for his early pioneering work on object-oriented programming and windowing graphical user interface design):

> *Simple things should be simple and complex things should be possible.*
>
> —Wikiquote

The POJO-based programming model that Spring uses is one of the most important concepts you should take away from this section. In other words, your applications can be completely coded by just using POJOs. When you're working with Spring, you don't need to worry about implementing specific interfaces or having to conform to a strict programming model (like, for instance, EJB 2*x*). You are able to create your business logic with basic Java classes.

This doesn't mean that you can't work together with these models. Spring has a number of utilities, templates, and more that can be used together with your POJOs to create advanced configurations, and thus allow you to apply enterprise services, such as transaction and security, to your POJOs. All this, however, is done nonintrusively, without tying your business logic to a certain technology. For instance, if you look back at the Mule architecture you'll see something similar. The Mule components, where we locate our integration logic, are just simple POJOs, without a dependency to Mule.

Inversion of control and dependency injection

Spring implements the inversion of control (IoC) and dependency injection (DI) paradigms to provide the flexibility we just described. Since this book isn't about design patterns, we don't spend too much time on these concepts, but we just give you a quick overview. Let's first look at IoC. The analogy people most often make when talking about IoC is called the Hollywood principle: "Don't call me, I'll call you." What this means is that you don't call the framework code, but the framework will call certain methods on your components. This isn't something new; for instance, when you look at the Servlet interface you can see that you must implement the init and destroy methods. These methods are called from the Servlet container on startup and shutdown of your servlet. This concept is also used in Spring to specify which methods to call on construction and destruction of your POJO.

DI is another important concept. This term, coined by Martin Fowler (http://martinfowler.com/articles/injection.html), describes a pattern for performing wiring between beans. This means that any dependencies your POJO might have are injected into your component, instead of you having to retrieve them. In J2EE (at least until Java EE 5) when you required a resource (e.g., a data source or another bean) you had to use the JNDI API to pull that resource in. With DI you don't have to do that anymore—your container will make sure you have the dependency pushed into your POJO by using getters and setters. In the new Java EE 5 specs, many of the same concepts are used.

Enough theory; let's now look at how Spring is used as a component framework. Then we describe how you can use Spring in combination with Mule and ServiceMix.

USING SPRING

In this section, we show how to use Spring to create a POJO-based application. First let's look at a couple of simple beans; the first one is shown in listing 3.1, which contains a simple service implementation.

Listing 3.1 `CustomerServiceImpl` bean that will be configured with Spring

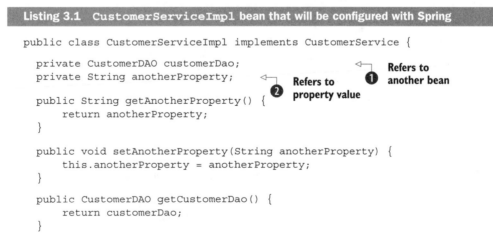

```
public class CustomerServiceImpl implements CustomerService {

    private CustomerDAO customerDao;                    Refers to
    private String anotherProperty;          Refers to  ❶ another bean
                                          ❷ property value
    public String getAnotherProperty() {
        return anotherProperty;
    }

    public void setAnotherProperty(String anotherProperty) {
        this.anotherProperty = anotherProperty;
    }

    public CustomerDAO getCustomerDao() {
        return customerDao;
    }
```

```
public void setCustomerDao(CustomerDAO customerDao) {
    this.customerDao = customerDao;
}
}
```

CustomerServiceImpl is a good example of a service bean implementation that we typically use with Spring. This service has two references: first to the CustomerDAO ❶, which we discuss in listing 3.2, and a second reference to a String property value ❷. In listing 3.3 you'll learn how these references are injected into this class.

In listing 3.2 you can see the CustomerDAO implementation, which is used in the CustomerServiceImpl service bean.

Listing 3.2   CustomerDAO that will be injected into the CustomerBean

```
public class CustomerDAOImpl implements CustomerDAO {

    private String name;
    private String address;
    private String clientnumber;

    public void save() {
    // persist logic
    }

    // getters and setters not shown
}
```

Listing 3.2 contains an implementation of the CustomerDAO interface. This is not a real-life example of a Data Access Object (DAO), but is just used to demonstrate Spring's functionality. The CustomerDAOImpl implementation defines a number of class attributes and a save method to persist a customer.

We configure Spring in such a way that this second bean will be injected in CustomerServiceImpl, as shown in figure 3.1.

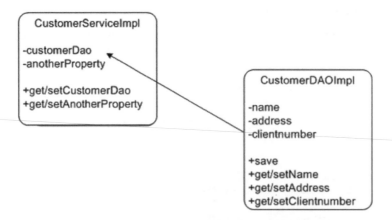

Figure 3.1   A schematic overview of a customer service bean and a customer DAO class implementation. The customer DAO class is injected into the customerDAO property of the customer service bean.

Now we have implemented two Java classes: a service bean and a DAO class. At this point we can use Spring to inject the property values and a bean reference. To implement the DI functionality, we must define a Spring configuration file (see listing 3.3).

Listing 3.3 Spring dependency injection example

```
<beans xmlns="http://www.springframework.org/schema/beans"
  xmlns:xsi="http://www.w3.org/2001/XMLSchema-instance">

  <bean id="customer" class="org.demo.CustomerServiceImpl">     <--(1)
    <property name="anotherProperty" value="someStringValue"/>
    <property name="customerDAO" ref="customerDAO"/>     <--(2)
  </bean>

  <bean id="customerDAO" class="org.demo.CustomerDAOImpl">     <--(3)
    <property name="name" value="Manning"/>
    <property name="address" value="Greenwich"/>     <--(4)
    <property name="clientnumber" value="12345"/>
  </bean>
</beans>
```

In listing 3.3 we configure two Spring beans: a customer bean ❶, which is the implementation of the CustomerServiceImpl class, and a customerDAO ❸, which points to the CustomerDAOImpl. The customer bean defines two properties; one property points to the customerDAO bean ❷ and the other is a simple String property. These two properties will map to the setters we define in our implementations. The customerDAO property maps to the setCustomerDAO method, and the anotherProperty property maps to the setAnotherProperty method.

When the customer bean is retrieved (we show you how later), Spring will make sure that an instance of the customerDAO is injected and that the other properties ❹ are set as well. So we as component developers don't need to worry about retrieving all kinds of dependencies using factories, singletons, and so forth; we just configure how everything is tied together and let Spring inject the dependencies.

USING SPRING WITH MULE AND SERVICEMIX

If you need to create extensions for Mule or ServiceMix (such as custom components or transformers), you can easily do so using standard POJOs and then define and configure those components with Spring, as you've seen in the previous samples.

Let's first look at how you can use Spring together with Mule. As we've already mentioned, everything configured in Mule 2 is configured in Spring. So whenever you configure Mule you're actually already using Spring. Let's start by looking at listing 3.4, which shows how you can create a Mule service that specifies a component directly by using a class name.

Listing 3.4 Using Spring together with Mule: an example service

```
<service name="FileService">
  <inbound>
    <file:inbound-endpoint path="work/in" />
  </inbound>
  <component class="esb.chapter3.Component1" />     <--| Defines component
                                                        using class name
```

```
  <outbound>
    <outbound-pass-through-router>
      <vm:outbound-endpoint path="comp2Queue" />
    </outbound-pass-through-router>
  </outbound>
</service>
```

This service in itself is already defined using Spring. You'll probably notice that this configuration looks very different from the beans we defined earlier. The reason for this is that with Spring 2, you can easily define your own custom XML configuration. We don't go into the details, but it's enough to know that even though it doesn't look like Spring, under the covers Spring is still used.

If we want to use our own Spring beans from this configuration, instead of using the <component> tag with a class attribute, we first need to make our Spring beans available to Mule. To do this, we simply add them to this file or import them from an external file (which is a nice way to keep your configuration files organized). To import them from an external configuration file, use the following statement:

```
<spring:beans>
  <spring:import resource="components.xml"/>
</spring:beans>
```

This will import the Spring beans you've defined in that file into the context of Mule. Note that if we copied all the Spring bean definitions from that file to the Mule configuration, the result would be the same. You can now reference those beans directly from Mule by using the <spring-object> child element of the <component> element, as shown in listing 3.5.

Listing 3.5   Mule component referencing a Spring bean

```
<spring:bean name="component1" class="esb.chapter3.Component1">
  <spring:property name="prop1" value="value1"/>
  <spring:property name="prop2" value="value2"/>
</spring:bean>

<service name="comp1service">
  <inbound>
    <file:inbound-endpoint path="work/in" />
  </inbound>
  <component>
      <spring-object bean="component1"/>          References
  </component>                                    component1
  <outbound>                                      Spring bean
    <outbound-pass-through-router>
      <vm:outbound-endpoint path="comp2Queue" />
    </outbound-pass-through-router>
  </outbound>
</service>
```

You will see this way of configuring components for Mule used throughout the examples in this book. Now that we've shown you how Spring is used and can be referenced from Mule, let's see how to use Spring beans from ServiceMix.

You'll recall from chapter 2 that in ServiceMix you've got a number of components to which you can deploy artifacts (in the form of service units). Those artifacts will then run inside the service engine or binding component. One of the JBI components to which you can deploy service units is the `servicemix-bean` service engine. This JBI component provides functionality to directly run POJOs using Spring, inside Service-Mix, without having to create components following the complete JBI spec. This is a simple way to add custom integration functionality.

POJO beans with servicemix-bean

Although the container is called a bean container and we talk about POJOs here, we do have to implement a specific interface when we want to deploy a Java class to the `servicemix-bean` service engine. As you might remember from chapter 2, in JBI we work with message exchanges. A JBI component doesn't just receive the message content; it receives additional information about the message exchange. So if we want to create a simple component using Spring, we have to tell the JBI container how our JBI component can receive these message exchanges. We've got two options for this. We can either annotate a specific method with the `@operation` annotation, or we have to implement the `MessageExchangeListener` interface. In upcoming chapters we show you how to do this.

Besides the bean component, there is another way of using POJOs in Service-Mix. In chapter 6 we show you how you can use the JSR181 service engine to expose POJOs in ServiceMix to be consumed by other services. However, with the `servicemix-bean` service engine, you have easy access to the JBI context, which in the JSR181 service engine is more difficult. So it's easier to use the JSR181 service engine when you already have functionality that doesn't need to know anything about JBI, and it's easier to use the `servicemix-bean` component when you require access to the JBI environment.

To use the `servicemix-bean` service engine, let's configure a specific ServiceMix configuration, the xbean.xml (see listing 3.6).

Listing 3.6   ServiceMix configuration that references a POJO bean defined in Spring

```
<beans xmlns=http://www.springframework.org/schema/beans
       xmlns:bean="http://servicemix.apache.org/bean/1.0"
       xmlns:esb="http://opensource.esb/jbi">

  <bean id="listenerBean" class="esb.chapter3.ListenerBean"/>      ◁──┐  Defines
                                                                      ❶  Spring
  <!--                                                                   bean
      This deploys to the bean SE. It registers itself
      as service: esb:bean and endpoint beanEndpoint.

      This can now be referenced by its service and endpoint name.
  -->
  <bean:endpoint service="esb:bean" endpoint="beanEndpoint"
        bean="#listenerBean"/>      ◁──┐  References
</beans>                             ❷  Spring bean
```

The one thing to notice in listing 3.6 is the `bean` attribute ❶, ❷. The `bean` attribute points to the `#listenerbean` Spring bean. You can also see that the `bean` endpoint that we defined here also defines service and endpoint names. The combination of the service and endpoint names uniquely identifies this bean in the JBI container.

We can also define the Spring bean in an external file to keep the servicemix-bean and the Spring bean configuration separated. To use this external file, we have to import it, just as we did for Mule. You can do this by adding the following to the XML configuration in listing 3.6:

```
<import resource="components.xml"/>
```

This will import the beans you've defined into the ServiceMix context. The components.xml file can be implemented with this code:

```
<?xml version="1.0" encoding="UTF-8"?>
<beans xmlns="http://www.springframework.org/schema/beans">
    <bean id="listenerBean" class="esb.chapter3.ListenerBean"/>
</beans>
```

And that's all there is to it. We've now shown how Spring can be used with Mule and ServiceMix. As you can see, both Mule and ServiceMix make working with Spring very easy, since both already use a Spring-based configuration. What you've seen here so far is only the most basic usage of Spring in Mule and ServiceMix. In upcoming chapters you'll see more complex examples.

Now that you know the basics of Spring and we've explored integrating Spring with Mule and ServiceMix, it's time to move on to JiBX.

Spring integration

We've only covered the basics of Spring in this section. Spring has grown from an IoC object container to a large framework that covers areas such as web services, front-end development, batch processing, and more. One of the newer Spring projects, which is closely related to Mule and ServiceMix, is called *Spring Integration*. With Spring Integration you get the basic building blocks, such as channels, queues, routers, and adapters, which you can easily use in your own applications. Spring Integration provides an easy way to connect message-driven environments to your own POJOs without you having to worry about the infrastructure, events, JMS, and other concerns. In other words, it provides an abstraction layer between your application and the messaging middleware.

Configuring Spring Integration is done in much the same way as configuring Mule and ServiceMix. It has its own XML configuration language that defines, for example, incoming channels and adapters and connects them to your POJOs. So if you understand the basic ideas behind Mule and ServiceMix, working with Spring Integration won't be too difficult. To see an example of how to use Spring Integration, see the end of chapter 4.

3.1.2 *XML marshaling with JiBX*

When you're working with integration tools, you're often working with XML. XML provides a standard format for exchanging information between systems. However, working with XML directly from Java is a bit cumbersome. In our integration logic, we want to work with standard Java objects, but we still need a generic format that can be sent between the various components. Many open source libraries are available that allow you to easily transform a Java object to XML and back again, such as Java Architecture for XML Binding (JAXB) and Service Data Objects (SDOs).

For this book we chose JiBX, an open source framework. Using JiBX you can create a mapping definition that provides the necessary functionality to map from XML messages to your existing Java objects and back again. The main reason why we chose this framework is its flexibility. You can easily reuse your existing Java classes and have full control of how the Java classes are mapped to XML, and vice versa.

Using JiBX together with Mule and ServiceMix will allow us to keep using Java objects inside our Java code instead of having to work with XML. In this section, we show you how JiBX works, and also how you can integrate JiBX into Mule and Service-Mix to provide easy mapping from and to XML.

DEFINING JiBX MAPPING CONFIGURATIONS

To get JiBX to work, you need to create a mapping definition. This definition tells JiBX how an XML message is mapped to a Java object. In this definition file, you specify the name of the element in the XML message and then specify the name of the field in the Java object it needs to be mapped to. Let's map the following XML message:

```
<person>
    <firstname>John</firstname>
    <lastname>Doe</lastname>
    <city>Amsterdam</city>
    <country>The Netherlands</country>
</person>
```

Of course, this is a simple XML message, but it's a good one to start with. This XML message has a Java class equivalent:

```
public class Person {

    private String firstName;
    private String lastName;
    private String city;
    private String country;

    // getters and setters
}
```

To map the person XML message to the Person Java class and back again, we need to create a JiBX mapping file (see listing 3.7).

> **Listing 3.7 JiBX mapping file of the `person` XML message to a `Person` Java class**

```
<binding>      <-- ❶
  <mapping name="person" class="org.demo.Person">      <-- ❷
```

```
      <value name="firstname" field="firstName" />
      <value name="lastname" field="lastName" />      ◄─❸
      <value name="city" field="city" />
      <value name="country" field="country" />
   </mapping>
 </binding>
```

In the JiBX mapping file you define the root element name of the XML message (person in this case) and the Java class we want to map it to ❷. Notice that there is a binding root element ❶, which is used by JiBX to represent the start of the mapping definitions. The next part involves defining the mapping between the message child elements and the properties of the Java class ❸. We do this by specifying the name of the XML element (e.g., firstname), and then in the field property we can specify the corresponding Java property (e.g., firstName). Figure 3.2 shows the mapping of a value from an XML file to a property in a Java object.

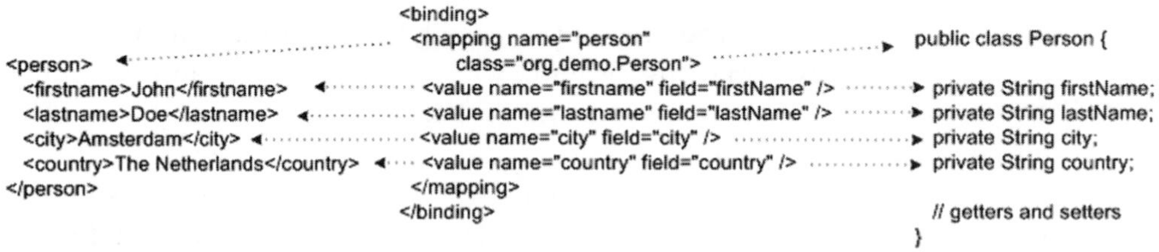

```
                                      <binding>
                                        <mapping name="person"                         public class Person {
<person>    ◄·······················      class="org.demo.Person">  ·······················►
  <firstname>John</firstname>    ◄·······    <value name="firstname" field="firstName" />  ·········►  private String firstName;
  <lastname>Doe</lastname>    ◄···········    <value name="lastname" field="lastName" />  ·········►  private String lastName;
  <city>Amsterdam</city>  ◄·············    <value name="city" field="city" />  ·····················►  private String city;
  <country>The Netherlands</country>  ◄····  <value name="country" field="country" />  ············►  private String country;
</person>                                    </mapping>
                                         </binding>                                        // getters and setters
                                                                                           }
```

Figure 3.2   An example of how JiBX maps the elements of an XML message to a Java object

The example shown in figure 3.2 is the most basic JiBX mapping. We show you a couple more binding options that will allow you to map most Java objects to XML, and vice versa. Let's start once again by showing you the XML message that we want to map in the following code snippet:

```
<person>
   <firstname>John</firstname>
   <lastname>Doe</lastname>
   <address>
     <city>Amsterdam</city>
     <country>The Netherlands</country>
   </address>
</person>
```

The corresponding Java object is shown in this code snippet:

```
public class Person {
   private String firstName;
   private String lastName;
   private Address address;
}

public class Address {
   private String city;
   private String country
}
```

As you can see, we can't map the XML message to a single Java object. Part of the XML message, the address elements, has to be mapped to a separate Java class. We can do this by introducing a structure element, as listing 3.8 shows.

Listing 3.8 JiBX mapping example with a structure definition

```
<binding>
  <mapping name="person" class="org.demo.Person">
    <value name="firstname" field="firstName" />
    <value name="lastname" field="lastName" />
    <structure name="address" field="address"      ❶
            class="org.demo.Address">
      <value name="city" field="city" />
      <value name="country" field="country" />      ◁—❷
    </structure>
    </mapping>
</binding>
```

In listing 3.8 we define a structure that maps the address element to the Java property in the Person class with the same name ❶. We also specify that the structure element be mapped to the Java class Address. This way, we can easily map an element in an XML message to a Java class other than the root element (in this example, the Person class). Inside the structure element, the same mappings we showed earlier are configured to map the address XML elements to the properties in the Address Java class, such as the country element ❷.

Figure 3.3 illustrates how the previous mapping file maps the structure to the Java object.

Now that you understand the structure definition of JiBX, you should be able to map complex XML messages to corresponding Java objects. However, we haven't discussed the use of namespaces yet.

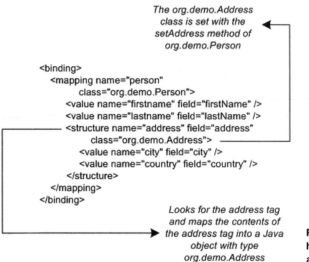

Figure 3.3 An example that shows how JiBX maps a structure element to a Java class

XML namespaces are used to uniquely identify a certain XML element, and you'll see these in most real-world XML usage. If you want to map an XML message that uses namespaces, you must configure these namespaces in the JiBX binding file. For our example, we use the same Java objects as we did in the previous example. But this time, we change the XML to use a namespace definition:

```
<ps:person xmlns:ps="http://demo/persons"
        xmlns:ad="http://demo/address">
  <ps:firstname>Jos</ps:firstname>
  <ps:lastname>Dirksen</ps:lastname>
  <ad:address>
    <ad:city>Eindhoven</ad:city>
    <ad:country>The Netherlands</ad:country>
  </ad:address>
</ps:person>
```

We add two namespaces to the person XML message: one for the person-specific elements, which uses the "ps" prefix, and one for the address-specific elements, which uses the "ad" prefix. We need to make some small changes to the binding file to support this (see listing 3.9).

Listing 3.9   An example of a JiBX binding file with namespaces

```
<binding>
  <mapping name="person" class="org.demo.Person">
    <namespace uri="http://demo/persons"          ▏ Defines person
        default="elements"/>                        ▏ namespace
    <value name="firstname" field="firstName" />
    <value name="lastname" field="lastName" />
    <structure name="address" field="address"
        class="org.demo.Address">
      <namespace uri="http://demo/address"         ▏ Defines address
          default="elements"/>                       ▏ namespace
      <value name="city" field="city" />
      <value name="country" field="country" />
    </structure>
  </mapping>
</binding>
```

With the changes we made to the binding file compared to the one in listing 3.8, JiBX is now configured to look for the person element and its child elements, in the http://demo/persons namespace, and the address elements and its child elements should be in the http://demo/address namespace.

USING JiBX TO TRANSFORM XML MESSAGES INTO JAVA

In the previous section you learned how to configure the mappings between Java objects and XML messages with JiBX, but we haven't shown you how to use these mappings. First you need to run the binding compiler, which will use the binding definition and compile it into your class files. In other words, your class files will be enriched with the information required to marshal XML objects to Java and back again.

Running this binding compiler isn't difficult. You have two options. The first is to run the binding compiler directly:

```
java -jar jibx-bind.jar yourbinding.xml
```

Remember that if you choose this approach you have to ensure that all the classes you're binding to (and superclasses as well) are on the classpath.

The second option is the one we use in this book. You can use an Ant task to run the binding compiler directly from your build file. To be able to run the binding compiler within an Ant build file, first create a new Ant task definition:

```
<!-- JiBX binding compiler task definition -->
<taskdef name="bind" classname="org.jibx.binding.ant.CompileTask"
    classpath="${jibx-lib}/jibx-bind.jar"/>
```

The JiBX task definition tells Ant which JiBX class should be executed to run the binding compiler and configures the classpath. With the JiBX task definition in place, we can define a bind configuration within an Ant target:

```
<!-- Run JiBX binding compiler -->
<bind verbose="true" load="true" binding="binding.xml">
  <classpath>
    <pathelement path="classes"/>
    <pathelement location="${jibx-lib}/jibx-run.jar"/>
  </classpath>
</bind>
```

Once you've run the binding compiler, you're ready to use the bindings from your application. The binding compiler processes the binding file and creates Java classes to execute the XML marshaling at runtime.

When we use JiBX in the examples in this book, you don't have to worry too much about running the JiBX binding compiler. The build files used to run and compile the examples in this book already use the previously shown JiBX Ant tasks.

Using JiBX from your application code is easy. Let's first see how to use JiBX to marshal a Java object to an XML file:

```
StringWriter outWriter = new StringWriter();
IMarshallingContext ctx = BindingDirectory.getFactory(Person.class)
    .createMarshallingContext();
ctx.marshalDocument(person, "UTF-8", null, outWriter);
```

You first need to get an `IMarshallingContext`. With this context you can use the `marshalDocument` method on your object instance to write the XML output to a `Writer` implementation—for example, a `StringWriter`.

When you want to go from XML to Java, you must use similar steps. But instead of using an `IMarshallingContext`, you should use an `IUnmarshallingContext`, as you can see in the following code snippet:

```
IUnmarshallingContext ctx = BindingDirectory.getFactory(Person.class)
    .createUnmarshallingContext();
Object obj = ctx.unmarshalDocument(new StringReader(data));
```

You've now seen how to configure binding files for JiBX, how to run the binding compiler, and how to invoke the JiBX bindings from Java. So if you want to use JiBX from your application code, you can use the code snippets we showed you to do so. In the next section, you'll learn how to use JiBX together with ServiceMix and Mule.

USING JiBX WITH MULE AND SERVICEMIX

JiBX is used in this book whenever a transformation is required from XML to Java or the other way around. In most examples, we send the data as XML between the various components. ServiceMix requires this, and it's generally considered good practice. Mule doesn't have any special requirements for the data sent between components; with Mule, you can just as easily send serialized Java objects between components.

Canonical data format and normalized messages

It's often a good practice to define a common format for the messages that are exchanged between the various components and services. This format is called a *canonical data format*. You might wonder why this is useful; why not simply apply a transformation between the formats and be done with it? Well, that approach works when you don't have to integrate multiple applications. If you have two or three applications to integrate, it's often not that hard to keep track of the different data format requirements of these applications. However, when the number of applications increases you have to write more and more transformations to keep all the applications talking to one another. If you add a new application and you use the canonical data format, you only need to write one transformation—the one from the canonical data format to the new application—instead of writing new transformations for all the applications that are already connected.

Note, though, that when using ServiceMix you don't automatically have a canonical data format. What you've got is a *normalized message*, which describes what the data that is sent over the line looks like—XML in the case of ServiceMix. A canonical data format goes one step further. It defines not only the type of the message, but also the format (and in the optimal case, the semantics as well). So if, say, we want to use a canonical data format, we also have to specify an XML Schema that exactly describes the XML format of the messages that we're sending over the line. As an example, consider the Universal Business Language (UBL) standard. This standard defines a number of XML Schemas and messages that you can use when you're working with orders, receipts, and invoices. You could choose to use UBL as the canonical data format you're using for your integration solution.

When there is already existing business logic implemented or when new business logic has to be included, you usually don't want to work with XML messages directly. From a developer perspective, it's much simpler to develop against Java objects. So we need an easy mechanism to transform the Java objects to XML messages, and vice versa.

Mule provides an easy access point for this with the transformer concept. Listing 3.10 shows an example of implementing a Java object–to-XML transformation step in Mule.

Listing 3.10 Implementation of the `ObjectToXML` transformer for Mule

```
public class ObjectToXML extends AbstractTransformer {      ◄─❶

  protected Object doTransform(Object payload)      ◄─❷
        throws TransformerException {
    try {
      StringWriter outWriter = new StringWriter();
      IMarshallingContext ctx = BindingDirectory.getFactory(      ❸
          payload.getClass()).createMarshallingContext();
      ctx.marshalDocument(payload, "UTF-8", null, outWriter);
      return outWriter.toString();
    } catch (JiBXException e) {
      throw new TransformerException(this, e);
    }
  }
}
```

In listing 3.10, we implement a transformer for Mule based on JiBX. In the previous examples we've shown how you can use JiBX to marshal an object to XML. We can use this functionality without any change in a Mule transformer ❶. When this transformer receives the message payload ❷, it checks the class of the object and retrieves the specific marshaling context for that class ❸. Then the JiBX context marshals the Java object contents to an XML String representation.

Of course, we also must be able to create a Java object from an XML message when we receive a message in a service bean. The Mule transformer implementation for the XML to Java marshaling is shown in listing 3.11.

Listing 3.11 Implementation of the `XMLToObject` transformer for Mule

```
public class XMLToObject extends AbstractTransformer {

private String targetClassName;      ◄─❶

  protected Object doTransform(Object xmldata)      ◄─❷
        throws TransformerException {
    try {
      IUnmarshallingContext ctx = BindingDirectory
          .getFactory(Class.forName(targetClassName))      ❸
          .createUnmarshallingContext();
      return ctx.unmarshalDocument(new StringReader(xmldata));
    } catch (Exception e) {
      throw new TransformerException (this, e);
    }
  }

  public String getTargetClassName() {
    return targetClassName;
  }

  public void setTargetClassName(String targetClassName) {
    this.targetClassName = targetClassName;
  }
}
```

The XMLToObject Mule transformer receives an XML String as input and transforms it into a Java object ❷. To be able to create the JiBX unmarshaling context ❸, we need to specify the class of the Java object we want to transform to ❶. This only works for objects for which we've created a mapping file and for which we've run the binding compiler.

Now that you've seen how to implement a Mule transformer based on JiBX to transform Java to XML and back again, let's implement a similar transformer for ServiceMix.

For ServiceMix we need to provide a helper class to implement the transformations. ServiceMix itself is JBI based, so all the data that's sent between the components needs to be in line with the JBI specification—which means it has to be XML. So when we create our custom components for ServiceMix, we can use a helper class that handles the transformation for us. Let's look at the servicemix-bean implementation that uses JiBX to marshal and unmarshal the XML messages (listing 3.12).

Listing 3.12 The servicemix-bean implementation, using the JiBX framework

```
public class SimpleListenerBean
    implements MessageExchangeListener {
                                                    Implements ❶
    @Resource                              MessageExchangeListener
    private DeliveryChannel channel;                  interface

    public void onMessageExchange(MessageExchange exchange)
        throws MessagingException {
      if (exchange.getStatus() != ExchangeStatus.ACTIVE)
        return;

      NormalizedMessage msg = exchange.getMessage("in");
      try {
        Person person = (Person)
          JiBXUtil.unMarshalDocument(msg)        Unmarshals XML
              .getContent(), Person.class);      to Java object

        person.setName("John Doe");
        exchange.getMessage("out").setContent(JiBXUtil.     Marshals Java
          marshalDocument(person, "UTF-8"));             object to XML

        MessageUtil.transferInToOut(exchange, exchange);
        channel.send(exchange);

      } catch (JiBXException e) {
        throw new MessagingException(
              "Error transforming object to or from XML");
      }
    }
}
```

The SimpleListenerBean implementation contains the onMessageExchange method of the MessageExchangeListener interface ❶. The incoming message of the JBI message exchange is unmarshaled to a Person Java object, using a JiBX utility class that we discuss in listing 3.13. Then the name of the person is changed on the Java object and the object is marshaled to an XML message again. The XML message is a `Source` instance; in this example we use a `StreamSource`.

The `SimpleListenerBean` uses a JiBX utility class for the JiBX-specific functionality. Let's look at the implementation of the `JiBXUtil` class in listing 3.13.

Listing 3.13 `JiBXUtil` class showing how to unmarshal and marshal XML messages

```
public static Object unMarshalDocument(Source source,
      Class targetClass) throws JiBXException {
  Object result = null;
  try {
    IUnmarshallingContext ctx = BindingDirectory
        .getFactory(targetClass)
        .createUnmarshallingContext();
    result = ctx.unmarshalDocument((InputStream) new         Unmarshals XML
      ByteArrayInputStream(getBytes(source)), "UTF-8");        to a Java object
  } catch (Exception e) {
    throw new JiBXException("Error unmarshalling", e);
  }
  return result;
}
public static Source marshalDocument(Object src)
      throws JiBXException {
  Source result = null;
  try {
    ByteArrayOutputStream bOut = new ByteArrayOutputStream();
    IMarshallingContext ctx = BindingDirectory.getFactory(
        src.getClass()).createMarshallingContext();
    ctx.marshalDocument(src, "UTF-8", null, bOut);          Marshals Java
    result = new StreamSource(                               object to XML
        new ByteArrayInputStream(bOut.toByteArray()));
  } catch (Exception e) {
    throw new JiBXException("Error marshalling", e);
  }
  return result;
}
```

The methods in listing 3.13 look much like the methods we've seen for Mule, only this time we use a `java.xml.transform.Source` object as our input and output for the JiBX methods. ServiceMix uses this class to represent the XML messages in a message exchange.

Well, that's it for our discussion on JiBX. For Mule we've defined transformers that take care of transforming a message into and from XML, and for ServiceMix we created a helper class that can, for instance, be used with the `servicemix-bean` service engine.

The final technology we discuss is ActiveMQ, which provides us with asynchronous communication and reliable messaging capabilities.

3.1.3   *Using JMS with the ActiveMQ broker*

ActiveMQ is an open source JMS broker that we use in our examples together with Mule and ServiceMix. You might ask yourself, "Why would we need a separate JMS broker, when we've already got a complete ESB?" The answer is rather simple. Mule doesn't focus on the transport layer; its focus is to provide ESB functionality such as routing and transformation. In other words, for Mule it doesn't matter whether all the messages are transported over HTTP, JMS, TCP, SMTP, or any of the other supported transports.

If you're in a production environment you want a reliable transport mechanism, and you may choose JMS. With JMS you can support reliable messaging and ensure that your messages arrive at the target destination. Another advantage of using JMS is that it's easily pluggable. You can, for instance, replace ActiveMQ with a different JMS-compliant broker such as Joram, WebSphere MQ, JBoss MQ, or any of the other dozen implementations.

So what about ServiceMix? Does ServiceMix also require a JMS broker for reliable messaging? Yes, it does. When you run ServiceMix using the default Staged Event-Driven Architecture (SEDA) flow, the message exchanges are routed using the default, nonpersistent, normalized message router. ServiceMix also has the option to run its normalized message router based on a JMS flow, which uses ActiveMQ. The JMS flow provides reliability, clustering, and fail-over capabilities to ServiceMix. ActiveMQ is delivered as part of the ServiceMix distribution, so you don't have to perform a separate installation as you would with Mule.

EXPLAINING THE JMS SPECIFICATION

For those of you not familiar with JMS, let's quickly discuss how JMS works (see figure 3.4).

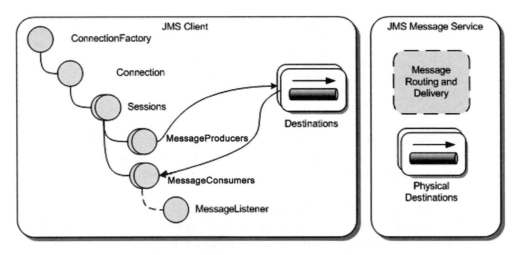

Figure 3.4   The important concepts of the JMS specification. The JMS classes that are common when developing JMS-based functionality are shown as well.

With JMS it's possible to create clients that *receive* messages from a JMS broker and clients that *put* messages on a JMS broker. These clients are called, respectively, `Message-Consumers` and `MessageProducers`. Before creating these clients, follow these steps:

1　*Obtain a* `ConnectionFactory`—There are two ways to get a connection factory. The official way is to use JNDI to look up a `ConnectionFactory` in a JNDI registry. We don't bore you with all the details, but this is the most flexible method and allows you to easily change the JMS broker without altering the client code. The other (not recommended) way is to create a `ConnectionFactory` programmatically. This may be easier to do, but you're pretty much wiring yourself to a specific JMS broker.

2　*Create a connection*—Once you have a `ConnectionFactory` you can use it to create a connection. The `ConnectionFactory` contains the information on how to connect to the JMS broker.

3　*Create a session*—Another abstraction layer used by JMS is the session. We can create multiple sessions on a connection, and sessions themselves can have multiple providers and consumers.

4　*Create the* `MessageConsumer` *or* `MessageProducer`—Now you can create a `MessageConsumer` (or a `MessageProducer`) to receive (or send) on a specific destination via the session instance.

In JMS we have two types of destinations. The first is a queue, which is used to implement point-to-point message channels. With a queue, you can have many different message producers and many different message consumers (though a JMS message can be consumed by only one consumer). In addition to queues, you can use topics, which can implement publish-subscribe message channels. You can have multiple publishers sending messages to a topic, and all the subscribers on that topic will receive the published messages. Note that when no subscribers are listening on the topic, the message may get lost.

We've only skimmed the surface of JMS, but this should be enough information to comprehend the JMS-related topics in this and upcoming chapters.

Apache ActiveMQ is a popular JMS broker, which can be used with both Mule and ServiceMix. The ServiceMix distribution even includes an ActiveMQ distribution out of the box. ActiveMQ is a very mature JMS broker and is simple to use and configure. We first look at some of the features of ActiveMQ, and then we show you an example configuration.

ACTIVEMQ FEATURES
So what are the features that are interesting to us?

- *Full support of JMS 1.1*—Since we'll be using the default JMS API, we need a JMS broker that supports the JMS specification; ActiveMQ provides full support for this specification.
- *Supports easy persistence*—We need a reliable transport to complement the Mule and ServiceMix ESBs. For a reliable transport, we need a way to persist messages so that when the ESB goes down, the messages on the JMS broker can be recovered. ActiveMQ provides an easy way to use JDBC for persisting messages.

- *Spring support*—This is a very important feature for us. Since we're going to specify most of our reusable components in Spring, being able to configure ActiveMQ with Spring makes it all a lot more understandable.
- *In-memory JMS provider*—ActiveMQ can be used as an in-memory JMS provider. This means we can easily start a complete JMS broker from our code. This approach makes testing much more efficient.

Now let's look at how we can configure ActiveMQ to be used as a reliable message broker.

EXAMPLE OF AN ACTIVEMQ CONFIGURATION
ActiveMQ is configured with an XML file named activemq.xml. Listing 3.14 shows an example ActiveMQ configuration using a PostgreSQL database for persistency.

Listing 3.14   ActiveMQ configuration using a PostgreSQL database for persistency

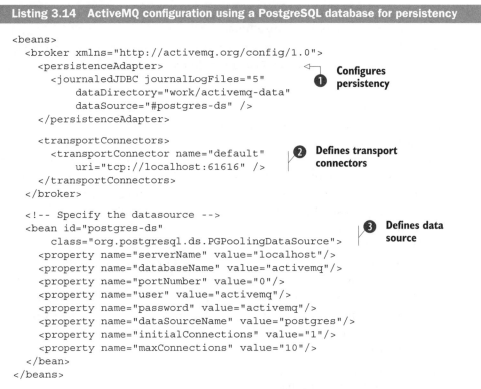

```
<beans>
  <broker xmlns="http://activemq.org/config/1.0">
    <persistenceAdapter>
      <journaledJDBC journalLogFiles="5"          ◁─┐  ❶ Configures
          dataDirectory="work/activemq-data"             persistency
          dataSource="#postgres-ds" />
    </persistenceAdapter>

    <transportConnectors>
      <transportConnector name="default"         ❷ Defines transport
          uri="tcp://localhost:61616" />            connectors
    </transportConnectors>
  </broker>

  <!-- Specify the datasource -->
  <bean id="postgres-ds"                          ❸ Defines data
      class="org.postgresql.ds.PGPoolingDataSource">   source
    <property name="serverName" value="localhost"/>
    <property name="databaseName" value="activemq"/>
    <property name="portNumber" value="0"/>
    <property name="user" value="activemq"/>
    <property name="password" value="activemq"/>
    <property name="dataSourceName" value="postgres"/>
    <property name="initialConnections" value="1"/>
    <property name="maxConnections" value="10"/>
  </bean>
</beans>
```

The example ActiveMQ configuration consists of the following parts:

- *Persistency configuration* ❶—This section specifies that ActiveMQ must persist the messages in the queues and topics. We also specify the working directory of ActiveMQ (work/activeMQ in this example) where the journal files are being stored. The final configuration here is the database that's going to be used to persist the messages.
- *Transport connectors configuration* ❷—In this section we define how to connect to the ActiveMQ broker. This is an important section, since it specifies how Mule

and ServiceMix connect to ActiveMQ as their JMS provider. In this example we show that we can connect to this broker over TCP using the port 61616 (this is also the default configuration of ActiveMQ).

■ *Data source definition* ❸—Finally, we configure how ActiveMQ can connect to our PostgreSQL database. These are the common properties you see with any data source configuration.

Because ServiceMix delivers ActiveMQ out of the box, a standard ActiveMQ configuration is already present. By default, ServiceMix doesn't use database persistency for its message exchanges. When you download ActiveMQ for use with Mule, the default configuration also doesn't include database persistency. Let's look at the details of using ActiveMQ with Mule and ServiceMix.

USING JMS AND ACTIVEMQ IN MULE AND SERVICEMIX
If you want to use ActiveMQ in Mule and Servicemix, we need to configure the ESBs in such a way that they can get a reference to the ActiveMQ connection factory. We need this functionality to be able to send and receive messages via a JMS transport.

Let's start by looking at how to do this in a Mule configuration (see listing 3.15).

Listing 3.15 Definition of an ActiveMQ connection in a Mule configuration

```
<mule xmlns="http://www.mulesource.org/schema/mule/core/2.0"
    xmlns:xsi="http://www.w3.org/2001/XMLSchema-instance"
    xmlns:jms="http://www.mulesource.org/schema/mule/jms/2.0"    ◁─❶
    xsi:schemaLocation="
      http://www.mulesource.org/schema/mule/core/2.0
        http://www.mulesource.org/schema/mule/core/2.0/mule.xsd
      http://www.mulesource.org/schema/mule/jms/2.0
        http://www.mulesource.org/schema/mule/jms/2.0/mule-jms.xsd">

  <jms:activemq-connector name="jmsConnection"
          brokerURL="tcp://localhost:61616"/>    ❷
</mule>
```

In listing 3.15 we specify the configuration of a connection to ActiveMQ by creating a connection factory specific for ActiveMQ ❷. We also configure the connection factory to connect to the default location ActiveMQ is running on: `tcp://localhost:61616`. Notice that the `activemq-conector` element is namespace-qualified with a Mule JMS namespace ❶, ❷. For each transport Mule provides a transport-specific set of elements and a corresponding namespace. Now we can use the JMS transport functionality to create JMS endpoints. (We show you how to do this in section 3.3, when we present an extensive Mule example.)

Configuring a connection to the ActiveMQ broker in ServiceMix isn't that much harder. Again we only need to configure a connection factory to use JMS functionality in the ServiceMix environment. Listing 3.16 shows how to configure a connection to ActiveMQ as part of a `servicemix-jms` xbean.xml configuration.

Listing 3.16 Defining an ActiveMQ connection in a `servicemix-jms` configuration

```
<beans xmlns:jms="http://servicemix.apache.org/jms/1.0">
  <bean id="connectionFactory"
      class="org.apache.activemq.ActiveMQConnectionFactory">
    <property name="brokerURL" value="tcp://localhost:61616" />    ◁─❶
  </bean>
</beans>
```

The ServiceMix configuration is quite similar to the Mule configuration we saw in list-ing 3.15. The main difference is that ServiceMix doesn't provide an element for defin-ing an ActiveMQ broker connection, but it uses a Spring bean to create the connection
❶. We show a detailed example of how to define JMS consumers and providers in a
`servicemix-jms` configuration in section 3.4.

In the last couple of sections, we've introduced three technologies: Spring, JiBX,
and ActiveMQ. This information provides a common background for the examples in
this book. In the next section, wel look at setting up the development environment to
be able to start working with the book's examples.

3.2   *Preparing the development environment*

Let's get started with setting up the environment that we use throughout this book.
We explain how you can run (and play with) the provided examples. Note that you
don't need to use Eclipse to run our examples. We provide Ant scripts so that you can
also run them from the command line or from other integrated development envi-ronments (IDEs) such as NetBeans or IntelliJ.

3.2.1   *Setting up ESBs, tools, and required libraries*

Before we get started, make sure you have the correct versions of Ant and Java
installed. Mule and ServiceMix can run with older versions of Java, but some of our
examples use Java 5 features, so make sure you've got an up-to-date Java version
installed. Besides an up-to-date Java version, we use Ant for automating download,
compile, build, and startup tasks, so we also require an up-to-date Ant version.

INSTALLING THE LATEST JAVA VERSION
To check your version of Java, run `java -version` from the command line. This com-mand should return something similar to this:

```
java version "1.6.0_06"
Java(TM) 2 Runtime Environment, Standard Edition (build 1.6.0_06-b02)
Java HotSpot(TM) Client VM (build 10.0-b22, mixed mode, sharing)
```

Notice that this is the output of a Java 6 runtime environment, but Java 5 is also
fine. If the Java version shown is below 1.5, then please install a newer version from
http://java.sun.com/javase/downloads/index.jsp.

INSTALLING THE LATEST ANT VERSION
Besides an up-to-date Java version, we also use Ant to run the examples. If you
don't have Ant installed, please download and install the latest version from

http://ant.apache.org. If you do have Ant installed, run the `ant -version` command to check the version of your installation. Verify that the version returned is at least 1.7. If you've installed an older version, go to http://ant.apache.org and download the latest version.

SETTING UP THE ENVIRONMENT WITH ANT

Now that you know that the correct versions of Java and Ant are installed on your system, let's get the libraries, servers, and tools used in this book. Some of the tools used in this book, such as the Apache Directory Server in chapter 8, need a separate installation. We've created an archive that you can download from this book's website, http://www.esbinaction.com/rademakers (if you haven't done so already in chapter 1). Unpack this archive into a directory of your choice, and you'll see that the following directory structure has been created:

```
-boxResources
-esb
-libraries
-prepareResources
-tools
-workspace
build.xml
```

In the esb subdirectory we'll install ServiceMix and Mule. If you've worked through the examples in chapter 1, you've already installed Mule and ServiceMix in this directory. In the libraries subdirectory, we'll store all the required libraries used in our examples. In the tools directory, we'll install various servers such as an EJB container, and an XML and relational database. The workspace directory contains the examples and resources shown in this book. If you look through the directories, you'll notice that most of them are still empty. This is because providing all the libraries would make the downloadable archive very large. So to get started, we'll use the Ant build file in the root directory, build.xml, to download all the libraries, servers, and tools and then store them in the right directory structure.

> ### Ant, Ivy, and Maven
>
> For this book we chose to use Ant for all the builds and examples, and we also use Ant to set up the initial environment. The reason we use Ant instead of Ivy or Maven is that with Ant we can easily get the installation archives and unpack them to specific directories. This would also be possible with Maven or with Ivy, but would involve a lot of work in getting all the dependencies correct and getting the dependencies in the proper target directory.
>
> The main reason to use Ant is that we're not forced into a specific directory structure or project setup (Maven does force that on you). However, when you're doing your own ServiceMix project, Maven might be a good option. The people behind ServiceMix have provided a nice set of Maven artifacts that you can use to set up and deploy service units and service assemblies to ServiceMix.

To get all the correct libraries (we list the versions in appendix G), you should run the ant script from the root directory where you unpacked the downloaded archive, which happens to be the directory where the Ant file is located. You do this by running the following command:

```
ant prepare-environment
```

When you run this example, you can get a cup of coffee, since this will start downloading all the required libraries, tools, and servers from various online repositories and websites. When you scroll back in your console, you'll see output in your console that looks similar to this:

```
init:
    [mkdir] Created dir: tools
    [mkdir] Created dir: libraries
get-mule:
    [echo] Downloading Mule.... (38MB)
    [get] Getting: http://snapshots.dist.codehaus.org/mule/org/mule/
    ➥distributions/mule-full/2.0.2/mule-full-2.0.2.zip
    [get] To: work/downloads/mule-full-2.0.2.zip
```

When the Ant build file has finished executing, you'll have a completely configured environment that you can use to run the book's examples and play around with the Mule and ServiceMix ESBs.

Navigate to the workspace folder and you'll see two subdirectories. One directory contains a Mule workspace and the other a ServiceMix workspace. In these workspaces you'll find all the examples from this book. So just navigate to the correct chapter in these workspaces and you'll find an Ant file there that you can use to run the examples from that specific chapter. In all the upcoming chapters we explain which Ant file and which target you need for a specific example.

So far we've only set up a command line–based environment. Since developing and experimenting with the code is much easier from an IDE, let's see how you can use Eclipse together with these examples.

3.2.2 *Running examples from Eclipse*

You don't have to do much to run our examples from Eclipse. In this section we show how to import the examples in Eclipse. To do this, start Eclipse and create a new workspace that points to the workspace/workspace-mule directory (where you unpacked the downloaded archive). When Eclipse has started, select File > Import from the Eclipse menu. This opens the screen shown in figure 3.5.

From this screen select Existing Projects into Workspace and click Next. This opens the Import Projects screen, shown in figure 3.6.

On the Import Projects screen, use the Browse button to navigate to the workspace/workspace-mule directory. After you've selected that directory, you can select the Mule project and import it into your own workspace. Make sure, though, that you

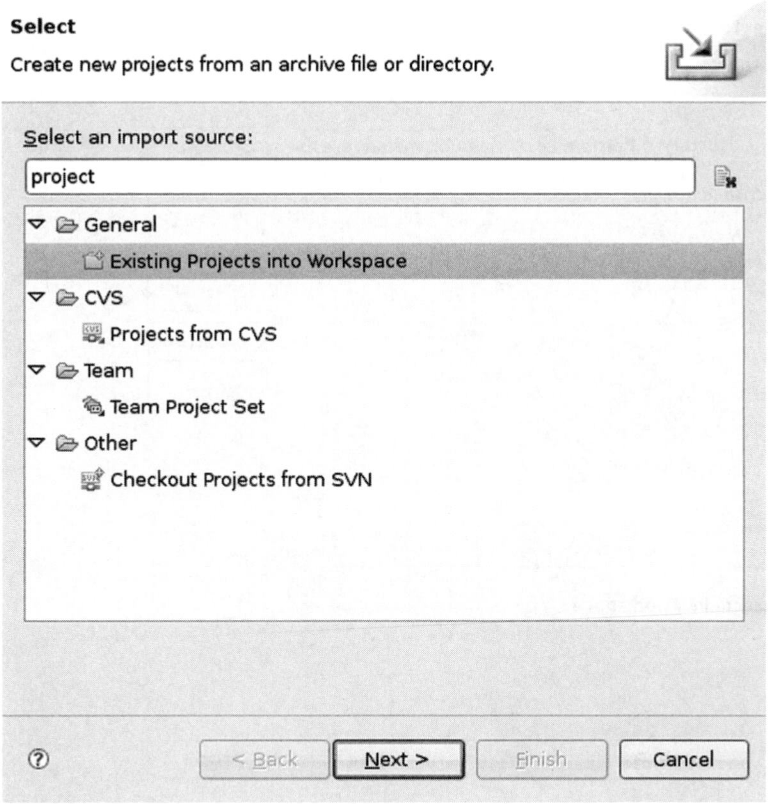

Select

Create new projects from an archive file or directory.

S̲elect an import source:

| project | |

▽ 🗁 General
     🗂 **Existing Projects into Workspace**
▽ 🗁 CVS
     🖳 Projects from CVS
▽ 🗁 Team
     🖼 Team Project Set
▽ 🗁 Other
     🖼 Checkout Projects from SVN

---

   ⑦   [< B̲ack]   [**N̲ext >**]   [F̲inish]   [Cancel]

Figure 3.5   Import an existing project into Eclipse using the Import wizard.

don't select the Copy projects into workspace option, since the project is already at the correct location.

And that's it! You now have a configured Eclipse workspace from which you can run and experiment with our Mule examples. You might wonder why you don't have to configure the classpath or do any other setup work. During the "prepare-environment" step, we also created the Eclipse-specific .classpath file to make it all a bit easier.

Now the Mule setup is finished, and we can do the same thing for ServiceMix. For this you can repeat the previously mentioned steps, but this time point the workspace to the workspace/workspace-servicemix directory instead of the workspace/workspace-mule directory. Then you can import the ServiceMix project in the same manner as we showed in figures 3.5 and 3.6.

The development environment is in place, and you can run the examples from both the command line and from Eclipse. Next let's look at an example where everything we've done so far comes together. We start with a Mule-based example, and after that we show you a ServiceMix-based example.

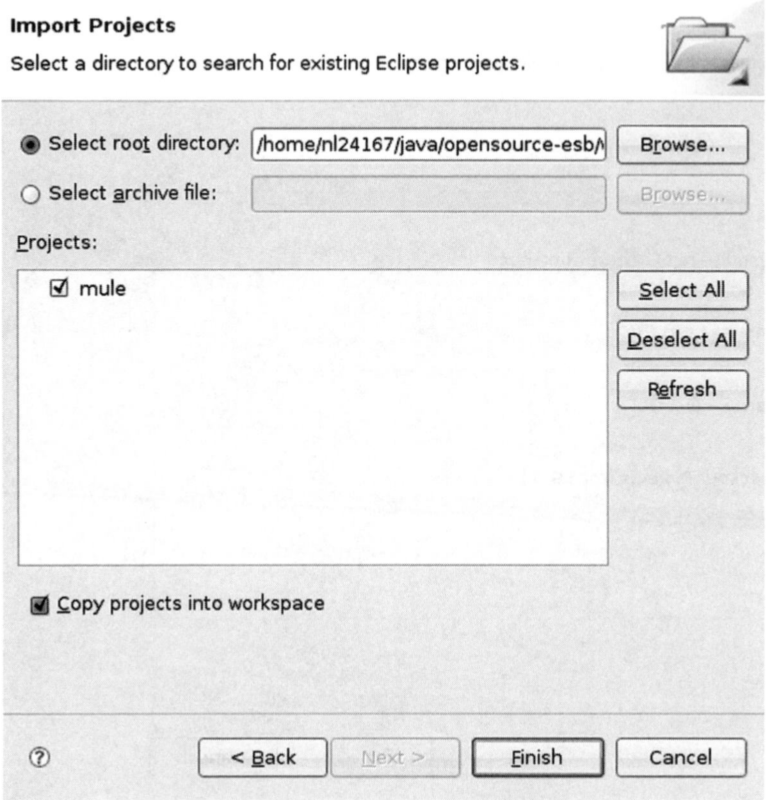

Import Projects

Select a directory to search for existing Eclipse projects.

○ Select root directory: /home/nl24167/java/opensource-esb/   Browse...

○ Select archive file: Browse...

Projects:

☑ mule

Select All

Deselect All

Refresh

☑ Copy projects into workspace

⑦   < Back   Next >   Finish   Cancel

Figure 3.6   Select a project to import from the file system.

3.3   *Inaugurate the Mule environment*

In this section we show how you can use the development environment created in the previous section and the technologies explained in the first part of this chapter together in a simple example.

We walk through a specific integration scenario with Mule. In this scenario you'll see how the technologies we've explained in the beginning of this chapter and Mule can work together. We first start with a general overview of the scenario in figure 3.7 and then dive into the various components and configurations.

As you can see in figure 3.7, we check a certain directory in the file system where we pick up a file (which in our example is an XML file). This file is transformed into a Java object and bridged to a JMS queue. In the next step, we receive this message from the JMS queue, pass the object into our logging service component, and send it to a JMS topic, which is read by two message listeners that store the message in the file system. One of them stores it directly; the other first transforms the message back to XML. There's a lot to do, so let's start by looking at all the configuration files we need for this process.

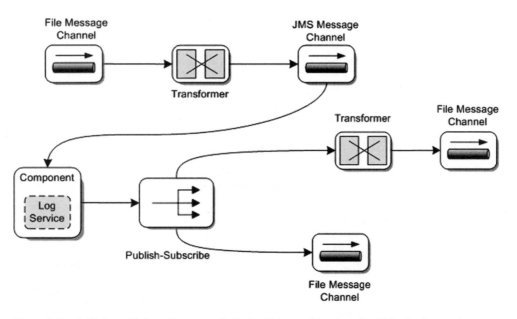

Figure 3.7 A file-based integration scenario that will be used to show the Mule development environment with Spring, JiBX, and ActiveMQ

3.3.1 Writing and configuring the Mule components

If you look at the example in figure 3.7 in the context of the Mule architecture, you'll see we need to configure a number of services and endpoints. Figure 3.8 shows what we need to configure.

Before we look at the services and endpoints defined in figure 3.8, let's examine some general configuration that we need to take care of. First, we have to configure the ActiveMQ connection, as described in listing 3.15. In addition, we need to define the transformers we'll be using. We've already explained this at the beginning of this

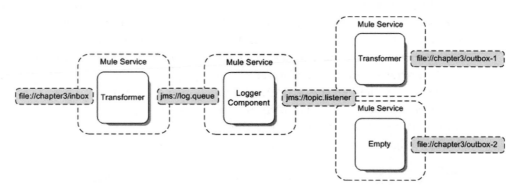

Figure 3.8 Mule services and endpoints required for the implementation of the integration scenario

chapter. Listing 3.17 shows the configuration of the ActiveMQ connection factory and the transformers.

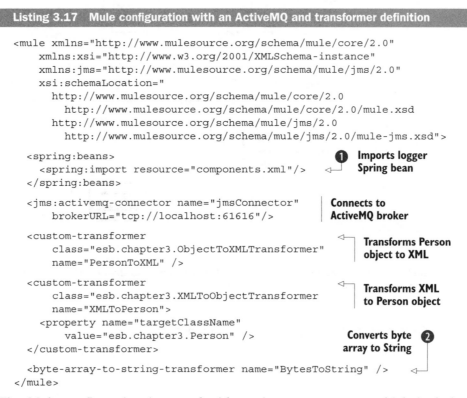

Listing 3.17   Mule configuration with an ActiveMQ and transformer definition

```
<mule xmlns="http://www.mulesource.org/schema/mule/core/2.0"
    xmlns:xsi="http://www.w3.org/2001/XMLSchema-instance"
    xmlns:jms="http://www.mulesource.org/schema/mule/jms/2.0"
    xsi:schemaLocation="
      http://www.mulesource.org/schema/mule/core/2.0
        http://www.mulesource.org/schema/mule/core/2.0/mule.xsd
      http://www.mulesource.org/schema/mule/jms/2.0
        http://www.mulesource.org/schema/mule/jms/2.0/mule-jms.xsd">
  <spring:beans>                                            ❶ Imports logger
    <spring:import resource="components.xml"/>      ⟵┘        Spring bean
  </spring:beans>

  <jms:activemq-connector name="jmsConnector"            Connects to
      brokerURL="tcp://localhost:61616"/>                ActiveMQ broker

  <custom-transformer                                 ⟵┐
      class="esb.chapter3.ObjectToXMLTransformer"        Transforms Person
      name="PersonToXML" />                              object to XML

  <custom-transformer                                 ⟵┐
      class="esb.chapter3.XMLToObjectTransformer          Transforms XML
      name="XMLToPerson">                                 to Person object
    <property name="targetClassName"
        value="esb.chapter3.Person" />                 Converts byte   ❷
  </custom-transformer>                                array to String  ┐
                                                                         │
  <byte-array-to-string-transformer name="BytesToString" />   ⟵┘
</mule>
```

The Mule configuration is started with an import statement, which includes the Spring bean definitions from the components.xml file ❶. In the components.xml file, we have defined a logger Spring bean, which we use to log the incoming person information.

The `byte-array-to-string-transformer` might seem a bit odd ❷. The reason we specify this transformer is that the default transformers are overridden when we add custom transformers on an endpoint. Because we'll define a custom transformer on a file endpoint, we also have to configure the default file transport transformer, which is the byte array–to-String transformer.

Now we've defined the ActiveMQ connection and the transformers, we can implement the first service (listing 3.18), which listens on a directory via the File transport and sends the message on to a JMS queue. Note that this listing is part of the same Mule configuration as listing 3.17.

Listing 3.18   Mule service definition forming a bridge between a file and a JMS endpoint

```
<mule>
<!-- ActiveMQ connection and transformer definition,
    see code listing 3.17). -->
```

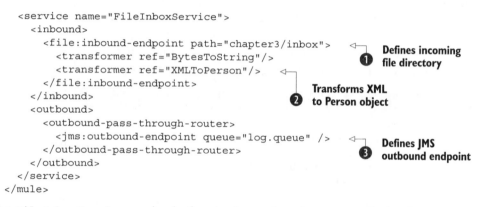

```
<service name="FileInboxService">
  <inbound>
    <file:inbound-endpoint path="chapter3/inbox">
      <transformer ref="BytesToString"/>
      <transformer ref="XMLToPerson"/>
    </file:inbound-endpoint>
  </inbound>
  <outbound>
    <outbound-pass-through-router>
      <jms:outbound-endpoint queue="log.queue" />
    </outbound-pass-through-router>
  </outbound>
</service>
</mule>
```

1 Defines incoming file directory

2 Transforms XML to Person object

3 Defines JMS outbound endpoint

The FileInboxService service is the starting point of our example implementation. In listing 3.18 we're reading messages from an inbox directory **1** and then transforming the incoming message in two steps. First, we transform the File instance to a String with the default byte array–to-String transformer, and then we transform this String, using our JiBX transformer **2**, to a Java object.

To bridge between a file and a JMS endpoint **3**, we don't have to configure any component implementation. This means that we don't execute any additional integration logic, but only pass the message from the file inbound endpoint to the JMS outbound endpoint. So after the message is transformed, it's sent to the specified JMS queue.

According to figure 3.8, the next Mule service is the logger service, which sends the incoming message from the JMS outbound endpoint defined in listing 3.18 to a JMS topic. Let's look at listing 3.19 for the configuration of this logger service. Note that this service is again part of the same Mule configuration as the previous code listings.

Listing 3.19 Mule service that bridges from a JMS queue to a JMS topic

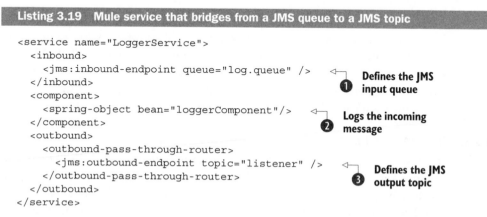

```
<service name="LoggerService">
  <inbound>
    <jms:inbound-endpoint queue="log.queue" />
  </inbound>
  <component>
    <spring-object bean="loggerComponent"/>
  </component>
  <outbound>
    <outbound-pass-through-router>
      <jms:outbound-endpoint topic="listener" />
    </outbound-pass-through-router>
  </outbound>
</service>
```

1 Defines the JMS input queue

2 Logs the incoming message

3 Defines the JMS output topic

As you can see here, we consume JMS messages from the log.queue queue **1**, and send the message on to the listener topic **3**. But before the message is sent to the JMS topic, it's logged and enhanced with the Spring bean loggerComponent **2**. In addition to logging the message, the incoming customer number is changed to another value.

The implementation of the logger is simple and therefore only included in the source code of this book.

The last two services we need to implement, shown in listing 3.20, are straightforward and just store the messages received from the topic in the file system.

Listing 3.20 Two Mule services listening on a JMS topic and logging to the file system

```
<mule>
  <service name="FileOutboxService1">
    <inbound>
      <jms:inbound-endpoint topic="listener" />          ❶ Defines the JMS
    </inbound>                                                topic subscriber
    <outbound>
      <outbound-pass-through-router>                     ❷ Writes transformed
        <file:outbound-endpoint                             message to file
            path="chapter3/outbox-1">
          <transformer ref="PersonToXML"/>
        </file:outbound-endpoint>
      </outbound-pass-through-router>
    </outbound>
  </service>

  <service name="FileOutboxService2">
    <inbound>
      <jms:inbound-endpoint topic="listener" />
    </inbound>
    <outbound>
      <outbound-pass-through-router>                     ❸ Writes message
        <file:outbound-endpoint                             as-is to file
            path="chapter3/outbox-2" />
      </outbound-pass-through-router>
    </outbound>
  </service>
</mule>
```

These last two Mule services of our example implementation are the services that subscribe ❶ to the topic defined as an outbound endpoint in listing 3.19. The first service, `FileOutboxService1`, uses a transformer to transform the message back to an XML format ❷. The second service, `FileOutboxService2`, outputs the message as received, which means it's serialized to the file system using standard Java-based serialization ❸.

3.3.2 *Running the Mule example*

It's easy to run the example by using the supplied Ant build file. Open a command console and go to the directory where you unpacked the downloaded archive. From there, navigate to the workspace/workspace-mule/mule/resources/chapter3 directory. From the console, run `ant -f ch3-examples.xml chapter3-combined`. When you run this command, Ant will start up the Mule container with the configuration shown in listings 3.17 through 3.20.

We can now put a file into the chapter3/inbox directory and look at the result files in the outbox-1 and outbox-2 directories, which are also located in the chapter3 subdirectory. If everything went well, you should see the input file in both of the output directories.

If you want to run this example from Eclipse instead of from a command console, just open the Ant view in Eclipse and add the ch3-examples.xml Ant build file to this view by dragging it to the window. Now you can start the `chapter3-combined` target by double-clicking, and you can once again put a file in the chapter3/inbox directory and see it being processed by Mule.

Now that you've seen how to use Mule with JiBX, Spring, and ActiveMQ, let's look at an example using ServiceMix.

3.4 Inaugurate the ServiceMix environment

The scenario we show you for ServiceMix will be a simple example that can help you get acquainted with the environment. This example will illustrate how Spring, ActiveMQ, and JiBX can be used with ServiceMix (see figure 3.9).

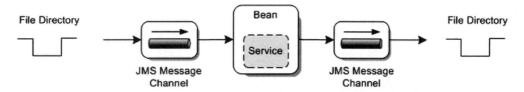

Figure 3.9 We use this scenario to show how ServiceMix can work together with Spring, JiBX, and ActiveMQ.

As you can see in figure 3.9, we listen to a certain directory and pick up any files put in there. These files, which should have an XML format, are sent to a bean via a JMS queue. In our custom bean, we transform the XML to Java, log some information, change the first name value in the input message, and send it again over JMS to another directory on the file system.

So to get this example to work, we must execute these steps:

1 Select the required binding components and service engines.
2 Configure the service units for this scenario.
3 Package all the service units into a service assembly, which we can deploy.
4 Deploy the service assembly to ServiceMix.

Let's start by selecting the right service engines and binding components for the functionality described in figure 3.9.

3.4.1 Select the necessary JBI components

Before we can configure service units for a specific JBI component, we need to select the necessary binding components and service engines. To get an overview of the available JBI components, look in the esb/apache-servicemix-3.2.1 directory. Here you'll find a directory named hotdeploy. Any JBI component or service assembly dropped into this directory is deployed automatically to ServiceMix. For our example we need these components available in the hotdeploy directory:

```
servicemix-bean-3.2.1-installer.zip
servicemix-file-3.2.1-installer.zip
servicemix-jms-3.2.1-installer.zip
```

You see more available JBI components in this directory. All the binding components and service engines available in ServiceMix are started automatically. If you want to speed things up when you start ServiceMix, you can remove unnecessary binding components and service engines from this directory. This is especially useful if you're debugging or working with a specific service engine or binding component and want to minimize ServiceMix's startup time.

Now it's time to start ServiceMix. To do this, navigate to the workspace/workspace-servicemix/servicemix/resources/chapter3 directory in a command console and run `ant -f ch3-build.xml start`. This command will start the ServiceMix container and automatically deploy all the service engines and binding components from the hotdeploy directory.

Once you have ServiceMix running, let's configure the service units that we'll deploy to this running ServiceMix instance. If you've already run the Mule example, you'll see there is a big difference in how the examples are started. With Mule we must specify the Mule configuration to run at startup time; for ServiceMix we start the container and can deploy our service assemblies at a later time. In short, ServiceMix is hot deployable and Mule, at the time of this writing, is not. The Mule project is working on an Open Services Gateway Initiative (OSGi) implementation of Mule that will be hot deployable.

3.4.2 *Configuring the ServiceMix example implementation*

In figure 3.9 you saw that we must read an XML file from the file system, and then put that XML message on a JMS queue for further processing. Another part of the example is listening on this queue and forwarding the message to our custom transformer component.

In the transformer component we use JiBX to transform the incoming message to a Java object, alter a value, and transform it back to XML. In the final step, we put the message on a JMS queue and bridge it to the file system. Figure 3.10 shows the example implementation in the context of the JBI architecture.

As you can see in figure 3.10, we have two binding components, which handle the communication from outside the container, and we have one service engine, which runs our own custom component that implements transformation functionality. In chapter 2 we defined a service unit as an artifact that can be deployed inside a JBI component. In this example implementation, we deploy four JBI services inside the JMS component—two consumers and two providers. We deploy two services inside the File component: a file sender and a file poller. Finally, we deploy one bean service into the `servicemix-bean` service engine.

Inaugurate the ServiceMix environment

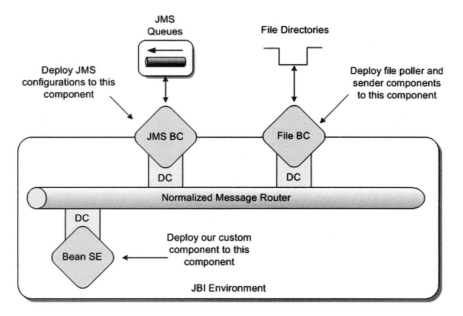

Figure 3.10   The binding components and service engines used in the implementation of our example

Let's see how we're going to implement all this. Before we dive into the XML configuration, check out our custom Java component in listing 3.21, which we deploy to the servicemix-bean service engine.

> **Listing 3.21   Bean implementation that defines transformation and routing logic**

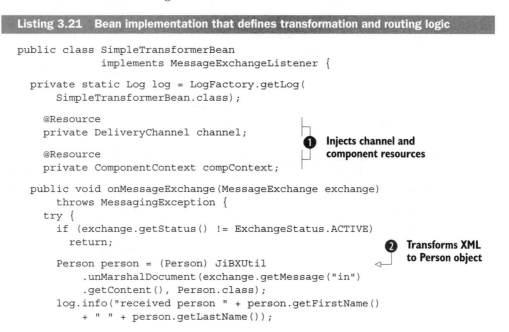

```
public class SimpleTransformerBean
            implements MessageExchangeListener {

  private static Log log = LogFactory.getLog(
     SimpleTransformerBean.class);

    @Resource
    private DeliveryChannel channel;              ❶ Injects channel and
                                                     component resources
    @Resource
    private ComponentContext compContext;

  public void onMessageExchange(MessageExchange exchange)
     throws MessagingException {
     try {
       if (exchange.getStatus() != ExchangeStatus.ACTIVE)
         return;                                  ❷ Transforms XML
                                                     to Person object
       Person person = (Person) JiBXUtil
         .unMarshalDocument(exchange.getMessage("in")
         .getContent(), Person.class);
       log.info("received person " + person.getFirstName()
         + " " + person.getLastName());
```

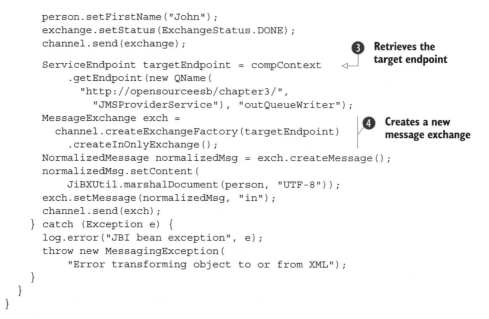

```
        person.setFirstName("John");
        exchange.setStatus(ExchangeStatus.DONE);
        channel.send(exchange);                             ❸  Retrieves the
                                                                target endpoint
        ServiceEndpoint targetEndpoint = compContext   ◁┘
            .getEndpoint(new QName(
              "http://opensourceesb/chapter3/",
                "JMSProviderService"), "outQueueWriter");
        MessageExchange exch =                              ❹  Creates a new
          channel.createExchangeFactory(targetEndpoint)        message exchange
            .createInOnlyExchange();
        NormalizedMessage normalizedMsg = exch.createMessage();
        normalizedMsg.setContent(
            JiBXUtil.marshalDocument(person, "UTF-8"));
        exch.setMessage(normalizedMsg, "in");
        channel.send(exch);
      } catch (Exception e) {
        log.error("JBI bean exception", e);
        throw new MessagingException(
            "Error transforming object to or from XML");
      }
    }
  }
```

A number of interesting things are going on in listing 3.21. You can see that the
`SimpleTransformerBean` implements the `MessageExchangeListener` interface. This
interface defines that this class is able to receive message exchanges. The next thing
you see is that the resources we need in this class are inserted by the ServiceMix container ❶. In this case, we inject the `DeliveryChannel`, which we use to send and
receive messages, and the `ComponentContext`, which we can use to search for registered JBI endpoints.

When we receive a message, we first check to see if it's part of an active exchange,
since we only need to process active JBI message exchanges. We then start to process
the message with JiBX to transform it to a Java object ❷. After that, we finish the current exchange, because we are done processing. To finish the current in-only message
exchange, the `channel,send(exchange)` is executed with a status of done. Then we
do a lookup ❸ for the target endpoint of the transformed message, which will be a
JMS queue defined in listing 3.23.

The last step is to create a new JBI message exchange ❹ to send an XML message,
transformed with JiBX, to the target destination.

Before we dive into the configuration of the ServiceMix JBI components we use in
this example, let's quickly look at the JiBX configuration in listing 3.22, which shows
how to map the incoming XML to a Java object.

Listing 3.22   JiBX mapping illustrating how to map between XML and Java

```
<binding>
    <mapping name="person"
            class="esb.chapter3.Person">
    <value name="customer-number" field="customerNumber"/>
```

```
      <value name="first-name" field="firstName"/>
      <value name="last-name" field="lastName"/>
      <value name="street" field="street"/>
      <value name="city" field="city"/>
      <value name="state" field="state"/>
      <value name="zip" field="zip"/>
      <value name="phone" field="phone"/>
      </mapping>
  </binding>
```

Listing 3.22 shows a basic mapping that transforms a simple XML message to the
esb.chapter3.Person Java class. We don't show the Person class, since this is just a
POJO with a getter and setter for all the fields specified in the mapping file. As we've
mentioned before, we need to run the binding compiler before we can use this JiBX
mapping configuration at runtime. All this is done automatically for you when you use
the supplied Ant build file in the servicemix/resources/chapter3 directory from the
servicemix-workspace to deploy this example to ServiceMix at the end of this section.

Now that the programming part is out of the way, the main thing missing is the
configuration of the three JBI components. Let's start with the JMS consumers and
providers. ServiceMix already starts up an ActiveMQ broker in its default configuration, so we don't have to start a separate JMS broker instance. We only have to configure the JMS consumers and providers and connect to this broker. We can do this by
creating an ActiveMQConnectionFactory, and since the ServiceMix configuration
already is based on Spring, this is easy to do:

```
<bean id="connectionFactory"
    class="org.apache.activemq.ActiveMQConnectionFactory">
  <property name="brokerURL" value="tcp://localhost:61616" />
</bean>
```

In this configuration, we define a connection to the ActiveMQ broker instance. This
code is added to the service unit configuration, which we deploy to the servicemix-jms
binding component. Listing 3.23 shows how we reference the ActiveMQConnection-
Factory.

Listing 3.23   ServiceMix JMS configuration

```
<beans xmlns:jms="http://servicemix.apache.org/jms/1.0"
    xmlns:esb="http://opensourceesb/chapter3/">

  <jms:consumer service="esb:JMSConsumerService"
      endpoint="inQueueReader"
      targetService="esb:beanService"          ◁─┐  ❶ Targets JBI service for
      targetEndpoint="endpoint"                      consumed message
      destinationName="inQueue"
      connectionFactory="#connectionFactory" />

  <jms:consumer service="esb:JMSConsumerService"
      endpoint="inQueueReader2"
      targetService="esb:fileSender"
      targetEndpoint="endpoint"
```

```
        destinationName="outQueue"
        connectionFactory="#connectionFactory"/>
    <jms:provider service="esb:JMSProviderService"
        endpoint="inQueueWriter"
        destinationName="inQueue"
        connectionFactory="#connectionFactory" />
    <jms:provider service="esb:JMSProviderService"
        endpoint="outQueueWriter"
        destinationName="outQueue"
        connectionFactory="#connectionFactory" />
    <bean id="connectionFactory"
        class="org.apache.activemq.ActiveMQConnectionFactory">
      <property name="brokerURL" value="tcp://localhost:61616" />
    </bean>
</beans>
```

2 Defines the consumer queue name

3 Defines the provider queue name

4 References the connection factory

We see two different types of JMS endpoints defined here: consumer endpoints and provider endpoints. A consumer endpoint listens on a specific JMS input queue **2**, and when a message is received, it invokes the specified target service, like, for example, the bean service **1**. A provider sends a message to a queue **3** using the ActiveMQ connection factory **4** defined at the bottom of the JMS service unit configuration. Table 3.2 shows the properties for a JMS endpoint.

Table 3.2   The ServiceMix JMS endpoint attributes

Attribute	Description
service	The name of the service this endpoint will be registered on.
endpoint	The name of the endpoint this service can be reached on.
targetService	If a message is received on the queue, it's sent to the service registered on this name.
targetEndpoint	The name of the endpoint we send the message to.
destinationName	The name of the queue a consumer listens to or a provider sends to.

In listing 3.23 we have two providers that send messages to the inQueue and outQueue queues, and two consumers that listen to those queues and forward the messages to the osesb:beanService JBI service and the osesb:fileSender JBI service.

The final items we consider for this scenario are the configuration of the service unit for the bean component and the configuration of the service unit for the file component. The file component is a simple configuration, as shown in listing 3.24.

Listing 3.24   File endpoints configuration for the ServiceMix example

```
<beans xmlns="http://xbean.org/schemas/spring/1.0"
  xmlns:file="http://servicemix.apache.org/file/1.0"
  xmlns:esb="http://opensourceesb/chapter3/">
```

```
<file:sender service="esb:fileSender"
    endpoint="endpoint"
    directory="chapter3/out"/>
```
❶ Defines output directory

```
<file:poller service="esb:filePoller"
    endpoint="simpleToJMSPoller"
    targetService="esb:JMSProviderService"
    targetEndpoint="inQueueWriter"
    file="chapter3/in"
    period="2000"/>
</beans>
```
❷ Defines directory to be polled

Listing 3.24 is pretty much self-explanatory. We have a file poller that listens on the chapter3/in directory ❷, and a sender that sends the received messages to the chapter3/out directory ❶.

The final JBI component that we have to configure is the servicemix-bean (its Java code appears in listing 3.21):

```
<beans xmlns:bean="http://servicemix.apache.org/bean/1.0"
    xmlns:esb="http://opensourceesb/chapter3/">

  <bean:endpoint service="esb:beanService"
      endpoint="endpoint"
      bean="#SimpleTransformer"/>

  <bean id="SimpleTransformer"
      class="esb.chapter3.SimpleTransformerBean"/>
</beans>
```

Here we define a JBI service bean by configuring the name and endpoint of the service and the implementation class. The #SimpleTransformer reference tells Service-Mix to look up the component in the Spring context.

The final step is packaging all these service units into a service assembly and deploying it to the ServiceMix container.

3.4.3 Running the ServiceMix example

You can now run our example by using the supplied Ant build file. Since we already started ServiceMix at the beginning of this section, we only need to create and deploy the service assembly. From a command console, go to the resources/chapter3 directory in the ServiceMix workspace and execute the deploy-chapter3-example Ant target (ant -f ch3-build.xml deploy-chapter3-example). This will start up the ServiceMix container and initialize the JBI service engines and binding components. When Service-Mix has started, you can execute the deploy-chapter3-example Ant target (ant -f ch3-build.xml deploy-chapter3-example). This command will first compile our Java classes and then run the JiBX binding compiler. In the next step, all the service units are packaged into a single service assembly. This service assembly is then deployed to the running ServiceMix container by copying it to the hotdeploy directory in the Service-Mix distribution.

We can now test this example by copying a test file (e.g., person.xml, available in the resources/chapter3 directory) into the chapter3/in directory (within the ServiceMix distribution). We should see the output logged from our custom component, and see the file being written to the chapter3/out directory.

If you want to start this example from Eclipse, just use the Ant view as we explained in the previous Mule section. Drag the ch3-build.xml file to the Ant view window and you will be able to execute the Ant target `deploy-chapter3-example` as we just described.

In this section we've shown how you can combine ServiceMix with JiBX, Spring, and ActiveMQ. We've implemented a simple integration example in which Spring is used for the configuration, JiBX for the transformation, and ActiveMQ as the messaging broker.

3.5   *Summary*

We introduced you to some new technologies in this chapter. We started by exploring the technologies used throughout this book to provide additional functionality for Mule and ServiceMix. We introduced the Spring framework, which is used as the object container in which we configure all the components we'll be implementing. We also described a Java-to-XML marshaling framework: JiBX. We'll use this framework when we want to map XML content to a Java object, and vice versa. Finally, we explored JMS and Apache ActiveMQ, which give us a simple way to enable our components to communicate with one another in a reliable way.

We also explained how to set up your development environment for the two ESBs. You can use Ant build files for all the examples when you're working from the command line. In addition, we demonstrated setting up an Eclipse environment. At this point you should have a fully configured Eclipse environment and a completely configured command-line environment from which you can run and experiment with our examples. In the last part of this chapter, you saw two examples of using the configured development environment together with Spring, JiBX, and JMS.

In the next few chapters, we investigate the core functionality of an ESB. This core functionality will be explored using the technologies and environments explained in this chapter, so if you have any difficulty while reading a specific section, you can always come back here for a short introduction.

The foundation of
an integration solution

4

Now that we've discussed the basics of Mule and ServiceMix, it's time to examine the foundational elements of a full integration solution: integration logic and message flows.

Integration logic is simply the logic you need to build your integration solution. Open source ESBs provide a lot of functionality out of the box, but most solutions need additional logic. This additional logic may involve something as simple as changing the content of an incoming message, but it can be as complex as including validation rules for EDI messages. One of the great features of open source ESBs is that implementing logic for your integration solution is fairly easy.

Writing components for specific integration logic is similar to writing components for Java or JEE applications. Open source ESBs such as Mule and ServiceMix are developed to make it as simple as possible to "click" your Java components in an integration solution. Because there's no large set of requirements, your Java

111

components can remain independent of specific Mule and ServiceMix classes. We look at the implementation of integration logic with Mule in section 4.1 and with ServiceMix in section 4.2.

Naturally, the development of integration logic isn't enough to get your integration solution running. To be able to implement an integration solution within an open source ESB, you must combine integration logic and functionality that's offered out of the box in so-called *message flows*. A message flow can be viewed as the final deliverable for an integration problem. Because the concept of a message flow is critical to understanding how you develop integration solutions, we look at the theory of message flows in section 4.3. Then we illustrate the theory with an example of a message flow for Mule in section 4.4 and for ServiceMix in section 4.5.

Let's kick off this chapter with a discussion on implementing your own integration logic with Mule.

4.1   *Implementing integration logic with Mule*

When you want to implement an integration solution with Mule, you can utilize all the out-of-the-box functionality that Mule provides. Don't make the mistake of underestimating this rich set of functionality, but implementing complex enterprise integration scenarios will require some custom logic. As you'll see in this section, applying custom logic with Mule is simple.

4.1.1   *Creating a logging solution with Mule*

Let's begin with developing a component that logs an incoming message to the console with the popular logging framework Log4j. Logging functionality is also provided out of the box with the LogComponent class, but this is a good starting point to learn about the development of custom logic in Mule. First, we have to develop the Java class that does the actual logging (see listing 4.1).

> **Listing 4.1   Simple logging implementation**

```
package esb.chapter4.component.simple;

import org.apache.log4j.Logger;

public class SimpleComponent {

  private final static Logger logger =            ❶
      Logger.getLogger(SimpleComponent.class);

  public void accept(String payload) {            ◁—❷
    logger.info("received payload " + payload);
  }
}
```

Well, this isn't hard, is it? The SimpleComponent class defines a Log4j Logger class instance ❶ that can be used to log the incoming message. There's just one method, accept ❷, that receives one String parameter logged to the console with the Log4j logger instance. As you can see, this Java class has no dependency to any Mule class at all. To be able to use our custom logic with Mule, we must define a Mule configuration that makes use of the `SimpleComponent` class.

The Mule configuration has to include a service definition with a component element that points to the `SimpleComponent` class we've just created. But before we can create the Mule configuration, we have to choose which transport protocol we'll define for incoming messages. For this simple example, we use the so-called stdio Mule transport, which is able to accept command-line user input. Now we can complete the Mule configuration for our logging example (see listing 4.2).

Listing 4.2   The command-line Mule configuration: mule-config.xml

```
<mule xmlns="http://www.mulesource.org/schema/mule/core/2.0"
  xmlns:xsi="http://www.w3.org/2001/XMLSchema-instance"
  xmlns:stdio="http://www.mulesource.org/schema/mule/stdio/2.0"
  xsi:schemaLocation="
    http://www.mulesource.org/schema/mule/core/2.0
      http://www.mulesource.org/schema/mule/core/2.0/mule.xsd
    http://www.mulesource.org/schema/mule/stdio/2.0
      http://www.mulesource.org/schema/mule/stdio/2.0/mule-stdio.xsd">

<stdio:connector name="inConnector"
    promptMessage="Enter a statement"/>

<model name="SimpleExample">
  <service name="SimpleComponent">
    <inbound>
      <stdio:inbound-endpoint system="IN"        <-- ❶
          connector-ref="inConnector"/>
    </inbound>

    <component                                                  ❷
        class="esb.chapter4.component.simple.SimpleComponent"/>
  </service>
</model>
</mule>
```

The main part of the Mule configuration in listing 4.2 is the component element ❷. Here we define the implementation class that will handle messages arriving at the defined inbound endpoint ❶. As you can see, the `SimpleComponent` that we created in listing 4.1 is configured as the implementation class. The inbound router contains an endpoint definition that uses a standard IO (stdio) connector. This connector accepts messages from the command-line equivalent to `System.in`. The input messages consist of the user's responses to the message "Enter a statement," which is configured on the connector definition.

With the Mule configuration ready, we can execute this simple logging example. You have to use the Ant build file in the resources/chapter4 directory of Mule's workspace in this book's source code. Run the component Ant target that's available in the ch4-examples.xml Ant build file to construct a JAR file with the Mule configuration file in listing 4.2 and a compiled `SimpleComponent` class. The component Ant target also deploys the JAR file to the lib/user directory in the Mule distribution so the example is available in the Mule classpath when Mule is started. At this point, from the command line you can run the example with the component script file (component.bat or component.sh) that's available in the resources/chapter4/component directory of the source code.

Running the example from the command line

Because of a conflict between using the stdio connector and running a Java program with Ant, we have to start Mule from the command line for the examples that involve the stdio connector. The stdio connector isn't able to accept user input when running Mule via an Ant startup script. When we start Mule with the standard mule.bat or mule.sh script file in the bin directory of the Mule distribution, the stdio connector works just fine.

When Mule is started and the "Enter a statement" line appears in the console, you can provide a statement. The same message is logged with Log4j to the console as implemented in the SimpleComponent class.

This means that we've developed a very simple custom logic component, and we've also been able to run this component within Mule. You may be wondering how Mule is able to call the accept method in the SimpleComponent class; we haven't instructed Mule to call this method. Here's the answer: Mule uses reflection to determine the correct method to invoke. Since our implementation has only one method, this seems to be pretty simple, right?

Mule tries to find the proper entry point (i.e., method) based on the payload type of the incoming message. Our SimpleComponent implementation has a method that accepts a String parameter, and this corresponds with the payload type of the Stream provider (stdio connector) configured as an inbound router. If we change the String parameter into an int parameter and rerun the example, we get a NoSatisfiableMethodsException, meaning that no entry point can be determined for our SimpleComponent.

Or suppose we define two methods in the SimpleComponent class with the same parameter(s). We can, for example, duplicate the accept method and rename the copied method to deny. When we rerun the example, Mule throws a TooManySatisfiableMethodsException. Therefore, be sure you carefully implement the proper entry points.

Mule provides other options for invoking the component's methods. If you use the org.mule.api.lifecycle.Callable interface, you'll need to include the onCall method. The onCall method will always be invoked if the component uses the Callable interface, so no reflection is used in that case. Another way to work with the method invocation logic is to specify the method to invoke in the endpoint URI. So if we have a component B with an inbound router that has a virtual machine (VM) inbound endpoint with path value componentB, we can invoke a specific method on component B. What's needed is an outbound router on, say, component A, with a VM endpoint that has a path value of componentB?method=methodABC. This means that the method `methodABC` is invoked on component B. The method invocation logic is quite flexible, and you can adapt it to fit your needs.

In addition to the `Callable` interface and the specification of the method name, Mule provides so-called entry point resolvers. In chapter 2 we mentioned a number of these entry point resolvers. If you want another option for resolving entry points, you can always implement your own logic by implementing Mule's `EntryPoint-Resolver` interface.

Because the entry point is, by default, determined based on the payload type of the incoming message, we seem to have a dependency between the transport provider and the custom logic implementation. But as you may recall, Mule provides transformers, which can be used to transform the payload of an incoming message to the expected payload type of the custom logic implementation. Mule offers a number of transformers out of the box with specific transport provider implementations, such as the `JMSMessageToObject` transformer for the JMS transport provider and the `FileTo-String` transformer for the File transport provider. You can even define your own transformer, as you'll see next.

4.1.2 *Developing a custom transformer with Mule*

Suppose that instead of a string, we want to use the `Integer` message type in the `SimpleComponent` class's accept method. There's no default transformer to transform a string to an integer in Mule, so we have to develop our own `StringToInteger` transformer. So our accept method declaration changes to this:

```
public void accept(Integer payload) {
```

Mule defines an `AbstractTransformer` class that you can extend to implement your own transformer. We can use this abstract class for the implementation of the `String-ToInteger` class (see listing 4.3).

Listing 4.3 Implementation of the `StringToInteger` transformer

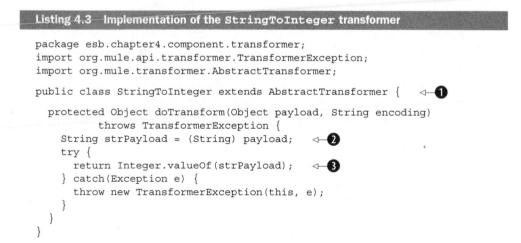

```
package esb.chapter4.component.transformer;
import org.mule.api.transformer.TransformerException;
import org.mule.transformer.AbstractTransformer;

public class StringToInteger extends AbstractTransformer {    ←❶

  protected Object doTransform(Object payload, String encoding)
        throws TransformerException {
    String strPayload = (String) payload;    ←❷
    try {
      return Integer.valueOf(strPayload);    ←❸
    } catch(Exception e) {
      throw new TransformerException(this, e);
    }
  }
}
```

In listing 4.3, the `StringToInteger` custom transformer extends the `Abstract-Transformer` abstract class ❶ provided by Mule. Our transformer is thus forced to implement the doTransform method. Because we know that in cases where this transformer will be used the message payload will be of type String, we can just cast the standard payload type object to a string ❷. We also expect that the payload is a number, and therefore we create an integer object out of the string payload right away ❸. When this conversion fails, we simply return a TransformerException that will contain the NumberFormatException.

We can now use our just created transformer in a Mule configuration similar to listing 4.2, but this one expects the user to provide a number via the console. Listing 4.4 shows this new Mule configuration.

Listing 4.4   Mule configuration for the simple logging example with a transformer

```
<mule>
  <stdio:connector name="inConnector"
      promptMessage="Enter a number"/>

  <custom-transformer name="StringToInteger"                        ←❶
      class="esb.chapter4.component.transformer.StringToInteger"/>

  <model name="SimpleIntExample">
    <service name="SimpleIntComponent">
      <inbound>
        <stdio:inbound-endpoint system="IN"
            connector-ref="inConnector">
          <transformer ref="StringToInteger"/>     ←❷
        </stdio:inbound-endpoint>
      </inbound>
      <component
        class="esb.chapter4.component.transformer.SimpleIntComponent"/>
    </service>
  </model>
</mule>
```

Notice in listing 4.4 that we left out the namespace configuration for the mule element. This is just for convenience; you can check listing 4.2 for the full namespace definition. The new Mule configuration begins by registering our custom transformer that we described in listing 4.3 ❶. The rest is similar to the previous example shown in figure 4.1, except for the definition of the registered transformer on the endpoint of the inbound router ❷. The transformer element on the inbound endpoint lets you register a number of transformers that must be applied before invoking the Java class SimpleIntComponent (shown in the following code snippet):

```
public class SimpleIntComponent {

private final static Logger logger =
    Logger.getLogger(SimpleIntComponent.class);

public void accept(Integer payload) {
    logger.info("received payload " + payload);
  }
}
```

You can build this example using the `component-transformer` target in the ch4-examples Ant build file that we also used in the previous example. The `component-transformer` Ant target builds the JAR file with the Mule configuration and the Java classes, and then copies this JAR file to the Mule lib/user directory. You can run Mule by executing the `intcomponent` script. The Mule server is started with the configuration shown in listing 4.4. When you respond with a number to the "Enter a number" prompt, you'll see that the number is logged to the console. If you respond with a non-number, Mule will log a transformer exception to the console. This behavior works as expected with the `StringToInteger` transformer, shown in listing 4.3.

You've already implemented two integration logic components in just a few pages, and you saw how easy it is to build your own components within Mule. Now let's look at using the Spring Framework to build our components.

4.1.3 *Integrating Mule and Spring*

In the previous examples we haven't yet utilized the Spring functionality to, for example, inject beans. So let's develop a simple addition to the logging example of listing 4.2 and configure a few possible responses to user input. We'll utilize Spring dependency injection for this purpose.

We need a Java class that's able to hold a collection of responses and that can determine the proper response based on the user input. To implement this neatly, we also need an interface that this Java class implements. Listing 4.5 shows this interface, `ResponseOptionsIF`, and the implementation class, `ResponseOptions`.

> **Listing 4.5 Java interface and class that return a response to a given user input**

```
public interface ResponseOptionsIF {
  public String getResponseOption(String word);     ←①
}

public class ResponseOptions implements ResponseOptionsIF {
  private Map<String, String> options;              ←②

  public String getResponseOption(String word) {    ←③
    if(options.containsKey(word)) {
      return options.get(word);
    } else {
      return options.get("other");
    }
  }

  public void setOptions(Map<String, String> options) {
    this.options = options;
  }
}
```

In listing 4.5, the `ResponseOptionsIF` interface defines one method ① that returns a response to the user input. In the implementation class, `ResponseOptions`, a `Map` with the name `options` ② is defined that's able to hold a number of key/value pairs, where the key is the user input and the value is the corresponding response. The little piece of logic to return the proper response to the user input is implemented in the getResponseOption method **❸**.

To use ResponseOptions, we have to adjust the component implementation from listing 4.1 a bit. In the previous examples, the component implementation didn't return a response. For this example, we need to return the response determined in the ResponseOptions class (see listing 4.6).

Listing 4.6   Component implementation using `ResponseOptions`

```
public class SimpleSpringComponent {
  private ResponseOptionsIF responseOptions;      ◁—❶

  public String generateResponse(String word) {
    return responseOptions.getResponseOption(word);      ◁—❷
  }

  public void setResponseOptions(      ◁—❸
      ResponseOptionsIF responseOptions) {
    this.responseOptions = responseOptions;
  }
}
```

As you can see in listing 4.6, this class isn't difficult to understand. The important part is that there's no dependency to the ResponseOptions implementation class but only to the ResponseOptionsIF interface **❶**. Therefore, the SimpleSpringComponent doesn't know which implementation class it will invoke when the getResponseOption method is called **❷**. This is a great way to reduce the coupling between these classes. The ResponseOptions class reference will be injected by Spring via the setResponse-Options method **❸**. This all happens automatically, so you don't need to do any additional coding for this.

The remaining part of our simple Spring example is the Mule configuration. We need to add the ResponseOptions configuration and an outbound router to give the response back to the user via the console. Listing 4.7 contains the full Mule configuration.

Listing 4.7   Mule configuration of the Spring example

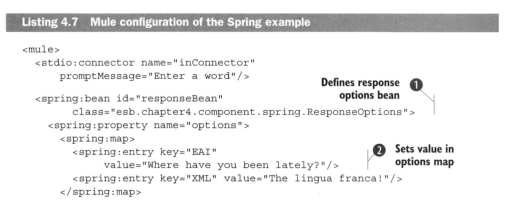

```
<mule>
  <stdio:connector name="inConnector"
      promptMessage="Enter a word"/>

  <spring:bean id="responseBean"
      class="esb.chapter4.component.spring.ResponseOptions">
    <spring:property name="options">
      <spring:map>
        <spring:entry key="EAI"
            value="Where have you been lately?"/>
        <spring:entry key="XML" value="The lingua franca!"/>
      </spring:map>
```

Defines response options bean ❶

Sets value in options map ❷

```
        </spring:property>
      </spring:bean>

      <spring:bean id="simpleBean"
            class="esb.chapter4.component.spring.SimpleSpringComponent">
        <spring:property name="responsOptions" ref="responseBean"/>
      </spring:bean>

      <model name="SimpleSpringExample">
        <service name="SimpleSpringComponent">
          <inbound>
            <stdio:inbound-endpoint system="IN"/>
          </inbound>
          <component
              <spring-object bean="simpleBean"/>       ◁⎤   Refers to
          </component>                                   ❸  Spring bean
          <outbound>
            <outbound-pass-through-router>
              <stdio:outbound-endpoint system="OUT"/>  ◁⎤   Defines response
            </outbound-pass-through-router>              ❹  destination
          </outbound>
        </service>
      </model>
    </mule>
```

The Mule configuration may seem somewhat large at first, but we also implement quite a bit of functionality here. First, we define a Spring bean with the `spring:bean` element that configures the `ResponseOptions` class ❶. The `spring` prefix points to the namespace of the Spring Framework defined at the root element `mule`. To keep the example readable we left out the namespaces, but you can look in the book's source code to see the entire configuration. As part of the response option bean definition, we configure the content of the options map. With Spring we can fill a `Map` instance with several key/value pairs ❷. To trim the configuration, we include only two possible user inputs and corresponding responses in listing 4.7.

The `SimpleSpringComponent` class defined as a Spring bean can be referenced in the component implementation with the `spring-object` element ❸. As you can see, it's easy to use a Spring bean as the implementation of the component part of a Mule service. The last part of our configuration shows an outbound router that passes the response value of the `SimpleSpringComponent` class to the console ❹.

To build and deploy this example to Mule, run the `component-spring` target in the ch4-examples Ant build file. You can then run this example with the springcomponent script (as we also did in the previous examples in this section). When Mule is started, enter a word in the console—for example, enter "EAI" and Mule should then respond with "Where have you been lately?" We've now explored three simple examples that use custom logic within Mule. Notice that it's not hard to include custom functionality and that you can easily use Spring functionality in your Mule configuration. Let's take a look at the possibilities for applying custom logic in ServiceMix.

4.2   *Implementing integration logic with ServiceMix*

Let's begin with a simple example similar to the first example in section 4.1.1. We implement a small piece of custom logic that just logs the content of the incoming message to the console with Log4j. However, we select another transport protocol for the incoming message, as ServiceMix has no stdio binding component capable of reading user input from a console. So we use the JMS transport protocol for the incoming messages.

An important difference with Mule is that the message format in ServiceMix is XML. The JBI specification and, in particular, the normalized message router are based on the WSDL and XML standards. Therefore, we use XML messages in these examples.

Because ServiceMix consists of binding components (BCs) and service engines (SEs), we first have to decide which JBI component we're going to use to implement the simple logging functionality. Because we want this example to be simple, a POJO implementation is the best choice. ServiceMix offers two POJO SEs: `servicemix-bean` and `servicemix-jsr181`. Both SEs are suited to show the logging example, but the `servicemix-bean` SE gives us better insight into the message exchange within Service-Mix. So we implement our example with the `servicemix-bean` SE.

4.2.1   *Creating a logging service assembly for ServiceMix*

Now let's tackle the actual coding. When using the `MessageExchangeListener` interface provided by ServiceMix, the entry point for the Java class that we need to implement is the `onMessageExchange` method. The downside is that our Java class isn't a real POJO anymore, and there is a dependency to the ServiceMix framework. But for now let's ignore this, and start implementing the logging functionality in listing 4.8.

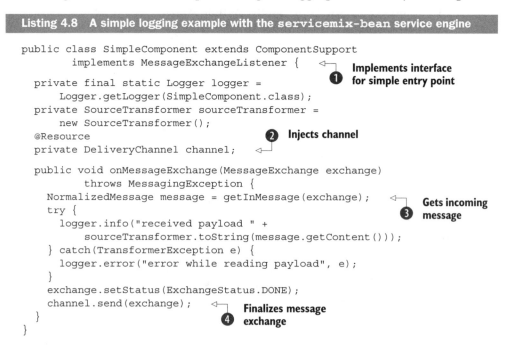

Listing 4.8   A simple logging example with the `servicemix-bean` service engine

```
public class SimpleComponent extends ComponentSupport
        implements MessageExchangeListener {          ◁— ❶ Implements interface
                                                           for simple entry point
  private final static Logger logger =
      Logger.getLogger(SimpleComponent.class);
  private SourceTransformer sourceTransformer =
      new SourceTransformer();
  @Resource                                    ❷ Injects channel
  private DeliveryChannel channel;          ◁—

  public void onMessageExchange(MessageExchange exchange)
          throws MessagingException {
    NormalizedMessage message = getInMessage(exchange);    ◁— ❸ Gets incoming
    try {                                                       message
      logger.info("received payload " +
          sourceTransformer.toString(message.getContent()));
    } catch(TransformerException e) {
      logger.error("error while reading payload", e);
    }
    exchange.setStatus(ExchangeStatus.DONE);
    channel.send(exchange);        ◁— ❹ Finalizes message
  }                                    exchange
}
```

In listing 4.8, the `SimpleComponent` class implements the `MessageExchangeListener` ❶ interface to produce a simple entry point for the message exchange with the `onMessageExchange` method. The `ComponentSupport` abstract class is the parent class, because this class provides convenience methods for working with the JBI message exchange. The `servicemix-bean` SE provides a way to inject the channel into the bean implementation ❷. For in-only exchanges, as we have in this example, this does nothing more than finalize the exchange and inform consumers that the exchange is over ❹. In the `onMessageExchange` method implementation, we first have to obtain the incoming message of the exchange. Because the `SimpleComponent` class extends the `ComponentSupport` abstract class, we can easily retrieve the incoming message with the `getInMessage` method ❸. The content of this message is logged with Log4j to the console.

4.2.2 *Creating service units and a service assembly*

With the implementation of the `SimpleComponent` class ready, we've finished the Java part of this simple logging example. What we have skipped so far, for convenience reasons, is the project structure. As you already saw in previous chapters, the connection between the JMS BC and the `SimpleComponent` `servicemix-bean` SE can be configured in several ways. We use the JBI-compliant approach to structure the distribution, using a service assembly and several service units. Figure 4.1 shows the `simple-sa` service assembly that we use for the logging example.

The `simple-sa` service assembly consists of two service units, as shown in figure 4.1. The `SimpleComponent` class from listing 4.8 is part of the `simple-bean-su` service unit. The other service unit, `simple-jms-su`, configures the JMS transport provider for the incoming message. Both service units have an xbean.xml file that configures the

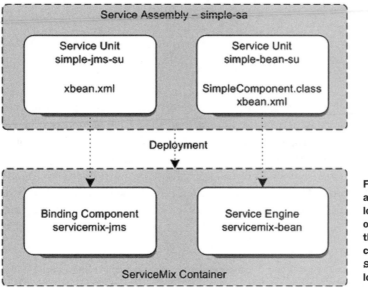

Figure 4.1 The service assembly for the simple logging example consists of two service units, and the `simple-bean-su` consists of the `SimpleComponent` logging implementation.

JMS BC and the `servicemix-bean` SE. This includes the configuration of the relationship between the JMS queue for the incoming message and the Java class that will be invoked when a message arrives at that queue. When the `simple-sa` service assembly is deployed to the ServiceMix container, the `simple-jms-su` service unit is deployed to work with the `servicemix-jms` BC and the `simple-bean-su` service unit works together with the `servicemix-bean` SE.

DEFINING THE PROJECT STRUCTURE

Fortunately, we can create the service assembly and the service units by using an Ant build file or a Maven plug-in provided by ServiceMix. The only thing we have to do is structure the project in such a way that this Ant build file or Maven plug-in is able to create the actual service assembly distribution.

> ### Using an Ant- or Maven-based project structure
>
> Because ServiceMix provides both an Ant- and a Maven-based build procedure to create service units and service assemblies and to deploy the distribution to the ServiceMix container, we have to choose between these two build procedures for our examples. Maven is growing in popularity and provides a great way to deal with library dependencies; Ant is a build tool that has been around for quite some time and is integrated quite nicely in IDEs like Eclipse and NetBeans.
>
> The downside of using Maven to build the ServiceMix distributions is, simply said, the time it takes to create the distribution and to deploy it to the ServiceMix container. The Ant build for ServiceMix takes considerably less time and works just fine for the build and deploy task. Therefore, we decided to use an Ant-based build procedure for our examples, although we know that not everybody will agree with our decision.
>
> Note that our choice doesn't impact the implementation of the examples; the implementation with a Maven-based build structure would include the same configuration files, except for the jbi.xml file generated only by Maven. Therefore, you can structure the examples in such a way that you can use Maven for the build and deploy task just as easily.

As explained in the previous callout, we use Ant to build and deploy the examples in this book. The project structure for the `simple-sa` service assembly is shown in figure 4.2. Note that the project structure of the other examples in the book use the same structure of service unit directories and XBean configuration files.

The project structure shown in figure 4.2 can be found in the ServiceMix code distribution for this book. The component directory is the starting point for the project structure of the `simple-sa` service assembly. In the jbi.xml file of the component directory, the service assembly's structure is defined, as you can see in the following code snippet:

```
<jbi xmlns="http://java.sun.com/xml/ns/jbi" version="1.0">
  <service-assembly>
```

```
<identification>
  <name>simple-sa</name>
  <description>OS ESBs - ServiceMix - Simple - SA</description>
</identification>
<service-unit>
  <identification>
    <name>simple-jms-su</name>
    <description>simple-jms-su</description>
  </identification>
  <target>
    <artifacts-zip>simple-jms-su.zip</artifacts-zip>
    <component-name>servicemix-jms</component-name>
  </target>
</service-unit>
<service-unit>
  <identification>
    <name>simple-bean-su</name>
    <description>simple-bean-su</description>
  </identification>
  <target>
    <artifacts-zip>simple-bean-su.zip</artifacts-zip>
    <component-name>servicemix-bean</component-name>
  </target>
</service-unit>
</service-assembly>
</jbi>
```

This jbi.xml file will be processed by the ServiceMix container to inspect the contents of the service assembly. Therefore, the jbi.xml file has to be part of the service assembly distribution file. The configuration of the service units is implemented with the xbean.xml files, as we see in more detail in the next section. ch4-examples.xml is an Ant build file for building and deploying the examples in chapter 4; you can also start the ServiceMix container with this file.

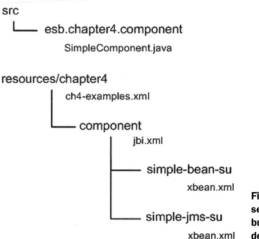

Figure 4.2 Project structure for the `simple-sa` service assembly used by the ch4-examples Ant build file to create the distribution that can be deployed to ServiceMix

CONFIGURING THE SERVICE UNITS

Now let's go back to the logging example. We have yet to discuss the configuration of the service units in the xbean.xml files. When we want to execute our simple logging example, the first configuration we have to implement is the JMS queue for the incoming message. In the xbean.xml file shown in listing 4.9, the JMS endpoints are configured.

Listing 4.9   ServiceMix configuration for the `simple-jms-su` service unit

```
<beans xmlns:jms="http://servicemix.apache.org/jms/1.0"
       xmlns:esb="http://esbinaction.com/examples">

  <jms:consumer service="esb:simpleConsumer"         ←1
      endpoint="simpleEndpoint"
      targetService="esb:simpleComponent"            ←2
      destinationName="simple.input"                 ←3
      connectionFactory="#connectionFactory"/>

  <bean id="connectionFactory"                                  ←4
      class="org.apache.activemq.ActiveMQConnectionFactory">
    <property name="brokerURL" value="tcp://localhost:61616" />
  </bean>
</beans>
```

The configuration of the JMS queue for the incoming messages of our logging example is implemented with the `jms:consumer` element ❶. The queue name is configured with the `destinationName` attribute and has a value of `simple.input` ❸. Because the endpoint is implemented as a consumer, it will listen for messages arriving at the `simple.input` queue. The connection factory used to connect to this queue is configured separately as a Spring bean, and points to the ActiveMQ broker that is part of ServiceMix ❹.

But what has to be done with the incoming messages? Well, the target destination for incoming messages is configured with the `targetService` attribute ❷. The destination for the incoming message is the `simpleComponent` service, which is configured in the `http://esbinaction.com/examples` namespace. The destination values correspond to the configuration of `simple-bean-su`, as shown in listing 4.10.

Listing 4.10   ServiceMix configuration for the `simple-bean-su` service unit

```
<beans xmlns:bean="http://servicemix.apache.org/bean/1.0"
       xmlns:esb="http://esbinaction.com/examples">

  <bean id="simpleBean"                                      1
      class="esb.chapter4.component.SimpleComponent" />

  <bean:endpoint service="esb:simpleComponent"      ←2
      endpoint="simpleEndpoint"
      bean="#simpleBean"/>
</beans>
```

Notice that the service value of the `bean:endpoint` ❷ matches the `targetService` value of the `jms:consumer` shown in listing 4.9. The `bean:endpoint` simply links the endpoint to a JavaBean implementation with id `simpleBean` ❶—in our case, the `SimpleComponent` class in listing 4.8.

We've now implemented all the pieces that accept a message from the `simple.input` queue, forward it to the `SimpleComponent` Java class, and log the message with Log4j to the console. All we have to do now is deploy the `simple-sa` service assembly to ServiceMix.

DEPLOYING AND TESTING THE LOGGING SOLUTION

The first step to deploy the service assembly is to start ServiceMix. As you'll recall from previous chapters, you must start the ServiceMix container with the default target in the Ant build file of this chapter (the ch4-examples.xml file).

Once you've started ServiceMix, you're ready to build and deploy the logging service assembly. Run the `deploy-simple` target in the ch4-examples.xml Ant build file. The service assembly is now deployed in the ServiceMix container, and the JMS and Bean service units are deployed to the corresponding JMS BC and Bean SE. This means that we are now ready to test the logging example. There are two options here; the first is to use the `SimpleComponentTest` JUnit test available in the source distribution in the test directory in the package `esb.chapter4.component.test`. The other option is to use the Swing test client application accompanying this book (see appendix F for more information) to put a message in the `simple.input` queue of the ActiveMQ broker. Regardless of the choice you make, you should see a logging statement in the ServiceMix console that displays the content of the message you've sent. If you use the JUnit test class provided in the source distribution, you should see the following log message:

```
INFO - SimpleComponent - received payload
<hello>world</hello>
```

If you see this message in the ServiceMix console, this means you have successfully completed the simple logging example. Let's now enhance this example a bit and include an example of Spring integration with the JavaBan component. The Spring integration with ServiceMix is provided automatically, because the ServiceMix configuration uses the Spring configuration. In the xbean.xml examples in listings 4.9 and 4.10, you can see that the root element name is `beans`. This element belongs to the Spring bean configuration namespace. In the next section, we see how Spring can be used with ServiceMix.

4.2.3   *Integrating ServiceMix and Spring*

We can easily enhance the simple logging example of section 4.2.1 with Spring functionality without doing a lot of extra work. In the source code for chapter 4, as shown in figure 4.2, the Spring example is already added to the xbean.xml files of the `simple-jms-su` and `simple-bean-su` service units. In the JMS configuration we add another endpoint definition that listens to another queue, `simpleSpring.input`, and forwards the incoming message to another service, `simpleSpringComponent`. The rest of the JMS configuration is the same as in listing 4.9. For the Spring example, we create a separate Java component, `SimpleSpringComponent`, shown in listing 4.11.

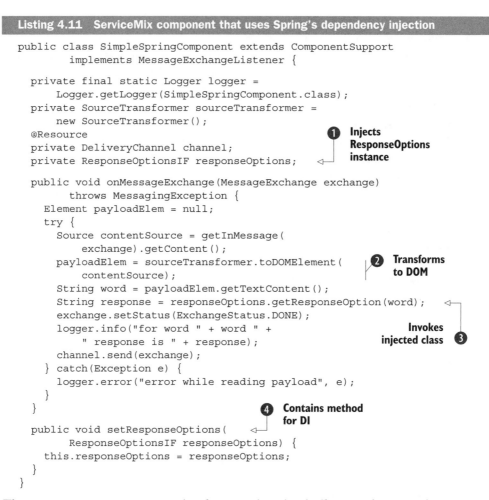

Listing 4.11   ServiceMix component that uses Spring's dependency injection

```
public class SimpleSpringComponent extends ComponentSupport
        implements MessageExchangeListener {

  private final static Logger logger =
      Logger.getLogger(SimpleSpringComponent.class);
  private SourceTransformer sourceTransformer =
      new SourceTransformer();
  @Resource
  private DeliveryChannel channel;                            ❶ Injects
  private ResponseOptionsIF responseOptions;                     ResponseOptions
                                                                 instance
  public void onMessageExchange(MessageExchange exchange)
        throws MessagingException {
    Element payloadElem = null;
    try {
      Source contentSource = getInMessage(
          exchange).getContent();
      payloadElem = sourceTransformer.toDOMElement(      ❷ Transforms
          contentSource);                                   to DOM
      String word = payloadElem.getTextContent();
      String response = responseOptions.getResponseOption(word);
      exchange.setStatus(ExchangeStatus.DONE);
      logger.info("for word " + word + "               Invokes
          " response is " + response);               injected class ❸
      channel.send(exchange);
    } catch(Exception e) {
      logger.error("error while reading payload", e);
    }
  }                                          ❹ Contains method
                                                for DI
  public void setResponseOptions(
        ResponseOptionsIF responseOptions) {
    this.responseOptions = responseOptions;
  }
}
```

The SimpleSpringComponent implementation is similar to the one for Simple-Component in listing 4.8. There are, however, a few important differences. The Response-OptionsIF and ResponseOptions classes used in the Mule example and shown in listing 4.5 are also used for this ServiceMix example. The ResponseOptions class is injected by Spring according to the configuration that we discuss in listing 4.12 ❶, ❹. Because we need to pass an incoming text message to the injected ResponseOptions class instance, the incoming message is transformed to a DOM element ❷. With the DOM element, we can easily get the value of the element with the getTextContent method. Because the input message will be similar to <word>ESB</word>, the get-TextContent method will return the value of the word element (ESB in the example given). The value of the word element is then passed on to the ResponseOptions class instance ❸ and the response value is logged to the console with Log4j.

You may wonder why we don't send the response value back to the sender of the text message. Because this needs some extra configuration (which we discuss in section 4.5), we just log the response to the console. The remaining part of the Spring integration example is the xbean.xml configuration of the `simple-bean-su` service unit. Listing 4.12 describes this configuration.

> **Listing 4.12   ServiceMix configuration that uses a Spring bean**

```
<beans xmlns:bean="http://servicemix.apache.org/bean/1.0"
    xmlns:esb="http://esbinaction.com/examples">

  <bean:endpoint service="esb:simpleSpringComponent"
      endpoint="simpleSpringEndpoint"
      bean="#simpleSpringBean"/>                          Injects        ❶
                                                     ResponseOptions
  <bean id="simpleSpringBean"                              instance
      class="esb.chapter4.component.SimpleSpringComponent">
    <property name="responseOptions" ref="responseOptionsBean"/>
  </bean>

  <bean id="responseOptionsBean"                   ❷ Constructs
      class="esb.chapter4.component.ResponseOptions">   options map
    <property name="options">
      <map>
        <entry key="EAI" value="Where have you been lately?"/>
        <entry key="XML" value="The lingua franca!"/>
      </map>
    </property>
  </bean>
</beans>
```

The ServiceMix configuration is similar to the one for Mule in listing 4.7. The `ResponseOptions` configuration is exactly the same, as we use Spring in both examples ❷. A `ResponseOptions` instance is injected by Spring in the `responseOptions` setter method of the `SimpleSpringComponent` class that we have just discussed ❶.

   Because we've already deployed the `simple-sa` service assembly to the ServiceMix container that also includes the Spring example, we can proceed to test the example. You can again use a JUnit test, `SimpleSpringComponentTest`, or use the Swing test client to put a message in the `simpleSpring.input` queue of the ActiveMQ broker.

   The result of the unit test or the Swing test client should be a log statement in the ServiceMix console. The log statement should reproduce the `word` element value you've sent and the corresponding response value as configured in the xbean.xml file shown in listing 4.12.

   With this final test, we've succeeded in implementing some custom logic in both Mule and ServiceMix. But the custom logic involved just one component—a real-world integration solution consists of more than one. In the next section, we look at how these integration solutions can be implemented with message flows.

4.3   *Constructing message flows with an ESB*

Now that you know how to build components in Mule and ServiceMix, you only need to learn how to connect these components into complete message flows. We talk about what a message flow is and which elements it consists of in section 4.3.1. But to grasp the basics of constructing message flows, you'll want to implement a message flow yourself. In section 4.3.2 we present a case study that involves implementing a message flow. This case study will be used in the remaining sections of this chapter (with Mule in section 4.4 and ServiceMix in section 4.5). But let's not rush and instead start off with some background.

4.3.1   What is a message flow?

Building an integration solution doesn't stop with developing components and connecting them to one another as we've done in sections 3.1 and 3.2. These sections were merely a ramp for the actual deliverable in an integration solution: the message flow. To avoid making our discussion too theoretical, we begin with a schematic overview of a message flow (figure 4.3).

In basic terms, a *message flow* provides an intermediary layer between a service consumer and a service provider. The terminology of *service consumer* and *service provider* is used in the web services and SOA world to indicate which application asks for information (the service consumer) and which application provides the information (the service provider). In chapter 1 we listed the benefits of an intermediary layer in a complex IT environment that needs to integrate applications. The implementation of the intermediary layer is the message flow, which makes sure that the request message is delivered at the service provider and the response message is sent back to the service consumer.

A typical message exchange between a service consumer and a service provider consists of a request and a response message. Although there are other message exchange patterns (MEPs), we use the request-response MEP to explain the concept of a message flow.

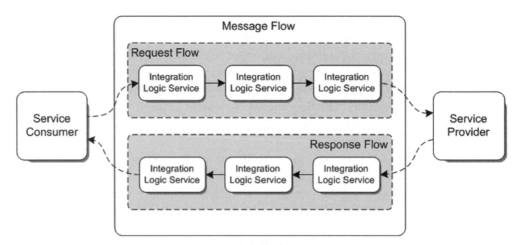

Figure 4.3   Schematic explanation of a message flow, which is the intermediary between a service consumer and a service provider

Message exchange pattern (MEP)

The exchange of messages between a service consumer and a service provider can be described with a message exchange pattern (MEP). Common MEPs are request-response and one-way in WSDL 1.1 terminology. In WSDL 2.0, request-response is referred to as in-out and one-way as in-only. MEPs are useful to provide additional details on the message interface a service provider offers.

A typical message flow consists of a request flow for handling the request message and a response flow for dealing with the response message. Because of the diversity of integration logic necessary for a particular implementation, it's not possible to define a standard structure for a request or a response flow. But as shown in figure 4.3, we can be sure that a request and a response flow consist of a number of integration logic services. You can think of an integration logic service as a piece of work that needs to be done as part of the request or response handling. This can, for example, be a transformation of the incoming message to the message format expected by the service provider. Another example is a message enhancement that consists of retrieving some extra information from a database. The integration logic services are the conceptual equivalents of the ESB components discussed in section 4.1.

In most cases, a message flow consists of multiple integration logic services, so there's a need for communication between these services. We look at the details of linking components in this section. Figure 4.3 shows a straightforward connection between the various integration logic services. In practice, there will be different paths for different messages.

What also needs explaining is the communication between the service consumer and the service provider. There should be a clear interface for both the message exchange between the service consumer and the message flow (the ESB), as well as between the message flow (the ESB) and the service provider. Often, a WSDL is regarded as the "silver bullet" of defining interfaces between applications. We, however, find one part of the WSDL vital: the message definition. Preferably, use XML as the message exchange format so the message definition can be implemented with an XML Schema Definition (XSD).

Besides the message definition, the message transport protocol should be determined. When dealing with legacy applications the choice of transport protocols is very limited, but when dealing with applications that are still under development multiple options exist. What's important here is that a transport protocol be chosen that matches the nonfunctional needs for the service. For example, don't use plain SOAP over HTTP when the messages to be exchanged are business critical and shouldn't be lost. Chapter 6 explains the various connectivity options, along with their advantages and disadvantages. Now, let's move on and discuss a message flow example that will be implemented in section 4.4 with Mule and in section 4.5 with ServiceMix.

4.3.2   A message flow case study

We've discussed a bit of theory about message flows, so we should be ready to make this knowledge a bit more practical.

The context for the case study will be the calculation of the cheapest price for a specific book at two bookstores, Amazon and Barnes & Noble. As you may recall from figure 4.3, a message flow can be divided into a request and a response flow. The request flow starts with sending a message with an International Standard Book Number (ISBN) to the open source ESB. The ESB will forward this message to the two bookstores and wait for a response message. The processing of the response message is part of the response flow of the message flow that we'll implement. The response flow is triggered when the two bookstores send a response message containing the price for the book back to the ESB. These messages are aggregated into one message and then the cheapest price is calculated. The name of the bookstore with the least expensive price and the price amount is then sent back to the initial requestor (see figure 4.4).

As you can see in figure 4.4, the book price case study is not that simple to implement in a message flow. But we don't want only simple examples like the ones in sections 4.1 and 4.2, do we? Let's walk through the important and complex parts of the book message flow. A virtual book customer will send a message containing an ISBN to the ESB. The transport protocol used here could be pretty much anything, but for this case study we use JMS. When an ISBN message arrives at the JMS queue, the ESB will log the message for auditing. Then we need to forward the message to the Amazon and

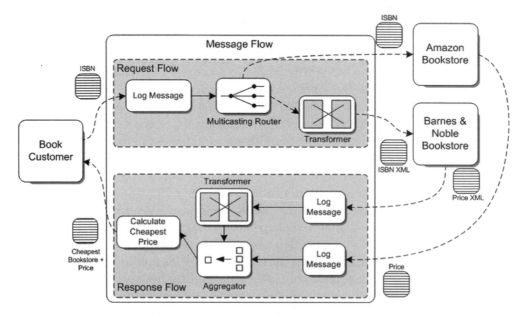

Figure 4.4   An overview of the message flow for the book price case study that involves communication with the Amazon and Barnes & Noble bookstores. The example shows a customer that requests the cheapest price for a specific book represented as an ISBN.

Barnes & Noble bookstores. Hohpe and Woolf's book on Enterprise Integration patterns (EIPs) has defined a number of patterns for these common integration problems. In figure 4.4, a multicasting router is shown that's referred to as the Recipient List pattern in the EIP book. This pattern simply distributes the same message to multiple endpoints—exactly what we need for our case study. We'll see later on how this pattern can be implemented.

The Amazon bookstore is able to process the message in the same format as the incoming message. The Barnes & Noble bookstore isn't capable of processing the incoming message. This bookstore expects a message in a specific XML format, and the incoming message has another message format. Therefore, the message is transformed to the XML format before it's sent to the Barnes & Noble bookstore.

When the bookstores have processed the ISBN message and found the listed price for the book corresponding to the ISBN, a response message containing the book price is returned to the ESB. As we did for the incoming message, we use a JMS transport protocol for communication with the two bookstores. When the response messages arrive, the messages are first logged for auditing purposes. The response message of the Amazon bookstore will contain the book price and the corresponding ISBN in a message format that the ESB is able to process. The Barnes & Noble bookstore message needs to be transformed to the same format as the Amazon response message before it can be processed.

Because we must be able to compare the two response messages, we must receive these two messages at the same time. Without implementing additional functionality, a message is commonly processed on an individual basis. To be able to combine the two messages, we can use an aggregator pattern, which is also defined in the EIP book. The aggregator is able to combine messages with unique element values into one message. The aggregator looks at incoming messages for unique values that you can specify and matches messages with the same unique values into one message. For the book price case study, we can use the ISBN message as a simple unique value for the aggregator. A condition to use the ISBN message is that only one input message with the same ISBN message can be processed at once. But for our simple example, this should be sufficient.

When the two book price messages are aggregated into one message, the lowest price can be determined. Eventually, when the lowest price is calculated, a response message containing the name of the bookstore with the lowest price and the corresponding amount is sent to the initial book customer.

Now that we've discussed the case study, we can proceed with the implementation. In section 4.4 we look at implementing the book price case study with Mule.

4.4 *Implementing a message flow with Mule*

In the examples in section 4.1, we've already implemented some simple message flows. The message flows consisted of only one Mule service that consumed user input from the console; in the last example, a response was also sent to the same console.

Therefore, these message flows lack a real request and response flow implementation. In this section, you'll learn how to implement a full message flow, based on the case study description given in section 4.3.2.

4.4.1   *Implementing the request flow with Mule*

The full implementation of the book price case study will consist of quite a number of Java classes and a large Mule configuration. As usual, the full source code is available at the book's website. Therefore, we don't show every bit of Java code and Mule configuration in this section, but we focus on the important parts. First we examine the processing of the incoming ISBN message and the forwarding of the ISBN to the Amazon and Barnes & Noble bookstores. Figure 4.5 shows the Mule configuration for the request flow.

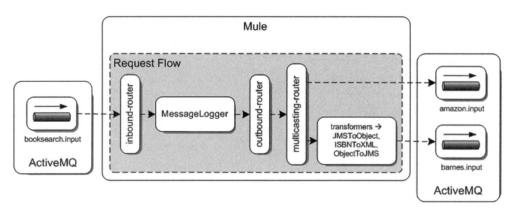

Figure 4.5   An overview of the Mule configuration of the request flow for the book price case study. The incoming message is logged and forwarded to two endpoints by the multicasting router.

Figure 4.5 shows a distinction between the Mule container and the ActiveMQ message broker. The JMS implementation that will supply the queues to communicate with the book consumer and the two bookstores is provided by ActiveMQ. In the Mule configuration bookquote-config.xml, a message logger class is configured as a Mule component that has an inbound router that polls the booksearch.input ActiveMQ queue. When a message arrives, it's simply logged with Log4j. This is probably quite familiar to you by now. The more interesting part of the request flow configuration is the implementation of the multicasting to the two bookstores. Let's zoom in to the outbound router configuration of the MessageLogger Mule component (listing 4.13).

Listing 4.13   Outbound routing configuration of the message logger service

```
<service name="BookQuoteLogger">
  <inbound>
    <jms:inbound-endpoint queue="booksearch.input"/>
  </inbound>
  <component class="esb.chapter4.messageflow.mule.MessageLogger" />
```

```
<outbound>
  <multicasting-router>
    <jms:outbound-endpoint queue="amazon.input"/>
    <jms:outbound-endpoint queue="barnes.input">
      <transformer ref="ISBNToXML"/>
      <transformer ref="ObjectToJMS"/>
    </jms:outbound-endpoint>
  </multicasting-router>
</outbound>
</service>
```

In the example in section 4.1 that also used an outbound router, a simple outbound-pass-through-router was used that just forwards the message to one endpoint. In this case we need a router that's able to forward a message to multiple endpoints. In listing 4.13, the `multicasting-router` is used to implement this functionality ❶. With this router, we can configure multiple endpoints to which the message is sent. For the Amazon bookstore, the message is forwarded to the ActiveMQ input queue, which will be read by an Amazon service that retrieves the book price for the provided ISBN. For the Barnes & Noble bookstore, the message is transformed into an XML message. Because the message just contains an ISBN, it is a simple XML message like this:

```
<isbn>ISBN number</isbn>
```

To be able to get the payload of the initial message as sent by the book customer and to not be dependent on a JMS message instance, the message is first transformed implicitly into a Java object at the inbound endpoint of the `BookQuoteLogger` Mule service. This transformer, `org.mule.transport.jms.transformers.JMSMessageToObject`, is provided out of the box, and just retrieves the actual payload of the JMS message. Because the transformed XML message is once again sent to a JMS queue, the message is changed back to a JMS message again at the outbound endpoint definition by another standard transformer, `org.mule.transport.jms.transformers.ObjectToJMSMessage`.

4.4.2 Implementing the response flow with Mule

More complex logic is implemented in the response flow of the book price case study. We have to implement functionality to aggregate the two response messages that contain the book prices and to calculate the lowest price of the responses. Let's start with a schematic overview of the Mule implementation of the response flow in figure 4.6.

As you can see in figure 4.6, this is different from the request flow we discussed in figure 4.5, isn't it? Let's break the response flow of figure 4.6 down to comprehensible portions. We begin with the two response messages that are received from the `amazon.output` and `barnes.output` queues. The same `MessageLogger` service used in the request flow is used to log the incoming messages from Amazon and Barnes & Noble that consist of a book price, the ISBN, and the bookstore company name. Before the message is routed to the next Mule service, it is transformed to a Java object, `BookQuote`, which has the three message attributes we just mentioned. For the response message from the Amazon bookstore, we can simply get the payload out of

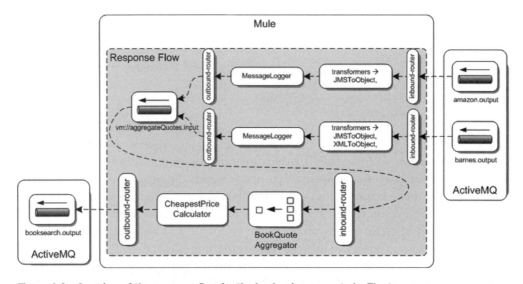

Figure 4.6   Overview of the response flow for the book price case study. The two response messages from Amazon and Barnes & Noble are logged and aggregated into one message. Then the prices are compared and the lowest price is sent back to the customer.

the JMS `ObjectMessage`, but for the Barnes & Noble bookstore, the response message has to be converted from an XML format to the `BookQuote` Java object. JiBX is used to do this transformation; for more details on JiBX, return to chapter 3.

CONFIGURING AND IMPLEMENTING THE AGGREGATOR

The two response messages that are both transformed into a `BookQuote` POJO are then sent to a so-called *virtual machine queue*, `vm://aggregateQuote.input`. This queue is hosted inside the Java Virtual Machine (JVM) Mule is running in, and is well suited for high-performance cases. In this case, the queue runs in-memory, but in cases where reliability is essential, the queue can also be made persistent. This virtual machine queue is defined in the `inbound` element of the `CheapestPriceCalculator` service.

But before the incoming message is routed to the component implementation, the two response messages are first aggregated into one message. Because the calculator must be able to get the book prices of both response messages in order to calculate the lowest price, the messages are combined into a collection of `BookQuote` POJOs. Before we look at the Java implementation of this aggregator component, let's see how this can be defined using the Mule configuration (listing 4.14).

Listing 4.14   Mule configuration for the cheapest price calculator

```
<service name="CheapestPriceCalculator">
  <inbound>
    <vm:inbound-endpoint path="aggregateQuotes.input"/>
    <custom-inbound-router
        class="esb.chapter4.messageflow.mule.BookQuoteAggregator"/>
  </inbound>
```
❶

```
  <component
      class="esb.chapter4.messageflow.mule.CheapestPriceCalculator"/>  ←❷
  <outbound>
    <outbound-pass-through-router>
      <jms:outbound-endpoint queue="booksearch.output"/>
    </outbound-pass-through-router>
  </outbound>
</service>
```

You've seen quite a few Mule configurations by now, so perhaps you notice that the main difference here is the use of a custom router ❶. Mule provides a number of inbound routers out of the box, but in this case we need some custom logic. We have to match two incoming messages with the same ISBN and aggregate them into one message. The aggregated message is eventually passed on to the Java class that calculates the lowest price ❷.

To implement the aggregator, a custom Java class is necessary, but luckily we can use an aggregator base class that Mule provides: `AbstractEventAggregator`. Before looking at the implementation of the `BookQuoteAggregator` in listing 4.15, remember that the incoming message for this aggregator is the `BookQuote` Java object that contains a book price, an ISBN, and a company name.

Listing 4.15 Implementation of a custom aggregator, the `BookQuoteAggregator`

```
public class BookQuoteAggregator extends AbstractEventAggregator {

  private static final Logger logger =
      Logger.getLogger(BookQuoteAggregator.class);

  protected EventCorrelatorCallback getCorrelatorCallback() {     ❶ Constructs
    return new EventCorrelatorCallback()   {                         aggregated
                                                                     message
  public MuleMessage aggregateEvents(EventGroup events)
      throws AggregationException {
    Iterator itEvent = events.iterator();
    Collection<BookQuote> quoteList = new ArrayList<BookQuote>();
    while(itEvent.hasNext()) {
      MuleEvent event = (MuleEvent) itEvent.next();
      BookQuote quote = (BookQuote)
          event.getMessage().getPayload();
      quoteList.add(quote);                    ❷ Returns
    }                                            aggregated
    return new DefaultMuleMessage(quoteList);    message
  }

  public EventGroup createEventGroup(MuleEvent event,
      Object correlationID) {
    return new EventGroup(correlationID, 2);
  }

  public boolean shouldAggregateEvents(EventGroup events) {
    Iterator itEvent = events.iterator();
    boolean isAmazonPresent = false;        Determines if
    boolean isBarnesPresent = false;      messages are present ❸
    while(itEvent.hasNext()) {
```

```
        MuleEvent event = (MuleEvent) itEvent.next();
        BookQuote quote = (BookQuote)
            event.getMessage().getPayload();
        String companyName = quote.getCompanyName();         ◁┐   Checks for both
        if("Amazon".equalsIgnoreCase(companyName)) {          ❹   company names
          isAmazonPresent = true;
        } else if("BarnesAndNoble".equalsIgnoreCase(companyName)) {
          isBarnesPresent = true;
        }
      }
      return isAmazonPresent && isBarnesPresent;
    }
  };}

  public MessageInfoMapping getMessageInfoMapping() {          ❺  Gets
      return new MuleMessageInfoMapping() {                        correlation
                                                                    identifier
    public String getCorrelationId(MuleMessage message) {    ◁┘
      BookQuote quote = (BookQuote) message.getPayload();
      return quote.getIsbn();
    }
  };}
}
```

The `BookQuoteAggregator` consists of quite a bit of code, but this class also provides a lot of functionality. The base class `AbstractEventAggregator` already includes the convenience methods to implement an aggregator, so we only have to implement the custom logic necessary for matching the two book price messages.

The first part of the custom aggregator is the aggregation process to create a new message ❶. Because we simply need to have the two messages available for the calculation of the lowest price, we create a collection of the two `BookQuote` Java objects and return them as the aggregated Mule message ❷.

The second piece of logic is the implementation of when the group of messages can be aggregated into one message ❸ and forwarded to the actual component implementation, in our example the `CheapestPriceCalculator`. The `shouldAggregateEvents` method returns true if all the messages of the same group have arrived and the aggregation can take place, and returns false if there are still messages to be processed. We're expecting two response messages, one from Amazon and one from Barnes & Noble, so we look at the company names of the messages in the group ❹ to determine whether the aggregation can already start.

The final part that we have to implement is the logic that matches corresponding response messages so that eventually the correct response messages are aggregated into one message ❺. In this example, the ISBN can be used to match the response messages. So when an event arrives at this aggregator, the ISBN of the message is returned as the group identifier. Based on this group identifier, the `AbstractEvent-Aggregator` implementation takes care of creating an `EventGroup` object instance, where corresponding messages are grouped together. So looking back at the custom aggregator we've just implemented, we think you'll agree it isn't as complex as you may have expected.

To provide a full overview of the functionality implemented to create the lowest price calculator functionality, listing 4.16 shows `CheapestPriceCalculator`. It shouldn't be too hard to follow, now that we've discussed the aggregator example.

Listing 4.16   Implementation of `CheapestPriceCalculator`

```
public class CheapestPriceCalculator {

  public BookQuote calculate(Collection<BookQuote> quoteList) {      ◁—❶
    BookQuote cheapestQuote = null;
    for(BookQuote quote : quoteList) {
      if(cheapestQuote == null ||
           quote.getPrice() <= cheapestQuote.getPrice()) {           ◁—❷
        cheapestQuote = quote;
      }
    }
    return cheapestQuote;
  }
}
```

The cheapest price calculator accepts a collection of `BookQuote` POJOs that were aggregated in the `BookQuoteAggregator` as input ❶. While looping through the list of `BookQuote` instances, the cheapest `BookQuote` instance is kept as a reference ❷. The lowest book price message is eventually returned as the output of the calculator component.

DEPLOYING AND TESTING THE MULE CHEAPEST PRICE CALCULATOR

We've implemented all parts of the book price case study for Mule, so we should be able to the test the whole message flow, right? Well, we're missing a few important conditions to be able to test the full message flow. We have no book consumer that sends an ISBN and eventually is able to receive the lowest book price. We also lack an implementation of the Amazon and Barnes & Noble price search services.

In the book's source code, you can find implementations for these three components. The book consumer is simulated with the Swing test client, and the two price search services, AmazonBookStore and BarnesBookStore, are implemented as JMS message listeners and producers. The AmazonBookStore and BarnesBookStore message listeners are started with the `messageflow-spring` target in the ch4-examples Ant build file.

You also need to start an ActiveMQ message broker by running the activemq script in the bin directory of the ActiveMQ binary distribution or by running the `start-activeMQ` target in the ch4-examples Ant build file. Go ahead and test this Mule message flow by executing the `messageflow-mule` target in the ch4-examples Ant script. This Ant script compiles the source code, creates and deploys a Mule-deployable JAR file, and starts Mule with the configuration of the cheapest price example.

Now we can execute the final step, which means running the Swing test client that's able to send a message to the `booksearch.input` queue. The input of the message should be an ISBN of 1010101010 or 9999999999. You can also use the JUnit test MessageFlowTest to test the message flow example.

The response message of the cheapest price message flow should eventually include a company name that equals to Amazon or BarnesAndNoble and the lowest price value. When you receive this message, this means that the full message flow has executed as designed. If you feel the need to dig into the processing path of the message flow, you can look in the console where Mule has started. You should find logging messages that describe the message flow path.

Take your time to explore all the parts of the message flow that we've just implemented with the Mule source code for this book. We implemented quite a bit of functionality in this section, and we focused on the difficult parts of the case study implementation. Now you're ready for more serious integration challenges with Mule in the chapters that follow. But first, we implement the same case study with ServiceMix. The ServiceMix case study implementation should give you a good feeling about the similarities and differences between Mule and ServiceMix. And it will make you even more knowledgeable about open source integration technologies in general.

4.5   *Implementing a message flow with ServiceMix*

In section 4.2 we implemented a small message flow. The example used a component that consumes messages from an ActiveMQ queue, and we included a small piece of custom logic that logged the incoming message to the console. When you look back at the theory behind the message flow concept, this functionality is similar to the request flow part of a message flow. So what's missing here is an endpoint where the request is sent to and a response flow that takes care of routing the response message produced by the endpoint back to the initial sender. In this section, we implement a full message flow, including a request flow and a response flow.

4.5.1   *Implementing the request flow with ServiceMix*

We use the price case study described in section 4.3.2 again as the integration problem that we need to solve, this time with ServiceMix. In section 4.2 we discussed the project layout and the JBI binding components and service engines, so we don't do that here again. Let's step through the ServiceMix implementation of the price case study by first discussing the request flow and then the response flow. Figure 4.7 kicks off the solution implementation with an overview of the request flow implementation.

The solution as shown in figure 4.7 is divided into the service unit packages as they will be deployed eventually on ServiceMix. The packages have the names of the service engines and the binding component to which the service units are deployed. One binding component and one service engine will be familiar to you: the `servicemix-jms` and the `servicemix-bean` JBI components. The request flow will start with an incoming message at the `booksearch.input` queue that you see in the left portion of figure 4.7. The numbers that are included in the figure can guide you with the execution order. We include them only as a functional guidance; the numbers don't represent the runtime execution order. For example, the message logger bean could be executed *after* the JMS provider for the Amazon service is executed.

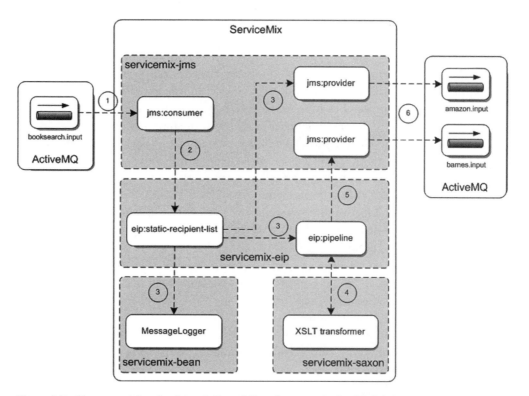

Figure 4.7 **The request flow implementation of the price case study with ServiceMix. The incoming message is logged and forwarded to the Amazon and Barnes & Noble endpoints.**

CONFIGURING A STATIC RECIPIENT LIST

A JMS endpoint is configured within ServiceMix that consumes the incoming message and passes it on to the `eip:static-recipient-list` component. This component uses the EIP package that ServiceMix provides with the `servicemix-eip` service engine. The static recipient list is able to send the same message on to multiple destinations, and that's exactly what we need here. The incoming message should be logged to the console and then forwarded to the Amazon and Barnes & Noble bookstores. The configuration of the static recipient list is shown in listing 4.17.

Listing 4.17 **ServiceMix configuration for the static recipient list**

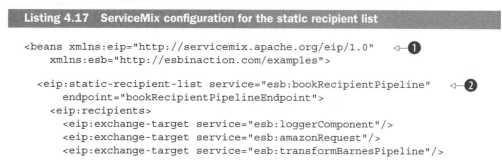

```
<beans xmlns:eip="http://servicemix.apache.org/eip/1.0"        ◄─❶
    xmlns:esb="http://esbinaction.com/examples">

  <eip:static-recipient-list service="esb:bookRecipientPipeline"   ◄─❷
      endpoint="bookRecipientPipelineEndpoint">
    <eip:recipients>
      <eip:exchange-target service="esb:loggerComponent"/>
      <eip:exchange-target service="esb:amazonRequest"/>
      <eip:exchange-target service="esb:transformBarnesPipeline"/>
```

```
        </eip:recipients>
      </eip:static-recipient-list>
    </beans>
```

The `servicemix-eip` service engine uses a separate ServiceMix namespace, `http://servicemix.apache.org/eip/1.0` ❶, as is common practice for every service engine or binding component within ServiceMix. The configuration of the static recipient list pattern is pretty simple in ServiceMix ❷. We only have to configure the list of destinations (called exchange targets) for the incoming message. The `service` attribute of the exchange target points to the destination where the message must be sent. You already learned how to use service names in section 4.2.

The `MessageLogger` implementation that takes care of the logging functionality is similar to the logging implementation in section 4.2. The message to the Amazon bookstore is just forwarded to a JMS endpoint that produces a new message on the `amazon.input` queue.

IMPLEMENTING AND CONFIGURING A MESSAGE TRANSFORMER

For the Barnes & Noble bookstore, we first have to transform the message into the proper XML message format. Because the XSLT transformation uses an in-out message exchange type, we have to deal with an in-only message exchange that's used by the JMS endpoint of the Barnes & Noble request message. Before we can execute the XSLT transformation, the message exchange type first has to be changed with a *pipeline component*.

> ### The ServiceMix pipeline component
> The pipeline component is able to accept an in-only message exchange to be forwarded to an in-out message exchange, where the result of the in-out call is forwarded to a destination that can be configured in the pipeline configuration. When you implement message flows with ServiceMix or JBI in general, the trigger of the flow can expect a response message (an in-out exchange), or the trigger expects no answer back (an in-only exchange). An asynchronous communication style is predominant in an enterprise integration environment, so the message exchange pattern is in many integration cases in-only. But some of the components that need to be used in the message flow implementation may require an in-out message exchange. For situations where you need to perform an in-out message exchange from an in-only message exchange, a pipeline can be used. The pipeline converts the in-only exchange into an in-out exchange and forwards the result of the in-out exchange to a configurable destination.

The pipeline component is an essential part when dealing with different types of message exchanges within ServiceMix. JMS endpoints typically use an in-only message exchange as they only accept incoming messages and don't give back a response message. On the other hand, a lot of the service engines use an in-out message exchange type as they accept incoming messages and return response messages. Listing 4.18 shows the configuration for the pipeline that calls the Saxon component.

Listing 4.18   Pipeline configuration for the in-out invocation of the Saxon component

```
<eip:pipeline service="esb:transformBarnesPipeline"
    endpoint="transformBarnesPipelineEndpoint">
  <eip:transformer>
    <eip:exchange-target service="esb:transformToBarnes" />    ⟵❶
  </eip:transformer>
  <eip:target>
    <eip:exchange-target service="esb:barnesRequest" />    ⟵❷
  </eip:target>
</eip:pipeline>
```

Notice that the service name for this pipeline corresponds with the last target of the static recipient list that was shown in listing 4.17. With the `transformer` element, the target service that requires an in-out message exchange is configured ❶. This service is implemented with the Saxon JBI component that we'll discuss shortly. With the `target` element, the target service for the response message of the Saxon JBI component can be configured ❷. The target service `barnesRequest` is implemented with a JMS endpoint.

Now that we've transformed the message exchange from in-only to in-out with the pipeline configuration, we're able to implement the actual transformation. Figure 4.8 shows the XSLT transformation performed here.

The XSLT transformation used in the book price case study is implemented with the ServiceMix Saxon JBI component. The Saxon JBI component is able to transform an incoming message based on a XSLT style sheet. Figure 4.8 shows a simple XSLT style sheet that transforms the incoming ISBN into an `isbn-number` element. The functionality implemented here is not so difficult, and the same setup could also be used to perform more complex XSLT transformations. Listing 4.19 shows the xbean.xml configuration for the XSLT transformation.

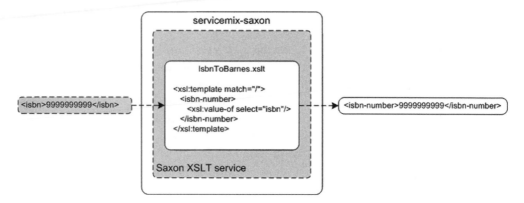

Figure 4.8   Transformation of the ISBN message incoming format to the message format as expected by the Barnes & Noble bookstore

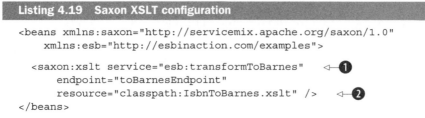

Listing 4.19   Saxon XSLT configuration

```
<beans xmlns:saxon="http://servicemix.apache.org/saxon/1.0"
    xmlns:esb="http://esbinaction.com/examples">

  <saxon:xslt service="esb:transformToBarnes"      ←❶
      endpoint="toBarnesEndpoint"
      resource="classpath:IsbnToBarnes.xslt" />     ←❷
</beans>
```

You can see that the value of the `service` attribute ❶ of this XSLT transformer, `esb:transformToBarnes`, is referenced from the configuration shown in the `trans-former` element in listing 4.18. Because the XSLT style sheet IsbnToBarnes.xslt is provided in the classpath of the service unit distribution, we can reference the IsbnToBarnes.xslt file directly ❷.

The result of the XSLT transformation will be sent to the target service configuration of listing 4.18, which is a JMS endpoint. You can find the configuration of the JMS endpoints and the `MessageLogger` bean in this book's source code. We've discussed the details of these configurations in section 4.2.

4.5.2   *Implementing the response flow with ServiceMix*

Let's move on to the response flow. This implementation must be able to consume the response messages of the Amazon and Barnes & Noble bookstores, log these messages, aggregate them into one message, calculate the cheapest offering, and eventually return this offering to the book customer. This is quite a lot of functionality, so let's begin the walkthrough of the response flow (figure 4.9).

The response flow in figure 4.9 consists of an impressive group of ServiceMix functionalities. When we compare the response flow with the request flow in figure 4.7, the main difference is the aggregator and the number of pipelines. Let's start with the order of functionality that's processed when the response flow is executed. The response flow is triggered by two response messages arriving from the Amazon bookstore at the `amazon.output` JMS queue and from the Barnes & Noble bookstore at the `barnes.output` JMS queue.

The incoming message from the Barnes & Noble bookstore is first transformed with an XSLT component. This is the same functionality that we saw in the request flow implementation. So again, we use a pipeline to transform the in-only message exchange of the JMS endpoint to an in-out message exchange needed by the Saxon XSLT transformer. (We don't discuss the details here again.)

IMPLEMENTING THE AGGREGATOR
You may be wondering why the message exchange with the `AggregateMessageLogger` is in-out and not in-only, as in the request message flow. Why is a pipeline component necessary to transform the in-only message exchange initiated by the JMS consumers to an in-out message exchange to invoke the logger component? In most cases, a logger component requires just an in-only as it consumes a message and doesn't produce

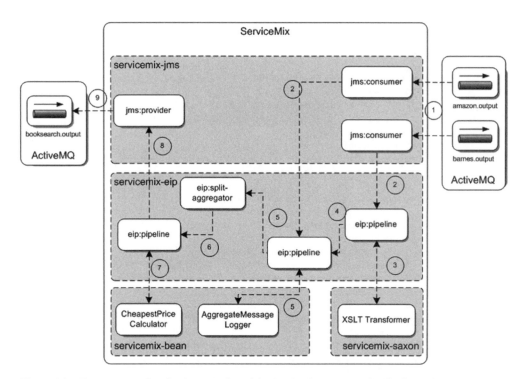

Figure 4.9   The response flow implementation of the book price case study. The incoming book quotes from Amazon and Barnes & Noble are logged and aggregated. Then the lowest price is calculated and sent back to the customer.

a response message. Well, `AggregateMessageLogger` does a bit more than just log the message contents.

Because we use a standard ServiceMix aggregator to group the two incoming response messages from Amazon and Barnes & Noble, we need to set some additional message properties. This standard aggregator is part of the splitter/aggregator functionality that ServiceMix provides. So messages are first divided into multiple smaller messages and eventually the aggregator groups the smaller messages into a large message again. Because we didn't have to use splitter functionality, we must set some message properties that otherwise the splitter would have done. (We could've also created a new aggregator implementation, but that approach would make this example unnecessarily complex.)

The `AggregatorMessageLogger` implementation uses the functionality of the servicemix-bean service engine. You saw some examples of such an implementation in section 4.2, but we're using different functionality this time (see listing 4.20).

Listing 4.20   `AggregatorMessageLogger` implementation

```
public void onMessageExchange(MessageExchange exchange)
    throws MessagingException {
```

```
if (exchange.getStatus() != ExchangeStatus.ACTIVE) {
  logger.info("state is not active so ignoring call");
  return;
}
Element payloadElem = null;
try {
  Source contentSource = getInMessage(exchange).getContent();
  payloadElem = sourceTransformer.toDOMElement(
      contentSource);
} catch(Exception e) {
  logger.error("error while reading payload", e);
  throw new MessagingException(e);
}
BookQuote bookQuote = QuoteMessageHelper.
    unmarshallQuote(payloadElem);
logger.info("received quote " + bookQuote.getIsbn() + ", "
    + bookQuote.getPrice() + ", "
        + bookQuote.getCompanyName());
NormalizedMessage outMessage =
    exchange.createMessage();
try {
  outMessage.setContent(new StringSource(
      QuoteMessageHelper.marshallQuote(bookQuote)));
} catch(Exception e) {
  logger.error("error while setting content in out message", e);
  throw new MessagingException(e);
}
outMessage.setProperty(
    "org.apache.servicemix.eip.splitter.corrid",
        bookQuote.getIsbn());
Integer aggregatorIndex = null;
if("Amazon".equalsIgnoreCase(bookQuote.getCompanyName())) {
  aggregatorIndex = new Integer(0);
} else if("BarnesAndNoble".equalsIgnoreCase(
    bookQuote.getCompanyName())) {
  aggregatorIndex = new Integer(1);
}
outMessage.setProperty(
    "org.apache.servicemix.eip.splitter.index",
        aggregatorIndex);
outMessage.setProperty(
    "org.apache.servicemix.eip.splitter.count",
        new Integer(2));
exchange.setMessage(outMessage, "out");
channel.send(exchange);
}
```

❶ Converts message to DOM object

❷ Transforms to BookQuote

❸ Creates response message

❹ Sets correlation identifier

❺ Sets message index

❻ Sets group size

Only the onMessageExchange method implementation is shown in listing 4.20. The logger, transformer, and channel instantiation were already shown in listings 4.8 and 4.11 in section 4.2. In this method implementation, the contents of the incoming message are first transformed to an XML representation as a Document Object Model (DOM) object ❶. This makes it easier to process the contents of the message for the rest of the method implementation. Then the DOM object instance is transformed to a `BookQuote` JavaBean with an `isbn`, a `price`, and a `companyName` attribute ➋. Now we can easily log the message contents with Log4j to the console.

To be able to set some message properties needed for the ServiceMix aggregator implementation, we created a response message ➌. First the contents of the incoming message are just copied to the outgoing message. We don't want to change this part of the message. What needs to be added are some message properties, including a correlation identifier for the group of messages that need to be aggregated into one grouped message ➍. As with the Mule implementation, we use the ISBN for the correlation identifier. For real-world implementations, you'd certainly choose a better and more unique correlation identifier here.

Another property that needs to be set for the aggregator is the message index. This is needed by the aggregator to determine whether every message of the group has been received. For this example, we just give the Amazon message a message index of 0 and the Barnes & Noble message a message index of 1. The index is then set with the `index` attribute ➎. The last property that needs to be set is the number of messages that have to be aggregated into one message. This is done by setting the `count` attribute ➏.

CONFIGURING THE SERVICE UNITS

We have yet to discuss configuring the pipeline that accepts messages from the Amazon response queue and the XSLT transformation, invokes the message logger, and routes the result to the aggregator component. This configuration is shown in listing 4.21.

Listing 4.21   Pipeline configuration for the message logger

```
<eip:pipeline service="esb:quoteLoggingPipeline"
    endpoint="quoteLoggingPipelineEndpoint">
  <eip:transformer>                                                ◁─➊
    <eip:exchange-target service="esb:aggregateLoggerComponent"/>
  </eip:transformer>
  <eip:target>                                                     ◁─➋
    <eip:exchange-target service="esb:quoteAggregator"/>
  </eip:target>
</eip:pipeline>
```

As shown with the `eip:transformer` element configuration ➊, the pipeline first invokes the `AggregatorLoggerComponent` from listing 4.9. With the `eip:target` configuration ➋, you can set the target service for the response message received from the `AggregatorLoggerComponent`. The pipeline component is used in many examples in this book as it is essential in invoking in-out components from an in-only message exchange.

The next component, the `split-aggregator`, is invoked in the response flow when the pipeline in listing 4.21 receives a response from the special logger component. Because we enhanced the logging component with the creation of three aggregator-related properties (the correlation identifier, message index, and group size), we can

use the standard aggregator provided by ServiceMix. We only need to configure this
aggregator (see listing 4.22).

Listing 4.22   ServiceMix aggregator configuration

```
<eip:split-aggregator service="esb:quoteAggregator"        ◁─❶
   endpoint="quoteAggregatorEndpoint">
 <eip:target>
   <eip:exchange-target service="esb:cheapestPricePipeline"/>    ◁─❷
 </eip:target>
</eip:split-aggregator>
```

The service name of the aggregator configuration ❶ corresponds to the target destination configuration of the pipeline in listing 4.21. This links the pipeline component
and the aggregator component to each other. There's no need to configure additional properties; we can just pass the result of the aggregation to the next component
in the response flow, which is another pipeline ❷.

The cheapestPricePipeline invokes the CheapestPriceCalculator bean component and passes the response message to the last point in the response flow, which is
the JMS endpoint that produces a JMS message to the booksearch.output queue. The
pipeline configuration is similar to the configuration in listing 4.21 and therefore isn't
included here. The configuration of all three pipelines and the aggregator are combined into one xbean.xml configuration for the servicemix-eip service engine. We
discussed the logic inside the CheapestPriceCalculator in the Mule example, but
because we have to deal with a message exchange for ServiceMix, we explore the
details in listing 4.23.

Listing 4.23   Implementation of the `CheapestPriceCalculator` bean

```
public class CheapestPriceCalculator extends ComponentSupport
     implements MessageExchangeListener {

  private static final Logger logger =
     Logger.getLogger(CheapestPriceCalculator.class);
  private SourceTransformer sourceTransformer =
     new SourceTransformer();
  @Resource
  private DeliveryChannel channel;

  public void onMessageExchange(MessageExchange exchange)
       throws MessagingException {
    if (exchange.getStatus() != ExchangeStatus.ACTIVE) {
      logger.info("state is not active so ignoring call");
      return;
    }
    Element payloadElem = null;                    Gets aggregated  ❶
    Source contentSource = null;                   message as DOM
    try {
      contentSource = getInMessage(exchange).getContent();
      payloadElem = sourceTransformer.toDOMElement(
          contentSource);
    } catch(Exception e) {
```

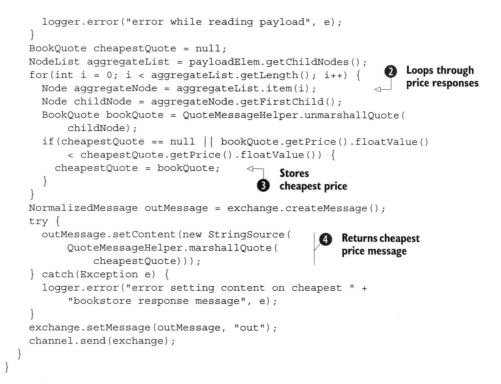

```
      logger.error("error while reading payload", e);
  }
  BookQuote cheapestQuote = null;
  NodeList aggregateList = payloadElem.getChildNodes();
  for(int i = 0; i < aggregateList.getLength(); i++) {      ❷ Loops through
    Node aggregateNode = aggregateList.item(i);                 price responses
    Node childNode = aggregateNode.getFirstChild();
    BookQuote bookQuote = QuoteMessageHelper.unmarshallQuote(
        childNode);
    if(cheapestQuote == null || bookQuote.getPrice().floatValue()
        < cheapestQuote.getPrice().floatValue()) {
      cheapestQuote = bookQuote;        Stores
    }                                 ❸ cheapest price
  }
  NormalizedMessage outMessage = exchange.createMessage();
  try {
    outMessage.setContent(new StringSource(
        QuoteMessageHelper.marshallQuote(    ❹ Returns cheapest
            cheapestQuote)));                   price message
  } catch(Exception e) {
    logger.error("error setting content on cheapest " +
        "bookstore response message", e);
  }
  exchange.setMessage(outMessage, "out");
  channel.send(exchange);
  }
}
```

Because the aggregated message produced by the AggregatorMessageLogger in listing 4.20 is sent across the ServiceMix container as a normalized message, we have to work with XML message content that contains both the price response from the Amazon as well as the Barnes and Noble bookstores. Therefore, we first transform the input message to a DOM structure ❶.

The root element of the input message contains two child elements that contain the price responses. So the next step is to loop through these two price responses to be able to determine which is the lowest ❷. When the price of the response message is the lowest, we store the unmarshaled BookQuote instance into a local variable ❸.

Now that we've determined the lowest price, the response message can be constructed and the message content must be filled. Therefore, we must marshal the lowest book quote message into an XML message ❹. Because we marshal the BookQuote instance to an XML String representation, we use the StringSource message type. The response message is then sent to the JMS output queue.

DEPLOYING AND TESTING THE SERVICEMIX CHEAPEST PRICE CALCULATOR

Let's proceed to the test phase of our solution. The test resembles the one we used in the Mule example. We also use two message listeners, AmazonBookStore and Barnes-BookStore, for testing our ServiceMix solution. To trigger the implemented message flow, we can also use a JUnit test case, MessageFlowTest, or we can use the Swing test client, which produces a message that includes a simple ISBN to the booksearch. input queue.

With all the code in place, we just have to deploy the solution to the running ServiceMix container. You can start the ServiceMix container with the default target in the Ant build file ch4-examples.xml. When the container has started, the `deploy-messageflow` target can be used to build and deploy the lowest price service assembly. To start the Amazon and Barnes and Noble JMS listeners, you have to run the `messageflow-spring` target.

Let's execute the JUnit test class `esb.chapter4.messageflow.MessageFlowTest`, available in the test directory of the book's source code. Alternatively, you can use the Swing test client to trigger the message flow. You should see logging statements in the console in your execution environment as well as in the ServiceMix container console. In the console of the JUnit test or in the Swing test client, you should eventually see a "received lowest quote" message with some contents displayed. This means that the message flow has executed successfully.

Take your time to examine the full implementation of this message flow in the source code. The implementation consists of many different parts, so it's a good idea to play with the source distribution for some time in order to fully grasp the details. Once you feel confident about all the parts of this message flow, you'll have made a giant step toward becoming a ServiceMix developer.

4.6   *Interlude: Spring Integration*

Before we end this chapter, we discuss another integration framework that contains some promising features: Spring Integration. We know it's already been a long ride so far; therefore, we'll keep the example simple and the level introductory. Spring Integration is a new framework provided by the Spring Framework; at the time of this writing, the project has released the fifth milestone for the 1.0 release. So the information in this section is a sneak preview of what you can expect of the Spring Integration framework.

We all know that Spring is an important and widely used framework for application development. The framework started as a dependency injection (DI) or inversion of control (IoC) project, but gradually a lot of other functionality was added, including web frameworks, web services support, persistency functionality, and messaging templates. And you've seen how Mule and ServiceMix also use Spring functionality—for example, for the XML configuration implementation.

What Spring lacked was an abstraction layer that made it easy to configure JMS or file listeners, for example, and to implement functionality like routing and transformation. Well, this is exactly what the Spring Integration framework offers. Based on the functionality already offered by the Spring Framework, an abstraction layer has been added to support the Enterprise Integration patterns defined by Hohpe and Woolf. Therefore, the Spring Integration framework fits quite nicely into the same area as Mule and ServiceMix, but it's still maturing. Let's take a quick look.

4.6.1   A quick example with Spring Integration

As you might expect, the Spring Integration configuration uses an XML file. In addition, a number of annotations are provided to define routing functionality. But just talking about a framework isn't a good way to gain insight into the functionality, so we show an example. We send a hello message to either Ross, the founder of Mule, or Guillaume, the project lead for ServiceMix. If the message is "hello Ross", it goes to Ross; if the message is "hello Guillaume", it goes to Guillaume.

First, let's implement the router that will send the hello message to the right person. Let's name this router `HelloRouter` and implement it according to listing 4.24.

Listing 4.24   Spring Integration Implementation of HelloRouter

```
@MessageEndpoint(input="hello")     ←--❶
public class HelloRouter {

  @Router
  public String resolvePerson(String message) {     ←--❷
    if(message.indexOf("Ross") != null) {
      return "ross";
    } else {
      Return "guillaume";
    }
  }
}
```

Notice that the router is a POJO component with two annotations provided by the Spring Integration framework. The `MessageEndpoint` annotation ❶ is used to relate the routing implementation class to a message channel. This message channel is defined in the Spring XML configuration that we see in listing 4.25. Then the `resolvePerson` method ❷ that determines the target channel is annotated with `Router`. This means that the Spring Integration framework knows that the output of this method will be a channel name where the incoming message must be routed. Now let's look at the XML configuration for this example (listing 4.25).

Listing 4.25   The XML configuration for the Spring Integration hello example

```
<beans:beans xmlns="http://www.springframework.org/schema/integration"
 xmlns:xsi="http://www.w3.org/2001/XMLSchema-instance"
 xmlns:beans="http://www.springframework.org/schema/beans"
 xmlns:context="http://www.springframework.org/schema/context"
 xsi:schemaLocation="http://www.springframework.org/schema/beans
   http://www.springframework.org/schema/beans/spring-beans-2.5.xsd
  http://www.springframework.org/schema/integration
   http://www.springframework.org/schema/integration/
     spring-integration-1.0.xsd
  http://www.springframework.org/schema/context
   http://www.springframework.org/schema/context/spring-context-2.5.xsd">

<message-bus/>
<annotation-driven/>        ←┐  Specifies message
                           ❶  bus container
```

```
<channel id="hello"/>
<channel id="ross"/>
<channel id="guillaume"/>

<beans:bean id="helloBean"
    class="esb.chapter4.springintegration.HelloBean">
  <beans:property name="helloChannel" ref="hello"/>
</beans:bean>
</beans:beans>
```

2 Defines hello channel

3 Defines hello bean with channel reference

The Spring XML file is where we configure the message bus and its message channels. The first element, message-bus **1**, instantiates the message bus container that will host the message channels to exchange messages. We also define a number of channels here, which we also used in listing 4.24. The hello channel **2** is used to send the hello message to the hello router. It's easy to define Spring beans and inject channels as properties in these beans **3**. We use the hello bean to send the hello message to the hello message channel according to this code snippet:

```
public class HelloBean {
  private MessageChannel helloChannel;
  public void setHelloChannel(MessageChannel helloChannel) {
    this.helloChannel = helloChannel;
  }
  public void sendHello(String message) {
    helloChannel.send(new GenericMessage(message));
  }
}
```

To complete the example, we need two beans to listen to the ross and guillaume channels. Here's a simple implementation of such a bean:

```
@MessageEndpoint(input="ross")
public class RossBean {

  public void hello(String message) {
    System.out.println("Ross received " + message);
  }
}
```

To be able to test the example, we can use a simple application that starts the Spring context and invokes the sendHello method of the HelloBean class, as in the following code snippet:

```
public static void main(String[] args) {
  AbstractApplicationContext context = new
      FileSystemXmlApplicationContext("hello.xml");
  context.start();
  HelloBean helloBean = (HelloBean) context.getBean("helloBean");
  // no offence to Guillaume intended here :-)
  helloBean.sendHello("Hello Ross");
}
```

Based on an XML configuration and a few Spring beans, we were able to implement the functionality. This simple example doesn't show complex enterprise integration functionality, but shows the foundation of the Spring Integration framework.

We'll keep an eye on the progress of the Spring Integration framework; because it's so easy to configure integration logic, it can be a suitable framework for integration challenges.

4.7 Summary

If you feel a bit overwhelmed by all the examples in this chapter, don't worry. In upcoming chapters, you'll see more examples that have many similarities with the examples from this chapter. As you progress in this book, you'll become familiar with configuring and using Mule and ServiceMix. You have already made a big step in this chapter.

We discussed how to develop custom logic in the first two sections of this chapter. The chapter started off by explaining how to implement your own components with Mule. As you may recall, this was fairly easy as the components are just simple POJOs. After examining a simple component implementation, we explored the integration with the Spring Framework. Because Mule 2.*x* uses Spring as its standard container, this integration is provided with no additional cost. So we were easily able to develop components with Spring's dependency injection.

In section 4.2, you saw that with the `servicemix-bean` service engine, developing custom logic with ServiceMix is not hard. The difference with the Mule approach is that the class implementation in ServiceMix has dependencies to the ServiceMix framework. We also examined JBI message exchanges, source transformers, and other JBI/ServiceMix logic. But as we progressed, you learned that the implementation isn't that difficult. And using Spring is also easy, because ServiceMix provides Spring integration out of the box.

You saw that it's not difficult to implement a challenging case study with Mule and ServiceMix. We were even able to test the implementation fairly easily. Now that we've reached the end of this chapter, you should be able to build a small solution by yourself.

We haven't discussed typical enterprise integration functionality like message routing yet. In the next chapter, we look at some interesting functionality that you'll need every time you implement message flows. We talk about the various kinds of routing functionality that Mule and ServiceMix offers, and we present some examples. Other topics we discuss are message validation, transformation, and enhancement. So take a breath and we'll hop on to chapter 5 and look at how you can work with messages in an open source ESB.

Part 2

Using ESB core functionalities

By now you have a basic understanding of open source ESBs—Mule and ServiceMix in particular—so it's time to take a closer look at the functionality an ESB can provide. In chapter 1, we described the core functionalities of an ESB; part 2 shows the practical usage of these functionalities. We start with a detailed description of routing, validation, and transformation functionality. Then we examine the connectivity options provided by Mule and ServiceMix.

Because web services connectivity is a subject on its own, we devote an entire chapter to this topic. We look at how to implement web services with Mule and ServiceMix, with a top-down as well as a bottom-up approach. We also look at support for WS-* standards, such as WS-Security and WS-Addressing.

Finally, we tackle more advanced topics, such as error handling, security, and transaction handling. By the end of part 2 you'll have a solid knowledge of the core functionalities Mule and ServiceMix have to offer, and you'll be ready to work with these open source ESBs in real projects.

5

Working with messages

As an open source ESB developer, you are dealing with messages in all kinds of different ways. For messages that arrive at the ESB, you'll have to determine where that message needs to be forwarded. And you must transform the message format to meet the requirements of the target service provider. In this chapter, we look at the various ways in which you can work with messages.

Because an ESB is a piece of middleware between service consumers and service providers, an essential part of creating an integration solution involves the determination of the target service provider(s). The logic related to this core functionality of an ESB is often referred to as message routing. We look at the theory of message routing and how it can be implemented in open source ESBs in section 5.1. With these examples, you'll be able to introduce complex routing functionality to both Mule and ServiceMix.

When messages flow through an ESB and are guided to the target service provider(s), we need to be sure that the message content meets its specification. When transforming and routing messages, we have to rely on the message specification to be able to execute the transformation and routing. When a message specification enforces the presence of a version attribute, we can develop routing rules that use this version attribute. It is a common practice to validate incoming messages against their message specification before logic like transformation and routing is performed. In section 5.2, we explore message validation and show how it can be implemented. We show Mule and ServiceMix examples that use XML Schema validation.

We already mentioned transformation a few times in this chapter introduction. Transforming the format of messages is common in integration solutions. In section 5.3, we look at message transformation in detail. With XSLT as the open standard for XML message transformation, we'll see how it can be used in a Mule and ServiceMix message flow.

By the end of this chapter, you'll have enough experience and knowledge of routing, message validation, and transformation that you'll be able to implement a large percentage of the real-life message flows for your projects.

5.1   Routing messages

Creating an integration solution always involves some kind of logic to determine the ultimate destination for an incoming message. Therefore, routing is an essential functionality that an ESB provides. As you can read in Hohpe and Woolf's Enterprise Integration Patterns, a distinction exists between different types of message routers. In this section, we look at examples of message routing that are common when implementing integration solutions. We begin with the most trivial case of a message router: the fixed router.

5.1.1   Fixed router

In some cases, the source application must simply be decoupled from the target application. When we don't use a message router between these applications, they are coupled via the message channel. The source application puts a message on a queue and the target application reads the message from this message channel. With a fixed message router, the source application places a message on a message channel; then the message is picked up by the fixed router and passed on to another message channel.

By decoupling the source from the target application, we can easily add functionality such as message transformation and a transport protocol conversion. Therefore, the addition of a message router can also be beneficiary for future integration needs. The downside of the fixed router is that the router configuration is only applicable to a specific source and target location. For the integration solutions that need a lot of routing, this message router is not the best choice. Figure 5.1 shows an example of a fixed router.

The example displayed in figure 5.1 shows an integration solution that uses a fixed router to send a JMS message to a web service. An adapter is used to read the JMS

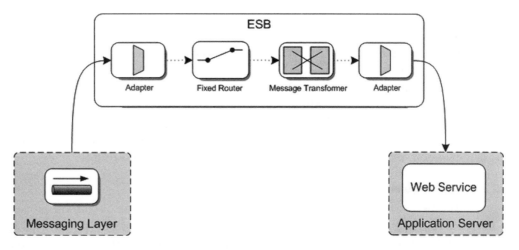

Figure 5.1 An example of a fixed router that moves the message from a messaging infrastructure to a web service

message from the queue, and then the fixed router sends the message to the web service. Before the web service is called, the JMS message is transformed to the message format defined in the WSDL file of the web service. A web service adapter eventually performs the web service invocation.

We've chosen to implement this example in Mule, because it has a clear definition of a fixed router. First, we have to define a service configuration with an inbound endpoint that listens for JMS messages on a specific queue and calls a web service via an outbound router. Let's look at a short example of a fixed router as it can be implemented with Mule (listing 5.1).

Listing 5.1 Service configuration of a fixed router implemented in Mule

```
<mule>
 <model name="FixedRouterModel">
  <service name="FixedService">
   <inbound>
    <jms:inbound-endpoint queue="fixed.input"/>      <--❶
   </inbound>
   <outbound>
    <outbound-pass-through-router>      <--❷
     <outbound-endpoint
       address="wsdl-cxf:http://test.org/test?wsdl&amp;method=test"/>   <--❸
    </outbound-pass-through-router>
   </outbound>
  </service>
 </model>
</mule>
```

The Mule configuration doesn't consist of any new elements. In the examples shown in this book so far, we've used a fixed router a few times. The inbound endpoint implements the adapter logic to get messages from the messaging infrastructure ❶.

The outbound router configures a web service destination using the Apache CXF web service adapter provided by Mule ❸. But where is the fixed router component configured within this listing? Well, it's defined by using Mule's outbound passthrough router ❷. This specific Mule message router forwards an incoming message to the defined endpoint, which is what a fixed router is supposed to do.

The fixed router is a trivial but common message router. Now let's look at another common, but less trivial, message router: the content-based router.

5.1.2 *Content-based router*

Another way to determine the ultimate destination for an incoming message is by looking at the content of that message. The content-based router interprets the incoming message against particular element values and forwards this message to the matching target endpoint. There are two main types of content-based routers, which differ as to where the ultimate destination is determined. The first type is the content-based router with domain logic, and the second is the router without domain logic.

For the first type of content-based router, the ultimate destination is determined in the ESB. The source application sends a message to the ESB, which consumes the message. The message is picked up by the content-based router, which reads message values based on predefined routing rules. For an insurance request, here's a sample routing rule: if the insurance type is car, the message is forwarded to the car insurance application. The content-based router will extract the insurance type from the incoming insurance request and fire the routing rule against the extracted value. The logic for determining the ultimate destination is therefore performed within the content-based router. The router needs to be configured with domain logic to determine the destination of an incoming message.

The other type of content-based router is ignorant of any domain logic. The source application itself determines the ultimate destination for the message that's waiting to be sent. The domain logic needed to execute this logic is then only required within the source applications. The message is enriched with a message header that contains the target destination and is then passed on to the ESB. The content-based router extracts the message header and sends the message to the destination as defined in this header value. The message header value typically isn't an endpoint definition that can be used directly to forward a message. In most cases, the message header contains some text value configured in the content-based router to represent a specific endpoint definition.

The content-based router with domain logic is the most common implementation. We'll look at an example with ServiceMix and Mule using this router. We'll show the other type of content-based router with an example using Apache Synapse.

CONTENT-BASED ROUTING WITH DOMAIN LOGIC IN SERVICEMIX-EIP

Let's implement the insurance request example that we discussed earlier with Service-Mix. To provide a better description of the insurance request example, figure 5.2 shows a schematic overview.

Figure 5.2 shows a simplified insurance request message that's sent to the ESB. The message contains an `insurance-type` element, which we can use to determine the destination service. In this simple example, we have two possible target applications: the car insurance application and the travel insurance application. The message in figure 5.2 is routed to the car insurance application because `insurance-type` equals `Car`.

To implement this example in ServiceMix, we have two main options. We can use the `servicemix-eip` or the `servicemix-camel` service engine. The `servicemix-eip` service engine is an implementation of a number of Enterprise Integration patterns from the Hohpe and Woolf book. Apache Camel is a subproject of the Apache ActiveMQ project, which provides a rich set of components that implement the same Enterprise Integration patterns. Future implementations of ServiceMix, starting at version 4.0, will be based on Apache Camel, so this service engine is our preference. We show listings for both service engines, though.

Let's first focus on the configuration with the `servicemix-eip` service engine. We've already used this service engine in chapter 4 to configure pipelines that transform an in-only to an in-out message exchange. Listing 5.2 shows the configuration of the content-based routing shown in figure 5.2.

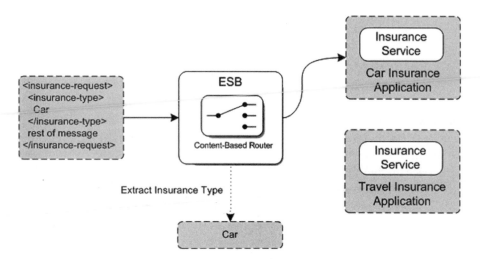

Figure 5.2 An example of the use of a content-based router with a car insurance request. The insurance request is routed to the car insurance application based on the insurance type element value.

Listing 5.2 Content-based router configuration with `servicemix-eip`

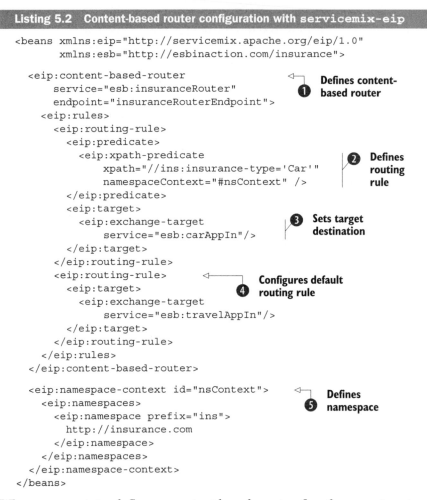

```
<beans xmlns:eip="http://servicemix.apache.org/eip/1.0"
       xmlns:esb="http://esbinaction.com/insurance">

  <eip:content-based-router
      service="esb:insuranceRouter"
      endpoint="insuranceRouterEndpoint">
    <eip:rules>
      <eip:routing-rule>
        <eip:predicate>
          <eip:xpath-predicate
              xpath="//ins:insurance-type='Car'"
              namespaceContext="#nsContext" />
        </eip:predicate>
        <eip:target>
          <eip:exchange-target
              service="esb:carAppIn"/>
        </eip:target>
      </eip:routing-rule>
      <eip:routing-rule>
        <eip:target>
          <eip:exchange-target
              service="esb:travelAppIn"/>
        </eip:target>
      </eip:routing-rule>
    </eip:rules>
  </eip:content-based-router>

  <eip:namespace-context id="nsContext">
    <eip:namespaces>
      <eip:namespace prefix="ins">
        http://insurance.com
      </eip:namespace>
    </eip:namespaces>
  </eip:namespace-context>
</beans>
```

- ❶ Defines content-based router
- ❷ Defines routing rule
- ❸ Sets target destination
- ❹ Configures default routing rule
- ❺ Defines namespace

When we want to define a content-based router for the `servicemix-eip` service engine, we have to create an xbean.xml file. The configuration for the router in this xbean.xml file uses the `content-based-router` element defined in the `servicemix-eip` service engine ❶. In this element, two common attributes, `service` and `endpoint`, have to be configured.

We can configure the logic in the content-based router by specifying routing rules. The insurance request message example consists of an `insurance-type` element that's important for the routing rule that we have to define. To implement the routing rule, we define a predicate that uses an XPath expression to check whether the insurance type is `Car` ❷. If necessary, it's also possible to define multiple predicate definitions as part of one routing rule. Besides the predicate definition, the routing rule must consist of a target definition, which configures the service destination if the routing rule evaluates to true ❸. Here we've defined a target service `carAppIn`, which represents the service location for the car insurance application.

For the insurance example, there are only two different insurance types that we need to address. Therefore, we can define a default routing rule that sends the incoming insurance request to the travel insurance application if the insurance type is not equal to Car. We can do this by leaving out the predicate definition in a new routing rule ❹. This default routing rule only consists of a target service configuration—travelAppIn for our example.

The last part of listing 5.2 defines a namespace context that can be used in the XPath expression we just discussed. Because the insurance-request message uses the namespace http://insurance.com, the XPath expression requires a namespace context definition. In the servicemix-eip service engine configuration, we can define a namespace-context element that consists of a number of namespaces ❺. For our example, we only need one namespace that has a prefix value of ins and a namespace URI of http://insurance.com. The prefix can then be used within the XPath expression, as we've done here ❷.

If you want to do a quick test with this content-based router configuration, you can use the service assembly implementation in the resources/chapter5/eip directory. Once you've started ServiceMix with the start target in the ch5-examples.xml Ant build file, you can deploy this insurance routing example with the deploy-insurance-eip target in the same build file. The example uses a file poller to trigger the content-based router and a file sender to simulate the car and insurance applications. With the Swing test client, you can trigger the routing example and check whether the content-based routing functionality is working.

CONTENT-BASED ROUTING WITH DOMAIN LOGIC IN SERVICEMIX-CAMEL

In addition to the servicemix-eip service engine, which can be used for content-based routing, ServiceMix also provides the servicemix-camel service engine. We already saw a quick example of using Apache Camel within ServiceMix in chapter 2. The main difference between these two service engines is that servicemix-eip was developed as part of ServiceMix and offers a small set of routers, and servicemix-camel provides integration with Apache Camel, which is a separate project that offers a large set of routers.

Apache Camel

Apache Camel is a subproject of the top-level Apache project ActiveMQ. Apache Camel provides an implementation of the Enterprise Integration patterns from the Hohpe and Woolf book with a Java-based Domain-Specific Language (DSL). Routing rules can be implemented with POJOs as well as an XML configuration. In addition to the Enterprise Integration pattern functionality, Apache Camel offers support for a lot of transports, such as HTTP, JMS, File, virtual machine queues, ActiveMQ, JDBC, JBI, and others. With this functionality, Apache Camel offers an ESB-like framework, but it's called a routing and mediation engine. Apache Camel can be easily integrated with other projects such as Apache ActiveMQ, Apache CXF, and of course Apache ServiceMix.

We can configure routing rules with a Java implementation as well as an XML configuration. We show both options in this section.

To provide an easier comparison between the servicemix-eip and the servicemix-camel configurations, let's start with an XML configuration. Just like the servicemix-eip service engine, we begin with a configuration file, named camel-context.xml, which is used to configure the routing rules (listing 5.3).

Listing 5.3   Content-based router XML configuration with servicemix-camel

```
<beans xmlns="http://www.springframework.org/schema/beans">
  <camelContext id="insuranceCamel"                           ←❶
      xmlns="http://activemq.apache.org/camel/schema/spring">
    <route>
      <from uri="jbi:service:#NS#/insuranceCamelRouter"/>      ←❷
      <choice>
        <when>
          <xpath>
            //insurance-type='Car'              ❸
          </xpath>
          <to uri="jbi:service:#NS#/carAppInCamel"/>
        </when>
        <otherwise>
          <to uri="jbi:service:#NS#/travelAppInCamel"/>       ←❹
        </otherwise>
      </choice>
    </route>
  </camelContext>
</beans>
```

The first difference compared with the servicemix-eip implementation in listing 5.2 is the number of lines. With Apache Camel, routing rules can be defined with just a few lines of code. To instantiate the Camel context for the routing rules definition, the camelContext element is the starting point ❶.

Within the Camel context, the trigger or originating service for the routing rules is configured with the from element ❷. To keep the listing compact, we've defined the namespace for the JBI service as #NS#, but in the book's source code this is replaced with http://esbinaction.com/insurance. In the URI definition of the from element, you can see how the integration between ServiceMix and Camel is implemented. The URI starts with jbi:service:, which tells the Camel runtime to look for a JBI service in the JBI runtime. Notice that you have to specify the full service name, including the namespace.

With a choice definition, a content-based routing configuration can be implemented in Camel. A choice consists of a number of when statements and one optional otherwise statement. Recall that in the insurance request example, insurance-type must be evaluated to be equal to Car. In Camel we can do this with an XPath expression, just as we did in the servicemix-eip configuration ❸. Camel, however, offers a richer set of options, such as JavaScript and Groovy scripts, to implement a routing rule. We can't use a namespace in the XPath expression, because namespace support for routing rules is supported within Camel starting from version 1.3, and ServiceMix is still on 1.2. In Camel 1.3, we can just define the namespace as part of the XML configuration with a common `xmlns` definition. In addition to the XPath expression, the target service definition is defined in the `when` statement.

The default target service, if `insurance-type` does not equal `Car`, can be easily configured with the `otherwise` element ❹. The URI definition is similar to the `from` element configuration we just discussed. The `#NS#` tag should also be replaced with the `http://esbinaction.com/insurance` namespace.

You can test the example with the service assembly in the directory resources/ chapter5/camel of the book's source code. To be able to run the Camel example, you'll have to implement a number of other service units. Of course, you need a way to trigger the routing functionality and to simulate the car and travel endpoints. In the example implementation, we used a file poller to trigger the Camel router, and two file senders to simulate the communication with the travel and insurance applications. Due to a problem with the message format in the exchange between ServiceMix and Camel, we also have to implement a bean service unit.

Use Camel XML configuration with ServiceMix

At the time of this writing, ServiceMix uses Camel 1.2 to implement the Camel service engine. Although ServiceMix and Camel are nicely integrated and both frameworks provide support for message exchanges, some inconveniences exist. For example, the file poller of ServiceMix parses the message as a `StreamSource`. A `StreamSource` can be accessed only once, and when the file message is sent to Camel, an `IOException` occurs, because the stream was already closed.

To prevent this `IOException` from occurring, we implemented a bean service unit, which transforms the `StreamSource` message type to a `StringSource` instance. And because the bean service unit needs an in-out message exchange to implement this functionality, we also need to use a pipeline component to convert the in-only exchange of the file poller to an in-out exchange. Although this sounds like complex functionality, you can look in the source code of chapter 5 to see that it's actually quite simple.

When you've started the ServiceMix container, you can deploy the Camel routing example with the `deploy-insurance-camel` target in the ch5-examples.xml Ant build file. Then you can use the Swing client to trigger the Camel routing example.

The Camel configuration can also be implemented with the Java DSL. This means that we implement a Java class that extends the `RouteBuilder` class, which consists of similar logic as the XML alternative that we have just discussed. Listing 5.4 shows the implementation of the insurance request content-based router with the `Insurance-Router` class.

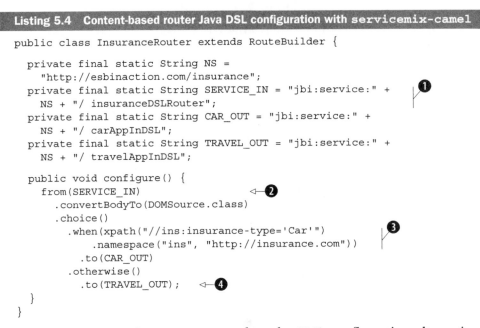

Listing 5.4 Content-based router Java DSL configuration with `servicemix-camel`

```java
public class InsuranceRouter extends RouteBuilder {

  private final static String NS =
    "http://esbinaction.com/insurance";
  private final static String SERVICE_IN = "jbi:service:" +
    NS + "/ insuranceDSLRouter";                              ❶
  private final static String CAR_OUT = "jbi:service:" +
    NS + "/ carAppInDSL";
  private final static String TRAVEL_OUT = "jbi:service:" +
    NS + "/ travelAppInDSL";

  public void configure() {
    from(SERVICE_IN)                          ◁ ❷
      .convertBodyTo(DOMSource.class)
      .choice()
        .when(xpath("//ins:insurance-type='Car'")    ❸
          .namespace("ins", "http://insurance.com"))
        .to(CAR_OUT)
      .otherwise()
        .to(TRAVEL_OUT);             ◁ ❹
  }
}
```

The `InsuranceRouter` is more compact than the XML configuration alternative in listing 5.3. To keep the routing logic clean, the class implementation starts with the definition of the incoming and outgoing services ❶. The `configure` method is called on initialization of the `RouteBuilder`, and is therefore the place to implement the routing logic. The service definition of the content-based router is defined by the `from` method and uses the `SERVICE_IN` attribute value for the configuration ❷. The `from` method returns a `RouteType` instance, which can be used to implement the routing logic.

In the Camel XML configuration example, we had to use an extra bean service unit to trigger the router due to usage of the `StreamSource` class by the file poller. In the Java DSL implementation a solution is available to transform the `StreamSource` instance to a `DOMSource` with the `convertBodyTo` method. The `convertBodyTo` method returns the same `RouteType` instance that the `from` method did. Only the incoming message type is transformed to a DOM structure.

The routing logic can be implemented with the `choice` method that is available on the `RouteType` class. With the `choice` method, we get a `ChoiceType` instance that can be used to implement content-based routing logic. We can now add a `when` predicate, which consists of an XPath expression ❸. The `xpath` method is a static method of the `XPathBuilder` class that can be used for XPath expressions. Notice that we've used a static import for the `xpath` method in this code example, which is a Java 5 feature. To support namespaces in the XPath expression, a `namespace` method is available in the `XPathBuilder`. The `when` method returns the same `ChoiceType` instance, so we can add a `to` method to register the target service for a `Car` insurance message.

The `to` method also returns the `ChoiceType` instance, which can be used to add an `otherwise` statement. The `otherwise` method again returns the `ChoiceType` instance, and we can add the target service for messages for which the XPath expression evaluates to false ❹.

This example shows that the Camel Java DSL is a nice alternative to the more verbose XML configuration. Maybe you have to get used to the concatenation of methods, but it provides a great way to specify routing rules in Java code. To run this example, we need a bit of XML configuration in addition to the Java code. This XML configuration is used by Camel to initialize the context with the right Java classes:

```
<camelContext id="camel"
      xmlns="http://activemq.apache.org/camel/schema/spring">
  <package>esb.chapter5.camel.router</package>
</camelContext>
```

As you can see, the XML configuration needed is quite minimal; only the Java packages for the Camel router classes have to be configured. In this case, we have only one router, so we have to include the package for the `InsuranceRouter`. Also notice that because we use the `convertBodyTo(DOMSource.class)` method in listing 5.4, we don't have to implement the additional service units that we saw in the Camel XML example.

To test the example, you can deploy the service assembly with the `deploy-insurance-camelDSL` target of the ch5-examples.xml Ant build file. Be sure that ServiceMix has been started before you execute this deploy target. Again, you can test the example using the Swing test client.

CONTENT-BASED ROUTING WITH DOMAIN LOGIC IN MULE

To be able to compare the content-based routing functionality of ServiceMix and Mule, we implement the insurance routing example with Mule (listing 5.5).

Listing 5.5 Mule content-based router implementation

```
<mule>
  <xm:xml-to-dom-transformer name="FileToDOM"/>      ⟵❶

  <model name="RoutingExample">
    <service name="InsuranceService">
      <inbound>
        <file:inbound-endpoint path="insuranceInbox" fileAge="500"
            pollingFrequency="2000" transformer-refs="FileToDOM"/>
      </inbound>
      <outbound>
        <forwarding-catch-all-strategy>
          <file:outbound-endpoint                      ❷
              path="insuranceException"/>
        </forwarding-catch-all-strategy>
        <filtering-router>
          <file:outbound-endpoint path="insuranceCar"
              outputPattern="car-${DATE}.xml"/>
          <xm:jxpath-filter                             ❸
              pattern="//ins:insurance-type='Car'">
            <xm:namespace uri="http://insurance.com" prefix="ins"/>
```

```
            </xm:jxpath-filter>
          </filtering-router>
          <filtering-router>
            <file:outbound-endpoint path="insuranceTravel"
                outputPattern="travel-${DATE}.xml"/>
            <xm:jxpath-filter                                     ❹
                pattern="//ins:insurance-type='Travel'">
              <xm:namespace uri="http://insurance.com" prefix="ins"/>
            </xm:jxpath-filter>
          </filtering-router>
        </outbound>
      </service>
    </model>
  </mule>
```

Listing 5.5 uses a file inbound and outbound endpoint with a content-based router, the filtering-router, defined on the outbound router. Filtering routers consist of an outbound endpoint and a filter implementation. If the filter evaluates to true, the message is sent to the outbound endpoint configured for the corresponding filtering router. To implement the filter, Mule offers several filter types, including a payload type, a regular expression, a wildcard, and an XPath filter. Because the insurance request message uses an XML format, the XPath filter is best suited to implement the content-based routing logic for this example.

The XPath filter is implemented with the Apache Commons JXPath library. The JXPath filter is part of the Mule XML module, and the XPath expression can be configured with the pattern attribute ❸ ❹. The XPath expressions for this example evaluate if the insurance-type element in the XML message equals Car or Travel. Because the insurance-type element has a namespace of http://insurance.com, we also have to configure the namespace and the namespace prefix as part of the JXPath filter definition. When the XPath filter evaluates to true, the message is sent to the Car or Travel file outbound endpoint, with the current date and time as part of the filename.

The ordering of the filtering routers can be important, because only the first filtering router that evaluates to true will be executed by default. If you want all of the filtering routers that evaluate to true to be executed, then configure a matchAll attribute value of true on the outbound element. We also have configured a catchall router, which handles the message ❷ when both filters evaluate to false.

Because the JXPath filter expects the payload type to be an XML document, an XML string, or a Java object, we need to transform the input stream payload of the incoming message to a string or document. Therefore, we've defined a Mule transformer for this purpose ❶.

To run the example, execute the routing-mule target in the ch5-examples.xml Ant build file in the resources/chapter5 directory. When Mule has started, use the example files in the resources/chapter5/routing directory as input for the insuranceInbox directory in the Mule distribution. Of course, you can also use the Swing test client to trigger this routing example.

CONTENT-BASED ROUTING WITHOUT DOMAIN LOGIC IN APACHE SYNAPSE

So far, we've discussed routers that use domain logic to determine the target end-point. Next, we look at content-based routers that don't include domain logic. We show an example with Apache Synapse, an open source ESB that is part of Apache's web services project.

Apache Synapse is based on the well-known Apache Axis2 web service container framework. With the wide variety of complex standards and specifications in the web service world today, such as WSDL, SOAP, XSD, WS-Addressing, WS-ReliableMessaging, and WS-Security, there is a need to simplify the usage for developers. Apache Synapse provides an abstraction layer that supports a lot of the web services standards but keeps it simple for developers to implement solutions, based on these standards. Figure 5.3 shows an overview of the Apache Synapse framework.

We focus on the Synapse processing model shown in figure 5.3. The functionality that Apache Synapse provides is implemented with so-called mediators. A mediator is a component that performs a specific kind of functionality on a message, such as message validation, XSLT transformation, logging, and message header processing. Another important component in the Synapse processing model is the endpoint, which represents an address for incoming and outgoing messages. By using mediators and endpoints, we can build mediation logic to send an incoming message to the right target endpoint, as we'd like to do with content-based routing.

In the previous section, we used the `insurance-type` element in the XML message to define routing rules. That was a simple example, but you can imagine that if routing rules become complex, the amount of domain-specific logic will increase. An alternative solution is to add some extra logic when creating the insurance request message in the originating application. This is typically the place where

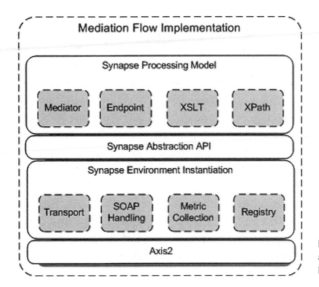

Figure 5.3   The Apache Synapse architecture, showing the different layers and Axis2 foundation

the domain logic about insurance requests is implemented, so why not add a small piece of extra logic to it?

A common way to implement this kind of functionality is by adding a header element to the message that defines the target destination with a keyword. The keyword is then matched in the ESB to the actual target endpoint address. This means that we still have the advantage of decoupling the originating application from the target application, but we don't have to implement domain-specific logic in the ESB. There is a web service standard that standardizes the header elements for a SOAP message: WS-Addressing.

WS-Addressing

The Web Services Addressing, or WS-Addressing, 1.0 standard specifies how address-related information, like the destination address, the reply endpoint, and the fault endpoint, can be specified. After a long process of standardization, the W3C standardization organization declared the WS-Addressing 1.0 specification to be a W3C recommendation (which means it is a standard). WS-Addressing uses SOAP header elements to define the address information, so intermediaries like ESBs don't have to look at the whole message. The SOAP headers defined in the WS-Addressing specification are quite similar to the JMS headers of the JMS specification. For example, both specifications have a message identifier and correlation identifier header that can be used to uniquely identify and correlate messages. A number of other web services specifications, including WS-ReliableMessaging, use WS-Addressing headers as a foundation.

We could use the WS-Addressing standard for the insurance request example, without having to use domain-specific logic inside the ESB. A WS-Addressing header element well suited for our purpose is the `Action` header. This element specifies the action related to the message, such as which service method needs to be called. We could use the `Action` header to specify the destination of the insurance request in our application. Figure 5.4 shows an overview of how WS-Addressing can be used as a foundation for our content-based routing implementation.

The insurance request message is wrapped in a SOAP envelope that includes a WS-Addressing `Action` header, as described in figure 5.4. The keyword `Travel-Insurance` maps to the endpoint address of the travel insurance application, so the content-based router in the ESB can send the insurance request to the proper target application.

With the incoming insurance request message structure defined, we can look at the routing implementation within Apache Synapse. The routing implementation is defined with the Synapse Configuration Language, an XML-based configuration language that specifies the necessary mediators. Listing 5.6 shows the XML configuration that implements the example in figure 5.4.

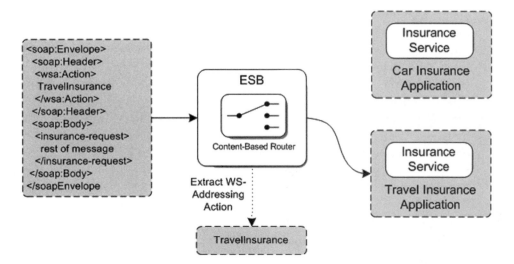

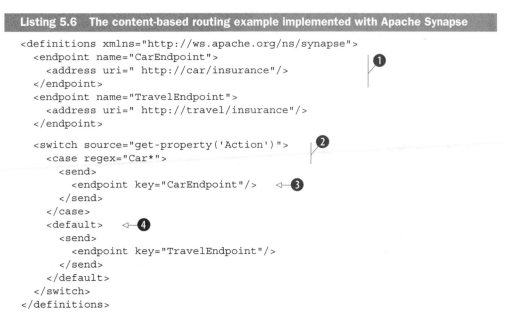

Figure 5.4 Example of content-based routing without domain logic using the WS-Addressing `Action` header element. The WS-Addressing `Action` header value defines a keyword that can be used to select the target endpoint for the insurance request message.

Listing 5.6 The content-based routing example implemented with Apache Synapse

```
<definitions xmlns="http://ws.apache.org/ns/synapse">
  <endpoint name="CarEndpoint">                              ❶
    <address uri=" http://car/insurance"/>
  </endpoint>
  <endpoint name="TravelEndpoint">
    <address uri=" http://travel/insurance"/>
  </endpoint>

  <switch source="get-property('Action')">        ❷
    <case regex="Car*">
      <send>
        <endpoint key="CarEndpoint"/>      ⬅❸
      </send>
    </case>
    <default>      ⬅❹
      <send>
        <endpoint key="TravelEndpoint"/>
      </send>
    </default>
  </switch>
</definitions>
```

A Synapse configuration starts with a definitions element. The endpoint addresses of the car and travel insurance applications can be registered quite simply with a name and address URI ❶. The endpoint name is the identifier that can be used within the Synapse configuration.

The actual routing logic is implemented with a switch mediator ❷. This mediator requires a source attribute that consists of an XPath expression that selects a message element. In this case, the `get-property` expression is used, which is a Synapse-specific expression to retrieve a SOAP message header. Because we want to select the WS-Addressing `Action` header, the literal 'action' is used. In addition to the switch mediator, a `case` element is used to complete the routing rule. The regular expression in the `case` element specifies the value for the `message` element that is selected in the switch mediator. So in this example, we check to see whether the WS-Addressing `Action` header value starts with `Car`. If this routing evaluates to true, the incoming message is routed on to the car insurance application ❸. We can simply reference the endpoint that we defined at the top of the configuration ❶.

We know that if the message should not be sent to the car insurance application, it's targeted for the travel insurance application. The switch mediator provides the default element for this purpose ❹. We can simply reference the `TravelEndpoint`, which points to the endpoint address of the travel insurance application.

You've seen that implementing routing rules within an ESB like Mule and Service-Mix is quite easy. You only have to specify XPath routing rules or Camel DSL logic to route the message to its destination. Doing this manually would mean a lot of extra coding. The provided routing functionality in Mule and ServiceMix can be an important reason to choose an open source ESB implementation if you have an integration issue, instead of developing your own custom routing logic.

In the next section, we look at another important capability of the open source ESB: message validation. To ensure that the incoming and outgoing messages are structured as agreed on by the involved application owners, message validation is critical. We discuss the details about this important step in a message flow with some interesting examples.

5.2 *Validating messages*

The Society for Worldwide Interbank Financial Telecommunication (SWIFT) standard is a widely adopted message standard for exchanging messages reliably and securely between banks and other financial institutions. When sending a message to the SWIFT network, the sending financial institution is responsible for the validity of that message. When a financial institution sends invalid messages to the SWIFT network, this results in penalties. Therefore, the messages are validated before they are sent out. This not only includes validation on the message format, but also the validity of the content of the message against all kinds of complex rules.

The validation of messages is not only important when sending messages between organizations, or financial institutions as in the SWIFT example. Within any organization message validation is important, because sending invalid messages between internal applications can result in storing invalid information about clients or a failure of processing messages in the receiving applications. Repairing this damage can be costly.

Message validation can be categorized into two types of validation functionality: validation of message format and validation of message content. Validating the format of a message is simpler than checking the message content against complex rules. An open standard is available to validate XML messages with the XML Schema Definition (XSD) specification. This type of validation is well supported within ESB products, and we'll look at how it can be implemented with Mule, ServiceMix, and Apache Synapse. For the validation of message content, custom solutions exist for specific message standards (like SWIFT for the financial market and Health Level 7 [HL7] for healthcare). There are JBI components available as part of the open source OpenESB and ChainBuilder that provide support for HL7. In this section we focus on validating the message format, because message content validation is a topic on its own.

Let's consider a small example about message validation before we look at the implementation details. Assume that we have an incoming message from a messaging provider. The message is picked up by the ESB and will be routed to a web service, just as in figure 5.1. Before the message is transformed to the message format of the web service, we must be sure that the incoming message is formatted as expected. Therefore, the incoming message is validated against an agreed-on XSD. Figure 5.5 shows these steps.

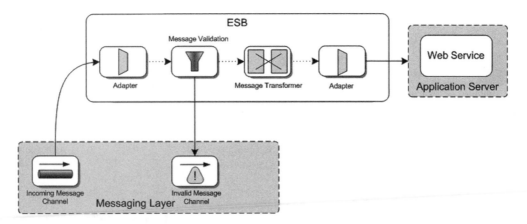

Figure 5.5   The incoming message from the messaging layer is validated against an XSD. When the message is invalid, it will be forwarded to an invalid message queue. When the message validation succeeds, the basic flow is processed.

Figure 5.5 shows how messages that don't pass the validation step are sent to the invalid message channel. This is a common way to deal with invalid messages. The invalid message channel is used as a storage mechanism so ESB administrators can be alerted when invalid messages arrive at the ESB. Now let's see how this kind of message validation can be implemented with Mule.

5.2.1   Validating messages with Mule

As message validation is a common step in the implementation of message flow for a specific integration solution, you'd expect that Mule would provide a standard message validation component. This is not the case, but when you look a bit further at the functionality provided by the inbound and outbound routers available in Mule, you'll see that the `FilteringXmlMessageSplitter` message router has an option for validation. In this section, we copy the validation functionality implemented in this router in our `ValidationRouter` class (see listing 5.8).

CONFIGURING MESSAGE VALIDATION FOR MULE

For the implementation of a message validation example in Mule, we need a simple inbound and outbound endpoint definition. Because JMS messaging is a common transport type for Mule, let's define a JMS input queue, `validation.in`, and a JMS output queue, `validation.out`. With this choice made, we can configure most of the necessary Mule elements (see listing 5.7).

Listing 5.7 Mule validation configuration

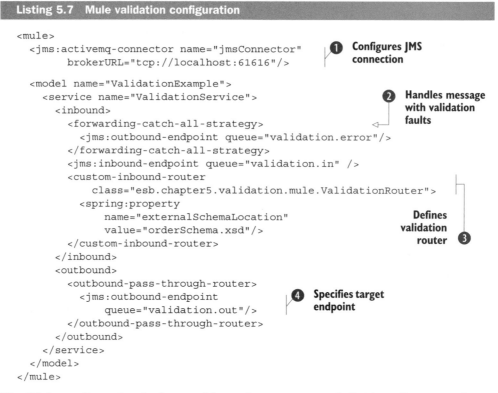

```
<mule>
  <jms:activemq-connector name="jmsConnector"              ❶ Configures JMS
      brokerURL="tcp://localhost:61616"/>                     connection

  <model name="ValidationExample">
    <service name="ValidationService">                     ❷ Handles message
      <inbound>                                                with validation
        <forwarding-catch-all-strategy>                        faults
          <jms:outbound-endpoint queue="validation.error"/>
        </forwarding-catch-all-strategy>
        <jms:inbound-endpoint queue="validation.in" />
        <custom-inbound-router
            class="esb.chapter5.validation.mule.ValidationRouter">
          <spring:property
              name="externalSchemaLocation"                       Defines
              value="orderSchema.xsd"/>                         validation
        </custom-inbound-router>                                   router  ❸
      </inbound>
      <outbound>
        <outbound-pass-through-router>
          <jms:outbound-endpoint                 ❹ Specifies target
              queue="validation.out"/>              endpoint
        </outbound-pass-through-router>
      </outbound>
    </service>
  </model>
</mule>
```

The Mule configuration is shown without the namespace definitions for convenience reasons. Because we are using the ActiveMQ message broker as the hosting environment for the JMS queues, the configuration starts with the JMS connector definition ❶.

There is one service defined called `ValidationService`, which configures the inbound and outbound router. The message validation functionality is implemented with a custom inbound router, named `ValidationRouter` ❸. This router consumes the incoming JMS message and performs an XSD validation against this message. The implementation of this router will be discussed in listing 5.8. The XSD file order-Schema.xsd, which is used for the validation step, is injected with a Spring property into the validation router. When the XSD validation returns no errors the message is forwarded to the outbound router ❹.

But what happens when the message validation step returns errors? An inbound router in Mule has to implement a method named isMatch, which specifies whether the message can be consumed by this inbound router. If the message validation step fails, this method should return false to prevent the incoming message from being forwarded to the endpoint defined in the outbound router. To be able to route a message to another endpoint when no inbound routers accept the incoming message, Mule provides a catchall strategy ❷. In this example, the incoming message that doesn't pass the validation step is routed to the validation.error JMS queue.

DEVELOPING A MULE VALIDATION COMPONENT

We still have to implement the actual validation logic in the custom inbound router used in the Mule configuration. This inbound router will be based on the Forwarding-Consumer inbound router provided by Mule, because we want to forward the incoming message directly to the outbound router when the validation step returns no errors. The inbound router will also use the same validation functionality as the Filtering-XmlMessageSplitter router, which is provided by Mule. So we are copying validation functionality here from an existing Mule router. Listing 5.8 shows the implementation of the isMatch method in the ValidationRouter.

Listing 5.8   Custom inbound router with XSD validation

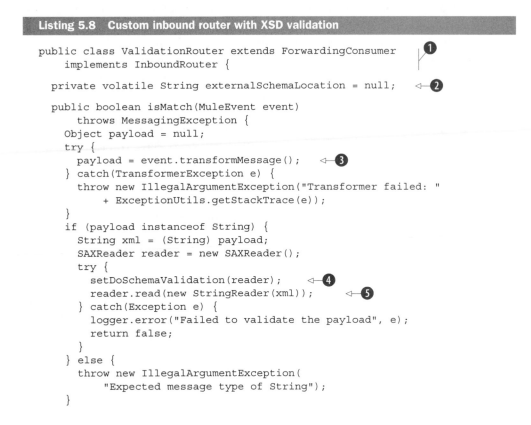

```
public class ValidationRouter extends ForwardingConsumer         ❶
    implements InboundRouter {

  private volatile String externalSchemaLocation = null;      ❷

  public boolean isMatch(MuleEvent event)
      throws MessagingException {
    Object payload = null;
    try {
      payload = event.transformMessage();       ❸
    } catch(TransformerException e) {
      throw new IllegalArgumentException("Transformer failed: "
          + ExceptionUtils.getStackTrace(e));
    }
    if (payload instanceof String) {
      String xml = (String) payload;
      SAXReader reader = new SAXReader();
      try {
        setDoSchemaValidation(reader);       ❹
        reader.read(new StringReader(xml));       ❺
      } catch(Exception e) {
        logger.error("Failed to validate the payload", e);
        return false;
      }
    } else {
      throw new IllegalArgumentException(
          "Expected message type of String");
    }
```

```
        return true;
    }
}
```

The `ValidationRouter` uses the functionality provided by the `ForwardingConsumer` message router by extending this class ❶. This means that the `process` method, which forwards the message from the inbound router directly to the outbound router, is already implemented.

The XML Schema used to validate the incoming message is injected with Spring into the `externalSchemaLocation` attribute ❷. The injection is done by calling the setter method for this attribute. We don't show the setter method in listing 5.8 to reduce the amount of Java code.

Before the `process` method (implemented in the `ForwardingConsumer` class) is called, the `isMatch` method is called by the Mule container. Because we only want messages without any validation errors to be forwarded to the outbound router, we have to implement the validation logic in this method. To be able to perform the message validation, we must first retrieve the incoming message from the `MuleEvent` instance. Notice that we use the `transformMessage` method in this example ❸, and not the more obvious `getMessage` method. When we use the `getMessage` method, we get a JMS message. JMS messages can be transformed to the payload type with the default transformer of the JMS endpoint, but we have to use the `transformMessage` method to execute this transformation step.

In this example we expect the JMS message payload to be of type `String`. A simple `SAXReader` is used to perform the parsing of the String to an XML structure. The `set-DoSchemaValidation` method sets the necessary properties on the `SAXReader` instance to enable validation when parsing the message ❹. The location of the XML Schema file is also defined on the `SAXReader` instance in this method. The implementation of this method is left out of the listing, because it's a trivial step for Java developers. For the full Java code overview of the `ValidationRouter` class, you can look at the book's source code.

Now that all the necessary parameters are set, we can parse the string with the read method of the `SAXReader` ❺. When an exception is thrown while parsing the string, a boolean value of false is returned to trigger the catchall strategy. If the validation step returns no errors, a boolean value of tr165

ue is returned and the process method is executed to forward the message to the outbound router.

Before we can start the example implementation in Mule, we first have to start the ActiveMQ broker. In the resources/chapter5 directory of the source code, you'll find the ch5-examples Ant build file, which you can use to build and deploy this validation example to Mule with the `validation-mule` target. This target also starts Mule with the validation Mule configuration. With the Swing test client, we can now send a message that passes the validation test and a message that will return a validation error.

Although Mule has no default message validation component available, we've built our own inbound validation router with code that's already implemented in the `FilteringXmlMessageSplitter` and we used the `ForwardingConsumer` as our base class. This isn't a difficult task, as you've seen in this section. This simple validation component could be enriched with additional functionality, such as storing the validation error messages in the message that's returned. Let's see how we can implement validation functionality in ServiceMix.

5.2.2 Validating messages with ServiceMix

ServiceMix provides a number of components that are JBI compliant and one deprecated component, the lightweight container, which isn't JBI compliant. The lightweight container provides some additional functionality, including validation, which cannot be found in the JBI-compliant components (a validation service engine will be provided in ServiceMix 3.3). When no JBI-compliant component is available that provides the desired functionality, the ServiceMix project's recommended approach is to develop a Java bean with, for example, the `servicemix-bean` JBI component. But for this section we've chosen to use the validation functionality provided by the lightweight container, to also provide some insight into the lightweight container implementation.

CONFIGURING MESSAGE VALIDATION FOR SERVICEMIX

Now let's look at how we can use the validation functionality of the lightweight container with JMS input and output queues. We have to define JMS endpoints within the `servicemix-JMS` binding component, and we have to configure a `servicemix-lwcontainer` service engine for the validation functionality. This isn't enough to implement the validation example, though. With the validation component, validation errors are sent back to the endpoint where the incoming message arrived—in this example, the `validation.in` JMS queue. We want the message that doesn't pass the validation step to be forwarded to the `validation.error` JMS queue. To take advantage of this functionality, we have to include a custom bean service engine implementation. Figure 5.6 shows an overview of the ServiceMix components for this example.

The JMS message consumed from the `validation.in` queue is forwarded to the `ErrorHandlerComponent`, as shown in figure 5.6. This custom bean component is responsible for the message exchange with the validation component configured in the lightweight container. When the validation component returns validation errors to the `ErrorHandlerComponent`, the message is forwarded to the `validation.error` queue; if there are no errors, the message is sent to the `validation.output` queue.

We've already configured a couple of JMS endpoints in earlier examples, so we'll focus on the implementation of the `ErrorHandlerComponent` and the configuration of the validation component. Let's start with the validation component configuration shown in listing 5.9.

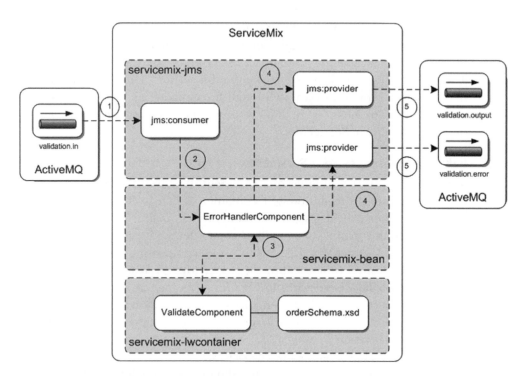

Figure 5.6   The JBI components needed to implement a validation example with JMS input and output queues. The `ErrorHandlerComponent` is a custom-developed bean component that forwards the response message to the proper JMS endpoint.

Listing 5.9   servicemix.xml of the validation component in the lightweight container

```
        <property name="rootPath"
                value="Fault/payload/messages"/>
        <property name="namespace"
                value="http://www.servicemix.org/fault"/>
        <property name="includeStackTraces"
                value="false"/>
    </bean>
  </beans>
```

In listing 5.9, the configuration for the lightweight validation component is implemented with the servicemix.xml file. For lightweight components, a different kind of configuration is used, based on the embedded ServiceMix configuration style. With the configuration of activation specifications, lightweight components can be defined with a service and endpoint name ❶. The service name can be used to call the validation component from the ErrorHandlerComponent (which we discuss in listing 5.10).

The validation component, org.apache.servicemix.components.validation. ValidateComponent, is configured with the bean element ❷, just as you saw in the servicemix-bean JBI component configuration. The location and name of the XSD file that will be used to validate the incoming message is injected with the schema- Resource property ❸.

When the validation component encounters validation errors, the default error handler just sends a fault message to the calling component. To format the fault message with an XML structure that lists all encountered validation errors, we inject another error handler ❹. This error handler is provided with the org.apache.servicemix. components.validation.MessageAggregatingErrorHandlerFactory class ❺. With the rootPath attribute, the root element for the validation errors can be configured, and the namespace property is used to specify the namespace for the fault message. It's possible to include the full stack trace of the validation error, but in this example we only want to include the validation error message.

DEVELOPING A SERVICEMIX VALIDATION ERROR HANDLER

Now we've configured the lightweight validation component and defined the JMS endpoints, we should be able to implement the custom bean. The bean implementation has to include an in-out message exchange with the validation component and forward the response or error message to the proper JMS queue. Listing 5.10 shows the implementation of the ErrorHandlerComponent.

Listing 5.10 Java implementation of the ErrorHandlerComponent

```
public class ErrorHandlerComponent implements MessageExchangeListener {

    @Resource
    private DeliveryChannel channel;
    private String NAMESPACE = "http://esbinaction.com/order";

    public void onMessageExchange(MessageExchange exchange)         ❶ Creates
        throws MessagingException {                                   client for
      if (exchange.getStatus() == ExchangeStatus.ACTIVE) {           validating
        ServiceMixClient client = createClient();
```

```
          Destination destination =
              client.createDestination(                        ❷  Defines
                  "service:" + NAMESPACE + "/validation");         validation
          InOut validationExchange =                               service
              destination.createInOutExchange();
          NormalizedMessage message =
              validationExchange.getInMessage();
          message.setContent(                                  ❸  Copies incoming
              exchange.getMessage("in").getContent());             message content
          client.sendSync(validationExchange);
          client.done(validationExchange);
          NormalizedMessage outMessage =
              validationExchange.getOutMessage();
          Fault fault = validationExchange.getFault();
          if(outMessage != null) {
            sendSuccessMessage(client,                         ❹  Returns validation
                outMessage.getContent());                         success message
          } else {
            sendErrorMessage(client, fault.getContent());    ◁
          }                                                      ❺  Sends
        }                                                         validation
        exchange.setStatus(ExchangeStatus.DONE);                  error message
        channel.send(exchange);
      }
      private ServiceMixClient createClient() {
        try {
          ClientFactory factory = (ClientFactory) new InitialContext()
              .lookup(ClientFactory.DEFAULT_JNDI_NAME);
          return factory.createClient();
        } catch(Exception e) {
          e.printStackTrace();
          return null;
        }
      }
      private void sendSuccessMessage(ServiceMixClient client,
          Source source) throws MessagingException {
        sendMessage(client, source,
            "service:http://esbinaction.com/order/validationSuccess");
      }
      private void sendErrorMessage(ServiceMixClient client,
          Source source) throws MessagingException {
        sendMessage(client, source,
            "service:http://esbinaction.com/order/validationError");
      }
      private void sendMessage(ServiceMixClient client, Source source,
          String destination) throws MessagingException {
        Destination returnDestination =
            client.createDestination(destination);
        InOnly inOnlyExchange =                                ❻  Creates in-only
            returnDestination.createInOnlyExchange();             exchange
        NormalizedMessage inMessage = inOnlyExchange.getInMessage();
        inMessage.setContent(source);
        client.send(inOnlyExchange);
      }
    }
```

The message exchange received in the ErrorHandlerComponent is the in-only exchange from the JMS consumer endpoint for the validation.in queue. Because the validate component exchange needs to be an in-out exchange, we have to instantiate a client ❶. A ServiceMix client can be used to start a new message exchange in your own bean implementation.

To configure the ServiceMix client with the target service details, we have to create a destination ❷. The full service name used here is configured in listing 5.9. Notice that the namespace of the service definition must be included in the destination. The destination instance can then be used to create the message exchange. Because we want the response of the validation component to be sent back to this bean component, we use an in-out MEP.

The input message for the validation component should be the received JMS message payload. So we just have to copy the incoming message content to the message exchange ❸. With the in message filled, the validation component can be invoked with the sendSync method on the ServiceMix client. The done method can be invoked right after the send method to finish the message exchange within the ServiceMix container. When we don't invoke the done method, the output or fault message is not yet filled and the message exchange is still running.

The response message of the validation component can be a copy of the incoming message or a fault message that contains the validation errors. Therefore, the getOut-Message and the getFault methods are both used. If the output message is filled with content, we know that there are no validation errors. In that case, we can forward the message to the validation.out message queue ❹. If the output message is empty, we can be sure that validation errors exist and the fault message content is forwarded to the validation.error queue ❺.

The logic needed to send the message to the JMS queues is quite similar to the message exchange we just discussed to communicate with the validation component. The main difference is that the MEP is in-only ❻. The content of the response or fault message is copied to the input message of the in-only exchange, and the ServiceMix client sends the message to the proper JMS queue.

To test the ServiceMix validation example, you can use the service assembly provided in the resources/chapter5/validation directory. First, you have to start the ServiceMix container with the ch5-examples build file, and then the deploy-validation target has to be executed to deploy the validation service assembly. The esb.chapter5.validation.test.ValidationJMSTest JUnit test case or the Swing test client can be used to put messages on the validation.in queue to test the validation example with and without validation errors.

We've implemented two validation examples with Mule and ServiceMix. In both cases, we had to use a bit of custom logic to implement the example to work according to our demands. In the next section, we look at another approach to message validation with Apache Synapse.

5.2.3   *An alternative way to perform message validation using Synapse*

Because Mule and ServiceMix don't provide a validation component out of the box that works without additional logic, we look at how message validation is supported within another open source ESB: Apache Synapse. We chose Apache Synapse because it provides good support for message validation based on an XML Schema definition. You've seen a Synapse configuration with content-based routing and endpoint functionality in section 5.1.2. We also talked about WS-Addressing and the `Action` header element in particular. For the message validation example, we use an endpoint definition and another WS-Addressing header, named `FaultTo`.

Because Apache Synapse is a web service mediation framework, we show the same order validation example as used for Mule and ServiceMix with web service endpoints instead of JMS queues. Apache Synapse does, however, also support JMS transport functionality.

With Synapse we can also use WS-Addressing header elements for our message validation example. When an incoming message fails the XSD validation step, we've used a JMS error queue in the previous examples. With the WS-Addressing `FaultTo` header element, clients that send SOAP messages to the ESB have a way to configure an endpoint address where faults should be sent. Now let's look at the Synapse configuration with message validation support (listing 5.11).

Listing 5.11 Message validation example with Apache Synapse

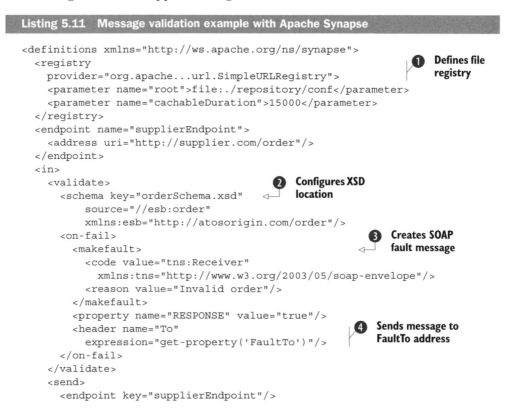

```
<definitions xmlns="http://ws.apache.org/ns/synapse">
  <registry                                              ❶ Defines file
    provider="org.apache...url.SimpleURLRegistry">         registry
    <parameter name="root">file:./repository/conf</parameter>
    <parameter name="cachableDuration">15000</parameter>
  </registry>
  <endpoint name="supplierEndpoint">
    <address uri="http://supplier.com/order"/>
  </endpoint>
  <in>
    <validate>                             ❷ Configures XSD
      <schema key="orderSchema.xsd"          location
        source="//esb:order"
        xmlns:esb="http://atosorigin.com/order"/>
      <on-fail>                              ❸ Creates SOAP
        <makefault>                            fault message
          <code value="tns:Receiver"
            xmlns:tns="http://www.w3.org/2003/05/soap-envelope"/>
          <reason value="Invalid order"/>
        </makefault>
        <property name="RESPONSE" value="true"/>
        <header name="To"                    ❹ Sends message to
          expression="get-property('FaultTo')"/>  FaultTo address
      </on-fail>
    </validate>
    <send>
      <endpoint key="supplierEndpoint"/>
```

```
      </send>
    </in>
    <out>
      <send/>
    </out>
  </definitions>
```

Besides the message validation functionality, we've used a registry in listing 5.11 **❶**. Synapse provides an easy-to-configure URL-based registry, which can be used to store XML Schemas and other definitions. In this example, the registry URL points to a local directory with the cache timeout set to 15,000 milliseconds.

The message validation functionality is configured with the `validation` element. The location of the XSD file is configured with the `schema` element **❷**. The key attribute value points to the XSD file location in the registry. The root element of the XML structure that must be validated is specified with the `source` attribute with namespace declaration.

When the XML parser encounters any validation errors, the `on-fail` element is executed. Synapse provides a simple mediator to construct a fault message, the `makefault` element **❸**. The `makefault` mediator creates a SOAP message with a SOAP `fault` element. The `code` and `reason` element values in the fault message can be easily configured with the same elements in Synapse.

Because the validation step is defined as part of the incoming message sequence, we have to instruct Synapse that the fault message should be sent back as a response. Therefore, the property `RESPONSE` is set to true. We also have to specify the endpoint address to which the fault response message should be sent. Here we can use the `FaultTo` WS-Addressing header element value that we expect the client application to set. With the header mediator and an expression that retrieves the `FaultTo` value, we can set the response destination address **❹**. This is all we have to do to implement message validation within Apache Synapse.

You've seen three approaches to message validation in this section. In all three open source ESBs, we can implement message validation pretty easily. Mule doesn't provide a standard validation component, but with the aggregation of two provided routers we're able to implement an inbound validation router. ServiceMix does provide a validation component as part of the lightweight container, but this component has limited error-handling functionality. With the addition of a custom bean component, we can implement the order validation example, though. With Apache Synapse, implementing message validation was the easiest, because of its support for fault handling and WS-Addressing.

Before a message can be sent to a service or application, we must be sure that the message conforms to the expected target message format. In many message flows, we need to transform the message to this message format, as you'll see next.

5.3   *Transforming messages*

As you've learned, message transformation cannot be neglected. Using an ESB means that different applications and services have to be integrated and information has to be shared. Because application and service development is usually not done with the same business object model in mind, developing integration solutions means that messages have to be transformed from one application model to another. In this section, we see how message transformation can be implemented with Mule and ServiceMix.

With message routing we saw that XPath is an important open standard for implementing routing rules and that XML Schema is an often used open standard for implementing message validation. To include a message transformation step in your integration solution, the XSLT open standard is a common choice. The assumption is that the messages exchanged via the ESB are in XML format. With ServiceMix you're forced to XML, although you can build transformers to, for example, change a text-based message to an XML format. But the message format inside ServiceMix is, according to the JBI specification, XML. For Mule there is no need to use XML messages inside the bus. We already saw in previous chapters that you can also exchange POJOs over the Mule bus, but the industry is more and more standardizing on XML for exchanging messages because it's technology and platform independent. So for the topic of message transformation, we'll assume that the message format is XML.

Although the concept of message transformation may already be quite familiar to you, let's look at a quick example of a message flow that involves a transformation step. Let's assume that a message is arriving from a JMS queue and that this message needs to be sent to a web service that has a WSDL with a different message format (see figure 5.7).

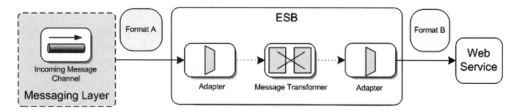

Figure 5.7   A message flow that transforms an incoming JMS message to the message format as defined in the WSDL of an external web service

The message transformer shown in figure 5.7 will consume the JMS message and transform the format with an XSLT style sheet to the web service format. Now let's look at how to implement such an example with Mule.

5.3.1   *Implementing message transformation in Mule*

Because transformation is such an essential piece of functionality within an ESB, Mule provides all kinds of out-of-the-box transformers. In order for Mule users to deal with

Table 5.1 Mapping of Java objects to JMS message types

Message payload type	JMS message type
java.lang.String	javax.jms.TextMessage
byte[]	javax.jms.BytesMessage
java.util.Map	javax.jms.MapMessage
java.io.InputStream	javax.jms.StreamMessage
java.lang.Object	javax.jms.ObjectMessage

building message flows that involve various transport protocols, Mule also uses the concept of transformation on a transport level. To make this easier to comprehend, let's focus on Mule's JMS transport.

Every developer who has coded a JMS consumer and/or producer knows that you have to deal with the javax.jms.Message interface and one of its subclasses: Text-Message, BytesMessage, MapMessage, StreamMessage, or ObjectMessage. These classes are used as message container objects. For XML and simple text-based messages, the TextMessage class is often used. So when you have a String representation of an XML message, you have to create a TextMessage and set the string as the message content before the message can be put on a JMS queue.

To facilitate using JMS transport within Mule, two transformers are available that handle this functionality for you. The ObjectToJMSMessage transformer accepts a Java object, creates the correct JMS message class, and sets the Java object as the message content. The JMSMessageToObject transformer does the exact opposite: it takes the payload out of a JMS message and returns the corresponding Java object type. Table 5.1 shows how the Java objects are mapped to JMS messages.

Because mapping the other way around is not the same, table 5.2 shows the mapping of JMS messages to Java objects.

Table 5.2 Mapping of JMS messages to Java objects

JMS message type	Java object
javax.jms.TextMessage	java.lang.String
javax.jms.ObjectMessage	java.lang.Object
javax.jms.BytesMessage	Byte[] (Note that the transformer will check whether the payload is compressed and automatically uncompress the message.)
javax.jms.MapMessage	java.util.Map
javax.jms.StreamMessage	java.util.Vector of objects from the stream message

The JMS transport support of Mule doesn't stop with availability of these two transformers. By default, these transformers are executed automatically. So when an inbound router is configured with a JMS transport URI, by default when an incoming `TextMessage` is consumed, the payload is extracted and passed on as a `String` object. For an outbound router with a JMS queue, a `String` object is automatically transformed to a `TextMessage`. Figure 5.8 shows a message flow that consumes messages from a JMS queue and then forwards this message to another JMS queue.

The example in figure 5.8 provides an overview of the default JMS transformers for both an incoming JMS message and an outgoing JMS message. Before the component is called, the payload is first extracted and a Java object of the payload is created. The component is then called with this Java object. When the component returns a Java object, the outbound router is called. The JMS transport connector then transforms the Java object to a JMS message again and the message is forwarded to the JMS queue. Note that this is the default behavior of the JMS transformers, but it can be overridden in every Mule configuration by implementing a `transformer-ref` attribute on an inbound or outbound endpoint. When a router contains this attribute, the listed transformers are executed instead of the default transformers that we've described.

The default transformers are provided by Mule to make it easier for Mule users to deal with various transport types. This isn't the type of transformer that we want to discuss in relation to message transformation, however. With message transformation, the message format is actually changed, and this isn't what happens with the transport transformers. Why discuss the previous JMS example, then? Well, the transformer architecture in Mule is based on this type of transformer, including the message transformation support. The `XsltTransformer` class that we use in the next example must also be

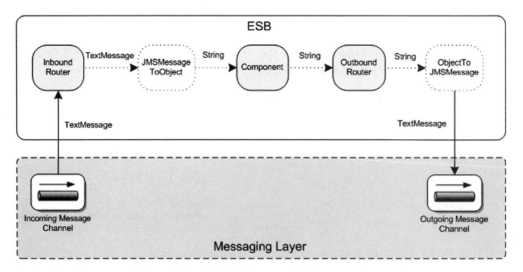

Figure 5.8   A message flow example showing the usage of default transformers within Mule. In this example, the default JMS transformers are shown that transform the JMS message type to a Java object, and vice versa.

configured in the `transformer` element, and therefore the default transformers are overridden. So you should know the concept of default transformers before using the `Xslt-Transformer`. Now let's take a look at an example of message transformation in Mule.

CONFIGURING THE WEATHER SERVICE INVOCATION IN MULE

We implement a message flow that listens for console user input, then calls a weather service and gives the response to the user via the console. The website WebserviceX.NET (http://www.webservicex.net) provides a number of free web services that are great to use for examples. One of these web services is a weather service that takes a city and country as input and responds with a number of weather parameters for that city. This means that we ask a user to enter a city and country in the console, then call the web service; then we send the response back to the console. But because we're only interested in the temperature and humidity, we first transform the web service response to a message format with these weather parameters before sending the message to the console.

To make it easy to comprehend the Mule configuration, we begin by retrieving the city and country via the console and calling the weather web service first. This part of the Mule configuration is shown in listing 5.12.

Listing 5.12   Mule configuration that calls the weather web service

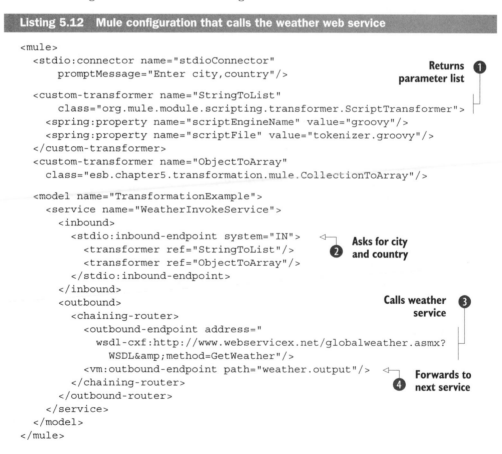

```
<mule>
  <stdio:connector name="stdioConnector"
     promptMessage="Enter city,country"/>                    Returns       ❶
                                                           parameter list

  <custom-transformer name="StringToList"
      class="org.mule.module.scripting.transformer.ScriptTransformer">
    <spring:property name="scriptEngineName" value="groovy"/>
    <spring:property name="scriptFile" value="tokenizer.groovy"/>
  </custom-transformer>
  <custom-transformer name="ObjectToArray"
    class="esb.chapter5.transformation.mule.CollectionToArray"/>

  <model name="TransformationExample">
    <service name="WeatherInvokeService">
      <inbound>
        <stdio:inbound-endpoint system="IN">        ◁┐  Asks for city
          <transformer ref="StringToList"/>         ❷  and country
          <transformer ref="ObjectToArray"/>
        </stdio:inbound-endpoint>
      </inbound>
      <outbound>                                          Calls weather  ❸
        <chaining-router>                                     service
          <outbound-endpoint address="
            wsdl-cxf:http://www.webservicex.net/globalweather.asmx?
              WSDL&amp;method=GetWeather"/>
          <vm:outbound-endpoint path="weather.output"/>   ◁┐  Forwards to
        </chaining-router>                                ❹  next service
      </outbound-router>
    </service>
  </model>
</mule>
```

Let's start with the inbound router that asks for user input via the `stdio` connector
❷. The user is asked to provide a city and country, using a comma as delimiter. This
means that we receive a `String` when the user provides this information. The web
service transport provider that we use later in the Mule configuration can accept multiple input parameters for a web service, but they have to be provided as a `List`. This
means that we have to transform the string message to a primitive list with two
entries: a city and a country.

We've used a Groovy script to transform the string message to a `List` ❶. We
could've implemented a small Java method with the same logic. The Groovy script
tokenizer.groovy consists of the following:

```
return src.toString().tokenize(",")
```

With this Groovy script, the incoming user input is transformed to a Java `List` object.
Because we need a primitive array to call the weather web service, we then have to
transform the `List` object to a primitive string array. We've implemented a simple
Mule transformer `CollectionToArray` that handles this conversion:

```
public class CollectionToArray extends AbstractTransformer {
   protected Object doTransform(Object src, String encoding)
      throws TransformerException {
    if (src instanceof Collection) {
      Collection collection = (Collection) src;
      return collection.toArray();
    } else {
      throw new TransformerException(this, new
         javax.xml.transform.TransformerException(
            "Only Collection payload is supported."));
    }
  }
}
```

We've configured the script and primitive array transformers on the inbound endpoint with the `transformer` elements. Because the `stdio` URI doesn't have any default
transformers, we only have to configure these two transformers.

With the user input converted to a primitive string array, we can invoke the weather
web service as an outbound endpoint ❸. Because we want to transform the response
of the web service, we use a chaining router to forward the web service response to
another Mule service. With a chaining router, the response of the first outbound endpoint is forwarded to the next configured outbound endpoint. We use a `wsdl-cxf`
transport URI to invoke the weather web service. The web service URI needs to point to
the WSDL of the web service. For the weather web service, this is the http://www.web-
servicex.net/globalweather.asmx?WSDL URI. We also have to provide the web service
operation to invoke: `GetWeather`. With this configuration, Mule will invoke the
`GetWeather` operation on the weather web service with the `city` and `country` parameters as input. The Apache CXF transport accepts the string array as input and puts the
first occurrence of the array in the first element of the input message for the web

service—in this case, the `city` value. Of course, the second occurrence in the string array is used as the second element: the `country` value.

The weather web service will then respond with the weather information, which includes a large number of weather-related elements. Because we're only interested in the temperature and humidity values, we've configured a message transformation step as a separate Mule service. The transformation service listens to the endpoint address of the second outbound router that's configured in the chaining router ❹.

CONFIGURING MESSAGE TRANSFORMATION IN MULE

The next part of the Mule configuration performs the message transformation step on the weather response message (see listing 5.13).

Listing 5.13 The message transformation service in the Mule configuration

```
<xm:xslt-transformer name="XSLT"
    xsl-file="weather.xslt" />              ❶

<model name="TransformationExample">
  <service name="WeatherResponseOutput">
    <inbound>
      <vm:inbound-endpoint path="weather.output">
        <transformer ref="XSLT"/>            ◁—❷
      </vm:inbound-endpoint>
    </inbound>
    <outbound>
      <outbound-pass-through-router>
        <stdio:outbound-endpoint system="OUT"/>   ◁—❸
      </outbound-pass-through-router>
    </outbound>
  </service>
</model>
```

Notice that normally we would've configured the XSLT transformation as part of the chaining router in listing 5.12. Then we wouldn't need an extra VM queue because the XSLT transformer would be part of the console response outbound endpoint. We chose to divide the functionality into two services to make it easier to show here. Also notice that we use the same model name here because the `WeatherResponseOutput` service is part of the Mule configuration shown in listing 5.12.

The first part of the Mule configuration defines an XSLT transformer with the `weather.xslt` style sheet ❶. This transformer converts an XML message with the XSLT style sheet to another message format. The style sheet consists of these transformation elements:

```
<xsl:stylesheet version="1.0"
    xmlns:xsl="http://www.w3.org/1999/XSL/Transform">
  <xsl:template match="/CurrentWeather">
    <weather-news>
      <temperature>
        <xsl:value-of select="Temperature"/>
      </temperature>
```

```
    <humidity>
      <xsl:value-of select="RelativeHumidity"/>
    </humidity>
  </weather-news>
</xsl:template>
</xsl:stylesheet>
```

The web service response has a root element with the name of CurrentWeather. We want to send two child elements back to the user: Temperature and RelativeHumidity. This style sheet extracts these two elements from the web service response message and converts the response message to a simple weather news message.

The XSLT transformer is configured on the inbound endpoint with the transformer-ref attribute ❷. The transformed message is then sent back to the console with the outbound endpoint ❸.

This means we've implemented the full weather integration solution. We should now be able to test this Mule example with the source code provided at the book's website. You can find the example in the resources/chapter5/transformation directory. Executing the transformation-mule target in the ch5-examples Ant build file builds and deploys the distribution to the Mule container. With the transformation script, Mule will start along with the example. The console should ask you to provide input for the city and country (in the format Amsterdam,Netherlands). You should receive a response with the temperature and humidity values for the city and country you entered.

We have seen how message transformation works in Mule with multiple transformer types. Now let's look at the message transformation functionality in ServiceMix.

5.3.2   *Implementing message transformation in ServiceMix*

We use the same weather service that has a city and country as input parameters and responds with weather information about this city. Because we've already discussed this example for Mule, let's jump straight to the ServiceMix configuration overview in figure 5.9.

The numbers shown in figure 5.9 reflect the runtime message flow of the weather service. The incoming JMS message is used to invoke the weather web service via the HTTP JBI component. A routing slip is used to configure a number of services that must be processed in a static ordering. The routing slip first invokes the weather web service via the HTTP binding component. Next, the web service response is handled by a Camel processor implementation and then transformed with an XSLT style sheet. (We discuss the Camel component later in this section.) Finally, the transformed message is sent to the outgoing JMS queue with the JMS consumer.

Using a JMS consumer to send the response message to the transformation.out queue may seem a bit strange—and it is, actually. In previous examples where we used a JMS consumer, we only took advantage of the message consumption functionality. Listing 5.14 shows how we can use a JMS consumer with an in-out message exchange pattern and a reply queue configuration.

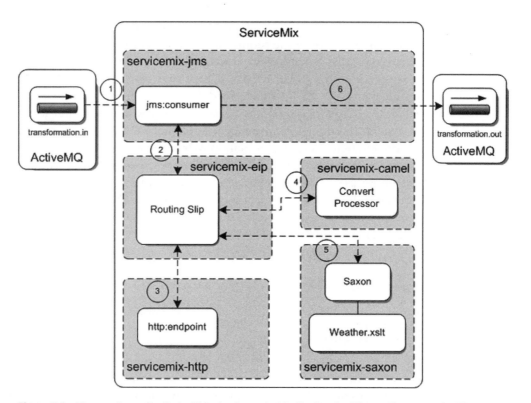

Figure 5.9 The service units that will be implemented in the ServiceMix weather example. We use a JMS message to invoke the weather web service. The web service response will be transformed with the Saxon component, and the transformed message will be forwarded to a JMS output queue.

Listing 5.14 Configuration of a JMS consumer with a reply destination

```
<beans xmlns:jms="http://servicemix.apache.org/jms/1.0"
    xmlns:esb="http://esbinaction.com/weather">

  <jms:consumer service="esb:weatherConsumer"
      endpoint="weatherEndpoint"
      targetService="esb:routingSlip"        ←❶
      destinationName="transformation.in"
      replyDestinationName="transformation.out"   ←❷
      connectionFactory="#connectionFactory"
      marshaler="#marshaler"/>                 ←
                                               ❸
  <bean id="marshaler"                        ←
    class="org.apache.servicemix.jms.endpoints.DefaultConsumerMarshaler">
   <property name="mep" value="http://www.w3.org/2004/08/wsdl/in-out" />
  </bean>
  <bean id="connectionFactory"
    class="org.apache.activemq.ActiveMQConnectionFactory">
   <property name="brokerURL" value="tcp://localhost:61616" />
  </bean>
</beans>
```

The JMS consumer sends the incoming message to the routing slip implemented in the
EIP service engine ❶. One of the requirements of a routing slip is that the incoming
message exchange must use an in-out message exchange pattern. By default, the JMS
consumer uses an in-only message exchange pattern, so we have to override the setting
in the default marshaler ❸. We have to define a Spring bean with the Default-
ConsumerMarshaler and then override the mep attribute with the in-out URI definition.
Now we've configured the JMS consumer to implement the in-out message exchange
pattern, we can configure a reply destination. When the routing slip has processed the
three services (as shown in figure 5.9), the response message is sent to the JMS consumer because we use an in-out message exchange pattern. We can easily configure
the reply queue with the replyDestinationName attribute ❷.

Since we haven't yet implemented a routing slip, let's quickly look at the configuration of the EIP service unit:

```
<eip:static-routing-slip service="esb:routingSlip" endpoint="endpoint">
  <eip:targets>
    <eip:exchange-target service="wws:GlobalWeather" />
    <eip:exchange-target service="esb:convertDSLRouter" />
    <eip:exchange-target service="esb:transformWeather" />
  </eip:targets>
</eip:static-routing-slip>
```

The configuration of the routing slip shows the ordering of the invocation of the different services. First, the weather web service is invoked via the HTTP service unit, and
in the other services the web service response is transformed so that the response message only includes temperature and humidity values. Let's take a look at the HTTP
endpoint configuration in listing 5.15.

Listing 5.15   Weather web service invocation configuration for ServiceMix

```
<beans xmlns:http="http://servicemix.apache.org/http/1.0"
    xmlns:wws="http://www.webservicex.net">          ←❶

  <http:endpoint service="wws:GlobalWeather"    ←❷
      endpoint="wsEndpoint"
      role="provider"                                ←❸
      locationURI="http://www.webservicex.net/globalweather.asmx"
      soap="true"
      soapVersion="1.1"
      soapAction="http://www.webserviceX.NET/GetWeather"/>
</beans>
```

This web service configuration for the invocation of the weather web service is quite
compact for the most part, but there are some caveats. The first thing to notice is that
the namespace of the target web service must be included in the service unit configuration ❶. We need this namespace declaration for the service name definition. The
name of the service as defined in the WSDL of the weather web service must be equal
to the service name of the HTTP endpoint ❷. This is something that you might over-
look when defining an HTTP endpoint for the first time.

Notice that we use a role of provider ❸ in this listing to invoke a web service. You may have expected a value of consumer, but that would mean ServiceMix would have to provide a web service that can be invoked from clients outside ServiceMix.

The WSDL file (which is very important to the HTTP endpoint configuration) can be configured with the wsdlResource attribute, but this attribute is not required. When the WSDL file is included in the service unit distribution, we can reference it by using the classpath: prefix. Because we want to use SOAP messages for the web service request and response, we have to define a soap attribute with a value of true. We also have to define the SOAP version to be used for the web service call because the default version is 1.2. The weather service only supports SOAP 1.1, so we have to provide a soapVersion attribute with a value of 1.1. The last attribute that we have to configure is the SOAP action. Because the weather web service needs a SOAP action specified in the request, we must define a soapAction attribute with the SOAP action for the GetWeather operation.

Another part that needs explaining is the need for a Camel component for this example. The response message of the HTTP weather service unit is marshaled into a result element, as shown here:

```
<soap:Envelope>
  <soap:Body>
    <GetWeatherResponse>
      &lt;?xml version="1.0" encoding="utf-16"?&gt;
      &lt;CurrentWeather&gt;
         Rest of message
      &lt;/CurrentWeather&gt;
    <GetWeatherResponse>
  </soap:Body>
</soap:Envelope>
```

Because the weather response message we're interested in is marshaled into the GetWeatherResponse message, the Saxon service engine is not able to transform this XML message. Therefore, we must first retrieve the actual response message, which has a root element of CurrentWeather. This is exactly why we introduced a Camel component in the example implementation. Let's look at the implementation of the Camel converter component in listing 5.16.

Listing 5.16 Implementation of the Camel converter component

```
public class ConvertRouter extends RouteBuilder {

  private final static String NAMESPACE =
     "http://esbinaction.com/weather";
  private final static String SERVICE_IN = "jbi:service:" +
    NAMESPACE + "/convertDSLRouter";

  public void configure() {
    from(SERVICE_IN)
      .convertBodyTo(DOMSource.class)     ◁—❶
      .process(new ConvertProcessor());   ◁—❷
  }
}
```

```
public class ConvertProcessor implements Processor {

  public void process(Exchange exchange) throws Exception {
    DOMSource payload = (DOMSource) exchange.getIn().getBody();
    Node resultNode =
      payload.getNode().getFirstChild();
    String weatherContent =
      resultNode.getTextContent();
    Message responseMessage = exchange.getOut();
    responseMessage.setBody(new StringSource(weatherContent));
  }
}
```

The Camel converter component is triggered after the weather web service has returned a response. The response message is parsed with a SAX parser by the HTTP service engine, and because we want to process the XML message in a tree structure, the XML message is first converted to a DOM structure ❶. After the message is converted to a DOM structure, the message is processed with the ConvertProcessor ❷.

The ConvertProcessor implements the process method of the Processor interface to process the message exchange. The weather response message is available as the first child, GetWeatherResponse, of the root element ❸. Then the content of the GetWeather-Response element ❹ is set as the body of the response message of the message exchange. This message is then sent on to the Saxon service unit by the routing slip.

The configuration of the message transformation is implemented in the Saxon service unit. This is also a small piece of XML configuration:

```
<beans xmlns:saxon="http://servicemix.apache.org/saxon/1.0"
    xmlns:esb="http://esbinaction.com/weather">

  <saxon:xslt service="esb:transformWeather"
              endpoint="transformWeatherEndpoint"
              resource="classpath:Weather.xslt" />
</beans>
```

You already saw an XSLT implementation in the message flow example in chapter 4, so this configuration may look familiar to you. Configuring an XSLT transformation step is quite easy in ServiceMix because we only have to provide an XSLT style sheet. This style sheet should be included in the service unit distribution and can then be referenced via the classpath. The style sheet is the same as the one we discussed in listing 5.13.

For a full insight into the example implementation, check out the resource/chapter5/transformation directory in the ServiceMix source code. Once you've deployed the service assembly to the ServiceMix container with the deploy-transformation target in the ch5-examples Ant build file, you can use the TransformationJMSTest in the chapter 5 test source folder to test the example. Of course, you can also use the Swing test client. You should receive a JMS response with the temperature and humidity values of the city and country you entered in the JMS input message.

5.4   *Summary*

In this chapter, we examined the ESB core capabilities of message routing, validation, and transformation. You learned how important open standards are for the configuration and implementation of these capabilities. Message routing is defined with routing rules that send messages to the proper target service. For content-based routing, the routing rules are defined with XPath expressions that include element values of the incoming message. When an XPath expression evaluates to true, the message will be sent to the target endpoint configured for that routing rule. Both Mule and ServiceMix provide solid support for message routing. We also saw that Apache Synapse provides routing capabilities with the WS-Addressing open standard.

Another capability, message validation, is also based on an open standard: XML Schema. Because Java provides out-of-the-box functionality that supports the parsing of XML messages with XML Schema validation enabled, implementing message validation in an ESB that uses Java is not so difficult. However, in section 5.2 you saw that there is no default message validation component in Mule. Yet, as you learned, implementing an XML Schema validation component is not hard. ServiceMix provides a message validation component, but this component doesn't provide the error-handling functionality that we needed for our example. With a bean component we easily implemented the necessary functionality. With the Synapse example, we showed how you can use the Synapse validation component to implement XML Schema–based validation.

The last section explored the implementation of message transformation with Mule and ServiceMix. We also used an open standard for this core capability: XSLT. Both ESBs provide support for XSLT style sheets with default components. We also discussed a different perspective on transformation with the Mule ESB. The Mule architecture defines transformers to make it easy to deal with messages from different transport protocols. We showed an example of these transport related transformers with the JMS transport. Support for message transformation (such as the XSLT transformer) is implemented in the same way as these transport transformers.

Next, we'll look at the connectivity functionality provided by Mule and ServiceMix. We used quite a few connectivity options in this and the previous four chapters, but both ESBs provide many more options. In the next chapter, we'll illustrate the various connectivity options for Mule and ServiceMix.

Connectivity options 6

When dealing with integration projects, you are bound to encounter many different types of technologies and standards. You have to be able to use older integration methods, such as file-based integration and FTP, as well as more modern integration mechanisms, such as web services and JMS. In this chapter, we show you how to use Mule and ServiceMix to connect to various transports and technologies and how Mule and ServiceMix can help you solve connectivity problems.

We describe the most common connectivity options and include examples using both Mule and ServiceMix. We don't discuss complex integration challenges, but we focus on how to implement connectivity functionality in open source ESBs. In part 3 of this book we delve into the more complex integration challenges, using the connectivity functionality you'll learn in this chapter. Here are the options you'll learn about:

- *File connectivity*—Files aren't really a technology, but file-based integration is a common way to communicate between applications. We look at the specific features Mule and ServiceMix offer related to file connectivity support.

File-based integration

In the early days of application integration, most integration solutions used simple files. One application stored a file in a specific directory in, say, a batch interval and another application picked up the file and processed it. There was no common standard to deal with this style of integration, so every integration solution required specific knowledge to implement the solution. File-based integration is still used a lot, especially when you're communicating with mainframes, old proprietary software, and the older UNIX systems.

- *Java Message Service (JMS)*—JMS is a standard way to connect applications based on the messaging paradigm. You learned about JMS in chapter 3, where we discussed ActiveMQ and JMS, so we don't go into greater detail here. We show various ways to connect and use JMS with the ActiveMQ message broker.
- *Java Database Connectivity (JDBC)*—In many integration scenarios, you need to either store or retrieve information from a database. For instance, storing logging information or retrieving data for message enhancement requires database connectivity. JDBC is the standard Java technology used to connect and query against relational databases. Since we don't want to install a complete MySQL, PostgreSQL, or other database server, we included HSQLDB in the book's source code. HSQLDB is a relational database management system written in Java, which requires no additional installation.

Shared databases

Before people started integrating applications using messaging and web services, data was often shared between applications using databases. One application would serve as the "master" of a certain part of data, and other applications could then connect to the database and just read that data.

The biggest issue with a shared database approach is that it's hard to define a database schema. Normally you'd create a schema made specifically for an application. With a shared database, you'll have to keep in mind that parts of the database schema are reused by other applications.

- *Mail integration*—A mail-based integration approach is an easy and asynchronous way to integrate applications—if performance and speed aren't an issue. Using POP3 and SMTP allows for easy communication between applications. Besides that, this approach offers an easy way to communicate with end users or the support staff about certain events. For instance, when an error occurs the support staff can be automatically notified by sending an email with a detailed error message as well as any additional information.

- *File Transfer Protocol (FTP)*—FTP is one of the older internet protocols, but is still used to communicate with legacy systems. We show you how the open source ESBs can log on to an FTP server to retrieve and store files there, and what advanced options Mule and ServiceMix support. We use the AnomicFTPD server to implement the examples. This open source FTP server requires no complex user management; you can start it and use it without having to create extensive configurations.

- *Enterprise JavaBeans (EJBs)*—EJBs are part of the JEE specification and provide functionality to create highly scalable and transactional service implementations. Many applications make use of EJBs, so it would be nice to be able to call these EJBs from Mule and ServiceMix. We show you how to connect to an EJB container and invoke the EJB methods with Mule and ServiceMix.

There is one important technology missing here: web service connectivity. For example, SOAP is increasingly used as a message standard to solve integration problems. Since integration with web services and SOAP is such a broad topic, we decided to dedicate an entire chapter to that subject (chapter 7).

Just a quick note before we start looking at the various options Mule and Service-Mix offer. You can play around with all the examples shown in this chapter—just navigate to either the Mule or the ServiceMix workspace and then go to the resources/chapter6 directory of the book's source code. Here you'll find an Ant build file, ch6-build.xml, that has targets for all the examples in this chapter.

6.1   *File connectivity*

Let's start with a simple connectivity option: the file connection. You've seen the file connection used in examples in previous chapters, so you already know the basics of this type of connection. Take a look at figure 6.1, which provides an overview of the example that we implement in this section.

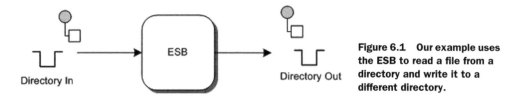

Figure 6.1   Our example uses the ESB to read a file from a directory and write it to a different directory.

In the example shown in figure 6.1, we read a file from the In directory and write it to the Out directory. Let's begin with Mule.

6.1.1   *Mule File transport*

When we want to implement integration logic in Mule, we have to define a Mule service as part of a Mule configuration. This Mule service reads files from the In directory and then writes them to the Out directory. The Mule configuration in listing 6.1 illustrates a number of features of the Mule File transport.

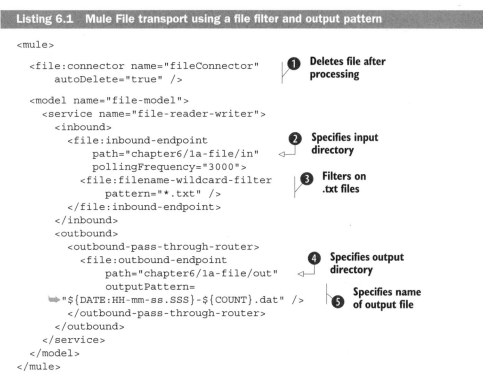

Listing 6.1 Mule File transport using a file filter and output pattern

```
<mule>
    <file:connector name="fileConnector"        ❶ Deletes file after
        autoDelete="true" />                       processing

    <model name="file-model">
        <service name="file-reader-writer">
            <inbound>
                <file:inbound-endpoint              ❷ Specifies input
                    path="chapter6/1a-file/in"         directory
                    pollingFrequency="3000">
                    <file:filename-wildcard-filter  ❸ Filters on
                        pattern="*.txt" />             .txt files
                </file:inbound-endpoint>
            </inbound>
            <outbound>
                <outbound-pass-through-router>
                    <file:outbound-endpoint         ❹ Specifies output
                        path="chapter6/1a-file/out"    directory
                        outputPattern=
    ➥"${DATE:HH-mm-ss.SSS}-${COUNT}.dat" />         ❺ Specifies name
                </outbound-pass-through-router>         of output file
            </outbound>
        </service>
    </model>
</mule>
```

In listing 6.1, we listen for new files in the chapter6/1a-file/in directory ❷. We don't process all the files that are put in this directory—just the ones that match the *.txt configuration of the file filter, which we define with the filename wildcard filter ❸. We also tell the endpoint to poll the chapter6/1a-file/in directory every 3 seconds, and once the file that matches the *.txt filter is consumed, it should be deleted ❶.

The outbound endpoint ❹ is specified in the same manner. The only property we define here is the filename to be used for the output file ❺. When Mule writes the file to the chapter6/1a-file/out directory specified in the outbound endpoint, it replaces the placeholders with real values, such as the date value. You can run this example with the chapter6-file-example-1a target in the ch6-build.xml Ant build file located in the resources/chapter6 directory of the book's source code.

There are a couple of properties of the Mule File transport we have yet to show you. Listing 6.2 is an example with more advanced properties.

Listing 6.2 Mule File transport using a backup directory

```
<mule>
    <file:connector name="fileConnector"        ❶ Appends file
        outputAppend="true" />                     content
```

```
<model name="file-model">
  <service name="file-reader-writer">
    <inbound>
      <file:inbound-endpoint path="chapter6/1b-file/in"
          pollingFrequency="3000"
          fileAge="10000"
          moveToDirectory="chapter6/1b-file/bak"
          moveToPattern="${UUID}.bak"/>
    </inbound>
    <outbound>
      <outbound-pass-through-router>
        <file:outbound-endpoint
            path="chapter6/1b-file/out"
            outputPattern="${DATE:yyyy-MM-dd}.dat"/>
      </outbound-pass-through-router>
    </outbound>
  </service>
</model>
</mule>
```

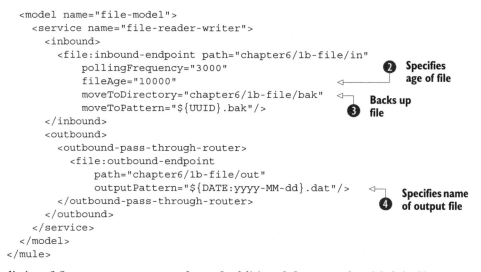

❷ Specifies age of file

❸ Backs up file

❹ Specifies name of output file

In listing 6.2, you can see a number of additional features that Mule's file connector provides. As you can see, we now specify a `fileAge` attribute ❷, which defines how old a file must be in relation to the current date and time before we start processing it. We also add a `moveToDirectory` ❸ and a `moveToPattern` property. We can use these properties to tell Mule to make a copy of our file and save it to a specific directory (with the `moveToDirectory` attribute) and with a specific name (with the `moveToPattern` attribute) before the actual processing starts. The use of a `moveToDirectory` attribute is very helpful, since it prevents the incoming messages from getting lost.

Another option in listing 6.2 is the `outputAppend` attribute for the file connector definition ❶. Normally when Mule writes an output file and the file already exists, that file is overwritten. By specifying the `outputAppend` attribute on a file connector, we ensure output files won't be overwritten because the new file is appended to the end of the existing file. The name of the output file is specified with the `outputPattern` attribute ❹; in this example, it's the current date with a .dat file extension. You can run this example with the `chapter6-file-example-1b` target in the ch6-build.xml Ant build file located in the resources/chapter6 directory of the book's source code.

You've seen how easy it is to work with files and file systems in Mule. Now let's see how you can use ServiceMix to access a file system.

6.1.2   *ServiceMix file transport*

As we explained in chapter 5, you can configure the ServiceMix JBI components by creating service units and service assemblies using xbean.xml configuration files. These service assemblies are deployed to the ServiceMix container, and then the various service units are each deployed to a specific binding component or service engine.

Let's start with a basic example that shows some of the features the `servicemix-file` binding component provides. We split the listings into a sender part, which writes files to a directory (listing 6.3), and a poller part, which reads files from a directory (listing 6.4).

Listing 6.3 `servicemix-file` binding component using a filename marshaler

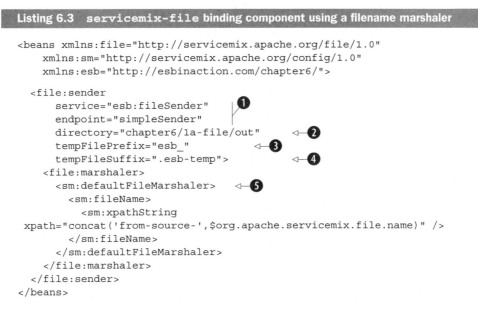

```
<beans xmlns:file="http://servicemix.apache.org/file/1.0"
    xmlns:sm="http://servicemix.apache.org/config/1.0"
    xmlns:esb="http://esbinaction.com/chapter6/">

  <file:sender
      service="esb:fileSender"
      endpoint="simpleSender"
      directory="chapter6/1a-file/out"
      tempFilePrefix="esb_"
      tempFileSuffix=".esb-temp">
    <file:marshaler>
      <sm:defaultFileMarshaler>
        <sm:fileName>
          <sm:xpathString
  xpath="concat('from-source-',$org.apache.servicemix.file.name)" />
        </sm:fileName>
      </sm:defaultFileMarshaler>
    </file:marshaler>
  </file:sender>
</beans>
```

As you can see in listing 6.3, part of a file sender implementation in ServiceMix is the definition of the file output directory ❷. And as with any JBI component, we also need to uniquely identify the file sender with a `service` and an `endpoint` name ❶ so that it can be registered in the JBI container. The other file properties listed here are optional. The `tempFile` properties ❸ and ❹ define the filename of the temporary file ServiceMix uses while writing the contents to the output directory.

Another part of the file sender is the configuration of the file marshaler ❺, which defines how the file output is written. In this example we only specify the filename of the output message, using the `fileName` element. The marshaler uses an XPath expression to create an output filename based on the original filename, prefixed with "from-source-."

If you want to use the `fileSender` service to write a message to the file system, you just need to send an in-only message exchange to this service endpoint ❶. The file poller in listing 6.4 demonstrates how you can do just that.

Listing 6.4 ServiceMix file poller that implements a custom file filter

```
<beans xmlns:file="http://servicemix.apache.org/file/1.0"
    xmlns:esb="http://esbinaction.com/chapter6/">

  <file:poller service="esb:filePoller"
      endpoint="simplePoller"
      targetService="esb:fileSender"
      targetEndpoint="simpleSender"
```

```
        file="chapter6/1a-file/in"          ◄─❷
        archive="chapter6/1a-file/archive"      ◄─❸
        delay="5000"
        period="2000">              ❹
    <file:filter>                   ◄┘
      <bean class="esb.chapter6.file.StartsWithFilter">
        <property name="startsWith" value="deploy_me" />
      </bean>
    </file:filter>
  </file:poller>
</beans>
```

In listing 6.4, we start the file poller configuration with a service name and an endpoint name definition, as you'd expect in a JBI service configuration. The two file attributes ❶, targetService and targetEndpoint, define which JBI service (the file sender from listing 6.3) will be called when a new file is found in the polled directory ❷.

The file poller also allows you to define an archive ❸ attribute. This archive will contain copies of all the files that the poller processes. That way, you can be sure that files are never lost, should something unforeseen happen during later processing. You can also define how the directory is polled. The delay attribute tells ServiceMix to wait 5 seconds before polling begins, and the period property sets the polling frequency for the input directory.

The last item shown in this configuration is a simple custom filter that only reads files whose names start with "deploy_me" ❹. As you can see, we used a standard Spring bean to define this filter. Since this is a custom bean implementation, let's just look at the code for this component in listing 6.5.

Listing 6.5 Filter implementation that checks the beginning of a filename

```
public class StartsWithFilter implements FileFilter {

    private String startsWith;                  ❶  Implements
                                            ◄┘      FileFilter interface
    public boolean accept(File file) {
        boolean result = false;
        if (file.getName().startsWith(startsWith)) {    ◄┐  Evaluates
            result = true;                          ❷  filename
        }
        return result;
    }

    public String getStartsWith() {
        return startsWith;
    }
    public void setStartsWith(String startsWith) {
        this.startsWith = startsWith;
    }
}
```

The filter implementation in listing 6.5 is applied to each file found in the polled directory. As you can see, the filter implements the standard FileFilter interface ❶, which is part of the Java IO package of the JDK. If the filename equals the value of the injected class attribute `startsWith`, the file is accepted by this file filter ❷.

To get the ServiceMix container started, you'll first have to run the default Ant target `start` of the ch6-build.xml build file in the resources/chapter6 directory of the book's source code. Then you can deploy the service assembly with the `deploy-1a-file-example` target in the same Ant build file. A test XML file is provided in the resources/chapter6/1a-file directory, which you can copy to the chapter6/1a-file/in directory in the ServiceMix installation directory.

So far you've learned how to write a file to a directory and how to read files from a directory. This doesn't mean, though, that you can process all the different types of files you might need in an integration project. Using the previous setup, for example, we can only process files that are valid XML. The reason is that the JBI specification defines the use of XML as the normalized message format. Luckily, we have a solution to consume non-XML file messages in the form of attachments.

JBI and attachments

When we discussed JBI in chapter 2, we mentioned that the payload of a JBI message should always be XML. So how can you send binary files? Well, a JBI message contains a bit more than just the message payload. It contains a set of message properties where you can set some metadata for the message, and it can also include attachments. These attachments can store pretty much everything and therefore can be used to transfer binary data.

However, take care when using these attachments, since not all the binding components and service engines in ServiceMix can deal with them. When you want to use attachments, be sure that the JBI service(s) know how to process them. Listing 6.6 shows how to configure the `servicemix-file` binding component to process non-XML files.

Listing 6.6 File sender configuration showing how to send binary files

```
<beans xmlns:file="http://servicemix.apache.org/file/1.0"
    xmlns:sm="http://servicemix.apache.org/config/1.0"
    xmlns:esb="http://esbinaction.com/chapter6/">

  <file:sender service="esb:fileSender"
      endpoint="binarySender"
      directory="chapter6/1b-file/out"
      tempFilePrefix="esb_"
      tempFileSuffix=".esb-temp">
    <file:marshaler>                          ❶ Writes a
      <sm:binaryFileMarshaler />                  binary file
    </file:marshaler>
  </file:sender>

  <file:poller service="esb:filePoller"
      endpoint="binaryPoller"
      targetService="esb:fileSender"
```

```
      targetEndpoint="binarySender"
      file="chapter6/1b-file/in"
      period="2000">
   <file:marshaler>
      <sm:binaryFileMarshaler />
   </file:marshaler>
</file:poller>
```

② Reads a binary file

This time, we add a different file marshaler **①** and **②**. The binary marshaler of the file poller **②** won't set the content of the polled file in the JBI message body, but it will add the file content as an attachment so it can be processed in ServiceMix and still conform to the JBI standards.

Of course, we also need to set the binary marshaler for the file sender so that the attachment can be written to the file system. Keep in mind, though, that not all the available service engines and binding components can deal with attachments. The JBI specification doesn't specify how attachments should be addressed.

To run this example, make sure that the ServiceMix container is started (the start Ant target of the ch6-build.xml build file can be used to start ServiceMix). Then you can deploy the binary file service assembly with the deploy-1b-file-binary-example Ant target available in the same Ant build file. We provide a graphics file, front.jpg, in the resources/chapter6/1b-file directory, which you can use to copy to the directory that's polled by ServiceMix.

As you'll recall, file-based integration is a common way to integrate two applications. An advantage of file-based integration is that it's asynchronous: the applications you're integrating don't have to wait for each other, or even be available at all times.

However, a more modern method of asynchronous integration is message-based integration. With message-based integration, there is also no direct communication between two applications, as the messages are sent to a message broker asynchronously. Java uses JMS as the standard API to access and communicate with message brokers. In the next section, we show how we can use JMS in Mule and ServiceMix.

6.2   Connecting to JMS

To demonstrate JMS's functionality, we present two different examples for Mule and ServiceMix. One example shows how to use the JMS queuing functionality, and the other shows how to use JMS topics. Let's first look at the queuing example (shown in figure 6.2).

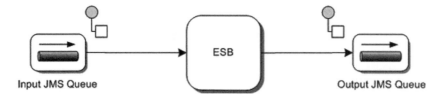

Figure 6.2   This JMS example shows how to use the ESB to consume a message from a JMS queue and produce the message for another JMS queue.

In the example in figure 6.2, the ESB consumes a message from a JMS queue. The ESB can then use integration logic to transform and route the message, but in this example we simply forward the message to another JMS queue.

The other example implementation using JMS topics is shown in figure 6.3.

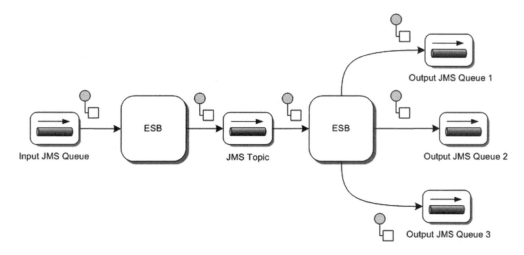

Figure 6.3   This JMS example shows how to use the ESB to consume a message from a JMS queue and send the message to a JMS topic. Then the ESB implements three topic subscribers that each forwards the message to a JMS queue.

For the topic example shown in figure 6.3, we start with consuming a message from a JMS queue. The ESB then forwards the consumed JMS message to a JMS topic. You may remember from the previous chapter that a topic follows the Publish/Subscribe principle. So in other words, all the topic subscribers of a JMS topic receive the message. So when we run this example and put a JMS message in the input queue, it should eventually result in three copies of the message being sent to a different JMS queue. Now let's examine our first example, which uses Mule.

6.2.1   *Connecting Mule to JMS*

This example forwards a message consumed from a JMS queue to another JMS queue, as shown in figure 6.2. When you want to run this example, just go to the resources/chapter6 folder in the Mule workspace. The ch6-build.xml Ant file available in that folder provides you with an Ant target named `chapter6-jms-example-2a` to run this example.

Now let's look at the Mule service we need to define to implement this simple JMS queue example. Listing 6.7 shows the Mule configuration that forwards a message to another JMS queue.

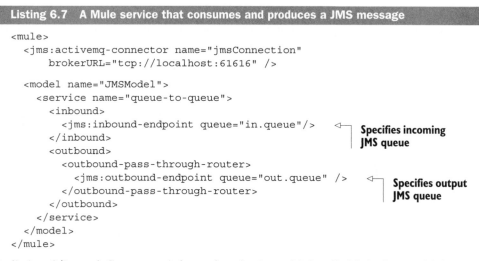

Listing 6.7   A Mule service that consumes and produces a JMS message

```
<mule>
  <jms:activemq-connector name="jmsConnection"
      brokerURL="tcp://localhost:61616" />

  <model name="JMSModel">
    <service name="queue-to-queue">
      <inbound>
        <jms:inbound-endpoint queue="in.queue"/>     ◁—┐ Specifies incoming
      </inbound>                                           JMS queue
      <outbound>
        <outbound-pass-through-router>
          <jms:outbound-endpoint queue="out.queue" />  ◁—┐ Specifies output
        </outbound-pass-through-router>                     JMS queue
      </outbound>
    </service>
  </model>
</mule>
```

In listing 6.7, we define a JMS inbound endpoint, which tells Mule from which queue the message should be consumed. Before you can run this example, make sure that you have started ActiveMQ, for example, with the ext:start-activeMQ Ant target in the ch6-build.xml. Then you can use the Swing test client to send a test message to the in.queue and to receive that message on the out.queue.

Now let's see how to implement a Mule example with topics. In this example, Mule consumes a message from a JMS queue and sends this message to a topic. Then Mule will define three different topic subscribers, and each will send the message to a different JMS queue. To implement this example in Mule, we need to define four Mule services. The first service will define functionality similar to that of the JMS queue example in listing 6.7. The service will just consume a message from a JMS queue and send it to another JMS endpoint. But instead of sending the message to a queue, we send the message to a topic (listing 6.8).

Listing 6.8   A Mule service that sends the incoming message to a JMS topic

```
<mule>
  <jms:activemq-connector name="jmsConnection"
      brokerURL="tcp://localhost:61616"
      acknowledgementMode="DUPS_OK_ACKNOWLEDGE"   ◁—┐ Specifies
      specification="1.1"                              acknowledgment
      maxRedelivery="1" />                             mode

  <jms:activemq-connector name="topicConnection"
      brokerURL="tcp://localhost:61616" />

  <model name="TopicModel">
    <service name="queue-to-topic">
      <inbound>
        <jms:inbound-endpoint queue="topic.in.queue"
            connector-ref="jmsConnection" />
      </inbound>
```

```
    <outbound>
      <outbound-pass-through-router>
        <jms:outbound-endpoint topic="topic1"        | Configures
            connector-ref="topicConnection" />        | topic name
      </outbound-pass-through-router>
    </outbound>
  </service>
</model>
</mule>
```

In listing 6.8, we show some additional configuration attributes for Mule's ActiveMQ connector. For example, we can specify the acknowledgment mode for the JMS consumer. The default value is AUTO_ACKNOWLEDGE, which means that so-called "exactly once delivery" is guaranteed by the JMS provider. If exactly once delivery isn't needed, we can also specify a value of DUPS_OK_ACKNOWLEDGE as we did in this example. By allowing duplicate messages, the JMS provider guarantees "at least once" delivery of the message.

We can also specify a maxRedelivery attribute, which configures the number of redeliveries in case of an error during the message processing for the ActiveMQ connector. Chapter 8, where we talk about error handling and transactions, provides more details about this topic.

We also changed the queue attribute on the JMS endpoint to a topic attribute, to instruct the Mule container to send the message to a JMS topic. Let's also look at one of the Mule services that subscribes to this topic (listing 6.9).

Listing 6.9 A Mule service that subscribes to a JMS topic

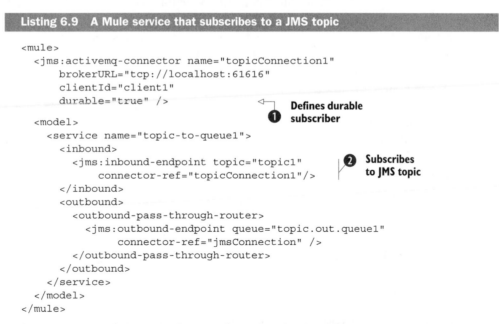

```
<mule>
  <jms:activemq-connector name="topicConnection1"
      brokerURL="tcp://localhost:61616"
      clientId="client1"
      durable="true" />                         ◁─┐  ❶ Defines durable
  <model>                                                subscriber
    <service name="topic-to-queue1">
      <inbound>
        <jms:inbound-endpoint topic="topic1"           ❷ Subscribes
            connector-ref="topicConnection1"/>            to JMS topic
      </inbound>
      <outbound>
        <outbound-pass-through-router>
          <jms:outbound-endpoint queue="topic.out.queue1"
              connector-ref="jmsConnection" />
        </outbound-pass-through-router>
      </outbound>
    </service>
  </model>
</mule>
```

In listing 6.9, we define another attribute for the ActiveMQ connector, the durable attribute ❶. This attribute is only applicable to topic subscriber endpoints, such as the one in this example ❷. A durable topic subscriber can receive messages published to the topic even if the topic subscriber wasn't active at that moment. The JMS provider will hold the message until the topic subscriber becomes active again. Notice that we need to specify a unique `clientId` for every durable topic subscriber.

Because this ActiveMQ connector configuration is only valid for the topic subscriber (the inbound endpoint definition in this example), we need two ActiveMQ connector configurations. The topic subscriber uses the `connector-ref` attribute to point to the durable subscriber connector configuration, and the JMS outbound endpoint points to the `jmsConnection` connector configuration (listing 6.8).

We don't show the other two Mule topic subscriber services since they are the same, except for the name of the service and the name of the outbound JMS queue. If you run this example with the `chapter6-jms-example-2b` Ant target, you'll see that if you put a JMS message onto the `topic.in.queue` JMS queue with the Swing test client, this will result in three messages on different JMS queues. Mule's JMS transport has more options than we have shown thus far in the code listings. All these properties, together with the properties for the other connectors, can be found in appendix D.

Implementing the same JMS examples in ServiceMix is quite similar to the Mule examples, as you'll see in the next section.

6.2.2   *Connecting ServiceMix to JMS*

With ServiceMix we have the concept of a message sender (or a *provider* in JBI terms) and a message reader (also called *consumer* in the JBI specification). The message sender provides the functionality, as a proxy, for other components to send a message to the configured JMS destination. The message reader consumes a message from its configured JMS destination and passes it on to another JBI service endpoint.

If you want to run the examples of this section yourself, go to the resource/chapter6 directory in the ServiceMix workspace. You have to start ServiceMix from the ch6-build.xml Ant build file. When ServiceMix is running, use the JMS deploy targets to try out the examples.

For this example, we read an XML message from a JMS queue and forward this message to another JMS queue. The required JBI services and components appear in figure 6.4.

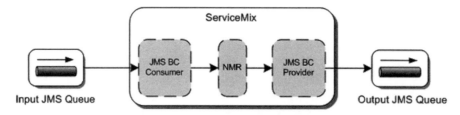

Figure 6.4   An example showing the ServiceMix JMS functionality for consuming messages from a JMS queue and producing messages for a JMS queue

Now let's look at the configuration of the JMS services shown in figure 6.4 (listing 6.10).

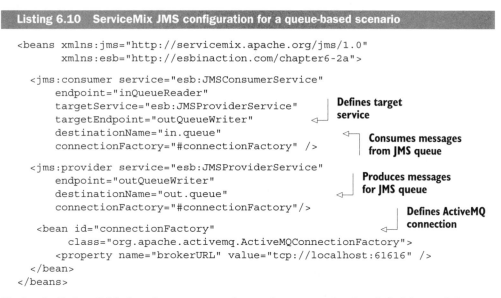

Listing 6.10   ServiceMix JMS configuration for a queue-based scenario

```
<beans xmlns:jms="http://servicemix.apache.org/jms/1.0"
       xmlns:esb="http://esbinaction.com/chapter6-2a">

  <jms:consumer service="esb:JMSConsumerService"
      endpoint="inQueueReader"
      targetService="esb:JMSProviderService"        Defines target
      targetEndpoint="outQueueWriter"               service
      destinationName="in.queue"
      connectionFactory="#connectionFactory" />      Consumes messages
                                                     from JMS queue

  <jms:provider service="esb:JMSProviderService"
      endpoint="outQueueWriter"                      Produces messages
      destinationName="out.queue"                    for JMS queue
      connectionFactory="#connectionFactory"/>

                                                     Defines ActiveMQ
  <bean id="connectionFactory"                       connection
      class="org.apache.activemq.ActiveMQConnectionFactory">
      <property name="brokerURL" value="tcp://localhost:61616" />
  </bean>
</beans>
```

Notice in listing 6.10 that the target service and target endpoint definitions of the JMS consumer point to the service and endpoint definition of the JMS provider. That's it—we've implemented the JMS queue example in ServiceMix by creating two JBI services: a JMS consumer and a JMS provider.

To test the example, first start the ServiceMix container with the `start` Ant target of the ch6-build.xml build file. Then deploy the JMS queue service assembly with the `deploy-2a-jms-queue-example` Ant target of the same Ant build file. Then you can use the Swing test client to send and receive messages with the JMS functionality of this example.

The previous example only showed how to use JMS queues in ServiceMix. In the next example, we show how to configure JMS topics in ServiceMix. We start with the definition of the JMS provider that writes to a topic (listing 6.11).

Listing 6.11   ServiceMix configuration showing how to write to a topic

```
<beans xmlns:jms="http://servicemix.apache.org/jms/1.0"
       xmlns:esb="http://esbinaction.com/chapter6-2b">

  <jms:consumer service="esb:JMSConsumerService"
      endpoint="inQueueReader"
      targetService="esb:JMSProviderService"
      targetEndpoint="topicWriter"                   Consumes messages
      destinationName="topic.in.queue"               from this queue
      connectionFactory="#connectionFactory"
      sessionAcknowledgeMode="1"                     Defines AUTO_
      jms102="true" />                               ACKNOWLEDGE mode
```

```
<jms:provider service="esb:JMSProviderService"
    endpoint="topicWriter"
    pubSubDomain="true"
    destinationName="topic1"
    connectionFactory="#connectionFactory"/>

<bean id="connectionFactory"
    class="org.apache.activemq.ActiveMQConnectionFactory">
    <property name="brokerURL" value="tcp://localhost:61616" />
</bean>
</beans>
```

Configures topic
subscriber

Defines topic
name

Note the use of the `pubSubDomain` attribute, which specifies that the JMS provider writes to a topic. The name of the topic is still configured with the `destination-Name` attribute.

We also configured some additional attributes for the JMS consumer. For example, we configured the acknowledgment mode for the JMS consumer with the `session-AcknowledgeMode` attribute. The default value is the `AUTO_ACKNOWLEDGE` mode, which has a value of 1, as we also configured in this example. But you can also configure the consumer to use the `DUPS_OK_ACKNOWLEDGE` mode (value of 3), which is an "at least once" delivery mode.

Listing 6.12 shows the configuration of the topic subscriber and one of the three JMS provider definitions.

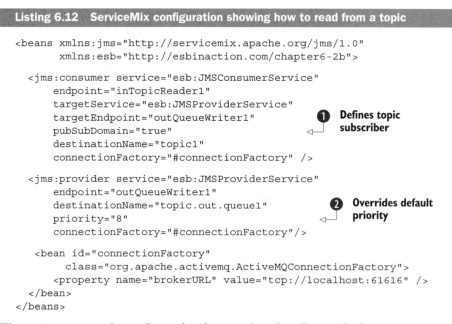

Listing 6.12   ServiceMix configuration showing how to read from a topic

```
<beans xmlns:jms="http://servicemix.apache.org/jms/1.0"
    xmlns:esb="http://esbinaction.com/chapter6-2b">

    <jms:consumer service="esb:JMSConsumerService"
        endpoint="inTopicReader1"
        targetService="esb:JMSProviderService"
        targetEndpoint="outQueueWriter1"
        pubSubDomain="true"
        destinationName="topic1"
        connectionFactory="#connectionFactory" />

    <jms:provider service="esb:JMSProviderService"
        endpoint="outQueueWriter1"
        destinationName="topic.out.queue1"
        priority="8"
        connectionFactory="#connectionFactory"/>

    <bean id="connectionFactory"
        class="org.apache.activemq.ActiveMQConnectionFactory">
        <property name="brokerURL" value="tcp://localhost:61616" />
    </bean>
</beans>
```

❶ Defines topic
subscriber

❷ Overrides default
priority

The JMS consumer is configured to be a topic subscriber with the same `pubSubDomain` attribute ❶ that we saw for the JMS provider in listing 6.11.

When this topic subscriber receives a message, it's forwarded to the JMS provider (also shown in listing 6.12). We configured a higher-priority value for the outgoing message using the `priority` attribute ❷. Note that a JMS provider isn't obliged to deal with higher-priority values in JMS messages.

We mentioned earlier that this example would include three JMS topic subscribers. But all three consumers have the same configuration as the JMS consumer defined here, except for the `endpoint` property value. Therefore, we show only one JMS consumer and provider definition here.

If you run this example with the ch6-build.xml Ant build file and the `deploy-2b-jms-topic-example` target, all three JMS queues will receive the message that was consumed by the topic subscriber in listing 6.11. Of course, you'll first have to send a message to the `topic.in.queue` (for example, with the Swing test client) to trigger the example.

And that's it. Just by adding the `pubSubDomain` property, we're now able to work with topics in ServiceMix.

So far we've explored file-based integration and message-based integration. In the next section, you'll learn how to connect to databases directly from an open source ESB, without having to write any JDBC code.

6.3 Connecting to a database using JDBC

Next, we show you how to use the open source ESBs to read from and write to a relational database. We introduce two types of examples, one that queries data from the database and another that manipulates data in the database. We use the HSQL database to implement the examples, because it requires no installation and yet still provides full relational capabilities. Before we delve deeper into these examples, let's take a quick look at the database table we use to query and store data:

```
Table name: person
id:         long primary key
name:       varchar[255]
processed:  boolean
```

The rows in the `person` table are identified by the `id` field. They contain a `name` column as well as a `processed` column (to indicate that the person has been processed). In the first example, shown in figure 6.5, we read the rows of the `person` table and send them to a file endpoint, where they'll be stored on the file system.

The second example, shown in figure 6.6, is the reverse functionality of the first. This time we read a file from the file system, process the contents from the file, and store the file contents as a new record in the database.

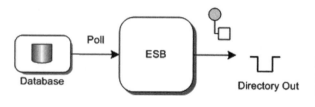
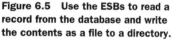

Figure 6.5 Use the ESBs to read a record from the database and write the contents as a file to a directory.

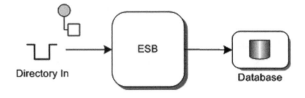

Figure 6.6   Use the ESBs to read a file from the file system and store its contents in the database.

Before we begin, we have to fill the HSQL database with some initial data. To do so, just run the `chapter6-jdbc-setup-database` Ant target from the ch6-build.xml Ant build file located in the resources/chapter6 directory. Note that you first have to start the HSQL database with the `ext:start-hsqldb` Ant target in the same Ant build file. Also note that this step is necessary for both the Mule as well as the Service-Mix examples.

6.3.1   *Connecting Mule to JDBC*

In this section, we implement the examples shown in figures 6.5 and 6.6 with Mule. For the first example we need to configure a JDBC connection to tell Mule how to connect to the HSQL database and which queries should be executed (listing 6.13).

Listing 6.13   Mule JDBC configuration for querying and updating a database table

```
<mule xmlns="http://www.mulesource.org/schema/mule/core/2.0"
  xmlns:spring="http://www.springframework.org/schema/beans"
  xmlns:jdbc="http://www.mulesource.org/schema/mule/jdbc/2.0">

  <spring:bean name="datasource"                              ◁─❶
      class="org.enhydra.jdbc.standard.StandardDataSource">
    <spring:property name="driverName"
        value="org.hsqldb.jdbcDriver" />
    <spring:property name="url"
        value="jdbc:hsqldb:hsql://localhost/xdb" />
    <spring:property name="user" value="sa" />
  </spring:bean>

  <jdbc:connector name="hsqldb-connector"
      dataSource-ref="datasource">
    <jdbc:query key="get"                                     ◁─❷
      value="SELECT * FROM person where processed=false" />
    <jdbc:query key="get.ack"                                 ◁─❸
        value="UPDATE person SET processed=true WHERE id=${jxpath:id}" />
  </jdbc:connector>
</mule>
```

In listing 6.13, we define a common JDBC data source ❶, which is used to connect to the HSQL database. We also define the JDBC queries that will be executed in order to read and update the `person` table in the HSQL database. The first query ❷ is used to get the data from the database; every row that is read is processed as a separate message. So if this query returns five rows, five different messages are sent to the Mule container.

The get.ack query ❸ is used to update the person table. Mule invokes the get.ack query automatically after the get query is executed. Mule tries to find a query with the same name as the get query, but now with ack appended. If Mule finds such a JDBC query definition, that JDBC query will be automatically executed. This functionality is useful for updating an indicator column, such as the processed column in this example.

The get query in listing 6.13 will first read all the rows that haven't been processed yet, as defined in the where clause: processed=false. For each row in the result message, the get.ack query is executed. One thing to notice about the get.ack query is the ${jxpath:id} placeholder. This expression uses JXPath to query the returned object from the database. So in this case, the id, retrieved from the returned rows of the get query, is used to specify which table row to update.

Now let's configure a Mule endpoint that uses this JDBC connector definition (listing 6.14).

Listing 6.14 Mule service showing how to query a database table

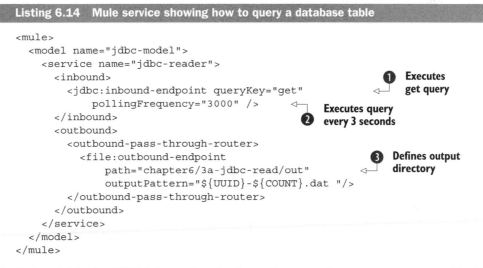

```
<mule>
  <model name="jdbc-model">
    <service name="jdbc-reader">
      <inbound>
        <jdbc:inbound-endpoint queryKey="get"
            pollingFrequency="3000" />
      </inbound>
      <outbound>
        <outbound-pass-through-router>
          <file:outbound-endpoint
              path="chapter6/3a-jdbc-read/out"
              outputPattern="${UUID}-${COUNT}.dat "/>
        </outbound-pass-through-router>
      </outbound>
    </service>
  </model>
</mule>
```

❶ Executes get query

❷ Executes query every 3 seconds

❸ Defines output directory

In listing 6.14, the JDBC inbound endpoint references the get query we specified in listing 6.13 ❶. This query is executed every 3 seconds ❷ by the Mule container. Every row retrieved with the get query is then sent to a file endpoint ❸, which stores the message in the file system. Note, though that the generated files contain serialized Java objects holding the result of the database query. You can run this example with the Ant target chapter6-jdbc-read-3a in the ch6-build.xml file.

In the second example, we show how to use Mule to write data to an HSQL database. Let's start with configuring the JDBC connector definition (listing 6.15).

Listing 6.15 Mule JDBC connector definition to insert data into a database

```
<mule>
  <file:connector name="fileConnector" streaming="false"/>

  <jdbc:connector name="hsqldb-connector"
      dataSource-ref="datasource">
```

```
      <jdbc:queries>
        <entry key="write"
          value="INSERT into person (id, name, processed)
              VALUES(NULL, ${payload}, false" />
      </jdbc:queries>
    </jdbc:connector>
  </mule>
```
❶

This configuration is quite similar to the JDBC connector definition in listing 6.13, except for the `write` query definition ❶. In the `write` query you see a placeholder: `${payload}`. This value will be replaced with the payload of the message. You can also use other placeholders that are retrieved from the payload. For instance, if your message is a simple JavaBean that has a `name` property, you can reference that property by using the `${name}` placeholder.

Next we have to configure the Mule service that uses this JDBC connector definition. Remember that we want to read from the file system and write that message to the database. Listing 6.16 shows the implementation of this Mule service.

Listing 6.16   Mule service showing how to write to a database

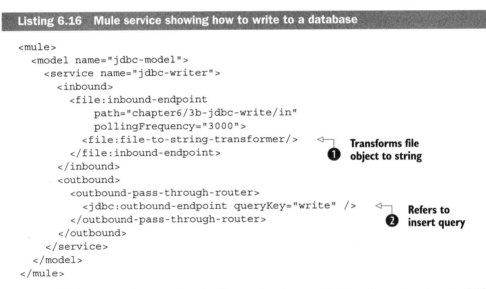

```
<mule>
  <model name="jdbc-model">
    <service name="jdbc-writer">
      <inbound>
        <file:inbound-endpoint
            path="chapter6/3b-jdbc-write/in"
            pollingFrequency="3000">
          <file:file-to-string-transformer/>        ◁───  Transforms file
        </file:inbound-endpoint>                      ❶   object to string
      </inbound>
      <outbound>
        <outbound-pass-through-router>
          <jdbc:outbound-endpoint queryKey="write" />  ◁─  Refers to
        </outbound-pass-through-router>                ❷   insert query
      </outbound>
    </service>
  </model>
</mule>
```

In listing 6.16, we configure a simple file reader that reads files from the chapter6/3b-jdbc-write/in directory. We also add a transformer, which is needed since the default format for the Mule file transport is a byte array. By using the `file-to-string` transformer ❷, we ensure that the file contents are transformed to a `String` object.

The outbound endpoint uses the `write` query we specified in listing 6.15 and replaces the `${payload}` placeholder with the content of the file ❸.

To run this example, execute the `chapter6-jdbc-write-3b` Ant target in the ch6-build.xml Ant build file. You can then test this example by dropping a text file with only a person name as content into the chapter6/3b-jdbc-write/in directory ❶. This file is read by Mule, transformed to a `String`, and passed on to the outbound endpoint, which uses the contents of this file to create and then execute the `insert` query. We configured the table with a unique primary key that will be generated, so the result is a new record inserted into the HSQL database, based on the contents of the input file.

We've now shown that you don't need to configure too much to get these examples running. You can now easily combine these two examples. If you run the JDBC write example first and then the JDBC read example, you can see that files dropped in the input directory of the JDBC write example will eventually be processed by the JDBC connector and stored in the output queue of the JDBC read example.

Now that you've seen them work successfully in Mule, let's implement the same examples in ServiceMix.

6.3.2 *Connecting ServiceMix to JDBC*

ServiceMix doesn't provide a binding component to connect to a database using JDBC. There are, however, other JBI-compliant ESBs available that do provide this functionality. For the implementation of the JDBC connectivity, we use the JDBC binding component provided by the Open JBI components project (https://open-jbi-components.dev.java. net). This project was started as a subproject of the Open ESB project (http://open-ESB.dev.java.net), which is the Sun open source implementation of the JBI standard (see chapter 1).

> **Interoperability between JBI ESBs**
>
> One of the goals of the JBI specification was to allow components from one ESB to run on another ESB. So in theory you could take any of the components from PEtALS or Open ESB, deploy them to ServiceMix, and instantly use the functionality provided by these components. However, in practice you're bound to run into issues. These issues usually are caused by different library versions on the classpath. For instance, the JDBC component in this section uses a patched version of the wsdl4j library. So when you initially deploy this binding component in ServiceMix, you'll get all kinds of strange errors. By replacing the wsdl4j supplied by ServiceMix with the version provided by the component, we easily solved this problem.

In the ServiceMix examples so far, you've seen how to configure binding components and service engines in the ServiceMix-specific way using xbean.xml configuration files. The JDBC binding component provided by Open ESB, however, requires your service units and the configuration to be in a different format.

Therefore, this section is a bit longer than other sections in this chapter, but it provides insight into deploying other JBI components to ServiceMix. We need to implement the following steps to get the JDBC functionality to work in ServiceMix:

1 *Register a data source in JNDI*—The JDBC component uses JNDI to retrieve its database connection, so we need to register a data source in JNDI for this.
2 *Create a database mapping*—The component also needs to know how its database columns are mapped to XML. In this step we configure this mapping.

3   *Configure the operations in a WSDL file*—The insert and polling operations are configured in a WSDL file. In this step we show you how to configure these operations.

4   *Create a jbi.xml file*—The jbi.xml file will tell ServiceMix how the operations can be accessed. In this step we show you how, for each operation, the jbi.xml file must be defined.

5   *Define file pollers and senders*—This is just a simple step where we connect the JDBC component to a file sender and a file poller so that we can test this component.

Let's start with the first step: defining the data source in JNDI.

REGISTER A DATA SOURCE IN JNDI

The JDBC binding component requires the JDBC data source to be defined in a JNDI provider. So before we can start configuring the JDBC component, we need to set up a data source in ServiceMix. Luckily for us, ServiceMix provides its own JNDI implementation, based on Spring. In the ServiceMix installation directory you'll find a conf directory containing a file named jndi.xml. In this file, add the code fragment in listing 6.17 as a child element of the `<util:map id="jndiEntries">` tag.

Listing 6.17   Adding a JDBC datasource to the JNDI registry

```
<entry key="java:comp/env/jdbc/defaultDS">
  <bean class="org.hsqldb.jdbc.jdbcDataSource">
    <property name="database"
        value="jdbc:hsqldb:hsql://localhost/xdb" />
    <property name="user" value="sa" />
    <property name="password" value=""/>
  </bean>
</entry>
```

Here, we register the data source for our database in the JNDI provider of ServiceMix. To be able to query the HSQL database we use in this example, we need to make the hsqldb.jar file available in the lib directory of the ServiceMix installation. This is already done by the Ant build script for the environment setup, which we showed in chapter 3. You can then start the database from the ch6-build.xml Ant build file with the `ext:start-hsqldb` target and create the database. Do this by running the `chapter6-jdbc-setup-database` target from the same Ant build file.

CREATE A DATABASE MAPPING

To illustrate how to configure this JDBC binding component, we create an example where the input of a file will be stored in a database and another example where database information is sent to the file system. The configuration for these examples consists of three files: a database mapping file, a WSDL, and a jbi.xml file. We begin with the database mapping file (listing 6.18).

Listing 6.18   Database mapping that maps the columns to an XML Schema

```
<?xml version="1.0" encoding="UTF-8"?>
<xsd:schema elementFormDefault="qualified"
    targetNamespace="http://j2ee.netbeans.org/xsd/tableSchema"
```

```
   xmlns="http://j2ee.netbeans.org/xsd/tableSchema"
   xmlns:xsd="http://www.w3.org/2001/XMLSchema">
<xsd:element name="PERSON" type="PERSON"/>
<xsd:complexType name="PERSON">
  <xsd:sequence maxOccurs="unbounded">
    <xsd:element name="ID" type="xsd:string"/>
    <xsd:element name="NAME" type="xsd:string"/>
    <xsd:element name="PROCESSED" type="xsd:boolean"/>
  </xsd:sequence>
</xsd:complexType>
</xsd:schema>
```

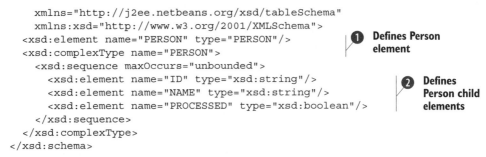

1 Defines Person element

2 Defines Person child elements

The person and child elements **1**, **2** we defined in listing 6.18 have the same names as the columns of the person table we defined at the beginning of this section. The data types of the columns are mapped to an XML Schema type equivalent. This schema will be used in the WSDL file to define the input format for the service implementation. So with the database mapping file, we ensure that the fields of the message sent to our service contain the correct information and have the correct format. To learn more about this database mapping, check out the Open ESB website (http://open-ESB.dev.java.net).

CONFIGURE THE OPERATIONS IN THE WSDL FILE

Now that we've defined the XML definition for the data source and the person table mapping, let's look at the WSDL that defines how and which queries are executed. Before we examine the code of this WSDL itself, let's look at the different elements of the WSDL file for database functionality (figure 6.7).

As you can see in figure 6.7, the WSDL file has five parts. In the first part, we import the file from listing 6.18. This database-mapping file defines how the input XML should look when we want to store data using this JDBC component in the database. The second part defines the operation arguments and the operations' results. In the

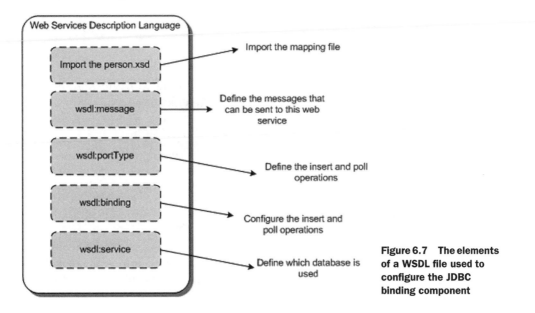

Figure 6.7   The elements of a WSDL file used to configure the JDBC binding component

next part of the WSDL, the interface, also called the portType, of the service is defined. Here we configure the names of the operations as well as the messages they take as parameters and return values.

Now that we've defined the service interface, which is also called the *abstract* part of the WSDL, we'll define the service implementation, or *binding*, of the interfaces we defined in the portType section. In this example, we create a binding to SQL, but usually you see bindings to SOAP over HTTP here. In the last part of the WSDL, we have to configure the service section. In this example, we define which data source will be used to execute the queries in the service section, but a more common usage of the service part of a WSDL is the definition of the web service location.

Let's look at the full implementation of the WSDL file for the JDBC component. Because the WSDL file is quite large, we split this up into five sections, as shown in figure 6.7. Listing 6.19 shows the first section of the WSDL file, where we import the XML Schema definition in listing 6.18.

Listing 6.19   WSDL configuration for JDBC component: import section

```
<?xml version="1.0" encoding="UTF-8"?>
<definitions name="jdbc-example"
  xmlns="http://schemas.xmlsoap.org/wsdl/"
  xmlns:xsd="http://www.w3.org/2001/XMLSchema"
  xmlns:wsdl="http://schemas.xmlsoap.org/wsdl/"
  xmlns:jdbc="http://schemas.sun.com/jbi/wsdl-extensions/jdbc/"
  xmlns:ns="http://j2ee.netbeans.org/xsd/tableSchema"
  xmlns:tns="http://opensourceesb/chapter6/"
  targetNamespace="http://opensourceesb/chapter6/">

  <types>                                           Imports database  ❶
    <xsd:schema>                                    mapping definition
      <xsd:import
        namespace="http://j2ee.netbeans.org/xsd/tableSchema"
        schemaLocation="PERSON.xsd" />
    </xsd:schema>
  </types>
```

We import the previously defined database mapping with the XML Schema import element ❶. The person element defined in the PERSON.xsd file is used in listing 6.20 to define the WSDL messages.

Listing 6.20   WSDL configuration for JDBC component: message section

```
<message name="inputMsg">
  <part name="part" element="ns:PERSON" />    ◁—❶
</message>
<message name="insertRetMsg">
  <part name="part" type="xsd:int" />          ◁—❷
</message>
```

The WSDL message section specifies the input and output messages for the operation part of the WSDL definition. The messages defined in this listing ❶, ❷ are used in listing 6.21 to define the operations for the JDBC service.

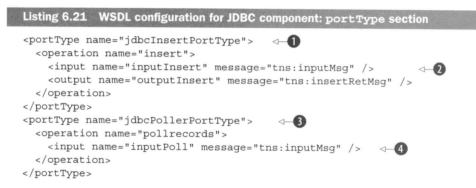

Listing 6.21 WSDL configuration for JDBC component: `portType` section

```
<portType name="jdbcInsertPortType">     ←❶
  <operation name="insert">
    <input name="inputInsert" message="tns:inputMsg" />      ←❷
    <output name="outputInsert" message="tns:insertRetMsg" />
  </operation>
</portType>
<portType name="jdbcPollerPortType">     ←❸
  <operation name="pollrecords">
    <input name="inputPoll" message="tns:inputMsg" />    ←❹
  </operation>
</portType>
```

We defined two interfaces, each with one operation. In the poller operation definition ❸, you might expect an output element instead of the input element `inputPoll` ❹, because when you poll a database you get a result. That's true, but keep in mind that the poller is a service that sends messages to the normalized message router. It reads data from a database and sends that data to a JBI service running in ServiceMix. The operation shown here specifies how the receiving service looks. So a receiving service must be able to handle the operation specified here.

For the insert operation ❶, it's the exact opposite. The insert operation can be directly invoked by other JBI services within ServiceMix. It receives an input message, `inputInsert` ❷, and sends a response back. This difference between a service provider (the insert operation) and a service consumer (the poll operation) is also the reason we created two different `portTypes`.

Let's look at how the WSDL operations are bound to the JDBC implementation (listing 6.22).

Service provider and service consumer

As you've seen so far, ServiceMix hides a lot of the inner details of JBI. JBI components from other JBI containers, however, don't necessarily do that, as you can see from this JDBC configuration and later in this chapter in the mail configuration. When you're working with components from other ESBs, and specifically when working with binding components, it's a good idea to have a clear understanding of service providers and service consumers. A binding component basically provides a service to other JBI services by serving as a proxy to a specific technology.

For our JDBC example, for instance, the JDBC binding component provides a service to the other JBI services that can insert a record in the database. Besides providing a service, a binding component can also allow a non-JBI component to call JBI services. In this case, the binding component serves more as a façade. If we look at this from the context of our JDBC example, we have a database, the non-JBI component, which wants to send a message to a specific JBI service. So every time a new record is found, a JBI service will be consumed.

Listing 6.22   WSDL configuration for JDBC component: `binding` section

```
<binding name="insertBinding"
      type="tns:jdbcInsertPortType">                    Defines JDBC
  <jdbc:binding />                              ❶      write interface
  <operation name="insert">
    <jdbc:operation/>
    <input name="inputInsert">
      <jdbc:input PKName="ID" TableName="PERSON"          Configures insert
        Transaction="NOTransaction"              ❷      query attributes
        operationType="insert"
        paramOrder="NAME"
        sql="INSERT into PERSON (id, name, processed)
            VALUES (NULL, ?,FALSE)" />
    </input>
    <output name="outputInsert">
      <jdbc:output returnPartName="part" />
    </output>
  </operation>
</binding>

<binding name="pollerBinding"                    ❸    Defines JDBC polling
      type="tns:jdbcPollerPortType">                    interface
  <jdbc:binding />
  <operation name="pollrecords">
    <jdbc:operation />
    <input name="inputPoll">
      <jdbc:input PKName="ID"
        PollMilliSeconds="5000"
        PollingPostProcessing="MarkColumn"              Updates
        MarkColumnName="PROCESSED"               ❹      PROCESSED
        MarkColumnValue="1"                             column
        TableName="PERSON"
        numberOfRecords="1"
        operationType="poll"
        Transaction="NOTransaction"
        sql="SELECT * FROM person where processed=false" />
    </input>
  </operation>
</binding>
```

The `binding` section starts with the definition of the insert binding ❶. When this binding is invoked by the ServiceMix container, the SQL insert query ❷ is executed. As you can see, this query is a common JDBC `PreparedStatement`. The ? in this statement will be replaced by the supplied parameters, based on the `paramOrder` attribute. In other words, the `NAME` element of the input message will be used as an input parameter for the prepared statement.

The second binding that's defined is the poller operation ❸. The poller operation will poll the database at an interval specified with the `PollMilliSeconds` attribute to determine if new records are inserted. If there are any new records, they will be processed and sent to a JBI service, which implements the `tns:jdbcPollerPortType` interface.

In this example, we defined a poller operation, which executes the query specified with the sql attribute every 5 seconds. We also specified what to do after we've processed a row. We configured a MarkColumn postprocessing operation ❹. This means that when we've read a row from the person table, we can update a specific column to a certain value. In this case, we set the PROCESSED column to a value of 1. This sets the PROCESSED column to true so it won't be processed the next time. The polling query defined with the sql attribute is simple; it just reads all the unprocessed rows.

Listing 6.23 defines the final part of the WSDL file.

Listing 6.23 WSDL configuration for JDBC component: `service` section

```
<service name="jdbc-service">
  <port name="insertPort" binding="tns:insertBinding">          ◄─❶
    <jdbc:address jndiName="java:comp/env/jdbc/defaultDS" />
  </port>
  <port name="pollerPort" binding="tns:pollerBinding">          ◄─❷
    <jdbc:address jndiName="java:comp/env/jdbc/defaultDS" />
  </port>
</service>
```

The service section of the WSDL file relates the two bindings of listing 6.22 with the JDBC JNDI configuration we implemented in listing 6.17. In this example, both port definitions ❶, ❷ work on the same data source. What's also important in listing 6.23 is the port name. If we want to reference the services defined here from other JBI services, we should use this port name as the endpoint name, since multiple ports can be defined on a service.

CREATE A JBI.XML FILE

We're ready to start with the last piece of the JDBC configuration: the jbi.xml file. This file maps the service definitions from the WSDL file to JBI services, which are available in the JBI container. Listing 6.24 shows the configuration of the jbi.xml file for our JDBC example.

Listing 6.24 JBI services configuration for the services described in the WSDL

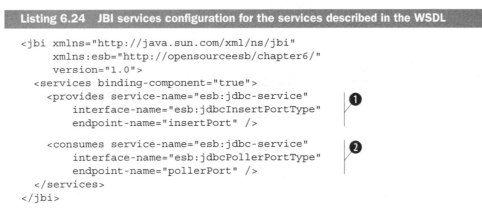

```
<jbi xmlns="http://java.sun.com/xml/ns/jbi"
     xmlns:esb="http://opensourceesb/chapter6/"
     version="1.0">
  <services binding-component="true">
    <provides service-name="esb:jdbc-service"                    ❶
        interface-name="esb:jdbcInsertPortType"
        endpoint-name="insertPort" />

    <consumes service-name="esb:jdbc-service"                    ❷
        interface-name="esb:jdbcPollerPortType"
        endpoint-name="pollerPort" />
  </services>
</jbi>
```

In listing 6.24, you can see that the portType and the port name that we defined in listing 6.23 are referenced here. We defined one provides element and one consumes element. The `provides` element ❶ defines a service that can be used by other JBI services. In this example, it points to the service and port we defined in the WSDL for the insert operation. So if a JBI service wants to add a record to the `person` table in the HSQL database, this can be done by sending a message to the service endpoint specified with the `provides` element.

The other element is the `consumes` element ❷. As the name implies, this polling service can't be used from other JBI services; this is a service that consumes another service. This means that the poller will invoke the JBI service specified here. So every 5 seconds, assuming new database rows are present, this JDBC component will send a message to the JBI service endpoint specified here (which is a file sender JBI service we explain in the next section).

DEFINE FILE POLLERS AND SENDERS

Now that we've completed the JDBC configuration, let's summarize the whole example again. We'll begin with the first part, where we read from the file system and write to the database. To implement this functionality, we have to configure a JBI service that reads files from a directory and invokes the JDBC insert service we configured in listing 6.24. The file poller and file sender are shown in listing 6.25.

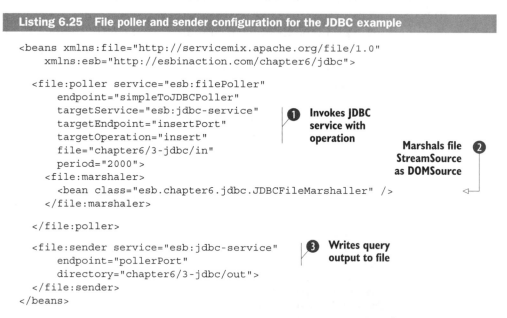

Listing 6.25   File poller and sender configuration for the JDBC example

```
<beans xmlns:file="http://servicemix.apache.org/file/1.0"
    xmlns:esb="http://esbinaction.com/chapter6/jdbc">

  <file:poller service="esb:filePoller"
      endpoint="simpleToJDBCPoller"
      targetService="esb:jdbc-service"          ❶ Invokes JDBC
      targetEndpoint="insertPort"                  service with
      targetOperation="insert"                     operation
      file="chapter6/3-jdbc/in"                               Marshals file ❷
      period="2000">                                          StreamSource
    <file:marshaler>                                          as DOMSource
      <bean class="esb.chapter6.jdbc.JDBCFileMarshaller" />
    </file:marshaler>

  </file:poller>

  <file:sender service="esb:jdbc-service"      ❸ Writes query
      endpoint="pollerPort"                       output to file
      directory="chapter6/3-jdbc/out">
  </file:sender>
</beans>
```

As you can see in listing 6.25, we reference the JDBC insert service ❶ provided by the JDBC binding component. The JDBC binding component also expects a method name to be specified, so we provide this with the `targetOperation` attribute. When a file is dropped in the chapter6/3-jdbc/in directory, the insert method, as specified in the WSDL file we discussed earlier, is invoked and the content of the input file is used as the argument.

We had to define an additional `marshaler` element ❷ in the file binding component configuration to get the example to work. By default, ServiceMix uses a `Stream-Source` instance as a container for the file message content that is consumed by the file poller. A `StreamSource` can only be processed once, and the Open ESB JDBC component processes the message payload more than once. Therefore, we created a custom marshaller, the `JDBCFileMarshaler` which transforms the `StreamSource` to a `DOMSource`, which can be processed more than once.

Notice that for the file sender definition, the service and endpoint name ❸ match the ones we specified in the jbi.xml file in listing 6.23. When the JDBC poller finds a new record to process, the resulting message is passed on to this file sender service, which writes the polled message to the file system.

To summarize, in order to work with the JDBC binding component provided by the Open JBI Components project, you first need to configure a database-mapping file that matches the JBI message to the database table. Then you need to create a WSDL file where you define the operations and how they map to JDBC queries. And finally, you tie everything together with the jbi.xml file and the file xbean.xml definitions.

Now let's deploy and test the example in your local environment. To get this example to run we have to walk through some additional steps. Make sure that the Service-Mix container isn't running and execute the following steps:

1 Copy the preparedResources/wsdl4j-sun.jar to the lib folder in your Service-Mix distribution.
2 Remove the wsdl4j-1.6.1.jar from the lib folder in the ServiceMix distribution.
3 Start ServiceMix with the `start` target in the ch6-build.xml Ant build file.
4 Copy the file boxResources/jdbcbc.jar to the ServiceMix hotdeploy directory to install the Open ESB JDBC component in ServiceMix.
5 Start the HSQL database with the `ext:start-hsqldb` target in the ch6-build.xml Ant build file.
6 Execute the `chapter6-jdbc-setup-database` target in the ch6-build.xml Ant build file to insert some test persons into the database.
7 Deploy the JDBC service assembly with the `deploy-3-jdbc-example` target in the ch6-build.xml Ant build file.

After executing these steps, you'll see messages arriving in the chapter6/3-jdbc/out directory in your ServiceMix installation directory. These messages include the persons we inserted with the database script in step 6. The person.xml file in the resources/chapter6/3-jdbc/jdbc/resources directory can be copied to the chapter6/3-jdbc/in directory to trigger the JDBC example to write a record to the `person` table.

This JDBC ServiceMix section has been a long one. Normally when you work with components from the Open ESB environment, you'll use the NetBeans IDE. NetBeans provides easy code completion and great visual wizards for these JBI components so configuration will be easier. This has been the most complex type of configuration for this chapter, and one of the most difficult ones in this book. Rest assured that the next sections will be much easier. Now let's see how to connect to mail servers to read and send mail.

6.4   *Connecting to mail servers*

Mail is a common way to integrate applications and to inform users and application maintainers of certain events. In this section we explain how to integrate Mule and ServiceMix with a mail server. We show how to use the SMTP and POP3 protocols from these two open source ESBs to communicate with a mail server. For the mail server we use Apache James, an open source mail server that supports all mail-related protocols. You could also use your own mail server for the examples in this section, but beware that mail which is read will be deleted by using the configuration shown here.

We once again focus on the connectivity functionality and only show you a couple of basic examples. The first one, as shown in figure 6.8, demonstrates how to send an email message to a mail server from Mule and ServiceMix.

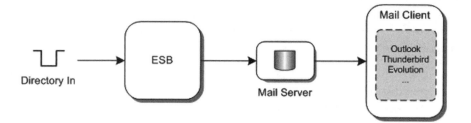

Figure 6.8   We read a file from the file system with the ESB and forward the message to a mail server using SMTP connectivity.

The other example we implement with Mule and ServiceMix shows how to receive email messages from a mail server, as shown in figure 6.9.

To implement examples as shown in figures 6.8 and 6.9, we use file connectivity to trigger or process the result of the Mail connectivity, because this is easy to test.

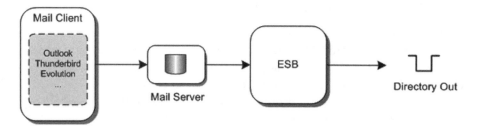

Figure 6.9   We receive an email from a mail server using the ESB with POP3 connectivity and send the email message to the file system.

The figures also show the use of a mail client; you can use your favorite mail client to work with these examples. Let's first look at configuring SMTP connectivity in Mule.

6.4.1 Connecting Mule to POP3 and SMTP

Our first task is to set up Mule so that we can send an email to a specific address from a Mule configuration. As we mentioned earlier, we read a file from the file system and send the file contents as the body of an email to a configured email address. The Mule configuration shown in listing 6.26 defines this SMTP connectivity.

Listing 6.26 Mule services configuration that sends mail using SMTP

```
<mule xmlns="http://www.mulesource.org/schema/mule/core/2.0"
    xmlns:file="http://www.mulesource.org/schema/mule/file/2.0"
    xmlns:smtp="http://www.mulesource.org/schema/mule/smtp/2.0">

  <file:connector name="fileConnector" streaming="false" />

  <model name="mail-model">
    <service name="file-to-mail">
      <inbound>
        <file:inbound-endpoint                      ❶ Specifies file input
            path="chapter6/4a-mail-smtp/in">           directory
          <file:file-to-string-transformer />
        </file:inbound-endpoint>
      </inbound>
      <outbound>
        <outbound-pass-through-router>
          <smtp:outbound-endpoint                   ❷ Defines SMTP
            to="mule@localhost"                        outbound endpoint
            cc="authors@localhost"
            from="authors@localhost"
            replyTo="authors@localhost"
            subject="You've got mail from Mule!"
            host="localhost"                        ❸ Configures SMTP
            port="25"                                  connection
            user="mule"                                properties
            password="mule" />
        </outbound-pass-through-router>
      </outbound>
    </service>
  </model>
</mule>
```

We only need to tell Mule how to connect to the SMTP server ❸ as part of an SMTP outbound endpoint definition ❷. In this case we connect to a local mail server (Apache James) using mule for the username and password.

Before you can start Mule with this configuration, start Apache James with the ext:start-james Ant target in the ch6-build.xml file. Now we need to add two email accounts to the Apache James server with these steps:

1 Open a telnet session with the following command: `telnet localhost 4555`.
2 In the James telnet session, log in with the username `root` and the password `root`.
3 Add a user mule by entering `adduser mule mule`.
4 Add a user authors by entering `adduser authors authors`.
5 Now exit using the `quit` command.

You can then run this example with the `chapter6-mail-smtp-4a` Ant target in the same Ant build file. To trigger the SMTP service definition in listing 6.26, you need to drop a file (such as the provided mail.txt file) into the chapter6/4a-mail-smtp/in directory ❶. Mule will send the file contents to the configured endpoint, with the file contents as the body of the email message. You can then use any mail client (for example, Mozilla Thunderbird) to receive the message, as shown in figure 6.10. Notice that you'll first have to configure the mule and authors email accounts in the mail client. You can use `localhost` as the POP and SMTP server and mule@localhost and authors @localhost as email addresses.

You know how to configure Mule to send emails, so now let's look at the next task: receiving email messages. To work with this example, we use a mail client to send a message, and then use the Mule POP3 transport to read the message from the mail server. We start again by looking at the Mule configuration (listing 6.27).

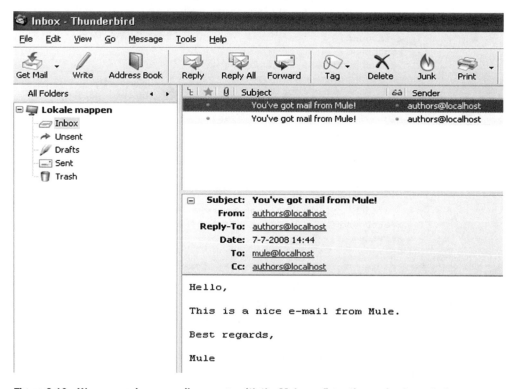

Figure 6.10   We can receive an email message with the Mule configuration we implemented.

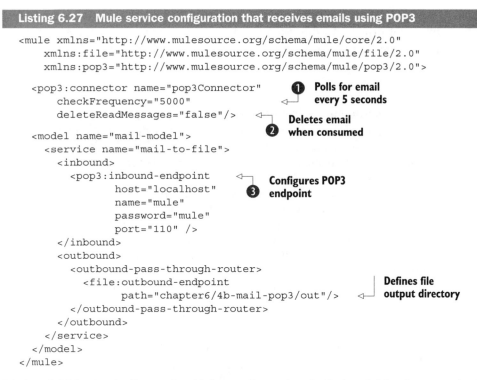

Listing 6.27 Mule service configuration that receives emails using POP3

```
<mule xmlns="http://www.mulesource.org/schema/mule/core/2.0"
    xmlns:file="http://www.mulesource.org/schema/mule/file/2.0"
    xmlns:pop3="http://www.mulesource.org/schema/mule/pop3/2.0">

  <pop3:connector name="pop3Connector"        ① Polls for email
      checkFrequency="5000"                       every 5 seconds
      deleteReadMessages="false"/>            ⎯ Deletes email
  <model name="mail-model">                   ② when consumed
    <service name="mail-to-file">
      <inbound>
        <pop3:inbound-endpoint               ⎯ Configures POP3
              host="localhost"               ③ endpoint
              name="mule"
              password="mule"
              port="110" />
      </inbound>
      <outbound>
        <outbound-pass-through-router>
          <file:outbound-endpoint                  Defines file
                path="chapter6/4b-mail-pop3/out"/> ⎯ output directory
        </outbound-pass-through-router>
      </outbound>
    </service>
  </model>
</mule>
```

Listing 6.27 looks similar to the Mule configuration in listing 6.26, where we showed you how to send email messages. We configured where the POP3 server is located and which username and password should be used to make the connection ③. We also specified some additional properties on the pop3:connector. In this case, we tell Mule to not delete messages it has received ②, and to check every 5 seconds for new email messages ①.

To test this code, use a simple mail client—just send a message to mule@localhost and you'll see that Mule will pick it up and process it. Make sure that you sent a plain text email message, as HTML-formatted messages can't be consumed by Mule's POP3 connector.

In addition to POP3 and SMTP, Mule supports the secure variants, POP3S and SMTPS, as well as IMAP. You use these secure transports in the same way, but you have to supply some additional security properties (such as certificates).

6.4.2 *Connecting ServiceMix to POP3 and SMTP*

To implement Mail connectivity with ServiceMix, we need a binding component to receive email messages using POP3 and a binding component that's able to send email messages using SMTP. A Mail binding component is available for ServiceMix, but only for version 3.3 and greater. We use a Mail JBI component provided by another JBI implementation.

In the JDBC example, we demonstrated how to use a JBI component from the Open ESB project. In this example, we use a JBI component provided by the PEtALS project (see chapter 1). When you created the environment in chapter 3 we provided this binding component, so no extra installations or downloads are needed.

> ## PEtALS components in ServiceMix
>
> The PEtALS components don't work out of the box in the ServiceMix container. We mentioned earlier that usually this is caused by incompatible JAR files or other library and classloading issues. In this case, however, the problems are simply caused by a bug in ServiceMix. If you look at the jbi.xml file from the JDBC example, you can see that we specify `consumes` and `provides` elements. These two elements are described in the JBI specification but don't allow service-specific configuration. ServiceMix uses Apache XBean for this configuration, and the Open ESB project configures services using a WSDL file. However, PEtALS uses the standard extension mechanism, which is described in the JBI specification. This allows additional configuration elements to be present in the jbi.xml file. In ServiceMix, however, only the first of these extension elements is processed. We provide you with a patched version to solve this issue.

We want to read a file from the file system and use ServiceMix to send an email message using the file contents to a certain email address. The first thing we've done is configure a simple file poller. This configuration is shown in listing 6.28.

Listing 6.28   File poller configuration that sends the message to the mail service

```
<beans xmlns:file="http://servicemix.apache.org/file/1.0"
    xmlns:esb="http://esbinaction.com/mail">

  <file:poller service="esb:filePoller"
      endpoint="simpleToMailPoller"
      targetService="esb:mail-service"
      targetEndpoint="mailEndpoint"        ❶
      file="chapter6/4a-mail/in"      ←—❷
      period="2000">
  </file:poller>
</beans>
```

In the file poller implementation, we just read a file from the file system ❷ and send the received file to the mail service endpoint ❶. Now let's focus on the mail service implementation.

We explained in previous sections that configuring service units in ServiceMix is done in the form of xbean.xml files. When you're working with PEtALS, you don't configure the service unit in an xbean.xml file—you use a jbi.xml file instead. Listing 6.29 shows the configuration of a PEtALS service unit that sends a message to an email address.

Listing 6.29   Configuration for sending emails using the PEtALS Mail binding component

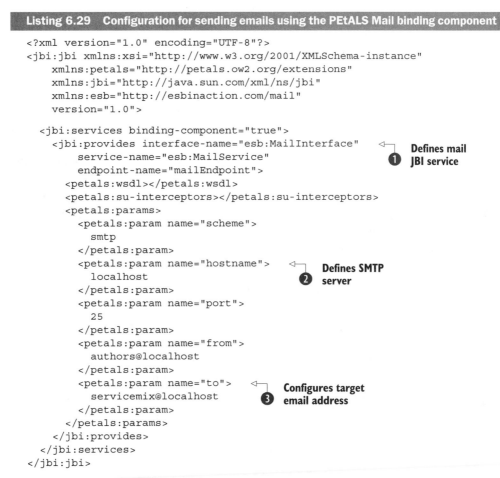

```xml
<?xml version="1.0" encoding="UTF-8"?>
<jbi:jbi xmlns:xsi="http://www.w3.org/2001/XMLSchema-instance"
    xmlns:petals="http://petals.ow2.org/extensions"
    xmlns:jbi="http://java.sun.com/xml/ns/jbi"
    xmlns:esb="http://esbinaction.com/mail"
    version="1.0">

  <jbi:services binding-component="true">
    <jbi:provides interface-name="esb:MailInterface"
        service-name="esb:MailService"
        endpoint-name="mailEndpoint">
      <petals:wsdl></petals:wsdl>
      <petals:su-interceptors></petals:su-interceptors>
      <petals:params>
        <petals:param name="scheme">
          smtp
        </petals:param>
        <petals:param name="hostname">
          localhost
        </petals:param>
        <petals:param name="port">
          25
        </petals:param>
        <petals:param name="from">
          authors@localhost
        </petals:param>
        <petals:param name="to">
          servicemix@localhost
        </petals:param>
      </petals:params>
    </jbi:provides>
  </jbi:services>
</jbi:jbi>
```

① Defines mail JBI service

② Defines SMTP server

③ Configures target email address

Adding the PEtALS Mail binding component for Mail support to ServiceMix is easy—all you have to do is configure the location of the mail server ②. Notice that we didn't set the subject. This is a limitation of the PEtALS Mail component: the subject of the email message sent is always set to the name of the service. So in this example where an email message is sent, the subject will be `mail-service`. Work is currently being done on this component to make the subject name configurable.

One more thing to notice about this configuration is the `provides` element ①. In chapter 2 we talk about consumers and providers. This example implements a provider, which can be accessed from other JBI services by sending a JBI message to this service endpoint.

To run this example, you first need to add an additional email account in Apache James and install the PEtALS Mail JBI component in ServiceMix. Execute these steps before you run the mail example:

1 Start Apache James with the `ext:start-james` target in the ch6-build.xml Ant build file.

2 Connect to Apache James with telnet in a command colsole: `telnet local-host 4555`.

3 Log into Apache James with the username `root` and the password `root`.

4 Add the user servicemix with the following command: `adduser servicemix servicemix`.

5 Exit the telnet session with the `quit` command.

6 Run the Ant target `gn:patchSMCore` in the ch6-build.xml Ant build file, which fixes a JBI deployment descriptor bug in ServiceMix.

7 Start the ServiceMix container with the `start` target in the ch6-build.xml Ant build file.

8 Copy the PEtALS JDBC component boxResources/petals-bc-mail-3.0-beta1.zip to the hotdeploy folder of the ServiceMix distribution; the JDBC component will be installed.

9 Run the Ant target `deploy-4a-mail-sender-example` in the ch6-build.xml Ant build file to deploy the mail sender service assembly.

Now you can drop a file (such as the provided test-mail.xml) into the chapter6/4a-mail/in directory specified in listing 6.27. ServiceMix will pick up this message and send it to the PEtALS Mail component. This component in turn will send an email message to the configured email address, `servicemix@localhost` ❸.

To receive email messages, you need to configure another jbi.xml file for the same PEtALS Mail binding component, only this time you'll consume a service endpoint provided by the ServiceMix file binding component. Let's first look at the service endpoint, which is provided by the servicemix-file component in the following code snippet:

```
<file:sender service="esb:mailFileWriter"
  endpoint="mailFileWriterEndpoint"
  directory="chapter6/4b-mail/out">
</file:sender>
```

This file binding component configuration provides a JBI service with the name `esb:mailFileWriter` and has an endpoint with the name `mailFileWriterEndpoint`. We use this service endpoint in our PEtALS Mail configuration (see listing 6.30).

Listing 6.30   PEtALS configuration for the Mail component to receive emails

```
<?xml version="1.0" encoding="UTF-8"?>
<jbi:jbi xmlns:xsi="http://www.w3.org/2001/XMLSchema-instance"
  xmlns:petals="http://petals.ow2.org/extensions"
  xmlns:jbi="http://java.sun.com/xml/ns/jbi"
  xmlns:esb="http://opensourceesb/mail/" version="1.0">

  <jbi:services binding-component="true">
    <jbi:consumes
      interface-name="esb:mailFileWriterInterface"           ◁⟶❶ Defines JBI
      service-name="esb:mailFileWriter"                           service
      endpoint-name="mailFileWriterEndpoint">
      <petals:mep>InOnly</petals:mep>
      <petals:operation>sendMessage</petals:operation>
```

```
      <petals:params>
        <petals:param name="period">10000</petals:param>
        <petals:param name="scheme">pop3</petals:param>
        <petals:param name="hostname">
          localhost
        </petals:param>
        <petals:param name="port">110</petals:param>
        <petals:param name="username">
          servicemix
        </petals:param>
        <petals:param name="password">
          servicemix
        </petals:param>
      </petals:params>
    </jbi:consumes>
  </jbi:services>
</jbi:jbi>
```

❷ Configures mail server hostname

❸ Provides username for authentication

The main difference compared to listing 6.29 is that here we specify a scheme of POP3 instead of SMTP. This will tell the PEtALS Mail component to start polling for mail messages. Whenever a message is received, it will be sent to the service endpoint configured in the `consumes` element ❶. In this example we specify the service and endpoint names for the File sender JBI service. So whenever a message is received, it will be passed on to the File sender JBI service, which writes it to the file system.

To deploy the mail receiver service assembly to the ServiceMix container, you can execute the `deploy-4b-mail-receiver-example` target provided in the ch6-build.xml Ant build file. Then you can send an email message with XML elements (for example, `<hello>world</hello>`) to the email address `servicemix@localhost` with the mail client of your choice. In the chapter6/mail-4b/out directory in the ServiceMix distribution, you should see files appearing with the content of the email message you sent. Notice that the files keep coming as the email message is not deleted on the email server.

Besides PEtALS, Open ESB also provides a Mail component. The Open ESB Mail component offers a lot of configuration options and has many features, but is somewhat harder to use since it requires the WSDL-based configuration we saw in the JDBC example in section 6.3. If you just want an easy way to connect to mail servers, the PEtALS component is probably the best solution; if you need more advanced features and don't mind the WSDL-based configuration, the Open ESB component would be a better choice. Of course, when ServiceMix version 3.3 is released, a Mail binding component will be available out of the box.

Now that we've seen how to connect to SMTP and POP3, let's look at another connectivity option that is still used often in enterprises: FTP.

6.5   *FTP connectivity*

FTP is one of the older transport protocols. It started back in 1971 and evolved in 1985 into the version that's currently used. Especially when communicating with mainframe systems or old UNIX environments, FTP is still used often. Just as with mail connectivity, FTP has its security-enhanced variants: SFTP and FTPS. Those variants aren't widely used, so we just focus on the basic FTP connectivity in this section.

We again show you a simple example, where we read a file from a directory and store it on an FTP server, as shown in figure 6.11.

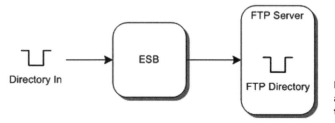

Figure 6.11   **We read a file from a local directory and send the file to an FTP server.**

And just as we did with the other connectivity examples, we also show the way back, where we read from an FTP server and write the contents to a local file (figure 6.12).

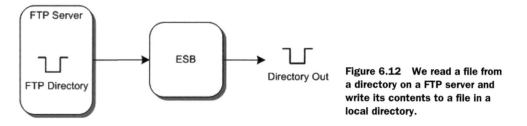

Figure 6.12   **We read a file from a directory on a FTP server and write its contents to a file in a local directory.**

As you'll see in the Mule and ServiceMix examples, the FTP connectivity looks a lot like the file connectivity. We begin by showing how Mule implements these examples.

6.5.1   *FTP and Mule*

Using FTP connectivity with Mule is pretty much the same as using basic file connectivity. We start with the example where we read a file from the file system and write its contents to a FTP server (listing 6.31).

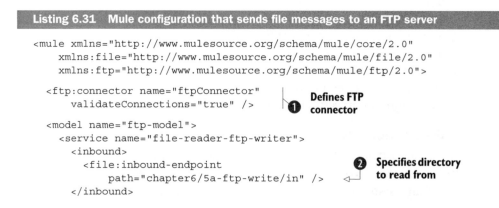

Listing 6.31   Mule configuration that sends file messages to an FTP server

```
<mule xmlns="http://www.mulesource.org/schema/mule/core/2.0"
    xmlns:file="http://www.mulesource.org/schema/mule/file/2.0"
    xmlns:ftp="http://www.mulesource.org/schema/mule/ftp/2.0">

  <ftp:connector name="ftpConnector"
      validateConnections="true" />

  <model name="ftp-model">
    <service name="file-reader-ftp-writer">
      <inbound>
        <file:inbound-endpoint
            path="chapter6/5a-ftp-write/in" />
      </inbound>
```

① Defines FTP connector

② Specifies directory to read from

```
<outbound>
  <outbound-pass-through-router>
    <ftp:outbound-endpoint
      user="bob"
      password="123password"
      host="localhost"
      port="2121"
      outputPattern="${ORIGINALNAME}-${SYSTIME}.dat"
      passive="false"
      path="/" />
  </outbound-pass-through-router>
</outbound>
    </service>
  </model>
</mule>
```

❸ Specifies FTP server to connect to

❹ Uses active mode

In listing 6.31 we poll for new files from a file system directory ❷. The FTP outbound endpoint tells Mule that we want to connect to the FTP server that is running locally on port 2121 ❸. It also tells Mule that we use bob as the username and 123password as the password to connect to the FTP server.

We also define some advanced properties on this endpoint. We define an output pattern that's used for the filename when we store a file on the FTP server. We also specify that we want Mule to check whether the connection is still valid before we attempt to upload a file ❶. So if the connection is lost, Mule will reconnect to the server and try again. Finally, we instruct Mule to use an active mode ❹ for file transfer instead of the passive mode.

Reading files from the FTP server is as simple as storing files on an FTP server. The only thing we need to do is switch the inbound and the outbound endpoints from our previous example (see listing 6.32).

Listing 6.32 Mule configuration that reads data from a FTP server

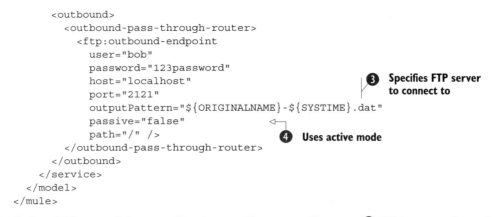

```
<mule xmlns="http://www.mulesource.org/schema/mule/core/2.0"
    xmlns:file="http://www.mulesource.org/schema/mule/file/2.0"
    xmlns:ftp="http://www.mulesource.org/schema/mule/ftp/2.0">

  <ftp:connector name="ftpConnector"
      validateConnections="true" />

  <model name="ftp-model">
    <service name="ftp-reader">
      <inbound>
        <ftp:inbound-endpoint user="bob"
            password="123password"
            host="localhost"
            port="2121"
            pollingFrequency="10000"
            passive="false"
            path="/" />
      </inbound>
      <outbound>
        <outbound-pass-through-router>
```

❶ Checks if connection is alive

❷ Configures FTP server

❸ Defines polling frequency

```
            <file:outbound-endpoint
                path="chapter6/5b-ftp-read/out" />
        </outbound-pass-through-router>
      </outbound>
    </service>
  </model>
</mule>
```

As you can see, we use the same configuration parameters ❷ for the inbound endpoint that we used for the outbound endpoint in listing 6.31. The only difference is the definition of a `pollingFrequency` attribute ❸ to indicate how often we'll check for files. When the FTP server is polled for new files, we first validate the FTP connection ❶.

When you want to run the FTP read and write examples, you'll first have to configure the AnomicFTPD server. First you need to configure the group authorization in the tools/AnomicFTPD_v0.93_build20080215/ftpd.groups file. Use the configuration as shown here. Notice that you need a different configuration for UNIX/Linux and Windows systems:

Unix/Linux

```
usergroup=rw-,00:01,/osesbinaction/ftproot/
guestgroup=r--,00:01,/pub
admingroup=rwx,00:01,/
```

Windows

```
dosusergroup=rw-,00:01,C:\\osesbinaction\\ftproot\\
dosguestgroup=r--,00:01,C:\\pub
dosadmingroup=rwx,00:01,C:\\
```

This code specifies the directory path for the `usergroup` (UNIX/Linux) and `dosusergroup` (Windows) FTP groups, which we use in this example. Of course, you can use another directory path if you like. Next you need to define the users for the AnomicFTPD server in the tools/AnomicFTPD_v0.93_build20080215/ftpd.accounts file. Use the configuration shown here to define these users:

UNIX/Linux

```
bob=usergroup,123password
anonymous=guestgroup,*
admin=admingroup,789password
```

Windows

```
bob=dosusergroup,123password
anonymous=dosguestgroup,*
admin=dosadmingroup,789password
```

Now you're ready to start the FTP server with the `ext:start-AnomicFTPD` Ant target in the ch6-build.xml Ant build file. You can use the `chapter6-ftp-write-5a` and `chapter6-ftp-read-5b` Ant targets in the same Ant build file to start Mule with the FTP read example (listing 6.31) and the FTP write example (listing 6.32). Next, let's move on to the implementation of the FTP connectivity in ServiceMix.

6.5.2 *FTP and ServiceMix*

Using FTP from ServiceMix is just as simple as using FTP from Mule. ServiceMix provides an FTP binding component that's able to read files from and write files to an FTP server. This BC uses the same concept as ServiceMix File BC. For the examples we explained in figures 6.12 and 6.13, we're going to create an FTP poller and sender. Let's first look at the FTP poller configuration (listing 6.33).

Listing 6.33 FTP binding component for ServiceMix with poller functionality

```
<beans xmlns="http://xbean.org/schemas/spring/1.0"
  xmlns:ftp="http://servicemix.apache.org/ftp/1.0"
  xmlns:esb="http://esbinaction.com/ftp">

  <ftp:poller service="esb:ftpPoller"
      endpoint="endpoint"
      targetService="esb:fileSender"
      targetEndpoint="simpleFromFtpSender"
      uri="ftp://bob:123password@localhost:2121"      <-- ❶
      deleteFile="true"/>                             <-- ❷
</beans>
```

We don't have to configure much to read files from an FTP server. We need to configure an uri ❶, which specifies where the FTP server is running and how to connect to this server. In this example, the server is running on localhost and on port 2121. This uri also specifies the credentials used to connect to this server.

Besides the connection uri, we also specify the deleteFile property ❷. With this property we instruct ServiceMix that when a file is processed from the FTP server, this file should be deleted. To complete the example where we pick up a file from the FTP server and write it to the file system, we also need to configure a file sender, shown in this code snippet:

```
<file:sender service="esb:fileSender"
    endpoint="simpleFromFtpSender"
    directory="chapter6/5-ftp/out" />
```

In the next example, we read a file from the file system and write that file to the FTP server. Again, we start by looking at the FTP configuration (listing 6.34).

Listing 6.34 FTP sender configuration for ServiceMix

```
<beans xmlns="http://xbean.org/schemas/spring/1.0"
  xmlns:ftp="http://servicemix.apache.org/ftp/1.0"
  xmlns:esb="http://esbinaction.com/ftp">

  <ftp:sender service="esb:ftpSender"
      endpoint="endpoint"
      uri="ftp://bob:123password@localhost:2121"      <-- ❶
      overwrite="true"                                <-- ❷
      uniqueFileName="osesb"
      uploadSuffix=".tmp" />      <-- ❸
</beans>
```

This FTP sender will send the messages it receives to the specified FTP uri ❶, which in this example is the same as our FTP poller shown in listing 6.33. Besides the uri attribute, we also specify an overwrite attribute here ❷. With this attribute we specify that if a file already exists at the FTP server and a file with the same name is uploaded, the file on the FTP server should be overwritten.

ServiceMix can't always determine the name of the file to use when uploading. If a file is first read from the file system before being sent to the FTP server, the FTP component uses the original filename. If the message originates from a JMS queue, the original filename isn't known. In that case, ServiceMix will use the uniqueFileName property to create a new filename: the uniqueFilename attribute value with a sequence number appended.

The final property shown here is the uploadSuffix ❸. This suffix is appended to the filename during upload, and once the file is completely uploaded, the uploaded file is renamed to the correct filename. This is done to prevent any processing of this file by other applications that are monitoring the upload site.

Of course, we need to define a file poller service to drive the FTP sender service. The definition of this service is shown in this code snippet:

```
<file:poller service="esb:filePoller"
    endpoint="simpleToFtpPoller"
    targetService="esb:ftpSender"
    file="chapter6/5-ftp/in"
    period="2000" />
```

To execute the FTP example, you should first start the FTP server with the ext:start-AnomicFTPD target of the ch6-build.xml Ant build file. Then you can start the ServiceMix container with the start target in the same Ant build file. Finally, you need to deploy the FTP service assembly with the deploy-5-ftp-example Ant target. There is a test file available, test-ftp.xml, which you can use to trigger the FTP example in the chapter6/5-ftp/in directory in the ServiceMix installation directory.

Mule and ServiceMix both make it easy to connect to FTP servers, and both have some advanced features (such as uploadSuffix, which you can use to indicate that the file being uploaded is not yet completely uploaded).

Let's now look at an old Java-based connectivity option: EJB 3.

6.6   *Connecting to EJB 3*

Enterprise JavaBeans (EJBs) are the standard JEE components to expose business functionality in a scalable, transactional, and distributed manner. Many enterprise applications use EJBs, and being able to connect to EJBs is an important feature for an ESB from a Java perspective. There are two different ways to implement EJB connectivity:

- Using RMI
- Adding a web service layer to the EJB and invoking the web service

In this section, we focus on the first option. We show how you can implement the example shown in figure 6.13.

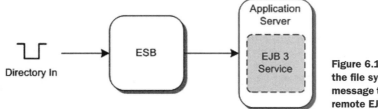

Figure 6.13   We read a file from the file system and use the message to invoke a method on a remote EJB.

In the example in figure 6.13, we use Mule and ServiceMix to connect to an EJB and use the content of the file as parameters for the EJB call. Before we dive into the Mule and ServiceMix configuration, let's create and deploy a sample EJB service that we use in this section.

We create a stateless session bean that can be used to search for individuals based on certain search criteria. Let's start by looking at the interface, shown in listing 6.35, of this session bean.

Listing 6.35   `PersonService` interface that defines the method of our EJB

```
@Remote
public interface PersonService {

  public List<Person> searchPersons(SearchQuery query);    ⬅—❶
}
```

The EJB 3 service interface implementation is straightforward: it consists of a single method, which takes a query as its input and returns a list of `Persons` ❶. The `SearchQuery` and the `Person` objects are both simple beans. These beans are shown in listing 6.36.

Listing 6.36   `Person` and `SearchQuery` objects used by the `PersonService`

```
public class Person implements Serializable {
  private String firstName;
  private String lastName;

  public Person(String firstName, String lastName) {
    this.firstName = firstName;
    this.lastName = lastName;
  }

  // ommitted getters and setters
}

public class SearchQuery implements Serializable {
  private String firstName;
  private String lastName;

  public SearchQuery(String firstName, String lastName) {
    this.firstName = firstName;
    this.lastName = lastName;
  }
```

```
  // omitted getters and setters
}
```

As you can see, these bean implementations are just basic POJOs. Let's move forward to the implementation of the EJB (listing 6.37).

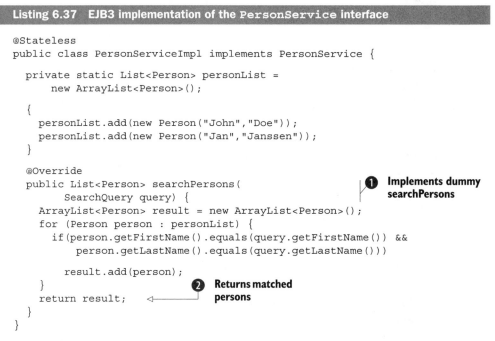

Listing 6.37   EJB3 implementation of the `PersonService` interface

```
@Stateless
public class PersonServiceImpl implements PersonService {

  private static List<Person> personList =
      new ArrayList<Person>();

  {
    personList.add(new Person("John","Doe"));
    personList.add(new Person("Jan","Janssen"));
  }

  @Override
  public List<Person> searchPersons(                    ❶ Implements dummy
        SearchQuery query) {                               searchPersons
    ArrayList<Person> result = new ArrayList<Person>();
    for (Person person : personList) {
      if(person.getFirstName().equals(query.getFirstName()) &&
          person.getLastName().equals(query.getLastName()))

        result.add(person);
    }                              ❷ Returns matched
    return result;    ⟵              persons
  }
}
```

Listing 6.37 is a dummy implementation, since we've implemented a static list of `Persons`. This, however, works great for testing. To start the OpenEJB container, use the Ant task `ext:start-openejb` in the ch6-build.xml file of the Mule or ServiceMix workspace. You can now use the Ant task `chapter6-ejb-deploy-ejb` in the same Ant build file to deploy this example to the OpenEJB EJB container. When you've done this, an EJB service bean becomes available that can be reached by using the JNDI settings shown in table 6.1.

Now let's see how to use Mule to implement the EJB connectivity in a Mule configuration file.

Table 6.1   Connection settings used to connect to the `PersonService` EJB

Property	Value
`jndiInitialFactory`	`org.openejb.client.RemoteInitialContextFactory`
`jndiProviderUrl`	`ejbd://localhost:4201`
`jndiName`	`PersonServiceImplRemote`

6.6.1 *Using EJB 3 from Mule*

Connecting to EJBs from a Mule configuration is just like using any of the other transports: you just need to configure an endpoint. To show the EJB connectivity in Mule, we implement the example shown in figure 6.13. We read a file from the file system that contains the arguments for the searchPersons method. Then we transform this file into a SearchQuery object and use that object to invoke the EJB method. The result from the EJB method will be stored on the file system.

The Mule configuration to implement this EJB connectivity appears in listing 6.38.

Listing 6.38   Mule configuration showing how to connect Mule to an EJB server

```
<mule>
  <file:connector name="fileConnector" streaming="false"/>

  <ejb:connector name="open-ejb"
    jndiInitialFactory=
      "org.openejb.client.RemoteInitialContextFactory"      ❶ Defines
    jndiProviderUrl="ejbd://localhost:4201"                    JNDI
    securityPolicy="wideopen.policy" />                        connection

  <model name="ejb-model">
    <service name="ejb-reader-writer">
      <inbound>
        <file:inbound-endpoint
            path="chapter6/6-ejb/in">
          <file:file-to-string-transformer />
          <custom-transformer                                ❷ Transforms String to
            class="esb.chapter6.QueryTransformer" />            SearchQuery object
        </file:inbound-endpoint>
      </inbound>
      <outbound>
        <chaining-router>
          <ejb:outbound-endpoint
              host="localhost"
              port="4201"
              method="searchPersons"
              object="PersonServiceImplRemoteHome" />    ◁┐ Specifies EJB
          <file:outbound-endpoint                        ❸   service home
              path="chapter6/6-ejb/out" />
        </chaining-router>
      </outbound>
    </service>
  </model>
</mule>
```

We just walk you through the interesting attributes of this Mule configuration step by step. The first thing we do is configure JNDI-related EJB properties on the EJB connector ❶; these properties will be used by all the EJB endpoints. The jndiInitialFactory property is used to connect to the JNDI server, and the securityPolicy defines the security policy we use. These are just basic EJB properties. The defintion of the EJB JNDI name is specified with the object attribute ❸ in the outbound-endpoint element. This

JNDI name is used to retrieve the home interface from the EJB container, so the searchPersons method can be invoked on the PersonServiceImpl EJB service.

The first endpoint we configured is a file inbound endpoint. This is a simple file endpoint that reads a file from the chapter6/6-ejb/in directory. When the file is read, it's transformed using a file-to-string transformer and a custom transformer ❷, which transforms the input string to a SearchQuery object. Let's look a bit closer at this custom transformer in listing 6.39.

Listing 6.39 Transformer that transforms a string to a `SearchQuery` object

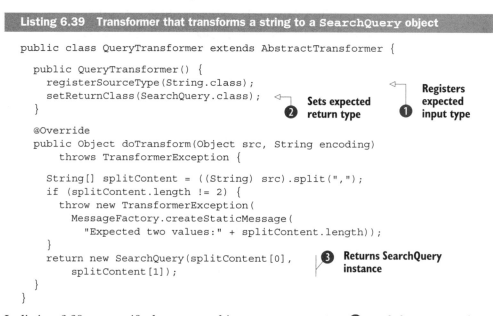

```
public class QueryTransformer extends AbstractTransformer {

  public QueryTransformer() {
    registerSourceType(String.class);
    setReturnClass(SearchQuery.class);                  Sets expected        Registers
  }                                                     return type ❷        expected
                                                                           ❶ input type
  @Override
  public Object doTransform(Object src, String encoding)
      throws TransformerException {

    String[] splitContent = ((String) src).split(",");
    if (splitContent.length != 2) {
      throw new TransformerException(
        MessageFactory.createStaticMessage(
          "Expected two values:" + splitContent.length));
    }
    return new SearchQuery(splitContent[0],          ❸ Returns SearchQuery
      splitContent[1]);                                instance
  }
}
```

In listing 6.39 we specify the expected input type, a String ❶, and the expected output type, a SearchQuery ❷, for this transformer. Mule will check whether the transformer is called with the correct source object and will also check whether the result from the transformer is of the type we specified. Adding these checks isn't necessary but will make our transformers more robust and will allow us to catch any problems immediately. The doTransform method performs the actual transformation by simply splitting the incoming String object and creating a new SearchQuery based on the resulting string array ❸. This SearchQuery is returned from this transformer and passed back to Mule.

If you return to listing 6.38, you can see that we use a chaining router. This chaining router calls the EJB and File endpoint sequentially and uses the output, if any, from each endpoint as input for the next. So in this case, the result of the EJB call is used as input for the next file endpoint, which writes the EJB result to a file.

As you can see, calling EJBs in Mule isn't that different from using Mule to connect to mail, file, or JMS servers. All we need to do is create an endpoint that shows us how to connect to the EJB. Let's look a bit closer at the properties defined on the EJB outbound endpoint in table 6.2.

Note that the default EJB connector in Mule doesn't support EJB 3, but only EJB 2.1. So the Mule EJB connector will expect an EJB home interface to be available. Luckily, we can easily make our EJB 3 implementation of the person service (listing 6.36) EJB 2.1–compliant by adding a `@RemoteHome` annotation, which references a `PersonServiceEJBHome` interface. We also need to implement an EJB object interface class with `PersonServiceEJB-Object`. Now our person service is EJB 2.1–compliant and we can invoke the EJB with the Mule EJB connector.

Table 6.2   The EJB outbound endpoint properties

Property	Description
host	The location where the JNDI registry is running
port	The port the JNDI registry is running on
method	The method to invoke on the remote EJB
object	The name under which the EJB is registered

Make sure the OpenEJB container is started (`ext:start-openejb`) and the EJB is deployed (`chapter6-ejb-deploy-ejb`). When you run this example with the `chapter6-ejb` Ant target and drop the test file, query-person.txt, into the chapter6/6-ejb/in directory, you'll see that this method is invoked and that the `Persons` found are stored in the directory specified by the last endpoint. Now let's move on to the last section of this chapter, where we implement the same example in ServiceMix.

6.6.2   EJB 3 and ServiceMix

ServiceMix doesn't provide a standard EJB binding component or service engine. Various JBI-based EJB binding components are available that we can use instead. However, in this section we show how you can use Spring with the ServiceMix JSR181 binding component to provide EJB 3 connectivity.

With this component, it's very easy to expose POJOs as services. To use this functionality to connect to EJBs, we use Spring's `JndiObjectFactoryBean`. With this component we can expose a remote EJB 3 bean and access it as a normal POJO, so with this Spring bean we can use the JSR181 component to expose remote EJBs. You might remember the `servicemix-bean` component from chapter 3, which could also be used to expose POJOs to ServiceMix. The main difference is that with the `servicemix-bean` component, we need to implement a couple of lifecycle methods and be able to handle the JBI-specific way services are called. When we use the JSR181 binding component, we can just expose a POJO and don't have to worry about the underlying JBI specifics.

Listing 6.40 shows how you need to configure Spring and this component so that you can access remote EJBS.

Listing 6.40   ServiceMix configuration that exposes EJBs as services to the NMR

```
<beans xmlns:jsr181="http://servicemix.apache.org/jsr181/1.0"
   xmlns:esb="http://esbinaction.com/ejb">

   <classpath inverse="true">          ❶ Defines inverse classpath
     <location>.</location>
```

```
      <location>aopalliance-1.0.jar</location>
      <location>openejb-client-3.0.jar</location>
      <location>geronimo-ejb_3.0_spec-1.0.jar</location>
      <location>spring-aop-2.0.6.jar</location>
      <location>spring-context-2.0.6.jar</location>
      <location>spring-remoting-2.0.6.jar</location>
    </classpath>

    <jsr181:endpoint annotations="none"
        service="esb:ejb"
        endpoint="ejb"
        serviceInterface="esb.chapter6.ejb.PersonService"     ◁─┐  Specifies exposed
        id="personService">                                   ❷ │ interface
      <jsr181:pojo>
        <bean id="myPojo"
            class="org.springframework.jndi.JndiObjectFactoryBean">
          <property name="jndiName"
              value="PersonServiceImplRemote" />
          <property name="proxyInterface"
              value="esb.chapter6.ejb.PersonService" />
          <property name="jndiTemplate" ref="jndiTemplate" />
        </bean>
      </jsr181:pojo>
    </jsr181:endpoint>

    <bean id="jndiTemplate"
        class="org.springframework.jndi.JndiTemplate">        ◁─┐  Configures JNDI
      <property name="environment">                           ❸ │ context
        <props>
          <prop key="java.naming.factory.initial">
            org.openejb.client.RemoteInitialContextFactory
          </prop>
          <prop key="java.naming.provider.url">
            ejbd://localhost:4201
          </prop>
        </props>
      </property>
    </bean>
  </beans>
```

In listing 6.40 we configure a JSR181 service you can use to invoke a method on the
PersonServiceImpl remote EJB. We do this by creating a Spring proxy to the remote
EJB. We use Spring's JNDI template ❸ to define how to connect to the remote EJB.

   With the JSR181 configuration in the listing, all the methods from the exposed
interface PersonService ❷ are automatically available on the ESB. So if you want to
call the searchPersons method on the remote EJB, you can just send a message to this
endpoint. We don't have to worry about the XML message exchange inside the Service-
Mix container and the use of Java objects in the PersonServiceImpl EJB; the ServiceMix
JSR181 component uses XFire to marshal and unmarshal the messages from XML to
Java and back again.

   Notice that we use an inverse classpath ❶ in listing 6.40. An inverse classpath
can be used to achieve a parent-last kind of classloading. So the libraries specified in

this ServiceMix configuration will be loaded first, before the libraries of the Service-Mix container.

So let's quickly look back at the scenario we want to implement. We want to read a file from the file system, invoke a call on the EJB, and send the result on to the file system. Let's first configure the file endpoints (listing 6.41).

Listing 6.41 A file sender and file poller configuration for the EJB example

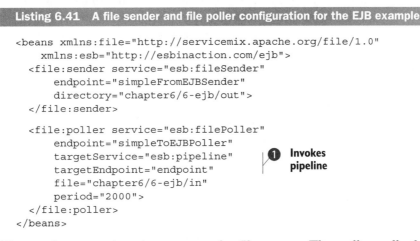

```
<beans xmlns:file="http://servicemix.apache.org/file/1.0"
    xmlns:esb="http://esbinaction.com/ejb">
  <file:sender service="esb:fileSender"
      endpoint="simpleFromEJBSender"
      directory="chapter6/6-ejb/out">
  </file:sender>

  <file:poller service="esb:filePoller"
      endpoint="simpleToEJBPoller"
      targetService="esb:pipeline"          ❶ Invokes
      targetEndpoint="endpoint"                pipeline
      file="chapter6/6-ejb/in"
      period="2000">
  </file:poller>
</beans>
```

The sender can write a message to the file system. The poller polls the file system every 2 seconds and uses the result to send a message to the pipeline service endpoint ❶. As you can see here, we don't directly invoke the EJB service, but we invoke a service called `pipeline`. We do this because we want to route the result of the EJB call to the file sender endpoint so it can be written to the file system. Listing 6.42 shows the configuration of this pipeline.

Listing 6.42 Pipeline configuration to connect the file endpoints to the EJB service

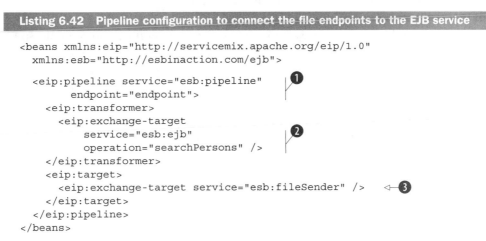

```
<beans xmlns:eip="http://servicemix.apache.org/eip/1.0"
  xmlns:esb="http://esbinaction.com/ejb">

  <eip:pipeline service="esb:pipeline"        ❶
      endpoint="endpoint">
    <eip:transformer>
      <eip:exchange-target
          service="esb:ejb"                    ❷
          operation="searchPersons" />
    </eip:transformer>
    <eip:target>
      <eip:exchange-target service="esb:fileSender" />   ←❸
    </eip:target>
  </eip:pipeline>
</beans>
```

With the configuration in listing 6.42, once this pipeline service ❶ is invoked, a call is made to the specified exchange target ❷, which in this case is the call to the EJB. The result of this call is then passed on to the file sender component ❸, which stores the EJB result on the file system.

You might wonder why we chose this odd construction. The reason is that we need to convert between different message exchange patterns. The file reader we specify reads a file from a directory and invokes a target service using the in-only pattern. The `PersonServiceImpl` EJB sends a response and thus only expects in-out exchanges. Using a pipeline, we can change the message exchange from an in-only pattern to an in-out pattern to invoke the EJB service and back to an in-only pattern to write the output to a file.

To execute the EJB example, you'll first have to start the OpenEJB container with the `ext:start-openejb` target in the ch6-build.xml Ant build file. Then you have to undeploy the EJB example of Mule with the `chapter6-ejb-undeploy-ejb` Ant target and deploy the ServiceMix EJB example (without the EJB 2.1 compliancy) with the `chapter6-ejb-deploy-ejb` Ant target. Finally, you start the ServiceMix container with the `start` Ant target and deploy the EJB service assembly with the `deploy-6-ejb-example` Ant target. With the PERSON.xml test file, you can trigger the EJB example by copying this file to the chapter6/6-ejb/in path in the ServiceMix installation directory.

6.7   *Summary*

In this chapter you learned how to use Mule and ServiceMix to connect to various technologies. You saw that the configuration of some of these technologies is straightforward, but some are a bit more complex and require an understanding not only of Mule and ServiceMix but also of how the underlying technology works.

Using ESBs such as Mule and ServiceMix facilitates working with all kinds of technologies and standards. Connecting to existing business logic using EJBs or JMS is as easy as adding a couple of lines of configuration.

The technologies in this chapter are just a selection of what's available. In appendices D and E, we list the available connectors and binding components, so if you want to use a technology not explained here, check out those appendices.

We covered a lot of ground in this chapter, and even though we skipped some technologies, you should now be able to work with other Mule transports and JBI components.

In the next chapter, we look at another popular integration technology. We show how you can use web services and two of the most important standards, WS-Security and WS-Addressing.

Web services support
7

In this chapter:

- Hosting web services
- Consuming web services
- Using WS-Security and WS-Addressing

Working with SOAP and web services is rather complex; for instance, you usually have to run a servlet engine in which you deploy your web services. In this chapter you'll learn how easy it is to use Mule and ServiceMix to connect to and host web services. We first show you how to connect to existing web services and how to create your own web services. Then we explain how to use two of the most important web services specifications in Mule and ServiceMix: WS-Security and WS-Addressing.

When creating web services you have three approaches:

- In the top-down approach, you write the WSDL file first and use it as the foundation for the Java service. This is usually the best approach since your WSDL file doesn't depend on the Java interface definition and you have total freedom in the way you create the messages and thus define the XML that is sent over the wire. This is especially useful when you want to interact with .NET web services. This option does, however, require some extra effort to get the web service implemented and running.

243

- In the bottom-up approach, you create a Java service and generate a WSDL file from that service. This approach is usually the quickest one and works pretty well if the web service consumers are also Java applications. But there is a risk that the generated web service won't interoperate correctly with .NET, although with the most modern web services frameworks, interoperability with .NET works well if you follow certain guidelines.

- In the meet-in-the-middle approach, you use an already existing Java model to create the foundation for the messages being sent in a WSDL file. You can then tailor the WSDL file to your liking.

In this chapter, we demonstrate the top-down and the bottom-up approaches; the meet-in-the-middle approach can easily be distilled from these two approaches.

The web service that we create is a simple service where we implement three operations that can be used to look up information about a company:

- *Get company*—Provides detailed information based on the name of a certain company. So when you look for information on MuleSource or IONA, you'll get the location of that company and the members of its board of directors.

- *Find companies*—Lets you search for companies based on street name and city name. This operation returns either an empty list (if no companies are found) or a list of companies.

- *Update company info*—Allows you to change an existing company's information by providing the name and new information.

We implement this web service using the bottom-up and the top-down approaches we've talked about. First let's look at implementing the web service using a top-down approach.

7.1   *Top-down approach web service*

For the top-down approach, we need to create a WSDL file that describes the type of messages that can be sent to, and received from, the web service and the operations this web service provides. A WSDL file is usually a large XML file, so we just look at the various parts that make up the WSDL file (figure 7.1). You've already seen the definition of a WSDL file in chapter 6 (when we discussed the JDBC connectivity of Service-Mix), but in this section we look at the parts of a WSDL file without the JDBC logic.

As you can see in figure 7.1, a WSDL version 1.1 file contains, among other things, XML Schema elements and type definitions.

Differences between WSDL 1.1 and WSDL 2.0

In this book, when we talk about WSDL, we're referring to the 1.1 version. A WSDL 2.0 specification is also available that is becoming popular. We don't go into the WSDL 2.0 details here but instead focus on the most visible differences between WSDL 1.1 and WSDL 2.0. The first thing you'll notice when you compare a WSDL 2.0 file to the WSDL 1.1 version is that the message constructs have been removed. In WSDL 2.0 they're instead defined using the standard XML Schema model in the `types` element. Another change is that some of the elements have been renamed. The `portType` element from WSDL 1.1 has been renamed to `interface` in WSDL 2.0, and the `port` element has been replaced with the `interface` element. As you may recall from chapter 2, the naming conventions of JBI match those of WSDL 2.0. The reason is that the JBI specification leans heavily on the WSDL 2.0 model.

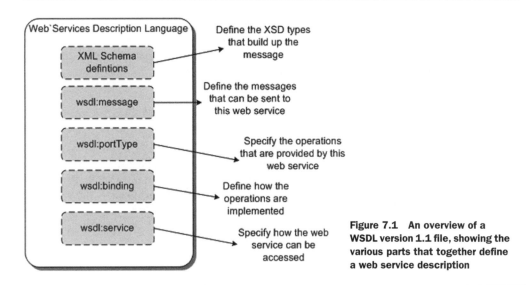

Figure 7.1 An overview of a WSDL version 1.1 file, showing the various parts that together define a web service description

These elements and type definitions describe the format of the XML messages used to communicate with the web service. Listing 7.1 shows the XML Schema definitions for the company web service we described in the introduction of this chapter.

Listing 7.1 XML Schema definition part of the WSDL file

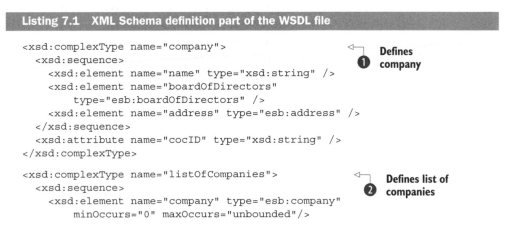

```
      </xsd:sequence>
    </xsd:complexType>                        ❸  Defines board
                                                  member
    <xsd:complexType name="director">    ◁┘
      <xsd:sequence>
        <xsd:element name="firstName" type="xsd:string" />
        <xsd:element name="lastName" type="xsd:string" />
        <xsd:element name="dateOfBirth" type="xsd:date" />
        <xsd:element name="address" type="esb:address" />
      </xsd:sequence>
    </xsd:complexType>                            ❹  Defines board
                                                      of directors
    <xsd:complexType name="boardOfDirectors">  ◁┘
      <xsd:sequence>
        <xsd:element name="director" type="esb:director"
            minOccurs="0" maxOccurs="unbounded" />
      </xsd:sequence>
    </xsd:complexType>                        ❺  Defines simple
                                                  address
    <xsd:complexType name="address">     ◁┘
      <xsd:sequence>
        <xsd:element name="street" type="xsd:string" />
        <xsd:element name="number" type="xsd:integer" />
        <xsd:element name="city" type="xsd:string" />
        <xsd:element name="state" type="xsd:string" />
        <xsd:element name="zipcode" type="esb:zip" />
        <xsd:element name="country" type="xsd:string" />
      </xsd:sequence>
    </xsd:complexType>                        ❻  Defines format
                                                  of zip code
    <xsd:simpleType name="zip">          ◁┘
      <xsd:restriction base="xsd:string">
        <xsd:pattern value="[0-9]{5}" />
      </xsd:restriction>
    </xsd:simpleType>
```

In listing 7.1, we define some XML Schema types that represent the objects we need for our company web service implementation: a company object ❶, which has a cocID; a name; an address; and a number of boardmembers. The director ❸, the boardmembers ❹, the address ❺, and its zipcode ❻ types are also defined in this listing. Since we have an operation that returns a list of companies, we also define a complex type for this result value ❷. These type definitions will define the format of the XML messages used to communicate with this web service.

When writing web services, it's a good thing to keep interoperability in mind. To ensure interoperability, you can use the document/literal wrapped approach.

With the document/literal wrapped approach, the parameters of the web service operation are wrapped in an XML element, which indicates the method to be called. So, for instance, when we invoke a findCompanies operation, the XML message that we send is

```
<findCompanies>
    <city>companyName</city>
    <streetName>companyName</streetName>
</findCompanies>
```

Document/literal wrapped

Document/literal wrapped is a SOAP style made popular by Microsoft and is now the de facto web service standard. With document/literal wrapped, we wrap the XML elements we want to send in a single element. So the input message for the web service will always contain a single XML element. This root element usually has the same name as the operation we want to invoke and isn't allowed to have any attributes. The name of this root element can then be used by the various web service frameworks to determine which method to invoke in the web service implementation. So in our example, our root elements will be called findCompanies, getCompany, and changeCompany, and the methods in our service implementation will have to have the same names.

The reason document/literal wrapped has become so popular is that we can now easily correlate the name of the method to invoke from the SOAP message. If we only used document/literal, we'd just send XML messages, without a wrapper, so we wouldn't be able to correlate the message directly from the XML received.

Document/literal wrapped does have some issues. The first is that you can't have overloaded methods, since the method name is used as a wrapper. The second problem is that since WS-Addressing is getting more popular, the use of the wrapped element to indicate the method to invoke is getting a bit obsolete. As we'll see in the last part of this chapter, we can do the same thing with WS-Addressing by specifying the wsa:action element, which is sent in the header of the SOAP message.

To be able to use this message definition for our company web service, we need to create the XML elements that represent this style. We don't explain all the element types, but focus on the request and response definition, shown in listing 7.2, for the find-Companies operation.

Listing 7.2 Wrapped element used for the findCompanies operation

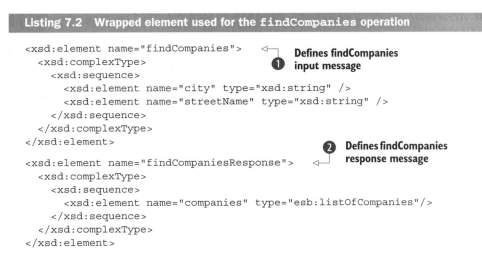

```xsd
<xsd:element name="findCompanies">          Defines findCompanies
  <xsd:complexType>                       1 input message
    <xsd:sequence>
      <xsd:element name="city" type="xsd:string" />
      <xsd:element name="streetName" type="xsd:string" />
    </xsd:sequence>
  </xsd:complexType>
</xsd:element>
                                            Defines findCompanies
<xsd:element name="findCompaniesResponse">  2 response message
  <xsd:complexType>
    <xsd:sequence>
      <xsd:element name="companies" type="esb:listOfCompanies"/>
    </xsd:sequence>
  </xsd:complexType>
</xsd:element>
```

In listing 7.2 we created a wrapper element, which contains all the parameters for the input message ❶ of the findCompanies operation, and we also created a wrapper element for the response message ❷. Now that we've defined the format of the input and response XML messages, let's define the messages and the operations (listing 7.3).

Listing 7.3   WSDL message and operations definition

```
<wsdl:message name="changeCompanyRequest">
  <wsdl:part element="esb:changeCompany" name="parameters" />       ◁─┐  Defines
</wsdl:message>                                                        │  message
<wsdl:message name="findCompaniesRequest">                          ❶  elements
  <wsdl:part element="esb:findCompanies" name="parameters" />
</wsdl:message>
<wsdl:message name="findCompaniesResponse">
  <wsdl:part element="esb:findCompaniesResponse" name="parameters" />
</wsdl:message>
<wsdl:message name="getCompanyRequest">
  <wsdl:part element="esb:getCompany" name="parameters" />
</wsdl:message>
<wsdl:message name="getCompanyResponse">
  <wsdl:part element="esb:getCompanyResponse" name="parameters" />
</wsdl:message>

<wsdl:portType name="CoCPortType">
  <wsdl:operation name="changeCompany">                      ◁─┐  Defines
    <wsdl:input message="esb:changeCompanyRequest" />          │  web service
  </wsdl:operation>                                          ❷  operations
  <wsdl:operation name="findCompanies">
    <wsdl:input message="esb:findCompaniesRequest" />
    <wsdl:output message="esb:findCompaniesResponse" />
  </wsdl:operation>
  <wsdl:operation name="getCompany">
    <wsdl:input message="esb:getCompanyRequest" />
    <wsdl:output message="esb:getCompanyResponse" />
  </wsdl:operation>
</wsdl:portType>
```

In listing 7.3, we defined five messages ❶, which serve as input or output messages for the WSDL operations ❷. Since we're implementing a document/literal wrapped web service, the messages just point to the XML elements defined in listing 7.1. The portType shown here ❷ specifies the operations this web service will provide. Note that at this point we haven't yet indicated how the operations are implemented or bound to a specific technology; this portType is the equivalent of a Java interface, where we just define the operations.

The final part of the WSDL is binding this portType to an actual implementation technology, where we define how this web service can be invoked. We use SOAP over HTTP and a document/literal style web service, as shown in listing 7.4.

Listing 7.4   WSDL part showing the binding implementation of the port type

```
<wsdl:binding name="CoCSoapBinding" type="esb:CoCPortType">
  <soap:binding style="document"
      transport="http://schemas.xmlsoap.org/soap/http" />
    <wsdl:operation name="changeCompany">
    <soap:operation
soapAction="http://esbinaction.com/CoC/changeCompany"/>
      <wsdl:input>
        <soap:body use="literal" />
      </wsdl:input>
  </wsdl:operation>
  <wsdl:operation name="findCompanies">
    <soap:operation
        soapAction="http://esbinaction.com/CoC/findCompanies" />
    <wsdl:input>
      <soap:body use="literal" />
  </wsdl:input>
    <wsdl:output>
      <soap:body use="literal" />
    </wsdl:output>
  </wsdl:operation>
  <wsdl:operation name="getCompany">
    <soap:operation
        soapAction="http://esbinaction.com/CoC/getCompany" />
    <wsdl:input>
      <soap:body use="literal" />
    </wsdl:input>
    <wsdl:output>
      <soap:body use="literal" />
    </wsdl:output>
  </wsdl:operation>
</wsdl:binding>
```

❶ Defines SOAP over HTTP

❷ Shows soapAction for this operation

An interesting aspect to notice in listing 7.4 is the soapAction attribute ❷. Earlier we mentioned that the name of the message can be used to determine which method needs to be invoked on the actual implementation. There's another common way to determine the method to invoke: the soapAction. Most modern web service frameworks allow you to specify which soapAction maps to which method in your web service implementation.

Also notice that we've specified that this company web service is bound to SOAP over HTTP ❶. In the JDBC connectivity example in chapter 6, you saw other options for implementing a WSDL definition. Another common binding is SOAP over JMS, which uses a reliable transport for a web service invocation.

Finally, we must define the web service location related to a binding definition (listing 7.5).

Listing 7.5   WSDL part showing the service location related to a binding definition

```
<wsdl:service name="CoCService">
  <wsdl:port binding="esb:CoCSoapBinding" name="CoCSoap">
```

```
<soap:address
    location="http://localhost:8080/services/coc" />
</wsdl:port>
</wsdl:service>
```
Defines web service location

So that's it. We've shown you the format of the XML messages and the operations definition, and explained how to bind them to use SOAP over HTTP. Now that we've created the web services definition, let's create a Java implementation that contains the business logic for the company web service.

7.1.1 Java implementation of the web service

For the Java implementation of the company web service, let's create an interface definition, as shown in the next code snippet, which contains the methods that match the names and the arguments in our WSDL definition:

```
public interface ChamberOfCommerceService {

    List<Company> findCompanies(String city, String streetName);
    Company getCompany(String companyName);
    void changeCompany(String companyName, Company companyInfo);
}
```

Back in listing 7.2, you can see that the findCompanies method shown here can be directly related to the WSDL definition. Note that we use a Company object in all three web service methods. A schematic overview of the Java objects related to the Company object is shown in figure 7.2.

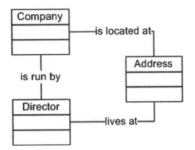

Figure 7.2 The data model used in the Company web service implementation. The Company object is used in the operations of the web service.

Figure 7.2 shows that both a company as well as a director have a relationship with an address. Listing 7.6 provides a more detailed description of these objects.

Listing 7.6 Domain objects by the company web service Java implementation

```
public class Company {
    private List<Director> boardOfDirectors;    ◁──┐  Lists company's
    private String cocID;                          │  directors
    private String name;           ┌ Shows company's
    private Address address;   ◁───┘  address
}
```

```
public class Director {
  private String firstName;
  private String lastName;
  private Date dateOfBirth;
  private Address address;          ◁─┐  Shows director's
}                                      │  address
public class Address {
  private String street;
  private int number;
  private String city;
  private String state;
  private String zipCode;
  private String country;
```

Now we that have implemented the Java interface definition and the domain objects needed as method parameters, we can implement the Java code for the company web service. The Java implementation of the ChamberOfCommerceService interface is shown in listing 7.7.

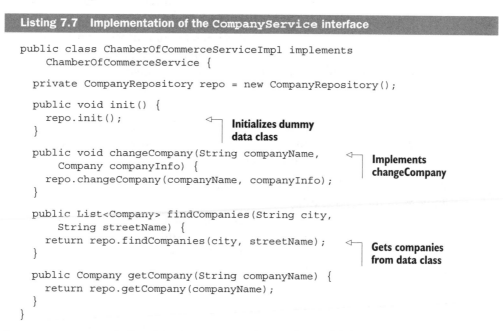

Listing 7.7 Implementation of the CompanyService interface

```
public class ChamberOfCommerceServiceImpl implements
    ChamberOfCommerceService {

  private CompanyRepository repo = new CompanyRepository();

  public void init() {
    repo.init();                    ◁─┐  Initializes dummy
  }                                    │  data class
  public void changeCompany(String companyName,     ◁─┐ Implements
      Company companyInfo) {                            │ changeCompany
    repo.changeCompany(companyName, companyInfo);
  }

  public List<Company> findCompanies(String city,
      String streetName) {
    return repo.findCompanies(city, streetName);    ◁─┐ Gets companies
  }                                                    │ from data class
  public Company getCompany(String companyName) {
    return repo.getCompany(companyName);
  }
}
```

As you can see, we defined a CompanyRepository class, which we use as a dummy data class. We don't show the implementation of this class, as it's just a simple class that stores a couple of companies in a map, which we use to retrieve the correct companies based on the operation parameters.

Now that you've seen the Java implementation and specified the WSDL, we show you how to use Mule and ServiceMix to host this company web service, based on the WSDL definition and the Java implementation.

7.1.2   *Implementing a top-down web service using Mule*

Mule has support for multiple frameworks that allow you to implement web services. It supports Apache Axis, Glue, and Apache CXF. Axis and Glue are mainly there for backward compatibility—for instance, when you need to connect to web services that support older standards such as Dime. Apache CXF is a modern, mature framework that implements the JAX-WS specification that's part of JEE 5. For the examples in this chapter, we use CXF, but the principles shown here also apply to Apache Axis and Glue.

To get this top-down approach (WSDL-first) working in Mule, we need to execute the following steps:

1   *Generate server stub*—This will create some Java files that map the incoming SOAP request to a Java operation. We do this to avoid having to write the conversion between the incoming XML and a Java operation ourselves. The result of this step is a basic Java class or a stub, which will already contain all the web service operations. We then just have to connect this class to our own implementation shown in listing 7.7.

2   *Implement the server stub*—In the implementation we map from the generated classes to our own JavaBeans and implementation. We need to do this since the classes generated in the first step won't be exactly the same as the ones we've created in section 7.1.1.

3   *Configure Mule to publish the WSDL as a web service*—The final step is publishing the WSDL and its generated implementation as a web service. When we do this, Mule will create a listener on a specific port, which web service clients can connect to, to invoke the web service we've just created.

We start with the first two items on this list and look at how we can generate and implement the server stubs.

GENERATING AND IMPLEMENTING THE SERVER STUB FOR MULE

We added a simple Ant target to the ch7-build.xml Ant build file of this chapter, which you can use to generate the server stubs. You do this by executing the cxf-generate-server-stubs task, which calls the Apache CXF WSDLToJava class to generate the Java code that maps the operations and types defined in the WSDL file to Java objects. When you run this Ant target, it will execute the following command:

```
<java classname="org.apache.cxf.tools.wsdlto.WSDLToJava"
        fork="true">
  <arg value="-server" />
  <arg value="-impl" />
  <arg value="-d" />
  <arg value="${workspace.home}/mule/src-generated" />
  <arg value="${chapter.home}/provide-wsdl-top-down/CoC.wsdl" />
  <classpath>
    <path refid="cxf.path" />
  </classpath>
</java>
```

We don't look at all the generated classes, since they are just basic JavaBeans, which use JAXB to map the incoming XML message to Java and back again. However, we look at the stub implementation since we need to connect the methods generated in that stub to our own Java implementation in listing 7.7. We don't show you the complete stub implementation but focus only on the parts that need to be changed (listing 7.8).

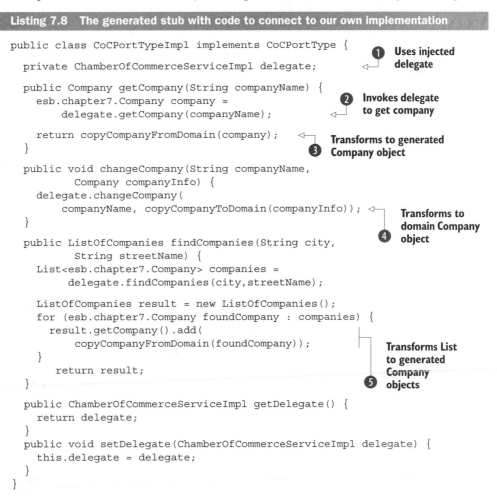

Listing 7.8 The generated stub with code to connect to our own implementation

```
public class CoCPortTypeImpl implements CoCPortType {        ❶ Uses injected
                                                                 delegate
  private ChamberOfCommerceServiceImpl delegate;

  public Company getCompany(String companyName) {
    esb.chapter7.Company company =                            ❷ Invokes delegate
        delegate.getCompany(companyName);                        to get company

    return copyCompanyFromDomain(company);                   Transforms to generated
  }                                                       ❸ Company object
  public void changeCompany(String companyName,
          Company companyInfo) {
    delegate.changeCompany(
        companyName, copyCompanyToDomain(companyInfo));      Transforms to
  }                                                             domain Company
  public ListOfCompanies findCompanies(String city,      ❹ object
          String streetName) {
    List<esb.chapter7.Company> companies =
        delegate.findCompanies(city,streetName);

    ListOfCompanies result = new ListOfCompanies();
    for (esb.chapter7.Company foundCompany : companies) {
      result.getCompany().add(
          copyCompanyFromDomain(foundCompany));           Transforms List
    }                                                        to generated
      return result;                                         Company
  }                                                     ❺ objects
  public ChamberOfCommerceServiceImpl getDelegate() {
    return delegate;
  }
  public void setDelegate(ChamberOfCommerceServiceImpl delegate) {
    this.delegate = delegate;
  }
}
```

The methods generated in this stub all delegate ❶ to the implementation ❷ we showed in listing 7.7. This way, we can easily regenerate the stubs or change the web service interface without having to touch our implementation. And in the same manner, our implementation can change without having to define a new WSDL every time our implementation changes.

In listing 7.8 you can also see a couple of copyXXX methods ❸, ❹, ❺. The implementation of those methods isn't shown, but the only thing these methods do is copy the generated domain objects to our own domain objects defined in listing 7.6 and back again.

Well, that's it for generating and implementing the web service stub. The final task is to configure Mule to publish the company web service we just created.

CONFIGURE MULE

All we need to do now is configure Mule so that we can access the web service using SOAP over HTTP. Figure 7.3 shows the example, which we implement using Mule.

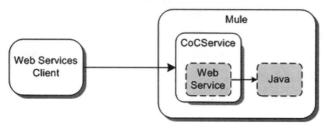

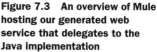

Figure 7.3   An overview of Mule hosting our generated web service that delegates to the Java implementation

Figure 7.3 shows that we want to use Mule to host a web service, which uses our Java implementation in listing 7.7. A web services client can then use the web service provided by Mule by just connecting to the port where Mule hosts this web service. To implement this web services functionality, we need to create a Mule configuration (listing 7.9).

Listing 7.9   Mule configuration that shows how Mule can host a top-down web service

```
<mule>
  <spring:bean name="ChamberOfCommerceServiceWebService"    ←─❶
      class="com.esbinaction.coc.CoCPortTypeImpl">
    <spring:property name="delegate"                        ←─❷
        ref="JavaChamberOfCommerceServiceImpl" />
  </spring:bean>

  <spring:bean name="JavaChamberOfCommerceServiceImpl"      ←─❸
      class="esb.chapter7.ChamberOfCommerceServiceImpl"
      init-method="init" />

  <model name="wsdl-model">
      <service name="cocService">
        <inbound>
          <cxf:inbound-endpoint
              address="http://localhost:8080/services/coc"    ❹
              wsdlLocation="CoC.wsdl"/>
        </inbound>
        <component>
          <spring-object                                      ❺
              bean="ChamberOfCommerceServiceWebService" />
        </component>
      </service>
  </model>
</mule>
```

We first specify two Spring beans. The first bean is the generated web service stub implementation, `ChamberOfCommerceServiceWebService` ❶, which we configured to delegate to the Java implementation from listing 7.7 ❷. The second Spring bean, `Java-ChamberOfCommerceServiceImpl` ❸, is our own Java implementation in listing 7.7.

You can also see that we created an `cxf:inbound-endpoint` ❹. This endpoint defines at which address the web service is hosted; in this example we also referenced the location of the WSDL file. Note that even though we specified the WSDL file here, this isn't really necessary. The stub that's generated by CXF contains a number of JAX-WS annotations. One of these annotations already specifies the WSDL file to use. Configuring it here, however, makes it clearer which WSDL is used. So if an external client looks up this address and appends `?wsdl`, the WSDL file we created at the beginning of this chapter is returned.

If a call is made to `http://localhost:8080/services/coc`, the message will be automatically marshaled to Java and a call on the generated stub is made ❺. The stub delegates the message on to the real implementation, which executes the query and returns the result. This result is finally returned to the requesting client. If you run this example from the supplied Ant build file with the `chapter7-top-down-provide` Ant target, you can use the Swing test client or, for example, SoapUI, to connect to this service and execute web service calls.

Message-based web services

Our example uses a binding library to automatically marshal Java to XML and back again. The CXF default binding implementation, and the one used here, is JAXB. We don't have to do anything for this since all the mapping is implemented when we generated our server stubs. Another popular approach to web services, which is especially promoted by the development team of Axis2, is message-based web services. With these kinds of web services, you don't create a binding to Java, but you just have a class that receives the XML payload of your SOAP message. You're then free to do with this what you want. CXF also provides support for this kind of web service.

As you've seen in this section, it's easy to provide a web service using Mule once you've got a WSDL file and a Java implementation. You only have to configure a CXF endpoint that points to the generated web service stub and Mule takes care of the rest. Since we're working top-down here, there's always some work required to connect the generated stub to your own implementation and also to convert the generated domain model to your own domain model.

Now that you know how to implement a web service in Mule, let's implement a simple top-down web service in ServiceMix.

7.1.3   *Implementing a top-down web service using ServiceMix*

ServiceMix also has support for multiple web services frameworks. It supports both XFire and CXF. Since CXF is the continuation of XFire and XFire itself isn't actively developed anymore, we show you how CXF can be used from ServiceMix. To implement web service functionality in ServiceMix, we need to repeat much the same steps we used for Mule:

1   *Generate server stub*—For ServiceMix we also need to have a server stub, which we can alter to delegate to our own implementation. So we need to generate a server stub, just like we did in our Mule example.

2   *Implement the server stub*—We map from the generated classes to our own Java-Beans and implementation. We can use exactly the same code that you saw in the previous section.

3   *Configure ServiceMix to publish the WSDL as a web service*—The final step is configuring a binding component to listen on an HTTP endpoint. We also need a service engine that contains our implementation. We configure this endpoint to work as follows: whenever a message is received on the binding component, the message will be forwarded to the JBI service endpoint defined in the service engine.

We start with the generation of the server stub, as we also did in the previous section on Mule.

GENERATING AND IMPLEMENTING THE SERVER STUB FOR SERVICEMIX

In the resources/chapter7 directory of the ServiceMix workspace is an Ant file, ch7-build.xml, which can be used to run all the examples in this chapter. This Ant file also contains a target called `cxf-generate-server-stubs`. When you run this target, it generates classes for all the types defined in the WSDL file introduced earlier in this chapter and a stub implementation, just as we've seen in the Mule example.

The implementation of the server stub looks exactly the same as in listing 7.8, so we don't go into more details here. Now that we have the same stub as the one in the Mule example, let's look at configuring ServiceMix to work with this web service stub.

CONFIGURE SERVICEMIX TO HOST A WEB SERVICE

With ServiceMix, it isn't possible to create a web service, which invokes a Java object as we did in the Mule example. This is related to the JBI specification. As we explained in earlier chapters, there's a distinction between binding components and service engines in JBI. The binding components handle the external communication, and the service engines consume and provide internal services. To get web services to work in ServiceMix, we need to do two things. We first need to configure a binding component so that the web service can be called from outside the JBI container, and secondly, we need to configure a service engine to provide the real implementation. Let's look at figure 7.4, which explains this in a bit more detail.

Whenever a message is received by the CXF binding component, we configure ServiceMix to forward the request directly to the Java implementation in the CXF service engine. The implementation will execute the call and return the optional result

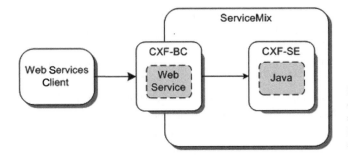

Figure 7.4 ServiceMix configuration for top-down web services showing how the CXF binding component calls the CXF service engine

back again to the binding component, which returns it to the client. We begin by looking at the configuration of the CXF binding component (listing 7.10).

Listing 7.10 CXF binding component configuration that publishes a web service

```
<beans xmlns="http://xbean.org/schemas/spring/1.0"
  xmlns:cxfbc="http://servicemix.apache.org/cxfbc/1.0"
  xmlns:coc="http://esbinaction.com/CoC/">

  <classpath>
    <location>.</location>
  </classpath>

  <cxfbc:consumer wsdl="classpath:CoC.wsdl"
    service="coc:CoCService"                            ❶
    interfaceName="coc:CoCPortType"
    targetEndpoint="CoCSoap"
    targetService="coc:CoCService"          ←❷
    targetInterface="coc:CoCPortType" />

</beans>
```

We defined a CXF JBI service, which can be deployed to the `servicemix-cxf-bc` binding component. This JBI service uses the information in the WSDL file to create a listener to which SOAP messages can be sent. The `service` and `interface` names ❶ should match the names used in the WSDL file. This information will be used by CXF to determine which service to expose. If you look back at the WSDL definition for the company web service, you'll see we defined the service element in the WSDL file, as shown here:

```
<wsdl:service name="CoCService">
  <wsdl:port binding="coc:CoCSoapBinding" name="CoCSoap">
    <soap:address location="http://localhost:8080/services/coc" />
  </wsdl:port>
</wsdl:service>
```

The elements used to determine where to expose the service are the `name` of the service, and the type of the `binding`. This `coc:CoCSoapBinding` is also defined in the WSDL file, and is of type `coc:CoCPortType`. Using this information, CXF exposes the service on the address `http://localhost:8080/services/coc`.

We also configured `targetEndpoint`, `targetService`, and `targetInterface` ❷.
This is the JBI service the message is sent to when a message is received on the web
service. Notice that we didn't specify where this service is listening. The CXF service
unit looks into the WSDL file and, based on information from the WSDL, exposes a
web service.

Let's now look at the real implementation of the service. This is defined in another
xbean.xml file, shown in listing 7.11, which is deployed to the `servicemix-cxf-se` service engine. Remember that this is the service the message will be sent to once it's
received by the previously configured binding component.

Listing 7.11   CXF service engine configuration, which calls a POJO class

```xml
<?xml version="1.0" encoding="UTF-8"?>
<beans xmlns:cxfse="http://servicemix.apache.org/cxfse/1.0"
  xmlns:coc="http://opensource.esb.org/CoC/"
  xmlns="http://xbean.org/schemas/spring/1.0">
                                                    Contains Java
                                                    implementation class
  <bean id="CocServiceImpl"
    class="esb.chapter7.ChamberOfCommerceServiceImpl"
    init-method="init"/>

  <classpath>
    <location>.</location>
  </classpath>
                                                    Specifies
                                                    generated web
  <cxfse:endpoint>                                  service stub
    <cxfse:pojo>
      <bean class="com.esbinaction.coc.CoCPortTypeImpl">
        <property name="delegate" ref="CocServiceImpl"/>
      </bean>
    </cxfse:pojo>
  </cxfse:endpoint>
</beans>
```

We use the generated stub as the implementation of the CXF service engine endpoint.
As you saw in listing 7.8, this implementation delegates all the calls to the Java implementation class we've written ourselves. And that's all you have to do.

You might wonder why we haven't specified an endpoint or service name here.
This isn't necessary in this case since this service engine uses information from the
generated web services stub to determine the service name and the endpoint name. It
does this by reading the JAX-WS annotations, which were also generated by CXF. We
haven't shown those yet, so let's quickly look at the JAX-WS annotations for the generated `CoCPortTypeImpl` Java class in listing 7.12.

Listing 7.12   JAX-WS annotations for the generated web services stub

```java
@javax.jws.WebService(
  name = "CoCPortType",
  serviceName = "CoCService",        ❶
  portName = "CoCSoap",              ❷
```

```
        targetNamespace = "http://opensource.esb.org/CoC/",
        endpointInterface = "org.esb.opensource.coc.CoCPortType")
public class CoCPortTypeImpl implements CoCPortType {    ←─❸
```

These annotations are used by the CXF service engine to determine how to register this service. The `serviceName` ❶ and `portName` ❷ together define the JBI service end-point name this JBI service is registered with in the JBI container. The `name` is used to indicate which interface is provided by this service. You can also see that this class implements the Java interface ❸ generated by CXF.

JSR-181: Web services metadata

JSR-181 is a specification started back in 2002 that specifies a set of annotations Java developers can use to easily create web services. When developing web services, you often have to write a whole set of artifacts: a WSDL describing the interface, a binding definition to marshal to and from XML, and maybe even some implementation-specific deployment descriptors. With JSR-181, a set of eight annotations have been defined that make it a lot easier for Java developers to write web services from a bottom-up approach.

Using this JSR-181, you can just annotate a POJO with the `javax.jws.Webservice` annotation, configure a web service framework (such as XFire, CXF, or any JEE 5–compliant application server), and the web service is created. This specification also gives you more fine-tuned control for mapping operations and messages using any of the other available annotations. Generally, not much fine tuning is needed, though, since the defaults chosen by JSR-181 fit most requirements.

When you deploy these two service units to ServiceMix, a web service will be started on the address specified in the WSDL file. This web service will be accessible by clients outside ServiceMix. This configuration will also start an internal service endpoint, which calls to the stub implementation. If you run this example from the supplied Ant build file, ch7-build.xml, with the `deploy-wsdl-top-down` Ant target, you can use the Swing test client or SoapUI to call this web service.

Next, let's discuss the bottom-up approach. We show you how to start from a Java class and expose it as a web service using Mule and ServiceMix.

7.2   Bottom-up approach

Another common approach to using web services is starting with a Java implementation, and generating a WSDL from the code. With modern web services frameworks such as CXF and Axis2, the WSDL files generated are of good quality, and this approach will get your web services up and running quickly. So if you already have numerous Java-based services, using a bottom-up approach you can quickly expose them as web services. In the upcoming sections, we show you how to use the bottom-up approach to provide web services in Mule and ServiceMix.

7.2.1 *Bottom-up approach using Mule*

We use the same service implementation from section 7.1.1. We want to expose as a web service the interface we implemented there. Let's quickly look at how this interface looks:

```
public interface ChamberOfCommerceService {

  List<Company> findCompanies(String city, String streeName);
  Company getCompany(String companyName);
  void changeCompany(String companyName, Company companyInfo);
}
```

Exposing this web service in Mule couldn't be easier. We use the CXF endpoint, shown in listing 7.13, to implement this functionality in a Mule configuration.

Listing 7.13   Mule configuration for providing a bottom-up web service

```
<mule>
  <spring:bean name="ChamberOfCommerceServiceImpl"           ◁─┐ Exposes service
      class="esb.chapter7.ChamberOfCommerceServiceImpl"         │ class as bean
      init-method="init"/>

  <model name="wsdl-bottom-up">
    <service name="cocService">
      <inbound>
        <cxf:inbound-endpoint address="                     │ Specifies address web
            http://localhost:8080/services/coc"/>            │ service listens on
      </inbound>
      <component>
        <spring-object
            bean="ChamberOfCommerceServiceImpl"/>            ◁─┐ References
      </component>                                              │ service bean
    </service>
  </model>
</mule>
```

If you compare listing 7.13 with the top-down approach, the only differences are that we didn't specify a WSDL file and that we point directly to our bean implementation. That's all you have to do: CXF will inspect the implementation, and based on the available methods, it will expose a web service on the specified address. Let's look at implementing the same example in ServiceMix.

7.2.2 *Bottom-up approach using ServiceMix*

For the bottom-up approach with ServiceMix, we start with the same implementation as in the previous Mule section. We create an endpoint in the CXF service engine (listing 7.14).

Listing 7.14   ServiceMix configuration for providing a bottom-up web service

```
<beans xmlns:cxfse="http://servicemix.apache.org/cxfse/1.0"
    xmlns:coc="http://opensource.esb.org/CoC/"
    xmlns="http://xbean.org/schemas/spring/1.0">
```

```
    <classpath>
      <location>.</location>
    </classpath>

    <cxfse:endpoint>
      <cxfse:pojo>
        <bean class="esb.chapter7.ChamberOfCommerceServiceImpl"     ◀━❶
              init-method="init"/>
      </cxfse:pojo>
    </cxfse:endpoint>
  </beans>
```

We only need to define the name of the class we want to expose as a web service ❶ and the CXF service engine will take care of the rest. In the previous section, we explained what JSR-181 does; this CXF service engine also uses JSR-181 to expose the methods from the implementation as a web service. We could customize the behavior of this implementation class with additional JSR-181 annotations. For this example, however, we only use the @Webservice annotation, which we defined on the implementation class:

```
@WebService(targetNamespace = "http://opensource.esb.org/CoC/" )
public class ChamberOfCommerceServiceImpl
    implements ChamberOfCommerceService {
```

If we could access internal ServiceMix endpoints from outside the container, we'd be finished at this point. But as we explained in previous chapters, to access internal JBI services, we need to configure a binding component that can serve as a façade to internal endpoints. So for this example we configure a CXF binding component that simply forwards the received message to this internal implementation (listing 7.15).

> **Listing 7.15 ServiceMix configuration for providing a web service externally**

```
<beans xmlns:cxfbc="http://servicemix.apache.org/cxfbc/1.0"

    xmlns:coc="http://opensource.esb.org/CoC/"
    xmlns="http://xbean.org/schemas/spring/1.0">

  <classpath>
    <location>.</location>
  </classpath>

  <cxfbc:consumer wsdl="classpath:coc.wsdl"       ◀━❶
      endpoint="ChamberOfCommerceServiceImplPort"                     ❷
      service="coc:ChamberOfCommerceServiceImplService"
      interfaceName="coc:ChamberOfCommerceServiceImpl"
      targetEndpoint="ChamberOfCommerceServiceImplPort"
      targetService="coc:ChamberOfCommerceServiceImplService"     ◀━❸
      targetInterface="coc:ChamberOfCommerceServiceImpl" />
</beans>
```

In listing 7.15 we define a web service that can be accessed from external clients. The first thing you see here is that we reference a WSDL file ❶. We don't write this WSDL file ourselves but generate it using the tools provided by CXF. For this we once again provide a simple target in the Ant build file for this chapter. When you run this target, cxf-generate-bottom-up, CXF will inspect the Java class we wish to expose, and based on the class, CXF will generate a WSDL file. In addition to the WSDL file, CXF will generate a set of JAXB classes that are used to go from XML to Java and back again.

The next thing we need to do is define the service and the endpoint for which we're going to provide a web service. This information can be found in the generated WSDL file, just as we did for the top-down web service earlier:

```
<wsdl:service name="ChamberOfCommerceServiceImplService">
  <wsdl:port name="ChamberOfCommerceServiceImplPort"
      binding="tns:ChamberOfCommerceServiceImplServiceSoapBinding">
    <soap:address location="http://localhost:9090/hello"/>
  </wsdl:port>
</wsdl:service>
```

The names that are generated for the WSDL are also used in the ServiceMix configuration to define which service and port combination we'd like to expose. This is done in the endpoint and service attributes ❷ in listing 7.15. If you look at the previous code fragment, you can also see a soap:address element. This element is used by Service-Mix to determine on which address it should expose the web service. You can see the default generated address in this fragment. If you want to expose the service on a different address, you can just change the value of the location attribute to the address you want to expose the web service on.

The final task is telling ServiceMix which internal service to invoke when a message is received on this binding component. We do this by specifying the targetEndpoint and targetService attributes ❸; as you can see in listing 7.15, these elements are the same as shown in the generated WSDL file.

That's all you have to configure. If you now run this example with the deploy-wsdl-bottom-up Ant target, the CXF binding component will start listening on http://localhost:9090/hello, or the address you specified in the generated WSDL file, and any call made to that HTTP endpoint will be forwarded to the internal running service inside the CXF service engine (listing 7.14). This service engine will then call to the POJO to execute the business logic. As you can see in this listing, the external exposed endpoint and service have the same name as the internal ones. As you'll recall from chapter 2, a service endpoint uniquely identifies a service within the JBI container, and therefore this might seem strange. The reason this can still work is that a difference exists between external service endpoints and internal endpoints. The first service endpoint in listing 7.15 defines an external endpoint ❷ and calls an internal endpoint ❸. Because ServiceMix knows when to call an internal endpoint and when to call an external one, these two endpoints with the same name can exist in the same JBI context.

So far you've seen how you can take advantage of the bottom-up and top-down approaches to use Mule and ServiceMix to provide web services that other parties can call. Let's now look at how we can use Mule and ServiceMix to consume web services. We begin by looking at Mule.

7.3   Consuming web services

Calling existing web services using Mule and ServiceMix is not that hard. They both provide various implementations that you can use to access these web services. The web service that we access in this example is the web service we created in section 7.2. So if you want to know which operations are available, check out the WSDL defined at the beginning of this chapter.

7.3.1   Consuming web services with Mule

You've seen how to host a web service in Mule using CXF—now let's look at consuming a web service using the same web services framework. The Mule configuration for consuming a web service is shown in listing 7.16.

Listing 7.16   Consuming web services using the CXF transport in Mule

```
<mule>
  <custom-transformer                   ◁─❶
      name="toStringTransformer"
      class="esb.chapter7.SimpleTransformer" />

  <file:file-to-string-transformer
      name="fileToString" />

  <file:connector streaming="false"
      name="fileConnector"/>

  <model name="consume-wsdl">
    <service name="cocServiceConsumeToJava">
      <inbound>
        <file:inbound-endpoint
            path="chapter7/consume-wsdl/in-to-java">
          <transformer ref="fileToString" />
        </file:inbound-endpoint>
      </inbound>
      <outbound>                            ❷
          <outbound-endpoint            ◁┘
            address="wsdl-cxf:http://localhost:8080/services/cocService
                ?wsdl&amp;method=getCompany">              ◁─❸
            <properties>
              <spring:entry key="service"                  ◁─❹
                value="{http://opensource.esb.org/CoC/}CoCService" />
              <spring:entry key="port"                     ◁─❺
                value="{http://opensource.esb.org/CoC/}CoCSoap" />
            </properties>
          </outbound-endpoint>
          <file:outbound-endpoint
              path="chapter7/consume-wsdl/out">      ◁─❻
            <transformer ref="toStringTransformer"/>
          </file:outbound-endpoint>
        </chaining-router>
      </outbound>
    </service>
  </model>
</mule>
```

The Mule configuration for consuming a remote web service based on a WSDL is quite large, so let's start at the top. First, we include a number of transformer definitions **❶**. The first transformer is used to create a readable string from a JavaBean and is used in the `file:outbound-endpoint` **❻**.

The outbound configuration shows a chaining router, which calls two endpoints. The first endpoint is the web service **❷** call. For this call we use Mule's wsdl-cxf **❸** endpoint. With this endpoint we can directly call an operation on a web service without having to generate any client code.

Calling web services using the CXF outbound endpoint

In our example we use the `wsdl-cxf` endpoint to directly call into a WSDL. Mule also provides an alternative way of calling web services. You can call remote web services using the `cxf:outbound` endpoint. The main difference between these two approaches is that when you use the `cxf:outbound` endpoint, you first have to generate the client classes from the WSDL file using the WSDL2Java tool provided by CXF. This generated client class is then used by the `cxf:outbound` endpoint to call the web service.

Notice that we also specifiy a `service` **❹** and a `port` **❺** attribute. Mule uses these values to determine which service and port from the WSDL file it should make the call to (since a WSDL file can contain multiple services and ports). Once the call is made, the result is sent to the next configured file endpoint **❻**, which writes the result from the web service to the file system.

To test this web service consumer, we also need a service provider. In listing 7.1 we showed you how you can use Mule to provide web services. If you run the `chapter-7-top-down` Ant task, you get a web service that you can use to test this example. Once you've started the web service, run the `chapter-7-consume-ws` target and drop the test file in the chapter7/consume-wsdl/in-to-java directory.

Before we discuss the WS-Security and WS-Addressing standards, we show you how to consume web services in ServiceMix.

7.3.2   *Consuming web services using ServiceMix*

When we want to consume web services in ServiceMix, we have to use a binding component since we're communicating with a service outside the ESB. For this we use the CXF binding component from section 7.1.3, where we used the `consumer` element of the binding component. In other words, we made a web service available to external clients over HTTP and consumed an internal service.

In this example, we want to provide a service to an internal service and consume an external web service, so we have to configure a `cxfbc:provider`. Listing 7.17 shows the CXF binding component for this example.

Listing 7.17 Calling web services using the CXF binding component in ServiceMix

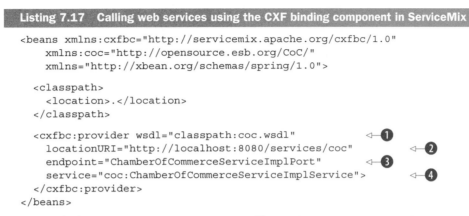

```
<beans xmlns:cxfbc="http://servicemix.apache.org/cxfbc/1.0"
    xmlns:coc="http://opensource.esb.org/CoC/"
    xmlns="http://xbean.org/schemas/spring/1.0">

  <classpath>
    <location>.</location>
  </classpath>

  <cxfbc:provider wsdl="classpath:coc.wsdl"                    ◄─❶
    locationURI="http://localhost:8080/services/coc"          ◄─❷
    endpoint="ChamberOfCommerceServiceImplPort"               ◄─❸
    service="coc:ChamberOfCommerceServiceImplService">        ◄─❹
  </cxfbc:provider>
</beans>
```

In listing 7.17 we specify a WSDL location ❶ for this CXF provider. This might seem strange, since we aren't offering a web service ourselves but are calling an external one. The reason is that all services and endpoints are self-describing in JBI. So with this WSDL specification, we provide the description of this service so that internal services know how to access this service. To specify where the service is running, we specify the `locationURI` ❷.

The attributes ❸ and ❹ identify the web service. It's good practice (and also enforced by CXF) to use the same names specified by the web service that we're calling, since this provider serves as a proxy between internal services and an external web service and as such provides exactly the same functionality. When you now send a message in the correct XML format to this service, the web service will be called.

Let's look at two other service units, which we use to read a file from the file system and use the file content to invoke the web service, and finally write the result of the web service call to a different directory. Let's begin with the `servicemix-file` binding component (listing 7.18).

Listing 7.18 File configuration for reading from and writing files to the file system

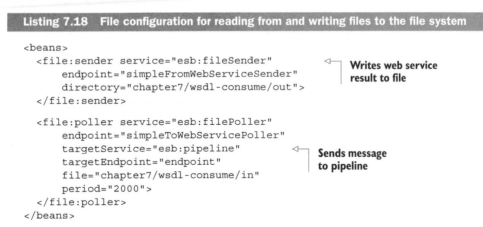

```
<beans>
  <file:sender service="esb:fileSender"
      endpoint="simpleFromWebServiceSender"       ◄─┐ Writes web service
      directory="chapter7/wsdl-consume/out">          │ result to file
  </file:sender>

  <file:poller service="esb:filePoller"
      endpoint="simpleToWebServicePoller"
      targetService="esb:pipeline"                 ◄─┐ Sends message
      targetEndpoint="endpoint"                        │ to pipeline
      file="chapter7/wsdl-consume/in"
      period="2000">
  </file:poller>
</beans>
```

Listing 7.18 configures a simple file poller that reads all incoming files from a directory and a file sender that writes files to a different directory. To connect the file sender and poller to the web service, we use a pipeline from the `servicemix-eip` component (listing 7.19).

Listing 7.19   EIP configuration that invokes the CXF service definition

```
<beans>
  <eip:pipeline service="esb:pipeline"
      endpoint="endpoint">
    <eip:transformer>
      <eip:exchange-target
        service="coc:ChamberOfCommerceServiceImplService"         Invokes CXF
        operation="coc:getCompany" />                             JBI service
    </eip:transformer>
    <eip:target>
      <eip:exchange-target service="esb:fileSender" />            Sends result
    </eip:target>                                                  to file sender
  </eip:pipeline>
</beans>
```

This pipeline definition in listing 7.19 is called from the file poller (listing 7.18) and makes a call to the service endpoint where the CXF web service provider is running. When the result from the web service comes back, it's sent to the file sender component, which is registered on `esb:fileSender`.

We need this `eip:pipeline` because we have to deal with two different MEPs. When a file poller reads a file and sends the content to a service, this is done using the in-only MEP. The web service, however, expects an in-out MEP, since it can return results. We use the `eip:pipeline` to bridge the in-only MEP to an in-out MEP.

If you want to run this example, go to the resources/chapter7 directory of the ServiceMix workspace and execute the `deploy-wsdl-consume` Ant target from the ch7-build.xml Ant build file. Just as for the Mule example we once again need a web service to call. We can use the ServiceMix bottom-up or top-down example, but let's use the Mule service. That way, you can see how easy it is to use web services as one way of integrating these two ESBs. Start up the `chapter-7-top-down` Ant task from the Mule workspace, and you get a web service that you can use to test this example. A test file is provided in the directory of this example.

So far you've seen how to provide and consume web services using Mule and ServiceMix. In the last part of this chapter, we look at two important web services standards: WS-Addressing and WS-Security. You'll learn how Mule and ServiceMix support these standards.

7.4   *Web service standards*

Our examples so far have demonstrated how to use web services together with Mule and ServiceMix. Web services, however, are much more complex than just sending plain XML messages wrapped in a SOAP envelope. Currently there are over one hundred web services specifications, and each governs a specific area. For instance, transactions are covered by the WS-Transactions specification, message encryption is covered by the WS-Security specification, and so on.

We don't have the space in this book to cover all these specifications, so we just focus on two important ones: WS-Security and WS-Addressing.

7.4.1 WS-Security

WS-Security is a standard that describes how to apply security to your SOAP messages. When we talk about security in this context, we're referring to these following four concepts:

- *Confidentiality*—The information we send to a certain party is only accessible by those authorized to have access. When someone sends a message to our web service, and we want to guarantee confidentiality, we have to encrypt the message.
- *Authenticity*—We want to verify that when someone sends us a message we're 100 percent certain that the sending party is who it claims to be. If we receive a message and let the sending party sign the message, we can use the signature to identify the sending party and be sure the message isn't being sent by someone else.
- *Integrity*—If someone sends us a message, the message is routed through firewalls, over the internet, and through some routers before it finally arrives at its destination. During transit, the message could have been changed. We want to guarantee that the message hasn't changed during transit. We can sign part of the data, and validate that data on the receiver end to determine whether the message has been tampered with.
- *Nonreputability*—When we receive and process messages—for instance, orders—the sending party shouldn't be able to deny it sent the message. This is easily accomplished by just storing the raw content of a message that's signed.

So how can we apply all of these requirements on a SOAP message that's sent to our service? The answer is by encrypting and signing the data, and the WS-Security specification tells us how to do it.

WS-Security specifies more than just encryption and signing; it also specifies, for instance, how you can use SAML, timestamps, and so forth together for authentication. However, we don't delve into those details in this section; we show how to use WS-Security to add encryption and signatures to SOAP message.

7.4.2 Using WS-Security with Mule

Mule supports WS-Security through the web service libraries it supports. So let's look at securing your web service and calling secured web services by using Mule's CXF support.

WS-SECURITY AND MULE FOR OUTGOING MESSAGES

Let's first look at how to apply WS-Security to outgoing messages. We don't show you the complete configuration in listing 7.20—just what you need to change in listing 7.16 to make the call secure.

Listing 7.20 Using Mule together with WS-Security for calling a secured web service

```
<mule>
  <cxf:connector name="wsdlCxfConnector">      ⊲—❶
    <property name="configurationLocation"                    ❷
      value="esb/chapter7/wss-cxf-config-client.xml" />
  </cxf:connector>

  <model name="consume-ws-security">
    <!—same as in listing 7.16 -->
  </model>
</mule>
```

The only configuration we add in listing 7.20 is a `cxf:connector` ❶. This CXF connector specifies how invocations to external web services using the CXF endpoint are made. The important part is the `configurationLocation` property ❷. This property points to an external CXF configuration file, where we indicate how CXF should deal with WS-Security (listing 7.21).

Listing 7.21 CXF configuration for securing outgoing web service calls

```
<beans xmlns="http://www.springframework.org/schema/beans">
  <bean name="SAAJOutInterceptor"                              ⊲—❶
    class="org.apache.cxf.binding.soap.saaj.SAAJOutInterceptor" />

  <bean name="WSS4JOutInterceptor"                             ⊲—❷
      class="org.apache.cxf.ws.security.wss4j.WSS4JOutInterceptor">
    <constructor-arg>
      <map>                                                    ⊲—❸
        <entry key="action" value="Signature Encrypt" />
        <entry key="passwordCallbackRef"
          value-ref="wsCallback" />
        <entry key="user" value="clientkey" />
        <entry key="encryptionUser" value="serverkey" />
        <entry key="decryptionPropFile"
          value="esb/chapter7/client.crypto.properties" />
        <entry key="signaturePropFile"
          value="esb/chapter7/client.crypto.properties" />
      </map>
    </constructor-arg>
  </bean>

  <bean id="cxf" class="org.apache.cxf.bus.CXFBusImpl">
    <property name="outInterceptors">                          ⊲—❹
      <list>
        <ref bean="SAAJOutInterceptor" />
        <ref bean="WSS4JOutInterceptor" />
      </list>
    </property>
  </bean>

  <bean id="wsCallback"
      class="esb.chapter7.TestPwdCallback" />    ⊲—❺
</beans>
```

To get WS-Security to be applied to all our outgoing messages, we add a WS-Security specific interceptor ❷. As you can see, we add two interceptors. This is necessary because the SAAJOutInterceptor ❶ prepares the content of the message so that the WSS4JOutInterceptor ❷ can work with it. Before looking at the details of the WS-Security configuration ❸, let's quickly examine the other parts.

As you can see, we add the configured interceptors to the CXFBusImpl ❹. By doing this, we ensure that all the outgoing web service calls use WS-Security. We also specify a password callback ❺, which is used when private keys need to be retrieved from the keystore. The most interesting part of this configuration, however, is ❸. This element contains WS-Security for Java (WSS4J)-specific properties (see table 7.1).

Table 7.1   An overview of WSS4J security properties

Name	Description
signaturePropFile	Defines the crypto properties for WSS4J. This file is used when signing a message or when checking a signature.
decryptionPropFile	Defines another set of crypto properties for WSS4J. Just as the signaturePropFile was used for the signing part, this file is used for encryption and decryption of the SOAP messages. In our case, this points to the same file.
action	Specifies what to do with the message. In this case, we specified Signature and Encrypt. As the name implies, this signs and encrypts the SOAP body.
user	Refers to the alias stored in the keystore, which is used for signing.
passwordCallbackClass	Returns the password for the specified user. This password is then used to get the correct key out of the keystore. This property is needed here since we want to retrieve the private key from the keystore.
encryptionUser	Indicates the name of the key used for encryption. No password is required, since this is just a public key.

Let's look at the properties described in table 7.1 in greater detail. We begin by looking at the client.crypto.properties file (listing 7.21). This file configures how we access the keystore where the certificates are stored:

```
org.apache.ws.security.crypto.provider =
    org.apache.ws.security.components.crypto.Merlin
org.apache.ws.security.crypto.merlin.keystore.type = jks
org.apache.ws.security.crypto.merlin.keystore.password = storePass
org.apache.ws.security.crypto.merlin.file =
    esb/chapter7/clientStore.jks
```

This file configures how WSS4J accesses the keystore. The first property you see here points to a WSS4J-specific implementation, which handles the encrypting and signing of the data. The other properties define where WSS4J can find the keystore and how the keystore is accessed. In this case, we have a Java KeyStore (JKS) store (the default format in Java) that's located in the classpath at esb/chapter7/clientStore.jks and that has a password of storePass.

Whenever WSS4J needs to access the keystore, it will use this information. As shown in table 7.1, the user property and the encryptionUser property must match a key's alias, which is stored in the keystore configured by the client.crypto.properties file. The keystore from the crypto.properties file also relates to the passwordCallback class; to access a private key, identified by the user property (which is used for signing), we require a password supplied by this passwordClass.

An action defines what needs to be done with the XML message. In this case, we want to add a signature to the message and encrypt the message, so we define that as the actions to execute: Signature and Encrypt.

When signing a message, we use a private key from the keystore to create a signature of the XML that we'll send. This signature can be validated by the server to check whether the message has been tampered with during transport, and whether the sender is who it claims to be. If the message is changed during transport, the signature check will fail, and if a different private key is used, which means someone is pretending to be someone else, the signature check will also fail, since we won't have that sender's public key inour keystore. Figure 7.5 summarizes the signing and encryption of messages.

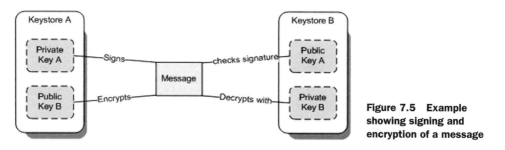

Figure 7.5 Example showing signing and encryption of a message

As shown in figure 7.5, for the encryption part the public key of the server is used, and the server decrypts the message using its own private key. This way, no one can read the message while it's in transit and only the intended recipient can decrypt the message.

Well, that was WS-Security for outgoing messages and an introduction to how WSS4J is configured. We'll see these same configuration elements in the sections that follow.

WS-SECURITY AND MULE FOR INCOMING MESSAGES
So far you've seen how to secure the outgoing messages. When we want to do this on incoming messages, we use a similar configuration, since we need the same information. We just show the changed code in regard to listing 7.13's Mule configuration (listing 7.22).

Listing 7.22 Using Mule and WS-Security to provide security to incoming messages

```
<mule>

  <cxf:connector name="cxfConnector">
    <property name="configurationLocation"
          value="esb/chapter7/wss-cxf-config.xml" />      ◁──❶
  </cxf:connector>

  <!-- not changed -->
</mule>
```

What you see in listing 7.22 is much the same as the outgoing configuration in listing 7.21. We point to an external file, which holds the WS-Security configuration ❶. Listing 7.23 shows the CXF configuration that is referenced here.

Listing 7.23 CXF configuration for securing incoming web service calls

```
<beans xmlns="http://www.springframework.org/schema/beans"
    xmlns:jaxws="http://cxf.apache.org/jaxws">
  <jaxws:server name=
    "{http://opensource.esb.org/CoC/}
                    ChamberOfCommerceServiceImplPort"      ◁   Specifies port
    createdFromAPI="true">                                    ❶ to enable
                                                                WS-Security on
    <jaxws:inInterceptors>
      <bean
        class="org.apache.cxf.binding.soap.saaj.SAAJInInterceptor" />
      <bean
        class="org.apache.cxf.ws.security.wss4j.WSS4JInInterceptor">
       <constructor-arg>
        <map>                                              ◁   Configures
          <entry key="action" value="Signature Encrypt" />     WS-Security
          <entry key="passwordCallbackRef"                  ❷ parameters
              value-ref="serverCallback" />
          <entry key="user" value="serverkey" />
          <entry key="decryptionPropFile"
              value="esb/chapter7/server.crypto.properties" />
          <entry key="signaturePropFile"
              value="esb/chapter7/server.crypto.properties" />
        </map>
       </constructor-arg>
      </bean>
    </jaxws:inInterceptors>
  </jaxws:server>

  <bean id="serverCallback"
      class="esb.chapter7.TestPwdCallback" />
</beans>
```

In listing 7.23, we specify WSS4J settings ❷ that define how to decrypt and validate a signature. The biggest difference here is that we don't apply these settings on all the CXF-provided web services, but only on the one with the specified fully qualified port name ❶. You can easily find out this name when you look at the WSDL file for the service you're providing.

The Mule support for WS-Security goes further than what we explain here, since WSS4J, which Mule use for WS-Security, has many more options. What we've seen so far however, are the most common WS-Security features. Let's look at the configuration of the same features in ServiceMix.

7.4.3   *Using WS-Security with ServiceMix*

To use WS-Security with ServiceMix, you use pretty much the same configuration you'd use with Mule—which isn't that strange since they both use CXF and WSS4J. Because we already created the initial example for ServiceMix with CXF, we don't have to change much of the configuration. We only have to extend the previous examples with some WSS4J-specific properties.

WS-SECURITY AND SERVICEMIX FOR OUTGOING MESSAGES

Listing 7.24 shows how we configure ServiceMix to consume messages based on a WSDL file.

Listing 7.24   Consuming web services using the CXF binding component

```
<beans xmlns:cxfbc="http://servicemix.apache.org/cxfbc/1.0"
  xmlns:coc="http://opensource.esb.org/CoC/"
  xmlns="http://xbean.org/schemas/spring/1.0">

  <classpath>
    <location>.</location>
  </classpath>

  <cxfbc:provider wsdl="classpath:coc.wsdl"
    locationURI="http://localhost:8080/services/coc"
    endpoint="ChamberOfCommerceServiceImplPort"
    service="coc:ChamberOfCommerceServiceImplService">
  </cxfbc:provider>

</beans>
```

To add WS-Security support to the CXF provider, we need to add a number of CXF interceptors, as shown in listing 7.25.

Listing 7.25   Consuming a web service that's secured using WS-Security

```
<beans xmlns:cxfbc="http://servicemix.apache.org/cxfbc/1.0"
    xmlns:coc="http://opensource.esb.org/CoC/"
  xmlns="http://xbean.org/schemas/spring/1.0">

  <classpath>
    <location>.</location>
  </classpath>

  <cxfbc:provider wsdl="classpath:coc.wsdl"
    locationURI="http://localhost:8080/services/coc"
    endpoint="ChamberOfCommerceServiceImplPort"
    service="coc:ChamberOfCommerceServiceImplService">
    <cxfbc:outInterceptors>                      Adds CXF out
      <ref bean="saajout" />          ❶           interceptors
      <ref bean="wss4jout" />
```

```
        </cxfbc:outInterceptors>
    </cxfbc:provider>

    <bean
        class="org.apache.cxf.binding.
                    soap.saaj.SAAJOutInterceptor"
        id="saajout" />
    <bean
        class="org.apache.cxf.ws.security.
                    wss4j.WSS4JOutInterceptor"
        id="wss4jout">
        <constructor-arg>
          <map>
            <entry key="action" value="Signature Encrypt" />
            <entry key="user" value="clientkey" />
            <entry key="signaturePropFile"
              value="esb/chapter7/client.crypto.properties" />
            <entry key="encryptionPropFile"
              value="esb/chapter7/client.crypto.properties" />
            <entry key="encryptionUser" value="serverkey" />
            <entry key="passwordCallbackClass"
              value="esb.chapter7.TestPwdCallback" />
          </map>
        </constructor-arg>
    </bean>
</beans>
```

2 Defines SAAJOutInterceptor

3 Defines WSS4J interceptor

4 Configures WSS4J interceptor

In listing 7.25, we add two interceptors ❶. The first one, SAAJOutInterceptor ❷, makes a DOM object from an XML message. This is needed for the WSS4JOut-Interceptor ❸, which handles the signing and encryption of the message. We also configure the actions ❹ that need to be applied—signing and encryption in this case—and we specify the property file that defines how the keystore is accessed.

We use the same password callback class as we did for the Mule example. This passwordCallback returns the password needed to access the private key in the keystore, which is used for signing the message. When you now run this example, the message that's sent will be signed with the private key (which has an alias named clientkey) and will be encrypted using the public key (which is stored as serverkey in the keystore).

WS-SECURITY AND SERVICEMIX FOR INCOMING MESSAGES
To enable WS-Security on the web services we offer, we use a similar configuration. This time, however, we define incoming interceptors, and we can remove the encryption alias. The CXF binding component configuration for this example is shown in listing 7.26.

Listing 7.26 Providing a web service that's secured using WS-Security

```
<beans>
  <cxfbc:consumer wsdl="classpath:coc.wsdl"
     endpoint="ChamberOfCommerceServiceImplPort"
     service="coc:ChamberOfCommerceServiceImplService"
     interfaceName="coc:ChamberOfCommerceServiceImpl"
     targetEndpoint="ChamberOfCommerceServiceImplPort"
     targetService="coc:ChamberOfCommerceServiceImplService"
```

```
        targetInterface="coc:ChamberOfCommerceServiceImpl">
    <cxfbc:inInterceptors>
      <ref bean="saajin"/>
      <ref bean="wss4jin"/>
    </cxfbc:inInterceptors>
  </cxfbc:consumer>

  <bean class="org.apache.cxf.binding.
                    soap.saaj.SAAJInInterceptor"
        id="saajin"/>

  <bean
      class="org.apache.cxf.ws.security.
                    wss4j.WSS4JInInterceptor"
        id="wss4jin">
    <constructor-arg>
      <map>
        <entry key="action" value="Signature Encrypt"/>
        <entry key="user" value="serverkey"/>
        <entry key="signaturePropFile"
           value="esb/chapter7/server.crypto.properties"/>
        <entry key="encryptionPropFile"
           value="esb/chapter7/server.crypto.properties"/>
        <entry key="passwordCallbackClass"
           value="esb.chapter7.TestPwdCallback"/>
      </map>
    </constructor-arg>
  </bean>
</beans>
```

❶ Defines interceptors

❷ Defines SAAJInInterceptor

❸ Defines WSS4JInInterceptor

❹ Configures WSS4J interceptor

We define two interceptors ❶ in listing 7.26. `SAAJInInterceptor` ❷ will transform the incoming message to a DOM message so that it can be processed by `WSS4J-InInterceptor`. `WSS4JInInterceptor` ❸ applies the specified WS-Security actions ❹ on the incoming message.

In this example, we specify the action as `Signature Encrypt`. This means that we first decrypt the message, using the private key with the alias `serverkey`, and then check the signature. We don't need to specify the key to check the signature with, since its serial identification is included in the XML message and is used to get the correct key from the keystore.

As you can see, using WS-Security on your messages from ServiceMix isn't difficult. The most difficult part is understanding all the private and public keys and the various configuration options.

In the last section of this chapter, we explore the WS-Addressing specification. This standard is becoming increasingly popular and provides great functionality.

7.4.4   *WS-Addressing*

WS-Addressing is a popular specification that can be used to specify addressing information using headers inside the SOAP message. One of the reasons this specification was created was because with web services, part of the addressing is normally done outside the message. For instance, when we send a SOAP message, the address where we sent the message is specified outside the message. This is an HTTP address or an SMTP address.

When we're doing direct point-to-point communication this isn't such big an issue, but when we have a number of intermediaries between the client and the server, this process can become a problem. The WS-Addressing specification identifies a number of SOAP headers that are used to address a message. In this section, we show you how Mule and ServiceMix handle the following headers:

- `wsa:To`—Specifies the destination where the message should be sent. For instance, when we have a central entry point for all our web services, we can route the message based on this header.
- `wsa:ReplyTo`—Allows the sending party to specify an URL where the response of the message will be sent to.
- `wsa:messageID`—Uniquely identifies the message.
- `wsa:relatesTo`—Used to indicate that this message is related to another message. When we use `replyTo` we can add this field to the response message and set the content to point to the `messageID` of the request. That way, the recipient can easily correlate the request to the response.
- `wsa:Action`—Defines the action that needs to be executed by the recipient. This could, for instance, be mapped to a certain operation on a web service.

Let's start by looking at Mule's support for WS-Addressing.

7.4.5 Using WS-Addressing in Mule

Mule supports WS-Addressing through its Apache CXF connector. If you want to use WS-Addressing in Mule, you have to create a CXF endpoint and specify a CXF configuration file that defines how you want to use WS-Addressing. Listing 7.27 shows how to configure an incoming web service endpoint that can process `ws:addressing` headers.

Listing 7.27   WS-Addressing–enabled inbound endpoint for Mule using CXF

```
<mule>
  <cxf:connector name="ws-addressing"
    configurationLocation="
        esb/chapter7/cxf-addressing-config.xml" />

  <spring:bean name="ChamberOfCommerceServiceImpl"
      class="esb.chapter7.ChamberOfCommerceServiceImpl"
      init-method="init" />

  <model name="cxf-ws-addressing">

    <!-- Calls directly to the service -->
    <service name="cocService">
      <inbound>
        <cxf:inbound-endpoint
            address="http://localhost:8080/services/coc">
          <custom-transformer
            class="esb.chapter7.WSAddressingTransformer" />
```

1 Defines WS-Addressing supporting

2 Configures CXF endpoint

```
          </inbound-endpoint>
        </inbound>
        <component>
          <spring-object bean="ChamberOfCommerceServiceImpl" />
        </component>
      </service>
    </model>
  </mule>
```

In listing 7.27, we use a CXF-based HTTP inbound endpoint ❷, which uses the CXF connector ❶. On this CXF connector, we override the default CXF configuration and specify our own: `cxf-addressing-config.xml`. The rest of this configuration is just the same as in the Mule bottom-up example. So when we make a call to the address specified with the inbound endpoint ❶, the call is routed to the specified component class. Let's look at the `cxf-addressing-config.xml` file, which specifies that we want to use WS-Addressing:

```
<beans>
  <jaxws:server name="{http://opensource.esb.org/CoC/}
        ChamberOfCommerceServiceImplPort" createdFromAPI="false">
    <jaxws:features>
      <wsa:addressing usingAddressingAdvisory="true" />
    </jaxws:features>
  </jaxws:server>
</beans>
```

In this code fragment, the WS-Addressing specific configuration for CXF is defined. With the CXF configuration, we can add features to a web service—in this case, the feature `wsa:addressing`. This feature is applied only to the web service that matches the specified name. For more detailed information on how to use WS-Addressing, check the CXF website (http://cxf.apache.org), which provides extensive demos on how to configure and use this feature. Before showing how you can use WS-Addressing in ServiceMix, let's quickly look at accessing the WS-Addressing headers from Mule.

Mule doesn't provide a standard transformer or filter for these headers, but creating one is easy, so that's what we do (listing 7.28).

Listing 7.28 Mule transformer that accesses the WS-Addressing headers

```
public class WSAddressingTransformer extends
    AbstractMessageAwareTransformer{

  @Override
  public Object transform(MuleMessage message,
      String outputEncoding) throws TransformerException {

    if ( message.getPayload() instanceof InputStream ) {
      ByteArrayOutputStream bOut = new ByteArrayOutputStream();
      try {
      IOUtils.copyLarge((InputStream)                  ❶ Gets SOAP
        message.getPayload(), bOut);                       message
    } catch (IOException e) {
```

```
        throw new TransformerException(this, e);
    }
    MessageImpl m = new MessageImpl();                    ❷ Creates new
    m.setContent(InputStream.class, new                      CXF message
            ByteArrayInputStream(bOut.toByteArray()));
    SoapMessage soapMessage = new SoapMessage(m);
    ReadHeadersInterceptor interceptor = new
        ReadHeadersInterceptor(BusFactory.getDefaultBus());  ❸ Uses CXF
    interceptor.handleMessage(soapMessage);                     interceptors

    List<Header> headers = soapMessage.getHeaders();
    for (Header header : headers) {
      String namespace = header.getName().getNamespaceURI();
      if (namespace.endsWith("addressing")) {
        message.setProperty(header.getName().getLocalPart(),   Checks for
            header.getObject());                               WS-Addressing
      }                                                     ❹ headers
    }
    message.setPayload(new ByteArrayInputStream(            Fills
        bOut.toByteArray()));                             ❺ MuleMessage
    return message;
  }
  else {
    return message;
  }
}
```

Listing 7.28 first uses CXF ❷ to parse the input message ❶ to a SOAP message. This SOAP message is again parsed by CXF to get to the headers of the SOAP message ❸.

Then we implement a bit of logic to check for WS-Addressing headers ❹. If any WS-Addressing headers are found, they're stored in the properties of the Mule message. Finally, we set a new stream in the Mule message ❺ so that further processing isn't interrupted. We can now configure this transformer on a web service–based endpoint. After this transformer is applied, we can access the WS-Addressing properties from everywhere, using them for content-based routing, for example.

Let's move on to the WS-Addressing functionality provided by ServiceMix.

7.4.6 Using WS-Addressing in ServiceMix

ServiceMix supports the WS-Addressing standard with its CXF binding component. This component automatically parses the WS-Addressing action and WS-Addressing To headers, and you can use them automatically for routing the incoming message to a service endpoint. So by specifying a specific wsa:to and wsa:action header in the incoming message, the service consumer can easily call different services provided by the JBI container:

- wsa:Action—Can be used to specify the target interface and the target operation
- wsa:To—Can be used to specify which service name and endpoint name to forward the message to

Both these headers use a custom format to determine either which interface/operation to send the message to, or to determine which service endpoint to invoke. Let's start by looking at the format used by the wsa:Action header:

```
[target namespace] [delimiter] [interface] [delimiter] [operation]
```

These elements are explained in detail in table 7.2.

Table 7.2   The wsa:Action header used in ServiceMix

Name	Description
Target namespace	The namespace of the interface that we want to call
Delimiter	Either : (if the namespace is a URN) or /otherwise
Interface	The name of the interface we want to call
Operation	The name of the operation on the interface we want to invoke

Here's an example:

```
<wsa:Action>http://osesb.org/CoCService/GetCompany</wsa:Action>
```

If we specify this action, the CXF BC will forward the message to a service endpoint that implements the CoCService interface and has a namespace equal to http://osesb.org. On this JBI service, the GetCompany operation will be invoked.

For the wsa:To header, the same construct is used, but now we specify the service and the endpoint name instead of the interface and the operation name:

```
[target namespace] [delimiter] [service] [delimiter] [endpoint]
```

Table 7.3 explains the background of these elements in more detail.

Table 7.3   The wsa:To header used in ServiceMix

Name	Description
Target namespace	The namespace of the service that we want to call
Delimiter	Either : (if the namespace is a URN) or /otherwise
Service	The name of the service we want to call
Endpoint	The name of the endpoint on the service that we'll invoke

Here's a simple example:

```
<wsa:To>urn:osesb:cocservice:simpleEndpoint</wsa:To>
```

The message will be automatically routed to a service with the name cocservice, which uses the namespace urn:osesb. On this service, the message will be sent to the simpleEndpoint endpoint.

Working with WS-Addressing in ServiceMix is easy. You don't have to configure any-thing, and you can use the WS-Addressing headers directly. For ServiceMix you can also use more advanced WS-Addressing features, but that topic is beyond the scope of this book. If you're interested in using these features, visit the CXF website.

7.5 Summary

This chapter described how to work with web services using Mule and ServiceMix. The top-down example illustrated how you can easily take a WSDL file and create a web ser-vice implementation from that WSDL using Mule and ServiceMix.

Even when you don't get the WSDL file from an external party, using a top-down approach is smart, especially when you're offering services to .NET consumers. Be sure to start with a good WSDL design to allow for easy integration.

Suppose you need to expose some functionality for other applications in your organization. The bottom-up approach is a quick way to get everything up and run-ning. Just use Mule or ServiceMix to expose a Java interface and you're done—but make sure the quality of the generated WSDL is sufficient.

Just providing web services isn't always enough. In a large organization, a number of different web services are available, such as web services that handle authentication or allow you to retrieve customer information. For these services, you're usually pro-vided with a WSDL file. You use this file to call the specific operation on the service. As you've seen in this chapter, this is easy to do using either Mule or ServiceMix.

In the last part of this chapter, we looked at two WS-* specifications. We started with WS-Security, which allows you to apply certain security aspects to your messages. Encrypting and signing your messages is a good thing, especially when you're calling or providing services that use the internet for communication.

Finally, we showed you how to work with WS-Addressing. The biggest advantage of this specification is that it allows you to specify all the routing information inside the message, independent of the transport used. With WS-Addressing it's easy to imple-ment web service proxies and expose certain operations based on the `wsa:Action` that was specified.

In this chapter we mainly talked about communicating with the outside world. In the next chapter, we'll dive into some more internal features of the ESB, such as error handling, transaction support, and security. These are features needed to run an ESB in an enterprise environment.

Implementing enterprise-quality message flows

In this chapter:

- Understanding error handling
- Using the Acegi framework
- Implementing an Apache LDAP server
- Using JAAS to secure ServiceMix
- Implementing transaction handling

Implementing message flows involves functionality such as routing, transformation, and connectivity. However, that's not enough to implement enterprise integration solutions in real-life integration projects. You also need to be able to deal with, for example, error handling, security, and transactions. In this chapter, you'll learn all the details.

Because message flows won't run as expected all the time, we start this chapter with a discussion on error handling. It is essential (for the implementation of security and transactions as well) to be able to handle errors on all parts of a message flow. Because integration solutions typically deal with numerous messages, addressing errors is often difficult. A common solution is to send messages to error queues or "dead letter" queues, where ESB administrators can be alerted when an error occurs. You'll see that implementing error-handling functionality is quite easy with Mule and ServiceMix.

Once error handling is in place, you can add security to a message flow. Error handling is a requirement when implementing security, because you encounter errors such as authentication and authorization failures. Security encompasses topics such as authentication, authorization, and message integrity. In the previous chapter, we discussed security in relation to web services, focusing on WS-Security. Because WS-Security deals with security on a message level, we focus in this chapter on security on an ESB container level. We look at the authentication and authorization of incoming messages in Mule and ServiceMix with security technologies like Lightweight Directory Access Protocol (LDAP) and Java Authentication and Authorization Service (JAAS).

In addition, we consider ways to implement transactional message flows in Mule and ServiceMix. A typical example of a transaction in a message flow is the consumption of a JMS message from a queue. The message will be consumed from the JMS queue only if the transactional processing of the message succeeds. If an error occurs, the transaction will be roll backed and the message will stay in the JMS queue. This is what was missing from the error-handling functionality that we just discussed. Although transaction handling is a complex topic, you'll see that Mule and Service-Mix make it easy to implement transactional message flows.

By the end of this chapter, you'll be able to implement complex message flows that take care of error handling, security, and transactions. Once you've experimented with the examples, you can consider yourself an integration professional!

8.1 Handling errors in your message flow

In the previous chapters you've seen a huge amount of functionality that can be used when implementing message flows in an open source ESB. But we've mainly talked about how to implement these message flows without taking into account possible errors and exceptions. When implementing message flows in real projects, error handling is an important part of the development work. In this section, we explore error handling in Mule and ServiceMix. First, let's address the exception strategies of Mule, which provide the error-handling functionality we're looking for.

8.1.1 Error handling with Mule

Mule features support to help you with handling errors during the runtime execution of a message flow. Errors and exceptions can occur at almost every step in the message flow, and therefore it's important to have a fine-grained error-handling model at your disposal. For Mule, this means that you can define exception strategies to handle errors.

Two types of exception strategies are available: component and connector. The component exception strategy can be used to handle exceptions that have been thrown in Mule components. And because you'll implement most Mule components yourself, this means that this exception strategy can be used to handle exceptions thrown by your own classes.

Connector exception strategies can be used to handle errors that are thrown by the connectors you use in your inbound and outbound endpoint definitions. For example, when an HTTP request fails in your outbound endpoint, the connector exception strategy can be used to handle this exception. Figure 8.1 shows a graphical overview of how you can use exception strategies in Mule.

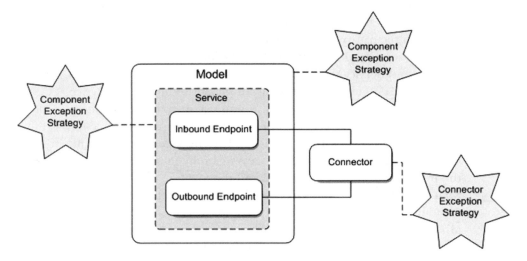

Figure 8.1   Mule offers component and connector exception strategies.

Notice that we can define exception strategies on three levels: the model, the service, and the connector levels. The model and service levels can be used for component exception strategies, and the connector level can be used for the connector exception strategy. If no exception strategies are defined in a Mule configuration, the Mule container automatically applies the default exception strategies. These exception strategies log the error stack trace with Log4j and just pass the exception on. When an exception occurs in an HTTP connector, this means that the message flow will just stop processing.

For a decent error-handling mechanism, it's therefore important to at least define an error queue or a dead letter queue to send error messages to. Listing 8.1 shows how easy the configuration of a dead letter queue is for handling component exceptions.

Listing 8.1   Configuring a dead letter queue

```
<mule>
  <model name="DeadLetterModel">
    <service name="ErrorService">
      <inbound>
        <jms:inbound-endpoint queue="test.input"/>      ◁─❶
      </inbound>
      <component class="ErrorGenerator">      ◁─❷
      <outbound>
        <outbound-pass-through-router>
```

```
            <jms:outbound-endpoint queue="test.output"/>
          </outbound-pass-through-router>
        </outbound>
        <default-service-exception-strategy>
          <jms:outbound-endpoint queue="test.error"/>
        </default-service-exception-strategy>
      </service>
    </model>
  </mule>
```
❸

Listing 8.1 shows a simple service definition that listens for new messages on a JMS input queue ❶. The incoming message is then passed on to the `ErrorGenerator` class ❷, which throws an exception during its message processing.

When an exception is thrown, the message isn't passed on to the configured outbound router. If an exception strategy is configured, as in this example ❸, the exception is processed by this exception handler. In this case, the default exception strategy is used, which means that the exception is passed on to the `Default-ComponentExceptionStrategy` class. This is the same class that handles the exception when no strategy is defined in the Mule configuration. The difference is that we define an outbound endpoint for this exception strategy. The error message will now be sent to the defined JMS queue.

The error message is a normal `MuleMessage` like every message that's sent within the Mule container. The difference is that the payload or the content of the message is an `ExceptionMessage`. This `ExceptionMessage` class is a wrapper for the exception, the name of the component, the endpoint URI that caused the error, and a timestamp. So when you want to build an error handler for an error queue like the `test.error` queue in listing 8.1, you'll receive a message with this content.

Now that you've seen an example of a component exception strategy, let's look at an example of a connector exception strategy. The exception handler for a connector is not that different from a component exception strategy, and you can also define an error queue with an outbound endpoint. But let's see how a connector exception strategy is configured (listing 8.2).

Listing 8.2   Configuring a custom connector exception strategy in Mule

```
<mule>
  <http:connector name="exceptionHTTP">
    <custom-exception-strategy
        class="HTTPExceptionHandler">
      <jms:outbound-endpoint queue="http.error"/>
      <spring:property name="status" value="500"/>
    </custom-exception-strategy>
  </http:connector>

  <model name="CustomExceptionModel">
    <service name="ConnectorExceptionService">
      <inbound>
        <jms:inbound-endpoint queue="test.input"/>
      </inbound>
      <outbound>
```

❶ Defines exception-handling logic

❷ Injects property value

```
        <outbound-pass-through-router>
          <http:outbound-endpoint
              address="http://localhost:8080/TestService"
              connector-ref="exceptionHTTP"/>           ◁┐   Uses exception
        </outbound-pass-through-router>                  ❸   HTTP connector
      </outbound>
    </service>
  </model>
</mule>
```

The exception strategy for a connector has to be defined as part of the connector configuration ❶. This custom exception strategy class must extend the `AbstractException-`
`Listener` or `DefaultExceptionStrategy` class. `AbstractExceptionListener` implements
the `ExceptionListener` interface and can be used as a base class for custom exception
strategies. `DefaultExceptionStrategy` implements the abstract methods of `Abstract-`
`ExceptionListener` and can be used as a base class when you don't want to implement a full-blown exception handler. For this example, it would be sufficient to
create a new class, which extends the `DefaultExceptionStrategy` and overrides the
`handleMessagingException` or the `defaultHandler` method.

In addition to the outbound endpoint definition used as an error queue for the
custom exception strategy defined in the `routeException` method of the `Abstract-`
`ExceptionListener` class, you can inject properties via the Spring Framework as you
can do with Spring beans ❷.

In listing 8.2, the message flow is triggered when a JMS message arrives at the
`test.input` queue. The message is then passed on to the outbound router, which
invokes a web service over HTTP. This is, of course, an oversimplified example, because
in a real implementation you'd have to transform the JMS message to adhere to the
message format expected by the web service. To use the custom exception strategy ❶,
we have to link the outbound endpoint to the connector definition with the `connector-`
`ref` attribute ❸. When the HTTP call to the web service fails, the custom exception
strategy is called with the exception message. The exception will eventually be sent to
an error queue, `http.error`, which can be used to trigger an error message flow or as
a logging mechanism for error messages.

In section 8.2, we use exception strategies to catch authentication and authorization exceptions, so we'll see some more examples later on. You now know how easy it
is to configure exception strategies within Mule, so you should be able to implement
error handling in your message flows as well. Next, let's explore implementing error
handling in ServiceMix.

8.1.2 *Error handling in ServiceMix*

You had a sneak preview of error handling in ServiceMix in chapter 5 (section 5.2),
when we discussed message validation. Because we needed a way to catch validation
errors in that example, we implemented a bean that caught fault messages and sent
them on to an error queue. In this section, we look in greater detail into dealing with
error handling in ServiceMix.

Let's begin by discussing error handling as part of the JBI specification. As you know, the choice of a message exchange pattern is important when implementing a message flow in a JBI container such as ServiceMix. Let's examine a typical example of error handling with an in-out message exchange (see figure 8.2).

Figure 8.2 shows a typical request/response message flow that uses an HTTP binding component (BC). In this message flow, the incoming HTTP request is routed to a bean. In the JavaBean, an exception occurs and a fault message is returned to the NMR. Because the message exchange uses an in-out message exchange pattern, this fault message is sent back to the HTTP client via the HTTP BC.

So for a default request-response message flow, the error message is simply sent back to the requesting application. This is not always the desired behavior; in some cases the error message needs to be caught and another response message must be sent back to the client application. This involves more complex error-handling logic and custom code development.

When using an enterprise service bus, the communication style is often asynchronous (with only an incoming message) instead of synchronous. So let's look at a typical example of an in-only message exchange with a JMS BC (see figure 8.3).

Notice that we use a JMS BC as a typical example of an in-only message exchange and an HTTP BC to explain an in-out message exchange. Both components can also be used with another message exchange pattern, but the common usage is shown in these figures. When an exception occurs in the bean component with an in-only message exchange, this still means that a fault message is sent to the NMR. However, the message flow will stop there because no routing path exists for the NMR to route the fault message to an endpoint. Therefore, the message flow is terminated and the exception is logged.

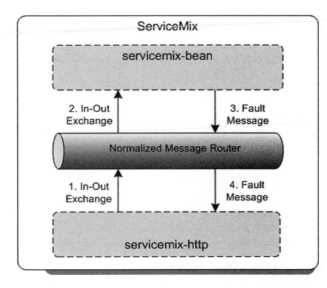

Figure 8.2   An in-out message exchange with a fault response message. The normalized message router (NMR) ensures that the messages are sent between the binding components and service engines in the JBI container.

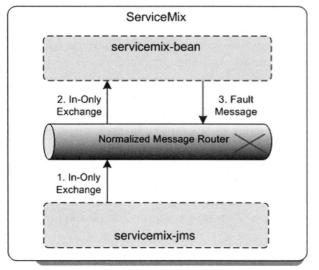

Figure 8.3   When a fault occurs in an in-only message exchange, the normalized message router doesn't know how to route the fault message.

The one-way message flow example of figure 8.3 is rarely the desired behavior. Incoming messages should never get lost and should at least be logged for tracing and auditing purposes. Therefore, we need another component in the message flow that provides error-handling capabilities. There are several options to implement an error-handler component in ServiceMix. We already implemented a bean component error handler in chapter 5. That example, however, involves custom development, which isn't necessary when you're using a Camel component. Figure 8.4 provides

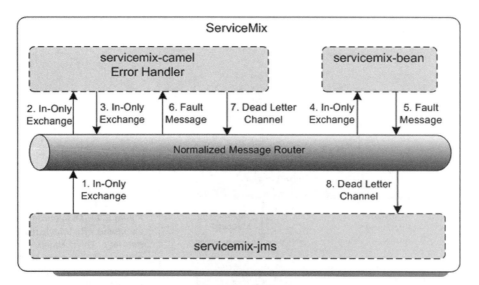

Figure 8.4   A one-way message flow implementation that uses the Camel component as an error-handling mechanism for the invocation of the bean component

an overview of the runtime message flow of a Camel error handler in a one-way message flow example.

The Camel component provides a default error-handling mechanism that also includes redelivery policies to define such parameters as the maximum number of redeliveries. When a fault message is sent to the Camel component, as shown in figure 8.4, the error handler processes the fault message. The default error handler tries to redeliver the message to the bean component six times. When the message isn't successfully consumed by the bean component after the sixth retry, the message is sent to the default dead letter channel, which is a log file. But you can also configure your own dead letter channel configuration to send the fault message to a JMS error queue (see listing 8.3).

Listing 8.3   Camel routing configuration with a custom dead letter channel

```
public class CamelErrorHandler extends RouteBuilder {

  private final static String NAMESPACE =
      "http://esbinaction.com/errorhandling";
  private final static String SERVICE_IN = "jbi:service:" +        ❶
      NAMESPACE + "/errorHandlerDSL";
  private final static String SERVICE_OUT = "jbi:service:" +
      NAMESPACE + "/errorComponent";
  private final static String ERROR_OUT = "jbi:service:" +         ❷
      NAMESPACE + "/errorStorageService";

  public void configure() {
    from(SERVICE_IN).
      errorHandler(deadLetterChannel(ERROR_OUT).               ❸
        maximumRedeliveries(2)).
    to(SERVICE_OUT);
  }
}
```

The Camel configuration can be implemented with a subclass of the RouteBuilder class. Because we use JBI services for the message flow implementation, we have to define a JBI service definition for the Camel routing implementation ❶. This JBI service name can now be used as a target JBI service for the JMS BC configuration.

In addition, we have to use the JBI service names. For example, the JBI service name for the error queue is configured as a JMS provider in the JMS BC ❷.

The message flow for the Camel component is defined in the configure method. Because the Camel component forwards the incoming message to the bean component, we can define a simple point-to-point flow with the from and to methods. The custom error-handler definition can then be configured within this point-to-point flow ❸. In listing 8.3, the error handler is configured as a dead letter channel which is actually a JMS queue. For this dead letter channel, we can define redelivery policy parameters, such as the maximum number of redeliveries. The invocation of the bean component will be retried twice, and then the message will be sent to the dead letter channel.

The full example, including the JMS and Bean JBI component configurations, is available in the resources/chapter8/errorhandling directory. When you've started the ServiceMix container with the `start` target in the ch8-examples.xml Ant build file (resources/chapter8), you can deploy the error-handling example with the `deploy-errorhandling` target. With the Swing test client, the error-handling example can be triggered. The incoming JMS message is forwarded to the Camel component presented in listing 8.3, which will invoke the bean component and eventually send the message to the JMS error queue.

Error handling in ServiceMix is tightly coupled to the message exchange pattern used within a message flow. To be able to catch faults in a message flow, ServiceMix requires an additional JBI component to function as an error handler. It's possible to implement an error handler in a bean component (as you saw in chapter 5), but Camel provides much more default error-handling functionality.

It's time to move on to another important aspect of making your ESB enterprise ready: security. In the next section you'll learn about different ways to implement security aspects such as authentication in Mule and ServiceMix. You'll benefit from the knowledge you've gained about error handling to deal with authentication and authorization failures.

8.2   *Securing the ESB environment*

A hot topic for every IT project is security. The IT infrastructure is increasingly exposed to external systems such as the internet. But security issues don't come only from the outside; some employees have a malicious intent while working with IT systems. So for both internal as well as external reasons, security is an important aspect. And because the ESB is a central system in an IT landscape, security is even more important when you're implementing integration flows.

Security is a difficult topic to grasp; it deals with the identification of users of a system, but also with securing messages that are sent from one application to another to prevent somebody from changing the message content. From an ESB point of view, security can be categorized as authentication and authorization, secure transport, and integrity of the message. Authentication and authorization deals with the identification of a user (or application) and the rights this entity has. Secure transport ensures that messages can only be read by the intended recipient. Message integrity ensures that a message can't be changed during the transport.

We now look at a number of examples showing how to implement authentication and authorization in Mule and ServiceMix. A number of handy configuration settings exist that let you easily configure an LDAP server and JAAS authentication and authorization rules in Mule and ServiceMix.

8.2.1   *Authentication and authorization with Mule*

The authentication and authorization model of Mule supports the Java Authentication and Authorization Service (JAAS) as well as Acegi. JAAS is the standard security framework of Java Standard Edition (SE), and Acegi is the security framework that's part of the Spring Framework. Because the support for Acegi provides a richer set of functionality and because the JAAS framework is discussed in the ServiceMix section (8.2.2), we choose Acegi to implement the security examples for Mule.

SIMPLE AUTHENTICATION WITH MULE AND ACEGI

Let's start with a simple example. For the input of the simple authentication flow, we use command line console input, which consists of a username and password. When the console input is processed by Mule, a security filter is executed to authenticate the username and password against an in-memory list of users. The result of the authentication step is sent back to the console (see figure 8.5).

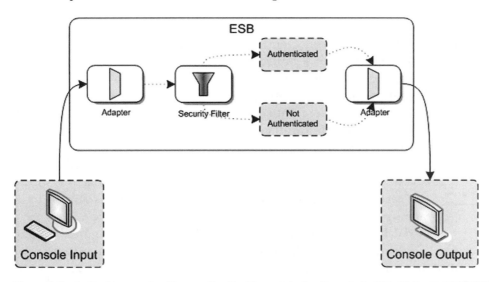

Figure 8.5 A simple example of how authentication can be implemented within Mule. A security filter will check the user credentials against an in-memory list of users.

As you can see in figure 8.5, the authentication credentials are validated with a security filter. This security filter is provided with the Mule framework. Because the full Mule configuration for this example is quite large, it's split into two parts. The first part (listing 8.4) contains the Acegi beans that are needed by the Mule container.

Listing 8.4 Part 1 of the simple authentication example showing the Acegi beans

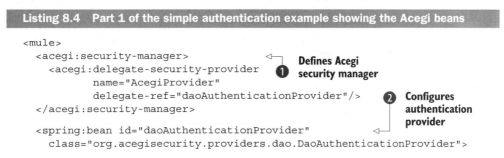

```
    <spring:property name="userDetailsService"
        ref="inMemoryDaoImpl"/>
  </spring:bean>

  <spring:bean id="inMemoryDaoImpl"
    class="org.acegisecurity.userdetails.memory.InMemoryDaoImpl">
    <spring:property name="userMap">
      <spring:value>
        admin=admin,ROLE_ADMIN
        johndoe=john,ROLE_USER
      </spring:value>
    </spring:property>
  </spring:bean>
</mule>
```

❸ Specifies in-memory user list

Security can be implemented in Mule by providing a security manager ❶. The security filter (see listing 8.5 in a moment) uses the security manager configured in listing 8.4. You could configure the security manager with a number of security providers, but since we use Acegi, this is the provider we use.

The integration between Mule and Acegi is achieved with the `AcegiProvider-Adapter` that's configured with the `delegate-security-provider` element. This adapter converts the Mule authentication model into an Acegi security model and passes further authentication processing on to the `delegate-ref`. This delegate provides the actual authentication implementation that will be used. In this example, a database authentication provider is configured, as you can see with the `dao-AuthenticationProvider` Spring bean, but Acegi also provides support for LDAP and JAAS, among others.

The database authentication provider of Acegi is also configured as a Spring bean ❷. This provider is normally used to retrieve user information from a database. A JDBC implementation class, `org.acegisecurity.userdetails.jdbc.JdbcDaoImpl`, is available in Acegi that implements default queries that can be overridden. But to simplify the example, we use an in-memory user list.

For testing and example purposes, Acegi provides an in-memory DAO implementation ❸. The `userMap` property can be used to inject a number of username/password/role combinations. In this example, we have two users, admin and johndoe, in the administrator and user roles, respectively.

With this simple configuration, we have created a Mule security manager that uses an Acegi in-memory user list to authenticate against. Now let's look at the second part of the configuration (listing 8.5).

Listing 8.5   Part 2 of the simple authentication example showing the message flow

```
<mule>
  <vm:connector name="exceptionVM">
    <default-connector-exception-strategy>
      <outbound-endpoint address="vm://security.error"/>
    </default-connector-exception-strategy>
  </vm:connector>
```

❶ Defines VM exception handler

```
<stdio:connector name="inConnector" promptMessage="Credentials"/>

<spring:bean id="keyEncryption"
    class="org.mule.extras.pgp.KeyBasedEncryptionStrategy"/>

<custom-transformer name="SimpleAuthTransformer"
    class="esb.chapter8...SimpleAuthenticationTransformer"/>

<model name="SimpleAuthExample">
  <service name="UserInputService">
    <inbound>
      <stdio:inbound-endpoint system="IN"/>
    </inbound>
    <outbound>
    <outbound-pass-through-router>
      <vm:outbound-endpoint path="security.in"
        transformer-refs="SimpleAuthTransformer"/>
      </outbound-pass-through-router>
    </outbound>
  </service>

  <service name="SimpleAuthService">
    <inbound>
      <vm:inbound-endpoint path="security.in"
          connector-ref="exceptionVM">
        <encryption-security-filter
            strategy-ref="keyEncryption"/>
      </vm:inbound-endpoint>
    </inbound>
    <component>
      <singleton-object
          class="esb.chapter8...AuthenticationService">
        <properties>
          <spring:entry key="authenticated" value="true"/>
        </properties>
      </singleton-object>
    </component>
    <outbound>
      <outbound-pass-through-router>
        <stdio:outbound-endpoint system="OUT"/>
      </outbound-pass-through-router>
    </outbound>
  </service>
  </model>
</mule>
```

❷ Sets credentials in message header

❸ Authenticates incoming message

❹ Returns "authenticated" to the console

The second part contains quite a lot of interesting elements. Let's look at the configuration in the order of the message flow definition. When console input has been sent, the message is transformed in the outbound router with the SimpleAuthTransformer ❷. The credentials that arrive via the console should be in the format username;password. The authentication transformer transforms that input into the message header credentials that Mule expects in its authentication filter. The esb.chapter8.security.transformer.SimpleAuthenticationTransformer class uses the following two lines of code to set the credentials:

```
String muleCredentials = MuleCredentials.createHeader(
    username, password.toCharArray());
message.setProperty(MuleProperties.MULE_USER_PROPERTY,
    muleCredentials);
```

The `MuleCredentials` class is used to create the `MULE_USER_PROPERTY` header property. The message variable is a `MuleMessage`, which can be used to set the credentials as a property in the message header. We have to implement this credential creation ourselves because the VM connector doesn't support authentication by default. With the `HttpBasicAuthenticationFilter`, Mule supports authentication without requiring you to customize the HTTP connector.

Now that the credentials have been set in the Mule message, we can authenticate the message with the security filter provided by Mule ❸. This security filter can only be used as an authentication filter for an inbound endpoint, so the message is forwarded to the `security.in` virtual machine (VM) queue. The security filter is implemented by `MuleEncryptionEndpointSecurityFilter`; this class extracts the credentials from the Mule message and performs a check against the configured security manager. For this example, this means that the username/password combination is checked against the in-memory user list (see listing 8.4).

We also have to define a `strategy-ref` attribute for the security filter that points to a Spring bean named `keyEncryption`. The `keyEncryption` bean defines an encryption strategy that will be used by the security filter to encrypt the credentials. However, the security filter only applies this encryption when it's configured on an outbound endpoint. Therefore, the encryption strategy isn't used in this example, but it must be set to let the security filter start up without errors.

When the authentication fails, the security filter throws an exception. With the default exception-handling strategy, this means that the exception is logged and that the message flow stops immediately. However, we want to return a message to the console indicating that authentication has failed. Therefore, we have to configure an endpoint on the exception handler for the VM connector ❶. This `security.error` VM queue is used by the default exception handler to forward the exception message without stopping the whole message flow. By linking the inbound endpoint of the Mule service `SimpleAuthService` with this VM connector, we can retrieve the exception message from the error queue.

When the authentication succeeds, the message is passed on to the `Authentication-Service`. This class returns a simple message of "Has the user been authenticated? Authentication result." The authentication result is injected with the `authenticated` property ❹. The same kind of configuration in another service definition has been implemented for the authentication failure flow, but we leave this out to reduce the number of code lines in the listing. (The `authenticated` property is set to false for the authentication failure service.)

You should now be able to test this example by executing the `simpleAuth` target in the ch8-examples.xml Ant script, which you can find in the resources/chapter8 directory. Then run the `simpleauth.bat` or `simpleauth.sh` script, available in the resources/chapter8/simpleauth directory, in a command console. When Mule starts, enter the credentials in the console. When you type admin;admin, the console should respond with "Has the user been authenticated? true." And when you enter a nonexistent user, you should get a detailed exception stack trace and the message "Has the user been authenticated? false."

In real life we don't want to use an in-memory database to authenticate against. In the next section, we discuss the use of an LDAP server with Mule.

LDAP AUTHENTICATION WITH MULE AND ACEGI

Authentication and authorization information is often stored in a Lightweight Directory Access Protocol (LDAP) server. LDAP is a standardized protocol for the exchange of data across a network in a hierarchical way. The directory-based structure of LDAP is handy for categorizing user data, such as user roles and organizational information. Products like Microsoft Active Directory and Tivoli Directory Server are commonly used LDAP servers. Very good open source LDAP servers are also available, such as OpenLDAP and Apache Directory Server.

In this section we use Apache Directory Server, because it's multiplatform and also provides a nice Eclipse-based administration tool. But does this mean that we have to implement a totally different Mule configuration than the example in the previous section? No, because we again use Acegi to provide a bridge between the Mule authentication functionality and the Apache Directory Server (see figure 8.6).

As shown in figure 8.6, the example will be implemented using an HTTP message channel. An HTTP adapter will accept HTTP requests that are expected to have credentials set in the HTTP header. Mule's HTTP security filter will then check whether

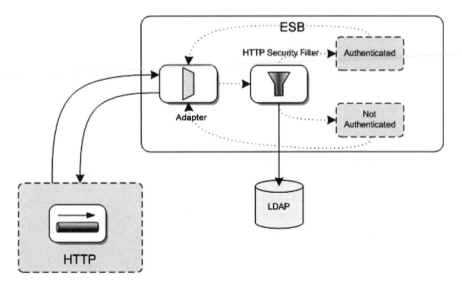

Figure 8.6 LDAP authentication implemented in Mule. Via HTTP, a request message with security context is consumed by the adapter, and the HTTP security filter validates the credentials against an LDAP server.

the credentials in the HTTP header are available in the LDAP server. Eventually a response is given back to the HTTP client with a message indicating whether the authentication has succeeded.

Let's start with the installation of the Apache Directory Server. Go to the http://directory.apache.org website and download the latest ApacheDS (we use 1.5.2) and Apache Directory Studio (1.1.0) products. The installation procedure is simple and thus requires no additional explanation. The Windows version of Apache Directory Server contains an apacheds.exe file that will install the LDAP server as a Windows service. For the Linux distribution, you can start the LDAP server with the following command:

```
/etc/init.d/apacheds start
```

Now that we've started the LDAP server, we can look at its initial contents with the Apache Directory Studio. This is a simple but efficient Eclipse tool that you can use to create a new connection to your local LDAP server. Use the configuration shown in table 8.1 to configure the connection.

Table 8.1   Connection configuration to the Apache Directory Server

Connection parameter	Parameter value
Connection name	`local` (or use your own name)
Hostname	`localhost`
Port	`10389` (or the port you configured during installation)
Encryption method	No encryption
Authentication method	Simple authentication
Bind DN or user	`uid=admin,ou=system`
Bind password	`secret`
Save password	`yes`

Once you've made the connection, you should be able to access the LDAP server. The contents of the LDAP server will be similar to figure 8.7.

The number of groups in your LDAP server will be different than shown in figure 8.7 because we added an extra group for the example. (We discuss this with the listings in this section.) For now, it's enough to see that we have a number of default users and groups available in the LDAP server.

Next let's look at configuring Mule to use this LDAP server to authenticate the incoming HTTP request. We again divide the configuration into two parts; the first part (listing 8.6) contains the LDAP integration.

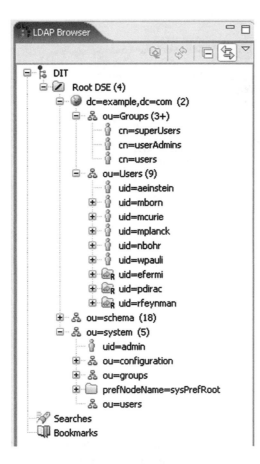

Figure 8.7 The initial contents of the Apache
Directory Server shown in the Apache Directory
Studio tool

Listing 8.6 Part 1 of the LDAP authentication example containing the LDAP integration

```
<mule>
  <acegi:security-manager>
    <acegi:delegate-security-provider name="AcegiProvider"
        delegate-ref="authenticationProvider"/>
  </acegi:security-manager>

  <spring:bean id="initialDirContextFactory"
      class="org.acegisecurity.ldap.DefaultInitialDirContextFactory">
    <spring:constructor-arg
        value="ldap://localhost:10389/dc=example,dc=com" />
    <spring:property name="managerDn">
      <spring:value>uid=admin,ou=system</spring:value>
    </spring:property>
    <spring:property name="managerPassword">
      <spring:value>secret</spring:value>
    </spring:property>
  </spring:bean>

  <spring:bean id="authenticationProvider"
      class="org.acegisecurity...LdapAuthenticationProvider">
```

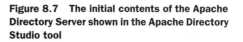

❶ Connects to LDAP server

❷ Defines LDAP provider

```
        <spring:constructor-arg>
          <spring:bean
              class="org.acegisecurity...BindAuthenticator">
            <spring:constructor-arg>
              <spring:ref local="initialDirContextFactory" />
            </spring:constructor-arg>
            <spring:property name="userDnPatterns">
              <spring:list>
                <spring:value>
                  uid={0},ou=Users                    Looks up user
                </spring:value>                      ❸ with uid
              </spring:list>
            </spring:property>
          </spring:bean>
        </spring:constructor-arg>
        <spring:constructor-arg>
          <spring:bean
              class="org.acegisecurity...DefaultLdapAuthoritiesPopulator">
            <spring:constructor-arg>
              <spring:ref local="initialDirContextFactory" />
            </spring:constructor-arg>
            <spring:constructor-arg>
              <spring:value>ou=Groups</spring:value>        Defines role
            </spring:constructor-arg>                    ❹ query
            <spring:property name="groupRoleAttribute">
              <spring:value>cn</spring:value>
            </spring:property>
          </spring:bean>
        </spring:constructor-arg>
      </spring:bean>
    </mule>
```

To use an LDAP server as the authentication mechanism in Mule, we need to start by configuring a security manager (just as we did in the in-memory authentication example). The main difference is that here we use another authentication provider in the `delegate-ref` attribute.

The first part that we have to configure is the connection to the LDAP server ❶. The Acegi framework provides a `DefaultInitialDirContextFactory` class that we can use to create this connection. This Acegi LDAP connection factory class needs a URI where it can find the LDAP server as a constructor argument. The default port for the Apache Directory Server is 10389, and we can also configure the default domain `dc=example,dc=com` in this URI. Then, we also need to provide a user with the `managerDn` property, so that the Acegi factory class can also authenticate the connection to the LDAP server.

With the LDAP connection information specified, we can configure the authentication provider ❷ that's linked to the Mule security manager. The Acegi `LdapAuthentication-Provider` class needs two constructor arguments: an authentication query bean (`Bind-Authenticator`) and a role query bean (`DefaultLdapAuthoritiesPopulator`).

The authentication query bean needs a connection to the LDAP server and a query to authenticate the user credentials against ❸. As you saw in figure 8.7, the users are categorized in the LDAP organizational unit (OU) called Users. To identify a unique user in the Users domain, we need to look for the uid attribute. Therefore, the query will look for LDAP users in the Users domain with a uid that equals the username of the provided credentials.

The role query bean also needs a connection to the LDAP server. In addition to this, we must specify an OU as a base group to look for user roles ❹. This group will be used by the Acegi LDAP authentication provider to look for the roles the authenticated user has been assigned to. The last configuration parameter that the role query bean needs is the attribute that contains the role name and the group of users belonging to that specific role. As you can see in figure 8.7, the roles have a cn attribute for the role definition, so the groupRoleAttribute property is configured with this value.

Another thing we have to do to be able to run the LDAP authentication example with role information is to add a new role in the LDAP server. In figure 8.7, you can see the cn=users role; let's add that role to your LDAP server now. Right-click on the ou=Groups attribute in the Apache Directory Studio and choose New Entry. Then, in the resulting window, choose the option "Create new entry from scratch," and in the next window you should add the groupOfNames attribute to the selected object classes. In the next step, use the configuration information shown in figure 8.8 to define the role name.

The last window of the role configuration is the specification of the role members via the DN editor. To add the default Albert Einstein user to the users role, specify the following entry in the drop-down field of the DN editor:

```
uid=aeinstein,ou=Users,dc=example,dc=com
```

With the addition of the users role and the membership definition, we've finished with the LDAP configuration. Next we can look at the second part of the LDAP Mule configuration (listing 8.7), which configures the message flow.

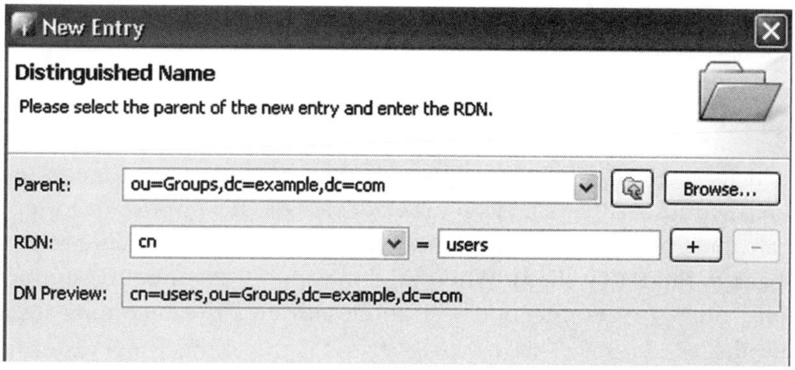

Figure 8.8   Use this information to add a new role, named users, to the Apache Directory Server.

Listing 8.7   Part 2 of the LDAP authentication example: the message flow definition

```
<mule>
  <http:connector name="exceptionHTTP">                    Defines HTTP
    <default-connector-exception-strategy>            ❶ exception handling
      <outbound-endpoint address="vm://ldap.error"/>
    </default-connector-exception-strategy>
  </http:connector>

  <model name="LDAPExample">
    <service name="UserHTTPService">
      <inbound>
        <http:inbound-endpoint                          ❷ Specifies
            address="http://localhost:8888/ldap"            synchronous
            synchronous="true">                             endpoint
          <acegi:http-security-filter              Filters on message
              realm="mule-realm"/>              ❸ credentials
        </http:inbound-endpoint>
      </inbound-router>
      <component>
        <singleton-object
            class="esb...authentication.service.AuthenticationService">
          <properties>
            <spring:entry key="authenticated" value="true"/>
          </properties>
        </singleton-object>
      </component>
    </service>
    <service name="LDAPFailedService">        ❹ Processes
      <inbound>                                   unauthenticated
        <vm:inbound-endpoint path="ldap.error"/>    message
      </inbound>
      <component>
        <singleton-object
            class="esb...authentication.service.AuthenticationService">
          <properties>
            <spring:entry key="authenticated" value="false"/>
          </properties>
        </singleton-object>
      </component>
    </service>
  </model>
</mule>
```

The defined message flow will be triggered when a request message is sent to the
`http://localhost:8888/UserHTTPService` address ❷. It's important to set the synchronous attribute on the HTTP inbound endpoint to true, because we want to send a
response back to the HTTP client. When we don't specify the inbound endpoint to be
synchronous, the HTTP connection will be closed after the incoming message has
been received.

Because Mule provides a default filter to implement HTTP authentication, we can
simply configure this filter on the inbound endpoint ❸. This filter will look for credentials in the HTTP header and will use the security manager (listing 8.6) to authenticate

these user credentials. Notice that we have to specify a `realm` attribute here. This realm must be specified for the credentials in the HTTP header or they will be ignored.

Because the Mule HTTP security filter will throw an exception when a user can't be authenticated, we must specify an outbound endpoint for the default exception handler ❶ to be able to catch this exception and return a response message to the HTTP client. `LDAPFailedService` is listening on the `vm://ldap.error` endpoint ❹ that has the same `AuthenticationService` component configured as the `UserHTTP-Service` shown in listing 8.7. The only difference is that the authenticated property is set to false.

With the configuration in place, we can start up Mule with the LDAP example by using the `ldap` target in the ch8-examples.xml Ant script in the resources/chapter8 directory. Make sure that the Apache Directory Server is running as well. When Mule has started, you can use the Swing test client to trigger the LDAP authentication example. In the Mule console, you should be able to see the LDAP connection details and the role information of the successful authentication message. The failed authentication request prints an error stack trace in the console with the root error message "Bad credentials."

Although these authentication examples have been complex, it's quite easy to add authorization rules to the Mule configuration once you define an authentication mechanism. In the next section, we look at an example that demonstrates how to use Acegi to configure authorization in Mule.

AUTHORIZATION WITH MULE AND ACEGI

Now that we're able to authenticate incoming requests against an in-memory database or an LDAP server, we can take it a step further and implement authorization rules. In addition to all kinds of authentication mechanisms, the Acegi framework supports authorization on Spring beans. Because Mule uses Spring as its default component container, we can easily utilize this Acegi authorization functionality.

So let's extend the LDAP authentication example with an authorization rule on the Mule component that processes the HTTP request message. We don't include the LDAP configuration in the authorization example; it's exactly the same as in listing 8.7. The first part of the authorization rule configuration, shown in listing 8.8, focuses on the Acegi authorization definition.

> **Listing 8.8 Part 1 of the LDAP authentication example with an authorization rule**

```
<mule>
    <spring:bean id="authorizationSecureComponent"
        class="org.acegisecurity...MethodSecurityInterceptor">   ❶ Defines AOP
        <spring:property name="authenticationManager">                authorization
            <spring:ref bean="authenticationManager"/>
        </spring:property>
        <spring:property name="accessDecisionManager">
            <spring:ref bean="accessDecisionManager"/>
        </spring:property>
        <spring:property name="objectDefinitionSource">
```

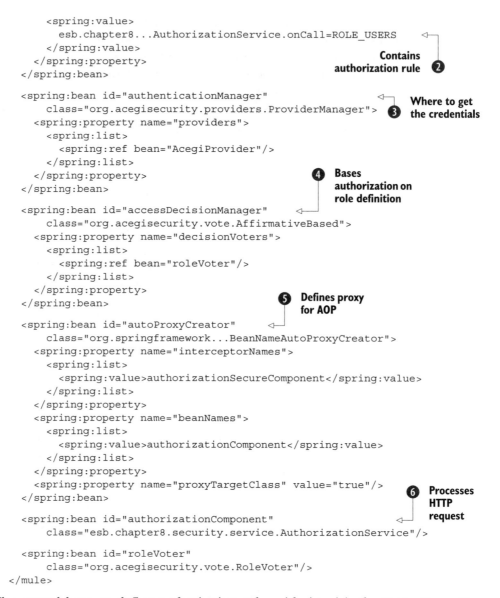

```
      <spring:value>
        esb.chapter8...AuthorizationService.onCall=ROLE_USERS      ◁
      </spring:value>
    </spring:property>                                        Contains
  </spring:bean>                                        authorization rule  ❷

  <spring:bean id="authenticationManager"               ◁        Where to get
      class="org.acegisecurity.providers.ProviderManager">  ❸    the credentials
    <spring:property name="providers">
      <spring:list>
        <spring:ref bean="AcegiProvider"/>
      </spring:list>
    </spring:property>                                    ❹  Bases
  </spring:bean>                                              authorization on
                                                             role definition
  <spring:bean id="accessDecisionManager"             ◁
      class="org.acegisecurity.vote.AffirmativeBased">
    <spring:property name="decisionVoters">
      <spring:list>
        <spring:ref bean="roleVoter"/>
      </spring:list>
    </spring:property>                             ❺  Defines proxy
  </spring:bean>                                      for AOP

  <spring:bean id="autoProxyCreator"          ◁
      class="org.springframework...BeanNameAutoProxyCreator">
    <spring:property name="interceptorNames">
      <spring:list>
        <spring:value>authorizationSecureComponent</spring:value>
      </spring:list>
    </spring:property>
    <spring:property name="beanNames">
      <spring:list>
        <spring:value>authorizationComponent</spring:value>
      </spring:list>
    </spring:property>
    <spring:property name="proxyTargetClass" value="true"/>    ❻  Processes
  </spring:bean>                                                    HTTP
                                                                   request
  <spring:bean id="authorizationComponent"              ◁
      class="esb.chapter8.security.service.AuthorizationService"/>

  <spring:bean id="roleVoter"
      class="org.acegisecurity.vote.RoleVoter"/>
</mule>
```

The central bean to define authorization rules with Acegi is the MethodSecurity-
Interceptor ❶. This bean needs an authentication context, an authorization mechanism, and a number of authorization rules that apply to a specific class. The
authorization rule is directly defined with the objectDefinitionSource attribute ❷.
This attribute can contain a list of fully qualified class and method names associated
with an authorization definition. In this case, we have just one method, onCall, that's
implemented in the AuthorizationService associated with the role users. Remember
that we added the default user Albert Einstein to a new group named users in the
LDAP example. Well, this authorization definition relates to this group. Because we

use a role-based authorization mechanism, `RoleVoter`, the users group needs to be prefixed with `ROLE_` and the group name needs to be uppercase.

The easiest part of the authorization definition is the authentication manager ❸, because we already defined the Acegi security provider in the in-memory and LDAP authentication examples. We can simply configure the authentication manager to use the `AcegiProvider` bean defined in listing 8.6.

To test the authorization rule with the credentials of the user, we define an `AccessDecisionManager` ❹. We use the `AffirmativeBased` Acegi class to process the authorization rule voters. This means that if any of the defined voters return a granted permission, the authorization is granted. We could've also used the `UnanimousBased` class, which only grants authorization when all defined voters are granted permission. We define only one voter here, the `RoleVoter`, which checks whether the defined role is in the list of roles of the authenticated user.

To be able to let Spring handle the authorization on the `AuthorizationService` ❻, we define a proxy class ❺ that tells Spring that if a call is made to this Spring bean it should execute the `authorizationSecureComponent` ❶.

With the proxy class defined, we can now implement the message flow that will invoke the `AuthorizationService`. The message flow shown in listing 8.9 is accepting HTTP requests, which are simply delegated to the Mule component.

Listing 8.9   Part 2 of the LDAP authentication example with an authorization rule

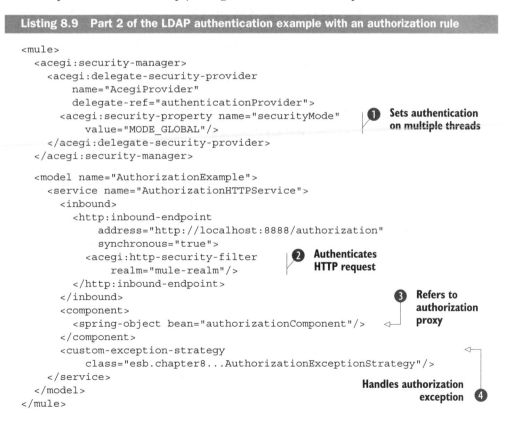

```xml
<mule>
  <acegi:security-manager>
    <acegi:delegate-security-provider
        name="AcegiProvider"
        delegate-ref="authenticationProvider">
      <acegi:security-property name="securityMode"          ❶ Sets authentication
          value="MODE_GLOBAL"/>                                on multiple threads
    </acegi:delegate-security-provider>
  </acegi:security-manager>

  <model name="AuthorizationExample">
    <service name="AuthorizationHTTPService">
      <inbound>
        <http:inbound-endpoint
            address="http://localhost:8888/authorization"
            synchronous="true">
          <acegi:http-security-filter          ❷ Authenticates
              realm="mule-realm"/>                 HTTP request
        </http:inbound-endpoint>
      </inbound>                                 ❸ Refers to
      <component>                                   authorization
        <spring-object bean="authorizationComponent"/>   ⬅  proxy
      </component>
      <custom-exception-strategy                                      ⬅
          class="esb.chapter8...AuthorizationExceptionStrategy"/>
    </service>                                  Handles authorization
  </model>                                               exception  ❹
</mule>
```

The first part of listing 8.9 shows the security manager definition we saw in the previous examples, but now with a securityMode attribute defined ❶. This property should be set to let all threads access the authentication realm. Particularly in an asynchronous message flow, not everything is handled by the same thread, so this is an important setting.

The authentication filter that retrieves the credentials from the HTTP header and processes the authentication against the LDAP server is no different than the previous examples ❷. The difference is in the Mule component that's invoked after the HTTP request has been authenticated. The AuthorizationService defined in listing 8.8 is referenced here ❸. During runtime, the class instance of the AuthorizationService is replaced by the proxy that authorizes the method invocation to onCall.

When the authenticated user is part of the users role, a message is returned by the AuthorizationService that the user was authorized. But when the authenticated user is not part of the users role, an AccessDeniedException is thrown. To be able to process this exception, we define a component exception strategy ❹. This can be a default exception strategy with an outbound endpoint where the exception message is sent to, but in this example we create a custom exception strategy. The AuthorizationExceptionStrategy class extends the DefaultComponentExceptionStrategy class provided by Mule.

The exception is simply passed on as a parameter of the defaultHandler method. In our exception strategy implementation, the AccessDeniedException is changed to a UnauthorizedException because of the HTTP status code of the response message. When the default AccessDeniedException is thrown, the status code is 501, which is an internal server error. We want to have a status code of 401, which is an authorization error and that can be realized with throwing the UnauthorizedException.

To run the authorization example, you can use the authorization target of the ch8-examples.xml Ant script in the resources/chapter8 directory. Make sure that the Apache Directory Server is also running. To send a successful and a failed authorization message, we include two test methods in the JUnit test case AuthorizationTest. The first message uses the credentials of the default Albert Einstein user that is part of the users group in the LDAP server. So this request message should receive an "authorization is granted" response message. The second message is also a valid user in the LDAP server, but this user isn't defined as a member of the users group. Therefore, this should result in an "authorization failure" response message with an HTTP status code of 401. You can also use the Swing test client to test the authorization example.

You've learned to implement authentication and authorization in Mule using the Acegi framework. So when your project needs a security model, you'll be able to guide your fellow team members to an excellent Mule security implementation. With Service-Mix, we look at an alternative way to implement authentication and authorization by using the JAAS specification.

8.2.2   *Authentication and authorization with ServiceMix*

Earlier you saw that integration with the Acegi framework is utilized to provide the necessary functionality to authenticate incoming requests and to define authorization rules. For ServiceMix, this functionality is provided with a Java Authorization and Authentication Service (JAAS) implementation. JAAS is the standard security framework of the Sun Java specification and is therefore a good foundation for authentication and authorization in ServiceMix.

The authentication options in ServiceMix available out of the box are pretty limited. The `servicemix-http` binding component provides HTTP header credentials authentication against the users defined in the ServiceMix configuration files. To authenticate against an LDAP server or a database, you must implement your own JAAS `LoginModule`. In this section, we first look at an example that uses the HTTP header credentials to authenticate an incoming request. Then we look at configuring authorization rules for services in the ServiceMix container.

SIMPLE AUTHENTICATION WITH SERVICEMIX

To help you better grasp ServiceMix's authentication implementation, we use a message flow that accepts HTTP requests on a specific endpoint URI. These HTTP requests will then be authenticated with the default ServiceMix JAAS login module, and the incoming message and authenticated principal will be logged in a bean component. The components that we use in this example are shown in figure 8.9.

As you can see in figure 8.9, the example is simple and consists of just two JBI components: the HTTP binding component and the Bean service engine. The authentication of the incoming HTTP request is configured in the HTTP binding component configuration. So let's start with a look at that configuration in listing 8.10.

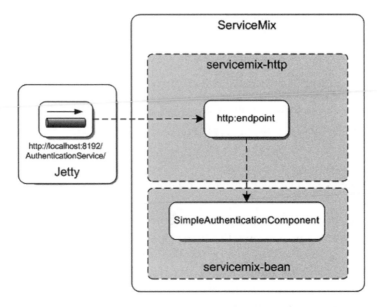

Figure 8.9 A simple example of a message flow that will authenticate an incoming HTTP request and forward the message content to a bean component, which in turn will log the security context and message content

Listing 8.10   HTTP endpoint configuration with authentication enabled

```
<beans xmlns:http="http://servicemix.apache.org/http/1.0"
    xmlns:esb="http://esbinaction.com/simpleauthentication">

  <http:endpoint service="esb:SimpleAuthentication"
       endpoint="authEndpoint"
       targetService="esb:simpleAuthComponent"        ◁─❶
       targetEndpoint="simpleAuthEndpoint"
       role="consumer"
       locationURI="http://localhost:8192/AuthenticationService/"
       authMethod="basic"                             ◁─❷
       defaultMep="http://www.w3.org/2004/08/wsdl/in-only"/>
</beans>
```

In listing 8.10, we define a target service ❶ pointing to the bean component that we discuss in listing 8.11. Also notice that the role attribute has a value of consumer; you might have expected a provider role since it's providing a web service endpoint. But instead this says that the HTTP endpoint is consuming HTTP request messages.

For our authentication example, the important attribute is the authMethod ❷. The only available authentication method is basic, but this can be extended to include LDAP and other authentication mechanisms. The basic authentication implementation will retrieve the HTTP header credentials and authenticate these values against the default JAAS login module.

The default JAAS login module is configured in the login.properties file in the conf directory of the ServiceMix distribution. There are two modules configured here, as you can see in the following code snippet containing the file's contents:

```
servicemix-domain {
  org.apache.servicemix.jbi.security.login.PropertiesLoginModule
    sufficient
    org.apache.servicemix.security.properties.user=
        "users-passwords.properties"
    org.apache.servicemix.security.properties.group="groups.properties";

  org.apache.servicemix.jbi.security.login.CertificatesLoginModule
    sufficient
    org.apache.servicemix.security.certificates.user=
        "users-credentials.properties"
    org.apache.servicemix.security.certificates.group="groups.properties";
};
```

Because we use a simple username/password combination in the HTTP header of the request message for this example, only the PropertiesLoginModule is relevant. The CertificatesLoginModule is used to process X509 certificates. The PropertiesLogin-Module uses two files to configure the users who have rights for the ServiceMix container: user-passwords.properties and the groups.properties. These files are also in the conf directory, and contain the username/password values (user-passwords.properties) and the groups or role definition (groups.properties). By default, there is only one user, smx, configured that has also smx as a password value. This user is configured to be part of one group (admin).

Now that you've seen the JAAS implementation ServiceMix provides and you've implemented the HTTP endpoint configuration, we just need to implement the Simple-AuthenticationComponent. Listing 8.11 shows the JBI service component, which will retrieve the authenticated user information from the incoming JBI message.

Listing 8.11 Bean component that logs the security context and the message content

```
public class SimpleAuthenticationComponent extends ComponentSupport
    implements MessageExchangeListener {

  private SourceTransformer sourceTransformer =
    new SourceTransformer();
  @Resource
  private DeliveryChannel channel;

  public void onMessageExchange(MessageExchange exchange)
      throws MessagingException {                                    ❶ Retrieves
    NormalizedMessage message = getInMessage(exchange);                 security
    Subject subject = message.getSecuritySubject();         ◄────────── context
    for (Principal principal : subject.getPrincipals() ) {
      if(principal instanceof UserPrincipal) {          ◄──┐ Contains
        logger.info("request made with username " +     ❷  username
            principal.getName());
      } else if(principal instanceof GroupPrincipal) {    ◄──┐ Contains
        logger.info("authenticated user belongs to group " +  user
            principal.getName());                         ❸  group
      }
    }
    logger.info("received payload " +
        sourceTransformer.toString(message.getContent())); ◄─┐ Logs
    exchange.setStatus(ExchangeStatus.DONE);                ❹  message
    channel.send(exchange);                                     content
  }
}
```

To retrieve the authenticated user information, we must invoke the getSecurity-Subject method on the incoming JBI message ❶. This will return a javax.security.auth.Subject class instance, where we can retrieve a set of Principal objects.

Every security aspect is represented by a different Principal object, so the username can be retrieved when we come across a UserPrincipal instance ❷. The groups where the user is configured as a member can be retrieved when we encounter a GroupPrincipal ❸.

The message content is logged by using a SourceTransformer to convert the incoming JBI message into a String representation ❹. Therefore, the bean will log both the security context values and the message content of the incoming JBI message.

To test the ServiceMix authentication example, you can use the service assembly provided in the resources/chapter8/simpleauth directory. First, you have to start the ServiceMix container with the start target in the ch8-examples.xml Ant file, and then you can use the deploy-simpleauth target in the same build file to build and deploy the authentication service assembly. When the example has been deployed, you can use the Swing test client to send an HTTP request message with the credentials of the smx user. When the authentication example is executed, the console of the Service-Mix container shows the log messages of the smx username and admin group and the message contents.

In addition to the authentication of an HTTP request, we can configure authorization rules in ServiceMix. In the next section you'll learn how to add authorization to JBI services.

IMPLEMENTING AUTHORIZATION IN SERVICEMIX

Adding authorization in ServiceMix is simple, so we won't go through another example but just extend the previous one with an authorization rule. The configuration of authorization rules is based on the group or role definitions defined in the groups.properties file. By default, only one group is defined: the admin group, and it has one member, smx.

The authorization rules can be configured in the security.xml file that is also in the conf directory of the ServiceMix distribution. The part that needs to be configured is the `authorizationMap`. In the following code snippet, an authorization rule is defined for the `SimpleAuthenticationComponent` bean that we implement in listing 8.11:

```
<sm:authorizationMap id="authorizationMap">
  <sm:authorizationEntries>
    <sm:authorizationEntry
        service="*:simpleAuthComponent"
        roles="admin" />
  </sm:authorizationEntries>
</sm:authorizationMap>
```

Multiple authorization entries can be defined, which link a service to a number of roles. In this example, the `simpleAuthComponent` JBI service name is linked to the admin role and therefore indirectly to the smx user. The asterisk states that this role definition is applicable to every JBI service with the name of `simpleAuthComponent` independent of the service namespace.

Before we test this configuration, add another user to the user-passwords.properties file and make this user a member of a new group named *users* in the group.properties file. We now have two users and only smx is authorized to invoke the bean component that's part of our simple authentication example. So when you execute the Swing test client again, you should see the same result you got before we defined the authorization rule. But when you change the HTTP credentials in the Swing test client to the just-created user, you'll receive an error HTTP status code from the ServiceMix container. In the ServiceMix console you'll see an error message, which means that the bean component hasn't been invoked due to an authorization failure.

Of course, this is a fairly simple way of configuring authorization rules, but you don't have to do more in most circumstances. When you want to implement more complex authentication and authorization functionality in ServiceMix, doing so is not too difficult. You can easily implement your own JAAS login module that, for example, will query an LDAP server using the Acegi framework. This login module can then be configured in the login.properties file, and that's all you have to do to authenticate against an LDAP server. With the knowledge of the JAAS implementation within Service-Mix, you'll be able to use much more complex security models than the example shown in this section.

The remaining pieces to implementing enterprise quality message flows are transactions. We dealt with error handling in the first section of this chapter, but we didn't address functionality to roll back database actions or consuming a JMS message from a queue in a transaction. Therefore, we explore transaction functionality in the next section so that you can implement transactional message flows.

8.3 *Making your message flows transactional*

The ESB is the heart of an integration solution, and therefore topics like error handling and security are important when implementing message flows. What's missing is the implementation of transactional message flows to ensure the ACID (atomicity, consistency, isolation, and durability) principle inside the ESB.

ACID principles

Atomicity means that the transaction will either perform all tasks of a transaction or none. So all tasks of a transaction will be performed without any exception, or all tasks will not be performed in case of an exception in one of the transaction tasks.

Consistency means that after a transaction has been executed, all resources are in a valid state without violating integrity constraints. This means that the tasks of the transaction are either fully performed without violating any integrity constraints, or the resources are rolled back into the state before the transaction began in the case of any exception or integrity violation.

Isolation means that the tasks performed in a transaction are completely separated from other operations that run on the same resources. So an intermediate state of a transaction shouldn't be visible to other operations or applications.

The last aspect is *durability*, which means that when a transaction is successful and the transaction manager has been notified, the transaction can't be undone. This implies that the transaction result should be available after a system or hardware failure.

When using database systems, the ACID properties are commonly used to ensure the integrity of the content of a database when lots of transactions are being processed. But transactions are also important in the implementation of integration flows. Imagine that a client application sends a JMS message to a queue where a message flow is listening. The message contains an important order that needs to be processed in a database and a back-office application. The message flow will first send a JMS message to the back-office application and then insert the order into the database. If an error occurs when the order is inserted into the database, we don't want the back-office application to receive the JMS message. If we'd started a transaction at the beginning of the message flow, all the tasks inside this flow would have been rolled back in case of a database exception at the end of the flow.

The following example deals with a special kind of transaction: an XA, or distributed, transaction. Non-XA (local) transactions only deal with a single resource. XA (global) transactions can deal with multiple resources. For distributed transactions, there is a coordinating transaction manager, which uses the Two-Phase Commit (2PC) protocol to be able to coordinate all local transactions. (To learn more about the 2PC protocol, you can look in Wikipedia [http://en.wikipedia.org/wiki/Two-phase-commit_protocol] for a detailed description.) In general terms, the 2PC protocol consists of two phases: commit-request and commit. The coordinating transaction manager receives an agreement message from every resource that tries to commit the local transaction. If any agreement message informs the coordinating transaction manager that the local transaction has failed, the whole global transaction is rolled back. If all agreement messages are successful, the coordinating transaction manager instructs the resources to perform a final commit on the local transaction. Figure 8.10 shows an example of an XA transaction with a JDBC and a JCA resource.

The example shown in figure 8.10 describes a global transaction with a successful JDBC transaction and a failed JCA transaction. Therefore, the whole transaction is rolled back after the coordinating transaction manager receives the failed agreement message from the JCA local transaction manager. In this section, we explore non-XA transaction examples to understand the basics of transaction handling in Mule and ServiceMix. For XA transaction examples, be sure to check out our website (http://www.esbinaction.com).

To introduce the basics of transaction handling in Mule, let's look at a local or non-XA transaction. A single resource transaction is the most common type of transaction and also easier to implement. An example of a single resource transaction is a

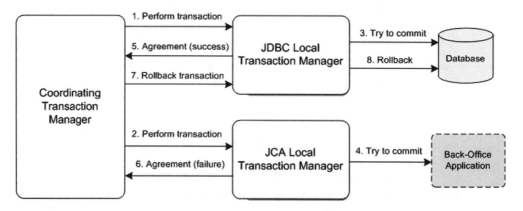

Figure 8.10 Example of an XA transaction that involves a JDBC and a JCA resource. In this example, the JCA transaction fails and therefore the global transaction is rolled back.

web application that updates information in a database with a JDBC transaction. For message flows, the use of JMS transactions is common to ensure that a message is only consumed when the JMS transaction succeeds. Next we look at the implementation of a single-resource JMS transaction in a Mule configuration.

8.3.1 *Implementing transactional message flows in Mule*

Implementing transactions in message flow definitions with Mule is not so difficult. There are, however, a few important aspects that you must know before you can work with transactions in Mule. The first thing to notice is that transactions can only be started on inbound endpoints. So when you define an inbound endpoint for a JMS queue, you're able to define a transaction configuration. The outbound endpoint automatically uses the transaction of the inbound endpoint if one is running. When you're using a single-resource transaction, this means that the transaction is committed or rolled back after the message is routed to the outbound endpoint. Note that only a few transports support transactions: JMS, JDBC, and VM.

To work with transactions in Mule, we have to know how to start or join a transaction on an inbound endpoint. There are five possible transaction properties that can be set on an inbound endpoint, as shown in table 8.2.

Table 8.2   The transaction properties, which can be configured on inbound endpoints in a Mule configuration

Transaction property	Description
NONE	The endpoint will not participate in any transaction.
ALWAYS_BEGIN	The endpoint will always start a new transaction. If a transaction already exists, an exception will be thrown.
BEGIN_OR_JOIN	The endpoint will start a new transaction if there is no existing transaction, or the endpoint will join the existing transaction.
ALWAYS_JOIN	The endpoint will always join the existing transaction. If no transaction exists, an exception will be thrown.
JOIN_IF_POSSIBLE	When a transaction exists, the endpoint will join the transaction. If no transaction exists, nothing will be done.

The best way to learn how to configure transactions within a Mule message flow is to implement a simple example. So let's start with a single-resource JMS transaction that's configured on an inbound endpoint.

The example that we implement in this section consumes a message from a JMS queue in a single-resource transaction. When an exception occurs during the processing of the message, in, for example, the Mule component, the transaction should be rolled back and the message should not be removed from the JMS queue. This ensures that the message is only consumed from the JMS queue when the transaction has succeeded and therefore the message processing has succeeded.

But what happens with the message that isn't consumed from the JMS queue? This message will be redelivered to the same Mule message flow to retry the transaction. To prevent the message from being redelivered over and over again when the transaction fails every time, we configure a maximum number of redeliveries. There is a maximum of six retries in a normal ActiveMQ connection. But we can also configure a different number of maximum retries in the JMS connector definition. After the maximum number of retries has been reached, the message will be sent to a dead letter queue. Let's look at the Mule configuration of the JMS transaction definition in listing 8.12.

Listing 8.12   Mule configuration with a JMS transaction definition

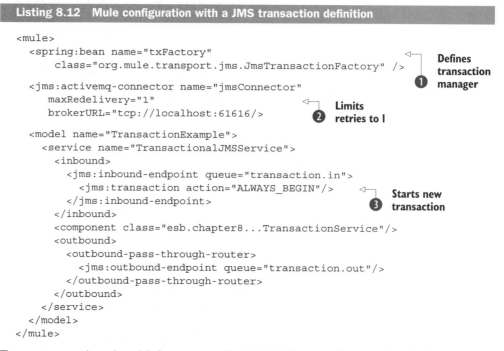

```
<mule>
  <spring:bean name="txFactory"
      class="org.mule.transport.jms.JmsTransactionFactory" />   Defines
                                                                transaction
                                                              ❶ manager
  <jms:activemq-connector name="jmsConnector"
      maxRedelivery="1"
      brokerURL="tcp://localhost:61616/>        Limits
                                              ❷ retries to 1
  <model name="TransactionExample">
    <service name="TransactionalJMSService">
      <inbound>
        <jms:inbound-endpoint queue="transaction.in">
          <jms:transaction action="ALWAYS_BEGIN"/>   Starts new
        </jms:inbound-endpoint>                     ❸ transaction
      </inbound>
      <component class="esb.chapter8...TransactionService"/>
      <outbound>
        <outbound-pass-through-router>
          <jms:outbound-endpoint queue="transaction.out"/>
        </outbound-pass-through-router>
      </outbound>
    </service>
  </model>
</mule>
```

To use transactions in a Mule message flow definition, we first need to define a transaction factory that Mule will use to perform the transaction management ❶. Mule provides a JMS transaction factory by default, and because we're using a single-resource JMS transaction, this factory class suits our needs.

As we've done in other examples using JMS endpoints, we define a JMS connector. We configure one additional attribute for the ActiveMQ JMS connector: maxRedelivery ❷. This attribute configures the maximum number of retries a JMS message will get when the transaction fails. When we don't specify a maximum number of retries, the default number of the ActiveMQ connection factory is used (6). Because we want to reduce the overhead of messages being redelivered, we use a value of 1.

The actual transaction configuration is defined at the inbound endpoint with the transaction element ❸. We define an action value of ALWAYS_BEGIN, which means that a transaction is always started when a new message is processed from the JMS queue.

Because we want to test this example with both a successful and a failed transaction, we configure a component that implements this functionality. The `Transaction-Service` class will fail the transaction when the message content is equal to "bad transaction"; otherwise the transaction will succeed. The following code snippet shows the implementation of the `TransactionService`:

```
public class TransactionService {
  public String processMessage(String message) throws Exception {
    if(!"bad transaction".equalsIgnoreCase(message)) {
      return "transaction succeeded";
    } else {
      throw new Exception ("The transaction will fail");
    }
  }
}
```

When the message content is equal to "bad transaction," the exception causes the current transaction to fail and the Mule container rolls back the running transaction, which leads to the JMS message not being consumed from the input queue.

We've already talked about the dead letter queue, where messages that have reached the maximum number of deliveries are sent. But where can we find this dead letter queue? The dead letter queue is configured in the JMS provider—in our case, ActiveMQ. In the ActiveMQ configuration file activemq.xml, which you can find in the conf directory of the ActiveMQ distribution, you can configure a policy definition that defines the dead letter queue. The following code snippet shows a policy definition that we can use for our JMS transaction example:

```
<destinationPolicy>
  <policyMap>
    <policyEntries>
      <policyEntry queue=">">
        <deadLetterStrategy>
          <individualDeadLetterStrategy queuePrefix="DLQ." />
        </deadLetterStrategy>
      </policyEntry>
    </policyEntries>
  </policyMap>
</destinationPolicy>
```

Notice that in the default activemq.xml file, there's already an example `destination-Policy` defined. Just overwrite this default `destinationPolicy` with the one we defined in the code snippet. This code snippet shows a policy entry with a dead letter strategy for all queues (the > notation). For every queue, the dead letter queue will have the same name with a prefix of DLQ. So the dead letter queue name of the `trans-action.in` queue from code listing 8.12 will be `DLQ.transaction.in`.

With the Mule and ActiveMQ configuration in place, we should now be able to the test the whole example with the `TransactionTest` JUnit test, which will test both a successful and a failed transaction. To deploy the example to the Mule container, you can use the `transaction` target in the ch8-examples.xml Ant build script. When you run the JUnit test, you'll see that a failed transaction will eventually result in a message to the dead letter queue `DLQ.transaction.in`. You can also use the Swing test client to test the transaction example.

This wraps up our discussion of how to implement transactional message flows in Mule. ServiceMix doesn't make use of the transactional properties shown in table 8.2 to configure transactions. We look at a new framework called Jencks to provide the transactional functionality in ServiceMix.

8.3.2   *Implementing transactional message flows in ServiceMix*

The support for transactions in ServiceMix is based on the Java Connector Architecture (JCA) flow implementation in combination with the JMS binding component. By default, ServiceMix uses the Staged Event-Driven Architecture (SEDA) flow implementation to process a message flow. This is also the model that Mule uses by default. But in addition to the SEDA flow model, ServiceMix provides a JMS and JCA model implementation. The differences between these models involve the quality of service support.

The SEDA model is the standard flow implementation that provides support for synchronous and asynchronous messaging. The JMS model adds support for clustering and persistency to the SEDA functionality. And the JCA model only supports asynchronous messaging, but it does provide clustering, persistency, and transactional capabilities. In this section, we focus on the JCA model due to its support for transactional message flows.

To illustrate the implementation of a transactional message flow in ServiceMix, we use an example similar to the Mule example in which we consume a JMS message and forward it to a bean component. The bean component will roll back the transaction if the message content is "bad transaction." Due to a problem with implementing transactions in a service assembly (namespace conflict with the ActiveMQ Resource Adapter), we implement this example with a stand-alone ServiceMix configuration. This means that we don't implement a full-service assembly, but we configure the message flow in one file that we also use to start up ServiceMix.

The ServiceMix configuration that we need to define consists of three parts. The first part (listing 8.13) defines the JMS consumer endpoint and the bean component. The second part configures the ActiveMQ broker that we use. The third part configures the transaction manager, the connection manager, and other resources.

Listing 8.13   Part 1 of the transactional message flow with the JMS and bean endpoints

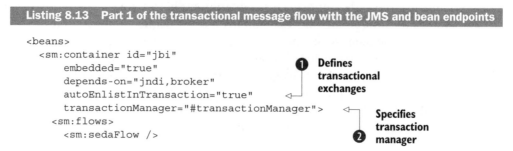

```
<beans>
  <sm:container id="jbi"
      embedded="true"
      depends-on="jndi,broker"
      autoEnlistInTransaction="true"
      transactionManager="#transactionManager">
    <sm:flows>
      <sm:sedaFlow />
```

❶ Defines transactional exchanges

❷ Specifies transaction manager

```
      <sm:jcaFlow connectionManager="#connectionManager"
          jmsURL="tcp://localhost:61616" />
  </sm:flows>
  <sm:endpoints>
    <jms:endpoint service="esb:JMSTransactionService"
        endpoint="jmsTransactionEndpoint"
        targetService="esb:TransactionService"
        role="consumer"
        defaultMep="http://www.w3.org/2004/08/wsdl/in-only"
        processorName="jca"
        connectionFactory="#connectionFactory"
        resourceAdapter="#resourceAdapter"
        bootstrapContext="#bootstrapContext"
        synchronous="true">
      <jms:activationSpec>
        <amqra:activationSpec
            destination="servicemix.transaction.in"
            destinationType="javax.jms.Queue"/>
      </jms:activationSpec>
    </jms:endpoint>
    <bean:endpoint service="esb:TransactionService"
        endpoint="transactionEndpoint"
        bean="#transactionBean"/>
  </sm:endpoints>
</sm:container>
<bean id="transactionBean"
    class="esb.chapter8.transaction.bean.TransactionComponent" />
</beans>
```

❸ Define transactional consumer

A stand-alone ServiceMix configuration includes a container definition with the container element. Because we want all message exchanges to be transactional, we define the `autoEnlistInTransaction` attribute ❶. The container will use the `transactionManager` bean to manage the transactions ❷. This transaction manager is defined in listing 8.14. Notice that there are two flow models defined for the container definition: a SEDA and a JCA flow. For the transactional exchange, the JCA flow will be used by the ServiceMix container.

The JMS consumer is defined with some extra attributes, which make the JMS consumer transactional ❸. The JCA message consumer processor is used, and the connection factory, resource adapter, and bootstrap context are configured. The attribute values refer to the bean definitions (listing 8.14). The connection factory is configured with an XA transaction and therefore the JMS consumer will be transactional.

Besides the JMS consumer, we define the bean component, which will process the incoming JMS message. The bean component is implemented with a simple Spring bean, which will roll back the transaction if the message content is equal to "bad transaction."

The message flow definition is quite simple, as you saw in listing 8.13. The transactional behavior is implemented in the second part of the transactional message flow example. The configuration shown in listing 8.14 uses the Jencks framework to provide a transactional connection factory and manager.

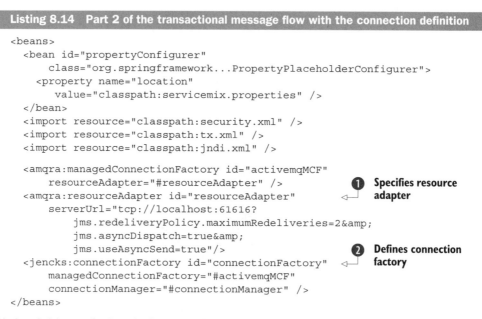

Listing 8.14   Part 2 of the transactional message flow with the connection definition

```
<beans>
  <bean id="propertyConfigurer"
      class="org.springframework...PropertyPlaceholderConfigurer">
    <property name="location"
      value="classpath:servicemix.properties" />
  </bean>
  <import resource="classpath:security.xml" />
  <import resource="classpath:tx.xml" />
  <import resource="classpath:jndi.xml" />

  <amqra:managedConnectionFactory id="activemqMCF"
      resourceAdapter="#resourceAdapter" />            ❶ Specifies resource
  <amqra:resourceAdapter id="resourceAdapter"             adapter
      serverUrl="tcp://localhost:61616?
          jms.redeliveryPolicy.maximumRedeliveries=2&amp;
          jms.asyncDispatch=true&amp;
          jms.useAsyncSend=true"/>                     ❷ Defines connection
  <jencks:connectionFactory id="connectionFactory"        factory
      managedConnectionFactory="#activemqMCF"
      connectionManager="#connectionManager" />
</beans>
```

Listing 8.14 uses the Jencks framework and the ActiveMQ Resource Adapter (RA). These managers are already configured in ServiceMix by default, so we can import the tx.xml and jndi.xml file. We also have to import the security.xml file and define the servicemix.properties file, because the configuration in these files is used in jndi.xml.

The resource adapter definition specifies the JMS connection used to connect to the ActiveMQ broker ❶. In the serverURL definition of the JMS connection, we can also specify the redelivery policy to be used. In our example, we specify a maximum number of redeliveries that will be processed before the JMS message will be sent to the configured dead letter queue. The configuration of the dead letter queue is defined in the ActiveMQ broker configuration that we discuss in listing 8.15.

The connection factory used in the JMS consumer definition in listing 8.14 indirectly uses the resource adapter definition ❷. The Jencks connection factory uses the managed connection factory defined with the ActiveMQ RA framework, which uses the resource adapter definition. The ActiveMQ connection is managed by the Jencks connection manager (which we discuss in a moment).

The one part remaining is the ActiveMQ broker configuration. Because we use the stand-alone ServiceMix configuration, ServiceMix won't be started with the configuration specified in the conf directory of the ServiceMix distribution. Therefore, the ActiveMQ broker won't be started without a broker configuration in our transactional message flow definition. Listing 8.15 shows part 3 of the transactional message flow example.

Listing 8.15   Part 3 of the transactional message flow with ActiveMQ broker definition

```
<beans>
  <bean id="jndi"                                      ❶ Defines
      class="org.apache...SpringInitialContextFactory"    JNDI
```

```
        factory-method="makeInitialContext"
        singleton="true" />

 <amq:broker id="broker">
   <amq:destinationPolicy>
     <amq:policyMap>
       <amq:policyEntries>
         <amq:policyEntry queue=">">
           <amq:deadLetterStrategy>
             <amq:individualDeadLetterStrategy
                 queuePrefix="DLQ." />
           </amq:deadLetterStrategy>
         </amq:policyEntry>
       </amq:policyEntries>
     </amq:policyMap>
   </amq:destinationPolicy>
   <amq:transportConnectors>
     <amq:transportConnector
         uri="tcp://localhost:61616" />
   </amq:transportConnectors>
 </amq:broker>
</beans>
```

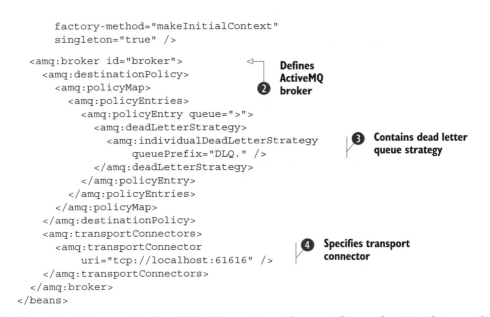

❷ Defines ActiveMQ broker

❸ Contains dead letter queue strategy

❹ Specifies transport connector

Besides the ActiveMQ broker definition, we need to configure the JNDI bean to be able to start the stand-alone ServiceMix container correctly ❶.

The ActiveMQ broker configuration starts with the broker element ❷, which is also referenced in the ServiceMix container configuration in listing 8.13. The broker configuration is similar to the activemq.xml file content in the conf directory of the ServiceMix distribution. This ActiveMQ configuration example is kept simple, but you can extend this configuration with, say, a persistency configuration.

Because we want to show a successful and a failed transaction, we include a dead letter queue strategy configuration ❸. A failed transaction causes the JMS message to be redelivered to the JMS consumer again. After the message has been redelivered two times, the message will be sent to a dead letter queue (according to the maximum redeliveries setting in listing 8.14). With this dead letter strategy, we specify that every queue has a corresponding dead letter queue with the same queue name prefixed by the DLQ queue prefix.

The last part of the ActiveMQ broker configuration defines the transport connector that will be used for the ActiveMQ broker ❹. Because we don't have specific needs for the transactional message flow implementation, we use the default TCP transport connector.

To test the transactional message flow configuration, you can use the servicemix.xml file available in the resources/chapter8/transaction-single/servicemix directory. To start the example, first execute the deploy-transaction target in the ch8-examples.xml Ant build file. This Ant target copies the TransactionComponent class in a transaction-example.jar file to the lib directory of the ServiceMix distribution. Furthermore, the Ant target extracts the libraries of the JMS BC, the Bean SE and a ServiceMix shared JBI component to the lib directory of ServiceMix. Because we run this example with a static configuration, we need these libraries in the lib directory of ServiceMix. To start up the ServiceMix container with the transaction example, you can use the following command script:

Windows:

```
%SERVICEMIX_HOME%/bin/servicemix.bat servicemix/servicemix.xml
```

Unix:

```
$SERVICEMIX_HOME/bin/servicemix.sh servicemix/servicemix.xml
```

When the ServiceMix container is started, you can use the Swing test client to send a message that will result in a successful transaction (with a `started` message content); any other message content will cause the transaction to roll back.

8.4   Summary

In this chapter you learned how to implement enterprise-quality message flows that are suited for real-life integration projects. Mule provides a number of exception strategies designed to handle errors at various points of a message flow. With the default and custom exception strategies, you can implement a fine-grained error-handling solution to meet your needs. ServiceMix doesn't provide a lot of error-handling capabilities besides the default MEP implementation. For in-out message exchanges, this means that fault messages are returned to the client application, but for in-only message exchanges this results in an exception that will stop the processing of the message flow. But with the addition of the Camel framework, errors can be easily managed in ServiceMix.

We also looked at how to implement security in your message flow. You saw that Mule nicely integrates with Acegi and therefore can leverage all the functionality that Acegi provides for authentication and authorization. Notice that Mule can also use JAAS to implement authentication and authorization functionality. It's quite easy to use authentication and authorization with an LDAP server. ServiceMix relies on JAAS for its authentication and authorization capabilities. The out-of-the-box functionality uses files to define users and groups or roles. You can easily implement an HTTP message flow with authentication and authorization capabilities.

We also showed you how to use JMS transactions in both Mule and ServiceMix message flows. You are now able to implement a transactional message flow with a JMS consumer and a bean component in both Mule and ServiceMix.

With the knowledge gained while reading this chapter, you're ready to start with the implementation of larger examples or case studies. Until now we've shown the functionality of open source ESBs with reasonably short examples, but in real life you'll be confronted with more complex situations. Therefore, we'll implement case studies that meet the complexity of real-life projects. In chapter 9 we discuss the full lifecycle of an integration project, from design to deployment. We use the Enterprise Integration patterns of Hohpe and Woolf to be able to create simple design models that provide much insight into the integration solution. You are just a few pages away from learning about a lightweight and fun way to implement integration solution.

Part 3

ESB case studies

We have worked with small examples in the previous two parts to introduce the basic concepts and the core functionalities of Mule and ServiceMix. In this part we work with larger examples to provide more insight in how to implement larger integration solutions.

In addition to the case studies, we also introduce a pattern-based design approach using the Enterprise Integration Pattern of Hohpe and Woolf. To be able to implement complex integration solutions, we need to have a sound design for the integration developers to work with and to have a clear picture of what will be implemented for all involved parties. Based on a case study, we use this design approach and then implement the case study with Mule and ServiceMix

When an integration solution is implemented and after several testing stages has been deployed on a production environment, we need ways to manage and monitor the ESB environment. We therefore show how we can monitor Mule and ServiceMix with JMX and manage the environment based on management patterns like a wire tap and a detour.

At the end of this part we introduce another interesting topic related to an ESB, which is a process engine. Process engines offer functionality to support service interactions which span more than one request-response flow. We look at how to integrate the jBPM process engine with Mule and the Apache Ode process engine with ServiceMix. By the end of this part you will have gained a lot of knowledge about implementing and designing integration solutions with Mule and ServiceMix and you will be experienced in using process engines together with an open source ESB.

Implementing a case
study using patterns

9

We've discussed a lot of different open source ESB technologies and capabilities throughout the previous chapters, but you may wonder where this leaves you when you need to implement a full-blown integration project. If you only understand the technical functionality of an open source ESB, you aren't ready to implement an integration project from beginning to end. You need some guidance to help you with all the phases of such a project.

In this chapter, we look the different phases of an integration project, from analysis and design to the deployment of the integration solution. The main part missing from the technical foundation we've discussed so far is a decent design approach. Luckily, we don't have to invent this, because a great foundational book about design patterns is available: *Enterprise Integration Patterns* by Gregor Hohpe and Bobby Woolf. We give you an overview of these integration design patterns and introduce a pattern-based design approach to help you in the design phase.

We use a case study about reserving restaurant tables at a large hotel to guide you through a typical integration project. We start with designing the integration solution using some of the Enterprise Integration patterns.

In addition to the project guidance we provide in this chapter, we show you some interesting functionality of Mule and ServiceMix. You'll design the table-reservation solution and also implement an integration solution with both Mule and ServiceMix. We discuss useful functionality provided by both these tools, like the easy way to implement a publish-subscribe mechanism and the powerful routing rules available.

9.1   Introducing a design approach for integration projects

Patterns are well known in the area of application architecture and design. If you talk to Java developers and ask whether they understand the Singleton or Proxy pattern, they'll think you're trying to make a joke. The Gang of Four patterns are mandatory literature, or at least should be, for every object-oriented developer.

In the world of integration, the use of patterns is less common. Integration specialists are less familiar with integration patterns. Why is this? Hohpe and Woolf's *Enterprise Integration Patterns* proves that a large number of patterns can be identified. Why aren't we integration specialists using these patterns in our projects?

Most developers have a tendency to start developing without designing the solution first. The integration specialist may take the patterns into account while developing an integration solution, but the implementation still may not contain any patterns. The implementation of the message flow depends on the flow elements that the enterprise service bus product provides. ESBs generally adhere to some of the Enterprise Integration patterns, and ESB products primarily implement a selection of routing patterns. Think of the Content-Based Router and Recipient List patterns as good examples of these routing patterns.

A number of routing patterns are part of ESB product functionality and are therefore also part of the common vocabulary of integration specialists. But other categories of patterns are also valuable when you're implementing integration solutions, such as Message Construction and Message Channel patterns. We present a restaurant case study, beginning with a pattern-based design phase and providing guidance throughout the integration project. In this section, we focus on introducing the Enterprise Integration patterns and the pattern-based design approach.

9.1.1   Introducing the Enterprise Integration patterns

Let's do a quick recap of the Enterprise Integration patterns. For more information, you can read *Enterprise Integration Patterns* or visit http://www.enterpriseintegrationpatterns.com, which lists and describes all the patterns of the book in detail.

The best way to start this discussion is to look at the six pattern categories. Figure 9.1 shows them in combination with a message flow definition.

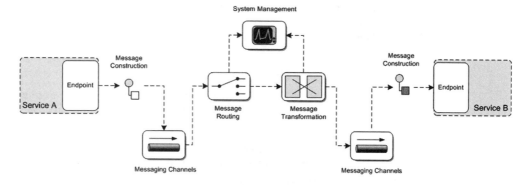

Figure 9.1 **An overview of the six Enterprise Integration pattern categories from the book by Hohpe and Woolf. Each category focuses on a different aspect of a typical message flow.**

The typical message flow definition shown in figure 9.1 consists of messaging elements similar to those in the examples in part 2 of this book. For example, we looked at message routing and transformation in chapter 5, and these ESB functionalities are also Enterprise Integration pattern categories. The flow definition in figure 9.1 starts with a messaging endpoint in service A. The endpoint dispatches a message that is constructed in the messaging endpoint to a message channel. Remember that a message channel can be, for example, a JMS queue, an HTTP URI, or even a file system. The message is then routed, transformed, and sent to the endpoint of service B via another message channel. The message flow is monitored with system-management patterns so you can administer the integration environment. Table 9.1 summarizes the six pattern categories.

Table 9.1 **The six Enterprise Integration pattern categories**

Pattern category	Description
Messaging endpoints	Patterns related to the production and consumption of messages from a messaging channel. Typical examples of endpoint patterns are the Idempotent Receiver and Selective Consumer patterns.
Messaging construction	Patterns that describe different kinds of message types and message elements. Typical examples are the Correlation Identifier and Document Message patterns.
Messaging channels	Ways to exchange messages between message flow elements. Typical examples are the Point-to-Point Channel and Guaranteed Delivery patterns.
Message routing	Ways to determine the target endpoint for an incoming message. Typical examples are the Content-Based Router and Aggregator patterns.

Table 9.1   The six Enterprise Integration pattern categories *(continued)*

Pattern category	Description
Message transformation	Patterns that transform the content of a message. Typical examples are the Message Translator and Content Enricher patterns.
System management	Patterns that deal with monitoring and administration functionality. Typical examples are the Wire Tap and Control Bus patterns.

The primary advantage of the Enterprise Integration patterns is their powerful expression in a message flow design. Complex integration problems like message splitting and aggregation or content-based routing can be simplified in a message flow design with one graphical element. In the next section, we discuss a design approach based on these patterns.

9.1.2   *Analyzing a pattern-based design approach*

To use the Enterprise Integration patterns, you must be able to incorporate them into your integration development process. Because the pattern descriptions are combined with a graphical element notation, the patterns are perfectly suited for the design phase of an integration project. You can use the Enterprise Integration patterns like you use the Unified Modeling Language (UML) for application development projects. The Enterprise Integration patterns can also be used as a Domain Specific Language (DSL), which is growing in popularity in the software development market. (A DSL combines the powerful functionality of a modeling language with a constraint set of modeling elements based on the target domain. For example, a DSL for developing a CRUD application is different from a DSL for an integration project.)

When you're ready to design an integration solution, you've already analyzed the integration problem area. This means you at least know the applications and services that are involved in the integration solution, and you know the format of the message exchanges between the applications and services. It's also nice to be familiar with any routing rules that are applicable to the integration problem domain and to be in contact with the application's and service's administrators and experts.

Imagine that you have an integration domain with three services, where service A sends a message to service B or C. When the message is a purchase order, it must be sent to service B with a transformation step; and when the message is an invoice, it must be sent to service C. If the incoming message is neither a purchase order nor an invoice, it can be considered invalid. The final requirement is that the message exchange between service A and the integration solution must be reliable.

This example consists of many requirements, and it's difficult to describe them all in one integration flow design. The Enterprise Integration patterns can help you design a simple diagram that explains the whole integration problem area; see figure 9.2.

Take your time as you analyze this design diagram, because it includes six Enterprise Integration patterns, a message flow definition, and a distinction in physical domains.

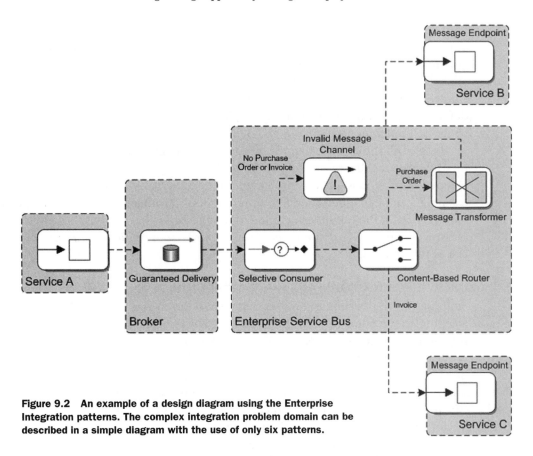

Figure 9.2   An example of a design diagram using the Enterprise Integration patterns. The complex integration problem domain can be described in a simple diagram with the use of only six patterns.

You can easily read the message flow definition by following the arrows. The first part of the message flow shows the Message Endpoint pattern that enables service A to send a message to a messaging infrastructure. The reliability requirement is covered by the Guaranteed Delivery pattern, which is implemented by a message broker (for example, ActiveMQ).

The functionality that is implemented by the ESB focuses on the implementation of the routing and transformation requirements. The message that is sent to the message broker is consumed by the Selective Consumer pattern, which makes it easy to only accept purchase orders and invoices. When another message type is consumed, the selective consumer sends the incoming message to an Invalid Message Channel. An ESB administrator is alerted via email or SMS message when a message arrives at the Invalid Message Channel.

Then a Content-Based Router pattern is used to route purchase orders to service B and invoices to service C, based on the content of the incoming message. This can, for example, be a message-type element or another combination of message elements to make a distinction between a purchase order and an invoice. Before the purchase order is sent to service B, the message is first transformed with a Message Transformer pattern. Eventually, the purchase order or invoice message is consumed by a message endpoint in service B or service C, respectively, which ends the message flow.

Most of this explanation can easily be determined from figure 9.2. This self-explanatory design makes it extremely useful for describing an integration problem. Another advantage of this design notation is that it's product independent. We don't define which ESB product we use to implement the design or which message broker we use to implement the guaranteed delivery.

It also isn't difficult to map the design to an integration implementation solution for Mule, ServiceMix, or any other ESB product. Most of the functionality can easily be mapped onto an ESB-specific implementation element. The content-based router, for example, can be mapped onto a filtering outbound router in Mule or onto a content-based router in the EIP service engine for ServiceMix.

Now let's use this pattern-based design approach to implement a case study in the rest of this chapter.

9.2   *Introducing a restaurant table reservation case study*

Suppose you're working as an integration specialist at the SleepingBeauty hotel. The SleepingBeauty wants to offer guests an easy way to reserve a table in one of its three restaurants: Lakeview, The Royal Duck, and Yokohama.

Because all rooms are equipped with LCD televisions, the hotel manager wants to provide a simple application that lets guests reserve a table via the TV menu. A guest should be able to ask the application which restaurants have a table available for a specific number of people and at a specified time. The guest can finalize the reservation by confirming one of the offered possibilities.

Because the hotel's restaurants are fully booked most days, the restaurant managers want to be sure that the table that's offered to a guest is valid only for a restaurant-dependent amount of time. Each of the three restaurants has a different validity time for table offerings; these values are provided by the restaurant managers.

The project started some weeks ago, and an information analyst has already created a high-level functional design diagram of the table-reservation functionality; see figure 9.3.

The case study overview in figure 9.3 focuses on the interaction between the different actors in the case study. The hotel guest starts by entering the number of people and the dinner time in the table-reservation menu on the TV. Eventually, the hotel guest has to confirm with one of the possible restaurants to reserve the table. Then the chosen restaurant responds with an acknowledgment of the confirmation.

Although this is a simple description, the implementation of such an integration solution is complicated. The hotel manager wants you, as the SleepingBeauty integration specialist, to start the implementation right away. But because your experience with other projects has taught you that a clear and well-considered design saves time later in the project, you decide to begin with a design.

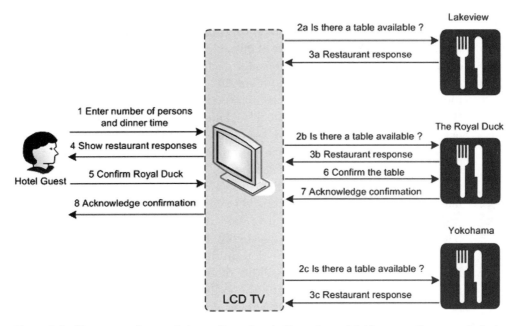

Figure 9.3   Message exchanges between the actors in the restaurant table reservation case study. In this example, the hotel guest reserves a table at The Royal Duck restaurant.

9.3   *Designing the restaurant table reservation solution*

The table-reservation integration solution consists of several message exchanges. It's wise to look for request/reply exchanges and combine them into one design. By looking at figure 9.3, you can see that one message exchange asks the restaurants if a table is available. Another message exchange involves the response messages from the restaurants saying whether a table is available for the specified number of people and at the specified time.

Because these are request/reply exchanges, you can combine them into one message flow design. The confirmation exchange can then be placed in a separate message flow design to improve the readability of the diagram.

9.3.1   *Designing a publish-subscribe message flow*

The first thing you have to decide is how the messages should be sent to the three restaurants. From section 9.1, you know that this decision area falls under the Message Channel patterns. The two patterns in the message channel category that can solve this problem are Point-to-Point and Publish Subscribe.

With the Point-to-Point pattern solution, you introduce three new message channels, which have a fixed message producer and consumer application. The Publish Subscribe pattern seems better suited because you publish a message to a topic, and subscribed consumers can consume the message. If you want to increase the number of restaurants that participate in the table-reservation application, you can easily do so with a publish-subscribe channel. So this case study implements the publish-subscribe channel to ask the restaurants for their table availability.

To implement the response-message exchange with the restaurants, it at first seems that you don't have to think about specific integration functionality. But if you look more closely at the requirements described in the previous section, you must consider the validity of the restaurant table availability response. When the hotel guest sends a confirmation message to reserve a table at one of the restaurants, you must be able to determine whether the confirmation message is still valid. One option would be to store the restaurant-response message with the current time in a database. You must also be able to correlate the confirmation message sent from the TV to the original restaurant response. To do so, you'll need to add a correlation identifier to the restaurant-response message before it's sent back to the TV menu. That Correlation Identifier pattern is part of the Message Construction pattern category.

You could use other options to determine the validity of the confirmation message. For example, you could send a validity time value in the response message to the TV and let the TV application handle the evaluation. But we're focusing on the implementation of integration functionality in this book, and therefore we implement the validity check in the open source ESB.

At this point, you can make a design of this part of the table-reservation solution; see figure 9.4.

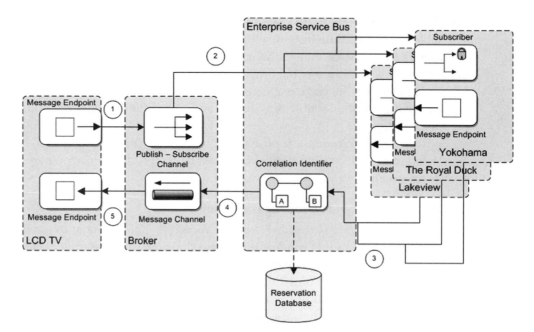

Figure 9.4 The message flow design diagram of the first part of the restaurant table application, using a number of Enterprise Integration patterns to visualize the integration solution

Notice that the graphical notation is similar to the example in figure 9.2, where we introduced the pattern-based design approach. The message flow starts with the message endpoint in the TV, which sends a table-availability inquiry message to a publish-subscribe message channel. Because you want the restaurant reservation applications to consume the messages from the topic, the ESB doesn't implement any additional functionality for this message exchange. The diagram uses the Durable Subscriber pattern to show the distinction between the consumption of a message from a normal queue and a topic.

But for this case study, the Durable Subscriber pattern isn't suitable, because the restaurant application has to respond quickly while the hotel guest is waiting; a durable subscriber means the subscriber can also be offline, and the message is delivered when the subscriber has started again. We've misused the graphical representation of this pattern to show that you're implementing a subscriber on a topic instead of a messaging endpoint. We've done this because no better-suited Enterprise Integration pattern is available.

To implement the restaurant responses, you use the Correlation Identifier pattern. The restaurant responses are persisted into the reservation database, and the database row identifier (the primary key) is set as a message header value in the restaurant-response message. Then the restaurant-response messages are sent to a default message channel, where the table-reservation menu shows the responses to the hotel guest.

9.3.2 Designing a filtering and routing message flow

The second message flow diagram that we need to discuss addresses the confirmation of the table reservation. This includes the functionality to determine the validity of the confirmation message. When the confirmation message is consumed by the ESB, the correlation identifier is retrieved from the message header, and the reservation database is queried for the stored restaurant-response message. Then the time that has passed between the persistence of the restaurant response and the confirmation from the hotel guest is compared to the validity time specified by the chosen restaurant. Remember that each restaurant can specify its own validity time for a table reservation. Only when the validity time hasn't been exceeded is the message sent further down the message flow.

When the message has exceeded the validity time, the message is forwarded to an invalid message channel. When the confirmation message is valid, a content-based router is used to route the message to the chosen restaurant application. The content-based router inspects the content of the message; based on the restaurant name, it determines the correct target endpoint. The TV receives a confirmation validity error message or a confirmation acknowledgment message, depending on the validity of the incoming confirmation message. Figure 9.5 shows an overview of this confirmation-message flow.

Notice that this confirmation message flow involves more functionality—which is implemented in the ESB—than the message flow we discussed in the previous section.

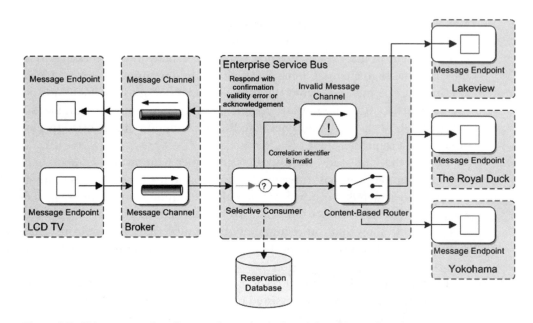

Figure 9.5   This message flow diagram shows the design of the table-confirmation message exchange. Only confirmations that haven't timed out are accepted by the ESB. A content-based router eventually sends the confirmation message to the correct restaurant application and an acknowledgment to the TV application.

A selective consumer is used to allow only valid confirmation messages in the remaining part of the message flow. The selective consumer queries the reservation database with the correlation identifier and determines the validity of the confirmation message.

We already discussed the remaining part of the message flow, so let's determine the next steps. You've been able to design the table-reservation system with two message flow diagrams, using the Enterprise Integration patterns. Next, you'll implement the message flows in the target platform. We show the implementation with both Mule and ServiceMix in the next section.

9.4   *Implementing the case study with Mule and ServiceMix*

One of the advantages of the design exercise in the previous section is that you can use it for both the Mule and ServiceMix implementations. The details of the implementations will be different, so this section is divided into three parts. We first look at the common building blocks you can use for both Mule and ServiceMix. Then we show you the details of the Mule and ServiceMix configurations separately.

9.4.1   *The Spring and Hibernate building blocks*

The common building blocks you need for each of the table-reservation implementations are the restaurant endpoints and the database persistency, designed in figures 9.4

and 9.5. The restaurant endpoints would in real life be reservation applications; but to simulate the interaction with these applications, you'll implement a stub. It's common in integration projects to implement stubs to simulate actual applications, to speed up the development process. Because Mule and ServiceMix both seamlessly integrate with Spring, we've chosen this container to facilitate the persistency and endpoint logic. And because Hibernate is the market standard for ORM frameworks, you'll use this framework to build the persistency logic.

THE RESTAURANT STUBS IMPLEMENTATION

To make it easier to implement the three stubs for the restaurant-reservation applications, you'll implement one Java bean that will be customized via dependency injection. For example, you'll inject the restaurant name into this Java bean, so you'll have three restaurant stubs at runtime. Listing 9.1 shows the bean implementation with the RestaurantServiceBean class.

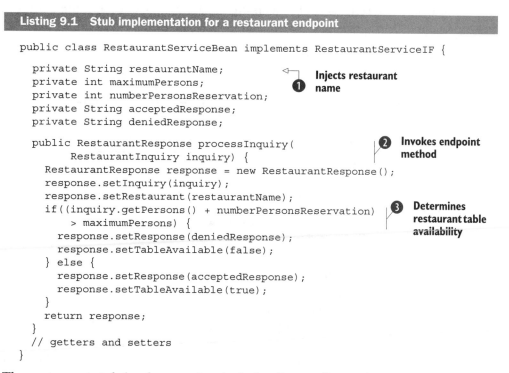

Listing 9.1 Stub implementation for a restaurant endpoint

```
public class RestaurantServiceBean implements RestaurantServiceIF {

    private String restaurantName;                    Injects restaurant
    private int maximumPersons;                     ❶ name
    private int numberPersonsReservation;
    private String acceptedResponse;
    private String deniedResponse;

    public RestaurantResponse processInquiry(          Invokes endpoint
            RestaurantInquiry inquiry) {            ❷ method
      RestaurantResponse response = new RestaurantResponse();
      response.setInquiry(inquiry);
      response.setRestaurant(restaurantName);
      if((inquiry.getPersons() + numberPersonsReservation)   Determines
          > maximumPersons) {                       ❸ restaurant table
        response.setResponse(deniedResponse);          availability
        response.setTableAvailable(false);
      } else {
        response.setResponse(acceptedResponse);
        response.setTableAvailable(true);
      }
      return response;
    }
    // getters and setters
}
```

The restaurant stub implementation includes five attributes that will be injected by the Spring container, including the restaurant name ❶. These values are used to customize behavior in, for example, the calculation to see whether the reservation can be accepted. The response that is sent back to the hotel guest can also be injected via a Spring property definition.

When the hotel guest sends an inquiry to see which restaurants have a table available, processInquiry ❷ must be invoked on this stub implementation. This means you need to implement logic in Mule and ServiceMix to invoke this bean from a publish-subscribe mechanism, as designed in figure 9.4. You'll see how you can easily configure this functionality later in this chapter when we discuss the Mule and ServiceMix configurations.

This stub implementation is kept simple, but you implement one piece of logic to determine whether a table is available for the requested number of people ❸. This is a simplification of the table-reservation process, but we're focusing on integration logic and not on the application logic.

DEFINING THE RESERVATION DATABASE MODEL

The other common building block is the persistency of the reservation, which lets you correlate the restaurant response to the confirmation message and calculate the validity of the confirmation message. To implement the persistence layer, you'll use an HSQL database. This database doesn't require a difficult installment procedure and is ready to go when you download the open source product. You'll use two simple tables to persist the reservation between the restaurant response and the guest's confirmation message, as shown in figure 9.6.

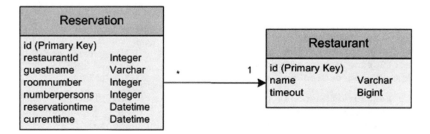

Figure 9.6   This is the database model for the restaurant-reservation case study; it enables the persistence of reservations. The `Reservation` table stores the restaurant reservation responses, and the `Restaurant` table holds the three restaurants with timeout values.

The `Reservation` table stores all the restaurant-response messages that are sent to hotel guests. You store the restaurant identifier and the current time with the guest information values. The current time value and the restaurant timeout value provide enough information to calculate the validity of the confirmation message. The identifier of the reservation table is used to correlate the restaurant-response message with the confirmation message. The `Restaurant` table holds the three restaurants with their names and corresponding timeout values, which are provided by the restaurant manager.

IMPLEMENTING THE RESERVATION DATA LOGIC

Now that you've defined the database model, you can implement the ORM logic with Hibernate. We won't go into detail about how to use the Hibernate framework, because two excellent books have been written about this topic by Hibernate's founders: *Java Persistence with Hibernate* (Manning: Christian Bauer and Gavin King, 2006) and *Hibernate in Action* (Manning: Christian Bauer and Gavin King, 2004). And because the ORM definition of these two tables is fairly simple, listing 9.2 shows the DAO that you'll use in the Mule and ServiceMix implementations. Remember that the entire example, including the mapping definition, is available at http://www.manning.com/rademakers and at http://www.esbinaction.com.

Listing 9.2 DAO to retrieve and store reservations; implemented with Hibernate

```
public class ReservationHibernateDAO extends
      HibernateDaoSupport implements ReservationDAOIF {

  public Reservation getReservation(                      Gets reservation
      long reservationID) {                           ❶  with ID
    return (Reservation) getHibernateTemplate().get(
      Reservation.class, reservationID);
  }
                                              ❷  Stores reservation
  public Reservation saveReservation(            object
      Reservation reservation) {
    String restaurantName = reservation.getRestaurant().getName();
    reservation.setRestaurant(getRestaurant(restaurantName));
    Long reservationId = (Long)
        getHibernateTemplate().save(reservation);
    return getReservation(reservationId);
  }
                                              ❸  Gets restaurant
  public Restaurant getRestaurant(String name) {   with name
    List restaurantList = getHibernateTemplate().find(
        "from Restaurant where name = ?", new Object[]{name});
    if(restaurantList != null)
      return (Restaurant) restaurantList.get(0);
    else
      return null;
  }
}
```

If you're familiar with the Hibernate framework, this DAO implementation class won't be difficult to understand. You use the Hibernate support class HibernateDaoSupport of the Spring Framework to handle the database connections and transactions, so you only have to implement the data-retrieval and -manipulation logic.

When the message flow in the ESB receives a confirmation message from the hotel guest, you need to retrieve the reservation based on the reservation identifier. The getReservation ❶ method implements this functionality in only one line of code.

You also need to persist a Reservation object to the HSQL database, so you implement the saveReservation method ❷. Because the message flow only sets a restaurant name in the Reservation object, you need to implement another method to retrieve the Restaurant object, including the restaurant identifier ❸. Then the reservation can be persisted to the database.

With these common building blocks in place, we can now look at the integration logic that you'll need to implement with Mule.

9.4.2   *Implementing the Mule message flow*

In the design phase, you separated the functionality into two design diagrams. This is also a good starting point for the implementation phase.

IMPLEMENTING A PUBLISH-SUBSCRIBE MECHANISM WITH MULE

The first part of the functionality involves implementing a publish-subscribe mechanism with the restaurant endpoints. You implemented a stub class to simulate the restaurant endpoints in the previous section; now you need to decide how you can use this class in your message flow implementation. Because you're using Spring as an object container for the restaurant endpoints, you can easily reference these beans from a Mule service definition. You must define three Mule services that are subscribed to a specific topic, which invoke the Spring beans that represent the restaurant endpoints. Figure 9.7 provides an overview of this publish-subscribe implementation for Mule.

Notice that you define three subscribers in the Mule configuration. This is different than the diagram in figure 9.4, due to the stub implementation of the restaurant endpoints. Stubs are useful in real-life projects, especially early on. But be sure to clarify the specification of the interface with the actual target applications as early as possible. The stub implementation should reflect the interface of the real target application. Figure 9.7 also shows the instantiation of the restaurant beans from the same restaurant service bean class, `RestaurantServiceBean`, which you implemented in listing 9.1. Listing 9.3 shows one of the subscriber service definitions configured in the Mule configuration.

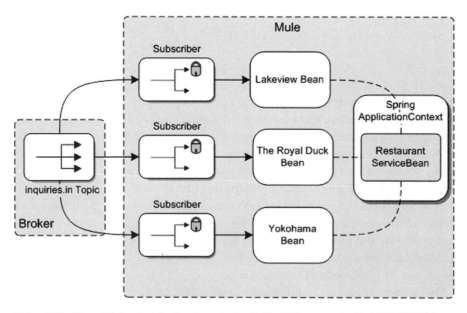

Figure 9.7   The publish-subscribe implementation in the Mule message flow definition. Three topic subscribers are defined; they invoke the restaurant beans that simulate the restaurant reservation applications.

Listing 9.3 Topic subscriber that invokes the restaurant bean

```
<mule>
  <spring:beans>
    <spring:import resource="restaurant-beans.xml"/>        ❶ Imports necessary
  </spring:beans>                                               Spring beans

  <jms:activemq-connector name="jmsConnector"              ❷ Defines JMS
      brokerURL="tcp://localhost:61616"/>                     connection

  <jms:endpoint name="inquiry-topic"                      ❸ Defines reusable
      topic="inquiries.in"/>                                  topic endpoint
  <vm:endpoint name="inquiry-out" path="restaurant.response"/>

  <model name="RestaurantModel">
    <service name="LakeviewRestaurantService">
      <inbound>
        <inbound-endpoint ref="inquiry-topic"             ❹ Wait for response
            remoteSync="true"/>                              with remoteSync
      </inbound>
      <component>
        <spring-object bean="lakeviewRestaurant"/>             References Lakeview
      </component>                                          ❺ Spring bean
      <outbound>
        <outbound-pass-through-router>
          <outbound-endpoint ref="inquiry-out"/>
        </outbound-pass-through-router>
      </outbound>
    </service>

    <service name="PersistResponse">
      <inbound>
        <inbound-endpoint ref="inquiry-out"/>
      </inbound>
      <component>                                          ❻ Injects DAO in
        <spring-object bean="expirationBean"/>                 ExpirationRouter
      </component>
    </service>
  </model>
</mule>
```

In addition to the definition of the publish-subscribe mechanism as shown in figure 9.7, this Mule configuration also describes the restaurant-response implementation shown earlier in figure 9.4. But let's first focus on the publish-subscribe functionality, because it's also the starting point for the message flow. The Mule configuration can become large, so it's a good practice to separate logical units of work in different files. You need to define the Spring restaurant beans and the Hibernate DAO in addition to the Mule message flow, so you'll divide these definitions into two files. It's easy to combine the two definitions with a simple import statement ❶. You can configure multiple import statements if necessary.

Because you want to implement three topic subscribers in this Mule configuration, you must first define a JMS connection ❷. You don't have to configure anything special to be able to subscribe to a topic, so you configure a default JMS connector.

To be able to reuse the topic endpoint definition for all three topic subscribers, Mule provides an option to define a reusable endpoint at the root level of the Mule configuration ❸. You can refer to the reusable endpoint with the inquiry-topic name. The JMS endpoint definition uses a prefix of `topic:`, which tells Mule that the JMS endpoint is a topic.

This Mule configuration defines just one of three restaurant subscribers, because the other two use the same configuration. The inbound router listens for new messages arriving at the topic endpoint. Because you eventually want to send the restaurant-response message to the JMS `ReplyTo` destination that is set in the incoming JMS message arriving at the topic, you use the `remoteSync` value of `true` in this configuration ❹.

Using the remoteSync attribute

The `remoteSync` attribute tells the Mule container to wait for a response on the outgoing message before responding to the incoming message. You can find information about the `remoteSync` attribute at http://www.mulesource.org/display/MULE2USER/Messaging+Patterns (login required). For this example, you want to send three restaurant-response messages to the TV application based on the JMS `ReplyTo` destination header value. Mule uses the `ReplyTo` destination transparently, without the need to define additional configuration parameters.

When you don't specify the `remoteSync` attribute, no response message is sent to the queue specified with the JMS `ReplyTo` header. By specifying the `remoteSync` value of `true`, the `expirationBean` response message is sent back to the `LakeView-RestaurantService` Mule service. So the response message of the `expiration-Bean` is processed by the `LakeViewRestaurantService` and sent to the destination defined by the JMS `ReplyTo` header value.

When the JMS message has been consumed from the `inquiries.in` topic, the Mule container invokes the restaurant service bean ❺. For the Lakeview topic subscriber, this means the Spring bean that is configured as the Lakeview stub implementation is invoked. The Lakeview restaurant service bean is configured in the restaurant-beans.xml file that you import ❶.

This concludes the definition of the publish-subscribe mechanism, but the Mule configuration example also shows the restaurant-response functionality. The restaurant responses are sent back to the hotel guest via the JMS `ReplyTo` header value. Before the message is sent, you need to add a correlation identifier to the outgoing message as designed in figure 9.4. This functionality is implemented with the `ExpirationBean` Spring bean, which is also imported from the restaurant-beans.xml Spring configuration ❻. We look at the implementation of this Spring bean in detail in listing 9.4. Because you need to store the restaurant-response message, you also inject the `Reser-vationHibernateDAO` class instance from listing 9.2 in this outbound router.

To set the restaurant identifier in the outgoing response message, you use a custom JMS header field named `restaurantResponseID`. The custom header field includes the reservation database identifier from the restaurant response in the confirmation message, which is sent back from the TV application. The details of the expiration Spring bean are shown in listing 9.4.

Listing 9.4 Expiration bean that stores the reservation message

```
public class ExpirationBean {

    public static final String RESPONSE_ID =
        "restaurantResponseID";                          ❶ Injects
    private ReservationDAOIF reservationDAO;                ReservationHibernateDAO

    public RestaurantResponse persist(RestaurantResponse response) {
        Reservation reservation = new Reservation();
        reservation.setRestaurantName(response.getRestaurant());
        reservation.setGuestName(
            response.getInquiry().getGuestName());
        reservation.setRoomNumber(
            response.getInquiry().getRoomNumber());
        reservation.setReservationTime(
            response.getInquiry().getReservationTime());
        reservation.setNumberOfPersons(
            response.getInquiry().getPersons());
        reservation = reservationDAO.saveReservation(   ❷ Saves
            reservation);                                   reservation
        MuleEventContext context = RequestContext.getEventContext();
        MuleMessage message = context.getMessage();
        message.setLongProperty(RESPONSE_ID,            ❸ Sets correlation
            reservation.getReservationID());                identifier
        return response;
    }
}
```

The reservation DAO is injected in the `ExpirationBean` via the `reservationDAO` attribute ❶. The `RestaurantResponse` message returned by the restaurant service bean consists of the restaurant name, a response message, and a Boolean value to indicate whether a table can be reserved. The response message also includes the inquiry message, which was received from the topic. To store the reservation, you need a restaurant name, the current time, and a number of guest-related values, as you may recall from figure 9.6. Because the current time is automatically set when a new `Reservation` object is instantiated, you only copy the other values. Then the `Reservation` instance can be persisted into the HSQL database via the Hibernate DAO ❷.

The `saveReservation` message returns the database-persisted `Reservation` values, which include the generated reservation identifier. This reservation identifier can now be set as a header property in the Mule message ❸. The header properties are automatically copied to the outgoing JMS message and returned to the TV reservation application.

With the publish-subscribe functionality in place, you can now implement the confirmation message functionality, which includes both a message filter and a content-based router implementation.

IMPLEMENTING THE ROUTING FUNCTIONALITY WITH MULE

The second part of the Mule configuration for the restaurant reservation application handles the confirmation message that the hotel guest sends to his or her chosen restaurant. You need to implement functionality that checks whether the confirmation message is still valid, and you must also determine which restaurant application is the target endpoint for the confirmation message. The best way to start the implementation of this functionality is to define the Mule configuration for this message flow. After that, you can implement the remaining functionality: in this case, the confirmation-validity check. Let's first look at the Mule configuration for the routing functionality, shown in listing 9.5.

> **Listing 9.5   Mule definition of the confirmation-message routing functionality**

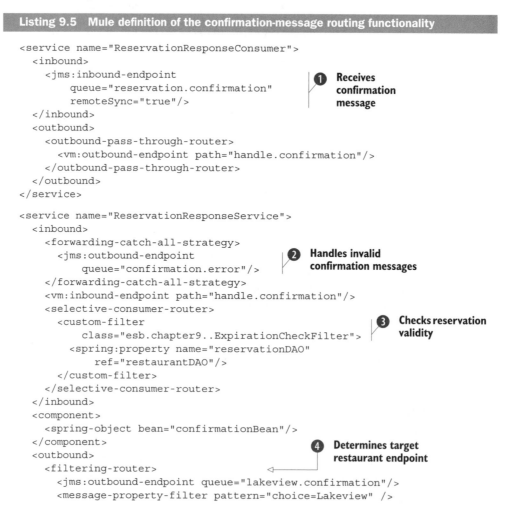

```
<service name="ReservationResponseConsumer">
  <inbound>
    <jms:inbound-endpoint
        queue="reservation.confirmation"
        remoteSync="true"/>
  </inbound>
  <outbound>
    <outbound-pass-through-router>
      <vm:outbound-endpoint path="handle.confirmation"/>
    </outbound-pass-through-router>
  </outbound>
</service>

<service name="ReservationResponseService">
  <inbound>
    <forwarding-catch-all-strategy>
      <jms:outbound-endpoint
          queue="confirmation.error"/>
    </forwarding-catch-all-strategy>
    <vm:inbound-endpoint path="handle.confirmation"/>
    <selective-consumer-router>
      <custom-filter
          class="esb.chapter9..ExpirationCheckFilter">
        <spring:property name="reservationDAO"
            ref="restaurantDAO"/>
      </custom-filter>
    </selective-consumer-router>
  </inbound>
  <component>
    <spring-object bean="confirmationBean"/>
  </component>
  <outbound>
    <filtering-router>
      <jms:outbound-endpoint queue="lakeview.confirmation"/>
      <message-property-filter pattern="choice=Lakeview" />
```

① Receives confirmation message

② Handles invalid confirmation messages

③ Checks reservation validity

④ Determines target restaurant endpoint

```
      </filtering-router>
      <filtering-router>
        <jms:outbound-endpoint queue="theroyalduck.confirmation"/>
        <message-property-filter pattern="choice=The royal duck" />
      </filtering-router>
      <filtering-router>
        <jms:outbound-endpoint queue="yokohama.confirmation"/>
        <message-property-filter pattern="choice=Yokohama" />
      </filtering-router>
    </outbound>
  </service>
```

The service that is configured in this example is part of the Mule configuration defined in listing 9.3. But to clarify the message flow, the configuration is split into two listings. The inbound router listens for confirmation messages arriving at the `reservation.confirmation` queue ❶. Again, you configure a `remoteSync` attribute value of `true` to use the JMS `ReplyTo` header value after the second service. If you didn't configure the `remoteSync` attribute value of `true`, no reply message would be sent to the JMS queue provided with the JMS `ReplyTo` header. Notice that even if you define an outbound router on the second Mule service, in this case the `reservationResponse-Service`, the response message of the component, in this case the `confirmationBean`, is also sent back to the inbound endpoint with the `remoteSync` attribute.

When a confirmation arrives, the validity of the message is checked with the `ExpirationCheckFilter` ❸. We look at the details of this filter in listing 9.6. Because you need to retrieve the persisted reservation based on the reservation identifier that is part of the confirmation message, the `ReservationHibernateDAO` class is injected in the filter instance.

Because you also need to deal with confirmation messages that are no longer valid, you implement a catch-all strategy ❷, which is invoked when the filter rejects the incoming JMS message. For this example, the invalid confirmation message is sent to a JMS queue, but in real-life implementations you could implement additional functionality here.

When the confirmation message is checked for validity, you need to forward it to the correct restaurant endpoint. In this example, you have three JMS queues, which represent the different restaurant applications. With a content-based routing implementation based on a filtering outbound router, you can forward the confirmation to the right JMS queue ❹. In the confirmation bean, the restaurant name is set as a message-header value. The message header `choice` is used to store the restaurant name. Therefore, you can use the message-property filter to implement the content-based router. The message-property filter evaluates the pattern attribute against the message headers in the outgoing message, which in this example is the `Restaurant-Confirmation` message.

The only part you need to implement to complete this integration solution is the filter to check the validity of the confirmation message. You check the time that has passed between the restaurant response and receipt of the confirmation message with the timeout value specified in the database for the chosen restaurant. The Java code implementation of the filter is shown in listing 9.6.

Listing 9.6   Filter implementation validating the confirmation message

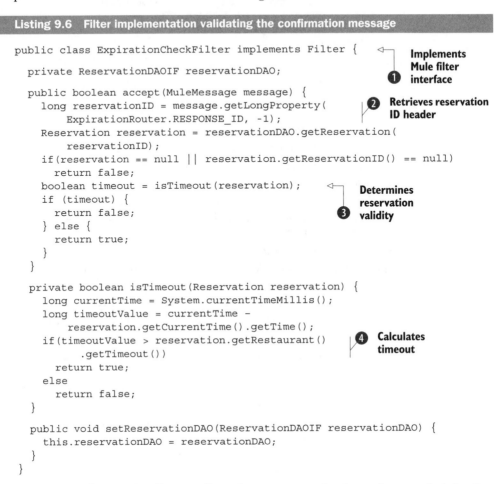

```
public class ExpirationCheckFilter implements Filter {          Implements
                                                                Mule filter
    private ReservationDAOIF reservationDAO;                  ❶ interface

    public boolean accept(MuleMessage message) {           ❷ Retrieves reservation
        long reservationID = message.getLongProperty(         ID header
            ExpirationRouter.RESPONSE_ID, -1);
        Reservation reservation = reservationDAO.getReservation(
            reservationID);
        if(reservation == null || reservation.getReservationID() == null)
            return false;
        boolean timeout = isTimeout(reservation);          Determines
        if (timeout) {                                     reservation
            return false;                                ❸ validity
        } else {
            return true;
        }
    }

    private boolean isTimeout(Reservation reservation) {
        long currentTime = System.currentTimeMillis();
        long timeoutValue = currentTime -
            reservation.getCurrentTime().getTime();
        if(timeoutValue > reservation.getRestaurant()    ❹ Calculates
                .getTimeout())                              timeout
            return true;
        else
            return false;
    }

    public void setReservationDAO(ReservationDAOIF reservationDAO) {
        this.reservationDAO = reservationDAO;
    }
}
```

Because you only want to allow confirmation messages that haven't exceeded the timeout value specified in the database for the chosen restaurant, you need a filter mechanism. Within Mule, this is easy to do by implementing the Filter interface ❶. Implementing the Filter interface means implementing the accept method. When a Boolean value of true is returned, this means the filter accepts the message; if the value is false, the message is rejected.

Because you want to check the time that has passed between the restaurant response and the confirmation message, you need to get the reservation identifier to retrieve the persisted time value. The reservation identifier is passed as a header property in the confirmation message, so you can easily retrieve this value ❷.

With the reservation identifier, you can retrieve the reservation from the HSQL database via the injected Hibernate DAO class. The last step is to compare the time that has passed between the restaurant response and the confirmation message and the timeout value that is specified for the chosen restaurant ❸. This is an easy calculation given the time values retrieved from the database and the current time value ❹.

You've implemented all the parts of the restaurant reservation solution in Mule. Because you started designing the integration solution by using Enterprise Integration patterns, you saw that the translation to an actual implementation isn't that difficult. You had to make some decisions about how to implement the publish-subscribe and selective-consumer functionality, but the foundation of the solution hasn't changed. More information about how to run this restaurant example on the Mule container can be found in section 9.5.1.

For the ServiceMix implementation of this case study, you'll have to make similar decisions. But you'll see that other options are available to implement the example, and this will help you on your quest to become an open source ESB specialist.

9.4.3 Implementing the ServiceMix message flow

You'll implement the same table reservation case study with ServiceMix as you did in the previous section with Mule. You'll see that the design that you made in section 9.3 is also great as a foundation for the ServiceMix implementation. You've kept the design product and technology neutral and therefore it's applicable for multiple ESB implementations. To make it easier to understand the ServiceMix integration solution, we split the solution description into a publish-subscribe and a filter and routing part just like you did for the Mule implementation.

IMPLEMENTING A PUBLISH-SUBSCRIBE MECHANISM WITH SERVICEMIX

The implementation of the publish-subscribe functionality in ServiceMix involves configuring a number of JBI components. You'll need to configure some JMS endpoints within the JMS binding component, but the incoming JMS messages also need to be routed to the three restaurant Spring beans you implemented in listing 9.1.

It's no problem to integrate Spring beans in a ServiceMix message flow, but you have to think about the marshaling and unmarshaling of the XML messages that flow through the JBI bus to the Java beans that are defined as the input parameters and return value for the Spring restaurant bean. Two components are applicable to implement the Spring bean invocation: the Bean service engine and the JSR-181 service engine. You'll use the JSR-181 service engine, because this component is capable of (un)marshaling the XML messages automatically. But the JMS binding component and the JSR-181 service engine are not the only JBI components you need: you also need to deal with routing the incoming message to the restaurant beans and handling the restaurant responses. This functionality will be implemented with the Camel service engine. Figure 9.8 shows all the JBI components required for the first part of the integration solution.

Figure 9.8 also shows the use of the Camel service engine. Why do you need this component? You also need to add a correlation identifier to be able to correlate the restaurant response to the confirmation message sent by the hotel guest. You use a Camel DSL router to invoke the JSR-181 component and handle the restaurant

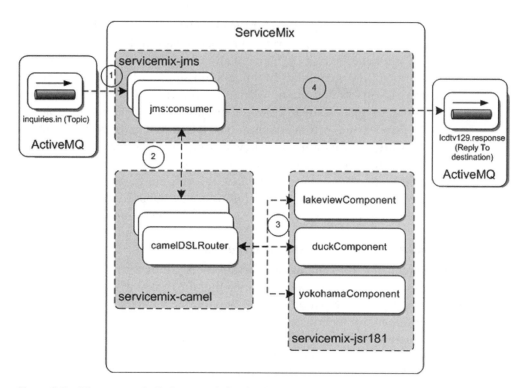

Figure 9.8 JBI components that are needed to implement the publish-subscribe functionality for the table reservation integration solution in ServiceMixBecause you'll use in-out JMS consumers, which consume messages from the `inquiries.in` topic and produce messages to the reply-to queue specified in the JMS `ReplyTo` header, you don't have to use the pipeline EIP component.

response by adding a correlation identifier to the outgoing restaurant-response message. You could also implement this functionality with a Bean service engine component, but the Camel framework provides some nice features, as you'll see later in listing 9.9.

You already saw how to configure JMS endpoints in a number of examples; listing 9.7 shows only one of the three JMS topic endpoints that you need in the solution implementation.

Listing 9.7 JMS endpoint configuration that listens for messages

```
<beans xmlns:jms="http://servicemix.apache.org/jms/1.0"
       xmlns:esb="http://esbinaction.com/restaurant">

  <jms:consumer service="esb:lakeviewTopicConsumer"
      endpoint="endpoint"
      targetService="esb:lakeviewDSLRouter"
      pubSubDomain="true"
      destinationName="inquiries.in"
      connectionFactory="#connectionFactory"
```

❶ Defines Camel router as target

❷ Configures a topic consumer

```
              marshaler="#replyInOutMarshaler"/>

    <bean id="replyInOutMarshaler"                    ❸ Sets reply-to
         class="esb.chapter9...servicemix.              destination
            ⮡ReplyToConsumerMarshaler">
      <property name="mep"
          value="http://www.w3.org/2004/08/wsdl/in-out" />
    </bean>

    <bean id="connectionFactory"
          class="org.apache.activemq.ActiveMQConnectionFactory">
      <property name="brokerURL" value="tcp://localhost:61616" />
    </bean>
</beans>
```

The difference between a queue listener and a topic subscriber is the pubSub-
Domain attribute value ❷. For topic subscribers, you have to specify a value of true
for this attribute.

The listing shows that this is a topic subscriber for the Lakeview restaurant. In figure 9.8, you saw that the message retrieved from the topic is forwarded to a Camel DSL
router, which in this case is the Lakeview DSL router ❶.

Because you want the consumer to use an in-out exchange pattern, you have to
configure a marshaler bean ❸. By default, the JMS consumer endpoint uses the
DefaultConsumerMarshaler class, which is provided by the ServiceMix JMS binding
component. The default marshaler uses an in-only exchange pattern. In addition, you
need to send the response message received from the DSL router to the queue specified in the JMS ReplyTo header of the incoming topic message. This functionality is
also implemented in the custom ReplyToConsumerMarshaler class. Listing 9.8 shows
the implementation of this class.

Listing 9.8   ReplyToConsumerMarshaler class implementation

```
public class ReplyToConsumerMarshaler
    extends DefaultConsumerMarshaler {              ❶ Passes JMS and
                                                       normalized message
  protected void populateMessage(Message message,   ◁─┘
      NormalizedMessage normalizedMessage) throws Exception {
    if (message instanceof TextMessage) {
      TextMessage textMessage = (TextMessage) message;
      normalizedMessage.setProperty(                      ❷ Copies JMS
          SimpleDestinationChooser.DESTINATION_KEY,          ReplyTo
              message.getJMSReplyTo());                      header
      Source source = new StringSource(textMessage.getText());
      normalizedMessage.setContent(source);
    } else {
      throw new UnsupportedOperationException(
          "JMS message is not a TextMessage");
    }
  }
}
```

Because you extend the `DefaultConsumerMarshaler` class, you can override the method where the ServiceMix normalized message is populated with the content of the incoming JMS message ❶. In this case, the incoming message is the restaurant inquiry message, which contains the guest name, room number, number of people, and reservation time.

Because you want to send the restaurant-response message to the JMS `ReplyTo` header destination, you need to extract this header from the JMS message ❷. This is easy; you can call the `getJMSReplyTo` method on the JMS message instance. Then you set this reply-to destination in the ServiceMix normalized message.

The ServiceMix JMS binding component uses a `SimpleDestinationChooser` by default to determine the target destination for an outgoing JMS message. This destination-chooser class is part of the ServiceMix JMS binding component and looks for a property in the normalized message header that's equal to the `DESTINATION_KEY` of the `SimpleDestinationChooser` class. When such a header is present, the JMS BC uses the value of this destination property as the target destination for the outgoing JMS message. When the destination header isn't present, the JMS endpoint looks for a statically configured destination value: for example, the destination configured with the `destinationName` attribute.

You set the reply-to destination on the message header of the normalized message. Because you specify that the JMS consumer uses an in-out message exchange pattern, the restaurant response message is returned to the JMS consumer. The `Simple-DestinationChooser` class inspects the response message for a destination header and uses this value as the target destination of the response message. The restaurant-response message is sent to the JMS `ReplyTo` header destination specified with the restaurant inquiry message.

ADDING A CORRELATION IDENTIFIER WITH APACHE CAMEL

Now let's move on to the next JBI component in the message flow: the Camel service engine. The three Camel components implement the most functionality of the publish-subscribe solution. First, the Camel router invokes the restaurant Spring bean via a JSR-181 endpoint; second, the Camel router adds a correlation identifier before the message is routed to the outgoing JMS endpoint. Listing 9.9 shows the Camel service engine configuration and the Lakeview Camel router.

Listing 9.9 Camel service engine with a router implementation

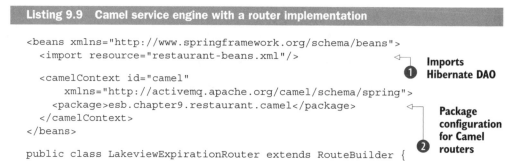

```
<beans xmlns="http://www.springframework.org/schema/beans">
  <import resource="restaurant-beans.xml"/>                      ◁─┐  Imports
                                                                  ❶ Hibernate DAO
  <camelContext id="camel"
      xmlns="http://activemq.apache.org/camel/schema/spring">
    <package>esb.chapter9.restaurant.camel</package>            ◁─┐  Package
  </camelContext>                                                   configuration
</beans>                                                            for Camel
                                                                  ❷ routers
public class LakeviewExpirationRouter extends RouteBuilder {
```

```
    private final static String SERVICE_IN =
        RestaurantRouter.JBI_PREFIX + "/lakeviewDSLRouter";
    private final static String LAKEVIEW_IN =
        RestaurantRouter.JBI_PREFIX + "/lakeviewComponent";

    public void configure() {
        from(SERVICE_IN).process(new InOutProcessor())
          .to(LAKEVIEW_IN).process(new ExpirationProcessor());
    }
}
```

❸ Routing logic

Listing 9.9 shows the configuration of the Camel service engine, camel-context.xml, at the top and below the Lakeview Camel router implementation. The only difference from the other restaurant Camel routers is the service-name configuration.

To be able to add a correlation identifier to the restaurant-response message, you first need to persist the reservation to the HSQL database with the Hibernate DAO from listing 9.2. The Hibernate bean configuration is split into a separate Spring bean file, which is imported in the Camel service engine configuration ❶.

For this implementation, you're implementing the router with the Java Camel DSL instead of the Spring XML configuration. So the Camel service engine configuration is short, and you only need to define the packages where the Camel router classes can be found ❷. When the Camel context is started, the Camel container instantiates the router classes that are available in the esb.chapter9.restaurant.camel package.

In the Camel router implementation, the routing rules are specified in the configure method, which is invoked by the Camel container. The routing rule definition starts with the service-name definition for the Camel router, so it can be invoked from the ServiceMix JBI container ❸. The service name lakeviewDSLRouter corresponds to the transformer-exchange target specified as the target service for the JMS consumer configuration in listing 9.7.

An InOutProcessor is defined as the first processor for the incoming message ❸. This processor is needed because the ServiceMix JBI and the Camel exchange have different views of message exchange patterns. In the ServiceMix container, message-exchange patterns are important definitions, because they specify whether a response message can be expected. Camel has a less strict definition of exchanges. In the JMS consumer definition in listing 9.7, you specify an In-Out Message Exchange pattern; but in the Camel router, this exchange pattern isn't copied from the ServiceMix message exchange and therefore the exchange pattern is equal to null. In the InOut-Processor, you must specify that the exchange is an in-out exchange so the outgoing message exchange to the JSR-181 component uses an in-out message exchange pattern. The implementation of the InOutProcessor is as follows:

```
public class InOutProcessor implements Processor {
    public void process(Exchange e) {
        JbiExchange exchange = (JbiExchange) e;
        exchange.setPattern(ExchangePattern.InOut);
    }
}
```

The second part of the routing rule specifies a target endpoint for the received message. This target endpoint is the JSR-181 service name for the restaurant Spring bean. When a response is received from the Spring bean, the correlation identifier is added in the `ExpirationProcessor` class. This processor lets Camel change the message exchange when required. You use the processor class to add a correlation identifier to the response message. Listing 9.10 shows the implementation of the `ExpirationProcessor` class.

Listing 9.10 `ExpirationProcessor` implementation, adding a correlation identifier

```
public class ExpirationProcessor implements Processor {

    public void process(Exchange exchange) throws Exception {
        StringSource payload = (StringSource)
            exchange.getIn().getBody();                           ❶ Gets restaurant
                                                                    response payload
        ReservationDAOIF reservationDAO =
            exchange.getContext().getRegistry().lookup(           ❷ Retrieves DAO
                "restaurantDAO", ReservationDAOIF.class);           instance
        Reservation reservation = createReservation(payload);
        reservation = reservationDAO.saveReservation(reservation);
        String responsePayload = addReservationID(
            payload.getText(),                                    ❸ Adds
                reservation.getReservationID());                    correlation
        Message responseMessage = exchange.getOut();                identifier
        responseMessage.setBody(new StringSource(responsePayload));
    }

    private Reservation createReservation(StringSource payload)
        throws Exception {
        Reservation reservation = new Reservation();
        XPath xpath = XPathFactory.newInstance().newXPath();
        NSContext ctx = new NSContext();
        ctx.setNamespace("esb",
          "http://message.service.restaurant.chapter9.esb");
        ctx.setNamespace("res", "http://esbinaction.com/restaurant");
        xpath.setNamespaceContext(ctx);
        InputSource payloadSource = new InputSource(
            new StringReader(payload.getText()));
        Node startNode = (Node) xpath.compile("//res:out").evaluate(
            payloadSource, XPathConstants.NODE);
        reservation.setRestaurantName(executeXPath(               ❹ Gets restaurant
            xpath.compile("//esb:restaurant"), startNode));         name
        reservation.setGuestName(executeXPath(
            xpath.compile("//esb:guestName"), startNode));
        reservation.setNumberOfPersons(Integer.valueOf(
            executeXPath(xpath.compile("//esb:persons"), startNode)));
        reservation.setRoomNumber(Integer.valueOf(
            executeXPath(xpath.compile("//esb:roomNumber"), startNode)));
        XsDateTimeFormat format = new XsDateTimeFormat();         ◁─┐ Uses
        Calendar reservationCal = (Calendar) format.parseObject(      XFire
            executeXPath(xpath.compile("//esb:reservationTime"),      DateTime
                startNode));                                       ❺ class
        reservation.setReservationTime(reservationCal.getTime());
        return reservation;
    }
```

```
      private String executeXPath(XPathExpression pathExpr,
         Node startNode) throws Exception {
      Node xpathNode = (Node) pathExpr.evaluate(
          startNode, XPathConstants.NODE);
      return xpathNode.getTextContent();
    }

      private String addReservationID(String payload, long reservationID) {
        StringBuffer payloadBuffer = new StringBuffer(payload);
        int outIndex = payloadBuffer.indexOf("<out");
        payloadBuffer.replace(outIndex, outIndex + 4,
            "<out reservationID=\"" +
                reservationID + "\"");
        return payloadBuffer.toString();
      }
    }
```

❻ Adds a correlation ID

This processor implementation performs the main part of the publish-subscribe and correlation-identifier functionality. The `Processor` interface prescribes the implementation of the process method, which gets the message exchange as an input parameter. The implementation of this processor starts with the retrieval of the restaurant-response message ❶. Because every message flowing through the JBI container is an XML message, you know that the payload content is an XML `String`. In ServiceMix, this means the payload is an instance of the `StringSource` class.

You saw in listing 9.9 that the Hibernate DAO, which you use to persist the restaurant-response message, is imported in the Camel configuration. Because you use a Spring context loader to start the Camel context, you can retrieve the Hibernate DAO instance via the registry instance in the Camel context ❷. The registry is implemented with a Spring registry class, so you can do a lookup for a bean with the identifier of `restaurantDAO`.

Before you can persist the reservation to the database, you first need to retrieve the restaurant and guest information from the restaurant-response message. Instead of an XML-to-Java deserializer like JiBX, you use XPath expressions to get the information from the response message. An example of retrieving such an element is the XPath expression for the restaurant name ❹.

Another example of an XPath expression is the retrieval of the reservation time. Because this is a `DateTime` value, you need to deserialize the element value to a Java Calendar object. The response message is received from the JSR-181 component, which we discuss later in this section, so the XML serialization is implemented with XFire and the Aegis binding. Because the `DateTime` serialization is implemented with a custom XFire and Aegis binding class, `XsDateTimeFormat`, you use this class to deserialize the `DateTime` value ❺.

With the Hibernate DAO and the restaurant and guest information retrieved, you can now store the reservation object in the HSQL database. The database identifier of the reservation table is used to correlate the restaurant-response message to the confirmation message sent by the hotel guest; you can add this identifier to the message ❸.

Because the JMS binding component doesn't provide functionality to copy a custom header from a JBI message to a JMS message, you need another solution to pass the correlation identifier back to the TV reservation application. You implement a quick-and-dirty way to add the reservation identifier to the response message as an attribute ❻.

One part of the publish-subscribe functionality remains to be implemented: the configuration of the JSR-181 service engine. But with the Camel component implemented, this should be a piece of cake. The JSR-181 endpoint is a wrapper to marshal and unmarshal the input and output XML messages for the restaurant Spring bean. Listing 9.11 shows one of the JSR-181 restaurant endpoints.

Listing 9.11   JSR-181 endpoint to wrap the restaurant Spring bean

```
<beans xmlns:jsr181="http://servicemix.apache.org/jsr181/1.0"              ❶ Defines
       xmlns:esb="http://esbinaction.com/restaurant">                        JSR-181
                                                                             service
  <jsr181:endpoint annotations="none"                                        name
      service="esb:lakeviewComponent"
      endpoint="endpoint"
      serviceInterface="..chapter9..RestaurantServiceIF"      ❷ Configures
      id="lakeview">                                            service
    <jsr181:pojo>                                               interface
      <bean id="lakeviewRestaurant"
          class="esb.chapter9..RestaurantServiceBean">
        <property name="restaurantName" value="Lakeview"/>
        <property name="acceptedResponse"
            value="The Lakeview has a table available with lake view"/>
        <property name="deniedResponse"
            value="The Lakeview is fully booked"/>              Implements
        <property name="maximumPersons" value="100"/>            wrapped
        <property name="numberPersonsReservation" value="50"/>   service  ❸
      </bean>
    </jsr181:pojo>
  </jsr181:endpoint>
</beans>
```

The configuration of a JSR-181 endpoint starts with the definition of unique service and endpoint names for the identification inside the JBI container, like any other JBI component ❶. The service name of the Lakeview JSR-181 component corresponds with the target endpoint for the Camel router shown in listing 9.9.

You configure the interface that must be used when calling this endpoint with the serviceInterface attribute ❷. RestaurantServiceIF specifies a processInquiry method, which expects a number of persons and a time parameter. This interface is transformed with the JSR-181 implementation into a WSDL counterpart, so that it can be used in the ServiceMix JBI container.

You can configure the service implementation in the pojo element with a normal Spring bean configuration ❸. With the property definitions, the RestaurantService-Bean is instantiated as a Lakeview restaurant endpoint. The implementation of the RestaurantServiceBean was discussed in listing 9.1.

You've covered a lot of functionality with the implementation of the first part of this solution, but you also need to implement the routing and filtering logic to handle the confirmation message from the hotel guest. The next section focuses on implementing a message filter and content-based routing functionality without introducing other JBI components to the integration solution.

IMPLEMENTING THE ROUTING FUNCTIONALITY WITH SERVICEMIX

In this section, we dive deeper into the Camel component as you implement filter, content-based routing, and error-handling logic. Let's start with a recap of what you need to implement according to the requirements from the design in section 9.3.

The hotel guest is presented with a number of restaurants that have a table available for this evening. When the guest chooses to confirm one the table reservations, a confirmation message is sent by the reservation application to the ServiceMix ESB. The ServiceMix message flow must first check the validity of the confirmation message with the persisted reservation and then route the confirmation to the correct restaurant endpoint if the message is still valid. If the confirmation message has timed out, the message is sent to an error queue. Figure 9.9 provides an overview of the message flow you need to implement and categorizes the functionality against the involved JBI components.

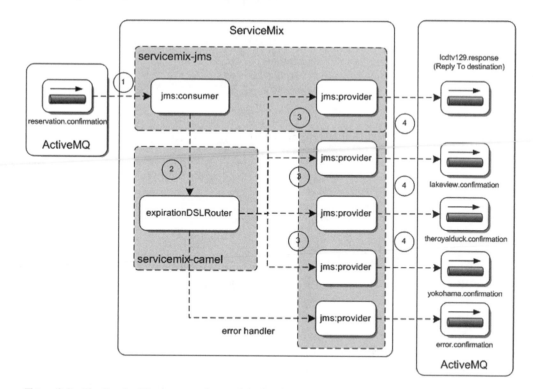

Figure 9.9 The ServiceMix message flow and the involved JBI components for the implementation of the confirmation message handler

The message flow shows that you use only two JBI components: Camel and JMS. The JMS component receives and sends JMS messages outside the JBI container, but the most interesting functionality is implemented in the Camel component. Listing 9.12 shows the Camel router implementation.

Listing 9.12 Expiration Camel filter and content-based router implementation

```
public class ExpirationCheckFilter extends RouteBuilder {

    private final static String SERVICE_IN =          ❶ Defines Camel
        RestaurantRouter.JBI_PREFIX +                    router service
            "/expirationDSLFilter";                      name
    private final static String REPLY_OUT =
        RestaurantRouter.JBI_PREFIX + "/lcdConfirmation";
    private final static String LAKEVIEW_OUT =
        RestaurantRouter.JBI_PREFIX + "/lakeviewConfirmation";
    private final static String YOKOHAMA_OUT =
        RestaurantRouter.JBI_PREFIX + "/yokohamaConfirmation";
    private final static String DUCK_OUT =
        RestaurantRouter.JBI_PREFIX + "/duckConfirmation";
    private final static String ERROR_OUT =
        RestaurantRouter.JBI_PREFIX + "/errorConfirmation";
    private final static String SEDA_CHOICE = "seda:restaurantChoice";

    public void configure() {
        from(SERVICE_IN)
          .errorHandler(deadLetterChannel(            ❷ Handles error
            ERROR_OUT).maximumRedeliveries(1))           messages
          .process(new ExpirationCheckProcessor())   ◁─┐ Checks message
          .multicast().to(REPLY_OUT, SEDA_CHOICE);    ❸   validity

        from(SEDA_CHOICE)
          .choice()
            .when(XPathBuilder.xpath(                 ❹ Defines
                "//restaurant='Lakeview'"))              restaurant
              .to(LAKEVIEW_OUT)                           routing rule
            .when(XPathBuilder.xpath("//restaurant='Yokohama'"))
              .to(YOKOHAMA_OUT)
            .otherwise()
              .to(DUCK_OUT);
    }
}
```

The implementation of the expiration Camel router starts with defining a number of JBI endpoints that are used in the routing implementation. One of the JBI endpoint definitions configures the service name for this Camel router ❶. The expiration-DSLFilter service name is configured as the target service for the JMS consumer endpoint, where the confirmation messages arrive.

The routing configuration starts with the definition of an error handler to handle exceptions that occur in the expiration processor ❷. The error handler specifies that the confirmation message must be redelivered only once and then sent to a JMS error endpoint.

The logic to check whether a confirmation message is still valid is implemented in the `ExpirationCheckProcessor` ❸. This processor implementation is invoked first when a messages is sent to this Camel router service. We explain this implementation after listing 9.13. When the reservation identifier in the confirmation message isn't valid, the expiration processor returns an error message, as you'll see in the implementation of the processor. A reservation timeout or a valid reservation results in a confirmation message being sent to the chosen restaurant and the TV application with the `multicast` method.

When the expiration processor has evaluated the validity of the message, the target restaurant endpoint is determined. This functionality is implemented with a number of content-based routing rules ❹. With the `XPathBuilder` class, you have an easy-to-use mechanism to use XPath expression in your routing rules. The routing rules defined in this example use the restaurant name in the message content to determine the correct target endpoint.

The logic to determine the validity of the confirmation message is implemented with a Camel processor class. The implementation of the `ExpirationCheckProcessor` is similar to the `ExpirationProcessor` shown in listing 9.10; the main difference is the validity check and the way error handling is implemented, as you can see in listing 9.13.

Listing 9.13 Camel processor, validating the confirmation message

```
public class ExpirationCheckProcessor implements Processor {
  public void process(Exchange exchange) throws Exception {
    String payload = getPayload(exchange);
    Reservation inputReservation = getReservation(          ❶ Retrieves reservation
      payload);                                                information
    ReservationDAOIF reservationDAO =
      exchange.getContext().getRegistry().lookup(
        "restaurantDAO", ReservationDAOIF.class);
    Reservation reservation =                               ❷ Gets
      reservationDAO.getReservation(                           reservation
        inputReservation.getReservationID());                 from database
    JbiExchange jbiExchange = (JbiExchange) exchange;
    JbiMessage message = new JbiMessage();
    message.setHeaders(jbiExchange.getIn().getHeaders());
    if(reservation == null ||
       reservation.getReservationID() == null) {
      exchange.setException(new ExpirationException(
        "reservation could not be found for ID " +
          inputReservation.getReservationID()));            ❸ Determines
    } else {                                                   reservation
      boolean timeout = isTimeout(reservation);                validity
      if (timeout) {
        message.setBody("<confirmation><invalid>" +            ◁─ Sets invalid
          "true</invalid><restaurant>" +                          confirmation
          reservation.getRestaurant().getName() +          ❹     message
          "</restaurant></confirmation>");
      } else {
```

```
          message.setBody(makeConfirmationMessage(         ❺  Forwards payload
            reservation));                                     as String
      }
    }
    jbiExchange.setIn(message);
}

private Reservation getReservation(String payload)
    throws Exception {
  XPath xpath = XPathFactory.newInstance().newXPath();
  InputSource payloadSource = new InputSource(
      new StringReader(payload));
  XPathExpression pathExpr = xpath.compile("//restaurant");
  Node restaurantNode = (Node) pathExpr.evaluate(
      payloadSource, XPathConstants.NODE);
  String reservationID =                                  ❻  Gets
      restaurantNode.getAttributes().getNamedItem(            reservation ID
        "reservationID").getNodeValue();                      attribute value
  Reservation reservation = new Reservation();
  reservation.setReservationID(Long.valueOf(reservationID));
  reservation.setRestaurantName(restaurantNode.getTextContent());
  return reservation;
}

private String makeConfirmationMessage(Reservation reservation) {
  return "<confirmation>" +
    "<restaurant>" +
      reservation.getRestaurant().getName() +
    "</restaurant>" +
    "<guestname>" + reservation.getGuestName() + "</guestname>" +
    "<roomnumber>" + reservation.getRoomNumber() + "</roomnumber>" +
    "</confirmation>";
}
// other helper methods
}
```

This processor implementation consists of quite a bit of logic, which is why we left some helper methods in listing 9.12. To determine the validity of the confirmation message, you first must get the reservation-identifier attribute value from the incoming message ❶ ❻. With an XPath expression, you can select the restaurant element and then the reservationID attribute.

We already discussed the way you can retrieve a Spring bean, in this case the restaurantDao, from the Camel context registry in listing 9.10; the same functionality is used here. With the Hibernate DAO instance available, you can get the reservation from the HSQL database with the reservation identifier ❷.

With the reservation available, you can calculate the time that has passed between the restaurant response that is stored in the database and the current time. This value is compared to the timeout value specified for the chosen restaurant to determine the validity of the confirmation message ❸.

When the message has timed out, you need to construct a confirmation message with an error indication so the application and the target restaurant are informed.

The response message includes an invalid indication of `true`. The confirmation message with the invalid element is set as the body on the message exchange ❹.

Because the incoming message payload is an instance of the `StreamSource` class, you must set a new message payload ❺. This is necessary because a stream can be processed only once; additional processing results in an exception. A new JBI message is created, and a String that represents the XML message is set as the payload.

As you may recall from figure 9.9, the JMS consumer uses an in-only message exchange pattern. To complete the example implementation overview, listing 9.14 shows the configuration of the JMS consumers and providers.

Listing 9.14   JMS consumers and providers for the expiration flow

```
<beans xmlns:jms="http://servicemix.apache.org/jms/1.0"
       xmlns:esb="http://esbinaction.com/restaurant">

  <jms:consumer service="esb:confirmationConsumer"
    endpoint="endpoint"
    targetService="esb:expirationDSLFilter"
    destinationName="reservation.confirmation"
    connectionFactory="#connectionFactory"          ❶ Creates ReplyTo
    marshaler="#replyInOnlyMarshaler"/>                 consumer

  <jms:provider service="esb:lcdConfirmation"         ❷ Uses ReplyTo
    endpoint="jmsEndpoint"                               destination
    connectionFactory="#connectionFactory"/>

  <jms:provider service="esb:lakeviewConfirmation"
    endpoint="jmsEndpoint"
    destinationName="lakeview.confirmation"
    destinationChooser="#verySimpleChooser"          ❸ Overrides
    connectionFactory="#connectionFactory"/>             ReplyTo header

  <bean id="replyInOnlyMarshaler"
    class="esb.chapter9...servicemix.ReplyToConsumerMarshaler"/>

  <bean id="verySimpleChooser"
    class="esb.chapter9...servicemix.VerySimpleDestinationChooser"/>

  <bean id="connectionFactory"
      class="org.apache.activemq.ActiveMQConnectionFactory">
    <property name="brokerURL" value="tcp://localhost:61616" />
  </bean>
</beans>
```

The JMS consumer that is defined uses the default In-Only message exchange pattern, but it needs to copy the JMS `ReplyTo` header to be able to send a response message to the LCD application. You define a custom marshaler that copies the JMS `ReplyTo` header value to the ServiceMix normalized message ❶. We discussed the implementation of this marshaler in listing 9.8.

Because you use an In-Only message exchange pattern, you need to define a JMS provider endpoint to send the response message to the LCD application. But as shown in the listing, no destination is specified for the JMS provider ❷. Because the default

SimpleDestinationChooser looks for a destination in the header of the normalized message, the message is sent to the ReplyTo destination specified by the input message sent by the LCD application.

For the restaurant JMS providers, you want to implement the opposite destination-resolving functionality. Although a destination is available in the header of the normalized message, you want the message to be sent to the destination specified with the destinationName attribute. So you implement your own destination chooser ❸. The implementation of VerySimpleDestinationChooser is short, as you can see in the following code snippet:

```
public class VerySimpleDestinationChooser
    extends SimpleDestinationChooser {

  public Object chooseDestination(MessageExchange exchange,
      Object message) {
    return getDefaultDestinationName();
  }
}
```

You've now implemented all the parts of the Mule and ServiceMix table-reservation solution, and you're ready to implement your own complex message flow in Service-Mix. You still need to do some testing and eventually a deployment before you're finished. The great thing about testing is that you can see your integration solution working in Mule and ServiceMix.

9.5   *Testing and deploying the integration solution*

You've implemented the case study in both Mule and ServiceMix, but you didn't yet test any part of the integration solution. In this section, we show how easily you can test an integration solution developed with Mule and ServiceMix with a JUnit test case on your development machine. After the testing phase, we discuss the deployment of the integration solution to the production environment.

9.5.1   *Using JUnit to test the Mule and ServiceMix flows*

JUnit is a well-known test framework for Java developers and is the industry standard to implement unit tests for Java applications. For message flows developed with Mule and ServiceMix, you need a way to unit-test the integration solution with different input messages. But to be able to unit-test a Mule or ServiceMix message flow, you need an environment where you have a Mule or ServiceMix installation, a message broker, and (if needed) a database, an FTP server, and a JEE application server. Figure 9.10 shows a developer machine environment that needs to be able to unit-test a Mule or ServiceMix integration solution.

The environment shown in figure 9.10 includes a number of open source integration products. The Other Tools category includes optional products that may be needed for a message flow that uses functionality like sending email messages (James mail server) and invoking EJBs (OpenEJB). The tools shown here can be replaced with

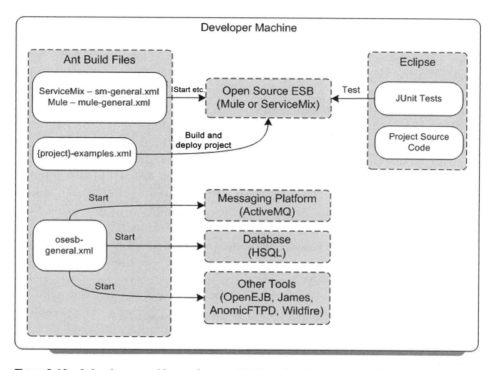

Figure 9.10 **A developer machine environment that needs to test message flows developed with Mule and ServiceMix. The Ant build files are provided as part of the source code distribution of this book.**

other products that provide similar functionality—instead of OpenEJB, you could use a JBoss or Geronimo application server to host the EJBs.

The minimal set of products required consists of an open source ESB and a messaging platform distribution. Note that a ServiceMix distribution contains the ActiveMQ messaging platform out of the box. To be able to test the table-reservation case study, you need a Mule and a ServiceMix distribution and also an ActiveMQ installation to provide the messaging functionality. You also need a database to persist the restaurant responses, so an HSQL installation is necessary.

To make it easier to work with the open source products in the developer machine environment, we provide a number of Ant build files with this book's source distribution. You can use the osesb-general.xml Ant build file to start a number of integration products. For example, with the `ext:start-hsqldb` target, you can start the HSQL database instance.

Another Ant build file can be used to interact with the open source ESB distribution: sm-general.xml for ServiceMix and mule-general.xml for Mule. The ServiceMix JBI container provides a number of management functions that you can use with the sm-general.xml Ant build file. ServiceMix can be started and stopped, but you can, for example, also view the installed service engines and deploy a service assembly. You can use the mule-general.xml Ant build file to start and stop Mule and also to deploy a message flow project to the Mule distribution.

The third Ant build file is a project-dependent file that contains the logic needed to build and deploy the integration solution. The build logic uses the targets in the sm-general.xml and mule-general.xml build files to build and deploy the project.

STARTING THE DEVELOPMENT ENVIRONMENT

Now let's use these Ant build files to get the development environment up and running for the table-reservation solution. First, start the HSQL database with the osesb-general.xml build file by executing the `ext-start-hsqldb` Ant target. When the HSQL database is running, you can run the database script defined for the solution by executing the `jdbc-setup-database` target in the chapter9-examples.xml build file available in the Mule and the ServiceMix source distribution in the resources/chapter9 directory.

Once the database is running with the necessary tables, you can start the ActiveMQ broker by running the `ext-start-activeMQ` target in the osesb-general.xml build script for the Mule example. Remember that for ServiceMix, ActiveMQ is started automatically with the ServiceMix container. Because ActiveMQ is configured to create queues on the fly when needed, you don't need to configure the queues and topic necessary for the solution beforehand.

Starting HSQL is no different from the Mule and ServiceMix implementations. But when you want to deploy the message flows to Mule and ServiceMix, you follow a different procedure. Because Mule needs to be started with the Mule configuration file and ServiceMix is hot-deployable and service assemblies can be installed when running, different steps are required when you deploy the message flow and start the ESB container.

For Mule, you first need to create the message flow jar and copy this file to the Mule distribution directory. The chapter9-examples.xml Ant build file in the resources/chapter9 directory of the Mule source distribution of this book can be executed with the default target jar to perform this first step. When the message flow jar is copied or deployed to the lib/user directory of the Mule distribution, you can start the Mule container. You do this by running the `restaurant-example` target in the chapter9-examples.xml file, because this target starts Mule with the Mule configuration file restaurant-config.xml. When you've executed all the previous steps, the Mule environment is ready for testing.

To start the ServiceMix environment, you first need to start the ServiceMix container by running the start target in the chapter9-examples.xml file in the resources/chapter9 directory of the book's ServiceMix code distribution. When the ServiceMix container has been started, you can create and deploy the service assembly for the case study implementation. To do so, execute the `deploy-restaurant` target in the chapter9-examples.xml file. Now the service assembly is deployed to the ServiceMix container, and the ServiceMix environment is ready for testing.

TESTING THE MULE AND SERVICEMIX CASE STUDY IMPLEMENTATIONS

To be able to communicate with the table-reservation message flows in Mule and ServiceMix, you should implement logic in the test case to send and receive JMS messages. Figure 9.11 shows the message exchange you should implement in the test case. The test case you need to implement simulates the TV reservation application. The test case sends, for example, a restaurant-inquiry message to the `inquiries.in` topic; you expect three restaurant-response messages back on the `lcdtv129.response` queue, which is the destination specified in the `ReplyTo` header of the inquiry message.

The `RestaurantTest` JUnit test case is pretty much the same for the Mule and ServiceMix implementations. The main difference is the format of the messages sent from and received by the test case. The ServiceMix messages are all sent in XML format, because this is the message format expected by the JBI container. The Mule messages are sent as Java objects, because this is an easy-to-use format for a Mule message flow. When you execute the `RestaurantTest` JUnit test case, no test errors should occur. When the test case has been executed without errors, this means that the message flow is acting as expected in different cases. The message flow is now ready for the next phase.

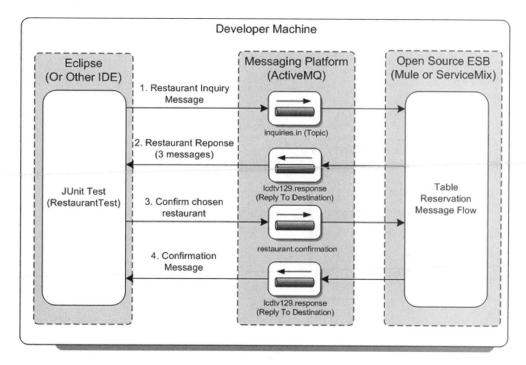

Figure 9.11 The messages that need to be sent from and received by the JUnit test case. With the JUnit test case, the reservation application is simulated.

9.5.2   *Deploying an integration solution to a production environment*

You've fully tested the case study on your development environment, and a common next step is to test the message flow in an integration stage environment. This means the message flow is tested with all the involved applications in a real-life environment. This kind of testing is more functionally focused and is often performed by test professionals and end-user groups. Because we focus on the technical aspects of an integration solution in this book, we skip this phase and go forward with deploying the integration solution to the production environment.

In most business environments, this isn't a task for the developer: it's a task for the administrative department responsible for the maintenance of the integration environment. But the administrators who execute the deployment of the integration solution will need a number of artifacts from the development team. Figure 9.12 shows what the administrators need in order to deploy the case study.

The production environment shown in figure 9.12 consists of three separate servers: the open source ESB, the messaging broker, and the database server. The actual server infrastructure depends on many aspects including the number of expected transactions and the organization's full production environment.

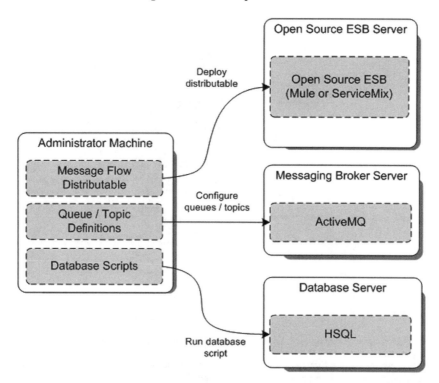

Figure 9.12 An example of a production environment consisting of the open source integration products necessary for the case study. The important artifacts needed by the administrator are shown as part of the administrator machine.

The figure also shows the important artifacts that an administrator needs in order to be able to deploy the solution. This isn't an exhaustive list of artifacts, but it gives some insight into the needs of an open source integration environment. The development team should at least provide a message flow distributable, such as a service assembly for ServiceMix or a message flow jar for Mule.

In addition to this artifact, the administrator requires an overview of the queues and topics used by the integration solution. If queues or topics don't exist yet on the messaging infrastructure, the administrator needs to add them to the broker with the configuration parameters specified by the development team. Think of parameters like the queue name and description, and persistent or nonpersistent settings. In this case, the administrator also needs to run some database scripts to create the necessary tables in the HSQL database.

This is just a quick overview of the deployment artifacts and the administrator tasks to deploy the integration solution to a production environment. The focus of this book is on developing integration solutions with Mule and ServiceMix and not on administering the production environment.

We've reached the end of the case study implementation. We've discussed the different phases of a typical integration project from design to deployment, and we've introduced a pattern-based design approach. To learn more about monitoring and managing an open source ESB environment, turn the page to the next chapter.

9.6   *Summary*

This chapter provides you with enough guidance to enable you to be part of a full-blown integration project with open source ESBs like Mule and ServiceMix. We've introduced the Enterprise Integration patterns in a compact way; you can also refer to http://www.enterpriseintegrationpatterns.com. Based on these patterns, we introduced a pattern-based design approach to be used in the design phase of an integration project. This isn't a heavyweight approach; it focuses on visualizing and describing the functionality of the integration solution in an easy way.

The case study introduced a lot of exciting integration functionality that you implemented with Mule and ServiceMix. You saw that it's easy to implement the Publish-Subscribe pattern in both Mule and ServiceMix, and you implemented content-based routing rules in just a few lines of code. We also showed you how easily you can add persistency to a message flow by using the Spring and Hibernate frameworks.

With the knowledge you've gained while reading this chapter, you can now guide your team members through the phases of an integration project. What we haven't yet discussed are the monitoring and management of integration solutions for Mule and ServiceMix. In the next chapter, you'll learn how you can monitor the flow of messages and you'll be introduced to some great management tools that make it easier to manage the integration environment.

10

Managing and monitoring the ESB

In the chapters so far, we've focused on ESB functionality such as routing, connectivity, support for Enterprise Integration patterns, and more. You've seen how easy it is to solve complex integration problems using the default building blocks these ESBs provide. We've mainly focused on the development part of integration; we haven't paid much attention to how you manage and monitor ESBs once your integration scenario is running.

Managing and monitoring integration products and running flows on them is a complex task. You have to work with a running system where messages are being sent between components and services and where it's difficult to debug and replay certain scenarios. This is especially difficult on a production system. In this chapter, we look at the options Mule and ServiceMix provide for managing and monitoring the ESB and how they let you monitor and control specific flows. We examine the following management and monitoring subjects:

- *System management Enterprise Integration patterns*—Before we dive into the management and monitoring features supplied by Mule and ServiceMix, we examine a couple of Enterprise Integration patterns that can help you monitor integration flows. We discuss the Wire Tap pattern, the Message Store pattern, and the Detour pattern.
- *Monitoring using JMX*—Java Management eXtensions (JMX) is a standard Java means of managing and monitoring applications. With JMX, you can track certain attributes of an application at runtime and invoke operations on exposed objects. Both Mule and ServiceMix provide a management API through JMX, which you'll use in this chapter.

In chapter 9, we showed how to implement an imaginary restaurant reservation service with Mule and with ServiceMix. We focused on how to create a design based on Enterprise Integration patterns and how to translate that design into an implementation using Mule and ServiceMix.

In this chapter, you'll take that example and add system-management and -monitoring functionality to it. You'll start by applying the Wire Tap, Message Store, and Detour patterns. Using these patterns, you can easily debug and monitor messages transmitted between the various components. We also discuss how you can manage ESBs using standard JMX-based tooling.

10.1 System-management Enterprise Integration patterns

The book *Enterprise Integration Patterns* describes many different system-management patterns. In this section, we examine three of them that can be useful when you're working with an ESB. You'll start by adding a wire tap to a specific channel of the message flow from chapter 9, which will let you see the content of the message that is sent over that channel.

10.1.1 The Wire Tap pattern

You place a wire tap on certain endpoints to let you see the messages received by those endpoints. A copy of each message is made and sent to a different endpoint so you can look at the message's content without having to pause the processing of the original message or do anything else that might disrupt the running system. When you add a wire tap to a production system, it lets you check the messages that are being sent and that might cause problems, without interfering with the messages' normal flow. Before we discuss the details of the wire-tap implementation, let's examine the restaurant example from chapter 9 and add a wire tap to it, as shown in figure 10.1.

We added a single wire tap that picks up all messages sent to the Lakeview endpoint, makes a copy, and sends it to the configured endpoint. The rest of the scenario stays exactly the same and the involved parties won't notice this change. Now, let's get

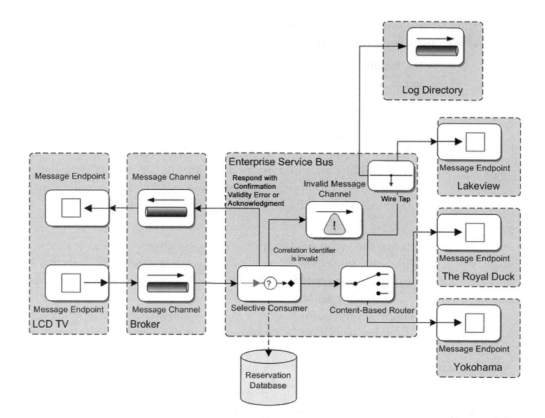

Figure 10.1   A design diagram showing the Wire Tap pattern being applied to the reservation example from chapter 9. All messages to the Lakeview restaurant service are also sent to the channel specified by the wire tap.

started with the Mule implementation of this scenario. After that, you do the same for ServiceMix.

MULE WIRE-TAP IMPLEMENTATION

Using the Wire Tap pattern in Mule is simple, because Mule provides a list of standard routers out of the box and one of them is a wire-tap router. All you have to do is add a configuration such as the one shown in listing 10.1 to the inbound section of a Mule service; a copy of all incoming messages will be made and routed to the specified endpoint.

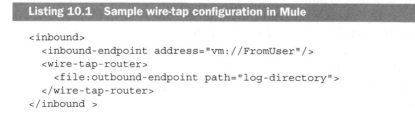

Listing 10.1   Sample wire-tap configuration in Mule

```
<inbound>
  <inbound-endpoint address="vm://FromUser"/>
  <wire-tap-router>
    <file:outbound-endpoint path="log-directory">
  </wire-tap-router>
</inbound >
```

Let's add this configuration to one of the services you saw in chapter 9. We don't show the complete configuration; we focus on how to apply this pattern to one of the services defined in the reservation example.

In chapter 9, you implemented an example that sent messages to different restaurants and waited for a reply. If a reply took too much time, a notification was sent to the client and the message could be ignored. Now, imagine that you want to monitor the incoming requests to one of those restaurants, because this restaurant claims it's not receiving any requests. Listing 10.2 shows how to apply the Wire Tap pattern to one of those services.

Listing 10.2   Mule restaurant service extended with the Wire Tap pattern

```
<service name="LakeviewRestaurantService">
  <inbound>                                        ❶ JMS topic
    <inbound-endpoint ref="inquiry-topic"    ⟵┘     subscriber
        remoteSync="true" />
    <wire-tap-router>                                       ⟵┐  Wire tap
      <file:outbound-endpoint                                │  copies the
          path="wireTap"  transformer-refs="jmsToObject" />  ❷  message
    </wire-tap-router>
  </inbound>
  <component>
    <spring-object bean="lakeviewRestaurant" />
  </component>
  <outbound>
    <outbound-pass-through-router>
      <outbound-endpoint ref="inquiry-out" />
    </outbound-pass-through-router>
  </outbound>
</service>
```

You alter the inbound part of the LakeviewRestaurantService and add a wire-tap-router to it ❷. This router sends a copy of each incoming message from the topic subscriber ❶ to the specified endpoint, which in this case is a directory on the file system. You also add a transformer to this endpoint, because the message you get here is still a JMSObject. We mentioned earlier that Mule doesn't use a specific normalized message format. You see this when you use this pattern. If a Java object is sent to the endpoint specified by the wire-tap-router, it's sent to the configured endpoint. If no transformers are specified on this endpoint, the Java object is serialized to the file system. If you want to view this data later, you have to deserialize this object before you can access its content. If you want to quickly test this, you can use the JavaToX-StreamTransformer, which is included in the sources. With this transformer, you can quickly serialize a Java object to an XML string without having to configure anything or create a mapping, as you would with JiBX.

If you run the example with the ch10-build.xml Ant build file and test the example with the Swing test client, you see that when a message is sent to LakeviewRestaurant-Service, a copy of the message is also be sent to the endpoint-configured wire-tap router. Let's now discuss how you can implement the Wire Tap pattern in ServiceMix.

SERVICEMIX WIRE TAP IMPLEMENTATION

For ServiceMix, you also have an out-of-the-box component that implements the Wire Tap pattern. This is provided by the servicemix-eip Service Engine. Listing 10.3 shows an example configuration of the Wire Tap pattern from the EIP service engine.

Listing 10.3 ServiceMix configuration for the Wire Tap pattern

```
<wire-tap service="test:exampleTap" endpoint="tapEndpoint">
  <target>
    <exchange-target service="test:target-service" />      ← ❶ Defines intended target
  </target>
  <inListener>
    <exchange-target service="test:trace-service" />       ← ❷ Defines wire-tap target
  </inListener>
</wire-tap>
```

The wire-tap component makes a copy of every incoming message and forwards the copy to a different Java Business Integration (JBI) service endpoint ❷, where you can, for instance, store it in the file system. The original message is sent to the intended target JBI service ❶, where it's processed as if nothing happened in the message-flow execution.

Now that you've seen how you can configure a wire tap, let's examine how to configure a wire tap for the reservation example from chapter 9. You first need to create a new service unit that implements the Wire Tap pattern configuration, as shown in listing 10.4.

Listing 10.4 ServiceMix wire-tap implementation in the EIP service unit

```
<beans>
  <wire-tap service="esb:lakeviewWireTapDSLRouter"
      endpoint="endpoint">                                  ← ❶ Service endpoint for wire tap
    <target>
      <exchange-target service="esb:lakeviewDSLRouter" />  ← ❷ Invokes intended target service
    </target>
    <inListener>
      <exchange-target service="esb:trace-service" />      ← ❸ Copies to trace service
    </inListener>
  </wire-tap>
</beans>
```

When this wire-tap service is called on its service endpoint ❶, it routes the message to the intended target lakeviewDSLRouter ❷ and sends a copy to the service specified in the exchange-target element ❸. We don't show the details of the esb:trace-service because it's a simple file sender that you've implemented a number of times before.

But you're not there yet. The wire tap you've created has a specific service endpoint ❶. You must make sure the service that called the esb:lakeviewDSLRouter service now calls the service with the wire tap you just created. The new JMS service configuration that calls the esb:lakeviewDSLRouter service is shown in listing 10.5.

Listing 10.5   Modified JMS consumer that calls the wire-tap service

```
<jms:consumer service="esb:lakeviewTopicConsumer"
    endpoint="endpoint"
    targetService="esb:lakeviewWireTapDSLRouter"      Calls wire tap
    pubSubDomain="true"                            ❶ service
    destinationName="inquiries.in"
    connectionFactory="#connectionFactory"
    marshaler="#replyInOutMarshaler"/>
```

When you run this example, the flow runs as if nothing has changed. The only difference is that now you get a copy of every message that passes through your wire tap, which you can use for debugging purposes. The advantage here is that the message is already in XML format so you don't have to apply an additional transformation to make it readable as we had to do with Mule.

The Message Store pattern does something similar to the Wire Tap pattern.

10.1.2 *The Message Store pattern*

The primary advantage of message stores is that you can store messages over a long period of time without interfering with their normal flow. Each message, or a selection of its properties, is copied to the message store, which can be analyzed at a more convenient time. The biggest difference between a message store and a wire tap is that with a message store, you can make sure the data stored is easily accessible. This can, for instance, be used to determine which messages cause performance issues, or which types of messages are sent the most often and are a target for optimization.

With a message store, you don't necessarily have to store the complete message; usually you store the message's most important properties—the properties for which you want to generate reports, or which are required for analysis.

For this pattern, we show you two implementations. The implementation with Mule will store the message's generated ID and timestamp properties in a JDBC database. You also store the reservation time and number of persons fields from the message. For the ServiceMix example, you use the normalized message (which is XML) and store the message's complete data in an XML database. Let's begin by looking at how you can configure the Mule scenario to store each message in a database.

MULE MESSAGE-STORE IMPLEMENTATION

For the Mule message-store implementation, you once again use the wire-tap concept to make a copy of the message and log that message. Instead of sending the copied message to a file endpoint, you send it to a JDBC endpoint, which will store the message in a database for later analysis. This Mule configuration is shown in listing 10.6.

Listing 10.6   Mule configuration, implementing the Message Store pattern

```
<mule>
  <jdbc:connector name="hsqldb-connector">
   <jdbc:dataSource                                  JDBC
     class="org.enhydra.jdbc.standard.StandardDataSource">  ❶ connector
                                                        configuration
```

```
  <properties>
    <entry key="driverName" value="org.hsqldb.jdbcDriver" />
    <entry key="url" value="jdbc:hsqldb:hsql://localhost/xdb" />
    <entry key="user" value="sa" />
  </properties>
  </jdbc:dataSource>
  <jdbc:queries>
   <jdbc:query key="write" value="INSERT
              into MSGSTORE (id, timestamp, persons, reservationtime)
              VALUES(NULL, NULL,
                     ${jxpath:persons}, ${jxpath:reservationTime})" />
  </jdbc:queries>
  </jdbc:connector>
                                                          Message store
                                                          insert query  2

  <model name="RestaurantModel">
    <service name="LakeviewRestaurantService">
      <inbound>
        <inbound-endpoint ref="inquiry-topic"
            remoteSync="true" />
        <wire-tap-router>                           3  Creates message
          <jdbc:outbound-endpoint queryKey="write">    store
        </wire-tap-router>
      </inbound>
      <component>
        <spring-object bean="lakeviewRestaurant" />
      </component>
      <outbound>
        <outbound-pass-through-router>
          <outbound-endpoint ref="inquiry-out" />
        </outbound-pass-through-router>
      </outbound>
    </service>
  </model>
</mule>
```

In this code, you configure a simple message-store implementation. You add a wire tap to the inbound configuration of a Mule service **3** and configure this wire tap to store information from the message in the HSQL database **1**.

With the JDBC connector definition, you can connect to an HSQL database **1** and use the insert query named write. The SQL for this query **2** is an insert into the MSGSTORE table. In the query, you also add a number of properties. Mule will replace these with properties from the received message using JXPath.

For this example, as in all the other examples in this chapter, an Ant build file is provided in the resources/chapter10 directory of the Mule workspace. You'll find targets in that build file to create the database and run the examples.

If you run the scenario a couple of times with various messages, you see the database being filled. Other applications can use the database to analyze the messages without interfering with the message flow.

Now that we've shown you how to create a message store in Mule using a relational database, let's implement the same pattern in ServiceMix.

SERVICEMIX MESSAGE-STORE IMPLEMENTATION

You could use the same setup you used for the wire-tap example to create a message store for ServiceMix. But for this example, you use a feature ServiceMix provides to add auditing functionality to the complete ServiceMix environment. You do this by adding a message listener to the Normalized Message Router (NMR). In chapter 2, we explained that internal message routing in ServiceMix is done via the NMR. If you send a message from a service consumer to a service provider, this message is first sent to the NMR, which passes it on to the service provider. Because all the messages are routed by the NMR, the NMR is a good place to add a message store without having to alter any of the service Units.

You use an open source eXist XML database to store the messages. Just as for all the other servers used in this book, you can start this database from the Ant build file for this chapter, which is in the resources/chapter10 directory of the ServiceMix workspace. The message store example you implement in this section is shown in figure 10.2.

To add a listener to the NMR, you must configure ServiceMix with an auditor. ServiceMix provides two auditors out of the box, which you could use for your message store: `JDBCAuditor` writes messages to a JDBC database, and `FileAuditor` stores messages in the file system. If you look back at the wire-tap example, you could also have used `FileAuditor` to implement the Wire Tap pattern. In this example, you won't use these auditors; instead, you provide a custom auditor to persist data to an XML database. This approach shows you how easy it is to create custom auditors and integrate various technologies.

To implement a custom auditor, you can extend from the `AbstractAuditor`, which is a base class that ServiceMix provides. Listing 10.7 shows how to create an auditor that can write to an eXist database.

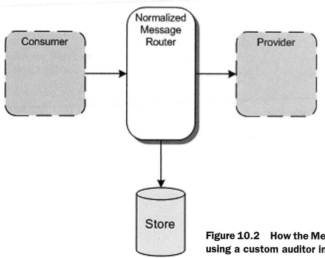

Figure 10.2   How the Message Store pattern is implemented using a custom auditor in ServiceMix

Listing 10.7   Auditor implementation that stores messages in a database

```
public class ExistAuditor extends AbstractAuditor {
  private static Log LOG = LogFactory.getLog(ExistAuditor.class);
  private String databaseName;
  private String url;
  private Collection collection;

  /**
   * This method will be called whenever the NMR receiver a message.
   */
  public void exchangeSent(ExchangeEvent event) {          NMR receives
    XMLResource document;                                ❶ message
    try {
      document = (XMLResource) collection.createResource(
          null, "XMLResource");
      Source source = event.getExchange()
          .getMessage("in").getContent();
      Transformer tr = TransformerFactory
          .newInstance().newTransformer();
      DOMResult result = new DOMResult();
      tr.transform(source, result);
      document.setContentAsDOM(result.getNode());
      collection.storeResource(document);
      event.getExchange().getMessage("in").setContent(
          new DOMSource(result.getNode()));
    } catch (Exception e) {
      LOG.warn("Error persisting message in database", e);
    }
  }

  public String getDescription() {
    return "Simple persister to eXist";
  }

  // lifecycle methods

  /**
   * Setup the connection to the collection
   */
  @Override                                          ❷ Called when
  protected void doStart() throws JBIException {          auditor starts
    super.doStart();
    try {                          ❸ Gets connection
      collection = getCollection();       to eXist
    } catch (Exception e) {
      throw new JBIException("Error setting up auditor: "
        + e.getMessage(), e);
    }
  }

  /**
   * Close the collection
   */
  @Override                                          ❹ Called when
  protected void doStop() throws JBIException {          auditor stops
```

```
      super.doStop();
      try {
        collection.close();
      } catch (XMLDBException e) {
        throw new JBIException(
          "Error closing auditing connection: "
            + e.getMessage(), e);
      }
    }
    private Collection getCollection() throws Exception {          ⑤  Connects to
      String driver = "org.exist.xmldb.DatabaseImpl";                  eXist database
      Class cl = Class.forName(driver);
      Database database = (Database) cl.newInstance();
      DatabaseManager.registerDatabase(database);
      return DatabaseManager.getCollection(url + databaseName);
    }
  }
```

You extend from the abstract class AbstractAuditor, provided by ServiceMix. To create a custom auditor, you have to implement a number of methods. This example only shows the implementation of the exchangeSent method ❶. This method is called whenever a message is received by the NMR.

Before we look at how the message is stored, let's first examine the lifecycle methods doStart ❷ and doStop ❹. The doStart method is called when the component is loaded, and doStop is called when ServiceMix shuts down. In these methods, you set up a connection to the XML database ❸ ❺. Without going into too much detail, you get a connection to a specific collection. You can see a collection as a schema within a relational database.

In the exchangeSent method ❶, you receive an ExchangeEvent and transform it in a DOM object that you can easily store in the eXist database. To store an object in eXist, you must first create an XMLResource. You set the DOM object as the content of this XMLResource and use the collection, which you created in the doStartup method, to store this XMLResource in the database.

The last thing you need to do to get ServiceMix to use your custom auditor is register it. You do this by editing the servicemix.xml file in the ServiceMix conf directory and adding the following Spring bean configuration:

```
<bean name="existAuditor" class="esb.chapter10.auditor.ExistAuditor"
    init-method="start"
    destroy-method="stop">
  <property name="container" ref="jbi"/>
  <property name="url"
      value="xmldb:exist://localhost:8080/exist/xmlrpc/"/>
  <property name="database" value="db"/>
</bean>
```

This configuration makes sure your auditor is started when ServiceMix starts and is stopped when ServiceMix shuts down. The configuration options for this auditor are the default settings that are used to connect to a running eXist database.

Start up the eXist database from the supplied Ant file and run the Wire Tap example a couple of times to get some messages stored in the database. You can use either the eXist XQuery tool or the webdav view to browse and query the messages. The easiest way to check whether the messages are stored is to open the webdav view, located at http://localhost:8080/exist/webdav/db.

To log in to this application, use admin/admin as the username and password. Figure 10.3 shows the browser view.

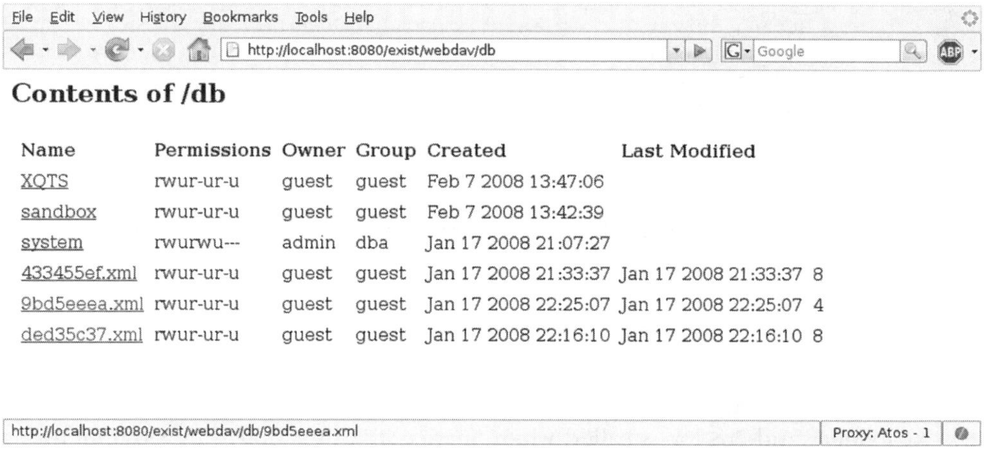

Figure 10.3   A screenshot of the webdav view of the eXist database where the messages are stored

You've now seen how to implement the Message Store pattern in Mule and in Service-Mix. For Mule, you extended the Wire Tap pattern to store important message properties into a database; with ServiceMix, you created an auditor that stored the content of each message in an XML database for later analysis. But there is a small difference between the two approaches: with Mule, each message is stored only once; and with ServiceMix, you store each message that is sent to the NMR. Depending on the scenario, with ServiceMix you may store some messages multiple times. If you don't want this, you can easily change your auditor to keep a table of correlationIDs for each stored message. If a new message arrives, you can take the correlationID, check whether you already stored it once, and, if you did, not store it again.

The last pattern we look at is the Detour pattern. With the Detour pattern, you reroute the message to alter some properties or log information. After you've changed the message, you re-insert the message in the flow at the same place to continue processing.

10.1.3   *The Detour pattern*

Finding problems in integration flows is often difficult. Messages flow from one component to another, making the flow hard to debug. You can choose to start Mule and ServiceMix in debug mode and use a Java debugger to check the messages that are sent between components, but you usually can't do this on production systems. With the Detour pattern, you reroute the message to a different endpoint, where you can examine and (optionally) alter the message. After you've made your changes, you put the message in a different channel, where it's picked up again and processed normally.

You again implement this pattern in Mule and ServiceMix. The functionality you implement is shown in figure 10.4.

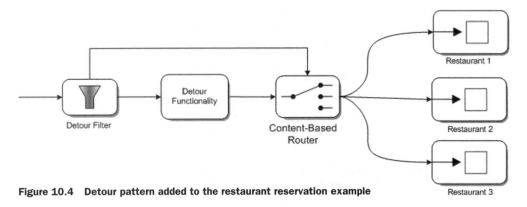

Figure 10.4   Detour pattern added to the restaurant reservation example

You add a Detour pattern which can be used to intercept all the confirmation messages. The Detour filter from figure 10.4 will determine when to send a message to the detour part of the message flow or send it directly to the Content-based router service. This may look a bit like the wire-tap example, but instead of making a copy of the original message, you intercept the complete processing of the message so you can alter the message before sending it further.

In this example, the intercepted message is sent to a Java bean where you can alter the message or let an administrator alter the message. This way, it will be easy to test different types of messages and determine how the system will react to specific content without having to change the configured components and services or change any of the message properties that are used for routing.

DETOUR PATTERN IN MULE

To implement the Detour pattern in Mule, you create a content-based router that determines, based on a filter's settings, whether to send a message to the detour flow or directly to the target component. You first add a new Mule service that will handle the detoured message. Listing 10.8 shows the Mule configuration of a basic detour service that allows you to process the detoured message in a Java class.

Listing 10.8   Mule configuration that implements the Detour pattern

```
<service name="detour-service">
  <inbound>
    <inbound-endpoint ref="confirmation-out-detour" />     ❶  Receives detoured
                                                                messages
```

```
      </inbound>
        <component class="esb.chapter10.DetourMessageProcessor" />
      <outbound>
        <outbound-pass-through-router>
          <vm:outbound-endpoint
            path="handle.confirmation" remoteSync="true"/>
        </outbound-pass-through-router>
      </outbound>
    </service>
```

Java bean handles detoured messages ❷

Forwards message to original endpoint ❸

The service from listing 10.8 receives detoured messages on the configured endpoint ❶ and processes the messages in a simple java class ❷. This class has only a single method in which you can alter the message or its properties. In this example, you don't do anything with the message; you just write it to System out. After you've processed the message, it's passed to the endpoint defined in ❸, where it's processed normally by the rest of the integration flow.

Now that you've seen how the message is processed, let's look at how you can determine whether to send the message either to the detour service or to the original service. This configuration is shown in listing 10.9.

Listing 10.9 Mule configuration for the Detour pattern

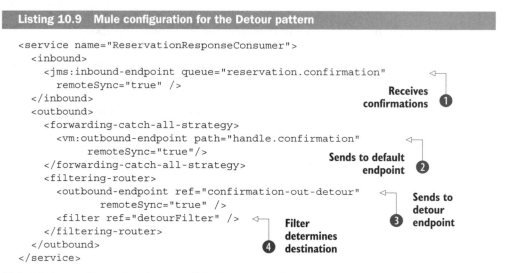

```
<service name="ReservationResponseConsumer">
  <inbound>
    <jms:inbound-endpoint queue="reservation.confirmation"
      remoteSync="true" />
  </inbound>
  <outbound>
    <forwarding-catch-all-strategy>
      <vm:outbound-endpoint path="handle.confirmation"
          remoteSync="true"/>
    </forwarding-catch-all-strategy>
    <filtering-router>
      <outbound-endpoint ref="confirmation-out-detour"
          remoteSync="true" />
      <filter ref="detourFilter" />
    </filtering-router>
  </outbound>
</service>
```

Receives confirmations ❶

Sends to default endpoint ❷

Sends to detour endpoint ❸

Filter determines destination ❹

This Mule configuration is a modified version of the reservation example implementation. You only have to make a couple of changes to add the Detour pattern. This services still receives all the confirmation messages ❶ from a JMS queue. The service then uses a filter ❹ to determine where to send this confirmation message. If the filter is enabled, the confirmation message is sent to the detour service from listing 10.8 ❸; if it's disabled, the message is sent to its original destination ❷. With this configuration you can, at runtime, turn on the filter and intercept and change any of the confirmation messages.

The last question that remains is how to turn the filter on and off at runtime. Let's start by looking at the detour filter implementation, shown in listing 10.10.

Listing 10.10   DetourFilter that can be enabled and disabled using JMX

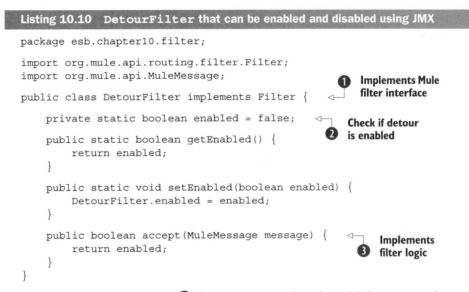

```
package esb.chapter10.filter;

import org.mule.api.routing.filter.Filter;
import org.mule.api.MuleMessage;

public class DetourFilter implements Filter {

    private static boolean enabled = false;

    public static boolean getEnabled() {
        return enabled;
    }

    public static void setEnabled(boolean enabled) {
        DetourFilter.enabled = enabled;
    }

    public boolean accept(MuleMessage message) {
        return enabled;
    }
}
```

❶ Implements Mule filter interface

❷ Check if detour is enabled

❸ Implements filter logic

This filter, which implements ❶ the Filter interface from Mule, returns the enabled property ❷ from the accept method ❸. If this property is set to true, the confirmation messages are sent to the detour endpoint; if the property is false, these messages are sent to their original destination. How can you set the property to the intended value, given that in its current state, it will never detour the messages?

You need a way to change the enabled property value. To do this, you use JMX. We mentioned that with JMX, you can manage applications if they expose this management information; you expose the filter settings to JMX. Spring makes this simple, as shown in listing 10.11.

Listing 10.11   Spring configuration exposing the detour filter to JMX

```
<spring:bean id="exporter"
    class="org.springframework.jmx.export.MBeanExporter">
  <spring:property name="beans">
    <spring:map>
      <spring:entry
        key="filter:name=detourFilter"
        value-ref="detourFilter"/>
    </spring:map>
  </spring:property>
</spring:bean>

<spring:bean id="detourFilter"
    class="esb.chapter10.filter.DetourFilter"/>
```

❶ Exposes Spring JMX

❷ Defines detour filter with Spring

You use the Spring MBeanExporter ❶ to expose all the public methods from your DetourFilter bean ❷ to JMX. You register the DetourFilter in the JMX registry as filter:name=detourFilter. If you start up a JMX console such as JConsole, which is available in the standard Java distribution, you can connect to the running Mule

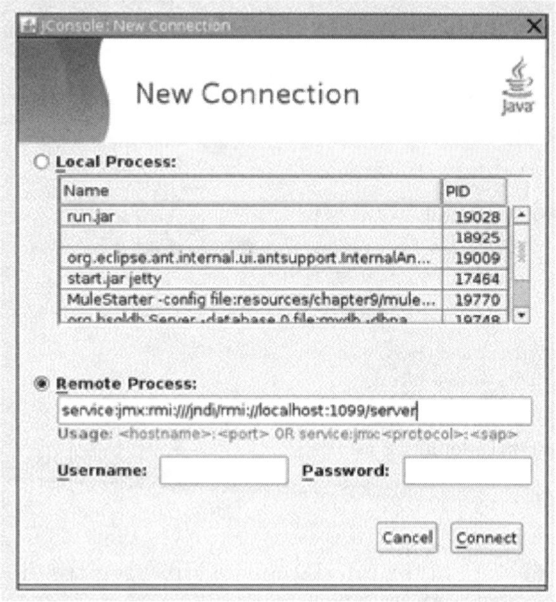

Figure 10.5   Connecting JConsole to Mule

instance. Figure 10.5 shows how to connect JConsole to Mule. For more information on how to use JMX with Mule, see section 10.2.

After you've made a connection to Mule, look for the filter node. You see a screen similar to figure 10.6.

As you can see in figure 10.6, the `DetourFilter` is registered in the JMX registry. Using JConsole, you can easily change the setting of the `enabled` property to enable the detour filter and also stop it later.

In the last couple of sections we've shown you how to implement the Detour pattern in Mule. The Detour pattern is more difficult to implement than the Wire Tap or Message Store pattern, because you must intercept a message before it's sent to a target service. With the routers available in Mule, and with the help of JMX, you can implement the Detour pattern in such a way that it's flexible and can be turned on and off at runtime.

In the next section, we examine how you can use the EIP Service Engine to implement the Detour pattern in ServiceMix.

DETOUR PATTERN IN SERVICEMIX

To implement a Detour pattern in ServiceMix, you can use the content-based router available in the servicemix-eip Service Engine. You configure this router to either send messages directly to the target configured service or send them to the service you've configured as the detour address. We start with configuring this router; first, you must create a new service Unit, as you had to do for the Wire Tap pattern. The EIP Service Engine configuration for the Detour pattern is shown in listing 10.12.

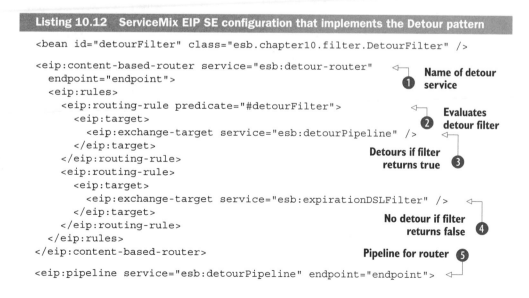

Figure 10.6 JConsole, showing the JMX property for the detour filter. With JConsole, you can enable and disable the detour filter.

Listing 10.12 ServiceMix EIP SE configuration that implements the Detour pattern

```
<bean id="detourFilter" class="esb.chapter10.filter.DetourFilter" />

<eip:content-based-router service="esb:detour-router"          ◁──  Name of detour
  endpoint="endpoint">                                          ❶   service
  <eip:rules>
    <eip:routing-rule predicate="#detourFilter">               ◁──  Evaluates
      <eip:target>                                             ❷   detour filter
        <eip:exchange-target service="esb:detourPipeline" />    ◁──
      </eip:target>                                                Detours if filter
    </eip:routing-rule>                                        ❸  returns true
    <eip:routing-rule>
      <eip:target>
        <eip:exchange-target service="esb:expirationDSLFilter" />   ◁──
      </eip:target>
    </eip:routing-rule>                                          No detour if filter
  </eip:rules>                                                 ❹  returns false
</eip:content-based-router>
                                                             Pipeline for router ❺
<eip:pipeline service="esb:detourPipeline" endpoint="endpoint">  ◁──
```

```
  <eip:transformer>
    <eip:exchange-target service="esb:detour" />
  </eip:transformer>
  <eip:target>
    <eip:exchange-target service="esb:expirationDSLFilter" />
  </eip:target>
</eip:pipeline>
```

Resumes normal ❻
processing

You configure a content-based router ❶ with a single routing rule. Each message received by this content-based router is checked against the specified predicate, which in this case is the custom `DetourFilter` ❷. This detour filter is exposed in the same manner as you saw for the Mule detour filter using the Spring `MBeanExporter` (not shown in the listing). If the result from this filter is true, the message is forwarded to the specified `exchange-target`, which is the detour pipeline ❸. If none of the predicates matches (in this example you have only one), the message is sent to the intended target specified in the default routing rule ❹. This listing also includes a pipeline ❺. This pipeline is called when the filter matches and calls a service where you can alter the message. We look at the configuration of this target service in listing 10.15. After this custom service, the `exchange-target` ❻ is called once again, and normal processing resumes.

Before we look at the changes you need to make to other service unit implementations from chapter 9, let's quickly examine the detour filter implementation shown in listing 10.13.

Listing 10.13   ServiceMix detour filter implemented as a ServiceMix predicate

```
public class DetourFilter implements Predicate {        ◁——  Implements ServiceMix
                                                              Predicate interface
    private boolean enabled = false;        ◁—— Check if
    public boolean getEnabled() {                detour is
        return enabled;                          enabled
    }

    public void setEnabled(boolean enabled) {
        this.enabled = enabled;
    }

    public boolean matches(MessageExchange exchange) {     ◁——  Evaluates
        return enabled;                                          filter logic
    }
}
```

If you've read the section on Mule, you can see that this is much the same as the filter you implemented in the Mule detour example and is exposed to JMX in the same manner.

You also need to change the JMS Service Unit, `esb:confirmationConsumer`, because you want this service to call your detour-enabled service instead of directly calling the `esb:expirationDSLFilter`. Listing 10.14 shows the changed `esb:confirmation-Consumer`.

Listing 10.14   Modified JMS consumer that calls the wire-tap service

```
<jms:consumer service="esb:confirmationConsumer"
    endpoint="endpoint"
    targetService="esb:detour-router"
    destinationName="reservation.confirmation"
    connectionFactory="#connectionFactory"
    marshaler="#replyInOnlyMarshaler"/>
```

❶ Calls JBI detour service

The only thing you change is the `targetService` attribute ❶. Instead of directly sending the incoming message to `esb:expirationDSLFilter`, it's now sent to `esb:detour-router`.

The last thing to do is create the service to which the detoured message is sent. The configuration of this service is shown in listing 10.15.

Listing 10.15   ServiceMix bean SU configuration to deal with the Detour pattern

```
<beans xmlns:bean="http://servicemix.apache.org/bean/1.0"
    xmlns:esb="http://esbinaction.com/restaurant">

    <bean:endpoint service="esb:detour"
                   endpoint="endpoint"
                   bean="#detourBean"/>

    <bean id="detourBean" class="esb.chapter10.detour.DetourBean"/>
</beans>
```

Invoked by detour service

You have to make sure the name of the sender service is the same as you configured in listing 10.12. This service will receive an exchange and can easily change the message or ask an administrator for input.

If you run this example and send a message, depending on the configuration of the `DetourFilter`, the message is sent either to this detour service or directly to the original destination. Because you exposed the detour filter to JMX, you can once again use JConsole to enable and disable the filter. For more information on how to use JMX, see section 10.2.

So far, we've focused on how you can debug and analyze messages that are sent over the ESB, and how you can monitor specific integration scenarios. In the second part of this chapter, we look at how you can monitor the complete ESB. To do this, you use the JMX support provided by both ESBs.

10.2   *Monitoring using JMX*

JMX was introduced by Sun in 2002 and was added to the standard Java runtime when Java 5 was released. With JMX, you have a standard model you can use to expose your own beans to be managed by external applications, and a standard model that external monitoring applications can connect to and use to control your exposed beans. Figure 10.7 gives an overview of the components and layers used in JMX.

Let's quickly examine each of the layers. The instrumentation level is where your applications reside. In your application, you define a number of MBeans, as you did with Spring in the previous section; these MBeans are registered in a registry called the MBean server. An MBean defines a number of operations and attributes from your beans that can be invoked by remote management applications.

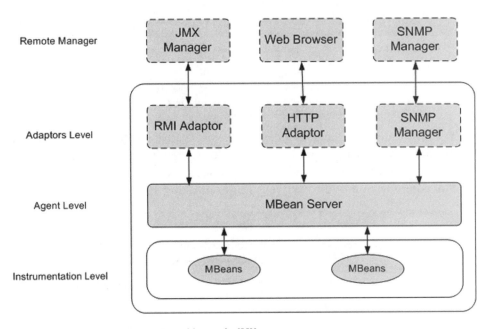

Figure 10.7   All the components and layers in JMX

You also need a way to access those MBeans. For this purpose, JMX uses an *adaptor*. An adaptor exposes the beans registered in the MBean server to external applications using a specific technology. For example, you can have an RMI adaptor that uses standard Java remoting to access the MBeans. Other adaptors expose MBeans using SOAP, plain HTTP, or the SNMP protocol.

Once the MBeans have been exposed using a specific technology, you can use a remote manager to access them using one of the registered adaptors. Many remote managers are available for this purpose. There are commercial managers, such as IBM Tivoli and HP OpenView, which can connect to JMX, and a number of open source tools are also available. The best known are Sun's JConsole, MC4J, and MX4J. MX4J provides Java libraries you can use to connect from Java to a JMX MBean server, so we won't look at that one here. In the following sections, we look more closely at how JConsole and MC4J can be used to monitor Mule and ServiceMix.

10.2.1   *Using JMX to administer Mule*

Before starting Mule, you need to tell it to expose its management functionality through JMX. To do this, add the following line to the Mule configuration:

```
<mgmt:jmx-default-config/>
```

Mule creates its own MBean server, register-management, and statistics MBeans, and adds an RMI connector. Add the previous line to the example from chapter 9, and fire up the ESB. Then, run JConsole by typing `jconsole` from the command line; doing so starts JConsole and shows you the startup screen, as shown in figure 10.8.

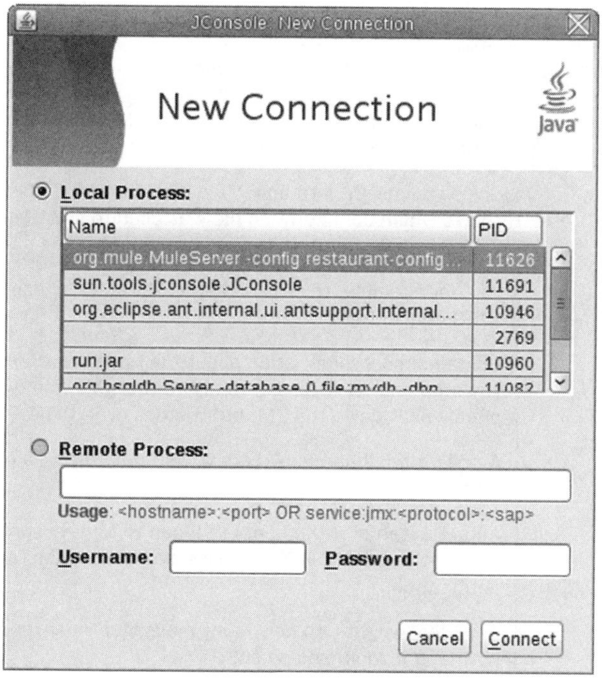

Figure 10.8 JConsole startup screen

From here, you can use JConsole to connect directly to any of the Java processes running on your machine or to a remote process. When Mule starts with JMX enabled, it starts up its own MBean server instead of registering all the beans in the JVM MBeanServer; so, you need to connect to Mule as if it were a remote process. If you connect to the local process, you get only the basic JVM MBeans instead of the Mule MBeans.

If you examine Mule's startup output, you see the address you need to use to connect. It looks something like this:

```
service:jmx:rmi:///jndi/rmi://localhost:1099/server
```

Copy this address into the remote process field, and click the Connect button. Doing so uses the RMI adaptor to connect JConsole to Mule's MBean server. You now see an overview of all the MBeans available in the MBean server, grouped per type, as shown in Figure 10.9.

As you can see, Mule provides access to a number of different types of objects. Table 10.1 gives a short summary of what each MBean type means.

We look more closely at the `org.mule.Service` MBean group and the `org.mule.Connector` group with JConsole, and you use MC4J to get some insight into the `org.mule.Statistics` group. Let's start by examining the `org.mule.Service` group.

We show you the attributes and operations defined on the `DuckRestaurant-Service` from the restaurant example in chapter 9. First, figure 10.10 shows the attributes, which are mostly about statistics for the Mule service and the lifecycle status for this component.

Table 10.1   JMX categories that Mule can manage

Type	Description
org.mule.Service	Contains all the services you define in Mule. You can see statistics, stop and start services, and more.
org.mule.Configuration	Gives you insight into how Mule was started. For instance, shows which configuration file was used to start Mule.
org.mule.Connector	Contains information about the defined connectors. Allows you, for example, to stop and start the JMS connectors and JDBC connectors.
org.mule.MuleContext	Contains more information about the Mule server and lets you stop and start the server. Note that this won't completely shut down the VM, but it stops everything.
org.mule.model	A collection of services. Lets you stop and start a complete model.
org.mule.Notification	Allows external JMX clients to listen to Mule-specific notifications. With JMX, it's possible to subscribe to received notifications.
org.mule.Statistics	Provides insight into how many messages were received, how long it took, and so on.
Log4j	Lets you alter the log levels. Not Mule-specific, but comes in handy.

Figure 10.11 shows the operations that can be executed on Mule; they're more interesting. You can use a number of methods to control this single Mule service. If you want to bring down a service, or temporarily pause it, you can easily do so using JConsole.

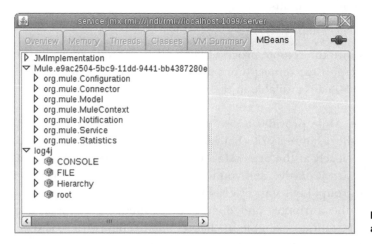

Figure 10.9   All the available MBeans for Mule

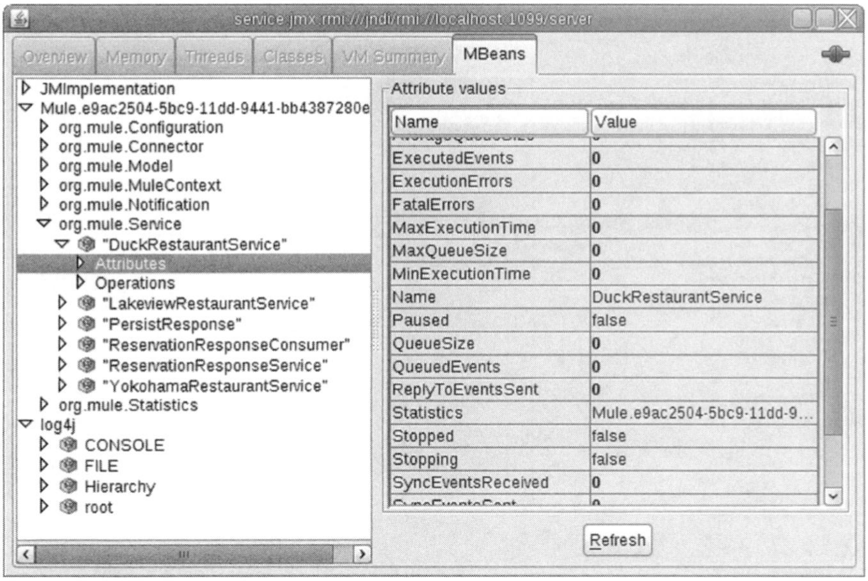

Figure 10.10 **JConsole showing all the attributes of the** `DuckRestaurantService`
Mule service

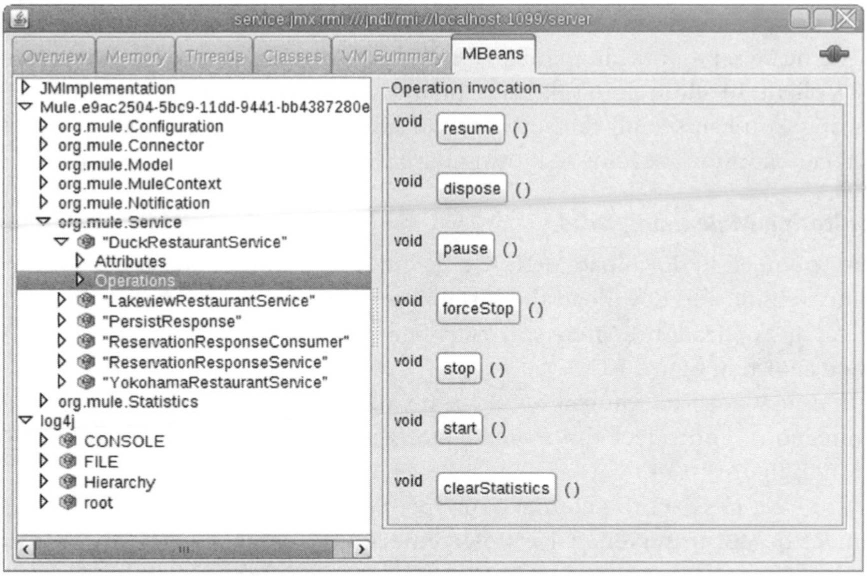

Figure 10.11 **JConsole showing all the methods of the** `DuckRestaurantService`

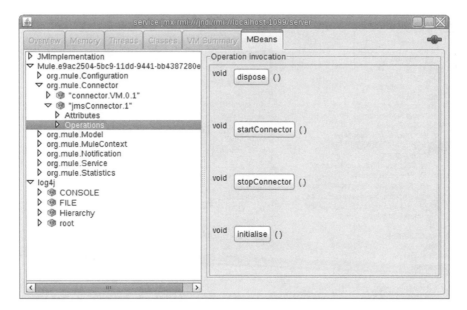

Figure 10.12 JConsole showing all the operations of the JMSConnector

The same functionality is available for the org.mule.Connector group. Figure 10.12 shows its operations, which can stop and start specific technology connectors.

As you've seen, you can manage the lifecycle of your services and connectors from a JMX client. In addition to this functionality, the JMX view also shows what is currently running; you can see all the services and all the connectors. Now, let's look at how MC4J can monitor the Mule ESB using the org.mule.Statistics group.

10.2.2 *Monitoring Mule using MC4J*

First, you need to download MC4J. Go to http://mc4j.org/confluence/display/mc4j/ Home website, and download the installation package. Run the package, and start up the MC4J application. When you start the application, you're presented with the screen shown in figure 10.13.

You now need to connect MC4J to the MBean server. To do this, right-click MC4J Connections, and select the Connect to Server option. Doing so starts the wizard shown in figure 10.14.

You have to select the connection type. Select JSR160, which is the default way to connect to MBean servers. Give this connection a name and fill in the server URL, which is the same one you used in JConsole: service:jmx:rmi:///jndi/rmi://localhost: 1099/server. Click Next, and on the next page click Finish. The Mule connection will be registered; when you expand it, you see the screen shown in figure 10.15.

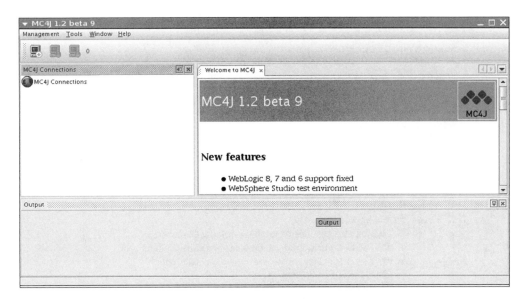

Figure 10.13   MC4J startup screen that you see when you start MC4J for the first time

Once you're connected, navigate to the org.mule.Statistics MBean, and from there select DuckRestaurantService. Open its attributes, and right-click average-ExecutionTime. From the resulting pop-up menu, select the Graph option. When you

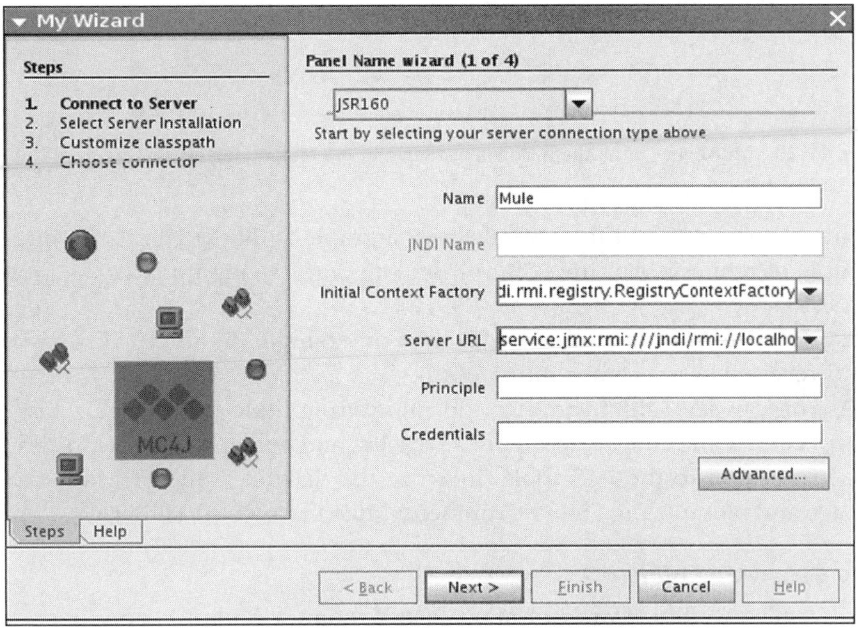

Figure 10.14   The MC4J connection wizard

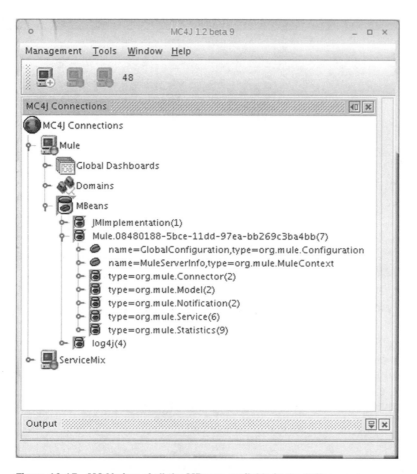

Figure 10.15   MC4J view of all the MBeans available in the MBean server

do this, the right side of the screen shows a graph of that attribute. If you now send a couple of requests over the ESB, you see the graph being updated, as shown in figure 10.16.

You can do this for all the attributes. For example, figure 10.17 shows the total events received by a certain component.

As you can see, administrating and monitoring Mule using JMX is easy. You can control connectors and components' lifecycles, and get all kinds of statistics from the ESB. In addition to the JMX tools shown in this section, Mule provides two tools to manage and monitor the ESB environment: Mule Galaxy and Mule HQ.

10.2.3   *Mule Galaxy and Mule HQ*

So far, you've seen how you can manage and monitor Mule by using open standards and applying common integration patterns. MuleSource, the company behind Mule, also offers two tools that can help you manage your Mule ESB:

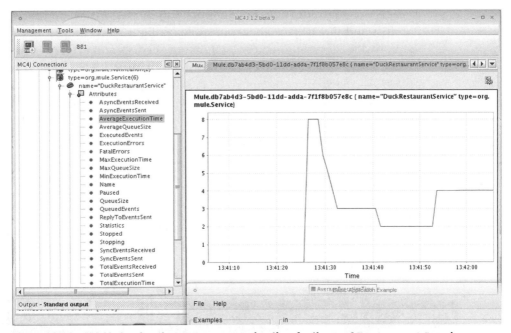

**Figure 10.16   MC4J showing the average processing time for the `DuckRestaurantService`
Mule service**

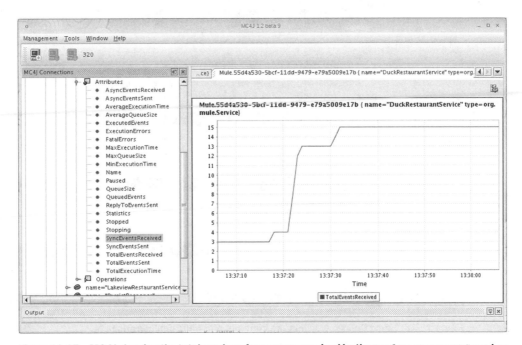

**Figure 10.17   MC4J showing the total number of messages received by the `DuckRestaurantService`
Mule service**

- *Mule Galaxy*—Provides a registry in which you can register your Mule configuration files and the artifacts that your Mule configurations use. Mule Galaxy can then provide lifecycle functionality for your services and artifacts. Mule Galaxy is open source and can easily be integrated with Mule 1.4 and Mule 2.0.
- *Mule HQ*—An extensive, commercial monitoring environment that you can use to monitor multiple Mule instances at the same time. You can use this tool to stop and start service, deploy new configurations, and check the health of your complete Mule environment.

In this section, we give you a quick overview of what these tools do and how you can use them. For more information about both these tools, visit the Mule website: http://www.mulesource.com.

MULE GALAXY

Mule Galaxy can serve as a service registry for your Mule instances. So, when you use Mule Galaxy, you don't have to start Mule with a configuration file. Figure 10.18 shows the look and feel of Mule Galaxy.

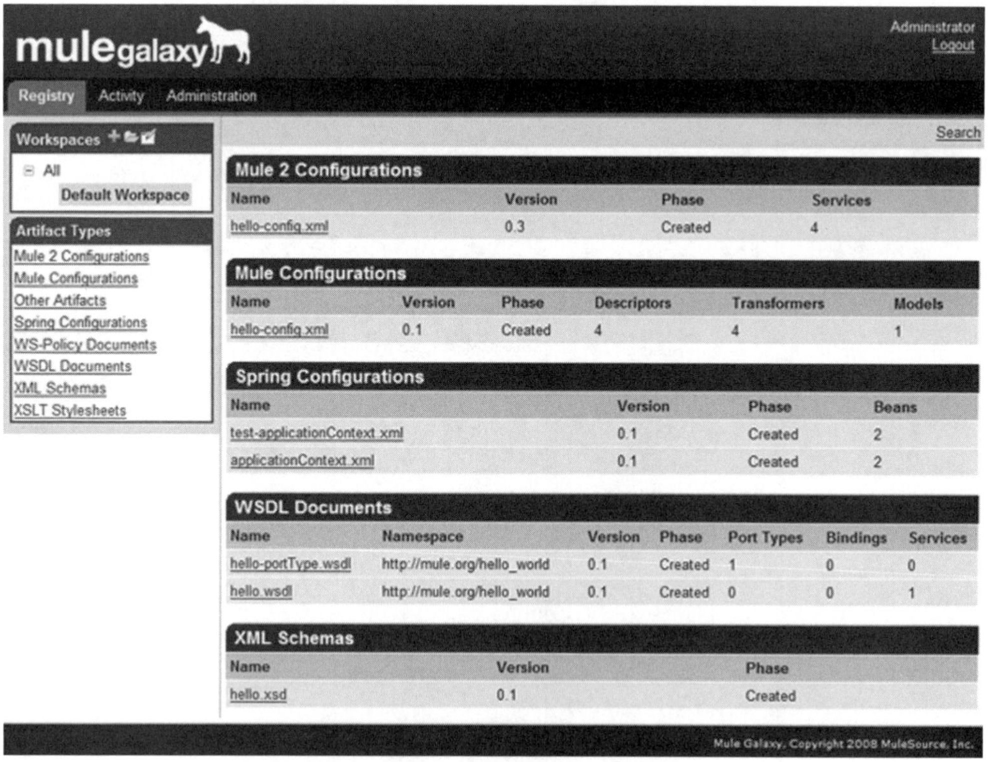

Figure 10.18 Mule Galaxy, showing the contents of a Mule configuration

In the figure, you can see all the artifacts managed by this instance of Mule Galaxy. You can also see that Mule Galaxy supports versioning on all these artifacts. This is especially useful when you're using XML Schemas for validation, or other artifacts that may change during runtime.

Mule Galaxy has only recently been released but already has a lot of functionality. If you want to try it, go to http://www.mulesource.com.

MULE HQ

You can get Mule HQ as part of a subscription package from MuleSource. It provides a single interface where you can monitor all the Mule instances you have running. If you're running Mule in a mission-critical production environment, using a tool like Mule HQ can be helpful. It can't monitor the runtime environment, but it can help you proactively detect issues so you solve them before they cause message loss or other serious problems.

Figure 10.19 shows an example of Mule HQ monitoring a Mule instance. All the Mule services are constantly monitored for health. You can also monitor the health of the platform Mule is running on. In figure 10.19, for instance, the system's free memory is also monitored.

Now that you're familiar with Mule's management and monitoring capabilities, let's see what ServiceMix exposes through JMX.

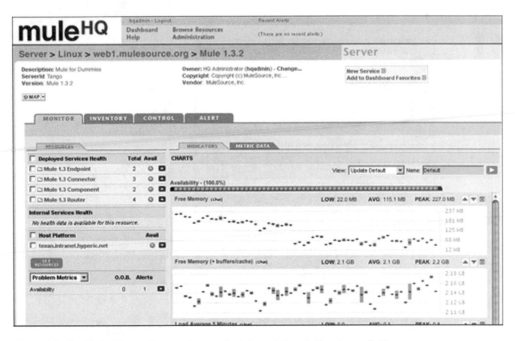

Figure 10.19   Mule HQ monitors various endpoints and the platform's available memory.

10.2.4   *Using JMX to administer ServiceMix*

When you use JMX with ServiceMix, you don't need to define any additional configurations. ServiceMix provides a number of MBeans you can use to monitor and administer the ESB. Let's start by using JConsole to connect to the MBean server and see what Service-Mix makes available to you.

Begin by starting up ServiceMix and JConsole. When JConsole starts, you're once again presented with the view shown in figure 10.20.

This time, you don't make a remote connection; you connect directly to the running process, because ServiceMix, in contrast with Mule, uses the default MBean-Server to register its beans. Select the `org.codehaus.class.Launcher` process and click Connect. Doing so connects you to the MBean server from the ServiceMix process and shows you the screen in figure 10.21.

As you can see, ServiceMix exposes a lot of its functionality through JMX. This isn't just a ServiceMix-specific feature: the JBI specification requires all the management functionality of a JBI container to be exposed through JMX. The primary advantage is that you get the same interface and the same type of options, regardless of the JBI implementation you use.

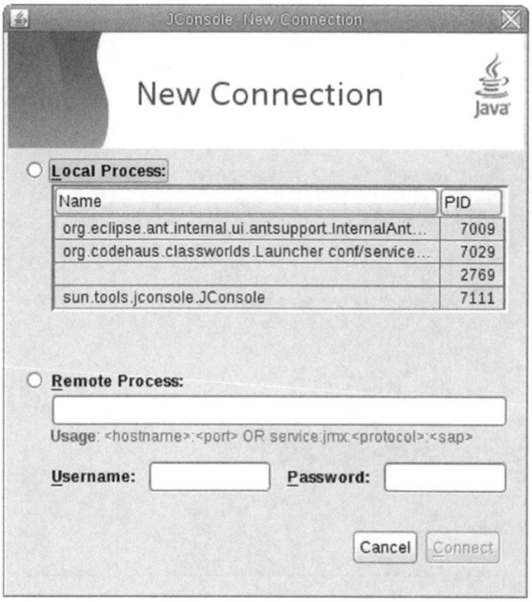

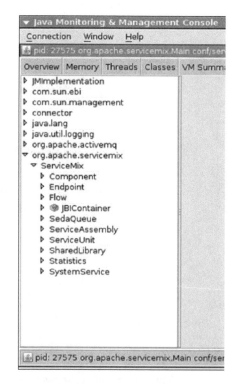

Figure 10.20   Connecting JConsole to ServiceMix

Figure 10.21   JConsole showing all the management options from ServiceMix

Let's quickly look at what the various MBeans let you do. Table 10.2 gives an overview of the categories and MBeans.

Table 10.2   MBean functionality provided by ServiceMix

Category	Description
Component	Shows all the deployed components (service engines and binding components) that are installed in the container. Also gives the option to stop and start each component.
Endpoint	Lets you view the endpoints that are registered whenever a service unit is deployed. You can also retrieve their WSDL contracts and send messages to those endpoints.
Flow	Contains ServiceMix-specific MBeans. For instance, you can stop and start the internally used transports.
JBIContainer	Allows you to stop and start the JBIContainer.
SedaQueue	Lets you stop and start internally used queues. Note that this category will only be visible when you have components that make use of these queues.
ServiceAssembly	Shows all the service assemblies deployed on ServiceMix. From here, you can stop and start a service assembly and get the JBI descriptor file.
ServiceUnit	Just as for ServiceAssembly, allows you to stop and start the deployed service units.
SharedLibrary	Gives an overview of all the shared libraries deployed in the JBI container. Shared libraries are another artifact you can deploy to a JBI container.
Statistics	Lets you access all the statistics of the components and endpoints running on the ESB.
SystemService	Gives you complete control over the JBI container. From here, you can deploy new service engines, binding components, and so on. You can also uninstall and remove these artifacts from here.

We look more closely at some of the SystemService functionality, because that service provides you with an interface to manage the ServiceMix container. The rest of the JMX MBeans provide stop and start functionality for the various artifacts.

MANAGEMENT FUNCTIONALITY EXPOSED BY THE ADMINCOMMANDSERVICE

Figure 10.22 shows most of the operations exposed through the AdminCommandService.

The AdminCommandService lets you control all your JBI artifacts. You can deploy new archives (by specifying an URI to the location of the archive), undeploy artifacts, and get an overview of all the artifacts currently available.

The next part of the SystemService that we examine is the DeploymentService, shown in figure 10.23.

The operations shown in figure 10.23 provide extra information about the link between a service assembly and the JBI component on which its service units are

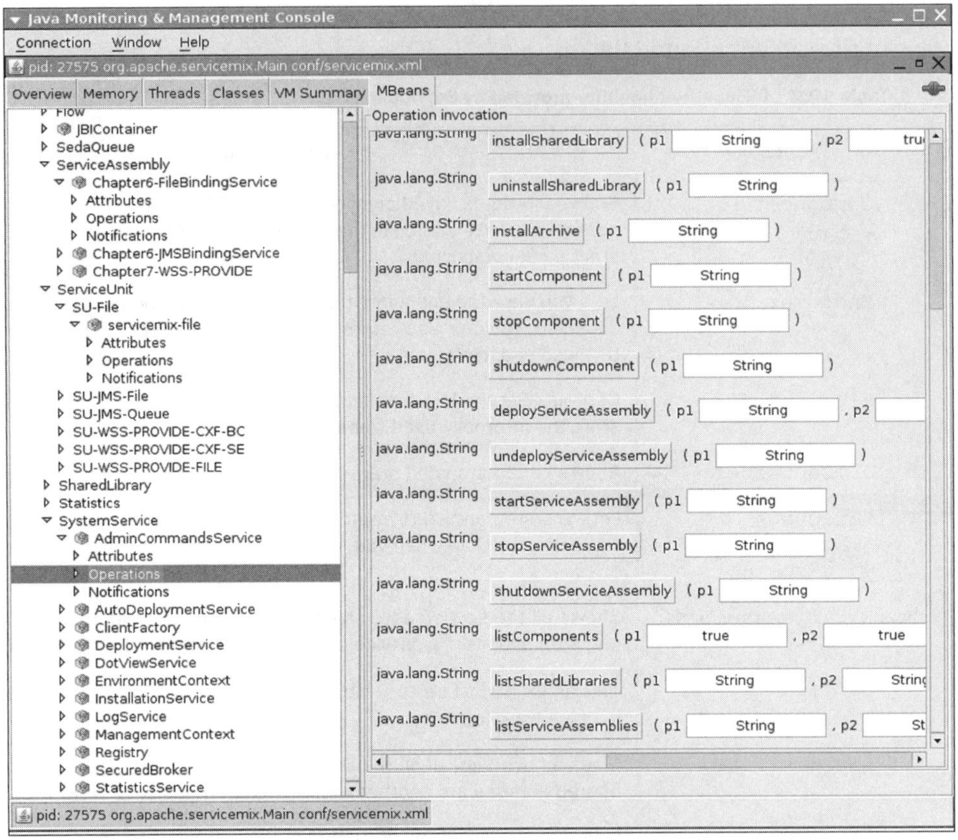

Figure 10.22   JConsole showing the operations exposed by the `AdminCommandService`

deployed. You can also check whether service units are deployed and whether it's possible to deploy to a certain component.

The last MBean we look at is the `LogService`, shown in figure 10.24.

`LogService` is a simple service with a single interesting method (besides its lifecycle methods): `reconfigureLogSystem`. When this method is called, ServiceMix reloads
the Log4j configuration. This allows you to change the log levels while the application
is running, which makes debugging live applications much easier.

10.2.5 *Monitoring ServiceMix using MC4J*

Just as you did with Mule, you use MC4J to monitor some basic statistics from Service-
Mix. If you haven't installed MC4J yet, you can download and install the latest version
from http://mc4j.org/confluence/display/mc4j/Home.

You have to connect to ServiceMix using a server URL. ServiceMix already supplies
an RMI-based connector you can use: right-click the connection label in MC4J, and
add a new connection. On the first screen of the wizard, shown in figure 10.25, use

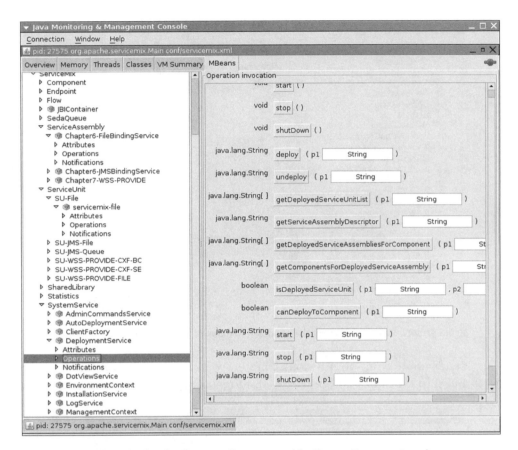

Figure 10.23   JConsole showing the operations exposed for the `DeploymentService`

service:jmx:rmi:///jndi/rmi://localhost:1099/jmxrmi as the server URL. ServiceMix also requires a username and password to access its MBeans. The default username is *smx*, and the default password is also *smx*. Fill in these values in the Principle (user) field and in the Credentials (password) field. Then, click Next; on the following screen, click Finish.

MC4J will connect to the running ServiceMix instance and provide an overview of all the MBeans deployed in the MBean container. For one of these beans, you add a graph with which you monitor the number of incoming messages. To do this, navigate to the Statistics MBean, and select the attribute you want to monitor. The example shown in figure 10.26 is monitoring the number of inbound messages for the file-binding component. If you set up this graph by right-clicking the attribute and choosing Graph from the context menu, you see that when you start sending messages from the file system, this action is reflected in the graph.

We've shown you some basic uses of JMX. We've explained how to use JConsole for easy access to all the management and monitoring functionalities the ESBs offer, and how easy it is to use MC4J to track of attributes and watch trends. If you think back to

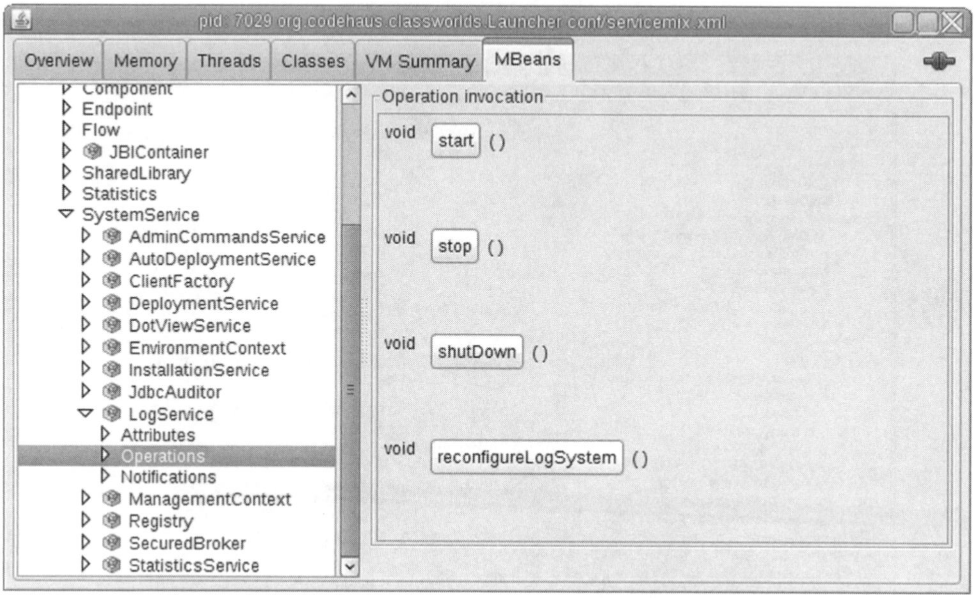

Figure 10.24   JConsole showing the exposed methods of the LogService

the example from the previous chapter, you can use this JMX functionality to stop and start the entire flow or to stop sending messages to certain restaurants. With this

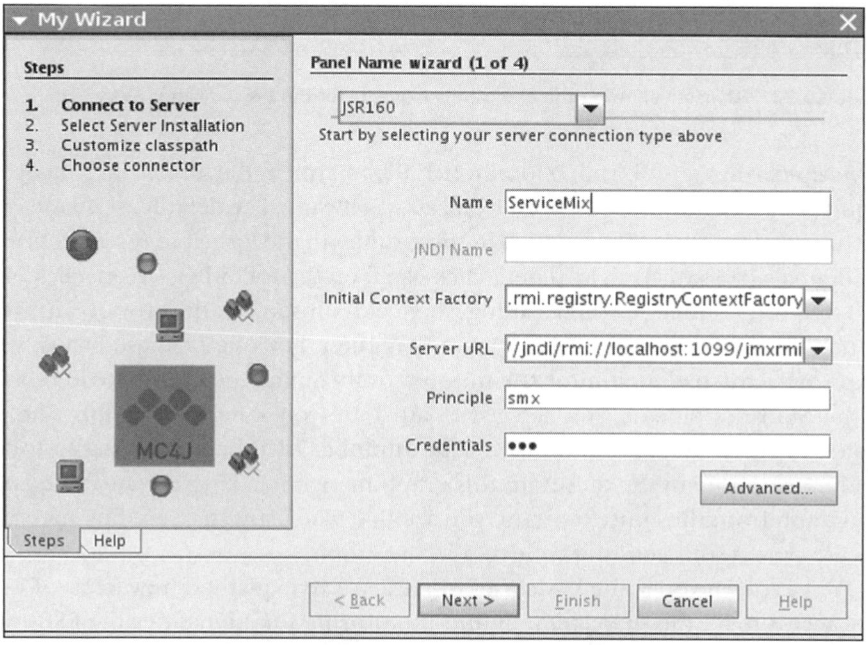

Figure 10.25   MC4J connection wizard with values set for ServiceMix

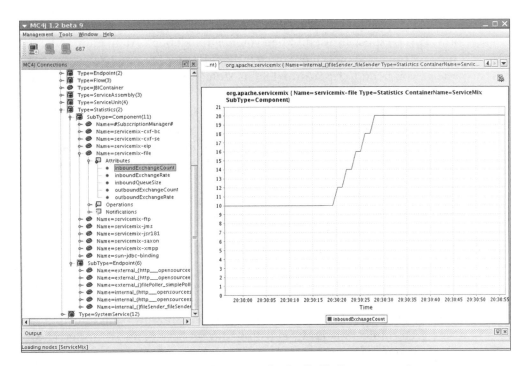

Figure 10.26 MC4J monitoring inbound messages for the file-binding component

functionality, it's also possible to monitor the number of messages sent to a specific endpoint and create statistics.

You can do a lot more with JMX than the functionality discussed in this chapter. For more information about JMX and how to use it, we recommend the Manning book *JMX in Action* (Benjamin Sullins and Mark Whipple, 2002).

10.3 Summary

In this chapter, we've focused on showing how you can manage and monitor two open source ESBs. We first showed how you can use some of the Enterprise Integration patterns to help you get more insight into the messages travelling over the ESB. You learned that with the Wire Tap pattern, it's easy to see the messages that are sent to certain endpoints. If you have an integration solution in which one of the components is having problems, you can easily add a wire tap that makes a copy of those messages for analysis. With ServiceMix, you can do this dynamically, because you can hot-deploy and restart service units. With Mule, however, you're forced to alter the configuration and restart Mule.

We also discussed the Message Store pattern, which allows you to store messages for later analysis. This is especially useful when you want to generate statistics or reports for your integration solutions. The last pattern on the list was the Detour pattern, which lets you stop message processing by sending the message to a detour endpoint. After the message is detoured, you can change the message and send it on in its changed form. This is especially useful when you need to debug certain endpoints, and when it isn't easy to create messages yourself. For the Detour pattern, as for the Wire Tap pattern, you need to restart the ESB in Mule; with ServiceMix, you can redeploy the new configuration.

We also looked at the management options provided by the ESBs. Both ESBs support the JMX standard, which allows you to connect to the ESBs in a generic way. But the ESBs don't provide the same management options: Mule only allows basic lifecycle management; ServiceMix, on the other hand, lets you control every aspect of the ESB from JMX.

In the section about JMX, you learned how you can manage the ESBs, stop and start components, and even create graphs by monitoring certain attributes. With JMX and the patterns shown in this chapter, you've got a fairly complete set of techniques with which you can manage and monitor the ESBs.

We've shown how to connect the ESBs to different transports, how transactions and security works, how routing is handled, and how you can work with web services. We have only one subject left to cover. In the next chapter, we examine how Mule and ServiceMix can support service orchestration. We show two different approaches: how to integrate Mule with jBPM, and how the services exposed in ServiceMix can be orchestrated using BPEL.

Implementing a process engine in the ESB

11

In the previous chapters, we've discussed different functionalities of open source ESBs including routing, transformation, connectivity, and transactions. These functionalities focus on integrating services and applications with message flows. Most of these message flows are *stateless*, which means that no state is preserved after the message has been routed through the open source ESB. The stateless characteristic of message flows is also an important aspect for an ESB to be able to scale when needed.

But in some scenarios, you want the state to be preserved during multiple message flow invocations. The time that passes between these message flow invocations can be days or even weeks in some environments, so you need an additional component to implement stateful flows.

In the integration market, these stateful flows are often implemented in *process engines*. Process engines are designed and implemented to be able to preserve state

393

between message invocations by using transactions and database persistency by default. Within a process engine, stateful flows are often called *processes*; you can implement these processes with a process-definition language, such as the Web Services Business Process Execution Language (WS-BPEL) OASIS standard.

In this chapter, you implement a case study in which hotel guests book scuba diving trips using WS-BPEL. This example shows the added value of a process engine. Multiple service invocations are required to book a scuba diving trip: a taxi reservation service, a lunch reservation service, and a booking service for the trip at a diving agency. Implementing such a case study with just ESB message flows would lead to a complex, difficult-to-maintain integration solution. By using a process engine, you can implement the service invocations with one process definition that takes care of the service orchestration.

We also look at an alternative to WS-BPEL: JBoss's jBPM initiative. jBPM is an open source framework that uses jBPM Process Definition Language (jPDL). jBPM also provides support for the WS-BPEL standard, but to show two different process-definition examples we focus on the jPDL implementation of jBPM. The main difference between WS-BPEL and jPDL is that WS-BPEL is more activity oriented and jPDL is more state and transition oriented, as we explain.

The foundations of the integration solution remain Mule and ServiceMix. In this chapter's examples, the added value of a process engine for products like Mule and ServiceMix will become clear.

Before we dive into the technical details of process engines, let's start with some theoretical background. We also discuss the differences in functionality between an ESB and a process engine.

11.1 *Introducing the process engine*

Before we talk about the scuba diving case study, we first discuss the concept of a process engine. A good place to start this discussion is to look at the Process Manager pattern from the book *Enterprise Integration Patterns*; it gives a good description of the functionality a process engine should provide. The Process Manager pattern is one of the routing patterns, because it orchestrates and routes messages to services as part of a process description.

What's the difference between the Process Manager pattern and the routing patterns we discussed in previous chapters, like the Content-Based Router and Message Filter patterns? The primary difference is that the examples so far have been stateless, whereas the Process Manager pattern is stateful. For example, the Content-Based Router pattern evaluates the contents of an incoming message and then routes this message to the correct service. When the message leaves the content-based router, no state is maintained in the ESB about this message.

With the Process Manager pattern, every incoming message other than the process-start message is matched against a specific process instance. Then, the process logic for this process instance is performed, and the next service call is made. This service call involves sending a message to a specific service. When this message leaves the process manager, the state is maintained; when the invoked service returns a response, the same process instance processes this response.

In this section, you see how a process engine can be integrated with an ESB, and we discuss a clear separation in functionality that should be implemented between a process engine and an ESB. We also discuss the use of the Process Manager pattern in a design diagram of a process engine–based integration solution.

11.1.1 The execution environment for processes

An integration solution should in one way or another contribute to an organization's business processes. Technicians sometimes forget why they're designing and developing a great technical solution, but the starting point of an integration solution involves a well-thought-out business case. With the rise of paradigms like Service Oriented Architecture (SOA) and technical vehicles like ESBs, a bridge has been built between the business and the IT departments. In our opinion, the key paradigm should be not SOA and the identification of services that perform business functionality, but Business Process Management, or BPM.

Business Process Management (BPM)

BPM is a paradigm that is widely used in the integration industry. According to Wikipedia (at the time of writing), "Business process management (BPM) is a method of efficiently aligning an organization with the wants and needs of clients. It is a holistic management approach that promotes business effectiveness and efficiency while striving for innovation, flexibility and integration with technology. As organizations strive for attainment of their objectives, BPM attempts to continuously improve processes—the process to define, measure and improve your processes—a 'process optimization' process" (http://en.wikipedia.org/wiki/Business_Process_Management).

And Gartner describes BPM as "a management discipline that requires organizations to shift to process-centric thinking, and to reduce their reliance on traditional territorial and functional structures" in the research report "Gartner's opinion on Business Process Management," 2006 (http://whitepapers.zdnet.com/abstract.aspx?docid=276439).

To narrow the meaning of this broad management discipline in the context of this book, we say that BPM uses process-centric thinking to manage and improve business processes for organizations. The Process Manager pattern can help translate this process-centric thinking for the IT world.

In the context of enterprise integration, processes are implementations of (part of) a business process. Examples of business processes are an ordering process, introducing a new customer, and handling an insurance claim. The IT implementation of a business process can be based on the Process Manager pattern. The Process Manager pattern is, as described in *Enterprise Integration Patterns*, a central processing unit that maintains the state of the sequence and determines the next processing step based on intermediate results.

A process manager is often implemented by a *process engine*, which is a product that executes in its own environment and is solely focused on the execution of processes. Examples of process engines include IBM WebSphere Process Server, Oracle BPEL Process Manager, Microsoft BizTalk, ActiveBPEL Engine, and two engines that we use in this chapter: JBoss jBPM and Apache ODE.

The process manager maintains the state of a sequence. A process implementation involves multiple steps or activities that need to be processed. The process manager or process engine makes sure that the state of the process (think of variables and correlation) is maintained between the steps or activities.

The next processing step is determined based on intermediate results. The process logic sometimes involves a choice between two or more activities to be executed. The process manager or process engine can evaluate this choice based on the execution path and the variables of the process's current state.

As we said, a process involves multiple steps or activities. These steps or activities can also involve the invocation of external services or applications. Considering that the process engine that provides the runtime environment for the processes executes in its own environment, how are these invocations implemented? Does the process engine invoke the external service or application? Technically, the process engine could perform the invocation of a service or application. But in the context of an organization's integration landscape, the process engine shouldn't implement this invocation or mediation logic. This is the task of the ESB.

In earlier chapters, you didn't use a process engine; the integration logic was implemented by Mule and ServiceMix. These two integration platforms provide the functionality needed to, for example, route, transform, and log a message. The introduction of a process manager or process engine doesn't change this. The added value of a process engine consists of the functionality to execute and monitor processes and to interact with the ESB. Figure 11.1 provides a schematic overview of an integration architecture with both a process engine and an ESB.

As figure 11.1 shows, the process engine provides an execution environment for processes. This example shows two different processes; process 1 has two instances running, and process 2 has one instance. It's important to notice that for process 1, each instance has its own state maintained by the process engine. For each invocation to an external service or application, the process engine uses the ESB for the integration logic.

The figure shows a number of patterns that can be implemented in the ESB environment. The ESB communicates with the external services and applications, and does the actual invocation. The optional response message is then routed back to the correct process instance in the process engine.

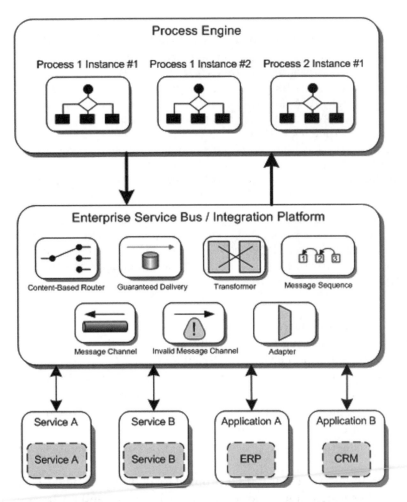

Figure 11.1 **Integration architecture that includes a process engine and an ESB. The process engine is responsible for managing the state of the process, and the ESB is responsible for technical integration aspects like routing, transformation, and connectivity.**

11.1.2 *Designing processes for a process engine*

We've discussed the execution environment for processes—the process engine—but we haven't talked about the construction of these processes: the process design. Before a process can be deployed on a process engine, it must first be designed. The industry standard to define a process is the Web Services Business Process Execution Language (WS-BPEL).

Many integration vendors provide a design tool to construct a WS-BPEL process. For example, IBM has the WebSphere Integration Developer product, Oracle has a BPEL Designer for JDeveloper, and Microsoft lets you import and export WS-BPEL

Web Services Business Process Execution Language (WS-BPEL)

WS-BPEL is an XML-based language that is standardized by OASIS. WS-BPEL 2.0 has been an OASIS standard since April 2007. The WS-BPEL 2.0 specification is based on the Business Process Execution Language for Web Services (BPEL4WS) specification by BEA, IBM, Microsoft, SAP, and Siebel. And the history doesn't stop here: The BPEL4WS specification is based on Microsoft's XLANG and IBM's Web Services Flow Language (WSFL). The foundation of the WS-BPEL specification is strong, and WS-BPEL is considered the standard technology to specify business processes. WS-BPEL is heavily based on WSDL and XSD; for example, these foundational technologies are used to define variables and partner links for a WS-BPEL process definition.

WS-BPEL defines a large number of activities that can be used to specify a business process. For example, a request/response process always has a *receive* activity for the incoming message and a *reply* activity for the outgoing message. But there are also activities to implement process logic, such as an *if* activity, a *while* activity, and a *forEach* activity.

from Visio. But there aren't many open source design tools for WS-BPEL. In section 11.5, we look in more detail at using WS-BPEL with Apache ODE; there you use the Eclipse BPEL plug-in as the open source WS-BPEL design tool.

Another example of a process definition language is jPDL, which is used by the JBoss Business Process Management (jBPM) product. jPDL is a graph-oriented programming model, which is based on states and transitions. The open source jBPM project provides an execution environment for processes defined in jPDL, along with an Eclipse-based plug-in to design processes and a web console to manage and monitor processes.

jPDL isn't an industry standard; it's a proprietary definition language that is only used in the jBPM project. But it's a powerful, simple language, and for Java developers it's a great option to implement a process engine because it's purely Java based. The jBPM project also provides support for the WS-BPEL standard, so people who are seeking industry standards can also choose this option. Because WS-BPEL support is also based on the Eclipse BPEL plug-in, it's similar to the Apache ODE example. In section 11.4, we provide a detailed case study implementation that uses Mule and jBPM with jPDL for the process definition.

Now that we've discussed two options to define processes with WS-BPEL and jPDL, we can examine the runtime implementation for such processes. Because the process definition involves the invocation of services, a lot of interaction takes place between the process engine and the ESB. Figure 11.2 shows a small implementation example of the interaction between the process engine or the process manager and the services.

We already looked at a more architectural overview of an integration environment with a process engine and an ESB in figure 11.1. Figure 11.2 provides another view of

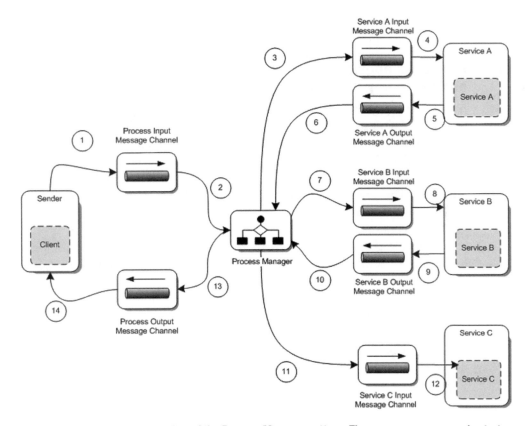

Figure 11.2 An abstract overview of the Process Manager pattern. The process manager orchestrates the involved services based on a process description.

such an environment with an example using the Process-Manager pattern. In this example, the process manager is invoked by a client application that sends a message to an input-message channel. The process implemented involves three external invocations to services A, B, and C. Services A and B use a request/response message exchange pattern; the process manager sends a request message to a specific message channel and waits on another message channel for the service's response message. The example also shows a fire-and-forget message exchange pattern with Service C. For this service invocation, the process manager sends a message to the input message channel for Service C but doesn't wait for an answer. This means step 12 in figure 11.2 may not be executed before step 13. (These steps aren't dependent on each other and therefore may not execute in the order shown.)

Note that this example is oversimplified and doesn't show the distinction in functionality between a process engine and an ESB as in figure 11.1. But imagine that the message channels are part of the ESB environment and may be enriched with transformations, routing, and message logging. This should give you a thorough overview of the functionality of the Process Manager pattern, so now let's look at a case study to implement a process engine. Let's go scuba diving!

11.2 A process engine case study: booking a day of scuba diving

A stay in Hawaii's SleepingBeauty hotel is an excellent opportunity to go scuba diving for a day. Hawaii provides a wide variety of scuba diving trips that include sharks, dolphins, wrecks, and caves. Currently, the hotel distributes flyers to guests, promoting the idea of booking a scuba diving day trip. This approach seems to be working well, because in the last few months the number of bookings has doubled. But there is one downside: The amount of time the hotel receptionist spends booking trips for hotel guests has also doubled.

The receptionist has to gather the booking request information from the hotel guest, including the date for the trip; the guest's name and room number; the number of divers; and the guest's preference for a shark, dolphin, or wreck-and-caves adventure. Then, the receptionist must make a phone call to the diving agency that provides the scuba diving trip of preference. The hotel guest can also request a lunch package for the group of divers, so the hotel's catering staff must be informed. And finally, a taxi reservation must be made to transport the guests to the diving agency and back. Figure 11.3 summarizes the current process for booking a scuba diving trip.

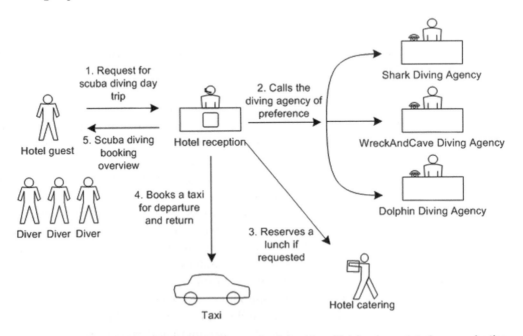

Figure 11.3 The current booking process for a scuba diving trip, which involves a lot of communication between the hotel receptionist and the other parties in the process

In addition to the amount of time the hotel receptionist has to spend booking each trip, hotel guests must also wait before the final booking information arrives. The hotel manager, Gregor Rest, has ordered your manager (John) to think of an IT solution. Because of your experience in solving integration problems in previous assignments, John has asked you to come up with a solution that requires far less of the receptionist's time. You asked John to book a room in the SleepingBeauty Hawaii hotel for a week so you can talk to the diving agencies and design a solution that will work for the hotel employees who are involved. John admitted that a stay in Hawaii would be necessary in order to come up with a good design; life as an integration specialist isn't so bad.

The starting point of your stay is a meeting with the three diving agencies shown in figure 11.3. Before you travelled to Hawaii, you thoroughly investigated the possibility of using a process engine. Because the desired solution includes a number of service invocations, and state must be maintained across these invocations, the choice to use a process engine seems obvious. To implement the same functionality with just ESB message flows would lead to a lot of unnecessary flow-configuration and state-management functionality. You come to the conclusion that the process engine will be used to orchestrate the service invocations and manage the state, and the ESB will be used to invoke the services.

But in order to design a process solution, the cooperation of the diving agencies and the taxi station is vital. During the meeting with the diving agencies, it becomes clear that they're all willing to invest in a booking service that can be used by Sleeping-Beauty. You suggest that you develop a booking-service solution that all three agencies can use. After an in-depth discussion, all parties agree on an XML message format and the contents of the request and response messages. Great!

In your meeting with the taxi station, things go even more smoothly. The taxi station is already busy developing a booking service that SleepingBeauty can use soon.

The last piece missing is the lunch service, which should be developed within SleepingBeauty. This service will be developed in the coming weeks so it can be implemented and integrated easily with existing applications.

After your stay in Hawaii—which of course included a day of scuba diving—you present your solution design to your manager, John, and hotel manager, Gregor, as shown in figure 11.4.

The high-level design shown in figure 11.4 introduces a booking process definition that defines the orchestration of the scuba diving, lunch, and taxi services. The diagram doesn't yet include the ESB, which takes care of the logic to invoke the services.

John and Gregor like your solution's process-based approach and are looking forward to the real implementation. You convince them that it would be wise to develop a quick proof-of-concept to choose between two popular open source process engines: jBPM and Apache ODE. You have only one week to develop this proof-of-concept, so you need to quickly move on to designing and implementing the messages and services that are necessary for the booking process.

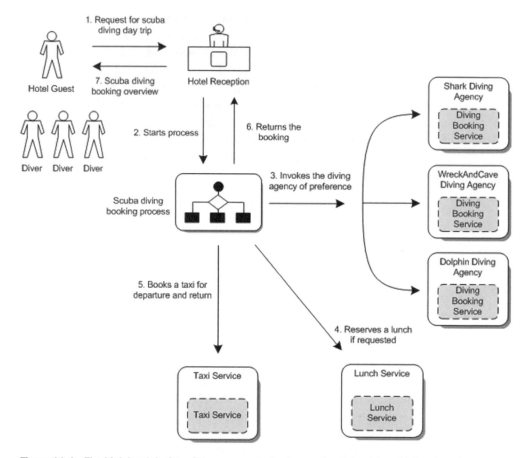

Figure 11.4   The high-level design of the process to book a scuba diving trip, which automates most communication with the involved parties. The hotel receptionist remains responsible for communicating with the hotel guest.

11.3   *Diving into the messages and services*

The booking process consists of multiple message exchanges: the scuba diving request message and the final booking response message are initiated and processed by an application at the reception desk, and there are also message exchanges with the diving agencies and the lunch and taxi services. You have quite a bit of work to do to construct these messages. You must design the request and response messages that you'll use to implement the message exchanges with the services and the booking process. Because the messages for the service invocations will be implemented with XML, you also need to develop a serialization strategy to marshal the messages to XML and unmarshal the XML messages back to Java objects.

In addition to the message definitions and the XML serialization, you also need to develop stub components to simulate the diving agencies and the lunch and taxi services. (You can't use the actual services during the proof-of-concept.)

11.3.1 *Designing the case study message definitions*

When a hotel guest asks the hotel receptionist to book a scuba diving day trip, information is needed to start the booking process. The hotel guest has to provide a name, a room number, the number of divers, the date for the trip, and whether a lunch is needed. The guest must also choose among the four kinds of diving trips: cave, dolphin, shark, or wreck. Note that there are four kinds of trips but only three diving agencies; one of the agencies provides two of the four kinds of trips.

The hotel receptionist enters this information into a simple booking application, which starts the process. The process invokes all the necessary services; the messages involved will be discussed later. The result of these service invocations is a scuba diving booking that holds all the necessary information. Figure 11.5 provides an overview of the scuba diving initial request and final booking messages.

The final booking message contains all the information related to the diving trip, including the name of the diving agency, the instructor name, the time slots for the taxi ride and the diving activity, and the total price.

The booking message consists of information gathered from the exchange of messages with the scuba diving agency, the lunch service, and the taxi station. Figure 11.6 summarizes the exchange of messages between these three services.

Let's look more closely at the three message exchanges involved in the booking process:

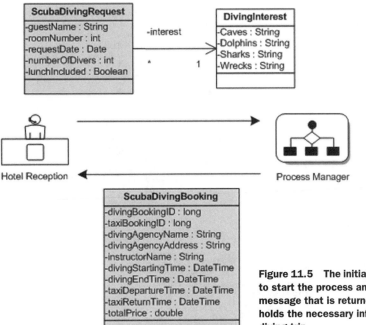

Figure 11.5 **The initial message that is needed to start the process and the final booking message that is returned by the process, which holds the necessary information for the scuba diving trip**

- *Booking the diving agency*—The request message holds, among other things, the number of divers and the requested kind of diving experience. The response message from the agency consists of information like a booking number, the starting and ending time of the diving trip, and the name of the agency and the diving instructor.

- *Booking lunch*—This one-way message exchange sends the guest's name and room number, the number of lunches, and the date on which the lunch must be prepared to the lunch service of the SleepingBeauty hotel.

- *Booking the taxi ride*—The request message from the booking process to the taxi station provides enough information to reserve a taxi on a particular date and time, taking into account the number of divers.

The message design described in figures 11.5 and 11.6 provides a good starting point for the implementation of the scuba diving booking process. But how are these messages

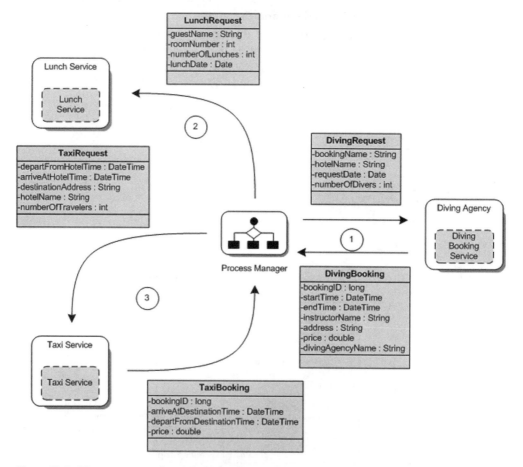

Figure 11.6   The message exchange between the process engine and the involved parties: respectively, the diving agency of choice, the lunch service, and the taxi service

exchanged with the involved applications and services? There are many different ways to exchange these messages, including the use of Java objects or XML messages.

The use of Java objects can be an efficient message format in a pure Java environment; but the booking process involves two external parties—the diving agencies and the taxi station—so the restriction of a pure Java environment isn't realistic. Some diving agencies will probably implement the booking service using .NET because their IT environments are Microsoft based. You decide that the message format will be XML. You'll use JiBX to serialize the Java objects from figure 11.5 and 11.6 into the correct XML format.

11.3.2 Serializing the case study messages to XML with JiBX

In a number of examples of the previous chapters, you used JiBX to serialize Java objects to XML messages and vice versa. In this chapter, the focus is on the implementation of the process engine, so we don't show JiBX mappings for all the messages defined in section 11.3.1. The other mappings are available as part of the source code distribution for this book. The JiBX mapping for the diving agency request and booking classes is shown in listing 11.1 as an example.

Listing 11.1 Scuba diving request and booking JiBX mappings

```
<binding>
  <mapping name="DivingRequest"
      class="esb.chapter11.scubadiving.model.DivingRequest"        ⟵  Maps the
      ns="http://divingagency.hawaii.com/xsd">                     ❶  diving request
    <namespace uri="http://divingagency.hawaii.com/xsd"               message
        default="elements"/>
    <value name="bookingName" field="bookingName"/>
    <value name="hotelName" field="hotelName"/>                    ❷  Serializes the
    <value name="requestDate" field="requestDate"              ⟵      request date
      serializer="esb.framework.util.DateJiBXSerializer.serialize"
      deserializer="esb.framework.util.DateJiBXSerializer.deserialize"/>
    <value name="numberOfDivers" field="numberOfDivers"/>
  </mapping>
  <mapping name="DivingBooking"                                  ⟵  Maps the
      class="esb.chapter11.scubadiving.model.DivingBooking"         booking
      ns="http://divingagency.hawaii.com/xsd">                   ❸  message
    <namespace uri="http://divingagency.hawaii.com/xsd"
        default="elements"/>
    <value name="bookingID" field="bookingID"/>
    <value name="endTime" field="endTime"/>
    <value name="startTime" field="startTime"/>
    <value name="instructorName" field="instructorName"/>
    <value name="address" field="address"/>
    <value name="name" field="name"/>
    <value name="price" field="price"/>
  </mapping>
</binding>
```

You keep the JiBX mappings for the booking process's messages easy. The Java objects' attributes are mapped to the same XML element name. The listing shows a diving request mapping ❶ and a diving booking message ❸. The only Java attribute that can't be mapped directly is the `requestDdate` ❷. For the deserialization of the request date, JiBX expects the request-date value to include a time property, as specified by the standard `dateTime` XML Schema type. Because you only use a date value for the `requestDate`, you need to define a `deserializer` method that converts a date `String` value in an XML message to a Java `Date` object.

This concludes the discussion of the message design and XML serialization for the scuba diving booking process. With the messages defined, you're missing two parts before you can start implementing the process: the technical design for the integration solution and the stub implementation for the involved services.

11.3.3 *Setting the stage for the case study implementation*

We introduced the Process Manager pattern earlier in this chapter, but we didn't yet relate it to the scuba diving case study. You'll make a design diagram for the case study that includes the Process Manager pattern as the foundation for the integration solution. In the next part of this section, we discuss the implementation of the service stubs that will let you test the case study implementation during the proof-of-concept phase.

MAKING A DESIGN DIAGRAM FOR THE SCUBA DIVING CASE STUDY

The process implementation for the scuba diving case study includes the invocation of two external services and one internal service. These services can be invoked directly by the process engine on which you'll deploy the process. Process engines can use common communication protocols and message formats; most process engines can communicate with SOAP over HTTP, SOAP over JMS, and other protocols and message formats. But process engines are primarily designed to provide an execution and maintenance environment for processes and not to integrate with the existing IT environment (for example, legacy applications). Integration with the IT environment is the main functionality of an ESB. You'll use this distinction between a process engine and an ESB in your technical design.

The process engine is responsible for implementing the process logic, and the ESB is responsible for integrating with the involved applications and services. Figure 11.7 provides an overview of the technical design for the scuba diving booking process, using this clear distinction between the ESB and the process engine.

Figure 11.7 lists the application and services and defines the messages exchanged with this application and these services. The names of the messages correspond to the names used in figures 11.5 and 11.6. The process engine is the environment where the process definition is deployed and the service instances are executed. The integration environment or ESB is used to communicate with the application and services.

The starting point for the scuba diving booking process is the hotel reception booking application. The receptionist uses this application to enter the necessary information provided by the hotel guest. When the booking information is entered, the application sends a scuba diving request message to the process-message channel

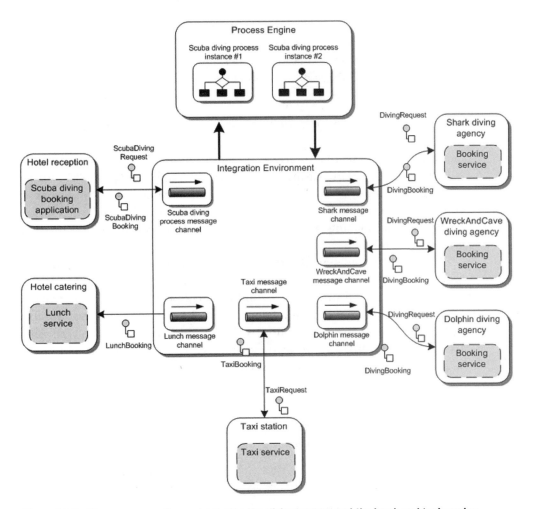

Figure 11.7　The process engine orchestrates the diving agency and the lunch and taxi service invocations while using the ESB as a connectivity layer. The ESB implements the functionality to route the messages to the correct service endpoints.

in the integration environment. The process engine retrieves the request message from the process message channel and then starts a new process instance based on the scuba diving booking process design. From there, the process instance completes the process as discussed in section 11.2.

Although you'll implement the design shown in figure 11.7 with two different process engines and ESBs, the design and implementation for the service stub can be similar. We start by looking at the implementation of these service stubs.

DEVELOPING THE SERVICE STUBS FOR THE CASE STUDY IMPLEMENTATION

The starting point of the scuba diving booking process is the booking application used by the hotel receptionist. You'll use the Swing test client provided with this book to simulate the request message sent by the hotel reception application. The booking process begins by using the diving agency booking services. Because you've convinced the diving agencies to use a common message design and protocol, you can use the same interface for all three diving agencies.

```
public interface DivingAgencyService {

    public DivingBooking processBooking(DivingRequest request);
}
```

The diving agency service interface provides one method with an incoming diving request and an outgoing diving booking. In the implementation class for this interface, the logic must be implemented to accept a diving request and to process that request into a booking. Because you have to simulate the three external diving agency services for the booking process, you must think of an easy solution to implement three service stubs.

You could implement the diving agency service interface with three different classes. But another way to do this is to define a number of attributes that are unique for one of the three diving agencies and use the Spring container to create three different instances for the same implementation class. Spring can inject the unique values based on the bean configuration; with that mechanism, you can easily simulate all three services. Listing 11.2 shows the diving agency service interface implementation that instantiates the three diving agencies.

Listing 11.2 The common diving agency service interface implementation

```
public class DivingAgencyBean implements DivingAgencyIF {

    private String divingAgencyName;
    private String endTime;
    private String instructorName;          ❶ Sets attributes with
    private double pricePerPerson;             Spring injection
    private String startingTime;
    private String address;

    public DivingBooking processBooking(DivingRequest request) {
        DivingBooking booking = new DivingBooking();
        booking.setBookingID(new Random().nextLong());
        booking.setStartTime(
            fillTime(request.getRequestDate(), startingTime));
        booking.setEndTime(
            fillTime(request.getRequestDate(), endTime));
        booking.setInstructorName(instructorName);
        booking.setPrice(request.getNumberOfDivers()    ❷ Simple price
            * pricePerPerson);                             calculation
        booking.setAddress(address);
        booking.setName(divingAgencyName);
        return booking;
    }
                                                    ❸ Parses time
    private Date fillTime(Date date, String time) {     String to Date
        GregorianCalendar calendar = new GregorianCalendar();
```

```
    calendar.setTime(date);
    calendar.set(Calendar.HOUR_OF_DAY,
        Integer.valueOf(time.substring(0, time.indexOf(":"))));
    calendar.set(Calendar.MINUTE,
        Integer.valueOf(time.substring(time.indexOf(":") + 1)));
    return calendar.getTime();
  }
}
```

The main part of the diving agency service implementation is the definition of the attributes that are injected by the Spring container ❶. These attributes can be used to uniquely identify the specific diving agency. The diving agency name is an important identifier for the service implementation, as is, for example, the price per person for the scuba diving trip. Listing 11.2 only shows the attribute definition, but the implementation includes getters and setters for all these attributes. The Spring container uses the attributes' setter methods to inject the values. The remainder diving agency service implementation is straightforward. A simple price calculation ❷ uses the price-per-person attribute value and the number of divers from the request message. To simplify the definition of the time values in the Spring bean configuration, it uses a `String` with the format `hh:mm`. The `fillTime` method ❸ converts the time `Strings` to a `Date` instance.

The Spring container can now use the implementation class for the diving agency service interface to create three different instances. In the Spring configuration, you can define property elements with name and value attributes that are mapped to the attributes in the Java implementation class. Spring uses the property elements to inject the Java attributes with the values defined in the value attribute. Listing 10.3 configures the three diving agency services with Spring bean configurations.

> **Listing 11.3   Spring configuration for the diving agencies**

```
<bean id="sharkDivingService"
      class="..chapter11...bean.DivingAgencyBean"       ❶ Defines shark diving
      singleton="false">                                  agency bean
  <property name="divingAgencyName"
            value="Shark Diving Agency"/>                ❷ Diving agency
  <property name="instructorName" value="Mr. Daredevil"/>   name
  <property name="pricePerPerson" value="123.56"/>
  <property name="startingTime" value="11:00"/>
  <property name="endTime" value="14:00"/>
  <property name="address" value="Sharkstreet 566"/>
</bean>

<bean id="wreckAndCaveDivingService"
      class="..chapter11...bean.DivingAgencyBean"
      singleton="false">
  <property name="divingAgencyName"
            value="Wreck and Cave Diving Agency"/>
  <property name="instructorName" value="Mr Ancient"/>   ❸ Defines
  <property name="pricePerPerson" value="110.90"/>          price
  <property name="startingTime" value="09:00"/>
```

```
    <property name="endTime" value="16:00"/>
    <property name="address" value="Cavestreet 4"/>
</bean>

<bean id="dolphinDivingBean"
      class="..chapter11...impl.DivingAgencyBean"
      singleton="false">
    <property name="divingAgencyName"
              value="Dolphin Diving Agency"/>
    <property name="instructorName" value="Mrs Romantic"/>
    <property name="pricePerPerson" value="70.40"/>
    <property name="startingTime" value="14:00"/>      ❹  Start and
    <property name="endTime" value="15:00"/>               end times
    <property name="address" value="Dolphinstreet 100"/>
</bean>
```

The three diving agency bean configurations start with a bean element that consists of an id, a class, and a singleton attribute ❶. The id attribute should have a unique identifier value within the Spring container. The class attribute provides the implementation class that Spring will instantiate. And the singleton attribute tells the Spring container whether multiple instances of the bean are allowed. The rest of the listing shows the property definitions for the three diving agencies. The divingAgencyName attribute, for example, is injected with the value "Shark Diving Agency" for the shark diving agency bean instance ❷. Another example is the pricePerPerson attribute, which is injected with a value of 110.90 for the wreck and cave diving agency ❸. This attribute is implemented in Java as a double, so the Spring container provides the conversion. A final example is the definition of the starting time and ending time for the scuba diving trip ❹.

Because the lunch and taxi services are implemented by one service provider in this case, the implementation of these services is simpler. But in order to provide a complete overview of the services, we discuss these service interfaces briefly. The lunch service uses a one-way interface, as you may remember from section 11.2. This interface is the simplest:

```
public interface LunchIF {

    public void processLunch(LunchRequestBooking lunchBookinglunchRequest);
}
```

The lunch-service interface accepts lunch requests and processes them so that on the requested date, the lunches are prepared for the hotel guests. The taxi service interface implements a request/response message exchange pattern and is similar to the diving agency service interface:

```
public interface TaxiIF {

    public TaxiBooking processTaxiRequest(TaxiRequest request);
}
```

The taxi service interface accepts requests for taxi rides and processes these requests into a taxi booking response. The implementation of this interface is similar to the diving agency service implementation shown in listing 11.2, except for the large number of attributes. In this book's source distribution, you can find the full implementation of the taxi service interface.

Now that you've defined the messages for the scuba diving booking process, outlined a high-level integration solution, and implemented the services, you can go further with the process engine implementation. In order to show you two process engines and process definition strategies, we've split the implementation of the process engine into two sections: section 11.4 discusses the jBPM process engine, and section 11.5 discusses a WS-BPEL implementation with Apache ODE.

11.4 Implementing a process engine with jBPM and jPDL

You can implement a process engine with many different products. To provide a good overview of the possibilities, we look at two different approaches to implementing the scuba diving booking process in the remaining part of this chapter. In this section, we focus on an implementation based on states and transitions with jBPM (http://labs.jboss.com/jbossjbpm), a process engine offered by JBoss. Because this may be your first introduction to jBPM, we start with an overview of how to define processes with the jBPM process definition language (jPDL).

11.4.1 Orchestrating services with jPDL

The jBPM product lets you implement processes that can consist of automatic steps as well as human workflow steps. The definition of these processes is based on jPDL. In addition, you can use WS-BPEL to define processes for jBPM. (We discuss WS-BPEL in section 11.5.) To get up and running with defining processes for jBPM, let's first look at some foundational concepts.

jPDL is based on a graph-oriented programming implementation technique. *Graphs* are also known as *states*; they can be modeled with UML state diagrams. The starting point for a graph or state is the relationship with transitions. When an application or service is in a particular state, you can use transitions to define the conditions required to progress to the next state. Figure 11.8 provides a schematic overview of the relationship between a node (or state) and a transition.

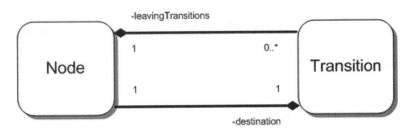

Figure 11.8   A schematic overview of the relationship between nodes and transitions. Nodes can have multiple leaving transitions; a transition always has one node as its destination.

By using nodes and transitions, you can model a basic process graph or state diagram. The nodes in this simple model can represent the current state of the process, and the transitions from one node to another can be used to define the order of states during execution.

But with this model, you can't easily define complex processes. There are no building blocks you can use to build a process. jPDL provides a basic set of nodes, including start and end states and a task state; see figure 11.9.

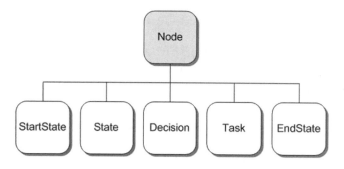

Figure 11.9   **The basic nodes you can use to define processes with jPDL. The difference between a *state* and a *task* is that the latter involves human interaction.**

Using the nodes shown in figure 11.9, you can model a more complex process graph or state diagram. For example, you can begin the process design with a StartState node and complete it with an EndState node. To implement logic to choose between three destination states, you can use a Decision node. The standard set of nodes implemented by jBPM also includes a Task node that can be used for workflow logic. With this set of standard nodes, you should be able to design a state diagram. But how can you include custom logic in the process graph? You can do this by using actions that can be defined for a node.

Custom logic can be implemented with an `ActionHandler` interface implementation that is invoked by the action. Actions can be attached to an event that is registered on a node. The most obvious events occur when the node is entered (`node-enter`) or left (`node-leave`) in the process graph. You can develop custom logic that is executed when the node for which you've registered the `node-enter` event is entered during the execution of a process instance. You can register an event for every node in jBPM, so this is the way to implement custom logic for your process. The node can be used as a process element as well; for such a node, you can attach an action implementation directly, without defining an event.

IMPLEMENTING A JPDL HELLO WORLD PROCESS

You can implement the process graph for jBPM using the jPDL XML Schema. This schema definition consists of the standard set of nodes that jBPM provides and the attributes and elements that can be specified for these nodes. We've looked at the theory behind this set of nodes and the use of actions and events, but the discussion will become clearer when we look at an example. Listing 11.4 shows a process definition for a hello world implementation.

Listing 11.4   Hello world implementation with jPDL

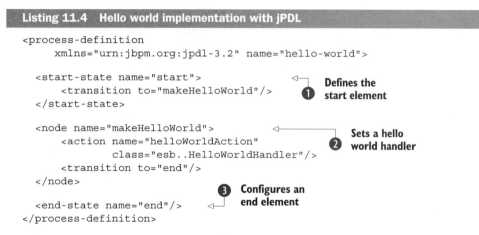

```
<process-definition
    xmlns="urn:jbpm.org:jpdl-3.2" name="hello-world">

  <start-state name="start">                        ◁         Defines the
    <transition to="makeHelloWorld"/>            ① start element
  </start-state>

  <node name="makeHelloWorld">                      ◁         Sets a hello
    <action name="helloWorldAction"                      ② world handler
            class="esb..HelloWorldHandler"/>
    <transition to="end"/>
  </node>
                                ③  Configures an
                                   end element
  <end-state name="end"/>          ◁
</process-definition>
```

The definition of the process graph starts with a process-definition root element that specifies the name of the process with the `name` attribute. But the starting point for the process is the `start-state` definition ①. For the hello world implementation, the start element doesn't have any logic implemented except a transition to the `makeHello-World` node. Note that for more complex processes, it's possible to define an event child element for a `start-state` where you can implement logic.

The start element only transitions the process state to the `makeHelloWorld` node, which defines some custom logic ②. The node definition has an `action` child element that is executed when the process state reaches the `makeHelloWorld` node. The `action` element defines a Java class that implements the `org.jbpm.graph.def.ActionHandler` interface provided by jBPM. We look at the implementation of this `ActionHandler` in a moment.

When the `ActionHandler` implementation is executed, the process state is transitioned to the `end-state` element ③. This is where the process instance ends. As you can see, the process definition is simple but powerful.

This `ActionHandler` interface defines just one method: `execute`. The current process state is passed on to the `ActionHandler` implementation with an `Execution-Context` object. The process state consists of information like the process identifier, the variables, and the execution path until this point in the process. Listing 11.5 shows the implementation of `HelloWorldHandler`, which is used by the `makeHelloWorld` node from listing 11.4.

Listing 11.5   jBPM `HelloWorldHandler` implementation

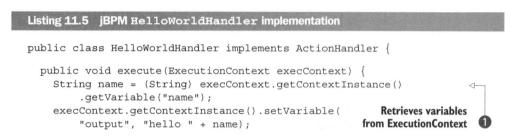

```
public class HelloWorldHandler implements ActionHandler {

  public void execute(ExecutionContext execContext) {
    String name = (String) execContext.getContextInstance()          ◁
      .getVariable("name");
    execContext.getContextInstance().setVariable(          Retrieves variables
      "output", "hello " + name);                       from ExecutionContext ①
```

```
        execContext.leaveNode();
    }
}
```

Triggers next transition

The ExecutionContext that is passed on by the jBPM container provides access to lots of information about the current process instance and the process template. For this example, the ExecutionContext is mainly used to retrieve and store variables. Assume that the hello world process instance is started with a variable name. With the ExecutionContext, you can get the ContextInstance variable that is primarily used for variable retrieval and storage ❶. The ContextInstance provides a getVariable method you can use to retrieve the name variable. With the setVariable method, you can just as easily store a new variable called output with a hello message to the process context instance.

The process instance must be notified that the makeHelloWorld node has finished and the process can be transitioned to the next node. To do this, you call the leave-Node method on the ExecutionContext ❷. When this line wasn't added to the HelloWorldHandler implementation, the process state got stuck in the makeHello-World node.

DESIGNING PROCESSES WITH THE jPDL DESIGNER

This concludes the hello world example. In the implementation of the scuba diving booking process, we look in more detail at the runtime execution of a process with jBPM. But jBPM includes another part: a jPDL designer. The jPDL designer is an Eclipse plug-in that you can use to graphically model a process that conforms to the jPDL schema. The jPDL designer consists of a palette where node types and transitions can be selected and provides a drawing canvas where you do the actual process modeling. Figure 11.10 shows the jPDL designer for the hello world process you just defined.

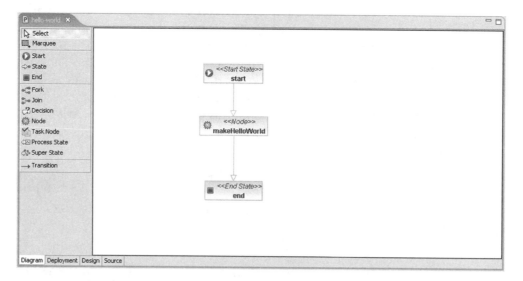

Figure 11.10   The hello world example in the jPDL designer

The palette appears on the left side and the drawing canvas on the right side. As you can see, the modeling elements are synonymous to the XML elements defined in listing 11.4. The graphical elements have a UML annotation–like way to specify the node type. Transitions between nodes are represented as arrows pointing from the leaving node to the target node. In addition to defining the nodes and transitions on the canvas, the jPDL designer provides a properties view that you can use to specify a node's details. For example, you can specify a node's action handler and the events configured for a process element. Figure 11.11 shows the properties view for the makeHelloWorld node.

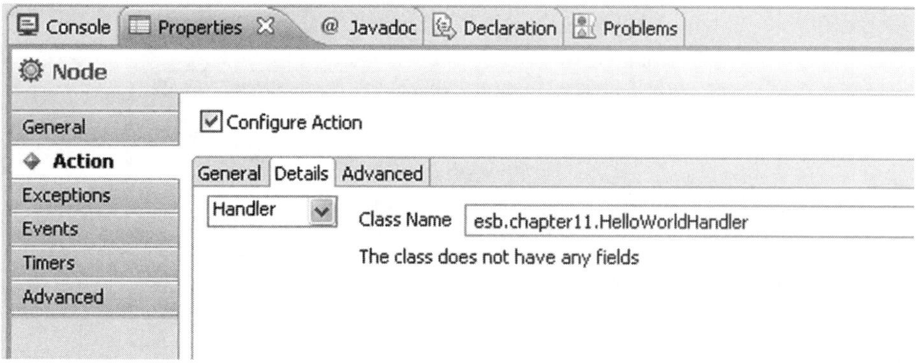

Figure 11.11 The properties view of the jPDL designer, where you can define the handler class to execute custom logic

The properties configuration for the makeHelloWorld node specifies the handler class that corresponds with the class shown in listing 11.5. In this view you can also configure other attributes for a node, such as the asynchronous attribute that specifies the way the node is invoked.

Now that you have some background knowledge of jBPM, let's continue with the design and implementation of the scuba diving booking process.

11.4.2 Implementing the case study with jBPM and Mule

The previous section presented a simple example of process design and implementation with jBPM. With the knowledge you've gained about jBPM, you should be able to design the scuba diving booking process implementation for the jBPM process engine. The design should also be based on the clear distinction between the process engine and the ESB, as discussed in section 11.3.3. Figure 11.7, shown earlier in that section, provides a good overview for this discussion.

When you translate this into an implementation with Mule and jBPM, Mule is responsible for the integration with the hotel reception application, the diving agency services, the lunch service, and the taxi service. jBPM will be used for the process definition and the execution of the process instance for the scuba diving booking process. Because

Mule comes with jBPM integrated out of the box, you can easily integrate the jBPM process engine with the Mule ESB. Figure 11.12 shows the design for the jBPM case study implementation.

Figure 11.12 can be overwhelming at first sight. Let's walk through all the aspects of this design for Mule and jBPM, starting with the definition of the process shown at left in the figure. These process elements don't make up the full process design; they only show the states that receive the first message (`ReceiveRequest`) and send messages to Mule. Later in this section, we look at the complete process design in the jBPM designer.

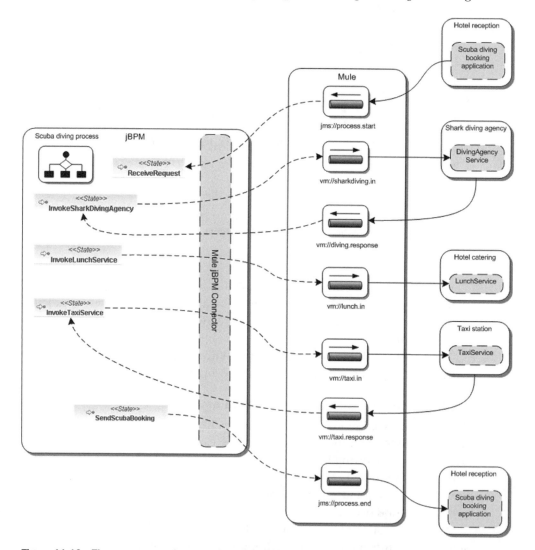

Figure 11.12   The message exchange between the jBPM process instance and the ESB services. The jBPM transport connector that is provided by Mule is used to implement the message exchange. Only one of the diving agency states is shown, because the other two agencies use the same invocation model.

The process elements shown here are all state nodes (the shark diving agency state also represents the two other diving agency states); each state invokes a service via the Mule ESB. As you saw in the implementation of the hello world example in section 11.4.1, invocation logic must be implemented in an `ActionHandler` interface implementation, which can be configured as an event handler for a particular state. Luckily, you don't have to develop this invocation logic yourself, because it's provided as part of the jBPM connector provided by Mule. The jBPM connector implements a number of `ActionHandler` interfaces to communicate with the Mule ESB. For example, `Invoke-SharkDivingAgency` uses a `SendMuleEvent` action handler to send a diving request to the shark diving agency. Because it's essential for the scuba diving case study implementation to understand how jBPM and Mule are integrated, let's discuss this topic in more detail.

INTEGRATING THE JBPM PROCESS AND THE ESB MESSAGE FLOWS

Your Mule distribution includes the jBPM library jbpm-jpdl-3.2.2.jar, which you can look up in the lib/opt folder, and a jBPM transport jar that you can find in the lib/mule folder. To integrate jBPM in a Mule configuration, you have to include a BPM connector definition such as the one shown in listing 11.6. The jBPM configuration for the scuba diving case study isn't easy to understand, but this simplified listing should make it clearer.

Listing 11.6 Definition of the jBPM transport in a Mule configuration file

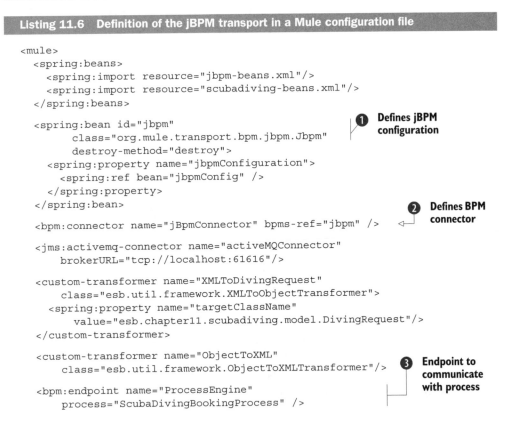

```
<mule>
  <spring:beans>
    <spring:import resource="jbpm-beans.xml"/>
    <spring:import resource="scubadiving-beans.xml"/>
  </spring:beans>

  <spring:bean id="jbpm"                                      ❶ Defines jBPM
        class="org.mule.transport.bpm.jbpm.Jbpm"                configuration
        destroy-method="destroy">
    <spring:property name="jbpmConfiguration">
      <spring:ref bean="jbpmConfig" />
    </spring:property>
  </spring:bean>
                                                             ❷ Defines BPM
  <bpm:connector name="jBpmConnector" bpms-ref="jbpm" />  ◁     connector

  <jms:activemq-connector name="activeMQConnector"
      brokerURL="tcp://localhost:61616"/>

  <custom-transformer name="XMLToDivingRequest"
      class="esb.util.framework.XMLToObjectTransformer">
    <spring:property name="targetClassName"
        value="esb.chapter11.scubadiving.model.DivingRequest"/>
  </custom-transformer>

  <custom-transformer name="ObjectToXML"                    ❸ Endpoint to
      class="esb.util.framework.ObjectToXMLTransformer"/>       communicate
                                                                with process
  <bpm:endpoint name="ProcessEngine"
      process="ScubaDivingBookingProcess" />
```

```
<jms:endpoint name="ScubaDivingRequest" queue="process.start"/>
<vm:endpoint name="SharkDivingIn" path="sharkdiving.in"/>
<vm:endpoint name="DivingResponse" path="diving.response"/>
<jms:endpoint name="ScubaDivingBooking" queue="process.end"/>

<model name="ScubaDivingModel">
  <service name="ToBPMS">
    <inbound>
      <inbound-endpoint ref="ScubaDivingRequest"/>
      <inbound-endpoint ref="DivingResponse"/>
    </inbound>
    <outbound>
      <filtering-router>
        <outbound-endpoint ref="ProcessEngine"
            synchronous="false" />
      </filtering-router>
    </outbound>
  </service>
  <service name="FromBPMS">
    <inbound>
      <inbound-endpoint ref="ProcessEngine"/>
    </inbound>
    <outbound>
      <bpm:outbound-router>
        <outbound-endpoint ref="SharkDivingIn"/>
        <outbound-endpoint ref="ScubaDivingBooking"/>
      </bpm:outbound -router>
    </outbound>
  </service>
  <service name="SharkDivingAgency">
    <inbound>
      <inbound-endpoint ref="SharkDivingIn">
        <transformer ref="XMLToDivingRequest"/>
      </inbound-endpoint>
    </inbound>
    <component>
      <spring-object bean="sharkDivingService"/>
    </component>
    <outbound>
      <outbound-pass-through-router>
        <outbound-endpoint ref="DivingResponse">
          <transformer ref="ObjectToXML"/>
        </outbound-endpoint>
      </outbound-pass-through-router>
    </outbound>
  </service>
</model>
</mule>
```

④ JMS endpoint that starts process

⑤ Calls process instance

⑥ Calls shark diving agency service

Listing 11.6 shows a simplified version of the Mule configuration for the scuba diving case study to make it easier to understand. Based on this discussion, you'll be able to understand the full Mule configuration that is part of this book's source distribution.

To be able to communicate with the process definitions and instances of jBPM from the Mule services, you must define a BPM connector **②**. And because the BPM connector is a common entrance to different process engines, you have to configure the bpms-ref attribute. Note that at the time of writing, Mule only provides a BPM connector implementation for jBPM.

The jBPM configuration is defined with a Spring bean that uses the Jbpm class of the jBPM transport to instantiate the jBPM connector ❶. The only property of the Jbpm bean definition is the jBPM configuration, which is defined in a separate Spring bean file jbpm-beans.xml; this file is imported at the top of the Mule configuration. We don't discuss this configuration in this book because this jBPM definition is too detailed and configures the Hibernate and the jBPM process angine settings. With this configuration, the jBPM container is instantiated when Mule is started.

Now that you have the jBPM transport connector configured, you can define an endpoint you can use to communicate with a jBPM process ❸. With the bpm prefix, the endpoint is configured to use the defined jBPM connector. The remainder of the endpoint address configures the process name of the process definition you want to communicate with—in this case, ScubaDivingBookingProcess.

Because you have incoming and outgoing messages for the scuba diving process instances, you define ToBPMS and FromBPMS services. ToBPMS defines all the messages sent to the scuba diving process instance, such as the initial request message ❹. When a JMS message arrives at this queue, the jBPM connector ❺ notices that no process instance is running for this message because no correlation identifier is present. The connector then starts up a process instance for the scuba diving process definition, and this message is sent to the first state in the created process instance. The Diving-Response endpoint is an example of an endpoint that communicates only with running scuba diving process instances, because this endpoint is used later in the process.

In the FromBPMS service, you see that the ProcessEngine endpoint is configured as the inbound endpoint. When you want to invoke a service via Mule from the process definition in jBPM, you can configure one of the outbound endpoints names ❻ as a target. Listing 11.6 only shows the endpoint for the shark diving agency, but the full implementation also configures the other diving agency services, the lunch service, the taxi service, and the final booking response endpoint.

CONFIGURING ACTION HANDLERS

To get a better overview of the scuba diving process implementation, let's look at the process configuration for one of the message exchanges. We focus on the invocation of the shark diving agency from the scuba diving process definition. You already saw in listing 11.6 how to configure the SharkDivingIn and DivingResponse endpoints; now, listing 11.7 shows how you can use these endpoint definitions in the jBPM process definition.

> **Listing 11.7 Snippet of the scuba diving process using action handlers**

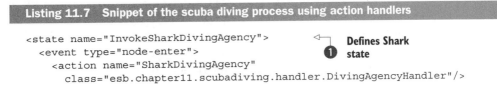

```
<state name="InvokeSharkDivingAgency">
  <event type="node-enter">
    <action name="SharkDivingAgency"
      class="esb.chapter11.scubadiving.handler.DivingAgencyHandler"/>
```

Defines Shark ❶ state

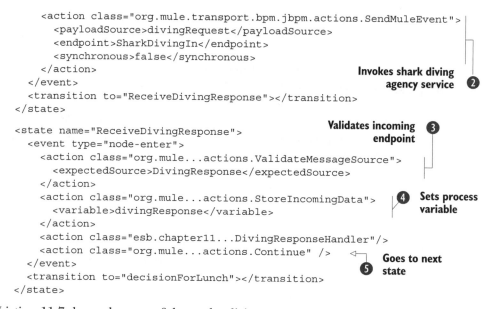

```
    <action class="org.mule.transport.bpm.jbpm.actions.SendMuleEvent">
      <payloadSource>divingRequest</payloadSource>
      <endpoint>SharkDivingIn</endpoint>
      <synchronous>false</synchronous>
    </action>
  </event>
  <transition to="ReceiveDivingResponse"></transition>
</state>

<state name="ReceiveDivingResponse">
  <event type="node-enter">
    <action class="org.mule...actions.ValidateMessageSource">
      <expectedSource>DivingResponse</expectedSource>
    </action>
    <action class="org.mule...actions.StoreIncomingData">
      <variable>divingResponse</variable>
    </action>
    <action class="esb.chapter11...DivingResponseHandler"/>
    <action class="org.mule...actions.Continue" />
  </event>
  <transition to="decisionForLunch"></transition>
</state>
```

Invokes shark diving agency service ❷

Validates incoming endpoint ❸

Sets process variable ❹

Goes to next state ❺

Listing 11.7 shows the part of the scuba diving process definition where the shark diving agency service is invoked and the response is handled. This snippet of the process definition starts with the declaration of the InvokeSharkDivingAgency state ❶. This state is triggered when the incoming booking request message consists of a diving interest element value of Sharks.

When the InvokeSharkDivingAgency state is activated by the jBPM process engine, the node-enter event is triggered. When the node-enter event occurs, two action classes are executed: DivingAgencyHandler is an ActionHandler interface implementation that creates the request message you want to send to the shark diving agency service, and SendMuleEvent sends a message to the Mule ESB ❷. This class is part of the jBPM connector provided by Mule; it expects an endpoint and a payload configuration. The SharkDivingIn endpoint that you define here corresponds with the outbound endpoint in the FromBPMS service from listing 11.6. And the payload source divingRequest relates to the process variable set in DivingAgencyHandler.

After the divingRequest variable is sent to Mule's SharkDivingIn endpoint, the scuba diving process remains in the InvokeSharkDvingAgency state. But when the shark diving agency service responds with a diving booking message in the DivingResponse endpoint, the scuba diving process is triggered again. This means the process state transitions to ReceiveDivingResponse.

When the node-enter event of the ReceiveDivingResponse state is triggered, four action classes are executed. The first, ValidateMessageSource, checks the inbound endpoint name where the incoming message arrives at the process instance ❸. This action handler is also part of the jBPM transport connector and checks whether the source indbound endpoint of the incoming message is equal to DivingResponse. When the endpoint-name check is valid, the payload of the incoming message is stored in the process variable `divingResponse` ❹. The `DivingResponseHandler` then uses the `divingResponse` variable to set the corresponding values for the process booking result variable `bookingResponse`.

The last action handler is also a class provided by Mule's jBPM transport. The `Continue` class does nothing more than instruct the process engine to transition the process instance to the next state ❺. In this case, this means the process instance transitions to the `decisionForLunch` state. Note that in the previous state, `Invoke-SharkDivingAgency`, the state transition is triggered not by an action handler but by receiving the diving response message. Because you don't expect a response message to arrive to transition the process instance for the `ReceiveDivingResponse` state, you automatically transition the state by using this `Continue` action handler.

We've discussed the details of integrating the jBPM process engine with Mule in this section. In addition to configuring jBPM in the Mule configuration, you now know how to invoke message flows in Mule from the jPDL process definition. In the next section, we look at the jDPL process definition for the scuba diving case study.

DESIGNING THE SCUBA DIVING PROCESS WITH jPDL

Now that we've discussed the integration between jBPM and Mule, let's look at the process definition for the scuba diving booking process. You already saw some of the process elements in figure 11.2, which focused on the communication between the jBPM process and the Mule message flows. In addition to the states that invoke services on the Mule ESB, you also need conditional logic. For example, you need to invoke the correct diving agency based on the hotel guest's diving interest.

To design a process definition with jPDL, you don't have to hand-code the XML definition as in listing 11.7. The jBPM project provides a jPDL Eclipse plug-in, which offers a graphical environment where you can drag and drop and configure the process elements into a process definition. To install the jPDL designer, first download the full jBPM jPDL suite from the jBPM website (http://labs.jboss.com/jbossjbpm). The suite contains the Eclipse plug-in as well as a JBoss server to run the jBPM container for jPDL processes. After you've unpacked the jDPL suite distribution, copy the contents of the designer/eclipse directory to your Eclipse installation directory. When you start up Eclipse, the jPDL designer will be available without any additional installation.

Figure 11.13 shows the whole process definition as designed with the jPDL designer.

Like every other process definition, the scuba diving booking process defines start and end states. They are the default starting and ending points for a process definition with jPDL. The first element that implements logic is the `ReceiveRequest` state, which handles the booking request message. The action handlers defined for this state are similar to the ones you saw in listing 11.7. Note that these action handlers can only be found by opening the resources/chapter11/jbpm/scuba-process.xml file in Eclipse with the jPDL designer installed. First the endpoint of the arriving message is checked, then the incoming message is stored as the booking-process variable, and finally the state of the process instance is forced to transition with the `Continue` action handler to the `decisionForDivingSchool` decision node.

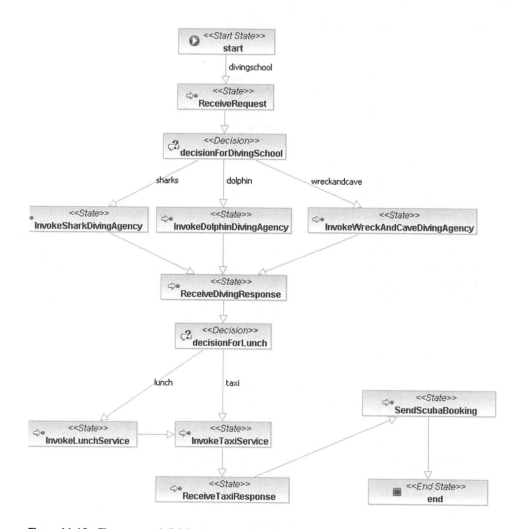

Figure 11.13   The process definition for the scuba diving booking process as designed with the jPDL Eclipse plug-in, which is provided by the jBPM project

Based on the hotel guest's interest, one of the diving agencies is invoked to book a scuba diving trip. Note that you set a booking variable in the process context in the `ReceiveRequest` state, which consists of the booking request that you can use to make this decision. With the `decision` element, you can set conditions on the transitions leaving the decision. To make it easy for the process developer, the jPDL designer of jBPM provides a properties view on a transition to set the condition. When you click the `wreckandcave` transition, you see a properties view similar to the one shown in figure 11.14.

On the Condition tab, you can set the condition type to Script and fill in the condition logic for the transition. Note that the decision is implemented with a structure

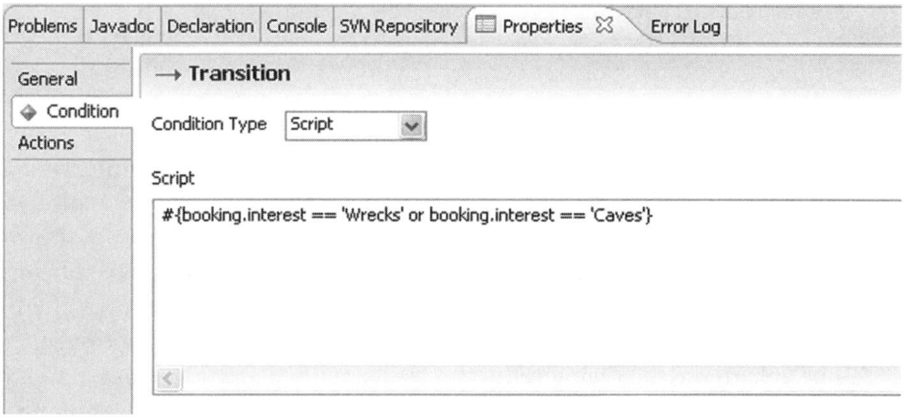

Figure 11.14　The properties view of a transition leaving a decision node. This example shows a script expression that checks whether the diving interest is equal to Wrecks or Caves. If the expression evaluates to `true`, then this transition is executed.

similar to the JSP expression language. The main difference is that the decision notation uses a #{..} structure, instead of the ${..} structure of the JSP expression language. The condition shown in figure 11.14 evaluates the interest attribute of the booking variable to see if its value equals Wrecks or Caves. You use a similar expression for the conditions of the shark and dolphin transitions that leave the decision-ForDivingSchool node (see figure 11.13). For the shark transition, the expression is #{booking.interest == 'Sharks'}, and for the dolphin transition it's #{booking.interest == 'Dolphins'}.

The decision node makes sure the scuba diving booking request is forwarded to the correct diving agency state. Three diving agency state nodes are included in the scuba diving process definition; you saw the action handlers for the InvokeSharkDiving-Agency state in listing 11.7. But we didn't discuss the custom action handler that fills and sets the request message process variable. Listing 11.8 shows the implementation of the DivingAgencyHandler.

Listing 11.8　`DivingAgencyHandler` implementation that sets the request message

```
public class DivingAgencyHandler implements ActionHandler {

    public void execute(ExecutionContext execContext) throws Exception {
        ScubaDivingRequest bookingRequest =
            (ScubaDivingRequest) execContext
                .getContextInstance()
                    .getVariable("booking");
        DivingRequest divingRequest = new DivingRequest();
        divingRequest.setHotelName("SleepingBeauty");
        divingRequest.setBookingName(bookingRequest.getGuestName());
        divingRequest.setNumberOfDivers(
            bookingRequest.getNumberOfDivers());
        divingRequest.setRequestDate(bookingRequest.getRequestDate());
```

❶ Retrieves booking variable

```
      execContext.getContextInstance().setVariable(
          "divingRequest", JiBXUtil.marshall(
              divingRequest));
  }
}
```
❷ **Sets diving
request in
XML**

The `DivingAgencyHandler` class implements the `ActionHandler` interface of jBPM,
because that's a requirement to be able to attach a handler implementation to a state.
The information needed in the request message to the diving agencies is provided by
the hotel guest's booking request, so first the booking object is retrieved from the process context **❶**. With the `ScubaDivingRequest` instance, you can copy the necessary
information from the booking request to the scuba diving request message.

To be able to use the diving request message in the `SendMuleEvent` action handler,
you must set the object in the process context **❷**. Because the communication
between the jBPM container and the Mule ESB is implemented with XML messages,
you use JiBX to serialize the request message to XML. Note that it's not necessary to
use XML messages here; it's an implementation decision. You also could use serializ-
able Java objects. But to have a clear distinction between the process engine and the
ESB, XML may be a good choice.

In listing 11.7, you saw the XML configuration of the `InvokeSharkDivingAgency`
state. This XML configuration provides a good overview of the events and action handlers configured for that state node. But with the jPDL designer, you don't have to
code this XML configuration yourself. The action handlers can be configured in the
properties view of the state node; for example, figure 11.15 shows the configuration
for the `InvokeSharkDivingAgency` state node.

The action handlers shown in figure 11.15 correspond with the XML configuration
from listing 11.7. First the `DivingAgencyHandler` action handler is executed, which
sets the diving request message; then, the `SendMuleEvent` action handler sends the
diving request to the Mule ESB. In this case, the actions are implemented with handler
classes, but an expression handler type option is also available. You can use the expression handler type for simple logic, like assigning a variable value.

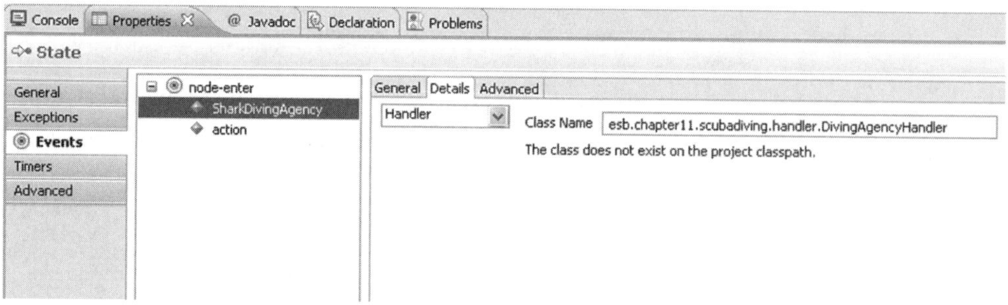

Figure 11.15 The properties view of the `InvokeSharkDivingAgency` state, which shows the
configuration of the action handlers executed for this state

The next part of the scuba diving booking process is a decision that determines whether the hotel guest requested lunch. Based on the outcome of this decision, the lunch handler is invoked or not. You can configure the lunch decision node like the decision example shown in figure 11.14. In the booking request, you use a lunch-included attribute to determine whether a lunch is requested. The decision is configured with the expression #{booking.lunchIncluded == true}. The implementation of the lunch handler is similar to the diving agency handlers, so we don't look at the details here. The code is included in the source distribution of this book.

The final part of the process definition as shown in figure 11.13 is the taxi node. Just like the diving agency nodes and the lunch node, the taxi node uses a number of handler classes to communicate with the taxi service via the Mule environment. For details about the taxi-handler class implementation, see the book's source distribution. The end state completes the scuba diving booking process definition.

We haven't discussed every part of the process implementation, but you're already familiar with the remainder, which includes the Mule configuration for the Spring bean invocation of the diving agencies and the lunch and taxi service. Because the full implementation code is available in the book's source distribution, we don't show listings of every part of the solution.

TESTING THE JBPM SCUBA DIVING PROCESS

The next step is to test the scuba diving process with the jBPM container and the Mule ESB. To use the jBPM transport provided by Mule, you have to deploy the process definition as part of the Mule message flow. Remember that you configured a jBPM connector as part of the Mule configuration in listing 11.6. With this configuration, the jBPM container will run in the same virtual machine as the Mule ESB container. Don't forget to start ActiveMQ before you start Mule.

The testing procedure for the scuba diving process isn't that different from previous examples. You can use the Swing test client to trigger the scuba diving process as a simulation of the hotel reception application. You can also use the unit test Scuba-DivingTest to trigger the process. But first, you must deploy the message flow deliverable to the Mule distribution by executing the scubadiving Ant target in the Ant build script available in the resources/chapter11 directory. This constructs a jar file that contains the Mule configuration as well as the jBPM process definition and starts the Mule container. When the Mule container is started, you can use the Swing test client to send the diving-request message.

The diving request message triggers the Mule message flow and the scuba diving process. Looking at the log output in the Mule command dialog, you see the execution of the process definition. Eventually, the booking response message of the scuba diving process is received in the Swing test client, which means the process has run successfully.

This is a good time to practice with the process definition of the scuba diving process. Try to change the process flow or add new action handlers to the process definition; doing so will help you to better understand how to use jBPM with Mule.

When you're ready, the next section contains a detailed description of the Apache ODE implementation. For Apache ODE, we look at an alternative process definition language, WS-BPEL, which is considered to be the industry standard for defining processes.

11.5 Implementing a process engine with Apache ODE and WS-BPEL

Implementing a process engine that can be integrated with ServiceMix is just as easy as integrating jBPM with Mule. The main difference is that ServiceMix implements the JBI specification and therefore provides a pluggable container for every process engine that can be deployed as a JBI service engine. The Apache ODE project provides such a JBI service engine for a WS-BPEL 2.0–compliant process engine.

In this section, we focus on implementing the scuba diving booking process with Apache ODE and WS-BPEL. First, we introduce the WS-BPEL specification for readers who aren't familiar with this specification. Then, we examine the implementation of the scuba diving process in WS-BPEL.

11.5.1 Orchestrating services with WS-BPEL

The WS-BPEL 2.0 specification is standardized by OASIS and reached the OASIS standard predicate in April 2007. WS-BPEL is a process definition language that is heavily based on XML standards like WSDL 1.1, XML Schema 1.0, and XPath 1.0. It's no surprise that the definition language is also specified in XML. As a process developer or designer, you're mainly interested in the WS-BPEL elements that you can use to define your processes. Figure 11.16 provides an overview of the WS-BPEL language constructs, with screenshots from the Eclipse BPEL designer we discuss later in this section.

As you can see, more process elements are available than in the jPDL language. jPDL only provides elementary process constructs like state and transition; the rest of the functionality can be implemented with handler classes. With WS-BPEL, you also have standard elements to validate messages and to assign message values to variables and vice versa.

Most of the process element names speak for themselves, but let's discuss the main elements in more detail. Every process definition needs to start with an element that receives a message. In most cases this is the Receive element, but when you need more

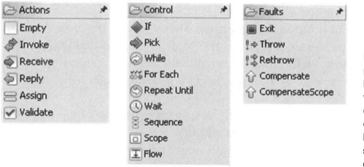

Figure 11.16 The primary WS-BPEL 2.0 language constructs, which you can use to define processes. These elementary elements can be nested within the sequence and flow control elements.

flexibility to distinguish between different types of incoming messages, you can also use the `Pick` element. The `Pick` element is able to receive messages from different parties. Another common construct is the `Reply` element, which sends a response message to the service that sent the message that started the process via the `Receive` element.

The best way to understand how to define a process with WS-BPEL is to look at a hello world example. This example uses the Eclipse BPEL designer plug-in, which is provided by the Eclipse project. You can install the plug-in by using the Eclipse BPEL project's update site, as described at http://download.eclipse.org/technology/bpel/update-site/. The installation procedure installs all the plug-ins and frameworks you need to run the BPEL designer plug-in from your Eclipse environment. The hello world example that we developed with this plug-in is shown in figure 11.17.

Figure 11.17 shows a `receiveInput` element of type `Receive`, which expects a message with only one string element. The interface of the `Receive` element is defined by the client-partner link shown at right. A partner link is linked to a WSDL definition—in particular, to the port type of a WSDL definition. A partner link has a clearly defined interface, with an incoming message and an optional response message. In addition to the interface definition, a partner link also specifies the role it plays for the process. The role can be a process role, which means an external partner sends a message to the process; or a partner role, which means the process invokes an external service partner. Remember that partner links are the way to define the interaction between the process and external services. Figure 11.18 shows the properties view of the client partner link.

You define two things for the client partner link: the role and the port type of a WSDL interface. In this case, you have an interface of an incoming and outgoing String message, just as you would expect for a hello world example. For the `receiveInput`

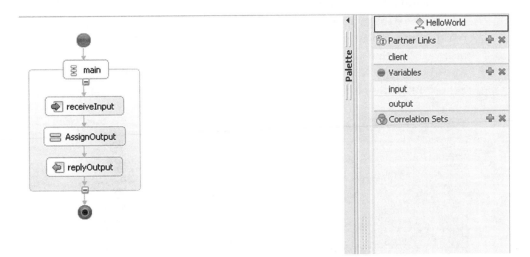

Figure 11.17   A hello world process, designed with the BPEL designer plug-in of the Eclipse BPEL project. The process copies the name of the incoming message to the response message with the prefix *hello*.

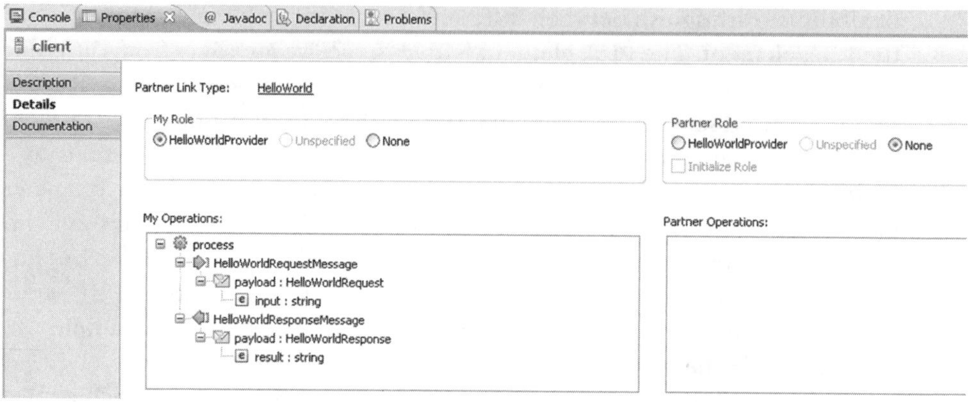

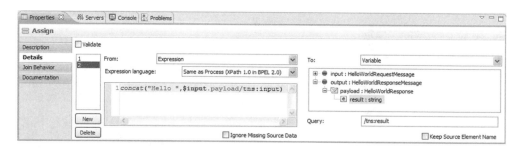

Figure 11.18   The properties view of the client-partner link defined as part of the hello world process definition. Notice that the role defines that an external partner will invoke the process.

activity in the hello world process, you configure the client partner link, the operation that is used (this can only be process for this interface), and the process variable input where you store the incoming message. When a `String` message arrives at this hello world process, the value is assigned to the input variable.

The next activity in the hello world process is the `assignOutput` element, which uses the `Assign` construct. With the `Assign` activity you can set a specific value for a variable and copy values from one variable to another. In this example, you want to copy the value of the input variable to the output variable and add the prefix *hello*. With the Eclipse BPEL designer, you can configure this functionality in the properties view of the `Assign` activity, as shown in figure 11.19.

In Figure 11.19, you can see that the output variable is presented in a tree structure in the `Assign` activity's properties view. In this case, you have a simple message, but this tree structure can become complex. This is an easy way to specify an element of a variable that you want to copy. On the `From` side of the `assign` statement, you can also use an XPath expression to retrieve a specific element of a variable. The Eclipse BPEL designer even provides code completion for the definition of the XPath

Figure 11.19   The properties view of the `Assign` activity that is used in the hello world process. In this example, you copy the input variable to the output variable with a *hello* prefix by using an XPath expression.

expression. With the $ prefix, you can retrieve the input variable and define the rest of the XPath expression.

The last part of the hello world process is the `Reply` activity, which also uses the client partner link, just as you saw with the `Receive` activity. The `Reply` activity also uses the process operation and is configured to return the output variable.

For now, this should provide enough background for you to be able to implement the scuba diving process case study. Let's not wait any longer and jump into the implementation of the case study with Apache ODE and ServiceMix.

11.5.2 *Implementing the case study with Apache ODE and ServiceMix*

As we stated earlier, Apache ODE provides a WS-BPEL 2.0–compliant process engine that can also be deployed as a JBI Service Engine on ServiceMix. The other deployment platform that Apache ODE supports is Axis2; it can also be deployed on application servers like Tomcat. In this section, we focus on the JBI service engine distributable of Apache ODE, because we want to have integration with the ServiceMix container.

The only thing you need to do to deploy the Apache ODE Service Engine in the ServiceMix container is to copy the ode-jbi-1.2.zip file from the libraries/apache-ode-jbi-1.2 directory, created by the setup script described in chapter 3, to the hotdeploy directory of the ServiceMix distribution, esb/apache-servicemix-3.2.1.

CHOOSING THE JBI COMPONENTS FOR THE SCUBA DIVING CASE STUDY

Before we look at the implementation of the scuba diving process, let's think about the different JBI components required for this solution and the message exchanges you need to implement. First, you must be able to send a scuba diving request message to the ServiceMix container from the hotel reception application. In the Mule implementation, you used JMS to provide asynchronous messaging capabilities for this message exchange; let's use the JMS binding component for the ServiceMix example.

The scuba diving process needs an in-out message exchange, because it sends a reply back to the requesting service. You need to add a pipeline that converts the JMS consumer's `InOnly` message exchange into an in-out message exchange for the BPEL process. The last thing you have to decide is how to provide connectivity to the diving agency, lunch service, and taxi service Spring beans. You defined JiBX mappings in section 11.3, so the easiest way to communicate with the Spring beans is to use the Bean Service Engine. Another option would be to use the JSR181 Service Engine, but this component uses its own marshaling and unmarshaling implementation; you use the ServiceMix Bean component for this example. Figure 11.20 provides an overview of the JBI components for the scuba diving process case study.

We've discussed most of the components shown in figure 11.20. Note that `divingAgencyService` represents the three Spring beans that implement the diving agencies. Some of the component implementations need no explanation, because you've used them in other examples. `ScubaDivingProcess` is the central component for this case study implementation, and we look at this implementation first.

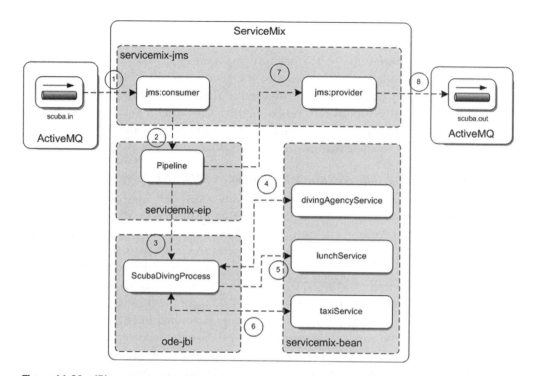

Figure 11.20   JBI components needed to implement the scuba diving process case study. This design diagram also shows the interaction and part of the component implementation.

DESIGNING THE SCUBA DIVING PROCESS WITH WS-BPEL

The first step in designing the scuba diving process with the Eclipse BPEL Designer is to define a WSDL interface for the BPEL process. In section 11.3, we defined the request and response messages for the process, so this shouldn't be a difficult exercise. With the Eclipse Web Tools Project (WTP) distribution, you have a fancy WSDL editor available, so you don't have to code the WSDL definition. Figure 11.21 shows the WSDL interface of the scuba diving process.

Figure 11.21 shows the input and output messages for the scuba diving process and a detailed view of the ScubaDivingRequest input message. In addition to the process interface, you also need to define the WSDL interfaces for the invocation of the diving agency and the lunch and taxi services. Luckily, you defined all the message definitions in section 11.3; you just have to create three additional WSDL interfaces that correspond with these message definitions.

Now that you've defined the WSDL interfaces for the scuba diving process, you can design the WS-BPEL process. In the hello world example, you saw the Eclipse BPEL Designer, which you can use to design the WS-BPEL process. Figure 11.22 shows the WS-BPEL process.

Figure 11.22 shows the complete WS-BPEL design for the scuba diving process, including the partner links and variables. You can look at the WS-BPEL scuba diving

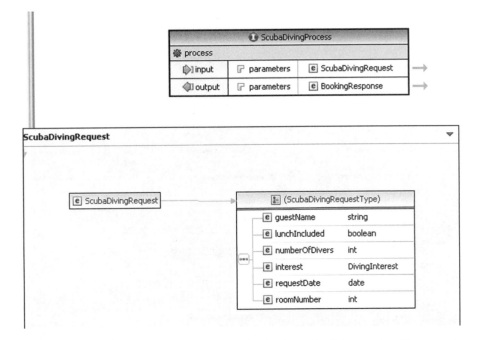

Figure 11.21 The WSDL interface you need to define for the scuba diving process. The message definition corresponds to the message design from section 11.3.

process in Eclipse (with the Eclipse BPEL plug-in installed) by opening the resources/ chapter11/scubadiving-bpel/resources/ScubaDivingProcess.bpel file. The primary part of the process implementation is a sequence of invocations that are executed. Every invocation needs its own set of variables for the input and output messages, and this is reflected in the names of the variables. You define partner links for every target service and for the process itself. Although most of the WS-BPEL implementation is self-explanatory, we need to discuss two parts.

First, we need to mention the pitfall of variable initialization required by the Apache ODE process engine. For example, when you want to invoke the shark diving agency service with the scubaDivingRequest variable, you must initialize the variable before you can copy values to its elements. Figure 11.23 shows the properties view of the AssignDivingValues activity where you initialize the scubaDivingRequest variable.

You have to initialize the scubaDivingRequest variable with a fixed string value that represents an empty diving-request message. After you've initialized the variable, you can copy values to it with an Assign activity.

Second, we need to discuss the implementation of the If element—for example, the CheckDivingPreference activity. The If activity is an if-elseif-else language construct that can be used to execute a different set of activities based on a condition. In the example, you need to determine the hotel guest's diving interest in order to invoke the correct diving agency. In the properties view of the if, elseif, and else

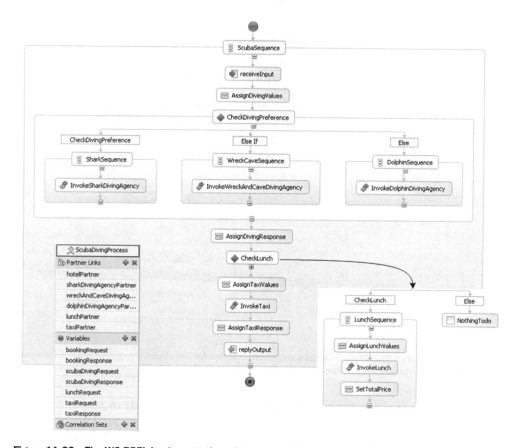

Figure 11.22   The WS-BPEL implementation of the scuba diving process in the Eclipse BPEL Designer. The WS-BPEL process diagram includes a smaller diagram of the partner links and variables.

transitions of the CheckDivingPreference activity, you can use XPath expressions to define the conditions. Figure 11.24 shows the XPath expression for the shark diving agency execution path.

The XPath expression shown in figure 11.24 is similar to the XPath expression in the Assign activity of the hello world example. The interest element is selected with an XPath expression, and the value is compared to the shark literal.

Figure 11.23   An example of the initialization of the scubaDivingRequest variable in the AssignDivingValues activity of the scuba diving process

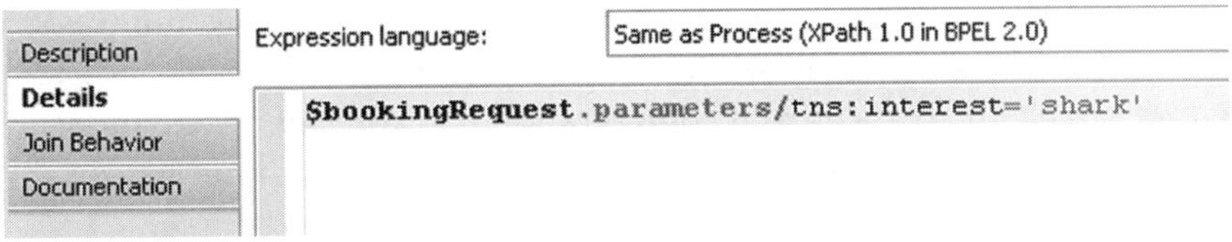

Figure 11.24   The definition of a condition for an `If` activity. This example checks whether the diving interest equals `shark`, to determine the correct diving agency to invoke.

With these additions, the process definition is straightforward and not much different from the hello world example. In addition to the WSDL interfaces and the BPEL process, you need to define the integration configuration with the ServiceMix container. This configuration file is named deploy.xml and defines the relationship between the partner links of the process and the ServiceMix services. The configuration of deploy.xml for the scuba diving case study is shown in listing 11.9.

Listing 11.9   Configuration to integrate Apache Ode with ServiceMix

```
<deploy xmlns="http://www.apache.org/ode/schemas/dd/2007/03"       ❶ Defines
        xmlns:esb="http://esbinaction.com/scubadiving">               process
                                                                      name
  <process name="esb:ScubaDivingProcess">
    <active>true</active>
    <provide partnerLink="hotelPartner">                          ❷ Configures the
      <service name="esb:ScubaDivingService"                         process JBI service
              port="ScubaDivingProcess"/>
    </provide>
    <invoke partnerLink="sharkDivingAgencyPartner">
      <service name="esb:sharkService" port="endpoint" />
    </invoke>
    <invoke partnerLink="wreckAndCaveDivingAgencyPartner">
      <service name="esb:wreckAndCaveService" port="endpoint" />
    </invoke>
    <invoke partnerLink="dolphinDivingAgencyPartner">            ❸ Invokes
      <service name="esb:dolphinService" port="endpoint" />          dolphin
    </invoke>                                                        diving
    <invoke partnerLink="lunchPartner">                             agency
      <service name="esb:lunchService" port="endpoint" />
    </invoke>
    <invoke partnerLink="taxiPartner">
      <service name="esb:taxiService" port="endpoint" />
    </invoke>
  </process>
</deploy>
```

The deployment configuration file begins with the definition of the WS-BPEL process that you need to integrate with the ServiceMix services ❶. The process name Scuba-DivingProcess and the corresponding namespace are declared as part of the WS-BPEL process definition.

The remainder of the configuration defines the relationship between a partner link of the scuba diving process and the corresponding ServiceMix service name. The first relationship is made between the hotelPartner partner link and the ServiceMix service name that you use to invoke the process ❷. By setting ScubaDivingService as the target service in an xbean.xml configuration file, you can invoke the scuba diving process from a ServiceMix JBI component. This service name must be used by the EIP Service Engine to call the process.

The configuration for the pipeline has one pitfall, as shown in the following code snippet:

```
<eip:pipeline service="esb:scubaPipeline" endpoint="endpoint">
  <eip:transformer>
    <eip:exchange-target  service="esb:ScubaDivingService"
                          operation="process"/>
  </eip:transformer>
  <eip:target>
    <eip:exchange-target service="esb:scubaResponse" />
  </eip:target>
</eip:pipeline>
```

In addition to the service name, you must specify the operation that you want to invoke on the process interface. As you saw in figure 11.21, only one operation is specified on the process interface, and that is the process operation. This operation name is also used in the pipeline definition.

The other partner links to ServiceMix service mappings are invocations from the process to ServiceMix services. An example of such a mapping is the invocation of the dolphin diving agency ❸. In the xbean.xml configuration file of the Bean Service Engine, dolphinService is configured as a service with an endpoint named endpoint. Notice that the port attribute refers to this endpoint name. We've now discussed all the aspects of the scuba diving WS-BPEL process.

TESTING THE APACHE ODE SCUBA DIVING PROCESS

Now that you've implemented all the JBI components for the scuba diving case study, you can think about testing the solution. We didn't discuss all the JBI components, but you can find the remaining configurations in the book's ServiceMix source distribution. With the knowledge you've gained by reading the previous chapters, it will be easy to understand the component configurations we didn't discuss in detail. Take your time and look at the all the configurations before you proceed with the testing activity.

Testing the scuba diving case study isn't that different from the previous examples in this book, although you do have to make sure you've installed the Apache ODE JBI distribution to the ServiceMix container as described in the case study implementation. When the Apache ODE JBI component is installed, you can start up the Service-Mix container, and the Apache ODE process engine will be available for deploying WS-BPEL processes.

To deploy the scuba diving integration solution to the ServiceMix container, you have to run the Ant script provided in the resources/chapter11 directory of the Service-Mix source distribution. This Ant build script creates a service assembly that contains all the service units from figure 11.20. The Ant script also deploys the service assembly to the ServiceMix container.

Now, you can use the Swing test client (also provided in the code distribution) to send a scuba diving request message to the ServiceMix container. Eventually, you'll receive a response message from the process containing detailed information about the scuba diving booking, including the total price and the start and end times for your trip.

11.6 Summary

This chapter provided a lot of information about process engines in general and jBPM and Apache ODE specifically. Because these process engines can be integrated easily with Mule and ServiceMix, respectively, you have a powerful integration environment in your hands. You saw much of the functionality an ESB can provide in the previous chapters; with the addition of the process engine, you can support stateful process flows, which provide state management, service orchestration, and versioning out of the box.

jBPM and Apache ODE both provide support for WS-BPEL, and jBPM also supports jPDL to define processes. WS-BPEL has the advantage of being an OASIS standard; it's widely supported in commercial process-engine products and a number of open source process engines. Because WS-BPEL is based on XML standards like WSDL, XSD, and XPath, incoming and outgoing messages should be defined with XML. The integration with ServiceMix is natural, because this ESB is also dependent on XML.

jPDL has no dependency on XML; you can also use Java objects to implement the request and response messages. But jPDL isn't an industry standard and is only supported by the jBPM process engine. Because Mule also supports multiple message formats, with Java objects and XML messages as the most obvious choices, the integration with jBPM is seamless. When you're in a Java environment, jPDL can be an excellent choice because you don't have to marshal and unmarshal XML messages. But the main objective of this chapter was to show two examples of process engines, integrated with an ESB environment; you should decide for yourself which process engine fits your needs. In the case study implementations, you saw that both process engines provide excellent tool support and nice ESB integration functionality.

The end of this chapter also means the end of this book. We've given you a good overview of the functionality Mule and ServiceMix can provide, including great routing, transformation, connectivity, and process-engine support. We've shown you that Mule and ServiceMix are good counterparts for commercial ESB products and deserve to be included in your short list when you're choosing an ESB product for your organization. Open source projects are changing at a fast pace, so we advise you to keep our website (http://www.esbinaction.com) among your favorites; we'll provide updates for the book examples when new versions of Mule and ServiceMix (and other open source ESBs, like Apache Synapse and Spring Integration) arrive.

ServiceMix 4.0

The examples in this book are based on ServiceMix version 3.2.1, which is the latest production release at the time of writing. But a milestone of the next version of ServiceMix is already available: version 4.0. This version of ServiceMix is based on a new architecture and therefore has many changes compared to version 3.x. We chose to use ServiceMix 3.2.1 in this book because ServiceMix 4 wasn't yet available. With ServiceMix 4.0, it will only become easier for integration developers to use ServiceMix in your integration projects.

Let's look at the new architecture of ServiceMix 4.0 in the first section. After that, we show you an example of how you can use ServiceMix 4.

The new architecture of ServiceMix 4

The new ServiceMix architecture tries to simplify the classloading mechanism, the development of (JBI) components, and packaging of your developed integration logic. The foundation of ServiceMix 4 is an OSGi container, which takes care of classloading and deployment of new or changed components. OSGi also provides a packaging structure that ServiceMix can use.

Before we dive into the details of OSGi in the next section, let's look at the revised architecture, shown in figure A.1, as described on the ServiceMix 4 website (http://servicemix.apache.org).

Figure A.1 shows the ServiceMix 4 architecture from three different viewpoints. The technology view has probably changed the least since version 3.x, because JBI 1.0 is still supported and JMS, JAX-WS, and Spring are important implementation technologies for ServiceMix. But the direct support for EJB3 components is new, and potential support for SCA looks promising.

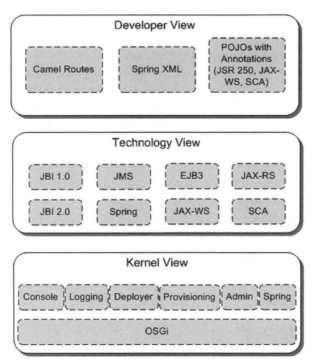

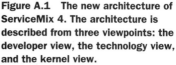

Figure A.1   The new architecture of ServiceMix 4. The architecture is described from three viewpoints: the developer view, the technology view, and the kernel view.

The developer view has changed quite a bit: The figure doesn't include service units and service assemblies, but only shows Camel routes, Spring XML configurations, and annotated POJOs. ServiceMix 4 provides the functionality to deploy a Spring XML configuration file or a Camel route configuration without any packaging required—you just copy the file to the ServiceMix container. But for more robust and enterprise-class deployments, ServiceMix 4 uses OSGi packages as its deployment model in addition to the (legacy) support for JBI 1.0 packaging with service assemblies.

The part that has changed the most is the kernel view. Let's look at this in some more detail.

A new project structure with Servicemix 4

Whereas ServiceMix 3.*x* consists of only one project and distribution, ServiceMix 4 consists of at least three projects:

- The *kernel* is an OSGi-based runtime that provides a lightweight container that enables the deployment of various bundles. The ServiceMix kernel provides functionality like hot deployment, dynamic configuration of property files, logging, and a security framework based on JAAS.
- *ServiceMix NMR* implements the Normalized Message Router based on Apache ActiveMQ and also provides the JBI 1.0 implementation. The ServiceMix NMR project provides a set of OSGi bundles that can be deployed on the ServiceMix

kernel. At the time of writing, you can deploy JBI components of ServiceMix 3 on the ServiceMix NMR, but the NMR doesn't yet fully implement the JBI specification. For example, using JMX for deployment and Ant tasks are missing.

- The ServiceMix *features* project provides a number of additional OSGi bundles, which can be deployed on the ServiceMix kernel. This project provides a distribution that includes the ServiceMix kernel and NMR. In this appendix, we use a milestone 2 SNAPSHOT version of the ServiceMix features project.

In addition to these three projects, the ServiceMix development team is preparing a restructuring of the entire ServiceMix project (including version 3.*x*). There are plans for each JBI component to be placed in a separate distribution, to allow a different release plan for every JBI component and, more important, to enable easy sharing of JBI components between ServiceMix 3 and 4.

The kernel is an essential part of ServiceMix 4: It provides important functionality like hot deployment and enables logging and security capabilities. As we've said, the foundation of the ServiceMix kernel is an OSGi container: Apache Felix. In the next section, we look at OSGi in more detail to help you understand this choice for the new architecture of ServiceMix 4.

A little background in OSGi

You may already have heard about the OSGi (an acronym of Open Services Gateway initiative) specification. OSGi is hot, and almost every self-respecting open source project is thinking about OSGi enablement, including ServiceMix. The article "OSGi for Beginners" by Joseph Ottinger, on theServerSide (http://www.theserverside.com/tt/articles/article.tss?l=OSGiforBeginners), gives a good, short explanation of OSGi:

> *OSGi is a framework for Java in which units of resources called bundles can be installed. Bundles can export services or run processes, and have their dependencies managed, such that a bundle can be expected to have its requirements managed by the container. Each bundle can also have its own internal classpath, so that it can serve as an independent unit, should that be desirable. All of this is standardized such that any valid OSGi bundle can theoretically be installed in any valid OSGi container.*

In essence, OSGi is a module system for Java. Modules are important as a solution to versioning and JAR dependencies. The OSGi specification describes a module system that can be used in a Java environment regardless of JEE version. In OSGi terminology, a module is called a *bundle*. A bundle is nothing more than a JAR with some extra meta information.

Let's implement a small OSGi bundle so you can see what we're talking about. A bundle typically implements a bundle activator interface named BundleActivator, which provides a hook into the lifecycle of an OSGi bundle. An overview of the OSGi bundle lifecycle is shown in figure A.2.

The OSGi bundle lifecycle is pretty much self-explanatory. When a new OSGi bundle is deployed to an OSGi container, its first state is always *installed*. Then, all

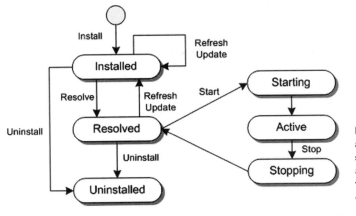

Figure A.2   The lifecycle of an OSGi bundle. The first state of an OSGi bundle is always *installed*, and from that state an OSGi bundle can eventually be started.

dependencies of the OSGi bundle are resolved by the OSGi container, and the bundle can be started. If necessary, an OSGi bundle can be stopped and uninstalled from the OSGi container.

Let's look at an example of a `BundleActivator` implementation class, which is invoked when the bundle is stopped and started:

```
public class SimpleActivator implements BundleActivator {

  public void start(BundleContext bc) {
    // do your bundle's startup logic
  }

  public void stop(BundleContext bc) {
    // shutdown your bundle
  }
}
```

As you can see, a `BundleActivator` interface isn't difficult to implement. The OSGi container calls the `start` method of the `BundleActivator` when all the dependencies have been resolved. It's now up to the bundle implementer to correctly start its service.

The `BundleActivator` also specifies a `stop` method. This method is called when you stop this bundle or want to uninstall the bundle. It's your job as bundle implementer to clean up the resources your bundle is using and make sure it shuts down neatly.

Getting started with ServiceMix 4

Now that you have a little background about ServiceMix 4 architecture and the OSGi specification, let's implement an example that shows some ServiceMix 4 functionality. The first step is to download ServiceMix 4.0 (we used a ServiceMix 4.0 M2 SNAPSHOT). You can also download the ServiceMix kernel and NMR separately, but for this example we use the ServiceMix 4.0 distribution, which includes both subprojects.

When you've extracted the distribution, start the ServiceMix container with the following script executed from the root directory:

```
bin\servicemix.bat (Windows)

bin/servicemix.sh (Unix/Linux)
```

When the ServiceMix 4 container starts, you see the following output in your console:

```
ServiceMix (1.0-m3)

Type 'help' for more information.
-------------------------------------------------
username@computer:/>
```

From this console, you can interact with the ServiceMix 4 container. The `help` command shows you the available commands. To show all the OSGi bundles installed in the ServiceMix container, you can use the command `osgi list`. By default, 81 OSGi bundles are installed and in the `active` state in the ServiceMix 4 container, including Spring and ServiceMix JBI bundles.

The JBI components that we describe and use in this book's examples, such as the JMS `binding` component and the `file binding` component, can also be deployed on the ServiceMix 4 container. Depending on the version you've downloaded, you may already have the JBI components installed and active. If you don't see the JMS and JBI components, execute the following OSGi commands to install them:

```
osgi install -s jbi:mvn:org.apache.servicemix/servicemix-shared-compat/
3.2.1/zip/installer
osgi install -s jbi:mvn:org.apache.servicemix/servicemix-jms/
3.2.1/zip/installer
osgi install -s jbi:mvn:org.apache.servicemix/servicemix-file/
3.2.1/zip/installer
```

The `jbi list` command lists all installed JBI components in the command console. With these JBI components installed, you can deploy any service assembly using the JMS and `file binding` components, as in the file or JMS queue example from chapter 6. You copy the service assembly file to the deploy directory of the ServiceMix distribution, and the integration logic is automatically deployed and started.

In addition to using service assemblies to deploy integration logic on the ServiceMix 4 container, you can also deploy an OSGi bundle. You can find OSGi bundle examples in the ServiceMix user guide (http://servicemix.apache.org/SMX4/users-guide.html).

Differences between
Mule 1.4.x and Mule 2.0.x

This appendix presents a high-level overview of the differences between Mule 1.4.*x* and Mule 2.0.*x*. If you want more information on this subject, the Mule site also provides information about what's new in Mule 2.0:

```
http://mule.mulesource.org/display/MULE2INTRO/Whats+New+in+Mule+2.0
```

We start with the biggest change, which is the way you configure Mule. If you're experienced with Mule 1.4, you probably know that Mule 1.4 used a DTD to validate the configuration and provide rudimentary code completion. In Mule 2.0, this is changed to an XSD-based configuration.

XSD-based configuration

With the XSD-based configuration, it's easy to create Mule configurations. You define in your XML header the schemas you wish to use, and you get automatic code completion in modern IDEs such as Eclipse, Netbeans, and IntelliJ's IDEA. Let's look more closely at this change in configuration. Listing B.1 shows an empty Mule 1.4.*x* configuration.

Listing B.1 Mule 1.4.*x*-based empty configuration file

```
<?xml version="1.0" encoding="UTF-8"?>
<!DOCTYPE mule-configuration PUBLIC
        "-//MuleSource //DTD mule-configuration XML V1.0//EN"
        "http://mule.mulesource.org/dtds/mule/mule-configuration.dtd">

<mule-configuration id="Mule_1.4.x_configuration" version="1.0">
</mule-configuration>
```

This configuration in Mule 1.4.*x* defines the DTD to use for this configuration file. The DTD contains all the descriptions of the elements you can use in the configuration. Although this provides some basic autocompletion, Mule 2.0.*x* has switched to using XSDs, which provide much more autocompletion functionality in the IDEs than the DTD does.

Let's look at the same empty configuration in Mule 2.0.*x*; see listing B.2.

Listing B.2   Mule 2.0.*x*-based empty configuration file

```
<?xml version="1.0" encoding="UTF-8"?>
<mule:mule xmlns="http://www.springframework.org/schema/beans"
  xmlns:xsi="http://www.w3.org/2001/XMLSchema-instance"
  xmlns:mule="http://www.mulesource.org/schema/mule/core/2.0"
  xsi:schemaLocation="
      http://www.springframework.org/schema/beans
      http://www.springframework.org/schema/beans/spring-beans-2.0.xsd
      http://www.mulesource.org/schema/mule/core/2.0
      http://www.mulesource.org/schema/mule/core/2.0/mule.xsd">
</mule:mule>
```

This XML file uses namespaces and references some external XSDs. These external XSDs contain all the information the IDE needs for autocompletion and which Mule 2.0.*x* uses internally to validate your configuration. Note that not all the elements are defined in a single file, as is the case with Mule 1.4.*x*; the Mule configuration is now split out over multiple XML schemas. For instance, file-specific elements are located in the http://www.mulesource.org/schema/mule/file/2.0/mule-file.xsd schema. For more information on these elements, see appendix D, where we list the most important schemas you can use to configure Mule 2.0.*x*.

Before we examine the configuration of the endpoints, let's quickly look deeper into the differences between a basic Mule 1.4.*x* configuration and a Mule 2.0.*x* configuration. In Mule 1.4, you configure services by using a `mule-descriptor`. Listing B.3 shows how to configure a service in Mule 1.4.

Listing B.3   Mule 1.4.*x* `mule-descriptor` configuration

```
<mule-descriptor name="simpleUMO"
    implementation="appendixB.SimpleComponent">

    <inbound-router>
       ..
    </inbound-router>
    <outbound-router>
       ..
    </outbound-router>
</mule-descriptor>
```

This listing contains the basic XML elements you use when you configure a `mule-descriptor` in Mule 1.4.*x*. You define the implementation class, an inbound router that contains `inbound-router` elements, and an outbound router that contains `outbound-router` elements. This is also changed in Mule 2.0.*x*; listing B.4 shows the same configuration, but using the Mule 2.0.*x* elements.

Listing B.4   Mule 2.0.*x* service configuration

```
<mule:service name="sample-service">
  <mule:inbound>
    ..
  </mule:inbound>
  <mule:component class="appendixB.SimpleComponent"/>
  <mule:outbound>
    ..
  </mule:outbound>
</mule:service>
```

The configuration for Mule 2.0.*x* is much the same as for Mule 1.4.*x*. All the elements from listing B.3 are still present—they've just been renamed. Another interesting thing to notice in listing B.4 is the sequence in which the elements are declared. In Mule 2.0.*x*, the elements are declared in the sequence in which a message is processed by this service. First the message is processed by the inbound element, then the message is processed by the component, and finally the message is processed by the outbound element.

Now that we've looked at the basic difference between the Mule 1.4.*x* configuration using a DTD and the Mule 2.0.*x* configuration using a number of XML schemas, let's examine the next big change: the way you can configure endpoints.

Transport-specific endpoints

In chapter 2, we explained how you can configure endpoints in Mule 2.0.*x*. We showed that you can use a specific endpoint URI to configure an endpoint or use the transport-specific endpoints. The transport-specific manner of endpoint configuration wasn't available in Mule 1.4.*x*, but it provides an easy way in Mule 2.0.*x* to configure endpoints, because it works with XSD-based code completion.

Changing from URI-based endpoints to the transport-specific endpoints isn't difficult, as we show in the next example. Let's start by looking at an SMTP endpoint that can be used to send mail using an SMTP server:

```
smtp://mule:pass@smtp.gmail.com?subject=HelloWorld&to=me@world.com
```

If you've worked with Mule 1.4.*x*, this will look familiar. Let's now look at this endpoint in Mule 2.0.*x*. It's configured in Mule's SMTP schema, which you can find here:

```
http://www.mulesource.org/schema/mule/smtp/2.0/mule-smtp.xsd
```

The previous endpoint now looks like this:

```
<stmp:outbound-endpoint
        user="mule"
        password="pass"
        host="smtp.gmail.com"
        subject="HelloWorld"
        to="me@world.com"/>
```

You specify the same endpoint but now use the SMTP-specific endpoint, which you can create using code completion. In Mule 2.0.*x*, transport-specific endpoints are provided for almost all the transports.

In addition to the XML configuration and endpoint changes, there are a couple of internal API changes that may affect you.

API changes

If you've written your own Mule 1.4.*x* components or extended the components provided by Mule 1.4.*x*, you'll have to rewrite them to work with Mule 2.0.*x*. The main reason is that the package names and some internal classes have been renamed or moved to different locations. The primary API changes are as follow:

- *Removed UMO prefix*—Many interfaces in Mule 1.4.*x* are prefixed with the UMO name. In Mule 2.0.*x*, this UMO prefix has been removed.
- *API moved to a different package*—In Mule 1.4.*x*, the API was mostly contained in the `org.mule.umo` package. In Mule 2.0.*x*, the API has been moved to the `org.mule.api` package.
- *Transport providers moved*—The name of the package where the providers are located has also been changed, from `org.mule.providers` to `org.mule.transport`.
- *General changes in API*—Internal API changes have been made to a number of classes.

These changes shouldn't be a reason not to switch to Mule 2.0.*x*. The issues that arise from them are usually easy to solve by changing to the new classes and interfaces.

Graphical tool support

You've seen quite a bit of XML configuration throughout the example implementations in this book. Open source products often lack graphical tool support for implementing functionality, but Mule and ServiceMix do provide graphical tool support, each with its own Eclipse-based implementation. In this appendix, we provide a short introduction to both these tools.

Graphical tool support with Mule IDE 2.0

The first step is to install Mule IDE 2.0 in your Eclipse environment. If you haven't already installed Eclipse 3.3.*x*, do so now. A good installation guide is available on the MuleSource website (http://www.mulesource.org/display/MULEIDE/Mule+IDE+2.0). Note that you have to deselect several parts of the EMF and GMF updates.

When you've installed all updates, including the Mule IDE 2.0 update, you're ready to begin modeling Mule configurations with Mule IDE 2.0. You can start a new Mule IDE 2.0 project by choosing File > New to start the New Project wizard, shown in figure C.1.

When you click the Next button in the New Project wizard, you can add a default Mule distribution. Click the Add button, and select the location of your Mule 2.0.2 distribution directory. When you've finished the New Project wizard, the libraries of the selected default Mule distribution are automatically added to your project's classpath. In addition, a conf directory is created automatically to host your Mule configuration files.

Click the conf directory and choose New > Other. Then, select Mule Configuration under the Mule directory, and a new Mule configuration is created. Eclipse automatically opens the Mule configuration canvas and palette, as shown in figure C.2.

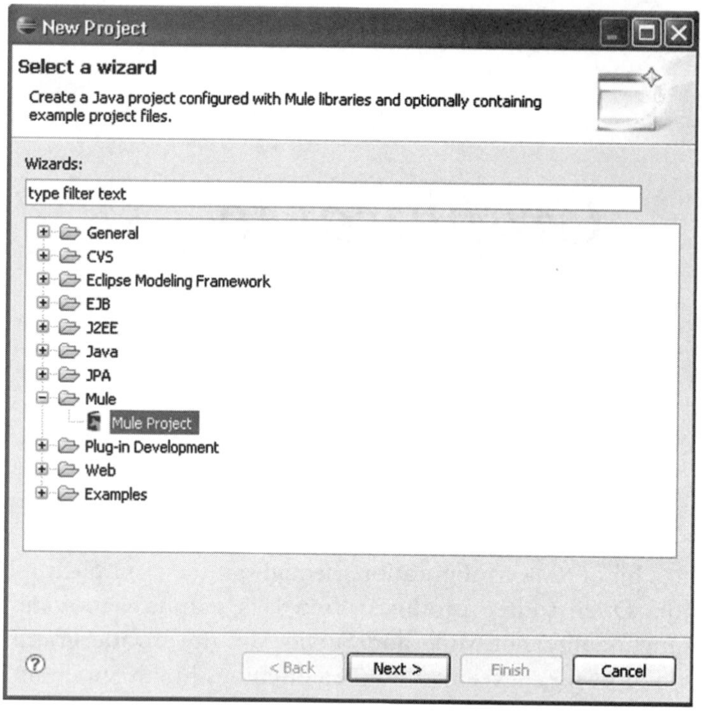

Figure C.1   The New Project wizard in Eclipse, showing the Mule Project wizard that's provided with the Mule IDE 2.0 Eclipse plug-in

The Mule configuration canvas and palette include familiar elements such as a component and an inbound and an outbound router. You can easily switch between the graphical view and the source code view of the Mule configuration by using the tabs at the bottom of the canvas.

Now, let's build a simple Mule service to show the look and feel of the Mule IDE. Follow these steps to design a hello world example:

1 Select Seda Service from the Services tab of the Mule IDE palette, click the Mule IDE canvas, and enter the name `HelloWorldService`. This translates to a normal Mule service definition, as in all of this book's Mule examples.

2 Select Java Component from the Components tab, and then click the component area of the Mule service you just created. A Java component is added to the service definition.

Enter `esb.appendixc.HelloComponent` in the Class property of the Eclipse properties view; this Java class returns a *hello* String with the input parameter name.

3 Switch to the Overview tab of the Mule IDE canvas to enable the JMS namespace. In the Namespace dialog box, select the JMS namespace.

4 To create a JMS ActiveMQ connector in the Overview tab, go to the Connectors window area and click Add. Choose the ActiveMQ connector at the top, and

name it `jmsConnector`. You've now added an ActiveMQ connector definition to your Mule configuration.

5 Switch back to the Services tab. You can now select a JMS inbound endpoint from the palette's Inbound tab. Click the JMS inbound endpoint, and then click the inbound area of the `HelloWorldService` in the canvas. In the Properties view of the JMS inbound endpoint, configure a JMS queue name, such as `hello.in`.

6 Complete the Outbound area of the Mule service. Add a pass-through router to the Outbound area from the Outbound palette, and then add a JMS outbound endpoint to this pass-through router.

You should now see a canvas similar to figure C.3.

Now, switch to the Source tab of the Mule IDE to look at the Mule configuration XML file. The XML configuration is similar to the configurations in this book's examples.

At the time of writing, the Mule IDE 2.0 is in its early stages, but you can see how easy it is to design a Mule configuration instead of typing XML yourself. The Mule IDE also provides support for deploying the Mule configuration on a Mule container. You can find more information on the Mule IDE website. But note that it's a work in progress—not everything will work as expected just yet.

Figure C.2 The Mule IDE configuration canvas and palette. The palette includes components and inbound and outbound routers, which are the fundamental elements of a Mule configuration.

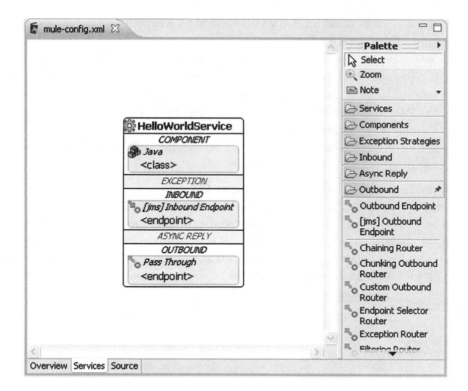

Figure C.3   Mule IDE canvas showing the hello world example you just created

Graphical tool support with the Enterprise Integration Designer

Graphical tool support for ServiceMix is part of the Eclipse SOA Tools Platform Project (Eclipse STP), in the Enterprise Integration Designer (EID) subproject. The EID plug-in is donated by Bull, the company that started the Cimero plug-in project to provide a visual tool to design JBI service assemblies for Apache ServiceMix and PEtALS. The current version of the EID plug-in adds generator support for Apache Camel distributions. For more information about the EID plug-in, see http://www.eclipse.org/stp/eid/index.php.

To download the EID plug-in, you can use the Eclipse software-update tool at the Eclipse STP update website: http://download.eclipse.org/stp/updates/ganymede. Choose to install the STP Enterprise Integration Designer Feature, and complete the installation wizard. Then, you can create a new Eclipse project and add an EID diagram by choosing New > Other. The resulting New dialog box looks similar to figure C.4.

Select Integration Patterns Diagram, and then choose ServiceMix (from the three options Camel, PEtALS, and ServiceMix) as the target ESB implementation and click the Next button. On the last screen of the New wizard, choose the filename of the

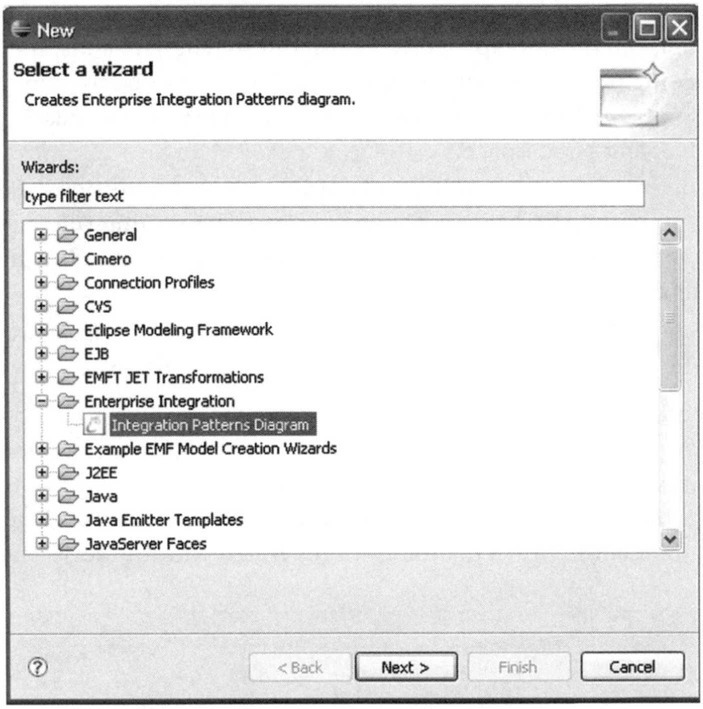

Figure C.4 The New wizard in Eclipse shows you how to create a new integration patterns diagram.

design diagram to be created, and click Finish. A canvas and a palette appear, as shown in figure C.5; you can use them to create a JBI service assembly for ServiceMix and PEtALS and a distribution for Apache Camel.

As you can see in figure C.5, you can use various integration functions of Service-Mix service engines and binding components to design an integration solution. Not all ServiceMix components are currently supported—for example, the Apache ODE service engine.

To demonstrate how to use the EID canvas and palette, let's work through a simple example. Follow these steps:

1 Click the JMS binding component in the palette, and then click the canvas. The JMS binding component appears on the canvas; you can configure it in the properties view.

   In the properties view, fill in the component name that will be used as the service unit name. In the Exclusive Properties – Consumer Property area, you can set many more properties. Be sure to complete at least the Endpoint, target-Service, targetEndpoint, destinationName, Service – Value, and Exclusive Properties, and the connectionFactory properties.

2 To implement some content-based routing logic, click Content-based-router in the palette, and then click the canvas. Using the palette's Connection element, you can connect the JMS consumer with the content-based router.

3 To configure the content-based router, you need to fill in quite a few properties. Enter the Component Name property, as you did for the JMS consumer. In the Namespace-context property, set an optional namespace to be used in the routing rules. Complete the Content-based-router properties, such as Endpoint, Service – Value, and Namespace.

You can define multiple routing rules using XPath expressions. For every routing rule, you must define an exchange target and a routing rule, just as you did in chapter 5 in the routing section. Define two routing rules for this example; just fill-in an XPath expression.

4 Add two JMS providers, which can be connected to the content-based router. As you did for the JMS consumer, you have to enter several properties.

The result of these steps should be similar to figure C.6.

You should now have three JMS binding components and one content-based router service engine. Now that you've designed the routing example, you can generate the JBI package by right-clicking the canvas and selecting Generate JBI package. When you refresh the Eclipse project, a folder is generated with the service assembly

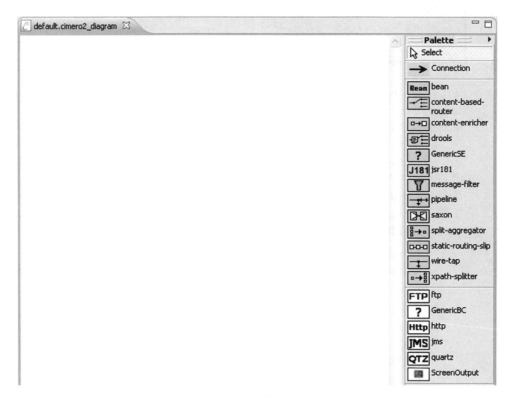

Figure C.5   The design canvas and palette of the Enterprise Integration Diagram plug-in

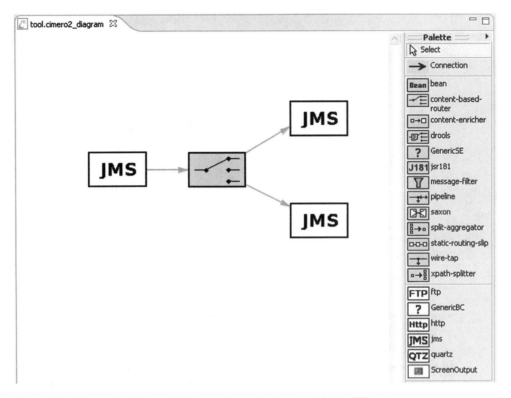

Figure C.6　The result of the routing example you implemented in the EID canvas

and the four service units. There is also an Ant build file that you can use to build the service assembly and deploy it to a ServiceMix container.

Note that the jbi.xml file in the service assembly is blank and doesn't include the service assembly and service unit configuration. But this example gives you a first look at the functionality of the EID plug-in.

Mule component overview

You can configure many different components in Mule 2.0: the basic Mule elements, as well as the connector-specific elements such as JMS connectors, file-specific transformers, and so on.

The following tables explain each element you can use in the Mule configuration file, beginning with the basic Mule elements and then continuing to the connector-specific configuration elements. Most of the descriptions are based on the XSD documentation and the Javadocs for the specific classes.

Mule core elements

The Mule core elements, listed in table D.1, form the basis of any Mule configuration file. These elements are from the http://www.mulesource.org/schema/mule/core/ 2.0 namespace.

Table D.1   Mule core elements

Name	Description
`and-filter`	Returns `true` only if all the enclosed filters return `true`.
`append-string-transformer`	A transformer that appends a string to a string payload.
`array-entry-point-resolver`	Delivers the message to a method that takes a single array as its argument. This element can be set on the model or component; the model value provides a default that individual component values can override. This element can also be used directly or as part of a set of resolvers; the resolvers in a set are used in turn until one is successful.

Table D.1   Mule core elements *(continued)*

Name	Description
auto-transformer	A transformer that uses the transform-discovery mechanism to convert the message payload. This transformer works much better when transforming custom object types rather than Java types because there is less chance for ambiguity.
base64-decoder-transformer	A transformer that base64-decodes a message to give an array of bytes.
base64-encoder-transformer	A transformer that base64-encodes a string or byte array message.
bridge-component	Transfers a message from inbound to outbound endpoints. This name is provided for backward compatibility—it's equivalent to not specifying any component.
byte-array-to-hex-string-transformer	A transformer that converts a byte array to a string of hexadecimal digits.
byte-array-to-object-transformer	A transformer that converts a byte array to an object (either deserializing or converting to a string).
byte-array-to-serializable-transformer	A transformer that converts a byte array to an object (deserializing the object).
byte-array-to-string-transformer	A transformer that converts a byte array to a string.
callable-entry-point-resolver	An entry point resolver for components that implement the Callable interface. This passes a MuleEventContext to the component. This element can be set on the model or component; the model value provides a default that individual component values can override. This element can also be used directly or as part of a set of resolvers; the resolvers in a set are used in turn until one is successful.
chaining-router	A router that sends the event through multiple endpoints using the result of the first invocation as the input for the next.
collection-aggregator-router	A router that returns the aggregated result as a MuleMessageCollection that contains all the events from the aggregation.
collection-async-reply-router	Configures a collection response router. This returns a MuleMessageCollection message type that contains all events received for the current correlation.
component	A simple POJO component that is invoked by Mule when a message is received. The instance can be specified via a factory or a class.
component-threading-profile	The threading profile to use on the component.
correlation-resequencer-router	A router that resequences events according to their dispatch sequence in the correlation group.

Table D.1 Mule core elements *(continued)*

Name	Description
custom-async-reply-router	Lets you specify your own custom `async-reply-router` instead of using the ones provided by Mule.
custom-catch-all-strategy	Lets you use a custom `catch-all-strategy` instead of using the Mule-provided ones.
custom-connector	A user-defined connector.
custom-correlation-aggregator-router	Lets you create a user-defined aggregator.
custom-entry-point-resolver	A custom entry point resolver that allows user-supplied code to determine how a message is passed to a component in Java. This element can be set on the model or component; the model value provides a default that individual component values can override. This element can also be used directly or as part of a set of resolvers; the resolvers in a set are used in turn until one is successful.
custom-entry-point-resolver-set	A custom entry point resolver set that allows user-supplied code to determine how a message is passed to a component in Java. This element can be set on the model or component; the model value provides a default that individual component values can override.
custom-exception-strategy	A user-defined exception strategy.
custom-filter	A user-implemented filter.
custom-forwarding-catch-all-strategy	Lets you create a user defined `custom-forwarding-catch-all-strategy`.
custom-inbound-router	Lets you use a custom `custom-inbound-router` instead of using the Mule-provided ones.
custom-lifecycle-adapter-factory	Lets you create a `custom-lifecycle-adapter-factory`.
custom-message-info-mapping	Allows the configuration of a custom implementation of `MessageInfoMapping`.
custom-outbound-router	Lets you use a custom `custom-outbound-router` instead of using the Mule-provided ones.
custom-service	A user-implemented service (typically used only in testing).
custom-transaction	Allow access to user-defined or otherwise unsupported third-party transactions.
custom-transaction-manager	A user-implemented transaction manager.
custom-transformer	A user-implemented transformer.
decrypt-transformer	A transformer that decrypts a message.

Table D.1 Mule core elements *(continued)*

Name	Description
default-connector-exception-strategy	Provides default exception-handling via an endpoint.
default-service-exception-strategy	Provides default exception-handling via an endpoint.
echo-component	Logs the message and returns the payload as the result.
encrypt-transformer	A transformer that encrypts a message.
encryption-security-filter	A filter that provides password-based encryption.
endpoint	An endpoint template that you can use to construct an inbound or outbound endpoint elsewhere in the configuration by referencing the endpoint's name. Each transport implements its own endpoint element with a friendlier syntax, but this generic element can be used with any transport by supplying the correct address URI. For example, vm://foo describes a VM transport endpoint.
endpoint-selector-router	A router that lets you route the event based on a certain property from the event.
entry-point-resolver-set	An extensible set of entry point resolvers that determine how a message is passed to a component in Java. Each entry-point resolver is tried in turn until one succeeds in delivering the message to the component. This element can be set on the model or component; the model value provides a default that individual component values can override.
exception-based-router	A router that lets you route an exception to a specific endpoint based on the type of exception.
exception-type-filter	A filter that matches the type of an exception.
expression-filter	A filter that can evaluate a range of expressions. It supports base expression types such as header, payload, regex, and wildcard.
expression-message-info-mapping	Allows expressions to be configured to extract the message information.
expression-transformer	A transformer that evaluates one or more expressions on the current event. Each expression equates to a parameter in the return message. The return message for two or more expressions is an Object[].
filter	A filter that is defined elsewhere (at the global level, or as a Spring bean).
filtering-router	A router that uses a filter to define where to route a specific message to.

Table D.1   Mule core elements *(continued)*

Name	Description
forwarding-catch-all-strategy	Acts as a catch-and-forward router for any events not caught by the router this strategy is associated with. Users can assign an endpoint to this strategy, where all events are forwarded.
forwarding-router	Forwards an incoming event over another transport without invoking a service. This can be used to implement a bridge across different transports.
gzip-compress-transformer	A transformer that compresses a byte array using gzip.
gzip-uncompress-transformer	A transformer that uncompresses a byte array using gzip.
hex-string-to-byte-array-transformer	A transformer that converts a string of hexadecimal digits to a byte array.
idempotent-receiver-router	A router that ensures that only unique messages are received by a service. It does so by checking the unique ID of the incoming message.
idempotent-secure-hash-receiver-router	A router that ensures that only unique messages are received by a service. It does so by calculating the SHA-256 hash of the message.
inbound-endpoint	An inbound endpoint that receives messages from the associated transport. Each transport implements its own inbound endpoint element with a friendlier syntax, but this generic element can be used with any transport by supplying the correct address URI. For example, vm://foo describes a VM transport endpoint.
inbound-pass-through-router	A router that allows inbound routing over all registered endpoints without any filtering. This class is used by Mule when a specific inbound router hasn't been configured on a UMODescriptor.
include-entry-point	A possible method for delivery.
jboss-transaction-manager	The JBoss transaction manager.
jndi-transaction-manager	Retrieves a named transaction manager factory from JNDI.
jrun-transaction-manager	The JRun transaction manager.
legacy-entry-point-resolver-set	An extensible set of entry-point resolvers (which determine how a message is passed to a component in Java) that contains resolvers to implement the standard logic. This is provided by default and is only needed explicitly if it will be extended with other entry point resolvers. This element can be set on the model or component; the model value provides a default that individual component values can override.

Table D.1 Mule core elements *(continued)*

Name	Description
`list-message-splitter-router`	A splitter that accepts a `List` as a message payload and then routes list elements as messages over an endpoint where the endpoint's filter accepts the payload.
`log-component`	Logs the message content (or content length if it's a large message).
`logging-catch-all-strategy`	A simple strategy that only logs events not caught by the router associated with this strategy.
`message-chunking-aggregator-router`	Aggregates the various chunks from `message-chunking-router` back together.
`message-chunking-router`	A router that breaks up the current message into smaller parts and sends them to the same destination. The Destination service needs to have a `MessageChunkingAggregator` inbound router in order to rebuild the message at the other end.
`message-properties-transformer`	A transformer that can add or delete message properties.
`message-property-filter`	A filter that matches properties on an event. This can be useful because the event properties represent all the meta information about the event from the underlying transport; for an event received over HTTP, you can check for HTTP headers, and so on. The pattern should be expressed as a key/value pair: for example, *propertyName=value*. To compare more than one property, use the logic filters for And, Or, and Not expressions. By default, the comparison is case sensitive; you can set the `caseSensitive` property to override this.
`method-entry-point-resolver`	Delivers the message to a named method. This element can be set on the model or component; the model value provides a default that individual component values can override. This element can also be used directly or as part of a set of resolvers; the resolvers in a set are used in turn until one is successful.
`model`	By default, a Staged Event Driven Architecture (SEDA) model.
`mule`	Either the root element of a Mule configuration or a top-level element in a Spring configuration that contains further Mule elements.
`multicasting-router`	A router that broadcasts the current message to every endpoint registered with this router.
`no-action-transformer`	A transformer that has no effect.
`no-arguments-entry-point-resolver`	Calls a method without arguments (the message isn't passed to the component).
`not-filter`	Inverts the enclosed filter (if it returns `true` for a message, this returns `false`, and vice versa).
`null-component`	Throws an exception if it receives a message.

Table D.1   Mule core elements *(continued)*

Name	Description
object-to-byte-array-transformer	A transformer that serializes all objects except strings (which are converted using getBytes()).
object-to-string-transformer	A transformer that gives a human-readable description of various types (useful for debugging).
or-filter	Returns true if any of the enclosed filters returns true.
outbound-endpoint	Sends messages to the associated transport. Each transport implements its own outbound endpoint element with a friendlier syntax, but this generic element can be used with any transport by supplying the correct address URI. For example, vm://foo describes a VM transport endpoint.
outbound-pass-through-router	Allows outbound routing over a single endpoint without any filtering. This class is used by Mule when a single outbound router is set on a UMODescriptor.
payload-type-filter	A filter that matches the type of the payload.
pooled-component	A pooled POJO component that is invoked by Mule when a message is received. The instance can be specified via a factory or class.
pooling-profile	Defines the object-pooling parameters for the service it's associated with.
properties	Sets Mule properties. These are name/value pairs that can be set on components, services, and so on, and that provide a generic way of configuring the system. In Mule 2, you typically shouldn't need to use generic properties like this, because almost all functionality is exposed via dedicated elements. But it can be useful in configuring obscure or overlooked options and in configuring transports from the generic endpoint elements.
property-entry-point-resolver	Uses a message property to select the component method to be called. This element can be set on the model or component; the model value provides a default that individual component values can override. This element can also be used directly or as part of a set of resolvers; the resolvers in a set are used in turn until one is successful.
prototype-object	Uses the defined component as a prototype.
queue-profile	Configures the queue profile used on a component.
recipient-list-router	A router that you can configure to send the received message to multiple endpoints at the same time.
reflection-entry-point-resolver	Generates a list of candidate methods from the component via reflections. This element can be set on the model or component; the model value provides a default that individual component values can override. This element can also be used directly or as part of a set of resolvers; the resolvers in a set are used in turn until one is successful.

Table D.1   Mule core elements *(continued)*

Name	Description
regex-filter	A filter that matches string messages against a regular expression. The Java regular expression engine (java.util.regex. Pattern) is used.
resin-transaction-manager	The Resin transaction manager.
security-manager	The default security manager.
seda-model	A SEDA model, which has separate threads and queues for each component.
selective-consumer-router	An inbound router used to filter out unwanted events. The filtering is performed by a Filter that can be set on the router.
serializable-to-byte-array-transformer	A transformer that converts an object to a byte array (serializing the object).
service	The standard SEDA service. A service describes how to receive messages, deliver them to a component, and handle the results (if any).
single-async-reply-router	Configures a single-response router that returns the first event it receives on a reply endpoint and discards the rest.
singleton-object	Uses the defined component as a singleton.
spring-object	Lets you reference a bean that is defined in Spring.
static-recipient-list-router	A router that is used to dispatch a single event to multiple recipients over the same transport. The recipient endpoints for this router can be configured statically on the router.
string-to-byte-array-transformer	A transformer that converts a string to a byte array.
template-endpoint-router	Allows endpoints to be altered at runtime based on properties set on the current event or fallback values set on the endpoint properties. Templated values are expressed using square braces around a property name, such as axis:http://localhost:8082/ service?method=[SOAP_METHOD]. Note that Ant-style property templates can't be used in valid URI strings; you must use square braces instead.
transformer	A reference to a transformer defined elsewhere.
weblogic-transaction-manager	The WebLogic transaction manager.
websphere-transaction-manager	The WebSphere transaction manager.

Table D.1   Mule core elements *(continued)*

Name	Description
wildcard-filter	A filter that matches string messages against wildcards. It performs matches with *. For example, `jms.events.*` will catch `jms.events.customer` and `jms.events.receipts`. This filter accepts a comma-separated list of patterns, so more than one filter pattern can be matched for a given argument: `jms.events.*`, `jms.actions.*` will match `jms.events.system` and `jms.actions` but not `jms.queue`.
wire-tap-router	An inbound router that can forward every message to another destination as defined in the `endpoint` property. This can be a logical destination or a URI. A filter can be applied to this router so that only events matching a criterion are tapped.
xml-entity-decoder-transformer	A transformer that decodes a string containing XML entities.
xml-entity-encoder-transformer	A transformer that encodes a string using XML entities.

Mule BPM elements

The elements in table D.2 are from the http://www.mulesource.org/schema/mule/bpm/2.0 namespace. You can use them to configure BPM support in Mule.

Table D.2   Mule BPM elements

Name	Description
connector	Lets you configure the behavior of Mule's BPM support.
endpoint	Defines a BPM endpoint that can be referenced from the inbound and outbound sections of a Mule service definition.
inbound-endpoint	Defines a BPM inbound endpoint. This endpoint can be used to receive messages from a running BPM flow, which can then be processed by Mule in the normal manner.
outbound-endpoint	Defines a BPM outbound endpoint that you can use in the outbound section of a Mule service definition. When a message is sent to this endpoint, a specific BPM flow can be started, and this message is inserted into that flow. You can also use this endpoint to further advance a running BPM flow.
outbound-router	A shortcut for an endpoint selector router that uses the following expression: `selectorExpression="header:MULE_BPM_ENDPOINT">`.

Mule EJB elements

The elements in table D.3 are from the http://www.mulesource.org/schema/mule/ejb/2.0 namespace. You can use them to configure EJB support in Mule.

Table D.3   Mule EJB elements

Name	Description
connector	A connector with which you can configure the behavior of Mule's EJB queues.
endpoint	Defines an EJB endpoint that can be referenced from the inbound and outbound sections of a Mule service definition.
inbound-endpoint	Defines an EJB inbound endpoint that you can use in the inbound section of a Mule service definition. This endpoint lets you poll a specific EJB.
outbound-endpoint	Defines an EJB outbound endpoint that you can use in the outbound section of a Mule service definition. This endpoint lets you make a call to an EJB.

Mule email elements

The elements in table D.4 are from the http://www.mulesource.org/schema/mule/email/2.0 namespace. You can use them to configure general email support in Mule. For more specific email support, see the IMAP, POP3, and SMTP configurations.

Table D.4   Mule email elements

Name	Description
bytes-to-mime-transformer	An email-specific transformer that transforms an incoming byte[] to a MIME message
email-to-string-transformer	An email-specific transformer that transforms an incoming String to an email message
mime-to-bytes-transformer	An email-specific transformer that transforms an incoming MIME message to a byte[]
object-to-mime-transformer	An email-specific transformer that transforms an incoming Object to a MIME message
string-to-email-transformer	An email-specific transformer that transforms an incoming String to an email message

Mule file elements

The elements in table D.5 are from the http://www.mulesource.org/schema/mule/
file/2.0 namespace. You can use them to configure file support in Mule.

Table D.5 Mule file elements

Name	Description
connector	A file-specific connector you can use to set file-specific properties that can be applied to the inbound and outbound file endpoints.
custom-filename-parser	Lets you specify a custom filename parser. The implementation has to implement org.mule.transports.file.FilenameParser.
endpoint	Defines a file endpoint that can be referenced from the inbound and outbound sections of a Mule service definition.
expression-filename-parser	Uses a Mule-supported expression to define how the name of the output file is constructed.
file-to-byte-array-transformer	A file-specific transformer that transforms an incoming File to a byte[].
file-to-string-transformer	A file-specific transformer that transforms an incoming File to a String.
filename-regex-filter	A regex-based filter to select which files are read from the file system.
filename-wildcard-filter	A wildcard-based filter to select which files are read from the file system.
inbound-endpoint	Defines a file inbound endpoint that you can use in the inbound section of a Mule service definition. This endpoint lets you poll a specific directory for new files.
legacy-filename-parser	Uses a limited set of tokens that you can use to construct the name of the output file.
outbound-endpoint	Defines a file outbound endpoint that you can use in the outbound section of a Mule service definition. This endpoint writes the received message to the file system.

Mule FTP elements

The elements in table D.6 are from the http://www.mulesource.org/schema/mule/ftp/2.0 namespace. You can use them to configure FTP support in Mule.

Table D.6   Mule FTP elements

Name	Description
connector	An FTP-specific connector that you can use to set FTP-specific properties that can be applied to the inbound and outbound FTP endpoints.
custom-filename-parser	Specifies a custom filename parser that you can use to create the name of the output file.
endpoint	Defines an FTP endpoint that can be referenced from the inbound and outbound sections of a Mule service definition.
expression-filename-parser	Uses a Mule-supported expression to define how the name of the output file is constructed.
inbound-endpoint	Defines an FTP inbound endpoint that you can use in the inbound section of a Mule service definition. This endpoint lets you poll a specific directory on an FTP server for new files.
legacy-filename-parser	Uses a limited set of tokens that you can use to construct the name of the output file.
outbound-endpoint	Defines an FTP outbound endpoint that you can use in the outbound section of a Mule service definition. This endpoint writes the received message to a specific directory on an FTP server.

Mule HTTP elements

The elements in table D.7 are from the http://www.mulesource.org/schema/mule/http/2.0 namespace. You can use them to configure HTTP support in Mule.

Table D.7   Mule HTTP elements

Name	Description
connector	An HTTP-specific connector that you can use to configure generic properties that can then be referenced by the HTTP endpoints.
endpoint	Defines an HTTP endpoint that can be referenced from the inbound and outbound sections of a Mule service definition.
http-client-response-to-object-transformer	An HTTP-specific transformer that transforms an HTTP client response to a Java `Object`.
http-response-to-string-transformer	An HTTP-specific transformer that transforms an HTTP response to a Java `String`.

Table D.7   Mule HTTP elements (continued)

Name	Description
`inbound-endpoint`	Defines an HTTP inbound endpoint that you can use in the outbound section of a Mule service definition. This causes Mule to listen for HTTP messages on the specific endpoint.
`message-to-http-response-transformer`	An HTTP-specific transformer that transforms a Mule message to an HTTP response.
`object-to-http-client-request-transformer`	An HTTP-specific transformer that transforms an `Object` to an HTTP client response.
`outbound-endpoint`	Defines an HTTP outbound endpoint that you can use in the outbound section of a Mule service definition. This lets you send HTTP messages to the configured endpoint.
`rest-service-component`	A built-in `RestServiceWrapper` that you can use to proxy REST-style services as local Mule components.

Mule IMAP elements

The elements in table D.8 are from the http://www.mulesource.org/schema/mule/imap/2.0 namespace. You can use them to configure IMAP support in Mule.

Table D.8   Mule IMAP elements

Name	Description
`connector`	An IMAP-specific connector that lets you configure common incoming mail settings. This connector can then be referenced from the IMAP endpoints.
`endpoint`	Defines an IMAP endpoint that can be referenced from the inbound section of a Mule service definition. Note that this can't be referenced from the outbound section because IMAP can only be used to receive messages. To send messages, use SMTP endpoints.
`inbound-endpoint`	Defines an IMAP outbound endpoint that you can use in the outbound section of a Mule service definition.

Mule JDBC elements

The elements in table D.9 are from the http://www.mulesource.org/schema/mule/jdbc/2.0 namespace. You can use them to configure JDBC support in Mule.

Table D.9 Mule JDBC elements

Name	Description
connector	A simple connector with which you can configure the behavior of Mule's JDBC endpoints. This connector is the best place to configure the queries the JDBC endpoints will use.
endpoint	Defines a JDBC endpoint that can be referenced from the inbound and outbound sections of a Mule service definition.
inbound-endpoint	Defines a JDBC inbound endpoint that you can use in the inbound section of a Mule service definition. This usually references a named query from the JDBC connector and executes a SELECT query.
outbound-endpoint	Defines a JDBC outbound endpoint that you can use in the inbound section of a Mule service definition. This usually references a named query from the JDBC connector and executes an INSERT or UPDATE query.
transaction	Specifies how the call to the JDBC datasource participates in a transaction.

Mule JMS elements

The elements in table D.10 are from the http://www.mulesource.org/schema/mule/jms/2.0 namespace. You can use them to configure JMS support in Mule.

Table D.10 Mule JMS elements

Name	Description
activemq-connector	A specific JMS connector that you can use to connect to the ActiveMQ JMS implementation
activemq-xa-connector	A specific JMS connector that you can use to connect to the ActiveMQ JMS implementation using an XA connection factory
client-ack-transaction	Serves as a simple transaction mechanism, where the client acknowledges the message
connector	A generic JMS connector that you can configure to connect to a JMS server
custom-connector	Lets you create a custom connector that you can use to connect to a JMS server
endpoint	Defines a JMS endpoint that can be referenced from the inbound and outbound sections of the Mule service definition

Table D.10   Mule JMS elements *(continued)*

Name	Description
inbound-endpoint	An incoming JMS endpoint that you can configure to listen to a JMS queue or topic
jmsmessage-to-object-transformer	A JMS-specific transformer that you can use to transform a JMS message to a Java `Object`
object-to-jmsmessage-transformer	A JMS-specific transformer that you can use to transform a Java `Object` to a JMS message
outbound-endpoint	An outgoing JMS endpoint that you can configure to send messages to a JMS queue or topic
property-filter	A JMS-specific filter that you can use to check whether specific properties on the JMS are set
transaction	Specifies how the call to JMS participates in a transaction
weblogic-connector	A specific JMS connector that you can use to connect to the WebLogic JMS implementation
websphere-connector	A specific JMS connector that you can use to connect to the WebSphere JMS implementation
xa-transaction	Specifies how the call to JMS participates in a distributed transaction

Mule POP3 elements

The elements in table D.11 are from the http://www.mulesource.org/schema/mule/pop3/2.0 namespace. You can use them to configure POP3 support in Mule.

Table D.11   Mule POP3 elements

Name	Description
connector	A POP3-specific connector that lets you specify common incoming mail settings. This connector can then be referenced from the POP3 endpoints.
endpoint	Defines a POP3 endpoint that can be referenced from the inbound section of a Mule service definition. Note that this can't be referenced from the outbound section because POP3 can only be used to receive messages. To send messages, use SMTP endpoints.
inbound-endpoint	Defines an SMTP outbound endpoint that you can use in the outbound section of a Mule service definition.

Mule Quartz elements

The elements in table D.12 are defined as XML elements from the http://www.mule-source.org/schema/mule/quartz/2.0 namespace. You can use them to configure Quartz scheduler support in Mule.

Table D.12   Mule Quartz elements

Name	Description
connector	A Quartz connector that you can use to specify generic Quartz settings that can then be applied to all the Quartz endpoints in the configuration
custom-job	Lets you create a custom Quartz job
custom-job-from-message	Lets you create a custom Quartz job based on a Mule message
endpoint	Defines a Quartz endpoint that can be referenced from the inbound and outbound sections of a Mule service definition
endpoint-polling-job	Creates a job that periodically polls an endpoint
event-generator-job	Creates a job that generates Mule events
inbound-endpoint	Defines a Quartz inbound endpoint that you can use in the inbound section of a Mule service definition
outbound-endpoint	Defines a Quartz outbound endpoint that you can use in the outbound section of a Mule service definition
scheduled-dispatch-job	Schedules a one-off or repeated message dispatch to a Mule endpoint

Mule RMI elements

The elements in table D.13 are from the http://www.mulesource.org/schema/mule/rmi/2.0 namespace. You can use them to configure RMI support in Mule.

Table D.13   Mule RMI elements

Name	Description
connector	An RMI connector that you can use to specify generic RMI settings that can then be applied to all the RMI endpoints in the configuration
endpoint	Defines an RMI endpoint that can be referenced from the inbound and outbound sections of a Mule service definition
inbound-endpoint	Defines an RMI inbound endpoint that you can use in the inbound section of a Mule service definition
outbound-endpoint	Defines an RMI outbound endpoint that you can use in the outbound section of a Mule service definition

Mule SMTP elements

The elements in table D.14 are from the http://www.mulesource.org/schema/mule/smtp/2.0 namespace. You can use them to configure SMTP support in Mule.

Table D.14   Mule SMTP elements

Name	Description
connector	An SMTP-specific connector that lets you set common outgoing mail settings. This connector can then be referenced from the SMTP endpoints.
endpoint	Defines an SMTP endpoint that can be referenced from the outbound section of a Mule service definition. Note that this can't be referenced from the inbound section because SMTP can only be used to send messages. To receive messages, use POP3 or IMAP endpoints.
outbound-endpoint	Defines an SMTP outbound endpoint that you can use in the outbound section of a Mule service definition.

Mule VM elements

The elements in table D.15 are from the http://www.mulesource.org/schema/mule/vm/2.0 namespace. You can use them to configure internal queue support in Mule.

Table D.15   Mule VM elements

Name	Description
connector	A simple connector with which you can configure the behavior of Mule's internal VM queues
endpoint	Defines a VM endpoint that can be referenced from the inbound and outbound sections of a Mule service definition
inbound-endpoint	Defines a VM inbound endpoint that you can use in the inbound section of a Mule service definition
outbound-endpoint	Defines a VM outbound endpoint that you can use in the outbound section of a Mule service definition

ServiceMix component overview

ServiceMix provides a number of service engines and binding components out of the box. You can configure all these components using a Spring-based XML file. In this appendix, we give you an overview of the components provided by ServiceMix and show you which elements you can use to configure these components.

The following tables describe each element you can use in the ServiceMix configuration file for a specific component. Most of the descriptions are based on the XSD documentation, ServiceMix's wiki, and the Javadocs of the specific classes.

ServiceMix bean elements

The elements in table E.1 are from the http://servicemix.apache.org/bean/1.0 namespace. You can use them to configure the ServiceMix bean service engine.

Table E.1 ServiceMix bean elements

Name	Description
component	Can be used when you want to use the bean endpoints in the lightweight container
defaultMethodInvocationStrategy	The default strategy for invoking methods on POJOs from a JBI message exchange
endpoint	Represents a bean endpoint that consists of a POJO together with a MethodInvocation-Strategy, so that JBI message exchanges can be invoked on the bean

469

ServiceMix cxf-bc elements

The elements in table E.2 are from the http://servicemix.apache.org/cxfbc/1.0 namespace. You can use them to configure the ServiceMix cxf-bc binding component.

Table E.2   ServiceMix `cxf-bc` elements

Name	Description
component	Can be used when you want to use the cxf-bc provider and consumer elements in the lightweight container.
consumer	Provides an HTTP web service that can be called from outside the JBI container. When a message is received on this endpoint, it's sent to a specific service endpoint.
provider	Calls an external web service. An internal component can use this service to call external web services.

ServiceMix cxf-se elements

The elements in table E.3 are from the http://servicemix.apache.org/cxfse/1.0 namespace. You can use them to configure the ServiceMix cxf-se service engine.

Table E.3   ServiceMix `cxf-se` elements

Name	Description
component	Can be used when you want to use the cxf-se endpoint and proxy elements in the lightweight container.
endpoint	Exposes a normal Java bean as a service in the JBI environment.
proxy	Lets you inject a service endpoint as a Java reference into a Java bean. This allows the Java bean to call JBI service endpoints as if it were a normal Java call.

ServiceMix drools elements

The elements in table E.4 are from the http://servicemix.apache.org/drools/1.0 namespace. You can use them to configure the ServiceMix drools service engine.

Table E.4   ServiceMix `drools` elements

Name	Description
component	Can be used when you want to use the drools endpoint element in the lightweight container.
endpoint	Specifies a drools rule file to be executed when a message exchange is received. The drools rule file can also access the JBI context to send new message exchanges or route the message to a different service endpoint.

ServiceMix EIP elements

The elements in table E.5 are from the http://servicemix.apache.org/eip/1.0 namespace. You can use them to configure the ServiceMix EIP service engine.

Table E.5   ServiceMix EIP elements

Name	Description
component	Can be used when you want to use the EIP elements in the lightweight container.
content-based-router	A content-based router you can use to route a message based on its content or its message properties.
content-enricher	A content enricher you can use to enrich the message with additional information.
default-comparator	Compares two MessageExchange sequence elements based on sequence numbers defined by a specific property in the NormalizedMessage. This comparator works on sequence numbers of type Long. Sequence numbers must be stored as NormalizedMessage properties. The property name under which the sequence number is stored is configured via this comparator's sequenceNumberKey property.
exchange-target	Specifies the target of an exchange while retaining all the JBI features (interface-based routing, service name–based routing, or endpoint routing).
message-filter	Determines whether to accept a message.
namespace-context	A NamespaceContext implementation that can be used to resolve namespaces.
pipeline	Transforms an In-Only message exchange to an In-Out message exchange.
recipient-list-aggregator	An aggregator that is specifically written to aggregate messages that have been sent using a StaticRecipientList pattern.
resequencer	Reorders incoming In-Only or Robust-In-Only exchanges and sends them synchronously to a target service. Synchronous sending ensures that messages arrive in correct order at the target service.
routing-rule	The RoutingRule interface is used by content-based routers. If the rule predicate matches the MessageExchange, the target defined on the rule is used as the destination for the given MessageExchange.
split-aggregator	Collects messages with count, index, and correlationId properties. These properties are automatically set by splitters. A timeout may be specified so that the aggregator won't keep data forever if a message is missing.
static-recipient-list	Forwards an input In-Only or Robust-In-Only exchange to a list of known recipients.
static-routing-slip	Routes an incoming In-Out exchange through a series of target services.

Table E.5   ServiceMix EIP elements *(continued)*

Name	Description
switch-predicate	A switch (on/off) predicate based on a property that can come from any of the following: • A system property • A property from a property file (specified as a Spring resource) • A property from the exchange This switch can also be switched on and off via JMX.
wire-tap	Forwards a copy of the input message to a different endpoint.
xpath-predicate	Routes and filters messages.
xpath-splitter	Splits messages based on an XPath expression.

ServiceMix file elements

The elements in table E.6 are from the http://servicemix.apache.org/file/1.0 namespace. You can use them to configure the ServiceMix file-binding component.

Table E.6   ServiceMix file elements

Name	Description
component	Can be used when you want to use the file elements in the lightweight container
poller	A polling endpoint that looks for a file or files in a directory and sends the files into the JBI bus as messages, deleting the files by default when they're processed
sender	An endpoint that receives a message and writes the content to a file

ServiceMix FTP elements

The elements in table E.7 are from the http://servicemix.apache.org/ftp/1.0 namespace. You can use them to configure the ServiceMix FTP-binding component.

Table E.7   ServiceMix FTP elements

Name	Description
component	Can be used when you want to use the FTP elements in the lightweight container
poller	A polling endpoint that looks for a file or files in a directory on an FTP server and sends the files into the JBI bus as messages, deleting the files by default when they're processed
pool	A pool of FTP clients for the Jakarta Commons Net library
sender	An FTP endpoint that receives messages from the JBI bus and stores them in a specific directory on an FTP server

ServiceMix HTTP elements

The elements in table E.8 are from the http://servicemix.apache.org/http/1.0 namespace. You can use them to configure the ServiceMix HTTP-binding component.

Table E.8 ServiceMix HTTP elements

Name	Description
basicAuthCredentials	Contains parameters needed to send basic authentication credentials
component	Can be used when you want to use the HTTP elements in the lightweight container
configuration	Lets you specify common settings such as connection limits, and so on
consumer	A plain HTTP consumer endpoint that can be used to handle plain HTTP requests (without SOAP) or process requests in a nonstandard way
endpoint	A generic endpoint that you can configure to act as an HTTP provider or an HTTP consumer
provider	A simple HTTP provider endpoint that can be used to make calls to a specific HTTP address
proxyParameters	Contains all the parameters needed to send HTTP requests through a proxy
serializedMarshaler	Handles Java serialized content from the InputStream of the HttpServletRequest object and to the OutputStream of the HttpServletResponse object
soap-consumer	A specific HTTP consumer that can parse the SOAP headers of an incoming SOAP call
soap-provider	A specific HTTP provider that is aware of a message's SOAP header and body
sslParameters	Contains all the parameters needed to create an SSL server or client socket

ServiceMix JMS elements

The elements in table E.9 are from the http://servicemix.apache.org/jms/1.0 namespace. You can use them to configure the ServiceMix JMS binding component.

Table E.9 ServiceMix JMS elements

Name	Description
component	Can be used when you want to use the JMS elements in the lightweight container
configuration	Lets you specify common settings such as username and password

Table E.9   ServiceMix JMS elements *(continued)*

Name	Description
consumer	A server-side HTTP endpoint that consumes plain JMS or JMS + SOAP requests and sends them into the NMR to a given JBI endpoint
endpoint	A generic endpoint that can be configured to act as a JMS consumer, JMS provider, JMS SOAP consumer, or a JMS SOAP provider
jca-consumer	A JMS consumer that can be configured as a resource adapter
provider	A client-side JBI endpoint that can receive requests from the NMR and send them to a given URL where the service is provided
soap-consumer	A specific JMS consumer that can parse the SOAP headers of an incoming SOAP call
soap-provider	A specific JMS provider that is aware of a message's SOAP header and body

ServiceMix JSR 181 elements

The elements in table E.10 are from the http://servicemix.apache.org/jsr181/1.0 namespace. You can use them to configure the ServiceMix JSR 181 service engine.

Table E.10   ServiceMix JSR 181 elements

Name	Description
component	Can be used when you want to use the JSR 181 elements in the light-weight container.
endpoint	Exposes a normal Java bean as a service in the JBI environment.
proxy	Lets you inject a service endpoint as a Java reference into a Java bean. This allows the Java bean to call JBI service endpoints as if it were a normal Java call.

ServiceMix Quartz elements

The elements in table E.11 are from the http://servicemix.apache.org/quartz/1.0 namespace. You can use them to configure the ServiceMix Quartz service engine.

Table E.11   ServiceMix Quartz elements

Name	Description
component	Can be used when you want to use the Quartz elements in the light-weight container
cron	Defines when the Quartz endpoint sends a new message exchange

Table E.11   ServiceMix Quartz elements *(continued)*

Name	Description
endpoint	Fires message exchanges at a given time or interval
jobDetail	Defines how the message looks when it's sent by the specified endpoint
simple	Defines when the Quartz endpoint sends a new message exchange

ServiceMix Saxon elements

The elements in table E.12 are from the http://servicemix.apache.org/saxon/1.0 namespace. You can use them to configure the ServiceMix Saxon service engine.

Table E.12   ServiceMix Saxon elements

Name	Description
component	Can be used when you want to use the XSLT elements in the light-weight container
xquery	Applies a specific XQuery on the input message
xslt	Applies a specific XML stylesheet on the input message

ServiceMix script elements

The elements in table E.13 are from the http://org.apache.servicemix/script/1.0 namespace. You can use them to configure the ServiceMix script service engine.

Table E.13   ServiceMix script elements

Name	Description
component	Can be used when you want to use the scripting elements in the light-weight container
exchangeHelper	Creates new message exchanges from your scripts
exchangeProcessor	Receives messages from the NMR, and invokes a specific script

ServiceMix TrueZIP elements

The elements in table E.14 are from the http://servicemix.apache.org/truezip/1.0 namespace. You can use them to configure the ServiceMix TrueZIP binding component.

Table E.14   ServiceMix TrueZIP elements

Name	Description
component	Can be used when you want to use the TrueZIP elements in the light-weight container
poller	A polling endpoint that looks for a file or files inside a zip file and sends the files into the JBI bus as messages
sender	An endpoint that receives a message and writes the content as an entry in a zip file

ServiceMix WSN-2005 elements

The elements in table E.15 are from the http://servicemix.apache.org/wsn/1.0 name-space. You can use them to configure the ServiceMix WSN-2005 service engine.

Table E.15   ServiceMix WSN-2005 elements

Name	Description
component	Can be used when you want to use the WS-Notification elements in the lightweight container
create-pull-point	Lets you create a WS-Notification pull point that can be used by a requestor to retrieve accumulated notification messages
publisher	Sends messages to a specific topic
register-publisher	An endpoint that can be used by publishers to register themselves
subscribe	Lets you create a subscription to a specific topic using the WS-Notification specification

ServiceMix XMPP elements

The elements in table E.16 are from the http://servicemix.apache.org/xmpp/1.0 name-space. You can use them to configure the ServiceMix XMPP binding component.

Table E.16   ServiceMix XMPP elements

Name	Description
component	Can be used when you want to use the XMPP elements in the light-weight container.
groupChatEndpoint	Represents a group chat endpoint that can be used to send messages to a group on an XMPP server.
privateChatEndpoint	Represents an endpoint for chatting to a single individual. This endpoint can be used to send messages to a single individual using the XMPP protocol.

The Swing test client

One of the great features of Mule and ServiceMix is testability, which lets you start up a Mule and ServiceMix container from, for example, a piece of Java code or an Ant build file. It's easy to get the developed message flows running, but what about the next step, flow testing? Because Mule and ServiceMix support a wide variety of connectivity options, there are several ways to test message flows, depending on the choice of connectivity for a specific message flow. For instance, when you use JMS, you can use Hermes JMS (http://www.hermesjms.com) to send a message to a specific queue or topic to trigger the message flow; and you can browse a queue or topic to look for messages arriving at the anticipated destination. You can also use Plain Old Unit Tests (POUT) to trigger a message flow and look for messages at specific endpoints.

This book offers another alternative for testing Mule and ServiceMix flows: the Swing test client. The Swing test client provides a wide variety of connectivity support and an easy-to-use graphical interface. For example, you can send messages to a JMS queue or a file directory and receive messages at their target destination. You need only one tool to support your unit testing.

Starting the Swing test client

You can start the Swing test client via a console or by using your IDE (such as Eclipse) to start an Ant target. To start the Swing test client via a console, go to the osesb-test-client directory, which is available in the root of the directory that you created to set up the book's working environment. Then, execute the following Java instruction in the console:

```
java -jar osesb-test-client.jar
```

The test client will start, and you'll see a screen similar to figure F.1.

In the Swing test-client screen, you can select most of the examples described in this book, categorized by open source ESB and chapter number. The Mule examples using the STDIO connector aren't available in the test client, because these examples should be tested via the console where Mule is started.

You can also start the Swing test client using the Ant build scripts for the book's different chapters. Eclipse provides a nice Ant view that you can use to easily start Ant targets. This Eclipse functionality can also be used to start the Swing test client in Eclipse. Once the Ant view is available in Eclipse (via the Windows > Show View > Ant menu options), drag the Ant build scripts for the various chapters (for example, resources/chapter8/

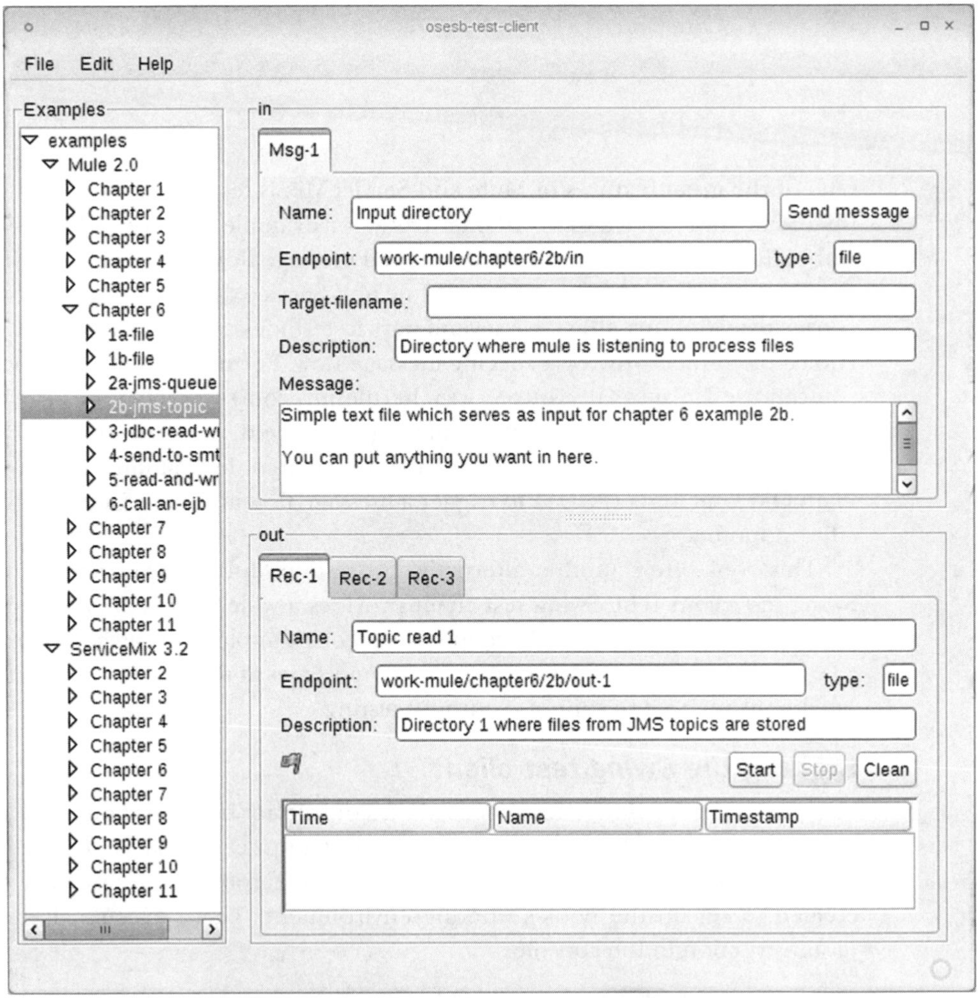

Figure F.1 The Swing test client, showing the available test configurations on the left. Depending on the connectivity configured in the examples, you'll see Send and Receive tabs on the right side of the screen.

ch8-examples.xml for chapter 8) to the Ant view. All the targets described in the Ant build file are available in the Ant view, as shown in figure F.2.

Figure F.2 shows that in addition to the ext:test-client Ant target, many other Ant targets are available for chapter 8's Mule examples. You can use these other Ant targets to start Mule, deploy the examples from chapter 8 to Mule, and start up additional tools such as Apache ActiveMQ. To start the Swing test client, double-click the ext:test-client Ant target to open a screen similar to figure F.1.

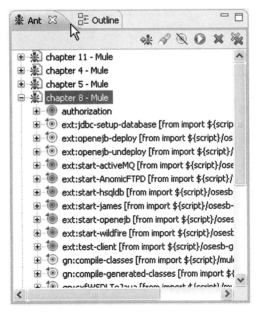

Figure F.2   The Eclipse Ant view showing the Ant build files for this book's Mule examples

Using the Swing test client

The Swing test client is categorized by Mule and ServiceMix chapter configurations. For each chapter, you can click the example you want to test. Because the examples described in this book use all kinds of connectivity, the Swing test client is able to send and receive messages from different message channels; it supports files, JMS, and web services.

For example, when you click the scuba diving example from chapter 11 for the ServiceMix ESB, two panels appear at right on the test client screen: an In panel for sent messages and an Out panel for received messages. The scuba diving example uses JMS to send and receive messages. Figure F.3 shows the panel that enables you to send a scuba diving request message.

This example's endpoint is configured to be the scuba.in JMS queue. Clicking the Send Message button sends the scuba diving request message to this JMS queue, which triggers the ServiceMix scuba diving message flow.

For other examples, different connectivity options are provided, such as file and web-services support. The panel shown in figure F.3 isn't that much different; the endpoint points to a file or directory for file connectivity and to an HTTP address for a web service. The message that is sent can be plain text (as shown in figure F.3) or a Java object instance.

The panel you use to receive messages from a specific message channel, shown in figure F.4, is similar to the panel that sends messages.

Clicking the Start button starts a listener or poller to receive messages. You can show the incoming message content by clicking a row in the messages table.

With the Swing test client, you can easily test all the examples in this book. To use the Swing test client in your own project, you can use the client-config.xml file

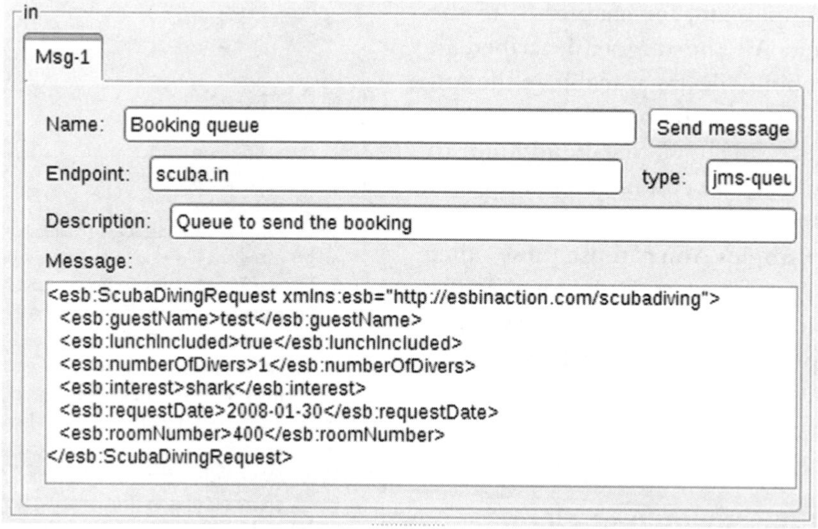

Figure F.3   The Swing test client panel that you can use to send a message to a message channel—in this case, a JMS queue

in the resources directory to configure the connectivity required to test your integration logic. Based on the available examples, you should be able to configure your own test easily.

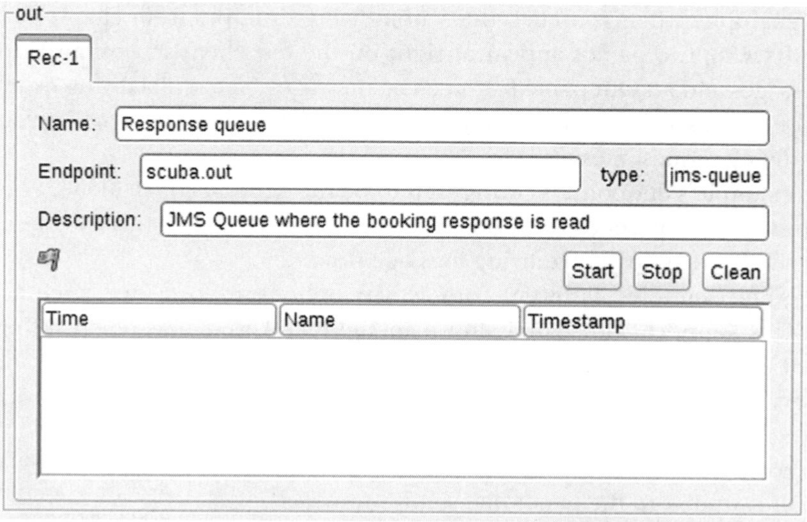

Figure F.4   The Swing test client panel that you can use to receive a message. If you double-click any of the received messages, the message's content is shown.

Overview of tools and libraries

You use many tools and libraries to implement this book's examples. This appendix lists specific versions and websites for these tools and libraries.

Tools

Table G.1 lists the name, version, and website of each tool used in the book and provides a short description.

Table G.1 Tools used in this book's examples

Tool name	Version	Website	Description
Anomic FTP Server	0.93	http://www.anomic.de/ AnomicFTPServer	A freeware FTP server implemented in Java (*not* an open source tool)
Apache ActiveMQ	4.1.2	http://activemq.apache.org	An Apache open source message broker implementation with full support for JMS 1.1
Apache Directory Server	1.5.2	http://directory.apache.org	An Apache open source LDAP server written in Java and fully LDAP v3-compliant
Apache Directory Studio	1.1.0	http://directory.apache.org	An Apache open source LDAP browser written in Java
Apache James	2.3.1	http://james.apache.org/	An Apache open source SMTP, POP3, and NNTP server written in Java

Table G.1   Tools used in this book's examples *(continued)*

Tool name	Version	Website	Description
Apache OpenEJB	3.0	http://openejb.apache.org/	An Apache open source EJB implementation with support for EJB 3.0, 2.1, 2.0, and 1.1
Apache ServiceMix	3.2.1	http://servicemix.apache.org	An Apache open source JBI implementation with full support for JBI 1.0
eXist	1.2.0	http://exist.sourceforge.net/	An open source native XML database
HSQLDB	1.8.0.9	http://www.hsqldb.org/	An open source 100% Java database
Mule	2.0.2	http://www.mulesource.org	A Java-based ESB implementation

Libraries

Table G.2 lists the name, version, and website of each library used in the book and provides a short description.

Table G.2   Libraries used in this book's examples

Library name	Version	Website	Description
Ant-Contrib	0.3	http://ant-contrib.sourceforge.net/	A collection of Ant tasks providing support for, for example, if statements
Apache CXF	2.0.7	http://cxf.apache.org	An Apache open source web-service provider
Apache ODE	1.1.1	http://ode.apache.org	An Apache open source BPEL server with support for WS-BPEL 2.0
BeanShell	2.0b4	http://www.beanshell.org/	A Java source interpreter with object-scripting language features, written in Java
Hibernate	3.2.6	http://www.hibernate.org/	A persistency framework that provides object-relational mapping (ORM) functionality
JavaMail API	1.4	http://java.sun.com/products/javamail/	A platform-independent and protocol-independent framework to build mail and messaging applications
JiBX	1.1.5	http://jibx.sourceforge.net/	A framework for binding XML data to Java objects

Table G.2 Libraries used in this book's examples *(continued)*

Library name	Version	Website	Description
Spring	2.0.8	http://www.springframework.org	A dependency-injection framework with a wide range of application functionality support
SVNKit	1.1.7	http://svnkit.com/	A pure Java toolkit that implements all Subversion features and provides APIs to work with Subversion working copies and access and manipulate Subversion repositories

index

MORE TITLES FROM MANNING

Open Source SOA
by Jeff Davis

> ISBN: 1-933988-54-1
> 350 pages
> $49.99
> March 2009

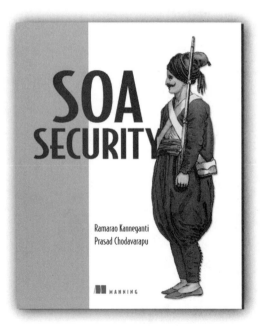

SOA Security
by Ramarao Kanneganti
  and Prasad Chodavarapu

> ISBN: 1-932394-68-0
> 512 pages
> $59.99
> December 2007

For ordering information go to www.manning.com